Pottery from Tell Khaiber

Archaeology of Ancient Iraq

In partnership with the State Board for Antiquities & Heritage,
Ministry of Culture, Republic of Iraq.

Pottery from Tell Khaiber

A Craft Tradition of the First Sealand Dynasty

Daniel Calderbank

Pottery from Tell Khaiber
A Craft Tradition of the First Sealand Dynasty
by
Daniel Calderbank

ISBN 978-1-910169-02-5

Archaeology of Ancient Iraq 1

Moonrise Press
Ludlow, UK
2021

www.iraqarchaeology.org

Acknowledgements

This book builds on the research presented in my doctoral thesis that I defended at the University of Manchester in 2018 to receive the degree of Doctor of Philosophy. It could not have been written without the guidance of my supervisor, Stuart Campbell, whose blend of knowledge and humour inspired my interest in the archaeology of Iraq and whose support has nurtured it ever since. My appreciation also goes to the core members of my supervisory team: Lindy Crewe, for theoretical and practical guidance (and for the many fun excavation seasons at Kissonerga-*Skalia*); and Ina Berg, whose expert advice on ceramic technologies has had a significant influence on the methods applied in this book; also to my external examiner, Augusta McMahon, whose insightful and probing questions have helped to shape my research.

I would also like to acknowledge the financial support I received from the Arts and Humanities Research Council (AHRC) North West Consortium Doctoral Training Partnership (NWCDTP), and from the University of Manchester President's Doctoral Scholarship (PDS) during my doctoral studies. The transformation of my thesis into the manuscript of this book was undertaken during my British Academy Postdoctoral Fellowship (2019–22) at the University of Glasgow.

It was a special experience to work at Tell Khaiber. My deep thanks go to the directors of the Ur Region Archaeology Project (URAP), Jane Moon and Robert Killick, for inviting me onto the project and for their support ever since; to Jane for coping patiently with the struggles of a young ceramicist dealing with such a large assemblage, and to Robert for being a constant source of knowledge as I navigated the stratigraphic and contextual complexities of the site. The other regular members of the URAP team, Mary Shepperson, Fay Slater, Adrian Murphy, Eleanor Robson, and Nick Overton, have all been wonderful colleagues and friends throughout. To the representatives of the State Board of Antiquities and Heritage of Iraq, local workers and friends, go gratitude for your hospitality, for planning and logistics, and for your tireless excavation and post-excavation work.

I also owe a significant debt to many fantastic colleagues who have supported me with their data, their time, and their advice: Abdulameer Al-Hamdani for his inspiring research on the Sealand, and his enthusiasm for building sustainable international collaborations; Odette Boivin for her extensive assyriological and historiographic knowledge of the Sealand; Flemming Højlund and Steffen Terp Laursen for introducing me to the archaeology of Dilmun and its Sealand connections, and for hosting me at Moesgaard Museum; Valentina Oselini, for discussions about the pottery of the Diyala; Katja Sternitzke for sharing her doctoral research re-analysing the pottery from Babylon; Elsa Perruchini for opening up opportunities for interdisciplinary collaboration; Claudia Glatz for always driving me to develop innovative and deeply human approaches to the past; and, finally, the two anonymous reviewers of the original book manuscript, whose suggestions have proven helpful in its final composition. Any errors or misjudgements made in this book are, of course, my own.

Especial thanks to my family, my friends, and my partner Synnøve, for seeing me through both the fun and difficult parts of this journey. Above all, this book is for Jürgen. Your belief in me is inspiring.

Contents

List of Illustrations

Figures

Tables

Plates

Abbreviations

AbB	Altbabylonische Briefe in Umschrift und Übersetzung (Leiden 1964 ff.)
AHw	Akkadisches Handwörterbuch (Wiesbaden 1959–81)
BM	British Museum Collection Number
CAD	The Assyrian Dictionary of the University of Chicago (Chicago 1956 ff.)
CDA	A Concise Dictionary of Akkadian (Black, J., George, A., and Postgate, N. 2000)
CDLP	Cuneiform Digital Library Preprints
CUSAS	Cornell University Studies in Assyriology and Sumerology (Bethesda 2007 ff.)
Ḫḫ	UR_5-RA = *ḫubullu* (Civil ed. 1996)
JASP	Jutland Archaeological Society Publications (Aarhus 1951 ff.)
MHEM	Mesopotamian History and Environment, Memoirs (Ghent 1987 ff.)
NAPR	Northern Akkad Project Reports (=MHEM Series 1; Ghent 1987–96)
ORACC	The Open Richly Annotated Cuneiform Corpus
SANER	Studies in Ancient Near Eastern Records (De Gruyter 2012 ff.)
UET	Ur Excavations. Texts (London 1928 ff.)

1. Introduction

The mid-second millennium BCE in southern Mesopotamia is characterised historically by the rise and fall of centralised state powers. The alluvial plains formed a dynamic region of urban city centres, rural hinterlands, marshlands, and contested spaces and frontiers, which alternated between periods of relative stability and episodes of disruption and conflict. The political events that traditionally bookmark accounts of this period are: (1) the First Babylonian Dynasty (ca. 1792–1595), the state formed when king Hammurabi unified the northern and southern plains under the control of the city of Babylon; (2) a so-called 'Dark Age' (ca. 1740–1450), in which Babylonian state control began to disintegrate and a period of political collapse gripped the region; and (3) the rise and expansion of the Kassite Dynasty (ca. 1450–1150), a group of uncertain origins, which assumed such power that they were able to correspond on equal terms with the Egyptian Pharaohs.

Episodes of ostensible collapse, while having far reaching social and material consequences, are rarely complete. Instead, they provide extensive opportunities for political and cultural reconfiguration (e.g. Yoffee 2014). Into the churning political milieu of the mid-second millennium stepped a series of shadowy kings of the 'Sealand' (ca. 1732–1450); these kings appear to have exercised some level of control over the marshy terrain of southern Mesopotamia, forming what Al-Hamdani (2015) has recently conceptualised as a 'shadow state' on the margins of centralised Babylonian control. Nevertheless, while recognised by Mesopotamian scholars for over a century (e.g. Dougherty 1932), an almost complete absence of new textual or material evidence has, until recent years, seen exceedingly little progress in our knowledge of the First Sealand Dynasty.

In 2013–17, the Ur Region Archaeological Project (URAP), attached to the University of Manchester, carried out five seasons of excavations at the site of Tell Khaiber, located in Dhi Qar province, southern Iraq, approximately 20km northwest of the ancient city of Ur (Fig. 1.1). These excavations, led by directors Professor Stuart Campbell, Dr Jane Moon, and Dr Robert Killick, are the first to provide secure, stratified architectural, textual, and material data which can be directly associated with the First Sealand Dynasty.[1]

1.1 Defining the Dataset

This volume deals with the extensive pottery assemblage generated from Tell Khaiber. All the ceramic data used to compile this report was recorded by the author at the team's Ur dig house alongside excavations. Although this volume will draw selectively on Tell Khaiber's wider contextual data, for more information on the results of these excavations, I refer all readers to the site's comprehensive excavation reports (Campbell et al. 2017; Moon ed., fothcoming).

The Tell Khaiber pottery presented in this volume was collected and recorded from excavations that focused on the site's Fortified Building, a large rectangular structure, 84 x 53m, which covers approximately 4,450 square metres (Fig. 1.2). Supplementary to this are also a few limited exposures at the Eastern Houses immediately to its southeast (Fig. 1.3). While the majority of the Fortified Building was surface scraped, revealing almost the entire architectural plan, comprehensive vertical excavation was carried out only in specific rooms and areas, totalling ca. 10% of the entire building.

Two levels of Sealand period occupation are recognised at Tell Khaiber. These are based on substantial architectural development of the Fortified Building, specifically the addition of the northern unit alongside remodelling and redevelopment of the southern unit for Level 2. It is in Level 2 that the Fortified Building assumed the layout in Fig. 1.2. The southern unit consisted of a clearly organised plan, with a central courtyard (Area 315) and several surrounding rooms (e.g. Rooms 314, 316, 600, and 601) including the Administrative Suite, a self-contained series of small rooms in the southeast corner of the building that housed the tablet archive (Rooms 299, 300, 301, 305, 309,

[1] The project was supported by Baron Lorne Thyssen-Bornemisza at the Augustus Foundation, the British Institute for the Study of Iraq, and others.

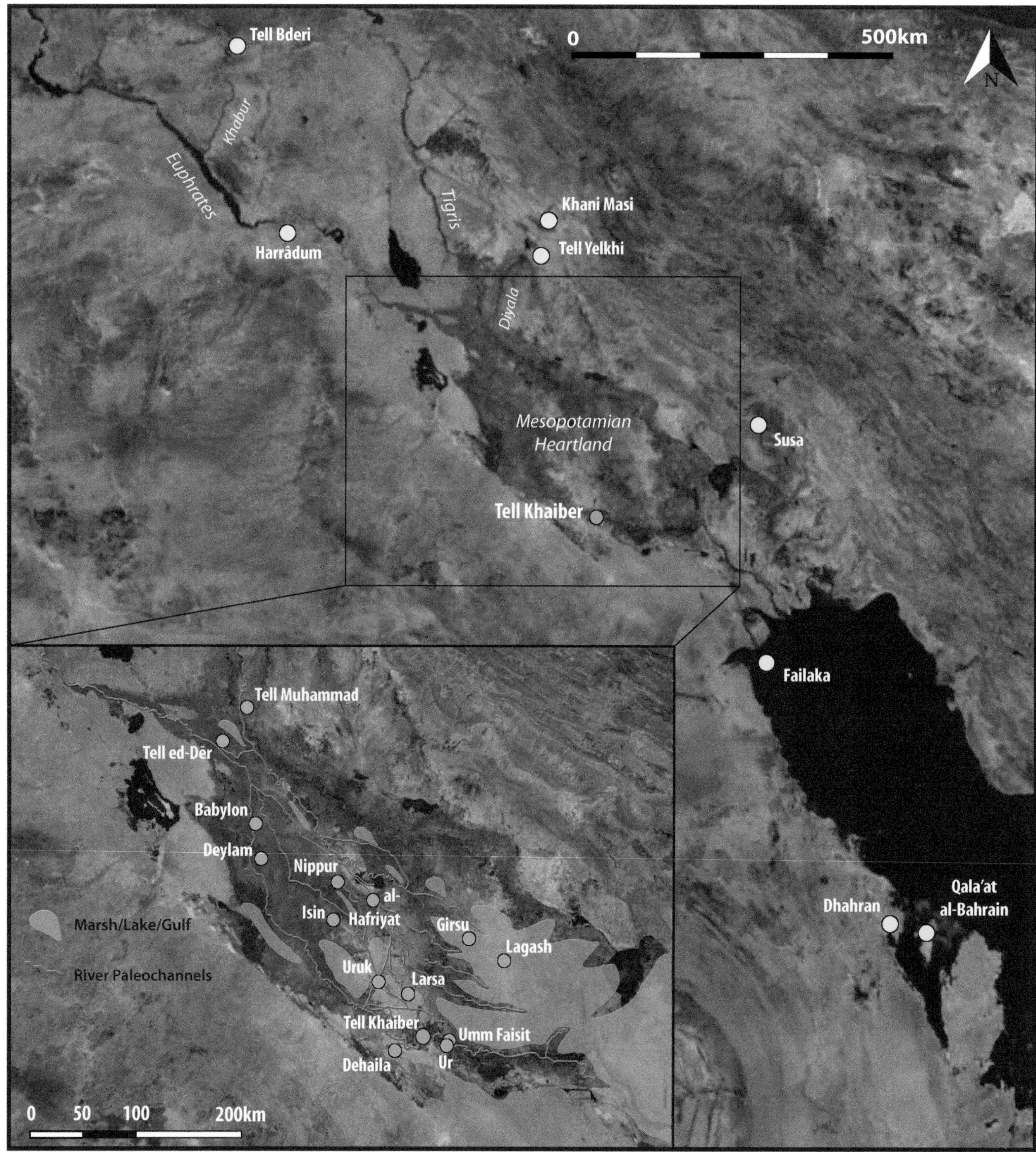

FIG. 1.1. Map of the region, with the Mesopotamian alluvial plains inset, containing the locations of key sites mentioned in the text: Tell Khaiber (red), southern/central plains (green), northern plains (orange), and beyond the Mesopotamian heartland (yellow). Location of ancient Gulf, wetlands, and river palaeochannels after Jotheri (2016: 172, fig. 5.1). Base map: © Bing Maps.

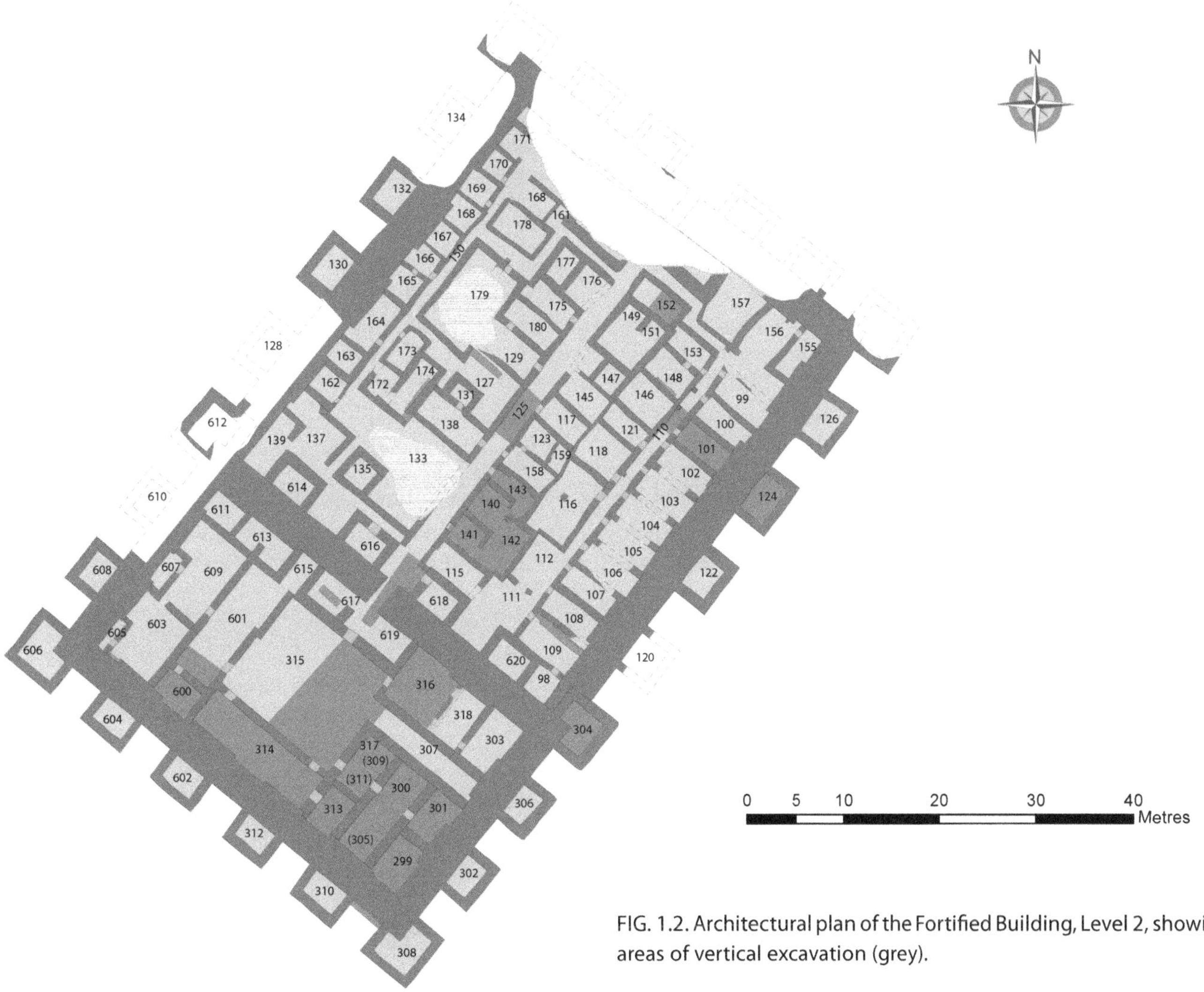

FIG. 1.2. Architectural plan of the Fortified Building, Level 2, showing areas of vertical excavation (grey).

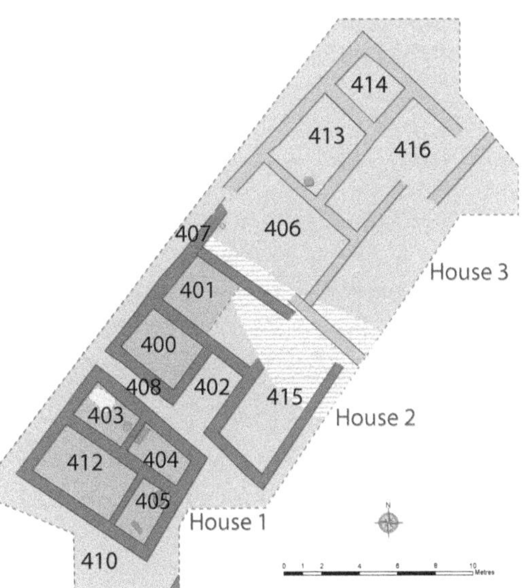

FIG. 1.3. Architectural plan of Eastern Houses to southeast of the Fortified Building.

and 313). The northern unit contained a series of identical rectangular rooms (Rooms 99–109) along the southeast side and a rather more complex and fluid architectural layout in the central area (e.g. Rooms 140–3).

Further phase separations are based on stratigraphic relationships within these relevant architectural levels (Level 1: Phase 1; Level 2: Phases 2.1–3). A chronological anchor for this relative sequence is the site's textual archive, which was produced and deposited in Phases 2.1–2 and dates to somewhere in the mid-16th century BCE (see Moon ed., fothcoming). The primary occupational sequence of the main building does, however, cover an uncertain chronological period for which we have no supplementary textual evidence, spanning a period of time before and after the deposition of the archive. Interpretations regarding the approximate period of time that elapsed between the start of Phase 1 and the end of Phase 2.3 must therefore be suggested based on the pottery evidence discussed in Chapter 3.

During this period of primary occupation, the Fortified Building appears to have operated as an administrative hub in control of the production and circulation of various goods, especially cereal products. It was inhabited by a semi-resident community of military personnel, administrators, and labourers. Tell Khaiber's 152 tablets and tablet fragments consist of ephemeral notes or memoranda, tabular accounts dealing with quantities of barley owed and received, numerical accounts tallying the receipt of other commodities, including pottery vessels (see §5.1), and a small collection of personal letters and scribal exercises. Together, these paint the picture of a light-touch administrative apparatus at Tell Khaiber, one that loosely tied approximately 150 named professional individuals into a broader palatial economic system (see Robson, forthcoming). The utilitarian identity of the building is supported by the material culture, which exhibits robust evidence for grain processing amongst other activities, yet offers little in the way of specialised high-status goods or items of personal ornament.

Later phases of more ephemeral reoccupation also occurred at Tell Khaiber. These are preserved only in small areas where the mound has suffered less erosion, and thus they offer little coherency for building an understanding of the nature of later associated occupation. These phases probably relate to ad hoc, perhaps episodic, re-use or squatting activities after the building's abandonment. The deposits are recorded within the site's Mixed Phase. Added to this Mixed Phase is the material generated from other deposits that cannot be reliably assigned to Levels 1 and 2: the accumulated deposits in the site's tower rooms, the surface scraped material from the upper ca. 10–20cm across the mound, several intrusive pot burials, as well as two exploratory soundings outside the Fortified Building.

It should be noted that, mixed in with almost all Sealand period deposits, were sherds dating to the late fourth and early third millennium BCE. Since the Fortified Building was positioned directly on top of a much earlier occupation mound, the various construction activities taking place no doubt served to disrupt and redistribute this earlier material. It seems likely, in fact, that much of this early material made its way into the building within the matrix of the mudbrick architecture, or as deliberate packing for the building's floors. The earlier ceramic material is not assessed in this volume, but these assemblages are examined elsewhere (Calderbank and Moon 2017; Calderbank in prep.).

Single context recording was used at Tell Khaiber. Each individual event horizon—a cut, a fill, a surface, a wall, a *tannur* etc.—received a *Context* number to which all finds and samples are associated. Context numbers always conform to a continuous four-figure system (e.g. 1001) and were assigned in a way that would minimise the potential for overlap in numbering; while one supervisor, for example, was assigned numbers in the 1000s, another received numbers in the 3000s. Once surface scraping of the site had revealed discrete rooms and spaces, *Room/Area* numbers were then also assigned, which conformed to a three-figure system (e.g. Room 101).

Throughout excavations at Tell Khaiber, all second millennium period pottery followed a consistent process of recording that was necessarily designed to maximise expediency. Pottery was brought back to the Ur dig house every day to be washed by Nasrullah Mohsen. Bulk sherds were laid to dry, before being sorted into several categories—diagnostic sherds, wasters,[2] and slag.[3] Sherds from secure contexts, such as discrete room surfaces, were kept in the short term, to maximise the chances of finding associated sherds for refitting. Once a context was fully excavated, these sorted categories were counted and recorded. While bulk body sherds were then securely discarded back on site, complete vessels and diagnostic sherds (rims, bases, and decorated sherds) were subjected to further analysis.

Each complete vessel and diagnostic sherd was entered into a Microsoft Access database, where it received its own unique *Pottery Number*. This pottery number was based on the context in which it was found, thus all pottery from context 1001 would take the initial designation p1001; each diagnostic item then took an additional, individual number based on the order in which it was recorded, for example p1001-1, p1001-2, and so on. In common with non-pottery finds, complete or almost complete vessels also received object numbers (e.g. 1001:1), which, when identified *in situ*, also have associated georeferenced find spot data, which provide an accurate coordinate and absolute height (above sea level).

For the sake of consistency and to avoid cases of duplication, only the pottery number will be used for reference throughout this volume. In the pottery database, several general features—shape type, rim/base diameter, fabric type, and texture—were recorded. If a new shape type, or a particularly good example of an existing shape type, was encountered, the sherd was illustrated and photographed, and more detailed description of the vessel colour and fabric type was conducted. Complete vessels were always illustrated and photographed, and a detailed macroscopic and microscopic analysis[4] of the vessel fabric was conducted where possible. Other morphometric measurements were also taken for complete vessels; these were specific to the type of vessel, but always included maximum height, maximum width, and volumetric capacity.[5]

Due to a lack of long-term storage space, Tell Khaiber's bulk and diagnostic sherds, once processed, were returned to the site for controlled discard. Complete vessels, on the other hand, were routinely taken to the Iraq Museum in Baghdad at the end of each excavation season, in accordance with the regulations of the Iraqi State Board of Antiquities and Heritage (SBAH).

2 Sherds rendered unusable due to being overfired to the point of vitrification and warping.

3 Vitrified waste material that gathers in a pottery kiln.

4 Using a digital microscope (Supereyes B008). Images were routinely taken at a magnification between ×100 and ×150.

5 Vessel volumes were measured using computer software named Pot_Utility v. 1.05 (©J.P. Thalmann & ARCANE).

1.2 Notes on Chronology and Terminology

The highly charged issue of the late third and early-to-middle second millennium Mesopotamian chronology has been a major research focus for over a century. Unlike later chronologies, which are fixed in calendar time, the precise reign dates of early second millennium kings, such as Hammurabi, or events such as the fall of Babylon, although anchored within a solid relative chronology, continue to float in calendar time. Depending on the chronological scheme one subscribes to, be it the High (HC), Middle (MC), Low (LC), or New Low (NLC), there can be a difference of up to 150+ years in calendrical date (see Hunger 2009, Pruzsinszky 2009 and Manning et al. 2016 for detailed overviews). This debate is pertinent to the content of this volume in that different dating schemes have a significant impact on the length of the so-called Mesopotamian Dark Age, the period in which Tell Khaiber was occupied.

Despite the growing body of textual, astronomical, and dendrochronological data, the chronological debate remains a contentious issue. As Roaf (2012: 170) states, each of the chronological systems 'can be made compatible with the 'givens' if the 'givens' are chosen appropriately'. Since the pottery examined in this volume does not fundamentally prove or disprove any of the main chronological schemes, I will follow Roaf's (2012: 171) view that the Middle Chronology is 'too convenient to discard'. Consequently, the Middle Chronology, which fixes the reign of Hammurabi at 1792–50 BCE and the fall of Babylon at 1595 BCE, will be used throughout.

Mesopotamian pottery, as a central source for dating, is often used to identify and frame political units e.g. Old Babylonian, Kassite, Mittani. Throughout this volume, I will be using these culture historical terms. In doing so, I do not intend to uncritically associate pottery types with political entities, or to view pottery as a passive materialisation of political power. When these terms are used to qualify pottery, for example Sealand pottery, they are done so simply to signify the general date of those vessels and, ultimately, to aid readability. Terms which carry less interpretive baggage, such as Middle Bronze Age or Late Bronze Age, do not currently bear the necessary level of chronological refinement.

The term Dark Age is commonly used as a label for the period falling between the end of the Old Babylonian period and the onset of the Kassite period (see, for example, van de Mieroop 2004: 122). Although there is extensive, if not complete, chronological overlap between this ostensible Dark Age and the Sealand period, they are not to be considered interchangeable. While the Dark Age is thought to encompass this period across most of Mesopotamia, the Sealand period is restricted to the southern plains, since this was the area covered by extensive marshland where the Sealand Dynasty exercised some degree of political sway. I will avoid the use of the term Dark Age in this volume, since it carries the misleading impression of sociopolitical and scribal collapse, which, given the evidence from Tell Khaiber, was evidently not the case.

1.3 Central Issues and Aims

There are two central aims of this volume: firstly, to establish a Tell Khaiber typology and relative chronology, and, secondly, to determine the *chaîne opératoire* underpinning Sealand period pottery, from clay collection through to vessel use and discard.

1.3.1 Typology and Relative Chronology

The chronological sequence for the middle centuries of the second millennium is extremely poorly understood. Precious little stratified archaeological material has been produced relating to this period. The major urban centres of the alluvial plains, which have traditionally formed the primary focus of archaeological investigations, all appear to demonstrate a complete break, or at the very least a dramatic downsizing, in occupation during the eighteenth and seventeenth centuries BCE. Historically, the cities of the southern alluvium, Ur, Uruk, Larsa, Girsu, and Lagash were abandoned by ca. 1740 BCE, while the cities in the central plains, Isin and Nippur, held out until ca. 1720 BCE (Stone 1977; Gasche 1989; Armstrong and Gasche 2014).

These dramatic changes have been attributed to various prime movers. Some scholars have focused on conflict, rebellion, and brutal Babylonian state retaliation as the central catalyst for settlement collapse. Indeed, the textual record for the period following Hammurabi's reign, although fragmentary, does speak to simmering tensions between Babylon and the southern cities, which resulted in centralised responses: King Samsuiluna destroying the walls of Ur, Larsa, and Uruk (Horsnell 1999: 185), Abi-ešuh's damming of the Tigris in a failed attempt to capture Iluma-ilu, the first King of the Sealand (Oates 1979: 84; Brinkman 2017), and the continuous construction of fortifications along major canal routes, such as at Dur-Abi-ešuh, in order to exercise control over the unruly countryside (Richardson 2005; van Leberghe and Voet 2009). Nevertheless, these textual-historical references to large-scale conflict do obscure the multiple internal stresses and systemic failures that also placed considerable strain on the Babylonian state. Environmental degradation, including a shift in the course of the Euphrates, certainly played a part (Adams and Nissen 1972: 39–41; Armstrong and Brandt 1994; Charpin et al. 2004: 342), as too did a failing economic system in which property became concentrated in the hands of a few wealthy individuals and families, leading to a dramatic polarisation of rich and poor (Stone 1977; see also Richardson 2002).

The picture of extensive change is largely supported by settlement data from the southern cities, which, as far excavation goes, demonstrate a period of hiatus, sometimes marked by signs of violence and conflict, for example at Ur (Woolley 1965: 1). It is also reflected in the survey data. A change in settlement pattern was identified in early surveys, such as Adams and Nissen's (1972), conducted in the area east of the Euphrates from Adab in the north to its southern point at Larsa. In the period concurrent with the Old Babylonian to Kassite transition, Adams and Nissen noticed two key changes: firstly, that there was severe disruption to the watercourses in this area, with the entire Euphrates system taking a decisive westward shift, extending as far south as Ur (Adams and Nissen 1972: 39–40, Fig. 18; Ur 2013: 147–8); and, secondly, that there was a small decrease in the number of sites attested (60 to 57) and a major drop in the area covered by these settlements. These patterns, they argued, was consistent with 'relatively sudden, catastrophic collapse' (Adams and Nissen 1972: 39).

Henry Wright (1981: 331) later extended the survey area to the Ur and Eridu areas, where he demonstrated a similar shift in settlement pattern. Of the 39 sites with identifiable Kassite remains, 79% had no previous Old Babylonian settlement (Adams: 1981: 332). This mid-second millennium switch from an agglomerated urban system to a dispersed pattern of smaller communities is reinforced by Al-Hamdani's recent surveys in the traditional marshland areas of southern Iraq.[6] Jason Ur (2013: 147) considers this change so profound as to describe it as 'the end of the Sumerian world'.

In the northern alluvium, traditional cities, such as Tell ed-Der and Deylam, were seemingly abandoned by ca. 1630 BCE. Babylon itself is traditionally considered to have formed the last bastion, its fate finally being sealed by a Hittite raid in 1595 BCE (Oates 1979). Significantly, however, recent analysis of the Babylonian textual evidence, alongside a reanalysis of material produced from the Merkes area of Babylon, suggests an almost continuous sequence of occupation throughout the centuries of the mid-second millennium (Sternitzke 2016a: 188–9), albeit a sequence that was not comprehensively recorded during Koldewey's excavations.

Several attempts have been made to integrate the fragmented pottery records produced from the sites outlined above into a unified typology of second millennium ceramics (e.g. Ayoub 1982). The most recent and remarkably comprehensive of these is Armstrong and Gasche's (2014) Mesopotamian Pottery volume. Unfortunately for any study of Sealand period pottery, Armstrong and Gasche's work is anchored by the occupational sequences of Tell ed-Der and Nippur, both of which demonstrate a break in occupation for the centuries of the mid-second millennium. In order to plug this chronological gap, they have drawn selectively on material from the problematic Susa sequence (Armstrong and Gasche 2014: 2), while largely overlooking reliably stratified material from sites in the Gulf, such as Failaka Island (Periods 3A–B) and Qala'at al-Bahrain (Period IIIa).

It is within this context that the assemblage from Tell Khaiber assumes pronounced archaeological significance. Tell Khaiber supplies us with the first securely stratified mid-second millennium pottery assemblage from southern Mesopotamia. Accordingly, this volume presents a comprehensive descriptive and illustrated typology (Chapter 2 and Plates). The illustrated typology departs from many previous Mesopotamian typologies, which have relied almost entirely on complete vessels and, in the case of early site reports, used individual and often highly stylised vessel drawings as representative of true vessel types. Instead, the Tell Khaiber typology appreciates the significant diversity within each vessel category and reflects this in the large number of vessels and diagnostic sherds chosen for illustration and publication. This volume uses this data to build a relative intra-site ceramic sequence (§3.1) which is placed within an inter-regional cultural and historical context (§3.2 and 6.2).

1.3.2 Chaîne Opératoire

Purely chronological and typological approaches to ceramics have formed the traditional backdrop to Mesopotamian archaeology. Yet, these approaches serve to position Bronze Age pottery vessels as passive elements of peoples' everyday lives, rather than as material assemblages that emerged in the complex relational engagements that produced and reproduced Mesopotamian society (after Duistermaat 2017; Hodder 2012).

In recent years, pottery studies have focused on the production sequence, or *chaîne opératoire* (e.g. Edmonds 1990; Gosselain 1999; 2000; Lemonnier 1983; 1993; Peña 2007; Roux 2019; Tite 1999), in its entirety, to understand the organisation of pottery production and the various decisions made by the potter—from collection of raw clay, through preparation, forming and finishing techniques, and to drying and firing. Ceramicists have regularly demonstrated the utility of such approaches in Aegean and Near Eastern contexts (e.g. Berg 2008; Choleva 2012; Duistermaat 2008; Knappett and Hilditch 2015; van As and Jacobs 2014). According to Roux (2016: 2), the *chaîne opératoire* provides a way to view pottery as 'part of a social and technological process and therefore as significant of the social groups behind them'. Consequently, production practices, or 'ways of doing' (Roux 2016: 2), that are routinely performed and are transmitted between generations can prove extremely resistant to change.

This volume will focus on the shared ways of doing that can be identified in the Sealand period pottery assemblage from Tell Khaiber. I will establish these aspects through detailed analysis of the production sequence (Chapter 4), from clay collection, through forming techniques, and to vessel firing. I will also extend the *chaîne opératoire* approach beyond production and into analysis of pottery circulation, use, and discard (Chapter 5), a method Duistermaat (2017: 122–3) has recently described as the 'holistic approach'. All aspects of Sealand period pottery production and use existed within a wider system of value production that linked the communities of southern Mesopotamia and beyond during this unstable period. This volume will present the first holistic approach to a southern Mesopotamian material assemblage and, in so doing, offer critical new insights into Sealand period chronology, politics, and economy, as well as some thoughts on the future direction of Mesopotamian pottery studies of the early historical periods (Chapter 6).

[6] Al-Hamdani's surveys took place between 2003 and 2010 and covered a 'triangle' between Larsa, Ur, and Eridu, east to Tell el-Lehem in the Hawr al-Hammār, including the plains between Lagash and Ur, and between Girsu, Lagash and Nina (Al-Hamdani 2015: 121).

2. The Typology

The Tell Khaiber typology is assembled from all second millennium ceramics found both within, and in the immediate vicinity of, the site's Fortified Building: over 150,000 sherds, 9,328 diagnostic sherds, and approximately 400 complete or mostly complete vessels.

The shape and fabric typologies presented in this chapter are built on complete vessels and diagnostic sherds produced from all contexts: floors, room fills, corridors, pits etc. Some vessel types, which are only represented by one or two examples, may not have been contemporary with the building's primary phases of use, but have been kept in the typology to allow for some level of chronological refinement; their infrequency is noted in the type descriptions and in the associated vessel statistics (Appendix A and Table 3.5).

It is important to clarify from the outset that the following shape and fabric typologies, as with all classificatory systems, are artificial constructs designed to aid interpretation of complex material patterning (after Adams and Adams 1991; Miller 1985). They are not intended to accurately reflect an emic Bronze Age, or indeed 'Sealand', classification of their own ceramic assemblage, or to determine the presence of any 'true type' (e.g. Ochsenschlager 1981: 79). Folk vessel typologies are complex and are often determined by the ways in which vessels were used (see Kempton 1981), rather than the subtle differences in shape and ware that structure most archaeological typologies. Alternative, functionally driven separations are presented in Chapter 5, in order to help inform upon the patterns of vessel use and deposition.

2.1 Shape Typology

The Tell Khaiber shape typology was initially structured in a sequentially numbered framework (1, 2, 3...), which did not distinguish between different categories of vessel—for example a bowl or a cup—or between each morphological feature—rim or base. However, as the assemblage grew, discrete patterns began to emerge. This enabled the formation of well-informed subdivisions, which subsequently resulted in a multi-level framework of classification.

Firstly, a series of essential shape-based separations (*Families*) were identified, which are broadly organised according to their degree of openness, with open shapes appearing before more closed vessel shapes. Families are designated by multiples of five (5, 10, 15...) and are labelled with commonly used ceramic terms, such as bowl, goblet, cup, and jar. These primary shape names are not intended to passively imply specific vessel functions (see Rice 1987: 211–2). Rather, because the use of these loaded terms is so widespread in archaeological discourse, I feel that the use of neutral geometric designations of shape (e.g. Ericson and Stickel 1973; Riemer 1997) would render the text incomprehensible.

Primary shape families are separated further by more small-scale variations in rim shape, base/foot shape, and occasionally body shape or decorative technique. These *Types* fit within the overarching family and are represented by single numbers (e.g. 5.1, 5.2, 5.3...), with the lowest numbers being reserved for complete shapes, where present, then rim shapes, body shapes, base/foot shapes, and miscellaneous features in ascending order. For example:

Family: Family 5. Bowls with plain, rounded rims.

Type: 5.1. Carinated body.

The typology was designed in this hierarchical manner and with the associated numbering system to correspond better with Armstrong and Gasche's (2014) influential second-millennium vessel typology, thus permitting ease of reference. Yet, unlike Armstrong and Gasche's typology, which also incorporates technical aspects of production, the Tell Khaiber typology follows a purely shape-based seriation. The central reason for this is that, while Armstrong and Gasche's typology deals only with complete vessels, where the signatures of production are easier to discern, the Tell Khaiber typology deals also with fragmentary diagnostic sherds, which can be more difficult to categorise technologically. Discussions of technical features, such as fabrics and forming techniques, will therefore be discussed in detail in Chapter 4. Similarly, regional and inter-regional vessel comparanda will not be presented in this typology. Instead, the chronological and cultural significance of relevant comparanda will be discussed in Chapter 3.

In total, eighteen vessel families have been identified, comprising seventy-seven constituent types, as well as one additional family of vessels that demonstrate re-use of other types (Family 95). Fifteen of these vessel families contain diagnostic types where the shape of the entire profile is known. These families therefore group together rims, bases, and occasionally also body sherds. A further three vessel families (15, 60, and 65), however, consist of rim and base sherds that could be associated with vessel shapes of more than one family, and are therefore kept separate. Inevitably, this skews the statistical counts; some vessel families are over-represented, since both base and rim sherds of the same vessel may occasionally have been recorded separately, while others are under-represented, as they were grouped in a miscellaneous family instead. We must accept that breakage biases will always exist when dealing with diagnostic sherd assemblages. In this volume, the biases in diagnostic counts are to some extent mitigated by providing relative frequency percentages for all families and types. Thus, assuming breakage biases remain consistent between phases and between each room/area, these relative frequencies provide reliable statistical information.

The accompanying plates provide a comprehensive illustrated shape typology for all vessel families and types, with accompanying tables that provide supplementary information regarding rim and base diameters, volumes, fabric types and the relevant phase from which the vessel/sherd was recovered, as well as other relevant qualitative information. The plates should be consulted in conjunction with the following vessel descriptions.

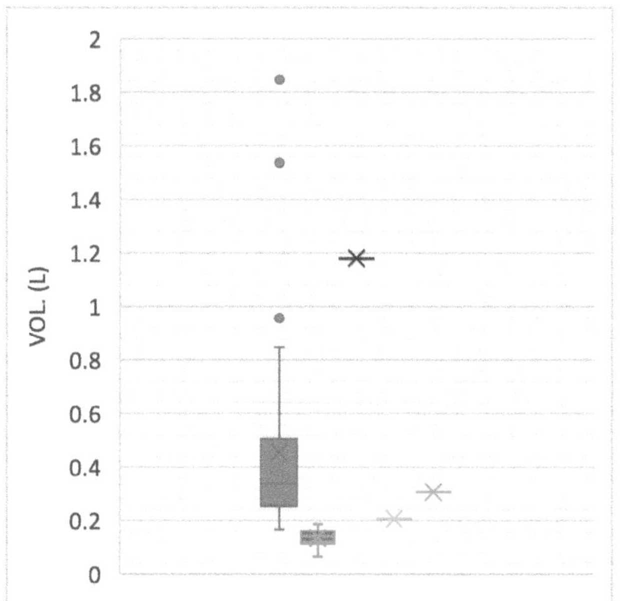

FIG. 2.1. Box and whisker chart demonstrating the distribution of vessel volumes of Family 5 Types: 5.1 (blue), Type 5.2 (red), 5.3 (green), 5.4 (yellow), and 5.5 (orange). Conventions: the middle line of the box represents the median; the X represents the mean; the bottom line of the box represents the median of the bottom half or 1st quartile; the top line of the box represents the median of the top half or 3rd quartile; the vertical lines extend from the ends of the box to the minimum and maximum values; isolated dots represent statistical outliers.

FIG. 2.2. Type 5.1 bowl (p3064-276).

Family 5 (Plates 1–4): Bowls with plain, rounded rims

(n=1312; 14.07% of the total assemblage)

Family 5 contains bowl types with plain, rounded rim shapes and undecorated bodies. It is the most frequently attested family in the Tell Khaiber assemblage, with five distinct types. The differences between these types is determined only by the shape of the body. 1312 diagnostic sherds, including 46 complete profiles, are attested across these five types. These vessels, as a rule, exhibit an open, shallow shape and flat string-cut bases. The low height–width ratio (Avg. 0.45) provides stability to these vessels. Rim diameters show great diversity (Range 70–370mm); the majority of these (71.5%), however, fall within a small–medium size range of ≤200mm (Fig. 2.6). Vessel volumes correlate well with rim diameters, with the majority yielding relatively small capacities (Avg. 0.41L; Range 0.07–1.85L; n=47), with 78.7% of measured vessels yielding volumes smaller than 0.5L (Fig. 2.1).

5.1. Carinated

This type is the most common type of Family 5 (60.9%; n=799). Its defining feature is a sharp carination of the body, presumably as a means of controlling spillage of liquid or semi-liquid contents. The carination varies somewhat in its sharpness, from angular to slightly more curved. The rim is generally oriented vertically, with a range of orientation of approximately 20° either outward or inward. The height from the carination to the rim also varies (Range 10–26mm; Avg. 14.6mm). Several examples demonstrate a lightly impressed band on the exterior surface between the carination of the body and the rim of the vessel. Bases are invariably of Family 15, but vary in their thickness (Range 4–17mm; Avg. 9.5mm; n=28). Rim diameters diverge markedly; although averaging 179mm, they generally fall within a range of 100–200mm (69.3%). Base diameters of complete examples average 53mm. Volumes for complete vessels range from 0.17 to 1.85L (Avg. 0.46L; n=36), with most clustering tightly between 0.2 and 0.4L (61%) (Fig. 2.1). Wall thickness is generally quite thin (Avg. 7.1mm; n=31), which contributes to the portability of these vessels.

5.2 Curved

The second most common constituent type of Family 5 is the bowl with a curved body shape (34.5%; n=452). The difference between this type and Type 5.1 is one of degree and depends largely on the relative sharpness of the body curve. In general, this type tends to be slightly smaller in size than those of Type 5.1. Although the average rim diameter (177mm) is almost identical, the average volume (0.14L; n=8) of complete examples is significantly lower than those of Type 5.1. Indeed, all eight examples fall within a tight range between 0.07 and 0.19L (Fig. 2.1). Bases are invariably of Family 15, but vary in their thickness (Range 6–14mm; Avg. 9.9mm; n=10). It is possible that most Type 5.2 bowls represent attempts to produce a carinated shape (Type 5.1), which is rendered difficult by the smaller size of these vessels. In accordance with this smaller size, average base diameters amongst the complete examples are also slightly smaller (50mm). The average wall thickness of 7.3mm falls in line with the other types of this family.

FIG. 2.3. Type 5.2 bowl (p3054-399).

5.3 Deep, curved

Only one complete example (p8029-3) constitutes Type 5.3. It is similar in general shape to Type 5.2, although its profile is much deeper and its walls much steeper (H–W Ratio: 0.53). The vessel has a larger volume (1.18L) than most other vessels belonging to this family. Its distinctive context, as part of a later, intrusive burial may account for its lack of parallels in the assemblage.

5.4 Wavy-sided

Type 5.4 bowls demonstrate a wavy, sinuous body shape. These vessels are rare at Tell Khaiber (2.1%; n=27). Unlike other constituent Types (5.1–3) of this family, the rim is turned outwards, rather than curving or carinating inwards, resulting in an everted rather than restricted shape. Bases for this type tend to be thicker, creating a higher platform more similar to Type 15.2 than Type 15.1. The only complete profile of this type (p6088-14), with a volume of 0.21L, was found in a surface scraped deposit directly to the south of the Fortified Building. This vessel is chronologically significant, since it has strong parallels with the ubiquitous wavy-sided bowls of the Kassite period.

FIG. 2.4. Type 5.4 bowl (p6088-14).

5.5 Straight-sided

This type is defined by a straight, sometimes faintly rippled, side that is usually quite roughly finished. Such straight sided bowls are particularly rare in the Tell Khaiber assemblage. One complete profile of this type, with a volume of 0.31L, is roughly finished and demonstrates a raised platform base (Type 15.2). Rim sherds of this type were only found in a specific area of mixed deposits at the very top of the mound.

Family 10 (Plates 5–6): Bowls with thickened rims and/or grooved bodies

(n=270; 2.9% of the total assemblage)

Less frequent than their plain counterparts, but nevertheless a distinct element of the Tell Khaiber assemblage, are bowls with shaped elements. Four types constitute this family. Each of these types demonstrates broadly the same carinated body shape, but vary both in the shape of the rim and the nature of treatment to the exterior surface during forming or finishing. No complete profiles were discovered, meaning it is difficult to be sure of the corresponding base shapes. However, it seems likely that complete profiles were essentially similar to Family 5. Thus, base Types 15.1 and perhaps also Type 65.1, should be associated with rim types of this family. Typical of this family are the extensive range of rim diameters (110–380mm). On the whole, they are somewhat larger than those vessels of Family 5, tending to fall into a medium–large size range (Avg: 235mm; n=213). Indeed, 73% of recorded sherds have a rim diameter of >200mm (Fig. 2.6).

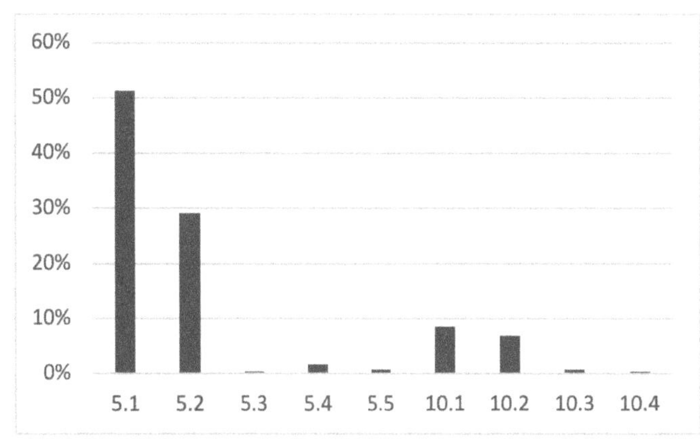

FIG. 2.5. Relative percentages of Family 5 and 10 bowl types.

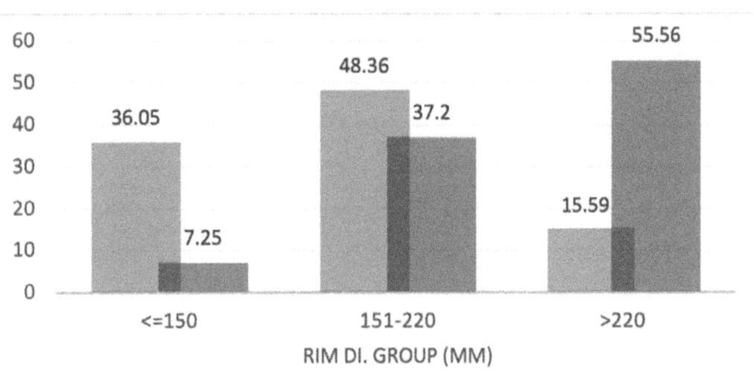

FIG. 2.6. Percentage of bulk bowl sherds fitting into three rim diameter categories (Small: ≤150mm; Medium: 151-220mm; Large: >220). Blue: Family 5 (n=821); Red: Family 10 (n=207).

10.1 Rounded rim, multiple grooved bands

Type 10.1 demonstrates a plain rounded rim, with multiple (usually 2–3, but sometimes as many as 5) impressed or incised grooves on the exterior surface, between the carination of the body and the rim. Type 10.1 is the most frequent present in this family, with 133 examples (49.3%) identified. Rim diameters vary from 120–370mm (Avg. 232mm).

FIG. 2.7. Type 10.1 rim sherd with impressed band decoration (p6059-31).

10.2 Squared/thickened rim, multiple grooved bands

This type demonstrates a flattened and thickened rim, with multiple (usually 2–4) impressed or incised grooves in the same position as Type 10.1. It is the second most common type in Family 10 (n=107; 39.6%). Rim diameters also vary greatly (110–380mm) with a high average diameter of 237mm (n=80).

10.3 Squared/thickened rim

Type 10.3 is identical in body and rim shape to Type 10.2, but does not exhibit impressed or incised bands on the exterior surface. The only decorated sherd of this type is p6175-39, which exhibits a relief band adorned with incised crescents. Type 10.3 is relatively uncommon, with just 13 diagnostic sherds attested. Rim diameters vary from 110–380mm (Avg. 249mm).

10.4 Thickened, everted rim, multiple grooved lines

Type 10.4 is the least common of Family 10 (n=6). For each example, the rim is thickened, rounded and everted. The profile is generally sinuous, and the exterior surface demonstrates multiple (2–5) impressed or incised bands directly beneath the rim. There is a relative lack of consistency in the degree of body curvature, as well as the rim orientation. Rim diameters range from 125–300mm (Avg. 209mm).

Family 15 (Plate 7): Bowl bases

(n=544; 5.83% of the total assemblage)

This family is comprised of those vessel bases that can be reliably associated with open bowls (Family 5 and probably also 10). It is these bases that are invariably present in the complete vessel profiles of Family 5. Two constituent types form this family, with the only difference lying in the thickness of the base platform. Bases are invariably 'string-cut', with the exterior exhibiting the concentric ellipsoidal markings indicative of the vessel's separation from the wheelhead using a string while still rotating (Fig. 2.8). Base diameters vary in size (Range 30–130mm: Avg. 61mm; n=492) and are no doubt linked to the size of the whole vessel. Even so, the majority of diameters cluster tightly between 40–70mm (83%). Some bases exhibit the incorporation of additional coarse, chaffy clay, in order to prevent cracking during drying (for more information on this technique, see §4.2.2).

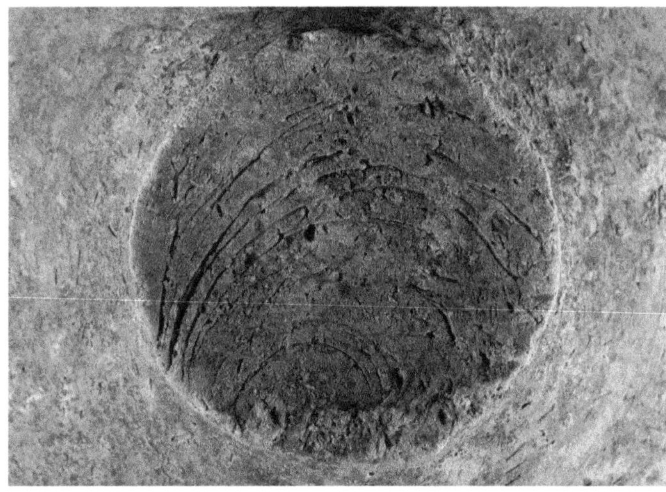

FIG. 2.8. Family 15 typical string-cut base (p3064-445). Not to scale.

15.1 Flat, string-cut

Type 15.1 is the typical open bowl base type, constituting 91% (n=493) of this vessel family. The shape is flat, and tapers sharply outwards directly above the base. The turn of the base is usually rather rough, indicating a lack of careful attention to finishing. Occasionally there are pronounced finger prints at this point where the vessel was lifted while still wet. The average base diameter is 61mm (n=444).

15.2 Pedestal, string-cut

More infrequent are flat bases with taller base platforms (n=50; 9% of family); this raised base can reach as high as 42mm. Despite this difference in base thickness when compared to Type 15.1, there is little corresponding difference in base diameter (Avg. 56mm; n=48). Where preservation allows, Type 15.2 tends to be more frequently associated with bowl Types 5.4 and 5.5, and is accordingly more common in the site's upper mixed deposits.

Family 20 (Plates 8–9): Trays/Basins

(n=47; 0.5% of the total assemblage)

Family 20 is comprised of a range of large, open vessel shapes with wide flat bases. These have been separated broadly into those with everted shapes (Type 20.1) and those with more restricted shapes (Type 20.2). These trays/basins are rare amongst the total assemblage and show little standardisation in comparison with other vessel families. There is substantial variability in rim diameters (Range: ca. 120–600mm; Avg. 379mm; n=28) and base diameters (Range: ca. 120–330mm; Avg. 252mm; n=6), as well as body shape (straight to curved) and rim shape. Indeed, accurate diameters are often not possible due to both the large size and irregularity of rim and base shapes. Vessels of this family are invariably coarse and thick walled (Avg. 23mm).

20.1 Open

Open trays/basins are the most common, constituting 87% of Family 20 (n=41). This type exhibits either a flat or curved base, and a plain straight or slightly curving body shape. The average height–width ratio of these vessels is 0.19 (n=4), meaning that they tend to be squat and shallow.

20.2 Restricted

Restricted types are comparatively rare (n=3). These vessels have a flat base and a vertical to slightly inwardly oriented profile. One complete example demonstrates a height–width ratio of 0.41 and a volume of 1.9L.

Family 25 (Plates 10–15): Pithoi

(n=603; 6.46% of the total assemblage)

The category of pithoi encompasses large barrel-shaped vessels, generally with rolled, thickened rims (Fig. 2.9) and applied ring bases (Fig. 2.12). Six constituent types make up this family: two of these are determined by rim shape (Types 25.1–2), one by body shape (Type 25.3), one according to size (Type 25.4), and another according to base type (Type 25.5). Depending on the constituent type, these vessels have either vertical, open body shapes (Types 25.1–2 and 25.4), or more rounded, slightly closed shapes (Type 25.3). Overall, the range of rim diameters measured presents great diversity (Range 200–825mm; n=328), although it must be noted that a high percentage of diagnostic rim sherds were too large for the recording chart.

Regardless of the more subtle shape changes, pithoi invariably have large volumes (Avg. 147.3L; Range 78–228L; n=6) and thick walls composed of a coarse chaffy clay matrix. Pithoi were usually so large, in fact, that they should perhaps be seen more as architectural features than as portable vessels. This emerges particularly clearly in an Old Babylonian letter, in which the sender laments his hopeless efforts to lift a pithos (Akk. *lahtanu*) (*AbB* 9 152: ll. 39–46, cited in Sallaberger 1996: 79).

FIG. 2.9. Cross-sections of rolled pithos rims: a) p5050-21; b) p8083-38). Not to scale.

Vessels of this type often have raised ridges, singly, in pairs, or multiple, and deep grooves, all located directly beneath the rim band. These were likely used to secure ropes for vessel closure. Indeed, the rim of vessel p8058-6 was found

FIG. 2.10. Examples of degraded fibres or cords coated in bitumen on the exterior of two pithos sherds: a) below the rim band (p8058-6); b) between the ribs on the body (p6125-1).

complete with preserved cord set in bitumen (Fig. 2.10a). Consistent with this, the bodies of pithoi often have applied ribs of chaffy clay running horizontally around the vessel circumference. Both surfaces of one pithos (p6125-1), for instance, were coated in bitumen; embedded within the bitumen on the exterior surface, between the applied ribs, was well preserved evidence for fibres (Fig. 2.10b). While the impermeability conferred by the bitumen would have made the vessel suitable for the storage of liquids, the application of wet cloths to the outside of the pithos, would, on evaporation, have served to cool the vessel's contents in a process known as 'sweating' (Skibo et al. 1989: 129–31).

25.1 Rolled/thickened rim

Vessels demonstrating rolled rim bands are the most frequently occurring type of Family 25 (n=279; 46.3%). Rim diameters are invariably large (Range: 240–825mm; n=164), even in comparison with other constituent types of this family. Walls are thick (Avg. 17mm) and overwhelmingly coarse in texture (87%; n=258). Type 25.1 is the only pithos type to yield complete profiles, and these always demonstrate open, straight sided shapes with an applied ring base of Type 25.5. The only exception is p3075-1, which possesses a rounded base, perhaps because this vessel was made purely for a burial context and was thus never designed to stand upright.

25.2 Rolled, thickened, grooved rim band

Less frequently attested in the assemblage (n=51; 8.5%) are pithoi demonstrating multiple grooves (usually three) on the exterior of the rolled rim band. In every other way, this type mirrors Type 25.1, with multiple ridges and deep grooves present beneath the rim. Rim diameters tend to be slightly narrower than Type 25.1 (Range 260–540mm; Avg. 378mm).

25.3 Rolled, thickened rim, closed body

Type 25.3 usually displays a rolled rim band, with impressed grooves directly beneath the rim, running down the upper body. The rim tends to be triangular in shape and the body flares outwards, usually directly beneath the rim. This creates a closed, more globular vessel shape. Consequently, rim diameters are narrower than Type 25.1–2 vessels (Range 220–480mm; Avg. 368mm; n=18). This type is encountered infrequently (6.6%; n=40) in comparison with the more open shapes belonging to this family.

25.4 Rolled, thickened rim, smaller body

This vessel type is almost identical in general shape to Type 25.1. The difference lies in its size. Examples of Type 25.4 are significantly smaller than Types 25.1. This is indicated both by rim diameters, which are significantly narrower (Range 200–400mm; Avg. 298mm; n=92), as well as wall thickness and texture, which is often medium (69%; n=77) rather than coarse. This vessel type does not exhibit the applied ribs or inset grooves on the exterior, as demonstrated by Types 25.1–3. Type 25.4 is quite a common element of this family (n=111; 18.4%). It is probable that at least some of these sherds had a complete profile more in line with vessels of Family 30 vessels rather than Family 25. However, because they do not preserve the distinctive perforated base shape of Family 30 (Type 30.2), it was deemed more appropriate to include them in Family 25.

FIG. 2.11. Type 25.3 (p5040-20).

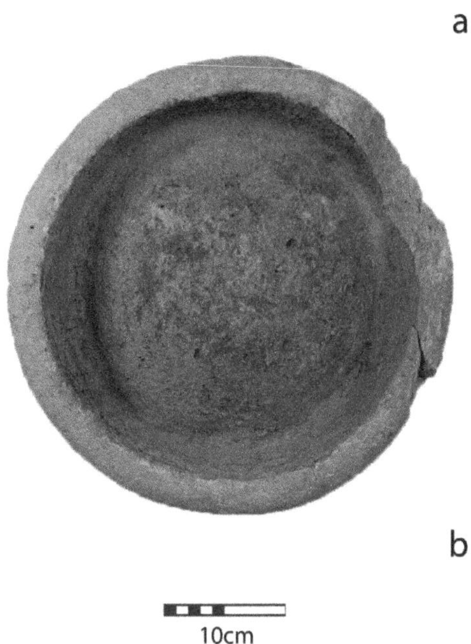

FIG. 2.12. Type 25.5 (p6125-1): profile (a) and base (b) views.

25.5 Applied ring base

The only reliably associated base type for Family 25 is an applied ring base, which is a common feature of the assemblage (n=103). These bases are made of thick, coarsely tempered pedestalled rings which were applied separately to the base of the pithos. The pedestals vary in height, but are necessarily wide in diameter (Avg. 289mm; n=71) in order to support the vast bulk of these vessels.

Family 30 (Plates 16–18): Pithoi with pierced bases

(n=26; 0.28% of the total assemblage)

This category consists of barrel-shaped vessels with open body shapes. Family 30 vessels are essentially identical in shape to vessels of Family 25 (especially types 25.1, 25.2 and 25.4). Due to these similarities, where rim sherds are ambiguous, they have been assigned to Family 25, thus at least partially resulting in the disparity in frequency between these two families.

FIG. 2.13. Type 30.1 rims: a) extended profile with incised arc decoration (p8082-42); b) relief band with incised crescent decoration (p3003-39).

The defining feature of Family 30 is the perforated 'bunghole' base (Type 30.2), which fundamentally separates the function of these vessels from that of regular pithoi (Family 25). These bunghole base vessels are commonly associated with filtering processes during beer brewing (Zarnkow et al. 2011). Accordingly, Family 30 vessels were never equipped with the ring bases of Type 25.5, but presumably instead sat in separate cylindrical pot stands (Types 85.2–3) from which they could be periodically removed. Another typical element of this vessel type is the regularity with which decorative features occur. Impressed bands are common on the exterior surfaces of these vessels, usually in specific fixed positions: directly beneath the rim, at the midpoint of the vessel, and directly above the perforated base. Other common features are wavy bands, which are usually faintly impressed around the vessel circumference. Incised line and crescent designs, although attested more infrequently, are located either directly beneath the rim of the vessel or at the base. Where volumetric measurements are possible, these vats show a great range (10.4, 15.3, and 60.6L). This is consistent with the range of rim diameters (230–430mm; Avg. 335; n=6), base diameters (45–110mm; Avg. 66.2mm; n=17), and perforation diameters (13–30mm; Avg. 22mm; n=16).

30.1 Rolled, thickened rim

Rims are rolled and thickened, either into a squared rim band, or into a grooved rim band. The reason two of these rim sherds have been assigned to this category and not Family 25 is that the nature of the body decoration (see Type 30.3) is consistent with known complete vessels of Family 30 (Fig. 2.13), yet is inconsistent with decoration known for Family 25.

30.2 Perforated base

This base type is the defining feature of Family 30. A circular clay coil is applied to the bottom of the vessel, moulded and pierced prior to firing, to create the typical 'bunghole' shape. Two general base sizes are identifiable: thicker, broader bases, usually manufactured of chaffier fabrics (Range 85–110mm; n=5), and narrower bases, generally made of relatively finer fabrics (Range 45–77mm; n=12) (Fig. 2.14). The former sometimes have bitumen covered interiors and exteriors to part way up the vessel, whereas the latter do not. Instead, the narrower-based vessels often have multiple impressed bands around the body, directly above the exterior base, most likely to help enable a secure fit within a pot stand (Type 85.2–3). The style of base does not, however, seem to affect the diameter of the base perforation, which averages ca. 22mm.

FIG. 2.14. Two main forms of Type 30.2 base: a) large and chaffy (p5060-1); b) smaller and finer (p5060-10). Not to scale.

30.3 Thick, vertical body, decorated

This type is constituted of body sherds that bear the typical decoration for this vessel family. This is usually a combination of decorated motifs, including incised lines or notches, as well as impressed wavy bands, which run around the vessel's circumference (Fig. 2.15). Just three sherds comprise this type, although the same decorative motifs are encountered in vessels of Types 30.1 and 30.2 too.

FIG. 2.15. Type 30.3 lower body sherd with notched ledges and impressed wavy band decoration (p5029-1). Not to scale.

Family 35 (Plates 19–22): Cylindrical beakers

(n=192; 2.06% of the total assemblage)

This vessel family is identifiable by its cylindrical shapes, with vertical to slightly concave profiles. The exterior surfaces of these vessels frequently exhibit concentric impressions or incisions, running around the vessel's circumference; these are present in isolation, in pairs, and even sometimes in sets numbering as high as nine. When present, these decorative elements tend to be placed in the same positions: beneath the rim, near to the midpoint of the body, and at the curve of the lower body. The manner of this regular, standardised spacing, is most likely associated with specific volumetric measurements. Amongst the Tell Khaiber assemblage, these volumetric measures are broadly consistent with different fractions of a *qa* (Table 2.1; Fig. 2.16), the common Sealand period measure that is broadly equivalent to a litre (Dalley 2009: 59).[7]

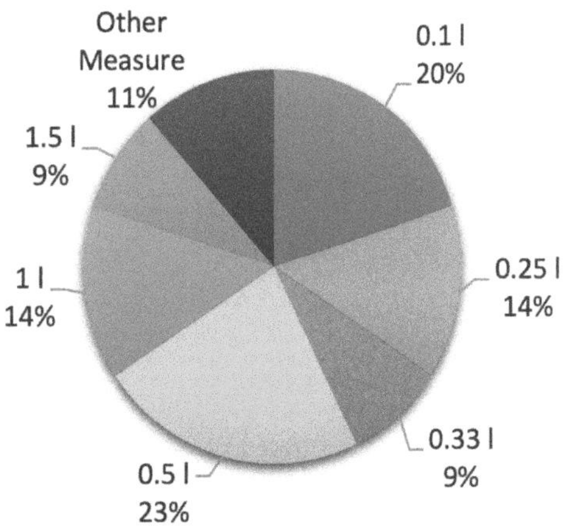

FIG. 2.16. Frequency of volumetric measures associated with individual sections of, or complete, cylindrical beakers (Family 35). Information taken from Table 2.1.

The differences between the constituent types of this family lie in the shape of the rim (Types 35.1–2) and the base (Types 35.4–5). One type is also reserved for decorated body sherds belonging to this family (Type 35.3). On the whole, vessels of this family demonstrate a good degree of differentiation in size: rim diameters range from 85–320mm (Avg. 189mm: n=112) and bases from 35–125mm (Avg. 61mm; n=45).

35.1 Plain, rounded rim

Type 35.1 demonstrates a simple, usually slightly everted, rounded rim, and is infrequently attested (n=6). However, one example is a complete, undecorated vessel with a flat disc base (Type 35.5) and a volume of 0.55L (Fig. 2.17). Rim diameters tend to be narrow, averaging 105mm (n=5). It is possible that some examples of ambiguous rim Type 60.1 might originally have been associated with Type 35.1 vessels, therefore resulting in the underrepresentation of this type.

FIG. 2.17. Type 35.1 (p1096-456).

35.2 Thickened/squared rim

Type 35.2 has a thickened, squared rim and is the most frequent type for this vessel family (n=117; 60.9%). Rim diameters are diverse (Range 110–320mm; Avg. 194mm; n=103), and, when extensive profiles are preserved, it is possible to see the variation in height between individual vessels. Whereas vessels p3088-20 and p5022-65 are tall, with several sets of concentric incisions and other impressed designs (Fig. 2.18), vessel p1139-125 is squat in shape, with just one incised groove on the lower body. Two complete volumes have been measured for vessels of this type (1.13 and 1.4L).

[7] See Powell 1987–90 for a comprehensive discussion of Mesopotamian weights and measures.

Vol. (L) / Sherd #	0.1 (1/10 *qa*)	0.25 (1/4 *qa*)	0.33 (1/3 *qa*)	0.5 (1/2 *qa*)	1 (1 *qa*)	1.5 (1 1/2 *qa*)	Other Measure
p1094-21					1 (1.05)		
p1096-456				0.55 Total			
p1139-125	1 (0.1)			0.43 Total			
p3054-394							1 (0.07)
p3059-16							1 (0.02)
p3085-125	1 (0.09)						
p3085-281	1 (0.08)			0.45 To Middle			
p3088-135		1 (0.24)					
p3088-182			3 (0.34, 0.32, 0.3)	1 (0.46)		1.42 Total	
p4036-20	1 (0.1)			0.49 To Middle			
p5016-12					1 (0.9)		
p5016-7					1 (0.87)		
p5022-65		3 (0.2, 0.2, 0.27)		1 (0.46)	1.13 Total		
p5022-66						2 (1.44, 1.6)	
p6058-104							1 (0.06)
p6166-40	1 (0.12)						
p8008-114				2 (0.54, 0.52)			
p8016-8	1 (0.09)						
p8074-17							1 (0.05)
p8083-21		1 (0.26)					
p8083-40	1 (0.1)						
p8083-41					1 (0.92)		

TABLE 2.1. Volumetric capacities of individual sections of, or complete, cylindrical beakers (Family 35), measured in litres (and corresponding *qa*).

FIG. 2.18. Type 35.2 (p5022-65).

FIG. 2.19. Type 35.5 beaker bases: small (p3085-125) and large (p1094-194).

35.3 Vertical body, decorated

Type 35.3 is comprised of those sherds that can only belong to this vessel family, on account of their vertical–concave body shape and incised or impressed decorative features, yet do not possess a preserved rim or base.

35.4 Ring base

Type 35.4 is one of two base types associated with cylindrical beakers and consists of a slightly pedestalled ring, which is finished and indented slightly in the centre. Above the ring base, the vessel body tends to project outwards slightly before reaching a sharp curve or carination, sometimes bearing an incised or impressed groove, which then graduates into the typical vertical-concave profile. Base diameters are slightly broader on average (Range 35–100mm; Avg. 64mm; n=14) than those of Type 35.5.

35.5 Plain, disc base

Type 35.5 bases are flat and unfinished. They are often string-cut and quite rough in appearance. Type 35.5 is the most common base type in this family (n=28; 14.6% of family). The profile shape above the base mirrors that of Type 35.4, with the body flaring out to a sharp curve or carination, which again regularly exhibits one or more incised or impressed grooves. Base diameters vary (Range: 35–125mm; Avg. 59mm; n=28), which is typical of the different sizes of cylindrical vessel attested in this family (Fig. 2.19).

Family 40 (Plates 23–5): Goblets

(n=67; 0.72% of the total assemblage)

Goblets have sharply defined flaring feet and tall, steep-sided bodies, which, where preserved, lead to clearly defined cylindrical necks. They occur rarely at Tell Khaiber and derive only from the mixed surface deposits from later, more ephemeral occupation. Three varieties of goblet have been identified amongst the diagnostic assemblage. Types 40.1 and 40.2 are similar in shape and style, but are differentiated in terms of body shape, while Type 40.3, although sharing similar flaring feet, are finer and taller than the other two types, with exaggerated necks and rims.

40.1 Flaring foot, steep-sided profile

Type 40.1 generally has a flaring, indented foot (Avg. diam. 67mm; n=10), which leads into a steep, straight sided profile (Fig. 2.20). The base is often very thick (usually 40–60mm). This is important for maintaining a low centre of gravity, thus maintaining some stability amongst goblets with such steep profiles, thick walls and tall necks. 65% of these vessels exhibit a coarse textured fabric.

40.2 Flaring foot, rounded profile

Although equipped with the same style of flaring, indented foot as Type 40.1, Type 40.2 has a thinner base. Furthermore, the average foot diameter for this type is slightly narrower at 53mm (n=40). It does not stand quite as tall as Type 40.1, but instead demonstrates a more rounded, squatter body with finer walls. The two complete examples of this type each demonstrate quite a high shoulder. Indeed, it is this high shoulder and elongated profile that separates this vessel type from cup Type 50.3. Although this vessel type is the most common form of goblet foot present in the assemblage (n=42; 62.7%), it may also be slightly underrepresented. Since the body shape is a defining feature, when extensive profiles were absent, these vessels may occasionally have been mistaken for Type 50.3 cups or Type 55.2 jugs.

FIG. 2.20. Type 40.1 (p0-1).

40.3 Neat pedestal foot

Type 40.3 differs considerably from the other types in this family and it is also the rarest (n=5). Type 40.3 is usually well defined and neatly finished, with a narrow foot diameter (Avg. 40mm). Where enough of the profile is present, these goblets appear to have short lower bodies, but very tall, well defined necks (Fig. 2.21). Indeed, the neck of one almost complete example (p6178-34) constitutes approximately two-thirds of the vessel's total height and boasts approximately half of its relative volume (0.23 of 0.5L).

Family 45 (Plates 26–7): Bottles

(n=24: 0.26% of the total assemblage)

Bottles are rare in the Tell Khaiber assemblage, yet this vessel family is comprised of a large concentration of complete specimens, meaning that we know a good deal about their entire profile shapes. These vessels invariably have tightly restricted necks and openings, and, apart from Type 45.3, demonstrate round, unstable bases. Bottles generally have squat, globular profiles. There is a clear preference for special surface treatments, such as slipping or extensive burnishing, amongst vessels of this family, practices which are exceedingly rare in the rest of the assemblage. Volumes vary significantly and are tightly associated with the specific bottle type.

45.1 Round base/body

This is the most commonly attested bottle shape (n=14; 58.3% of family). Specimens of this type are fairly consistent in shape, with squat bodies, narrow rounded bases (Avg. 8.5mm; Range 0–15mm), and restricted necks and rim diameters (Range 35–50mm; Avg. 44mm; n=10). Although they always have round bodies, the widest point shifts from the lower body in some examples to the upper body in others. The bases show some differences too; while some are barely perceptible, others possess a small point. Type 45.1 vessels have small, tightly restricted capacities (Range 0.04–0.24L; Avg. 0.1L; n=13).

FIG. 2.21. Type 40.3 (p6178-34) profile and base detail.

FIG. 2.22. Type 45.1 (p3124-18).

45.2 Round base, high shoulder

Type 45.2 bases are always completely rounded and neatly finished. Where preserved, the shoulders are high and turn sharply to meet narrow, cylindrical necks (Fig. 2.23). All three identified examples of this type were broken at the base of the neck. Exterior surfaces of Type 45.2 vessels demonstrate heavy burnishing or the application of a thick slip. In the two vessels measured, vessel volumes are much higher than those of Type 45.1 (0.52 and 0.88L).

FIG. 2.23. Type 45.2 (p8032-37).

45.3 Thickened rim, button foot

Type 45.3 is represented by only three examples at Tell Khaiber. Unlike the other bottle types, Type 45.3 has a narrow nipple or button foot, akin to cup Types 50.4–5. They are included in this family, however, due to their globular body shapes, narrow, well-defined necks, and restricted rim diameters (Avg. 49mm). One of these vessels (p1142-8) demonstrates a slipped exterior surface (Fig. 2.24). The volumes of the two measured vessels vary from 0.13 to 0.59L.

FIG. 2.24. Type 45.3 (p1142-8).

FIG. 2.25. Type 45.4 (p6175-40).

45.4 Button foot, sinuous body

Only one example of Type 45.4 is present in the Tell Khaiber assemblage. This unique vessel has a narrow button foot and a sinuous body, with no defined neck (Fig. 2.25). It has a small volume of just 0.07L and was found in a mixed surface deposit, alongside other vessels post-dating primary occupation at the site.

Family 50 (Plates 28–41): Cups

(n=1434; 15.37% of the total assemblage)

Cups are an extremely common component of the Tell Khaiber assemblage. They are often very well preserved in comparison with other vessel Families, with 157 vessels preserved at least up to the base of the neck. Cups are identifiable by their closed, round body shapes, and short, well-defined necks. These necks are vertical to slightly concave in profile and invariably end in rounded, slightly everted rims (Type 60.1). The widest point of cups tends to fall around the vessel's midpoint, but frequently falls slightly lower, and, less commonly, slightly higher, near to the shoulder. All cups show a high level of uniformity in morphological dimensions. Rim diameters always fall between 48 and 85mm (Avg. 74mm; n=71), while 63% of volumes fall between 0.2 and 0.4L (Range 0.06–0.88L; Avg. 0.33L; n=157) (Fig. 2.28). Regardless of overall size, the height–width ratio of vessels remains very consistent (Range. 1.18–1.52; Avg. 1.34; n=71).

The main differences between the constituent types of this family lie in the shape of the feet. Feet fall into two main categories: stable (Types 50.1–3) and unstable (Types 50.4–6). Further subcategories are then determined by more subtle differences in how the foot is finished (Fig. 2.26). Only Type 50.7 is separated based on the shape of the body.

Very few vessels in this family (3.9%; n=53) can be categorised as fineware. A number of vessels, predominantly of unstable footed Types 50.4–6, boast what appears to be a light slip (perhaps an incidental self-slip) on the vessel's exterior surface, and occasionally also the interior surface. Decoration is limited to incised and impressed concentric bands positioned around the shoulder of the vessel (usually of stable footed Types 50.1–3), and at the base of the neck (all types).

50.1 Flat pedestal foot

Type 50.1 is the most common stable footed cup type (20.2%: n=289). The foot is a flat, slightly pedestalled disc. Foot diameters vary (Range 10–50mm; n=276), but average at 29.5mm. The majority (76%), however, fall between 25 and 45mm. Volumes are generally higher than average for this family (Avg. 0.39L; Range 0.14–0.84L; n=38).

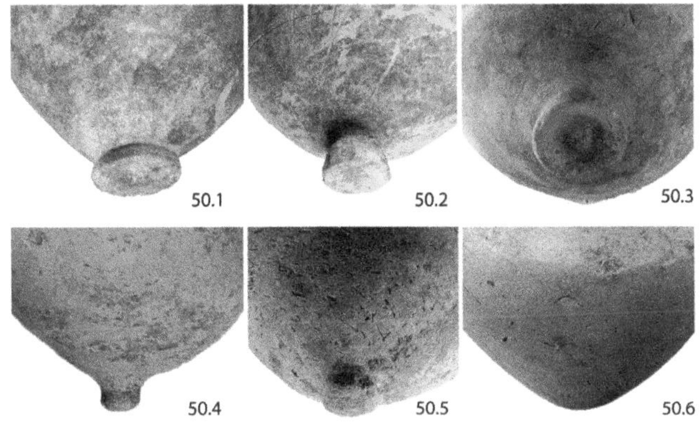

FIG. 2.26. The main Family 50 foot types. Not to scale.

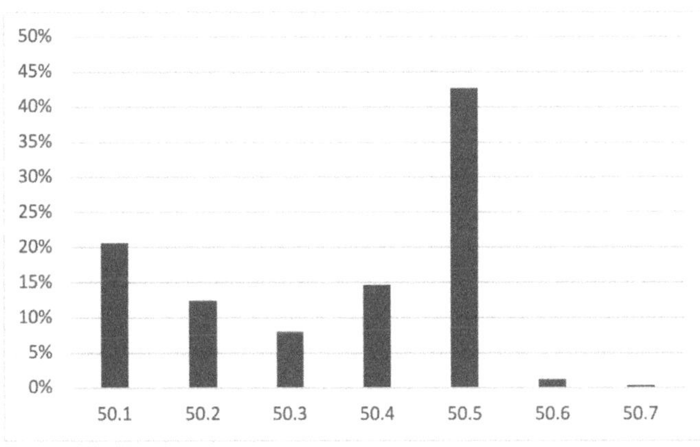

FIG. 2.27. Relative percentages of Family 50 types.

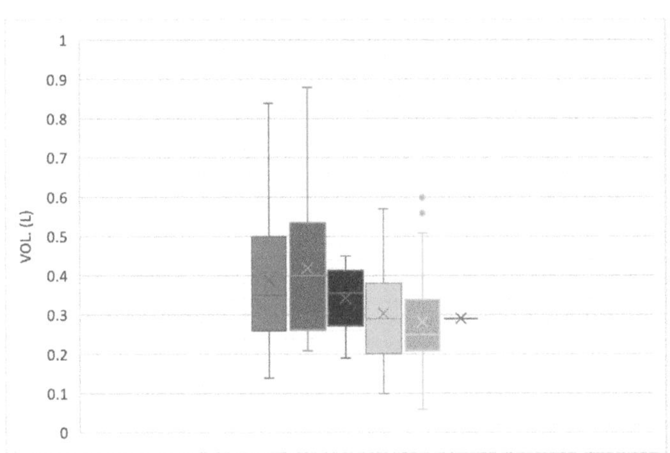

FIG. 2.28. Box and whisker chart showing the distribution of vessel volumes of different Family 50 Types: 50.1 (blue), 50.2 (red), 50.3 (green), 50.4 (yellow), 50.5 (orange), and 50.6 (grey). For conventions, see Fig. 2.1.

50.2 Angled pedestal foot

Type 50.2 is similar to Type 50.1, but has an angled pedestal disc foot. These are also common in the assemblage, constituting 12.2% (n=175) of this family. Foot diameters range from 15–65mm (Avg. 34mm; n=161). Volumes are higher than average for this family, yet are consistent with Type 50.1 (Avg. 0.42L; 0.21–0.88L; n=22). 32% of Type 50.2 vessels yield a capacity over 0.5L.

50.3 Indented pedestal foot

This type is identical in shape to Type 50.2, but has a finished, indented ring foot. It constitutes 7.8% of this family (n=112). Foot diameters are generally wider than any of the other types of this family (Avg. 40mm; Range 20–65mm; n=107), while volumes are relatively small in comparison to other stable footed types (Avg. 0.34L; n=6).

50.4 Nipple foot

Type 50.4 consists of an unstable, pointed nipple foot. This is sometimes neat and elegantly finished, but can occasionally be quite rough and hand moulded. It is a very common type, constituting 14.3% (n=205) of the family. Foot diameters are very narrow (Avg. 14.5mm; Range 10–25mm; n=190) and are therefore never able to stand alone without support. 96% of volumes fall under 0.5L (Avg. 0.3L; Range 0.1–0.57L; n=28).

50.5 Button foot

Type 50.5 is similar to Type 50.4 but has a swollen button foot rather than a pointed nipple foot. This is, by some margin, the most common type of cup in the assemblage (41.7%; n=598). Foot diameters are slightly broader than those of Type 50.4 (Avg. 20mm; Range 10–40mm; n=583). Even so, vessel volumes are very similar (Avg. 0.28L; Range 0.06–0.6L; n=62). 73% of these vessels yield capacities clustered between 0.2 and 0.4L.

50.6 Round base

Type 50.6 has no perceptible foot other than a small rounded point. It is a rare shape in the assemblage (1.2%; n=17). One volume has been measured (0.29L), which puts it in line with the other unstable footed types (50.4–5).

50.7 Flat pedestal foot, steep-sided

Type 50.7 demonstrates a flat, pedestal disc foot similar to Type 50.1. The foot is sometimes slightly indented, resulting in a small protruding point in the middle. The body of these vessels exhibits a steep, almost cylindrical profile, rather than the rounded shape shown by the other cup variants. This is a rare type (n=5), with examples invariably deriving from mixed surface deposits on the top of the mound.

Family 55 (Plates 42–6): Jugs

(n=412; 4.42% of the total assemblage)

As with cups, jugs are identifiable by their closed, round body shapes and well-defined necks. Indeed, these vessels share the majority of their morphological features with stable footed cups (Types 50.1–3). This is best observed by the height–width ratio of jugs (Avg. 1.33; Range 1.22–1.51; n=6), which is essentially identical to that demonstrated by stable footed cups. The main difference, however, is in the overall size of jugs compared to cups; rim diameters (Avg. 94mm; n=11), base diameters (Avg. 58.2mm; n=388), and volumes (Avg. 1.2L; Range 0.4–3.17L; n=25) are considerably larger in comparison (Figs. 2.29–30). At two ends of the spectrum, cups and a jugs

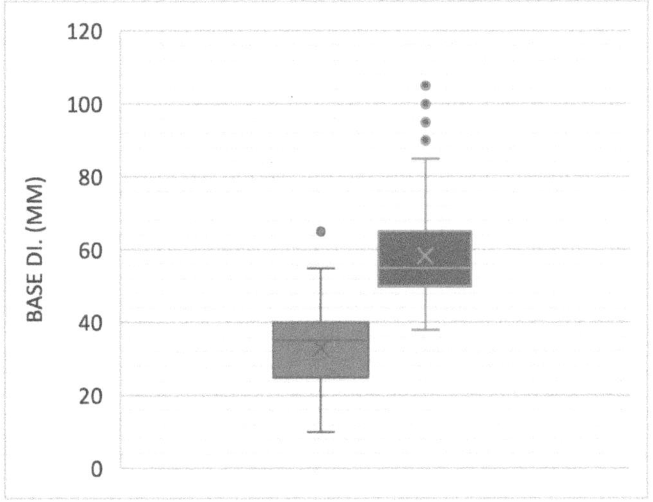

FIG. 2.29. Box and whisker chart showing the distribution of base diameters of stable footed cup types 50.1-3 (blue) and jug types 55.1-3 (red). For conventions, see Fig. 2.1.

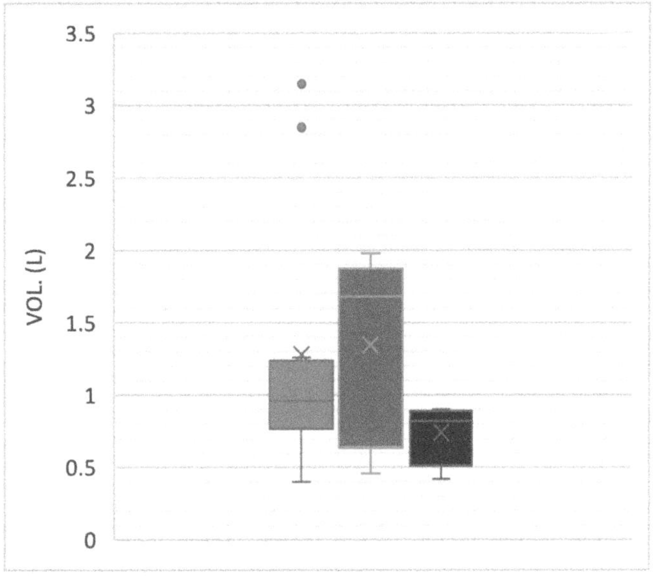

FIG. 2.30. Box and whisker chart showing the distribution of vessel volumes of Family 55 types: 55.1 (blue), 55.2 (red), and 55.3 (green). For conventions, see Fig. 2.1.

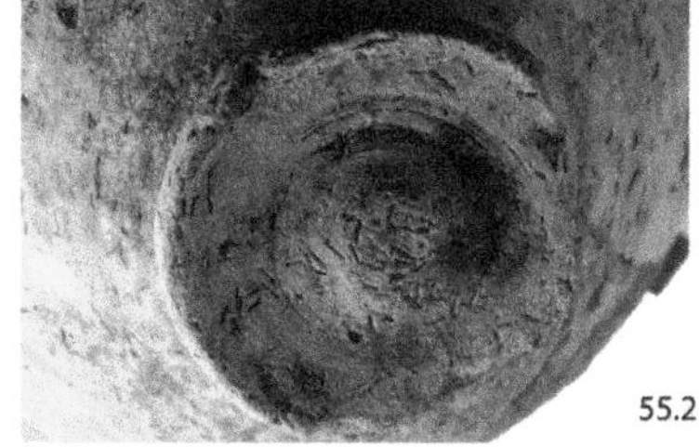

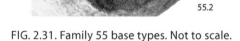

FIG. 2.31. Family 55 base types. Not to scale.

would have carried different functional identities, with a cup being used for consuming liquids and a jug probably for filling these cups. It was therefore important to keep these vessels separate typologically. There is, however, a significant grey zone between these two categories, which renders it difficult to establish hard and fast typological criteria to separate stable footed cups (Types 50.1–3) and jugs; generally, since foot/base diameter is shown to be a fairly good indicator of overall vessel size and volume, if the base diameter fell ≥45mm, and as long as the overall shape did not intuitively demonstrate otherwise, a vessel was categorised as a jug rather than a cup (Fig. 2.29).

Differences within this family are determined both by base shape (Types 55.1–2) and neck or rim shape (Type 55.3). Common among each of these types, however, is incised and impressed decoration. This usually takes the form of concentric lines or bands around the shoulder, singly, in pairs, or multiple. At the same time impressed bands at the base of the neck are also infrequent; the latter feature is most common on vessels of Type 55.3. As with some bowls, and many stable footed cups, a number of jug bases exhibit specific treatment with coarse, chaffy clay, in order to prevent cracking during drying. These are discussed further in §4.2.

55.1 Flat pedestal base

Type 55.1 is a flat, pedestal disc and is the most common type of jug base encountered (63.8%; n=263). Base diameters vary (Range 38–105mm; Avg. 55.3mm; n=249), with the majority (91%) falling between 45–70mm. Volumes are normal for the family (Avg. 1.28L; Range 0.4–3.17L; n=16), and usually fall between 0.7–1.3L (69%), which is approximately double that recorded for stable footed cups.

55.2 Indented pedestal base

Type 55.2 is similar to Type 55.1, but demonstrates an angled pedestal disc base, which is sometimes also finished and indented. These are also common in the assemblage (33.3%; n=137). Base diameters range from 40–100mm (Avg. 64.4mm; n=134). Volumes are normal for the family, but show a good deal of internal variability (Avg. 1.34L; 0.46–1.98L; n=5).

FIG. 2.32. Type 55.3 (p1137-35).

55.3 Pedestal base, tall neck

Type 55.3 is determined not by the base shape, which carry both base Type 55.1 and 55.2, but by the height of the neck. Vessels of this type have a neck that is almost twice the height (Avg. 61.3mm; Range 54–66mm; n=3) of a normal jug (Avg. 37.3mm; Range 33–42mm; n=4). The average volume of these vessels is 0.74L (Range 0.42–0.9L; n=4), with 75% clustered between 0.75 and 0.9L. Three of these vessels also exhibit matching impressed bands at the base of the neck. Although only four vessels of Type 55.3 have been identified, it is likely that they are slightly underrepresented. If the diagnostic neck was not well preserved, vessels of this type would be lumped in with Types 55.1–2, while, if the neck was present alone, it would have been recorded as Type 60.2.

Family 60 (Plates 47–8): Ambiguous rims

(n=1185; 12.7% of the total assemblage)

Family 60 is constituted of rim sherds that cannot be reliably attributed to one specific vessel family. Rather, they are ambiguous types that might be associated with several different vessel families.

60.1 Plain, rounded rim

Type 60.1 has a plain, rounded rim, with a flaring orientation and a vertical to slightly concave neck shape. This type dominates the vessel family (97.6%; n=1156), and is the typical rim sherd for most vessels of Families 50 and 55. Rim diameters accordingly average 81.7mm (Range 40–180; n=979), somewhere in between the average figures recorded for cups and jugs. Some of these sherds also have incised or impressed bands at the base of the neck and on the upper shoulder, which is, again, typical of the vessel families to which they would originally have related.

FIG. 2.33. Type 60.1 (p6127-1).

60.2 Plain, rounded rim, tall neck

Type 60.2 is identical to Type 60.1, except for its taller, vertical to slightly concave neck. This type is far less common than Type 60.1 (n=10). Rim diameters fall between 80–110mm (Avg. 95.6mm; n=9) and should almost certainly be associated with tall necked jug Type 55.3.

60.3 Thickened rim, wavy neck

Type 60.3 is identifiable by two specific features: its slightly thickened rim band and wavy sided neck. This shape is rare (n=7) and shows little uniformity between sherds. It is unclear to which vessel family these sherds should be associated, but, judging by the modest rim diameters (Avg. 127.9mm; Range 105–150mm; n=7), either large jugs (Family 55) or small jars (Family 70) would appear most likely.

60.4 Thickened rim, sharply defined shoulder

Type 60.4 is composed of just three individual sherds, each of which demonstrate a slightly thickened rim band, sometimes with a corresponding groove, and a well-defined neck. Where enough of the profile remains, there is a sharp carination at the base of the neck, moving into a vertical-sided body. One example is elaborately decorated with a complex series of impressed bands, wavy bands, and incised lines running around the circumference of the vessel (Fig. 2.34). The restricted rim diameters (Avg. 111.7mm; Range 100–125mm; n=3), vertical-sides, and elaborate decoration might suggest an association with Family 35. Sherds of this type are found only in the mixed deposits at the top of the mound.

FIG. 2.34. Type 60.4 (p6178-33).

Family 65 (Plates 49–51): Ambiguous bases

(n=757; 8.12% of the total assemblage)

Family 65 is constituted of base sherds that cannot be reliably attributed to one specific vessel family. Rather, they are ambiguous types that might be associated with several different vessel families.

65.1 Flat, pedestal base

Type 65.1 has a flat, pedestal disc base. This type is the most common amongst this family (72.9%: n=552). Base diameters vary widely (Range 40–290mm; Avg. 79.8mm; n=458). It is unclear whether these sherds belong to open vessels, such as bowls (Families 5–10), closed vessels, such as jugs (Family 55), or an unknown type of stable-based jar (Family 70). These bases are sometimes string-cut, and, when this is the case, it suggests their connection to open bowls (Families 5–10).

65.2 Indented ring base

Type 65.2 has a pedestal base, finished to form an indented ring base. Base diameters vary widely (Range 30–300mm; Avg. 88.4mm; n=153). Again, it is unclear whether these sherds belong to open vessels, such as large bowls (Families 5–10), closed vessels, such as jugs (Family 55), or an unknown type of stable-based jar (Family 70). The lack of preserved bowls with finished ring bases would, however, suggest the latter two families.

65.3 Rough, flat base

This type is similar to Type 65.1, but is generally quite roughly formed in comparison. These bases are also sometimes string-cut. Rather than flaring outwards from above the base, the body of this type tends to be steep sided. Base diameters are always large, but vary significantly (Range 95–240mm; Avg. 148mm; n=10). It is unclear whether these sherds should be associated with large bowls (Families 5–10), large cylindrical vessels (Family 35), an uncommon jar base, such as Type 70.8, or even a small hole-mouth vessel (Family 75).

65.4 Tall pedestal

Type 65.4 comprises tall, pedestal bases. These are sometimes neatly finished, but are also occasionally very rough. The pedestals are high (usually 30–60mm), yet with comparatively narrow base diameters (Range 40–55mm; Avg. 47.8mm; n=13). These vessels should most likely be associated with open bowl rims (Families 5–10), but no extended profiles have been identified to confirm this association.

Family 70 (Plates 52–61): Jars

(n=1862; 19.96% of the total assemblage)

Jars are extremely common in the Tell Khaiber assemblage. Although these vessels are usually encountered only in a fragmentary state, we do have a few complete examples from which to construct complete vessel shapes. Jars are identifiable by their rounded body shapes, and short, well-defined necks. Differences in type are determined by rim shape (Types 70.1–5), base shape (Types 70.7–8), as well as the presence of miscellaneous markings or decorative elements (Type 70.6).

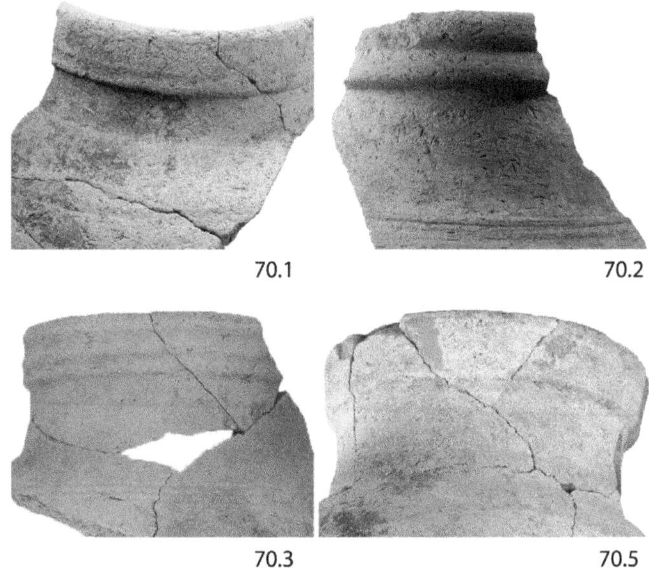

FIG. 2.35. The main Family 70 rim types. Not to scale.

Each of the different rim types has a thickened band, finished in a subtly different manner (Fig. 2.35). Presumably these thickened rims allowed for the secure fastening of a closure. A rounded base shape (Type 70.7) appears to have been by far the most frequent one amongst jars and is the only base shape that has been reliably associated with complete jar profiles. The high frequency of ambiguous base types (Family 65) in the assemblage might also designate these as potential jar bases. The best evidence for this would be a large Type 65.2 vessel base, which was re-used as a storage emplacement of Type 95.3 (p5019-2). The dimensions of this vessel strongly suggest that it would have originally belonged to a jar.

The widest point of jars tends to fall around the middle of the lower body, giving these vessels a bottom heavy, or 'baggy', appearance. Jars show a good deal of uniformity in size. Although rim diameters do vary across the entire assemblage (80–350mm; Avg. 155.6mm; n=1475), a sizeable majority of rim measurements (79.4%) fall in a tight cluster between 140–80mm (Fig. 2.37). Vessel volumes also show good consistency, falling into two corresponding sizes: two smaller vessels have an average capacity of 9.6L (9.33 and 9.9L) and four larger vessels yield an average capacity of 19.22L (Range 17.08–20.16L). Regardless of size, the height–width ratio of complete jars also shows a good degree of consistency (Range 1.31–1.54; Avg. 1.43; n=5).

All jar types regularly demonstrate incised and impressed decoration, in the form of single, double, or multiple concentric bands positioned around the shoulder of the vessel. It is difficult to establish any relationship between rim type and decorative type, other than that there does seem to be a general association between more elaborately formed rims (Types 70.2–3) and a higher number of impressed or incised bands.

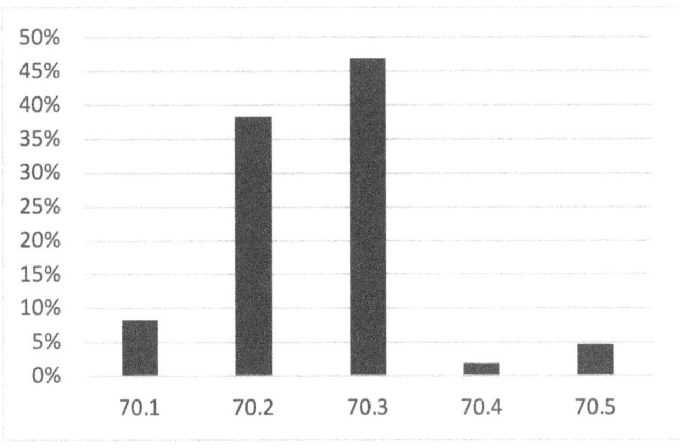

FIG. 2.36. Relative percentages of Family 70 rim types.

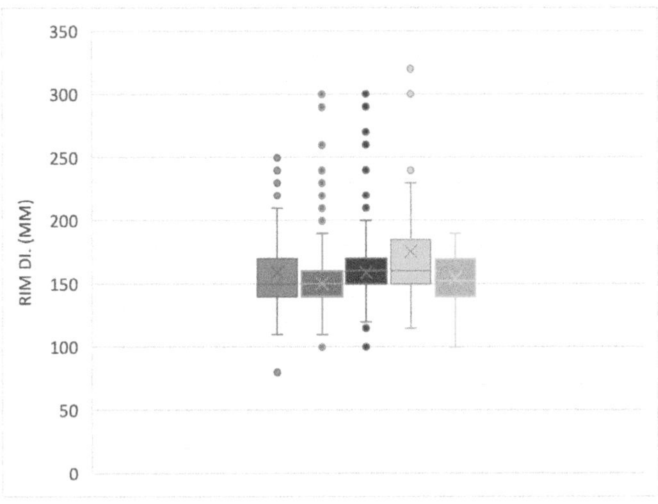

FIG. 2.37. Box and whisker chart showing the distribution of rim diameters for Family 70 types: 70.1 (blue), 70.2 (red), 70.3 (green), 70.4 (yellow), and 70.5 (orange). For conventions, see Fig. 2.1.

70.1 Thickened/squared rim band

Type 70.1 is a thickened, squared rim band. Although there is general consistency in the execution of this rim, minor variations are present between some squatter and thicker rims and other slightly longer and thinner rims. Type 70.1 is common (8.2%; n=152) and rim diameters for this type are typical for this family (Avg. 159.1mm; 80–250mm; n=128).

70.2 Thickened rim band, single groove

Type 70.2 consists of a thickened rim band, which has been waisted with a single groove. This is sometimes neatly done, but is often quite rough. This is the second most common type in this family (37.4%; n=696). Rim diameters are slightly below average for this family (Avg. 149.9mm; Range 100–300mm; n=565), but volumes of complete specimens are typical for the larger size range (17.08 and 19.98L).

70.3 Thickened rim band, multiple grooves

This type is similar to Type 70.2, but its rim bands are waisted multiple times. There are usually just two grooves, but more rarely also three or four. This is often neatly done, but is sometimes quite rough. Type 70.3 is the most common jar type (45.8%; n=853). Rim diameters are typical (Avg. 158.7mm; Range 100–300mm; n=668), and vessel volumes are associated with the larger size range (19.66L and 20.16L).

70.4 Round, thickened rim band

Type 70.4 is similar to Type 70.1, but exhibits a round rather than a squared rim band. Individual examples of this type do not show much consistency in the size or shape of the rim band. This type is only infrequently attested (1.8%; n=33) and rim diameters are on average quite large in comparison with other jar types (Avg. 175.5mm; Range 115–320mm; n=33).

70.5 Narrow, thickened rim band

This type is very similar to Type 70.1, but demonstrates a thinner, often elongated rim band. These are reasonably common in the assemblage (4.6%; n=86) and there is good consistency in the execution of individual examples. This consistency also carries through to the quite restricted rim diameters, which fall into quite a low and narrow range (Range 100–190mm; Avg. 154.7mm; n=72). One volume has been measured, which is typical of the smaller size range for jars (9.33L).

70.6 Incised/Decorated

Type 70.6 was created to accommodate a range of infrequent decorated jar sherds, such as those bearing relief bands with crescent incisions. This type category also includes body sherds with post-firing incised markings; for a further discussion of these, see §5.4.3.

70.7 Round base

This type consists of typical round bottom base sherds. These are hard to identify in the assemblage, as their lack of definition can easily be mistaken for the regular curvature of a body sherd. They are, therefore, vastly underrepresented here (n=4). The only way to reliably identify this shape type is by examination of the interior surface, which has a characteristic spiralling dimple (§4.2). In fact, as the vessel walls thin at this dimple, it often forms a point of weakness and results in vessel breakage and fragmentation.

70.8 Rough, flat base

Type 70.8 consists of only one example: an associated rim and base sherd. The base is of a flat, rough shape similar to ambiguous base Type 65.3, while the rolled, rounded rim is different to anything in the rest of the jar assemblage. Although the whole vessel could not be reconstructed, due to the coarse, friable nature of the fabric, it was probably larger than most other jar shapes, as demonstrated by the rim diameter of 350mm.

Family 75 (Plates 62–3): Hole-mouth, small

(n=46; 0.49% of the total assemblage)
Small, hole-mouth vessels are rare in the Tell Khaiber assemblage. These vessels have a round body shape, which flares outwards from directly below the rim, usually with no perceptible neck. This squat shape is reinforced by the height–width ratio of three complete vessels (Avg. 0.84: Range 0.69–0.93). Where bases survive, they are flat, rough, and usually string-cut (Fig. 2.38). The point of difference between the four different types in this family lies in the shape or orientation of the rim. Rim diameters are generally quite restricted (Avg. 102mm; Range 60–210mm; n=42).

75.1 Plain, round rim

This type demonstrates a plain, rounded rim that is oriented inwards. It is the most common type of this family (65.2%; n=30). Rim diameters have a narrow range, falling between 70 and 145mm (Avg. 101.7mm; n=29). One sherd (p6041-105) also has a small lug applied directly to the rim.

75.2 Thickened or squared rim

Type 75.2 is identical in shape to Type 75.1, but demonstrates a thickened, sometimes rolled rim band. There is little consistency in the shape of this band; it is sometimes triangular in shape and is sometimes squared and everted. Rim diameters vary (Range 80–210mm; Avg. 131.6mm; n=5). One volume has been measured at 0.76L.

FIG. 2.38. Type 75.2 (p8013-10).

75.3 Round, everted rim

Type 75.3 has a plain rounded rim, which projects outwards from the main body of the vessel. Just three sherds of this type have been identified, and these are always small and relatively fine in texture. Rim diameters are narrow and tightly clustered (Avg. 78.3mm; Range 60–95mm; n=3).

75.4 Uplifted neck, flat base

Type 75.4 is composed of vessels with short, vertically oriented necks. Three out of four examples of this type demonstrate 3–4 deep incised lines running around the neck. Rims are both simple and rounded, or are squared. Rim diameters are always narrow and tightly clustered (Avg. 88.2mm; Range 61–110mm; n=5), and the two volumes measured demonstrate restricted capacities (0.09 and 0.1L).

FIG. 2.39. Type 75.4 (p1167-6).

Family 80 (Plates 64–7): Hole-mouth, large

(n=228; 2.44% of the total assemblage)
Vessels of Family 80 are very similar in shape to those of Family 75. They are, however, larger in size, and are almost always produced of different fabrics (usually Fabric G). Vessels of this family always have inverted rim orientations with no perceptible neck, and, where preserved, demonstrate sharply curved or carinated lower bodies. This curve or carination leads to rounded bases with an interior dimple, similar to jar base Type 70.7. A number of vessels of this family carry one or more small, simple lugs, which are located irregularly around the circumference of the rim.

The exterior of these vessels is usually heavily wet-smoothed, as demonstrated by the heavy surface smudging. The three constituent types in this family are determined by rim shape (Types 80.1–2) and, where rims are not present, by the distinctive carinated body shape (Type 80.3). Regardless of rim shape, vessels of Family 80 exhibit comparatively large rim diameters (Avg. 203.4mm; Range 110–340mm; n=131) when compared to Family 75. Indeed, 84.2% (n=112) of Family 80 fall in a medium–large size range, between 140–260mm. The three volumes measured also show some consistency in size (Avg. 13.8L; Range 9.93–16.5L; n=3).

80.1 Plain, round rim

Type 80.1 has a plain, rounded rim, oriented inwards. It is the most common type of hole-mouth vessel, constituting 57% of the entire family (n=130). Yet, just one mostly complete profile has been identified, with a volume of approximately 15L. Rim diameters are consistent with the family as a whole (Avg. 210.4mm; Range 130–340mm; n=71).

FIG. 2.40. Types 80.1 (p1079-51), left, and 80.2 (p5063-1), right.

80.2 Thickened and squared rim

Type 80.2 has a thickened, squared rim band that tends to be roughly shaped. These vessels flare out directly below the rim to the vessel body. Occasionally, however, a small neck is perceptible below which the vessel projects outwards. This type is also common in the assemblage (32.5%: n=74). Rim diameters vary (110–280mm; Avg. 195.6mm; n=58). Two volumes have been measured (ca. 9.93 and 16.51L), which are consistent with that measured for Type 80.1.

80.3 Carinated body

Type 80.3 is composed of body sherds belonging to Family 80, which are identified purely on the basis of a typical sharp curve or carination on the lower body coupled with the distinctive cookpot fabric (Fabric G).

Family 85 (Plates 68–71): Vessel Stands

(n=272; 2.92% of the total assemblage)
Vessels in this family are always cylindrical in shape and generally demonstrate concave profiles, with the narrowest part of the vessel around the midpoint. Types 85.1–2 are hollow, with open bases, while Type 85.3 have flat, string-cut bases. Rim diameters tend to be slightly larger than base diameters, as is observed in the rim–base ratio for this family (Avg. 1.24; Range 0.9–1.62; n=67). Rims tend to be more neatly shaped and finished, while bases are often folded roughly on the interior, with little attention paid to finishing (see Fig. 4.6). Vessel stands are usually squat in shape, as is illustrated by the low height–width ratio (Avg. 0.66; Range 0.51–0.86; n=19).

FIG. 2.41. Types 85.1 (p6059-7), left, and 85.2 (p6136-90), right.

Separations between Types 85.1 and 85.2 are not based on the shape of the rim or base. Indeed, rim and base shapes within each type separation show a good deal of diversity. They are sometimes simple and rounded, but are often also thickened and shaped, sometimes with multiple grooves, similar to common jar rims (Type 70.1–3). Instead, the separation between Types 85.1 and 85.2 is made based on size (Fig. 2.41), while the separation of Type 85.3 is based on the shape of the base.

85.1 Small, cylindrical, open base

Type 85.1 constitutes cylindrical vessel stands with a rim and base diameter of <150mm. This type is the most common form of vessel stand (58.8%; n=160). Rims and bases are generally slightly thickened in comparison to the body. The average rim diameter of 104mm (Range 80–145mm; n=90) corresponds very well with the average maximum diameter of cups (Avg. 99.7mm; n=171), thus indicating the vessel family to which they were most likely functionally associated. Base diameters (Avg. 83.4mm; Range 70–110mm; n=53) are somewhat smaller than the average rim diameters; where both are preserved, the rim–base ratio average is 1.24 (Range 1–1.62; n=53).

85.2 Large, cylindrical, open base

Type 85.2 consists of cylindrical vessel stands with a rim and base diameter of ≥150. This type is less common than the smaller variant (35.7%; n=97). Rims and bases are usually thickened, and are sometimes also waisted in a similar manner to jar Types 70.2–3. This larger variant of vessel stand occasionally also exhibits impressed bands around the main body of the vessel. The curved, concave shape of the bodies can be exaggerated in comparison with Type 85.1. The average rim diameter of 235mm (Range 165–340mm; n=59) corresponds well with the average maximum diameter of jars (Avg. 287mm; Range 242–336mm; n=10) and even cookpots (Avg. 333mm; Range 310–346mm; n=3). Base diameters (Avg. 193.8mm; Range 155–245mm; n=20) of this type are marginally smaller than average rim diameters; where both are preserved, the rim–base ratio is on average 1.15 (Range 0.9–1.56; n=9).

85.3 Cylindrical, closed base

This type is constituted of cylindrical vessel stands with a flat, closed base. Type 85.3 is the most infrequent type of this family (n=10). Vessels of this type usually have a thickened, sometimes grooved, rim and a rough string-cut base. One individual example (p9020-114) also has five large applied lugs, positioned irregularly around the vessel's circumference, directly beneath the rim.

Unlike Types 85.1–2, which are separated based on rim diameter, variant Type 85.3 contains vessels of various sizes. Rim diameters are quite tight: smaller vessels, with an average rim diameter of 103mm (Range 96–110mm; n=2) and larger vessels with an average of 267mm (240–286mm; n=4). Base diameters correspond accordingly: smaller vessels have an average base diameter of 83.5mm (Range 82–85mm; n=2), while larger vessels have an average base diameter of 200mm (Range 175–280mm; n=8). Where both are preserved, the rim–base ratio is more pronounced than Types 85.1–2, averaging 1.38 (Range 1.17–1.52; n=6). As these vessels are closed and could potentially have held contents, volumes were also taken; the smaller variants yield an average capacity of 0.2L (Range 0.11–0.28L; n=2) and the larger variants hold an average of 1.8L (Range 1.11–2.25L; n=4).

Family 90 (Plates 72–5): Miscellaneous Types

(n=25; 0.27% of the total assemblage)

This vessel family represents several miscellaneous types that do not fit neatly into any of the other vessel categories presented above. Each individual type is represented by just a single example, or a small group of examples, that share specific similarities.

90.1 Lids and Stoppers

This type consists of small, shallow discs. These are infrequent in the assemblage (n=7) and show little internal standardisation. While some are clearly made or finished on the wheel, others are hand-moulded (Fig. 2.41). Each example has a flat or slightly curved bottom, sometimes indented in the centre, and a narrow point or platform on the top. The maximum diameter of these lids or stoppers is usually small (Avg. 71mm; Range 46–123mm; n=6) and corresponds well with the average rim diameters of bottles (Avg. 44mm), cups (74mm), jugs (94mm), and small hole-mouth vessels (102mm). They are generally too small to be associated with jars (Avg. 156mm). The upper platforms used for gripping the lid have an average diameter of 23mm (Range 5–35mm; n=7). Several examples of this vessel type show extensive wear, chipping, and even breakage around the maximum diameter, which is consistent with their proposed use.

FIG. 2.42. Type 90.1: wheel-made (p8008-9), left, and hand-moulded (p8013-9), right.

90.2 Sieves and Strainers

Type 90.2 is composed of small, shallow vessels with either a small perforation in the base or multiple small perforations in the walls (Fig. 2.43). They are extremely uncommon in the assemblage (n=3). The small size of these vessels is attested by the two recorded rim diameters (77mm and 130mm), and small volumes (0.04 and 0.24L). The perforated holes generally measure ca. 10–12mm.

90.3 Small, conical cup

This type is composed of just three small vessels, each formed into a small, roughly conical shape, with a flat string-cut base (Fig. 2.42). Rim diameters (Range: 56–79mm), base diameters (Range: 18–31mm), and volumes (0.03 and 0.06L) speak to this small size.

90.4 Miniatures

Type 90.4 is represented by miniature vessels. These vary significantly in their production: two have rough, rounded bases, and one has a neater, flat base. Each of these examples is manufactured of fragile, sunbaked clay.

90.5 Perforated cylinder

Only one vessel of Type 90.5 was found. It is a rough cylindrical vessel with an open base (68mm) and two perforations aligned horizontally on either side of the body (p3085-279). The vessel has a bitumen coated interior and is broken part way up the body.

90.6 Cylindrical, perforated base

Type 90.6 is represented by one vessel (p6163-34). It is a roughly cylindrical shape with a slightly inverted, straight sided body, which is broken, perhaps deliberately, part way up (Fig. 2.42). It has a perforated base (diam. 33mm), which is heavily worn on the interior surface. Around the exterior circumference of the base is an indented ledge (diam. 112mm), which is most likely designed to fit onto an associated stand.

90.7 Flasks

Type 90.7 is represented by two tall, steep-sided vessels with flat string-cut bases. One of these vessels flares outwards from the base to the widest point at the lower body (p9020-43) and has a small raised band that separates the neck from the body. The second vessel (p1078-76) tapers outwards from the base to reach its maximum width high at the shoulder, where it turns sharply inwards to the neck. Both vessels have similar capacities (0.36 and 0.44L).

90.8 Supported trays/basins

Two very different vessels constitute this type. The first is a fragment of a well-made vessel (p8021-11), with a very large rim diameter (>600mm) and evidence for a broken ring base. Stepped in from the thick squared rim is a ledge which steps down to an interior surface embedded with a large concentration of thick, coarse grit inclusions. This would have formed a very effective grinding platform. The second vessel of this type (p1080-14) is a rough, shallow basin with a thick rounded rim (diam. 310mm) and a curved body. On the exterior base, there is evidence for three irregular applied platforms, radiating from the centre, which have subsequently broken off. Just a few centimetres in from the rim, the interior surface is extremely worn, presumably as a consequence of extensive grinding activities; the vessel has a volume of ca. 2L.

FIG. 2.43. A selection of miscellaneous vessel types in Family 90.

90.9 Tripod

One finely manufactured vessel fragment represents this type (p3185-115). It is small and shallow, with a rim diameter of 150mm, and has the remnants of a broken leg just below the carination of the body; this would most likely have formed one of perhaps three legs of an original tripod base. The fine, dark fabric is unique in the Tell Khaiber assemblage, and its surfaces are heavily burnished (Fig. 2.43).

Family 95 (Plates 76–7): Re-used Vessels

(n=22; 0.24% of the total assemblage)

Family 95 is comprised of vessels that have been modified or manipulated so as to depart from their original form, presumably in order to be re-used for tasks that they were not initially designed to fulfil. Each type is represented either by an individual example, or a small group of examples that demonstrate specific patterns of manipulation or wear.

95.1 Lids or Stoppers

Type 95.1 consists of vessel bases that have been deliberately chipped around the circumference of the body to create shallow disc shapes (Fig. 2.44). Specific vessel bases are usually chosen for such treatment: cup or jug bases (n=5), and tall pedestal bases (n=2). Average maximum diameters for these vessels, once chipped to shape, is 73mm (Range 44–110mm; n=7). This is almost identical to the average maximum diameters of Type 90.1 lids and stoppers. The upper diameters of these reworked vessels, which represent the bases of original vessels, average 37mm (Range 11–55mm; n=7). This is also in line with diameters of the upper platforms of Type 90.1, thus suggesting an analogous function.

95.2 Grinding implements

This type is composed of just three sherds that have not necessarily been deliberately or strategically modified, but have been used as ad hoc grinding implements. One cup (p1094-192), which is preserved up to the neck, has a very heavily ground base (Fig. 2.44); the middle of the vessel is also smoothed and discoloured, perhaps consistent with the tight gripping of the vessel during such activities. The other two examples demonstrate heavy attritional wear on the interior surface of a complete base (p8013-7), as well as on the angle of a broken base sherd (p1079-494).

95.3 Open vessels

Type 95.3 consists of a number of different cup, jug, and jar bases that have been deliberately chipped around the body to create open vessels of various sizes (Fig. 2.44). Eight bases comprise this type, and these vary significantly in 'rim' diameter (Range 58–266mm; Avg. 109.6mm; n=8) and in volume (0.01–3.06L; Avg. 0.48L; n=8). This range most likely reflects the variety of uses to which these reworked vessels were put.

95.4 Supports

Three examples fit into this type. One is a pithos with an applied ring base (p6122-1; diam. 222mm) which was chipped directly above the ring base (Type 25.5) and re-used as a door socket. The other two examples are solid pedestal bases with incised relief bands and narrow maximum diameters (90mm and 120mm). These pedestal bases are chipped where the vessel originally flared out, and both demonstrate extensive wear on their upper platformed surface.

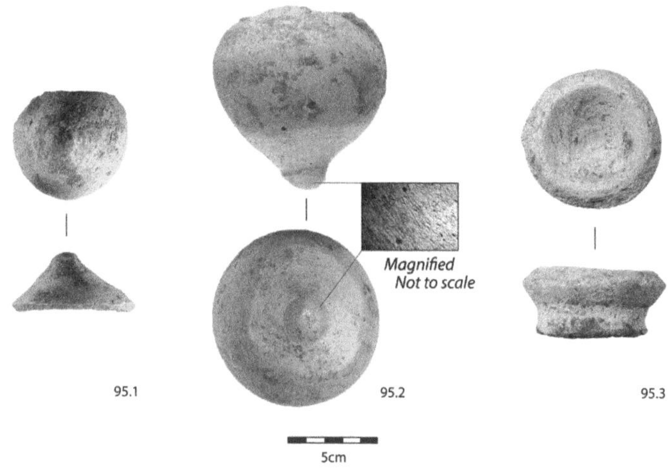

FIG. 2.44. A selection of re-used vessel types in Family 95.

2.2 Fabric Typology

The fabric of pottery vessels is composed of the fine mass of clay and the coarse fraction.[8] The fine mass is the raw clay body, while the coarse fraction is made up of non-plastic inclusions, either incidental to the clay or deliberately added (Roux 2019: 30–40). The nature and density of inclusions can not only help to inform upon the original clay source, and thus the places in which specific vessels were made (Orton and Hughes 2013: 187; Rice 1987: 31–79), but can also confer to us the choices made by ancient potters to instil their vessels with particular use-related properties: strength (e.g. Bronitsky and Hamer 1986; Rye 1976), (im)permeability (e.g. Rye 1981: 129–31; Skibo et al. 1989: 129–31), and thermal stress resistance (e.g. Frink and Harry 2008; Steponaitis 1984).

What is meant here by the term *inclusions* are those non-plastics—or the voids left by their original presence—in the cross-section of a fresh fracture. As a distinction could not always be made between non-plastic additives deliberately introduced by the potter, usually referred to as *temper*, and those present naturally within the clay matrix, it is considered safer throughout this volume to speak of inclusions.

Cross-sections of Tell Khaiber's fabrics were analysed both macroscopically and microscopically (×60 magnification). Initially, for expediency, bulk diagnostic sherds were separated into three broad fabric categories based on visual analysis: gritty, grit and chaff, and chaffy. This was considered to encompass the broad differences amongst what was a rather homogenous collection of fabrics. To capture finer differences, all illustrated sherds were also furnished with a more detailed qualitative description of inclusion types, which provided information on their approximate percentages within the clay matrix. In the 2016 and 2017 seasons, a digital microscope (Supereyes B008) was also employed in the analysis of vessel fabrics. Microscopic fabric photos were taken for a sample of approximately 500 vessels or diagnostic sherds.[9]

The following constituent inclusions were identified through both macroscopic and microscopic analysis of the Tell Khaiber assemblage:

Organics. Plant parts which, depending on the nature of the firing atmosphere, either remain present in the clay matrix as a white skeleton, or are attested by a void where they were burnt away. Although organics can occur naturally in the alluvial clays, they could form also deliberate additions to improve the clay's plasticity, and thus workability. Organics may have derived from farm waste, such as chopped straw, reeds, or manure, during the treatment and preparation of the clay body (van As and Jacobs 1992: 541).

Calcite. Small, white, rounded particles. These are present naturally in calcareous clays and are quite rare in the Tell Khaiber assemblage. When the firing temperature rises above a certain point (700–900°C), calcite minerals 'degass' and alter in colour and composition (Velde and Druc 1999: 103, 143–4, 253). These particles are therefore more difficult to identify in high-fired wares.

Fine Sand. Small, rounded mineral inclusions of an even size and in a range of different colours (red, brown, orange, black etc.). These inclusions are generally rounded in shape and occur naturally in riverine clays.

Coarse Sand. Appearance as with fine sand, but occur in larger sizes, often with angular to sub-angular edges. They sometimes also contain larger translucent particles.

'Grog'. Large particles of clay or crushed pottery, usually of a slightly different colour or texture to the surrounding clay body. When encountered at Tell Khaiber, this 'grog' tends to be composed either of added clay, or of incidental lumps of poorly worked clay, rather than crushed sherd material (Herbert and Smith 2010).

When the above inclusions regularly occurred in specific combinations and/or concentrations, they constituted a 'fabric type'. Eight fabric types were recognised in the Tell Khaiber assemblage, which can be summarised as follows:

Fabric A: well filtered, very fine sand;
Fabric B: medium–coarse sand;
Fabric C: fine–medium calcite;
Fabric D: fine sand, with some fine organics or voids;
Fabric E: coarsely chopped, well preserved organic 'skeletons';
Fabric F: dense, coarsely chopped organics or voids;
Fabric G: very coarse sand and/or grog;
Fabric H: soft fabric with fine sand, organics or voids, and often containing poorly mixed agglomerations of clay.

More detailed descriptions of these fabric types are presented below. Once identified from the microscopic images, these fabric types could be recognised macroscopically in the field. Consequently, recording of diagnostics according to the above categories was integrated into the bulk diagnostics database during the 2017 field season, replacing the initial, lower-resolution criteria previously discussed.

Fabric A

Fabric A contains very fine (<0.1mm) rounded to well-rounded sand particles. These particles comprise just <5% of the clay matrix and are distributed evenly. Particles are not generally visible to the naked eye, but are visible under a high-resolution microscope. This testifies to the fact that they occurred naturally within the source body, with the larger sand particles having likely been filtered during a careful process of levigation. The result is quite a fine

[8] The descriptive criteria and associated terminology in the following fabric descriptions are based on Orton and Hughes (2013: Appendix I, 275–85).

[9] Since the clarity of the image varied between sherds, it was necessary to adjust the scale of magnification for each image to compensate. Images were routinely taken at a magnification of between ×100 and ×150.

texture, which, when freshly broken, yields a smooth cross-section. No organics and few air pockets are present, which demonstrates that the clay was thoroughly worked.

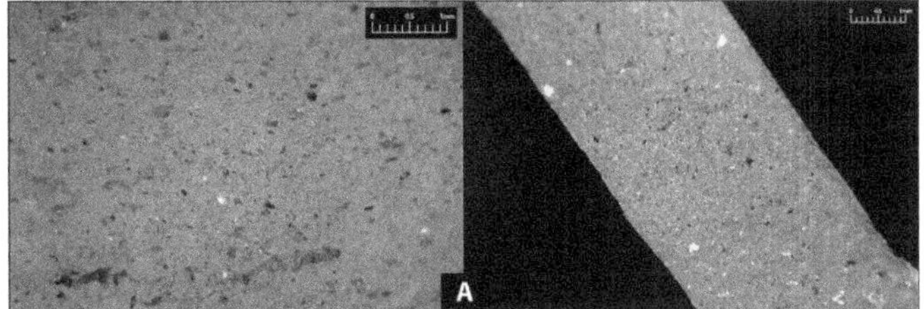

FIG. 2.45. Digital microscope images of Fabric A (p1079-98 and p3064-659).

Fabric B

Fabric B contains fine–medium (<0.5mm) rounded to sub-rounded sand particles. These particles comprise 10–20% of the clay matrix and are generally distributed evenly. Particles are just about visible to the naked eye. They likely occur naturally within the source body, and have not undergone the same level of careful filtering as specimens of Fabric A. The texture is fine–medium, and, when freshly broken, yields a smooth cross-section. Very few organics or air pockets are attested, suggesting that the clay body was thoroughly worked.

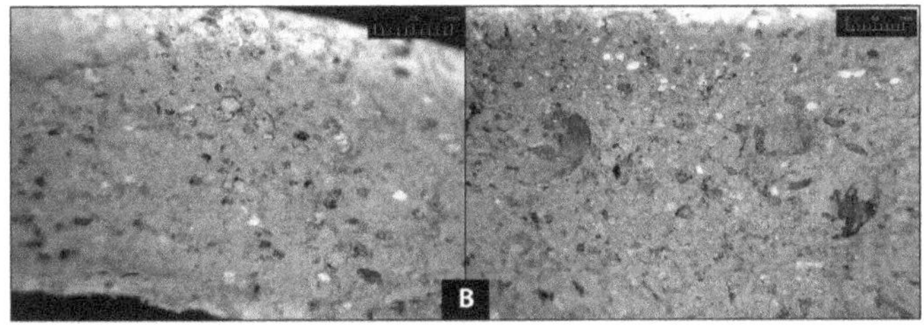

FIG. 2.46. Digital microscope images of Fabric B (p1094-280 and p3119-51).

Fabric C

Fabric C contains fine–medium (<0.5mm) rounded to sub-rounded sand particles. Amongst these inclusions are also white calcite particles. These are generally fine but occasionally take on a coarser form (0.5–1mm). Sand particles comprise 10–20% of the clay matrix, while calcite particles constitute ca. 5%. They are generally distributed evenly and are just about visible to the naked eye. Their size and shape suggests that they likely occurred naturally within the clay source body. The texture of this fabric is fine–medium, and, when freshly broken, yields a smooth cross-section. Very few organics or air pockets are attested, suggesting that the clay body was thoroughly worked. Calcite particles are only present in low-fired vessels with pink fabrics. In higher fired vessels, the chemical composition of the calcite is altered as it begins to decompose, with the consequent mutation no longer rendering it identifiable (Rye 1981: 33).

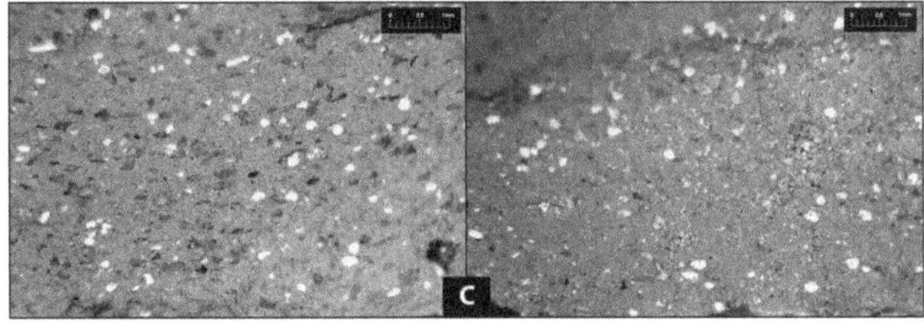

FIG. 2.47. Digital microscope images of Fabric C (p6150-299 and p1080-1).

Fabric D

Fabric D often contains fine–medium (<0.5mm) rounded to sub-rounded sand particles, as well as numerous fine–medium voids (<1mm). In combination, these elements comprise ca. 10–20% of the clay matrix. The sand particles occur naturally within the source body. The voids, on the other hand, might be the product of several processes: they could represent fine organics, occurring naturally in the source body, fine organics present in animal dung that was added during preparation of the clay, or they might simply represent incomplete working of the clay body, leaving air pockets in the final product. The texture varies: freshly broken examples of this fabric type usually yield a reasonably smooth cross-section, but can sometimes be more irregular and friable.

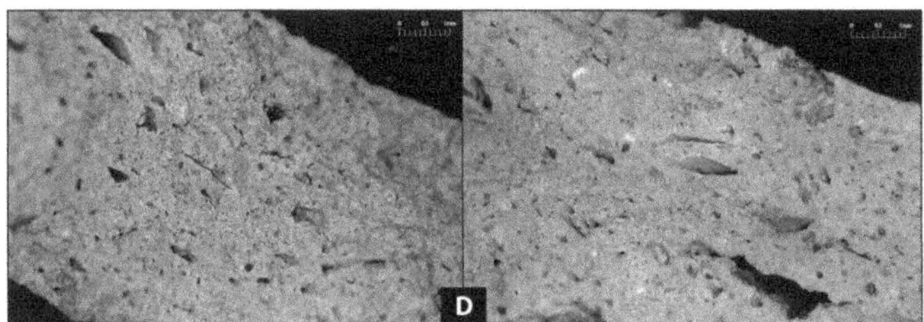

FIG. 2.48. Digital microscope images of Fabric D (p1096-462 and p8000-13).

Fabric E

Fabric E often contains fine–medium (<0.5mm) rounded sand and/or calcite particles, as well as rough straw or reed skeletons, occasionally reaching >2mm. The sand is usually evenly distributed, comprising 5–10% of the clay matrix, but the straw or reed inclusions are more irregular in their number and distribution. While the sand occurs naturally, the organic inclusions are roughly chopped and were likely added deliberately as temper. The texture is usually fine–medium

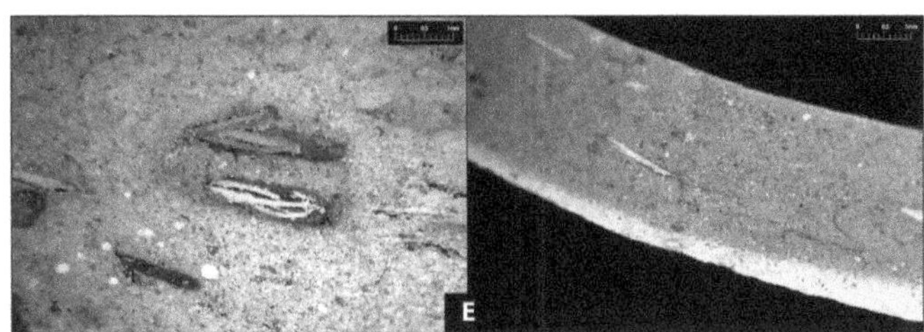

FIG. 2.49. Digital microscope images of Fabric E (p1080-6 and p3064-657).

and, when freshly broken, yields a smooth cross-section. The lack of air pockets suggests that the clay body was generally well worked. The skeletal straw or reed inclusions only tend to occur in low-fired vessels with a cream-pink colour. In higher fired vessels, the organic material can burn away, leaving large voids in its place.

Fabric F

Although some fine–medium sand particles are present, Fabric F predominantly contains a dense concentration of large, rough organic inclusions of ca. 1–5mm in length. Depending on the firing temperature, these organic inclusions are either preserved, or else are attested by large elongated voids. Generally, these organics or voids are irregularly distributed, and comprise >20–30% of the clay matrix. The roughly chopped material is no doubt deliberately added to the clay body as temper during preparation. The texture of this Fabric is friable, and, when freshly broken, exhibits a hackly, stepped cross-section. The numerous air pockets suggest that the clay body was not thoroughly worked.

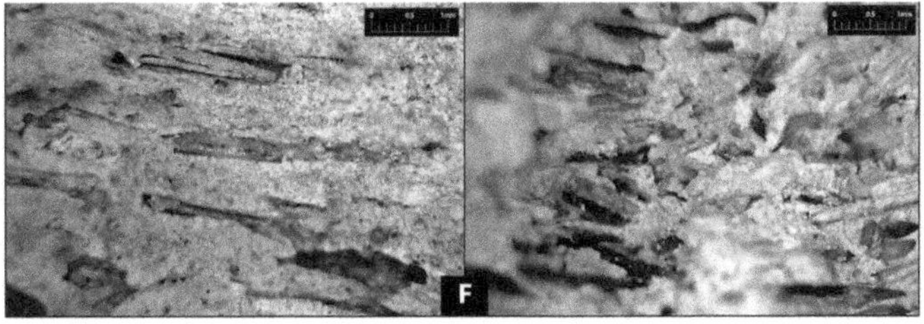

FIG. 2.50. Digital microscope images of Fabric F (p1092-42 and p3054-252).

Fabric G

Fabric G is significantly different from the other fabrics in that it is composed of a range of medium–very coarse, (ca. 0.25–3mm) non-plastic inclusions. These vary in their density. Some contain evenly distributed medium to coarse inclusions, comprising 20–30% of the clay matrix, while others demonstrate more irregularly distributed, coarse–very coarse inclusions, comprising just 5–10%. Inclusions are most commonly of a rounded, translucent (quartz?) material. However, sub-rounded to angular calcite, basalt(?), and undissolved clay inclusions are more infrequently attested. Rough organic inclusions and voids, both fine (<0.25) and coarse (>0.5mm), are occasionally also present.

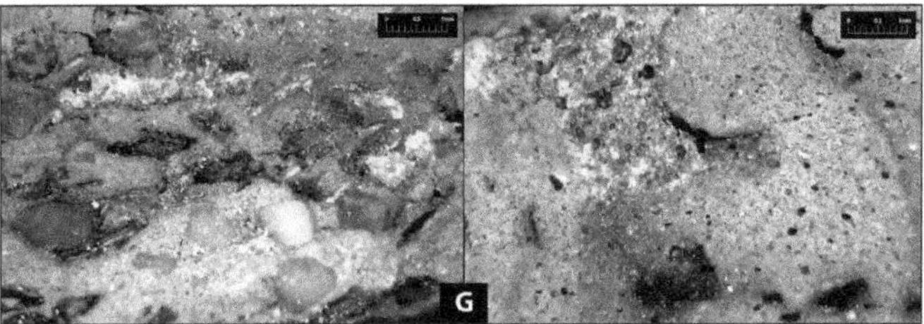

FIG. 2.51. Digital microscope images of Fabric G (p1139-105 and p3123-3).

The texture is rather friable, and, when freshly broken, exhibits a hackly, stepped cross-section.

Fabric H

Fabric H contains some fine (<0.1mm) rounded sand particles, as well as numerous fine–medium voids (0.1–0.5mm), and rough organic inclusions (>0.5mm). In some instances, there are also irregularly distributed coarse (0.5–1mm), rounded conglomerations of clay, of a different colour and consistency to the rest of the clay matrix. Combined, these elements comprise ca. 10–30% of the clay matrix. While the sand particles occur naturally within the clay source body, the voids could be the product of several processes: they could represent fine organics, occurring naturally in the source body, fine organics present in animal dung that was added during preparation of the clay, or they might simply represent incomplete working of the clay body which left air pockets in the final product. The rough organics, when present, were most likely deliberate additions by the potter, while the conglomerations of clay may represent particles that were not thoroughly dissolved during levigation (van As and Jacobs 1992: 533). When freshly broken, the texture exhibits an irregular hackly cross-section.

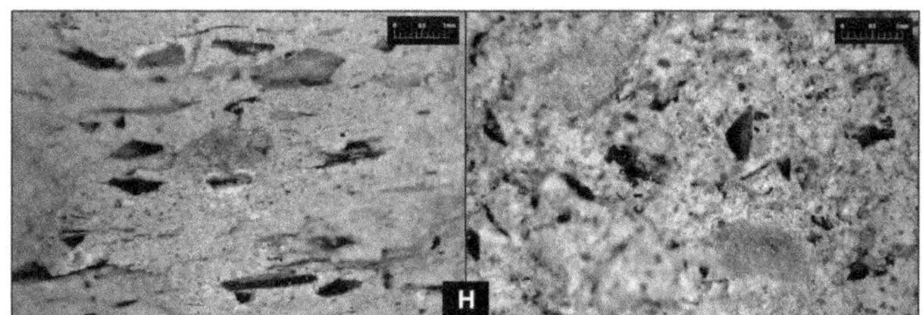

FIG. 2.52. Digital microscope images of Fabric H (p1114-26 and p8047-1).

3. Internal Chronology and Inter-Regional Connections

Past approaches have presented second millennium Mesopotamian pottery as a continuous and resilient craft tradition (after Armstrong and Gasche 2014; Ayoub 1982), which spanned the Old Babylonian and Kassite periods largely unchanged. The comprehensive Tell Khaiber typology presented in Chapter 2 and the plates, represents our first stratified evidence for the centuries of the mid-second millennium. This enables a detailed contextualisation of the Tell Khaiber material with regards to two central parameters:

- Internal shape development: how does the assemblage develop through the site's occupational sequence?
- Inter-regional context: how is the assemblage situated within its contemporary cultural context, on both a regional and interregional level?

3.1 Internal Shape Development

Tell Khaiber's primary occupation is separated according to two main levels (Level 1 and the later Level 2). This division is determined according to the main architectural developments of the Fortified Building, with the architectural reconfiguration of the southern unit and the addition of the northern unit marking the start of Level 2. Within these levels are further subdivisions—Level 1 (Phase 1) and Level 2 (Phase 2.1–3)—which are based on smaller-scale architectural developments and occupational build-up. The stratigraphic relationship between this primary sequence is therefore known. Less well understood are several further Mixed Phases, which consist of material generated from contexts that cannot be reliably positioned stratigraphically. These include: surface scraping of the upper deposits across the mound (=MSu), the deposits of the Tower rooms (=MT), intrusive burials across the Fortified Building (=MB), and two soundings in the direct vicinity (=MSo). The Eastern Houses (=EH) to the southeast of the Fortified Building are also included in this analysis.[9] The analysis in this section is based on statistics for all families and types presented in Chapter 2, which are separated according to the different phases of the site presented above (Table 3.5). In order to obviate the risk of confusion between functional and chronological variability, relative percentages of each family according to phase are presented in Table 3.1. Relative frequencies are used to mitigate potential biases in vessel count, as discussed in §2.1.

In general, vessel families demonstrate strong consistency in their chronological distribution, thus suggesting functional consistency through time (see Chapter 5). Any changes are therefore likely to be chronological, rather than functionally driven. In order to tease out chronological indicators, Table 3.2 presents the same data as Table 3.5, but in a compressed format. It omits those types that offer no significant temporal distribution, thus bringing to the fore those types that show notable temporal variability.

The types included in Table 3.2 can be roughly divided into two groups:

Type fossils. Those types that are restricted to one or two phases or do not occur before or after a given phase. These are the most useful for defining chronological differences, but are fairly rare in the Tell Khaiber assemblage.

Fluctuating types. Those types that occur in several contiguous periods, with a maximum frequency in one. Fluctuating types can only be effectively identified in relation to the wider type distributions. Accordingly, the maximum relative frequency of each type is highlighted in Table 3.2.

Before analysing the internal ceramic sequence for Tell Khaiber, it must be noted that the evidence available for each phase varies significantly. We have relatively little data for Level 1 (n=187), for instance, since it consists largely of incidental or deliberate packing material in preparation for Level 2. It is difficult to make meaningful assessments from this small sample. We do, however, have an abundance of varied material for the different phases of Level 2 (n=4688), which can be broadly associated with *in situ* depositions or

[9] For more detail on these levels and phases, see Moon ed., fothcoming.

	Phase 1		Phase 2.1		Phase 2.2		Phase 2.3		Stratigraphically Uncertain									
									MSu		MT		MB		MSo		EH	
Family	#	%	#	%	#	%	#	%	#	%	#	%	#	%	#	%	#	%
5	20	10.7	279	19.1	432	16.5	80	13.2	87	7.0	194	15.1	5	10.2	13	7.4	49	11.7
10	14	7.5	41	2.8	69	2.6	20	3.3	24	1.9	48	3.7	1	2.0	5	2.8	4	1.0
15	11	5.9	105	7.2	133	5.1	28	4.6	74	5.9	76	5.9	-	-	22	12.5	13	3.1
20	-	-	6	0.4	13	0.5	2	0.3	7	0.6	6	0.5	-	-	2	1.1	1	0.2
25	13	7.0	68	4.6	170	6.5	36	6.0	111	8.9	31	2.4	7	14.3	16	9.1	17	4.1
30	-	-	4	0.3	13	0.5	4	0.7	5	0.4	1	0.1	-	-	-	-	-	-
35	2	1.1	28	1.9	65	2.5	12	2.0	16	1.3	45	3.5	-	-	1	0.6	6	1.4
40	-	-	-	-	-	-	-	-	51	4.1	1	0.1	-	-	4	2.3	1	0.2
45	1	0.5	3	0.2	5	0.2	2	0.3	7	0.6	4	0.3	-	-	-	-	-	-
50	29	15.5	197	13.5	368	14.1	71	11.7	230	18.4	225	17.5	8	16.3	32	18.2	86	20.5
55	10	5.3	57	3.9	97	3.7	20	3.3	59	4.7	47	3.7	5	10.2	11	6.3	25	6.0
60	20	10.7	233	15.9	350	13.4	92	15.2	62	5.0	186	14.5	12	24.5	7	4.0	110	26.3
65	21	11.2	110	7.5	180	6.9	51	8.4	170	13.6	112	8.7	1	2.0	4	2.3	9	2.1
70	38	20.3	234	16.0	537	20.5	130	21.5	263	21.1	232	18.0	9	18.4	45	25.6	87	20.8
75	-	-	9	0.6	19	0.7	8	1.3	3	0.2	4	0.3	-	-	-	-	-	-
80	3	1.6	31	2.1	78	3.0	19	3.1	34	2.7	32	2.5	-	-	-	-	5	1.2
85	5	2.7	53	3.6	81	3.1	20	3.3	38	3.0	36	2.8	1	2.0	13	7.4	6	1.4
90	-	-	3	0.2	4	0.2	6	1.0	6	0.5	4	0.3	-	-	1	0.6	-	-
95	-	-	3	0.2	7	0.3	4	0.7	4	0.3	4	0.3	-	-	-	-	-	-
Total	187	100	1464	100	2621	100	605	100	1251	100	1287	100	49	100	176	100	419	100

TABLE 3.1. Count and relative percentages of each vessel family by phase.

incidental patterns of discard during the Fortified Building's primary period of occupation. We also have a substantial number of sherds (n=2759) from Mixed Deposits that are more difficult to determine stratigraphically.

The following discussion of phases will be based primarily on shape changes. As discussed in §2.2, analysis of fabrics was not consistently high-resolution enough from the onset of recording to enable a detailed and reliable breakdown. From the evidence available for Fabrics A–H (Table 3.3, Fig. 3.1), limited conclusions can be taken. These suggest a small *floruit* of finer wares (Fabric A) in Phases 2.1–2, as well as a broad uptick in heavily organic tempered vessels (Fabric F) and vessels with relatively poorly worked fabrics (Fabric H) throughout the site's occupational sequence, culminating in the high percentages observed in Phase 2.3 and the mixed surface deposits. Other than these observations, the relative percentages of different fabric types remain consistent throughout the site's occupational phases. This is likely the consequence of a tight link between clay preparation practices and vessel shape (§4.1.2), which renders fabric analysis a poorly refined chronological indicator in the mid-second millennium.

3.1.1 Levels 1–2 (Phases 1–2.3)

Few stylistic changes occur between the different primary phases of occupation at Tell Khaiber. Examining the difference in percentages of each family and type between Phase 1–2.3 provides a general picture of stylistic consistency. Two infrequently attested type fossils help to provide internal consistency to the sequence. The first is small, hole-mouth vessels of Type 75.4, which, although encountered in small numbers, are entirely restricted to Level 2 (Phases 2.1–3). Indeed, the two complete examples of this type are found at the onset of Phase 2.2 at opposite sides of the Fortified Building, lying on respective surfaces in Room 314 (p1167-6) and Room 152 (p8083-22). The second type is high-shouldered bottle Type 45.2, which occurs only in Phases 2.2 and 2.3.

Other than this, to identify chronologically fluctuating types we must rely on more subtle changes perceivable in the relative percentages of different shapes (Table 3.2). Larger vessels demonstrate the least change throughout the main occupational sequence. Pithoi, for instance, retained their squat, rounded shape, with large rim diameters, while most jars maintained a bottom-heavy, 'baggy' shape, with a defined neck and narrow rim diameter (Avg. 145–55mm). With jars, grooved Type 70.3 is the most common throughout these phases, and particularly

	Phase 1		Phase 2.1		Phase 2.2		Phase 2.3		Stratigraphically Uncertain									
									MSu		MT		MB		MSo		EH	
Family	#	%	#	%	#	%	#	%	#	%	#	%	#	%	#	%	#	%
5.1	17	9.1	146	10.0	303	11.6	66	10.9	52	4.2	113	8.8	3	6.1	9	5.1	24	5.7
5.2	3	1.6	127	8.7	122	4.7	7	1.2	11	0.9	77	6.0	1	2.0	-	-	23	5.5
5.3	-	-	-	-	1	0.0	2	0.3	-	-	-	-	1	2.0	4	2.3	-	-
5.4	-	-	1	0.1	3	0.1	-	-	11	0.9	3	0.2	-	-	-	-	2	0.5
5.5	-	-	-	-	-	-	-	-	12	1.0	-	-	-	-	-	-	-	-
10.1	10	5.3	14	1.0	36	1.4	11	1.8	13	1.0	22	1.7	1	2.0	3	1.7	2	0.5
10.2	4	2.1	24	1.6	27	1.0	7	1.2	5	0.4	19	1.5	-	-	1	0.6	1	0.2
15.1	11	5.9	105	7.2	125	4.8	24	4.0	49	3.9	69	5.4	-	-	17	9.7	13	3.1
15.2	-	-	-	-	8	0.3	4	0.7	25	2.0	6	0.5	-	-	5	2.8		
25.1	8	4.3	34	2.3	66	2.5	14	2.3	54	4.3	15	1.2	5	10.2	6	3.4	11	2.6
25.3	1	0.5	4	0.3	6	0.2	6	1.0	14	1.1	2	0.2	-	-	2	1.1		
40.1	-	-	-	-	-	-	-	-	17	1.4	-	-	-	-	-	-	-	-
40.2	-	-	-	-	-	-	-	-	29	2.3	1	0.1	-	-	4	2.3	1	0.2
40.3	-	-	-	-	-	-	-	-	4	0.3	-	-	-	-	-	-	-	-
45.2	-	-	-	-	1	0.0	2	0.3	-	-	2	0.2	-	-	-	-	-	-
45.4	-	-	-	-	-	-	-	-	1	0.1	-	-	-	-	-	-	-	-
50.1	7	3.7	47	3.2	54	2.1	18	3.0	62	5.0	46	3.6	1	2.0	2	1.1	16	3.8
50.2	2	1.1	11	0.8	24	0.9	8	1.3	30	2.4	25	1.9	2	4.1	14	8.0	33	7.9
50.3	2	1.1	3	0.2	23	0.9	2	0.3	15	1.2	14	1.1	3	6.1	15	8.5	13	3.1
50.4	1	0.5	26	1.8	89	3.4	9	1.5	16	1.3	16	1.2	-	-	-	-	9	2.1
50.5	14	7.5	105	7.2	167	6.4	29	4.8	86	6.9	120	9.3	2	4.1	1	0.6	14	3.3
50.6	1	0.5	-	-	5	0.2	-	-	4	0.3	2	0.2	-	-	-	-	1	0.2
50.7	-	-	-	-	-	-	-	-	5	0.4	-	-	-	-	-	-	-	-
55.3	-	-	-	-	1	0.0	-	-	3	0.2	-	-	-	-	4	2.3	-	-
65.1	8	4.3	86	5.9	141	5.4	44	7.3	134	10.7	70	5.4	1	2.0	4	2.3	7	1.7
65.2	13	7.0	19	1.3	32	1.2	4	0.7	29	2.3	36	2.8	-	-	-	-	2	0.5
70.1	-	-	17	1.2	41	1.6	9	1.5	26	2.1	12	0.9	1	2.0	3	1.7	5	1.2
70.2	21	11.2	79	5.4	206	7.9	40	6.6	80	6.4	71	5.5	4	8.2	34	19.3	49	11.7
70.3	14	7.5	123	8.4	241	9.2	67	11.1	124	9.9	127	9.9	3	6.1	6	3.4	31	7.4
75.4	-	-	1	0.1	2	0.1	1	0.2	-	-	-	-	-	-	-	-	-	-

TABLE 3.2. Condensed version of Table 3.5, containing only the types showing meaningful temporal patterns. The highest relative percentage of each type is shown in red.

so in Phase 2.3 (11.1%); Type 70.2 is also common (11.2 > 6.6%), while Type 70.1 shows consistently low, although increasing frequency (1.2 > 2.1%). Throughout these phases, there is also a noticeable increase in base Type 65.1 (4.3 > 7.3%), attendant with a decrease in the frequency of finished base Type 65.2 (7 > 0.7%). Type 65.2 may, in Phase 1, have been associated with jars (Family 70), as is the case with Late Old Babylonian jars, for example at Tell ed-Der (Armstrong and Gasche 2014: pl. 125–6). The diminishing occurrence of this type in Level 2 might therefore suggest that, after Phase 1, there was a general change in the style of jar base, moving from stable Type 65.2 to rough, unfinished Type 65.1 or, more likely, rounded Type 70.7.

Tablewares show more stylistic variation. While carinated bowl Type 5.1 remains the most common bowl form throughout Tell Khaiber's primary occupation, the frequency of bowls with a rounded body shape (Type 5.2) increases after Phase 1, particularly in Phase 2.1 (8.7%). Conversely, although bowl Types 10.1–2 are typical diagnostic features throughout, the frequency drops from a combined 7.4% in Phase 1 to 3% in Phase 2.3. Furthermore, while flat bowl bases (Type 15.1) decrease slightly (5.9–4%), platformed bowl bases (Type 15.2) start to appear in small numbers in Phases 2.2–3. Cups also provide fine-grained differences. Although almost all cups from Phases 1–2.3 show the same rounded body shape

Fabric	A		B		C		D		E		F		G		H		TOTAL	
Phase	#	%	#	%	#	%	#	%	#	%	#	%	#	%	#	%	#	%
1	1	0.9	7	6.2	2	1.8	17	15.0	38	33.6	32	28.3	-	-	16	14.2	113	100
2.1	19	4.5	22	5.2	19	4.5	51	12	166	39.0	112	26.3	4	0.9	33	7.8	426	100
2.2	39	3.8	45	4.3	40	3.8	137	13.2	386	37.1	297	28.5	15	1.4	82	7.9	1041	100
2.3	-	-	2	3.23	1	1.6	6	9.7	19	30.7	25	40.3	-	-	9	14.5	62	100
MT	6	2.5	23	9.6	2	0.8	30	12.6	120	50.2	34	14.2	5	2.1	19	8.0	239	100
MSu	4	1.2	13	3.9	9	2.7	57	17.1	97	29.1	82	24.6	2	0.6	69	20.7	333	100
MSo	5	2.8	5	2.8	6	3.4	21	11.9	60	34.1	54	30.7	-	-	25	14.2	176	100

TABLE 3.3. Relative frequencies of fabric types according to phase.

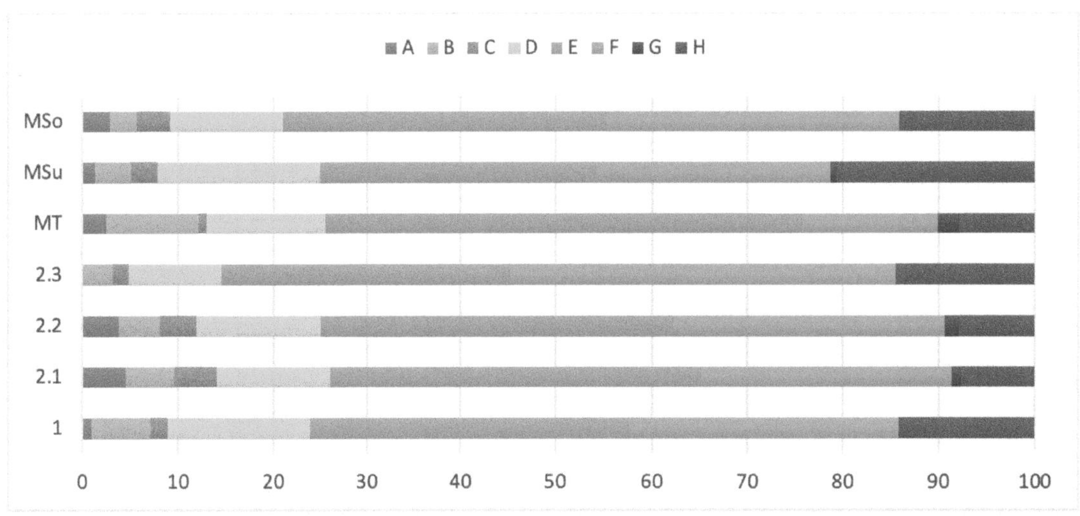

FIG. 3.1. Relative frequencies of fabric types according to phase, based on Table 3.3.

and short, well defined neck, foot shapes shift in relative frequency through time. While cups with unstable feet are common in all phases, the frequency of Type 50.4 reaches a peak of 3.4% in Phase 2.2, while Type 50.5 decreases slightly between Phase 1 and 2.3 (7.5 > 4.8%). Stable footed types (50.1–3) remain comparatively infrequent throughout these phases of primary occupation (combined 5.9 > 4.6%).

3.1.2 The Sealand Period Assemblage

Despite an episode of major architectural renovation between Levels 1 and 2, as well as substantial accumulation of occupation debris, only subtle stylistic changes can be identified between the earliest phase at Tell Khaiber (Phase 1) and those later in the primary occupational sequence (Phase 2.3) (Fig. 3.2). Likewise, there is no hint of those shapes typical of the Kassite period (see below) in these primary occupation deposits.

Since each particular phase was probably quite short lived, this supports a critically important resolution: that the Tell Khaiber evidence defines a coherent and homogenous 'Sealand Period' assemblage. The definitive shape types of this primary period of Sealand occupation are: carinated and rounded bowls (Types 5.1–2), bowls with grooves beneath the rim (Types 10.1–2), cups with unstable nipple and button feet (Types 50.4–5), and jars with grooved rim bands (Type 70.2–3) (Fig. 3.3).

Family	Number of Types
5	3
10	4
15	2
20	2
25	5
30	3
35	5
45	3
50	6
55	3
60	3
65	4
70	8
75	4
80	3
85	3
Total	63

TABLE 3.4. Number of different Sealand period types associated with each vessel family. Families and types associated with later periods, as well as miscellaneous families (90 and 95), are omitted.

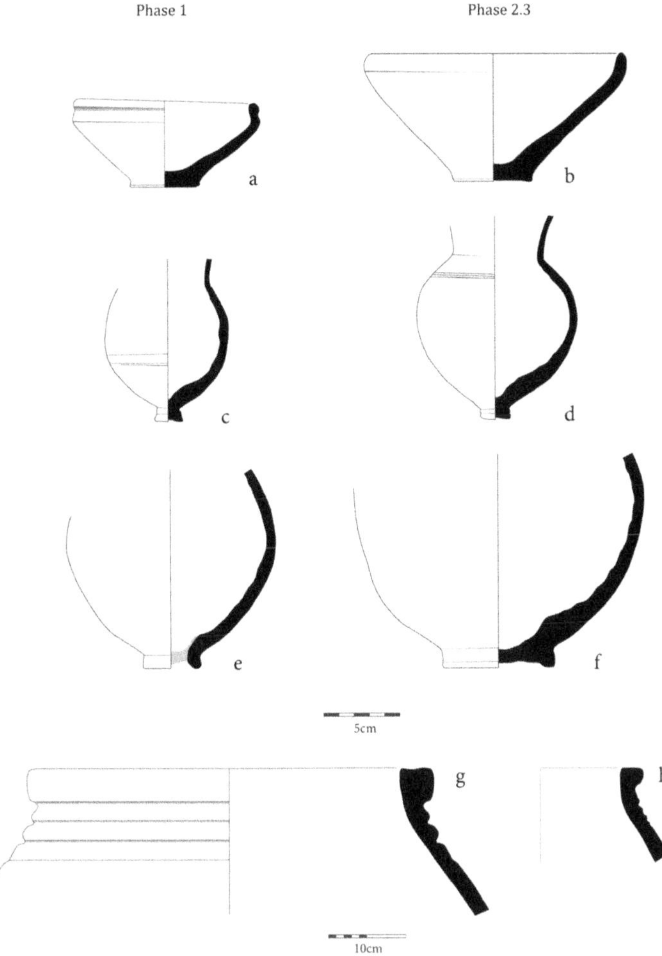

FIG. 3.2. A comparison between selected vessels from the earliest secure levels at Tell Khaiber (Phase 1), left, and the latest primary occupation levels (Phase 2.3), right: a) p3099-13; b) p5007-4; c) p3102-2; d) p8018-24; e) p3098-9; f) p5016-11; g) p3125-15; h) p8008-57.

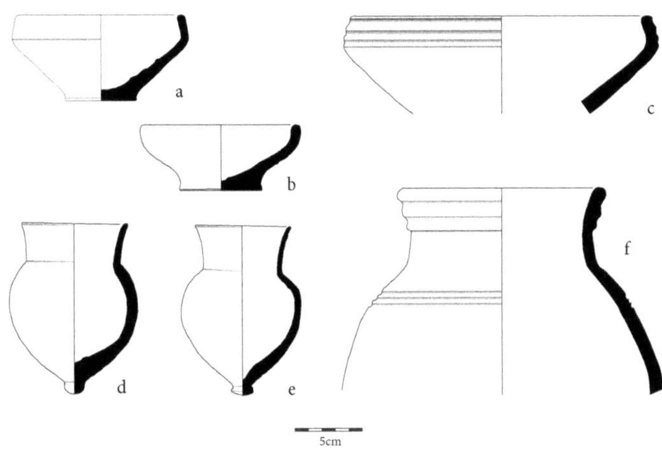

FIG. 3.3. Typical Sealand period vessel types: 5.1 (p3088-138); 5.2 (p1094-25); 10.1 (p1096-307); 50.4 (p1085-17); 50.5 (p3054-397); 70.3 (p6036-123).

Overall, each of the different vessel Families that comprise the entire Sealand Period typology at Tell Khaiber demonstrates a restricted number of associated shape types (Table 3.4). The differences between these shape types are not always clearly definable, but instead fall into groupings within a continuous spectrum. The precise number of these shape types does, however, vary according to vessel family. Bowls (Families 5 and 10), cups (Family 50), and jars (Family 70), for instance, show more variation than other vessel Families. This variation is to some extent a product of relative frequency; since these are the most archaeologically abundant vessel families, a higher number of minor variations within these categories were more likely to have been produced (and subsequently categorised). Even so, regarding tablewares in particular, the higher number of types might also have been determined, at least in part, by the intended contexts of vessel use. In arenas of commensality, for example, variations may also have functioned as subtle markers of individuality or as socially understood indicators of the contents designed to be consumed from those vessels.

3.1.3 Mixed Phases

It is only in the Mixed Levels that more extensive differences are identifiable. Although most deposits are composed of typical Sealand shapes, some of the areas of Mixed Phasing bring about significant changes in fluctuating types, while also marking the introduction of several distinct type fossils.

The tower rooms, for instance, demonstrate a regular mix of Sealand period types, which map very well in terms of relative percentages onto Phases 1–2.3 in the rest of the Fortified Building. This strongly suggests contemporaneity of the tower deposits and primary occupation, as discussed above.

In the surface scraped material, stable footed cups (Types 50.1–3) increase dramatically in frequency, composing 8.6% compared with 3.9–4.6% in the whole of Level 2. Similarly, Types 50.2–3 constitute 16.5% of the assemblage produced from the exploratory soundings directly outside of the Fortified Building, as well as in the disturbed deposits of the baked brick chamber to the east. In the same surface-scraped material and external soundings, there are also examples of flaring goblet feet (Type 40.2), a type not present in any of the primary occupational phases at Tell Khaiber. Indeed, this type is introduced in the same deposits that yielded an increased occurrence of wavy-sided bowls (Type 5.4), platformed bowl bases (Type 15.2), and Type 70.1 jar rims. These types in combination (Fig. 3.4) appear to be representative of restricted secondary re-use of the Fortified Building at a time most likely aligning with the Early Kassite period (ca. 1450–1300 BCE). If so, this would be among the earliest Kassite deposits in southern Babylonia, with the closest comparative material being found at Tell Yelkhi, Levels II–I (ca. 1500–1300 BCE; Valtz 2002–2003: pl. 142.21–23, pl. 148–9, and pl. 151.1–13).

It was probably during this period of secondary activity in and around the perimeter of the Fortified Building that the intrusive burials occurred, cut into primary occupational

	Phase 1		Phase 2.1		Phase 2.2		Phase 2.3		Stratigraphically Uncertain										TOTAL	
									MSu		MT		MB		MSo		EH			
Family	#	%	#	%	#	%	#	%	#	%	#	%	#	%	#	%	#	%		
5	-	-	5	0.3	3	0.1	5	0.8	1	0.1	1	0.1	-	-	-	-	-	-	15	0.2
5.1	17	9.1	146	10.0	303	11.6	66	10.9	52	4.2	113	8.8	3	6.1	9	5.1	24	5.7	733	9.1
5.2	3	1.6	127	8.7	122	4.7	7	1.2	11	0.9	77	6.0	1	2.0	-	-	23	5.5	371	4.6
5.3	-	-	-	-	1	0.0	2	0.3	-	-	-	-	1	2.0	4	2.3	-	-	8	0.1
5.4	-	-	1	0.1	3	0.1	-	-	11	0.9	3	0.2	-	-	-	-	2	0.5	20	0.2
5.5	-	-	-	-	-	-	-	-	12	1.0	-	-	-	-	-	-	-	-	12	0.1
	20	10.7	279	19.1	432	16.5	80	13.2	87	7.0	194	15.1	5	10.2	13	7.4	49	11.7	1159	14.4
10	-	-	1	0.1	4	0.2	2	0.3	3	0.2	-	-	-	-	1	0.6	-	-	11	0.1
10.1	10	5.3	14	1.0	36	1.4	11	1.8	13	1.0	22	1.7	1	2.0	3	1.7	2	0.5	112	1.4
10.2	4	2.1	24	1.6	27	1.0	7	1.2	5	0.4	19	1.5	-	-	1	0.6	1	0.2	88	1.1
10.3	-	-	1	0.1	1	0.0	-	-	-	-	6	0.5	-	-	-	-	1	0.2	9	0.1
10.4	-	-	1	0.1	1	0.0	-	-	3	0.2	1	0.1	-	-	-	-	-	-	6	0.1
	14	7.5	41	2.8	69	2.6	20	3.3	24	1.9	48	3.7	1	2.0	5	2.8	4	1.0	226	2.8
15	-	-	-	-	-	-	-	-	-	-	1	0.1	-	-	-	-	-	-	1	0.0
15.1	11	5.9	105	7.2	125	4.8	24	4.0	49	3.9	69	5.4	-	-	17	9.7	13	3.1	413	5.1
15.2	-	-	-	-	8	0.3	4	0.7	25	2.0	6	0.5	-	-	5	2.8	-	-	48	0.6
	11	5.9	105	7.2	133	5.1	28	4.6	74	5.9	76	5.9	-	-	22	12.5	13	3.1	462	5.7
20	-	-	1	0.1	-	-	1	0.2	1	0.1	-	-	-	-	1	0.6	-	-	4	0.0
20.1	-	-	5	0.3	11	0.4	1	0.2	6	0.5	6	0.5	-	-	1	0.6	1	0.2	31	0.4
20.2	-	-	-	-	2	0.1	-	-	-	-	-	-	-	-	-	-	-	-	2	0.0
	-	-	6	0.4	13	0.5	2	0.3	7	0.6	6	0.5	-	-	2	1.1	1	0.2	37	0.5
25	2	1.1	-	-	4	0.2	2	0.3	9	0.7	1	0.1	-	-	2	1.1	-	-	20	0.2
25.1	8	4.3	34	2.3	66	2.5	14	2.3	54	4.3	15	1.2	5	10.2	6	3.4	11	2.6	213	2.6
25.2	-	-	7	0.5	22	0.8	1	0.2	7	0.6	1	0.1	-	-	1	0.6	-	-	39	0.5
25.3	1	0.5	4	0.3	6	0.2	6	1.0	14	1.1	2	0.2	-	-	2	1.1	-	-	35	0.4
25.4	1	0.5	13	0.9	41	1.6	8	1.3	6	0.5	2	0.2	1	2.0	3	1.7	3	0.7	78	1.0
25.5	1	0.5	10	0.7	31	1.2	5	0.8	21	1.7	10	0.8	1	2.0	2	1.1	3	0.7	84	1.0
	13	7.0	68	4.6	170	6.5	36	6.0	111	8.9	31	2.4	7	14.3	16	9.1	17	4.1	469	5.8
30	-	-	-	-	-	-	-	-	-	-	-	-	-	-	-	-	-	-	0	0.0
30.1	-	-	-	-			-	-	2	0.2	-	-	-	-	-	-	-	-	2	0.0
30.2	-	-	4	0.3	11	04	4	0.7	2	0.2	1	0.1	-	-	-	-	-	-	22	0.3
30.3	-	-	-	-	2	0.1	-	-	1	0.1	-	-	-	-	-	-	-	-	3	0.0
	-	-	4	0.3	13	0.5	4	0.7	5	0.4	1	0.1	-	-	-	-	-	-	27	0.3
35	-	-	2	0.1	3	0.1	-	-	1	0.1	1	0.1	-	-	1	0.6	-	-	8	0.1
35.1	-	-	-	-	5	0.2	-	-	-	-	-	-	-	-	-	-	-	-	5	0.1
35.2	1	0.5	21	1.4	38	1.5	5	0.8	12	1.0	24	1.9	-	-	-	-	5	1.2	106	1.3
35.3	-	-	2	0.1	4	0.2	1	0.2	-	-	4	0.3	-	-	-	-	-	-	11	0.1
35.4	-	-	-	-	6	0.2	3	0.5	1	0.1	9	0.7	-	-	-	-	-	-	19	0.2
35.5	1	0.5	3	0.2	9	0.3	3	0.5	2	0.2	7	0.5	-	-	-	-	1	0.2	26	0.3
	2	1.1	28	1.9	65	2.5	12	2.0	16	1.3	45	3.5	-	-	1	0.6	6	1.4	175	2.2
40	-	-	-	-	-	-	-	-	1	0.1	-	-	-	-	-	-	-	-	1	0.0
40.1	-	-	-	-	-	-	-	-	17	1.4	-	-	-	-	-	-	-	-	17	0.2
40.2	-	-	-	-	-	-	-	-	29	2.3	1	0.1	-	-	4	2.3	1	0.2	35	0.4
40.3	-	-	-	-	-	-	-	-	4	0.3	-	-	-	-	-	-	-	-	4	0.0
	-	-	-	-	-	-	-	-	51	4.1	1	0.1	-	-	4	2.3	1	0.2	57	0.7
45	-	-	-	-	2	0.1	-	-	1	0.1	-	-	-	-	-	-	-	-	3	0.0
45.1	1	0.5	2	0.1	2	0.1	-	-	5	0.4	1	0.1	-	-	-	-	-	-	11	0.1
45.2	-	-	-	-	1	0.0	2	0.3	-	-	2	0.2	-	-	-	-	-	-	5	0.1
45.3	-	-	1	0.1	-	-	-	-	-	-	1	0.1	-	-	-	-	-	-	2	0.0
45.4	-	-	-	-	-	-	-	-	1	0.1	-	-	-	-	-	-	-	-	1	0.0
	1	0.5	3	0.2	5	0.2	2	0.3	7	0.6	4	0.3	-	-	-	-	-	-	22	0.3
50	2	1.1	5	0.3	6	0.2	5	0.8	12	1.0	2	0.2	-	-	-	-	-	-	32	0.4
50.1	7	3.7	47	3.2	54	2.1	18	3.0	62	5.0	46	3.6	1	2.0	2	1.1	16	3.8	253	3.1
50.2	2	1.1	11	0.8	24	0.9	8	1.3	30	2.4	25	1.9	2	4.1	14	8.0	33	7.9	149	1.9
50.3	2	1.1	3	0.2	23	0.9	2	0.3	15	1.2	14	1.1	3	6.1	15	8.5	13	3.1	90	1.1
50.4	1	0.5	26	1.8	89	3.4	9	1.5	16	1.3	16	1.2	-	-	-	-	9	2.1	166	2.1
50.5	14	7.5	105	7.2	167	6.4	29	4.8	86	6.9	120	9.3	2	4.1	1	0.6	14	3.3	538	6.7
50.6	1	0.5	-	-	5	0.2	-	-	4	0.3	2	0.2	-	-	-	-	1	0.2	13	0.2
50.7	-	-	-	-	-	-	-	-	5	0.4	-	-	-	-	-	-	-	-	5	0.1
	29	15.5	197	13.5	368	14.1	71	11.7	230	18.4	225	17.5	8	16.3	32	18.2	86	20.5	1246	15.5

TABLE 3.5. Shape types according to phase.

	Phase 1		Phase 2.1		Phase 2.2		Phase 2.3		Stratigraphically Uncertain: MSu		MT		MB		MSo		EH		TOTAL	
Family	#	%	#	%	#	%	#	%	#	%	#	%	#	%	#	%	#	%		
55	-	-	1	0.1	-	-	1	0.2	2	0.2	-	-	-	-	-	-	-	-	4	0.0
55.1	7	3.7	46	3.1	71	2.7	16	2.6	37	3.0	28	2.2	2	4.1	1	0.6	17	4.1	225	2.8
55.2	3	1.6	10	0.7	25	1.0	3	0.5	17	1.4	19	1.5	3	6.1	6	3.4	8	1.9	94	1.2
55.3	-	-	-	-	1	0.0	-	-	3	0.2	-	-	-	-	4	2.3	-	-	8	0.1
	10	5.3	57	3.9	97	3.7	20	3.3	59	4.7	47	3.7	5	10.2	11	6.3	25	6.0	331	4.1
60	-	-	-	-	-	-	-	-	-	-	-	-	-	-	-	-	-	-	0	0.0
60.1	20	10.7	228	15.6	345	13.2	92	15.2	57	4.6	183	14.2	12	24.5	7	4.0	109	26.0	1053	13.1
60.2	-	-	1	0.1	3	0.1	-	-	3	0.2	1	0.1	-	-	-	-	1	0.2	9	0.1
60.3	-	-	4	0.3	2	0.1	-	-	-	-	2	0.2	-	-	-	-	-	-	8	0.1
60.4	-	-	-	-	-	-	-	-	2	0.2	-	-	-	-	-	-	-	-	2	0.0
	20	10.7	233	15.9	350	13.4	92	15.2	62	5.0	186	14.5	12	24.5	7	4.0	110	26.3	1072	13.3
65	-	-	2	0.1	3	0.1	1	0.2	1	0.1	-	-	-	-	-	-	-	-	7	0.1
65.1	8	4.3	86	5.9	141	5.4	44	7.3	134	10.7	70	5.4	1	2.0	4	2.3	7	1.7	495	6.1
65.2	13	7.0	19	1.3	32	1.2	4	0.7	29	2.3	36	2.8	-	-	-	-	2	0.5	135	1.7
65.3	-	-	-	-	3	0.1	2	0.3	3	0.2	1	0.1	-	-	-	-	-	-	9	0.1
65.4	-	-	3	0.2	1	0.0	-	-	3	0.2	5	0.4	-	-	-	-	-	-	12	0.1
	21	11.2	110	7.5	180	6.9	51	8.4	170	13.6	112	8.7	1	2.0	4	2.3	9	2.1	658	8.2
70	-	-	2	0.1	8	0.3	7	1.2	5	0.4	2	0.2	-	-	1	0.6	-	-	25	0.3
70.1	-	-	17	1.2	41	1.6	9	1.5	26	2.1	12	0.9	1	2.0	3	1.7	5	1.2	114	1.4
70.2	21	11.2	79	5.4	206	7.9	40	6.6	80	6.4	71	5.5	4	8.2	34	19.3	49	11.7	584	7.3
70.3	14	7.5	123	8.4	241	9.2	67	11.1	124	9.9	127	9.9	3	6.1	6	3.4	31	7.4	736	9.1
70.4	-	-	3	0.2	6	0.2	-	-	9	0.7	2	0.2	-	-	-	-	2	0.5	22	0.3
70.5	2	1.1	9	0.6	32	1.2	7	1.2	11	0.9	17	1.3	-	-	1	0.6	-	-	79	1.0
70.6	1	0.5	-	-	3	0.1	-	-	5	0.4	-	-	-	-	-	-	-	-	9	0.1
70.7	-	-	1	0.1	-	-	-	-	2	0.2	-	-	1	2.0	-	-	-	-	4	0.0
70.8	-	-	-	-	-	-	-	-	1	0.1	1	0.1	-	-	-	-	-	-	2	0.0
	38	20.3	234	16.0	537	20.5	130	21.5	263	21.1	232	18.0	9	18.4	45	25.6	87	20.8	1575	19.6
75	-	-	-	-	1	0.0	-	-	1	0.1	-	-	-	-	-	-	-	-	2	0.0
75.1	-	-	6	0.4	14	0.5	4	0.7	1	0.1	3	0.2	-	-	-	-	-	-	28	0.3
75.2	-	-	2	0.1	1	0.0	2	0.3	1	0.1	-	-	-	-	-	-	-	-	6	0.1
75.3	-	-	-	-	1	0.0	1	0.2	-	-	1	0.1	-	-	-	-	-	-	3	0.0
75.4	-	-	1	0.1	2	0.1	1	0.2	-	-	-	-	-	-	-	-	-	-	4	0.0
	-	-	9	0.6	19	0.7	8	1.3	3	0.2	4	0.3	-	-	-	-	-	-	43	0.5
80	1	0.5	1	0.1	9	0.3	4	0.7	5	0.4	2	0.2	-	-	-	-	-	-	22	0.3
80.1	1	0.5	21	1.4	37	1.4	7	1.2	15	1.2	26	2.0	-	-	-	-	3	0.7	110	1.4
80.2	1	0.5	8	0.5	32	1.2	7	1.2	14	1.1	4	0.3	-	-	-	-	2	0.5	68	0.8
80.3	-	-	1	0.1	-	-	1	0.2	-	-	-	-	-	-	-	-	-	-	2	0.0
	3	1.6	31	2.1	78	3.0	19	3.1	34	2.7	32	2.5	-	-	-	-	5	1.2	202	2.5
85	-	-	-	-	-	-	-	-	-	-	2	0.2	-	-	-	-	-	-	2	0.0
85.1	1	0.5	34	2.3	55	2.1	13	2.1	18	1.4	26	2.0	1	2.0	2	1.1	5	1.2	155	1.9
85.2	4	2.1	17	1.2	23	0.9	7	1.2	17	1.4	6	0.5	-	-	11	6.3	1	0.2	86	1.1
85.3	-	-	2	0.1	3	0.1	-	-	3	0.2	2	0.2	-	-	-	-	-	-	10	0.1
	5	2.7	53	3.6	81	3.1	20	3.3	38	3.0	36	2.8	1	2.0	13	7.4	6	1.4	253	3.1
90	-	-	-	-	-	-	-	-	-	-	-	-	-	-	-	-	-	-	0	0.0
90.1	-	-	-	-	1	0.0	3	0.5	2	0.2	1	0.1	-	-	-	-	-	-	7	0.1
90.2	-	-	-	-	1	0.0	1	0.2	1	0.1	-	-	-	-	-	-	-	-	3	0.0
90.3	-	-	-	-	-	-	1	0.2	1	0.1	-	-	-	-	1	0.6	-	-	3	0.0
90.4	-	-	1	0.1	2	0.1	-	-	-	-	1	0.1	-	-	-	-	-	-	4	0.0
90.5	-	-	-	-	-	-	-	-	-	-	1	0.1	-	-	-	-	-	-	1	0.0
90.6	-	-	-	-	-	-	-	-	1	0.1	-	-	-	-	-	-	-	-	1	0.0
90.7	-	-	-	-	-	-	-	-	1	0.1	1	0.1	-	-	-	-	-	-	2	0.0
90.8	-	-	1	0.1	-	-	1	0.2	-	-	-	-	-	-	-	-	-	-	2	0.0
90.9	-	-	1	0.1	-	-	-	-	-	-	-	-	-	-	-	-	-	-	1	0.0
	-	-	3	0.2	4	0.2	6	1.0	6	0.5	4	0.3	-	-	1	0.6	-	-	24	0.3
95	-	-	-	-	1	0.0	-	-	-	-	-	-	-	-	-	-	-	-	1	0.0
95.1	-	-	1	0.1	2	0.1	1	0.2	1	0.1	3	0.2	-	-	-	-	-	-	8	0.1
95.2	-	-	1	0.1	-	-	1	0.2	-	-	1	0.1	-	-	-	-	-	-	3	0.0
95.3	-	-	1	0.1	2	0.1	2	0.3	2	0.2	-	-	-	-	-	-	-	-	7	0.1
95.4	-	-	-	-	2	0.1	-	-	1	0.1	-	-	-	-	-	-	-	-	3	0.0
	-	-	3	0.2	7	0.3	4	0.7	4	0.3	4	0.3	-	-	-	-	-	-	22	0.3
Total	187	100	1464	100	2621	100	605	100	1251	100	1287	100	49	100	176	100	419	100	8059	100

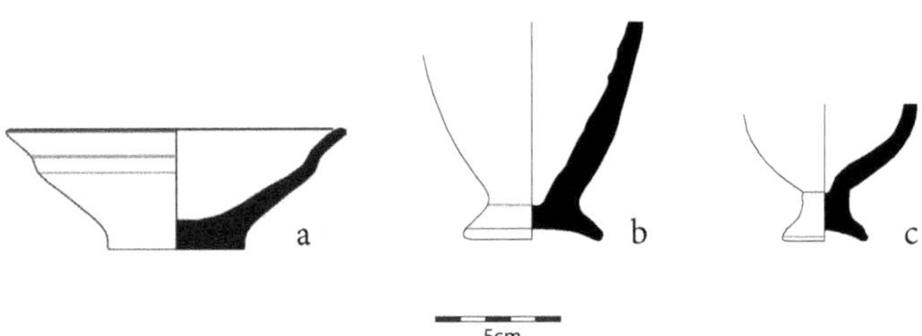

FIG. 3.4. Examples of 'Early Kassite' vessel types: 5.4 (p6088-14); 40.2 (p6088-12); 40.3 (p6088-1).

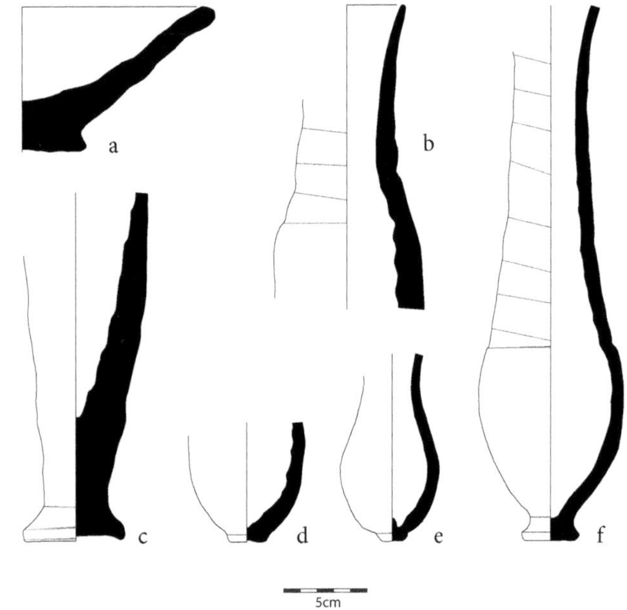

FIG. 3.5. Examples of 'Late Kassite' vessel types: 5.5 (p6175-22); 40.1a (p6183-18); 40.1b (p6183-20); 50.7 (p6178-25); 45.4 (p6175-40); 40.3 (p6178-34)

levels. This association is stratigraphic rather than stylistic, since the double-pithoi[10] and single jars[11] in which the bodies were interred allow for little chronological refinement; furthermore, the pots deposited as grave goods in Grave 6, including a Type 50.4 cup (p3079-9), as well as a Type 55.1 jug (p3091-2) found with Grave 8, are similar to those found in the primary occupational sequence. One exception is a deep, curved bowl (p8029-3) used to cap an infant burial jar (Grave 11), with a Type 50.5 cup found alongside (p8029-4); the former bowl is unique in the assemblage of the Fortified Building and finds only a few comparative sherds in the Mixed Soundings, while the latter cup exhibits a unique wavy neck. Given that the burials are dispersed across different areas of the Fortified Building and respect the original wall lines, this suggests two stratigraphic possibilities: 1) that they were intramural burials dug from now eroded floor levels while the building was still in use, or 2) that they were post-occupational interments at a point when the building was abandoned, but its walls were relatively intact and its various rooms were accessible. Either way, these burials must only slightly postdate the final secure primary occupational deposits of Phase 2.3.

Several other significant type fossils are limited to just a few contexts in the surface scrape,[12] located exclusively around the severely eroded north-eastern edge of the building, north of the main entrance to the Fortified Building and along the line of where the main northeast wall should have been. The type fossils found here include: ripple-sided bowls (Type 5.5), tall steep-sided goblets (Type 40.1), flare-footed goblets with tall necks (Type 40.3), button-footed bottles with sinuous bodies (Type 45.4), and flat-footed cups with steep sides (Type 50.7) (Fig. 3.5). These shapes are typical of the better known Late Kassite (ca. 1300–1100 BCE) assemblages at other sites in the region, for example at Uruk (van Ess 2014), Isin (Kaniuth 2017), Nippur (Armstrong 1993; 2017), and Khani Masi (Glatz et al. 2019: 454, Fig. 9), but are also identical to the shapes recovered from soundings at Tell Khaiber 2, a Kassite period mound located just one kilometre northwest of Tell Khaiber (Campbell et al. 2017). That this material was found within a later cut that destroyed this part of the building suggests not only that the building's occupation categorically did not continue into the Late Kassite period, but that its architectural integrity was, by this point, in a pronounced state of disrepair.

3.1.4 Eastern Houses

The Eastern Houses, located 38m southeast of the Fortified Building, sit in isolation from the other deposits discussed here. As such, any chronological associations must be made based on ceramic style rather than direct stratigraphic association.

As with the Mixed deposits within the Fortified Building, most shapes encountered in Houses 1–3 are generally typical of the broader Sealand period assemblage outlined in §3.1.2. Like the surface-scraped material and soundings, the presence of bowl Type 5.4, goblet Type 40.2, and the high percentage of stable footed cups (14.8%) compared with unstable footed cups (5.6%) are significant chronological indicators. Further to this, the shape of a small sample of stable footed cups (Fig. 3.6), which demonstrate elongated profiles and funnel necks, are subtly different from the remainder of the cup assemblage and find better comparisons at Early Kassite Tell Yelkhi, Levels II–I (Valtz 2002–2003: pl. 149.10–19), as well as in Kassite deposits at Uruk (van Ess 2014: pl. 10.2–3) and Babylon (Sternitzke, 2016: tables 105–6). Together, this ceramic evidence suggests that the Eastern Houses assemblage falls in line with the latest phases of primary use of the Fortified Building and may perhaps also overlap with the onset of secondary, Early Kassite period, re-use.

---

[10] Grave 6: pithoi p3075-1 and p3075-2; Grave 10: p6092-1 and p6093-1

[11] Grave 3; fragmentary unrecorded jar; Grave 7: jar p1097-1 capped by bowl p1098-1; Grave 8: jar p3091-3 capped by bowl p3091-1; Grave 11: fragmentary unrecorded jar capped by bowl p8029-3; Grave 13: fragmentary unrecorded jar: Grave 14: jar p6141-1.

[12] Contexts 1078, 6175, 6178, and 6183.

FIG. 3.6. Tall, funnel-necked cups: a) p4006-12; b) p4084-1.

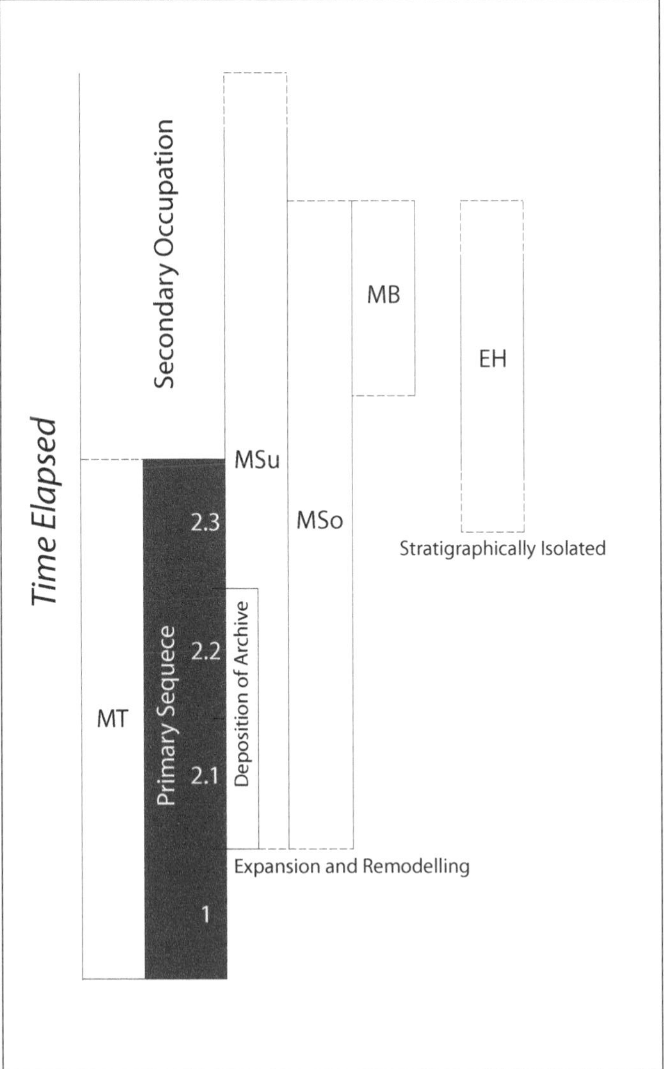

FIG. 3.7. A hypothetical model of the Fortified Building's main sequence (grey) and its relative temporal associations with the various Mixed deposits (white). Temporal associations are based on stratigraphic information as well as ceramic similarities discussed in the text. Dashed lines mark less certain temporal boundaries.

The latest pottery evidence from the Eastern Houses was produced from an intrusive double-pithos burial in House 1 (Grave 5), an interment which was most likely subsequent to the use of this area as residential space while still continuing to respect the lines of the house walls. As with those in the Fortified Building, the burial pithoi (see p4038-1) are themselves chronologically undiagnostic. Interred alongside this individual, however, was a particularly finely made jug (Type 55.1: p4041-1) alongside other burial goods, including an elaborate necklace of semiprecious stones. Since this vessel exhibits strong parallels with Early Kassite jugs found elsewhere in the alluvial plains (see §3.2), it should provide a relative termination point for the use of the Eastern Houses of somewhere between 1450 and 1300 BCE.

3.2 Regional Context: The Mesopotamian Heartland

Each major site in the Mesopotamian heartland is traditionally considered to demonstrate a break in occupation corresponding precisely to the period during which Tell Khaiber was occupied. Notwithstanding, Ayoub emphasised the diachronic predictability of second millennium Mesopotamian pottery development, stating that 'one can determine precisely how types emerge, and how they will develop further' (1982: 9, author's translation). Armstrong and Gasche's (2014) recent compendium advances a similar narrative of stylistic continuity. The Tell Khaiber assemblage provides a secure Sealand period assemblage with which to test this long held assumption of craft resilience.

Analysis of many Tell Khaiber vessel types does indeed show clear similarities with those of the Late Old Babylonian and Early Kassite periods. The main ones are with larger vessel types: jugs, jars, pithoi, and cookpots. Jugs at Tell Khaiber, for instance, show similarities to those found in Late Old Babylonian contexts at Tell ed-Der (Gasche 1989: pl. 36.1–10) and Deylam (Armstrong 2001: Fig. 5 and 10d). Yet the Late Old Babylonian examples tend to have a more rounded, globular shape than those found at Tell Khaiber. The closest comparison is a vessel produced from Burial 392 at Tell ed-Der (Armstrong and Gasche 2014: pl. 83.2). This vessel, dating to the Early Kassite period (ca. 1450 BCE), is held as the earliest evidence for reoccupation at any site in the alluvial plains following the so-called Dark Age (Gasche et al. 1998: 15; Pons 1989: 22–3). It is therefore significant that this vessel is almost identical to one found in the mixed surface deposits at Tell Khaiber (Fig. 3.8a–b). Equally, a vessel from Nippur is similar to a jug found in intrusive burial, Grave 5, cut into House 1 of Tell Khaiber's Eastern Houses (Fig. 3.8c–d).

Larger jars from Tell Khaiber also demonstrate consistency with those of the Old Babylonian and Kassite periods. The bottom-heavy shape of Late Old Babylonian and Kassite jars is mirrored in the Tell Khaiber assemblage. While there is a general similarity in shape, a notable difference is that the earlier examples tend to favour a

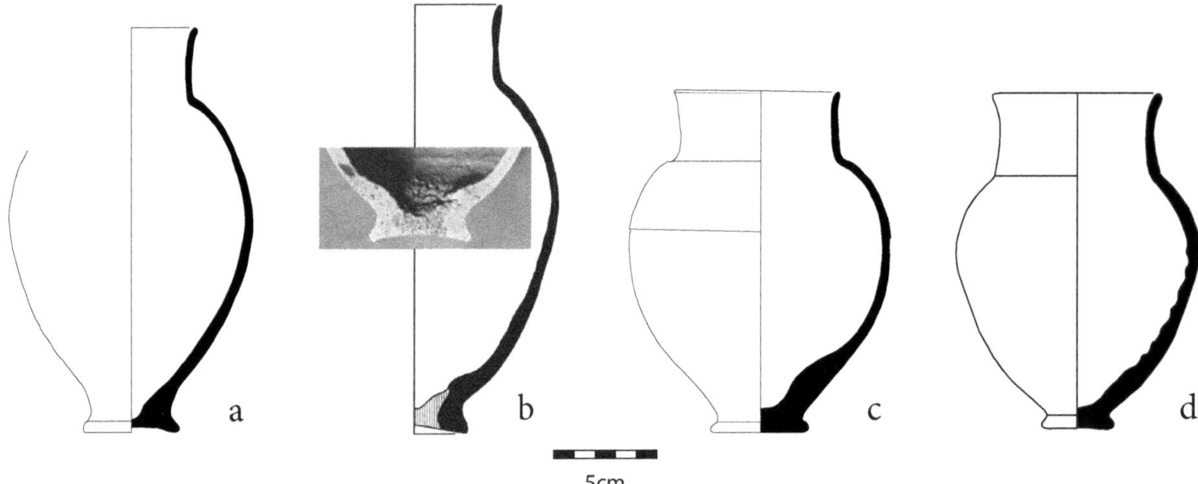

FIG. 3.8. Jugs from Tell Khaiber alongside close external parallels. a) Tell Khaiber (p3009-17); b) Tell ed-Der (Armstrong and Gasche 2014: pl. 83.2). Image courtesy of the Oriental Institute of the University of Chicago; c) Tell Khaiber (p4041-1); d) Nippur (Armstrong 1993: pl. 82a).

simple, slightly everted, thickened rim band, whereas Kassite jars yield vertically oriented, thickened rim bands with grooves. At Babylon, grooved rims develop during the Early Kassite period (Sternitzke 2016a: 602) (Fig. 3.9). Significantly, it is these grooved rims that dominate at Tell Khaiber and are common features from the onset of the site's occupation.

Cookpots and pithoi also show consistency through time. Late Old Babylonian and Kassite period cookpots, from Nippur (McCown et al. 1967: pl. 94.1) and Uruk (van Ess 2014: pl. 4.84 and pl. 7), for instance, are practically identical to those found at Tell Khaiber. Pithoi are similarly consistent: they invariably occur in large, squat shapes, with a thickened rim band and applied ribs running down the body. Since examples from Tell Khaiber always have applied ring bases rather than platform bases, and are very rarely painted, they align more closely with the features of Kassite pithoi rather than with earlier Old Babylonian examples (Armstrong and Gasche 2014: pls. 116–19).

Some of the more infrequent vessels from Tell Khaiber also show robust similarities with selected Old Babylonian and Kassite shapes. These include small storage bottles, a shape that has a long currency across Mesopotamia, and which are commonly found not only in the northern plains (Armstrong and Gasche 2014: pl. 88) but also in the Sîn-kāšid palace at Uruk (van Ess 2014: pl. 7). Likewise, a tall beaker with elaborate impressed wavy and horizontal bands from Old Babylonian Uruk (van Ess 1988: 199, Fig. 34) bears a striking resemblance to a decorated beaker from Phase 2.2 at Tell Khaiber (p5022-65).

It is therefore clear that many larger vessels shapes, as well as some more infrequent types, suggest a general

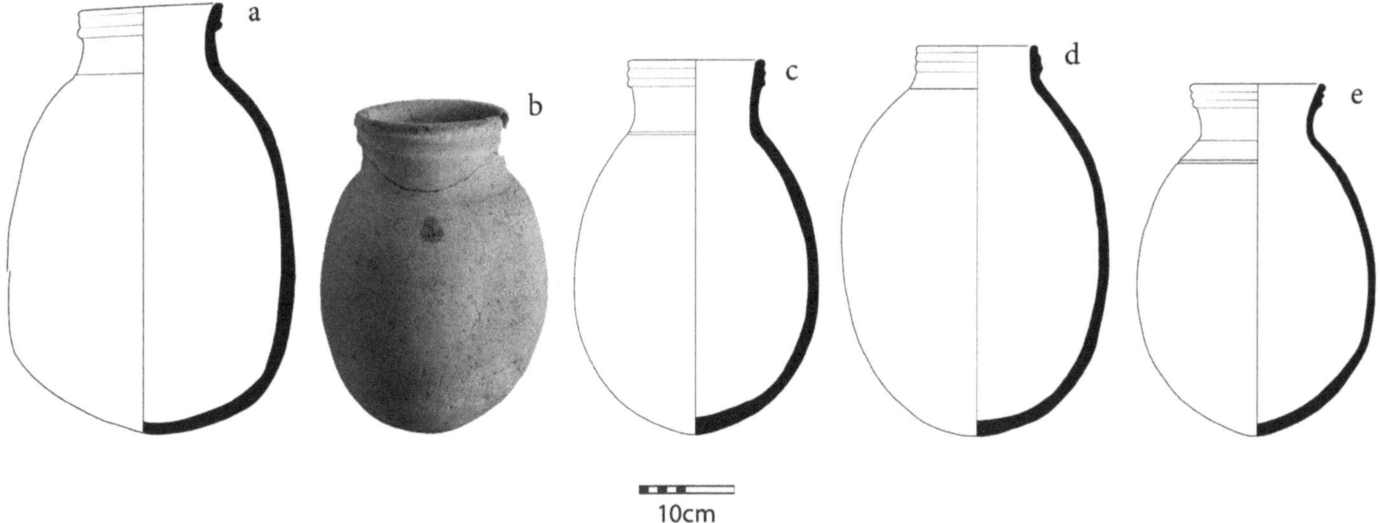

FIG. 3.9. Jars with grooved rim bands. a) Tell Khaiber (p6141-1); b) Umm Faisit (BM_U1665); c) Babylon (after Sternitzke 2016a: KG-5.f.4); d) Failaka Island (after Højlund 1987: 62, fig. 215); e) Tell Yelkhi (after Valtz 2002–3: table 153.13). Photo: Trustees of the British Museum.

picture of continuity between the Late Old Babylonian and Kassite periods across Mesopotamia, with the Tell Khaiber assemblage neatly slotting into the sequence.

However, with analysis of the smaller and more common tablewares, this thread of seamless continuity starts to fray. Shallow carinated bowls, for instance, both plain and grooved, are almost completely absent elsewhere in the Mesopotamian plains. Rare examples of plain carinated bowls have been identified from Tell Muhammad (Metab 1989–90), as well as from ostensibly Kassite dwellings at Uruk (van Ess 2014: pl. 2.51–53). Significant too are a couple of complete bowls with impressed decoration beneath the rim found at Tell ed-Der, in the house of Ur-Utu (Gasche 1989: pls. 25.46 and 28.2), as well as at Harrâdum, on the Middle Euphrates (Kepinski-Lecomte 1992: figs. 108.2–13 and 124.11). Both these contexts date to the reign of Ammisaduqa (ca. 1646–1626 BCE). Similar examples also derive from Tell Muhammad (Metab 1989–90; Metab and Hamza 2003–4). This is the only comparative evidence for what would become typical Sealand types at Tell Khaiber.

Nevertheless, these similarities are the exception. Late Old Babylonian and Kassite assemblages across Mesopotamia are dominated by shapes that are not present at Tell Khaiber. These include shallow straight-sided bowls and steep-sided bowls, painted bowls (Gasche 1989: pl. 27.23–31), and shallow platters (Gasche 1989: pl. 25). Kassite assemblages are similarly replete with typical wavy-sided bowls and ripple-sided bowls (e.g. Armstrong 1993: pls.72–7), each of which occur in the later mixed assemblages at Tell Khaiber. Common too in both Late Old Babylonian and Kassite assemblages are large, open bowls with thickened rim bands (Armstrong 1993: pl. 78.a–c and pl. 84; van Ess 2014: pl. 3.58–9). None of these vessels are found within the primary occupational sequence at Tell Khaiber.

Similar inconsistencies can be seen from the shape of Tell Khaiber's cups, the most common vessel category at the site. Late Old Babylonian cups from Tell ed-Der show broadly similar shapes to Tell Khaiber, with a well-defined neck and base, separated from a round, globular body (Gasche 1989: pl. 35.1–17). Yet a defining feature of Late Old Babylonian cups is the tall elegant neck, often equivalent in height to the rest of the body. This preference for extravagant necks is also well attested in the Kassite period, although in an even more exaggerated fashion, with the necks of many cups far exceeding the height of the rest of the vessel body (Armstrong 1993: pl. 80). The two elongated cups with funnel necks from the Eastern Houses (see Fig. 3.6) find the most extensive parallels at Tell ed-Der, again from the house of Ur-Utu (Gasche 1989: pl. 33.6–8), as well as from Late Old Babylonian contexts at Deylam (Armstrong 1992; Armstrong and Gasche 2014: pl. 62.1–9). They are also similar in style to the so-called *Trichterhalsbecherflaschen* encountered in the reanalysed data from Babylon (Sternitzke, 2016a: plates 105–6). In general, however, these two Tell Khaiber vessels are slightly squatter than their northern counterparts.

Far more frequently encountered at Tell Khaiber are those cups with unstable feet (Types 50.4–5). Individual cups with unstable button feet have been identified from Isin (Armstrong and Gasche 2014: pl. 90.17) and Babylon (Sternitzke 2016a). The most significant parallels, however, derive, firstly, from grave AHG/202 at Ur (Fig. 3.10d), which may have been associated with the 'squalid houses' that Woolley (1954: 197–8) reports as post-dating the Old Babylonian period destruction at the site, and, secondly, from Woolley's soundings at Umm Faisit (Fig. 3.10a and c). Umm Faisit is a small mound that, unfortunately, we have exceedingly little information for, other than the fact that it was located '6 miles NNE of Ur' (Woolley and Mallowan 1976: 190).

Other significant ceramic indicators derive not from positive diagnostic similarities, but from negative evidence. Absent entirely from the primary occupational sequence at Tell Khaiber are typical Babylonian goblets. According to Gasche et al. (1998: 26), the goblet 'is the most frequently and widely attested shape in the whole of the second-millennium Babylonian ceramic corpus, having been produced by the tens of thousands.' Since these vessels were considered 'essential to every second-millennium Babylonian household' (Gasche et al. 1998: 26), they dominate archaeological assemblages of both the Old Babylonian and Kassite periods across the alluvial plains. It is therefore significant that goblets of Type 40.1 only begin to appear sporadically at Tell Khaiber in the mixed deposits associated with ad hoc re-use of the Fortified Building.

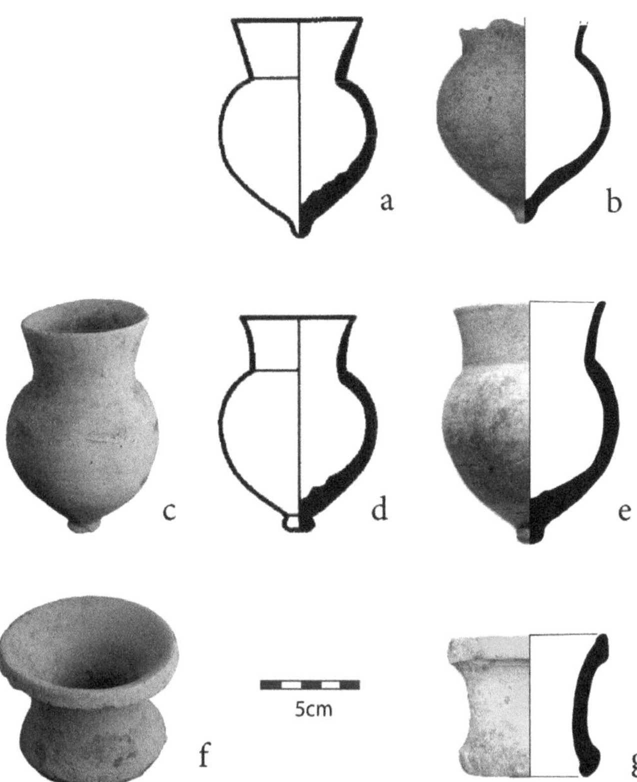

FIG. 3.10. Unstable footed cups: a) Umm Faisit (Woolley and Mallowan 1976: pl.106: 58a); b) Tell Khaiber (p4067-34); c) Umm Faisit (BM_U2901B); d) Ur (AHG/202; Woolley and Mallowan 1976: pl.106: 58b); e) Tell Khaiber (p1085-17); f) Umm Faisit (BM_U2922); g) Tell Khaiber (p6059-7). Photos: Trustees of the British Museum.

3.3 Inter-Regional Context: Beyond Babylonia

It is vital to also consider those sites distributed along the traditionally defined fringes of the Mesopotamian political sphere, which also demonstrate relevant contemporary sequences. These are: Susa (Chantier A: Levels AXII–XI), the capital of the Elamite kingdom in Susiana; Tell Yelkhi (Level II), located in the Hamrin basin of the Middle Diyala; Tell Bderi in the Khabur river valley in the Syrian Jazirah; Failaka Island (Periods 3A–4A) at the head of the Gulf; and Qala'at al-Bahrain (Period IIIa), situated in the heart of the Gulf, the centre of ancient Dilmun.

3.3.1 Susiana

Susa, lying in the southeast Iranian plains, right at the core of second millennium Elam, yields an extremely complex stratigraphic sequence (Deschesne 1996: 37; Ghirshman 1964; 1967), the grappling with which has recently been extended further by Gasche et al. (1998: 22–6). Using mainly ceramic similarities with the Mesopotamian heartland, they identify a continuous period of occupation at the site throughout the mid-second millennium. This is represented by material from *Chantier A* (Levels XI–XV, particularly XII–XI) and to a lesser extent that from *Chantier B* (Level VI–V) in the *Ville Royale* area of the site (Gasche 1973). Indeed, it is this sequence from Susa that Armstrong and Gasche (2014: 2) believe to provide the only 'useful ceramic evidence to fill this gap at the mid-millennium'. Accordingly, sixty-one vessels from these deposits were chosen for inclusion in their recent Mesopotamian pottery typology (2014: 12) as a means of filling the developmental gap in the mid-second millennium.

Susa's goblets in particular (from Levels AXII–XI; ca. 1600–1400 BCE) have been used to help bridge this gap (Gasche et al. 1998: 21–6 and pl. 1.31–37; see also Gasche 1973). However, the Susa type goblets that are highlighted as transitional shapes (Gasche et al. 1998: pl. 3) show little similarity to any contemporary shapes found in the Tell Khaiber assemblage. It is of course possible that the Mesopotamian tradition of goblet manufacture that existed in the northern and central plains during the Late Old Babylonian period passed into Susiana at this point, but subsequently developed in a way that was isolated and divergent from Mesopotamia (Gasche et al. 1998: 38). Even so, the lack of direct parallels challenges the utility of Susa material as a valid source of comparative material for the Sealand period in Mesopotamia.

3.3.2 The Hamrin Basin

Following a period of abandonment after Level IIIa (ca. 17th century BCE), Tell Yelkhi demonstrates a continuous ceramic sequence, which encompasses its resettlement in Level II (ca. 1525–1400 BCE) and all of Level I (ca. 1400–1100 BCE).[13] While the Level I assemblage consists largely of typical Kassite period vessel types, some of the shapes that are unique to Level II fit well with those from Tell Khaiber. These include cylindrical beakers (Valtz 2002–3: table 147), jugs (table 152), and pithoi (tables 143–6). Grooved-rim jars especially (table 153.13) are identical with examples found both at Tell Khaiber and across the wider region (see Fig. 3.9).

Most cups identified from Level II at Tell Yelkhi (Valtz 2002–3: 290–3, tables 148–9), although bearing similarities with those at Tell Khaiber, generally have taller, funnel shaped necks, and almost always demonstrate stable pedestal feet; the only cups from Tell Khaiber that seem to reflect this shape are the two funnel-necked vessels from the Eastern Houses (Fig. 3.6). Other than these, Tell Yelkhi's cups seem to represent a more direct derivation from some of the Late Old Babylonian cups of the northern alluvium, such as those found at Tell ed-Der and Deylam (Armstrong and Gasche 2014: pl. 62.1–9; Gasche 1989: pl. 33). The common unstable footed cups from Tell Khaiber, on the other hand, are almost completely absent at Tell Yelkhi and carinated bowls (Valtz 2002–3: table 142.1-7), so typical of the Tell Khaiber assemblage, while present in Tell Yelkhi Level II, are also uncommon.

3.3.3 The Syrian Jazirah

Tell Bderi, located along the Khabur river valley, was re-occupied at the onset of the Late Bronze Age, as part of the newly emergent Mitanni state; occupation then continued throughout the Mitanni and Middle Assyrian periods (ca. 1500–1100 BCE) (Pfälzner 1990). At the point of re-occupation, the ceramics, although mostly different from those of Tell Khaiber, share infrequent stylistic traits. Several sharply carinated bowls, often with ring bases but sometimes with flat pedestal bases (Pfälzner 1995: pl. 9) and grooved bodies (pl. 14e, pl. 140c–d), as well as rounded cups with nipple or button feet (pl. 63c–k, pl. 157e–f), and a grooved rim jar (pl. 155c), are all evidence of these similarities. Each of these examples derives from contexts dating to the Middle Jazirah IA–B (ca. 1550–1300 BCE). Nevertheless, despite these selective parallels, none of the most common shapes found at Tell Bderi find comparisons at Tell Khaiber, but instead conform to a broader Syrian Jazirah style (Pfälzner 2007).

3.3.4 The Gulf

The resettlement of Failaka Island in Period 3A (ca. 1650–1600) took place at a time broadly contemporaneous with the First Sealand Dynasty's emergence in southern Mesopotamia. With resettlement came a distinctive Mesopotamian feel to the material culture of the island. This can clearly be observed in the sharp increase in Mesopotamian influenced pottery styles found at Tell F3 and F6 in the 1958–63 excavations (Højlund 1987) (Table 3.7). While Mesopotamian styles constituted just 1–2% of the assemblage in Periods 2A/2B (ca. 1900–1720 BCE), this reached 50% during Period 3A resettlement (ca. 1650–1600 BCE), and rose to 60% (Tell F3) and 91% (Tell F6) during

[13] Gasche et al. (1998; see also Armstrong and Gasche 2014: 11–12) have attempted to recalibrate the relative ceramic chronology for Tell Yelkhi. This, however, was met with a robust defence by Gentili (2012; see also Oselini 2018), who argued in favour of the original chronology proposed by Bergamini et al. (2002–3). It is the original chronology that is used here.

Approximate Date	Mesopotamian Political Dynasty	Failaka (Tells F3 and F6) 1958-63 Excavations				Failaka (Tell F6) 2008-12 Excavations	Qala'at al-Bahrain (Associated Period)
		Period	Sherd #	Mesopotamian Pottery	Local Pottery		
1900-1800	Old Babylonian	2A	132	1%	99%	Phase 2-5	IIb-c
1800-1720		2B	256	2%	98%		
1650-1600	First Sealand Dynasty	3A	174	50%	50%	N/A	IIIa
1600-1450		3B (F3)	237	60%	40%	Phase 6	
		3B (F6)	212	91%	9%		
1450-1375	Early Kassite	4A (F3)	352	90%	10%	Phase 7	IIIb1
		4A (F6)	471	99%	1%		
1375-1200	Late Kassite	4B	171	89%	11%	Phase 8	

TABLE 3.6. Percentage of pottery styles present in the different periods excavated at Failaka Island (after Højlund 1987: 112, fig. 460) with relevant further information.

Period 3B (ca. 1600–1450 BCE). These styles are represented both by Mesopotamian shapes as well as fabrics containing organic temper (Failaka Fabric Types E–G).

Failaka's Mesopotamian wares show significant shape parallels with Tell Khaiber's assemblage (Table 3.7), particularly during Period 3B. It is at this time that jars with grooved rim bands (Type 56) (Fig. 3.9d) were found in significant numbers in Rooms 4 and 5 of the Tell F6 'palace' storehouse (Højlund 1987: 140–3). Other clear parallels occur with the tablewares, which commonly include carinated bowls, plain (Type 67A) and with grooved decoration (Types 67B/C), and cups with nipple and button feet (Type 78) (Fig. 3.11). These typical 'Sealand' shapes, very common in Tell Khaiber's primary occupational sequence, were found in similar frequencies at Failaka. Likewise, more infrequent features of the Failaka 3B assemblage, such as a miscellaneous squat beaker (Fig. 3.12) and vessel pot marks (§5.4.3), also find excellent parallels at Tell Khaiber. The same pattern of Mesopotamian influence has also been demonstrated in more recent excavations at Failaka, Tell F6 (Phases 6–7: 1600–1450 BCE) (Højlund 2016), while results from 2012–17 excavations at Tell F3, which will provide a more refined chronological sequence for the critical Period 3B, are currently in preparation (Højlund in prep.).

Other notable similarities at Failaka are wavy-sided bowls (Type 69), ripple-sided bowls (Type 68), tall goblets (Type 81), and finer pedestal-footed goblets (Type 86), which occur only in Periods 4A–4B (ca. 1450–1200 BCE) (Fig. 3.8); since these vessels generally appear at Tell Khaiber only in the Eastern Housing and in pockets of surface scraped material, it provides further support for the slightly later sequencing of these deposits, as discussed in §3.13–4.

Approximately 300km further south at Qala'at al-Bahrain, reoccupation of that site in Period IIIa (ca. 1600–1450 BCE) yields very similar material changes (Højlund 1987: 157–62; Højlund 2019: 43–9, 161–2; Højlund and Andersen 1994: 179–81; Højlund and Andersen 1997: 50–62). The same Sealand period tablewares, so common at Tell Khaiber and Failaka Island, dominate the ceramic assemblages of the Dilmunite capital too (Fig. 3.13). Højlund's (1987: 158–60;

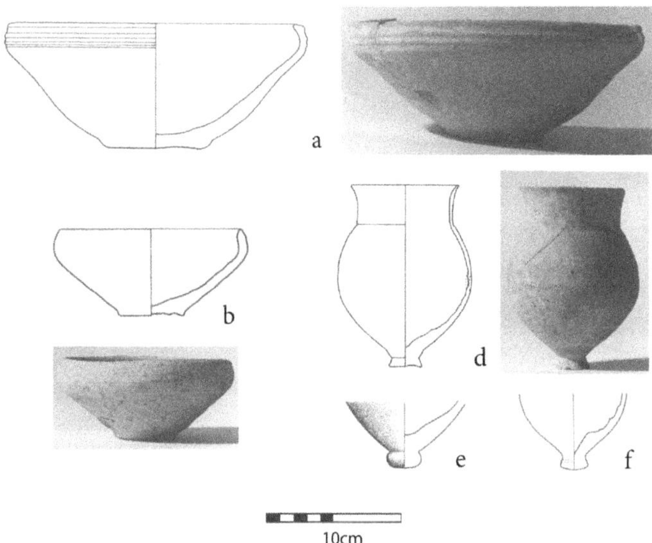

FIG. 3.11. A selection of table wares from Failaka Island (Periods 3B), showing similarities with those common at Tell Khaiber. From Højlund 1987: a) = 78, figs. 299–300, b) = 77, figs. 294–5, c) = 74, figs. 271–2, d) = 85, fig. 235, e) = 85, fig. 236.

FIG. 3.12. Miscellaneous Type 90.7 vessel from Tell Khaiber (a: p9020-43) alongside a similar vessel from Failaka Island, Period 3B (b: Højlund 1987: 75, fig. 280, and 85, fig. 332).

TK Type	Count/Percentage of Phase Total						Failaka Type	Count/Percentage of Phase Total					
	1 (n=187)	2.1 (n=1464)	2.2 (n=2619)	2.3 (n=605)	EH (n=419)	MSu (n=1248)		3A (n=174)	3B (F3) (n=237)	3B (F6) (n=212)	4A (F3) (n=352)	4A (F6) (n=471)	4B (n=171)
5.1–2	20 (10.7%)	273 (18.7%)	425 (16.3%)	73 (12.1%)	47 (11.2%)	63 (5.1%)	67A	-	9 (3.8%)	10 (4.7%)	-	-	-
5.4	-	1 (0.1%)	3 (0.1%)	-	2 (0.5%)	11 (0.9%)	69	-	-	-	13 (3.7%)	5 (1.1%)	3 (1.8%)
5.5	-	-	-	-	-	12 (1%)	68	-	1 (0.4%)	-	29 (8.2%)	5 (1.1%)	13 (7.6%)
10.1–2	14 (7.4%)	38 (2.6%)	63 (2.4%)	18 (3%)	3 (0.7%)	18 (1.4%)	67B/C	8 (4.6%)	17 (7.2%)	11 (5.2%)	1 (0.3%)	1 (0.2%)	-
40.1	-	-	-	-	-	17 (1.4%)	81	-	-	-	14 (4%)	-	2 (1.2%)
40.2	-	-	-	-	1 (0.2%)	29 (2.3%)	82	-	-	1 (0.5%)	-	-	-
40.3	-	-	-	-	-	4 (0.3%)	86	-	-	-	1 (0.3%)	-	2 (1.2%)
50.1–3	11 (5.9%)	61 (4.2%)	101 (3.9%)	28 (4.6%)	62 (14.8%)	107 (8.6%)	61B/79/80	-	2 (0.8%)	5 (2.4%)	2 (0.6%)	3 (0.6%)	-
50.4–5	15 (8%)	131 (9%)	256 (9.8%)	38 (6.3%)	23 (5.4%)	102 (8.2%)	78	-	13 (5.5%)	27 (12.7%)	5 (1.4%)	1 (0.2%)	1 (0.6%)
70.1	-	17 (1.2%)	41 (1.6%)	9 (1.5%)	5 (1.2%)	26 (2.1%)	54B/C	47 (27%)	5 (2.1%)	2 (0.9%)	1 (0.3%)	-	-
70.2	21 (11.2%)	79 (5.4%)	206 (7.9%)	40 (6.6%)	49 (11.7%)	80 (6.4%)	55A/B	-	3 (1.3%)	-	6 (1.7%)	3 (0.6%)	10 (5.9%)
70.3	14 (7.5%)	123 (8.4%)	241 (9.2%)	67 (11.1%)	31 (7.4%)	124 (9.9%)	56	2 (1.2%)	25 (10.6%)	65 (30.7%)	9 (2.6%)	7 (1.5%)	1 (0.6%)

Table 3.7. Counts and relative percentages by phase of the main chronologically diagnostic vessel types from Tell Khaiber, alongside comparative types and their occurrence by period from Failaka Island, Tells F3 and F6. Multiple types have been grouped into a single field when they match with a single type in the comparative typology. Tell Khaiber statistics taken from Table 3.5; Failaka statistics taken from Højlund 1987: 109, fig. 455.

1989: 12; 2007: 14–15; 2016: 257) long-held assertion that the influences that suffused the Failaka and Qala'at al-Bahrain assemblages undoubtedly emanated from a southern Mesopotamian tradition during the so-called Dark Age, has therefore been validated. The cultural and political implications of these remarkable material connections are discussed further in §6.2.

Højlund (2016: 256) has attributed these extensive similarities to a 'marked reliance on the import of Mesopotamian pottery, especially drinking and serving vessels' into the Gulf. However, while organic tempered fabrics (Failaka Ware G), typical of those in Mesopotamia, do begin to emerge in Periods 3A–B at Failaka (Højlund, 1987: 105–6), typical Sealand shapes at Qala'at al-Bahrain (Period IIIa) were regularly produced in local sandy fabrics too. These Sealand shapes were occasionally very finely manufactured, something that is not attested at Tell Khaiber (e.g. Fig. 3.13f). This mixture of clay preparation traditions at play in both the Failaka and Qala'at al-Bahrain assemblages suggests a complex picture of importation as well as emulation and assimilation that merits further analysis.

Adding further to the complexity of these emergent Gulf connections is a small sample of similar vessels from less well-stratified deposits at the mainland Saudi Arabian site of Dhahran (Zarins 1989: 81, 98, fig. 12). Parallels include typical carinated bowls, both plain and grooved (fig. 12.5 and 12.10), alongside some more peculiar hybrid types: a carinated bowl with painted decoration around the rim (fig. 12.4) and two jars with typical grooved rims but stable platform bases (fig. 12.14–15).

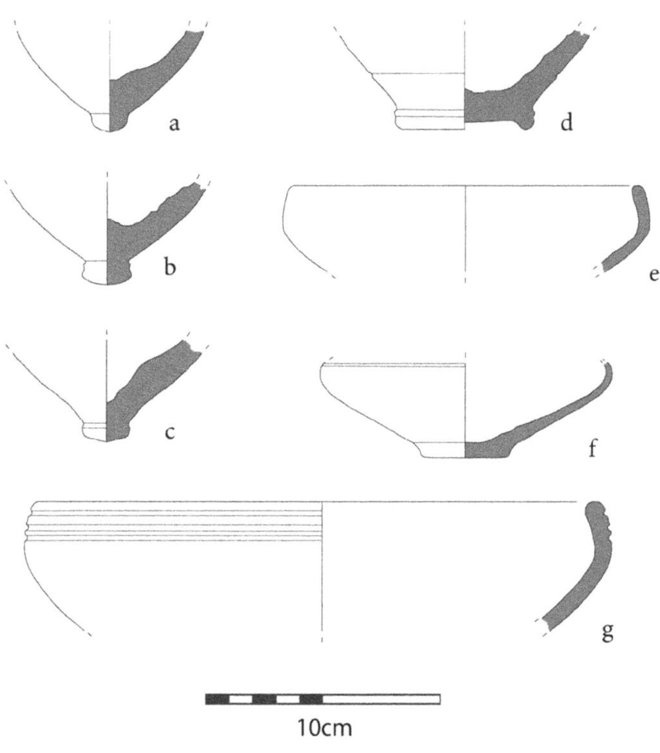

FIG. 3.13. A selection of table wares from Qala'at al-Bahrain, Period IIIa (Layers 12-14). a) 420.AB-B1-1; b) 420.BJ-BP-3; c) 420.AF-AU-5; d) 420.AF-BI-7; e) 420.AF-BP-4; f) 420.AF-AU-9; g) 420.BJ-BP-1.

4. The Sequence of Production

Two central forms of evidence—cuneiform texts, as well as macroscopic and microscopic analysis of the ceramic material itself—allow for a detailed understanding of the stages of the *chaîne opératoire* underpinning the production of the Tell Khaiber assemblage. Three sequential stages: clay collection and preparation, forming techniques and secondary treatments, and, finally, drying and firing are the key elements in the process of production.

4.1 Clay Collection and Preparation

4.1.1 Historical Background

Although there are no direct written sources that address clay collection and preparation techniques in the Mesopotamian context, these activities are hinted at in several texts of different genres, including lexical lists, literary epics, and incantations. Some of these are as follows.

Collection of (riverine) clay

In a Sumerian poetic debate between Summer (*emeš*) and Winter (*enten*), the work of the potter is presented as a summer activity and is characterised as follows: 'the potter who digs out clay, lights a fire and stokes it with wood, [...] the pot' (ETCSL 5.3.3 l. 210; see also Sallaberger 1996: 13). The summer months would have been ideal for clay extraction, since the river floods have by then abated, and the deposited clay is easy to obtain. That clay digging fell under the remit of potters themselves is reinforced by a personnel list from the Ur III period Temple of Inanna at Nippur, where a potter is listed as working in the 'clay pit of the god Iškur' (6N-T 454, rev. ii 10 in Zettler 1992: 157, 285; see also Sallaberger 1996: 13).

Levigation in soaking pits

The 'clay pit of the god Iškur' mentioned above suggests the use of soaking and levigation pits to remove heavy particles and produce finer clays, thus making clays more workable. Another document from Ur III Umma takes this further, stating that 14 men for one day 'stirred the clay' for king Shulgi's temple (RTC 402, rev. 3–4 in Sallaberger 1996: 14, author's translation). Although this activity is commonly attested as a stage in brick rather than pottery manufacture, it does show that clay extraction and preparation could be an intensive operation carried out at significant scales. An incantation in a Neo-Assyrian ritual for the manufacture of protective figurines instructs the Apsû, god of fresh and sweet waters, to consecrate and purify the clay pit, followed by an incantation: 'Clay pit, clay pit, you are the clay pit of Anu and Enlil, the clay pit of Ea, lord of the deep, the clay pit of the great gods; you have made the lord for lordship, you have made the king for kingship, you have made the prince for future days...' (*Šep lemutti ina bīt amēli parāsu*, ll. 151–4, transl. Wiggermann 1992: 13; see also Sallaberger 1996: 9). This passage demonstrates the ritual and even cosmological significance of these clay bodies and the craft activities which surrounded them.

Tempering of raw clay

Little is known from texts of clay tempering practices. Clay tempering practices did, however, provide a common source of metaphorical inspiration in Mesopotamian literature (Foster 2010: 142). The Old Babylonian creation epic Atrahasis, for instance, recites:

> Nintu shall mix clay
> With his flesh and his blood.
> Then a god and a man
> Will be mixed together in clay.
>
> Atrahasis, I iv (Dalley 1989: 15)

Foster (2010: 142) describes this literary scene in typically vivid and poetic manner, saying that 'just as shells, grit, and vegetal matter may give added plasticity and durability to clay, so man's physiological and psychological complexities are paradoxically the sources of his flexibility and strength.' It is clear then that the tempering of clay as a process was widely understood in Mesopotamian society and formed a potent allegorical device.

From the early first millennium, the lexical list UR$_5$-RA = *ḫubullu* (henceforth Ḫḫ) provides a scholarly perspective on what was mixed with raw clay. At the start of a section of terms referring to the processing of suitable clay, the following terms are listed:

> 484' **im in-nu** *ṭīṭ tibni*, 'clay with straw'
> 485' **im in-nu**-RI MIN *ilti* 'the same with chaff'
> 489' **im in bul-bul ḫi-a** *ṭīṭ pî*, 'clay with chaff' (Akk.)
> (Ḫḫ X, ed. Landsberger 1959: 104; cf. Sallaberger 1996: 14)

It is significant that subtle distinctions are drawn between these organic additives. These differences also seems to be reflected to some extent in the Tell Khaiber ceramic evidence, as will be discussed below.

Working of the clay body

Ḫḫ X (lines 422–38) also provides several verbs associated with clay working and preparation: *karāṣu*, 'to cut off, pierce (and form)' from the clay mass; *balālu*, 'to mix'; *mahāṣu*, 'to beat'; and *ruqququ*, 'to reduce and thin/stretch'. Further words associated with clay preparation include *kupputu*, 'lump forming', and *pišiltu*, 'clay lump' (Landsberger 1959: 101; Sallaberger 1996: 11–13). Several of these verbs are present in an Old Babylonian bilingual writing exercise from Ur (UET 6/3 673, transl. Peterson 2019: 829), an unusual text that details the steps to be followed when producing a clay tablet. It instructs the scribe to:

1. Take hold of the clay
2. Pinch off the clay/soften the clay(?)
3. Beat the clay
4. Thin it out
5. Set the 'head turning'(?) in motion(?)
6. Build up the middle, twist it/turn it around
7. Create the tablet (using a wooden tool)
8. Lengthen it/thicken it(?)
9. ...
10. Write/incise the rulings(?)
11. Stand it up(?)

Several of these stages of working and folding have been identified through material analysis of the British Museum's tablet collection (Taylor 2011: 7–12). The process of working clays fit for tablet production was presumably not far removed from the processing of clays suitable for the production of fine ware pottery; no doubt at least some of these actions were used to prepare regular potting clays too.

4.1.2 Clay Preparation at Tell Khaiber

Many of the processes outlined above are too ephemeral or transitory to leave permanent archaeological or architectural traces that can be easily identified. Consequently, the only evidence we have to understand the ways in which Sealand period potters processed their clays are the finished products. Tell Khaiber's vessels were manufactured from alluvial Euphrates clays. In some cases, these clays were used with little modification, as seen by the fine natural sand present in the matrix (Fabrics C and D). The natural composition of these riverine clays does, however, mean that they had little inherent plasticity or strength (van As and Jacobs 1992: 535). The predominant additive was therefore organic material, either in the form of fine chaff (Fabrics D and H) or rough straw or reed (Fabrics E, F, and H), the very same additives outlined in the lexical lists. These organics were present to some degree in at least 84% of the examined vessels (Fabrics D, E, F, and H), 62% of which were deliberate additions (Fabrics E and F), since they contain large amounts of organic matter that are unlikely to have been found in naturally occurring clays.

Shrinkage during drying and firing was a significant problem with natural Euphrates clays. This process affected the adherence of the clay body, causing catastrophic cracks and fissures to occur (van As and Jacobs 1992: 535–6). Since organic additives hold water for longer than the surrounding clay matrix, the consequent slower drying inhibits rapid shrinkage, thus offsetting or even preventing the formation of cracks, while also increasing the coherence and plasticity of the clay mass (Rye 1981: 33–4). It is for this reason that organic material forms the most common additive to Tell Khaiber's vessels.

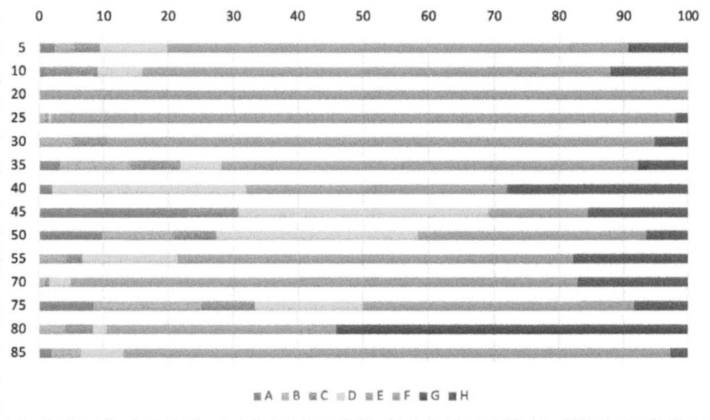

FIG. 4.1. Relative percentages of fabric types according to vessel family. Families composed of anomalous shape types are not included.

The size and concentration of these organic inclusions appear to have been determined mainly by the size of the intended vessel. Large vessels, such as pithoi (Family 25) and jars (Family 70) almost invariably demonstrate higher concentrations of rough organics or large voids where these inclusions once were (Fabrics E and F). Organics were probably added in the form of agricultural waste, perhaps following the year's harvest. Smaller vessels, such as bowls (Family 5), bottles (Family 45), and cups (Family 50), generally exhibit sparser, finer chaff and/or reed inclusions (Fabric D and E), maybe added in the form of dung or manure, which would not have been as heavily dependent on seasonal availability. Van As and Jacobs (1992; 2014) observed similar mixed tempering practices carried out by modern potters in the vicinity of Baghdad, where, in order to regulate the performance of riverine Euphrates clays, both manure and fine fibrous material (*Typha latifolia*) formed common additives to the clay matrix.

Each vessel category at Tell Khaiber appears to be formed of reasonably well-worked and levigated clays, visible in the even cross-sections of most sherds. The clearest exception to this rule is Fabric H, which contains undissolved clay inclusions, varying from small to large in size and pale pink to light brown in colour. This fabric type is present amongst a range of vessel types at Tell Khaiber and seems to occur naturally in the raw clay body. They are thus preserved in ceramic vessels when the clay was inadequately filtered or manually worked.

Almost all sherds in the assemblage contain naturally occurring non-plastics, such as fine grains of sand and calcite, albeit in differing concentrations. In some instances, such as Fabric A, the infrequency and relative fineness of these particles (<0.1mm) suggests that the potter was careful to filter out most of the naturally occurring minerals. This process, however, is quite rare in the assemblage (ca. 4%) and does not appear to correspond to a discernible fine ware tradition. The presence of calcite (Fabric C) is also quite rare and is for the most part limited to smaller vessels, such as bowls and cups. It is unclear if this represents an alternative pattern of raw clay sourcing for these vessels types, or whether the identification of calcite in these vessels is in fact a product of different firing practices, with calcite particles reacting differently when exposed to different temperatures; they remain largely unchanged at low temperatures (ca. 650–750 °C), but melt and fuse with the clay matrix at temperatures over ca. 1000 °C (Quinn 2013: 191–8).

Very few vessels demonstrate the clear and deliberate addition of mineral temper, as recognised by the shape and frequency of these particles. This is probably because increased non-plastic additives could have further affected the coherence of a clay body that was already difficult to work, thus further increasing the likelihood of cracking during drying and firing (van As and Jacobs 1992: 535–6). Only one vessel family (Family 80) contains extensive non-plastic inclusions (Fabric G), the high concentration and angular shape of which mark them as deliberate additions. These angular mineral inclusions were added in association with the intended function of these vessels as cooking wares. Production of these clay bodies may have formed a particularly specialised task, restricted to itinerant potters or specialised workshops.

Just a few vessels seem to demonstrate noticeably anomalous fabrics. One is composed of finely worked clay matrix containing only medium to large, angular, black mineral temper (p8032-37), which sets it apart from the rest of the assemblage. Another vessel (p5016-3) has a grey-black coloured fabric with a high density of calcite inclusions, as well as visible mica particles. Both of these vessels are Type 45.2, a rare type of bottle with heavily burnished exterior surfaces. These vessels may represent imports from a different production unit from that or those which usually serviced the Fortified Building at Tell Khaiber.

Overall, a small number of broadly defined fabric groups have been identified amongst the Tell Khaiber assemblage. These are constituted mainly of different concentrations of the same inclusion types coupled with some variation in the processes of filtering and levigation (see Fig. 4.2). These correspond well with the general differences in the various processes of clay preparation outlined in the Mesopotamian texts (see §4.1.1). The general consistency in fabrics across the assemblage was also borne out in pXRF analysis carried out on ca. 500 sherds, which did not provide any significant separations or chemical groupings.[14]

Variation in fabric composition was determined mainly by vessel shape type, over any other factor. The tight clustering of fabric types identified at Tell Khaiber could, therefore, be the result of two potential factors:

1. A clear tradition of clay preparation shared and adhered to by potters from different Sealand period workshops.

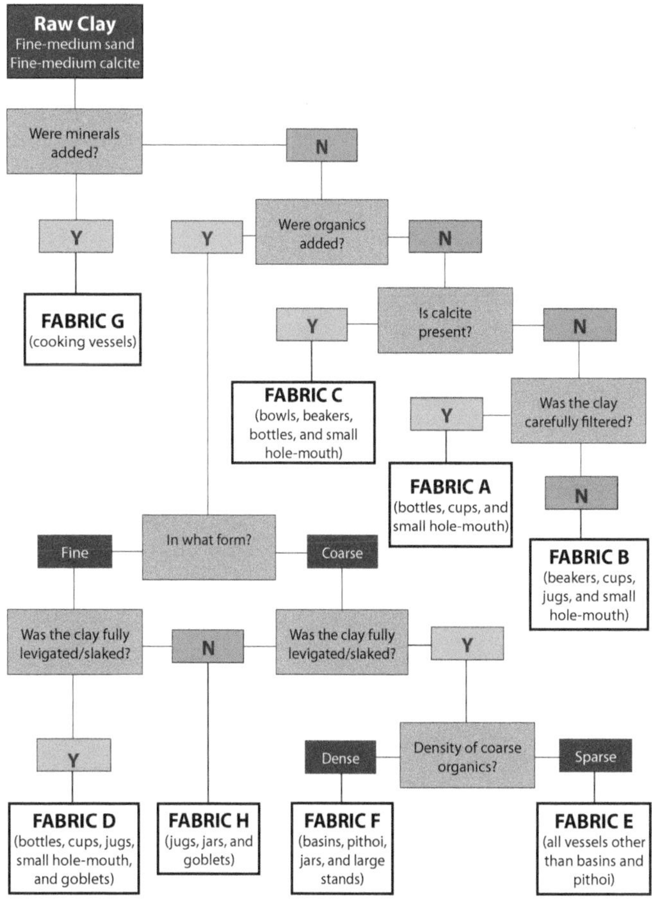

FIG. 4.2. Flowchart mapping the actions involved in the preparation of the clay body and the resulting fabric and vessel types.

[14] This may also be a result of the deposition of homogenous secondary clays covering large areas of the southern Mesopotamian alluvial zone (Campbell, S. 2016, pers. comm.), a factor also noted by van As and Jacobs (2014: 87).

2. A small number of production units responsible for manufacturing the entire Tell Khaiber assemblage throughout its occupational sequence.

I would suggest that we are probably seeing a convergence of both these elements. As is increasingly the case throughout the second millennium, there is a habit of clay preparation that focuses particularly on the use of different concentrations and sizes of organic inclusions (van As and Jacobs 1992; 2014). Yet, within this overarching tradition, the more nuanced differences in fabric types between smaller vessels (bowls, cups, and jugs) and larger vessels (jars, cookpots, and pithoi) evidenced at Tell Khaiber may be the result of different producer or workshop specialisms.

4.2 Forming Techniques and Secondary Treatments

4.2.1 Background and Methods

Forming technique refers to the methods by which the walls of a vessel are raised and shaped. Studies of forming techniques in Mesopotamian pottery studies have typically designated two mutually exclusive categories: handmade and wheel-thrown vessels. However, there exists a spectrum of intermediate techniques that incorporate aspects of both hand and wheel manufacture to fashion a vessel's profile and manipulate its shape (Roux 2019: 54–95). The differences between these various techniques are contingent upon whether or not rotative kinetic energy (henceforth RKE) was used. While wheel-throwing raises the vessel walls and rapidly forms the vessel's rough-out or preform by means of continuous, generally high-speed RKE, wheel-coiling refers to the creation of a rough-out via coil building,[15] before discontinuously applying RKE to create the finished shape (Roux and Courty 1998: 748; Velde and Druc 1999: 164).

Wheel-coiling can be performed in several different ways, depending on the stage of the forming process at which RKE is applied. Roux and Courty (1998: 749, fig. 1) have designated four primary methods of wheel-coiling: RKE used only for shaping (Method 1); RKE used for thinning and shaping (Method 2); RKE used for joining, thinning, and shaping (Method 3); RKE used for joining, thinning, and shaping successive coils in turn (Method 4). While mastery of any technique that utilises RKE requires cumulative bimanual skills that can be attained only through an extensive and intensive period of apprenticeship (Choleva 2012; Roux and Corbetta 1989), wheel-coiling is comparatively less demanding than wheel-throwing (Berg 2020: 10).

As a sequential process, wheel-coiling techniques can be executed in short bursts, utilising interrupted rotation rather than continuous rotation of the wheelhead (Berg 2013: 117). This aligns well with some of the key material, climatic, and technological limitations faced by Sealand period potters:

- The lack of natural plasticity in Euphrates clays.
- The dry heat of southern Iraq, which would have dried the clay very quickly.
- The discontinuously turning wheelhead, if an apprentice was not present to keep it spinning (e.g. Berg 2007: 246, fig. 11).

Although the range and complexity of wheel-based forming techniques has long been recognised (e.g. Rye 1981), the difficulty of identification amongst archaeological ceramic assemblages has formed a central point of debate. This is particularly the case when identifying the differences between wheel-throwing and wheel-coiling, processes that often leave very similar visual signatures on finished vessels (Courty and Roux 1995; Roux and Courty 1998).

Contemporary texts offer little in the way of resolution when it comes to understanding the precise forming techniques employed by Sealand potters. As Sallaberger (1996: 15, author's translation) has previously noted, 'the sources tell us practically nothing about the central work of potters at the wheel, or of their equipment.' Although the group of verbs in the lexical lists, discussed in §4.1.1, could justifiably also be linked to forming processes, these terms ('to pierce', 'to cut', or 'to pinch') could just as easily be applied to numerous other activities, such as baking or bread making. The lack of detailed reference to wheel-based production, I would suggest, reflects the specialised skills that were involved in these processes. Use of the potter's wheel involved a restricted skillset, with which the general populace would largely have been unfamiliar. Gosselain (1992; 2000) echoes these thoughts, stating that because forming processes are usually the least visible stage of the *chaîne opératoire*, they are consequently the least understood by non-potters: 'Relatives, neighbours, or customers who do not engage in pottery making or observe potters at work tend to remain oblivious to technical peculiarities…' (Gosselain 2000: 192).

Scientific techniques permit finer-grained identifications of diverse forming techniques. X-ray analyses of pottery vessels, for instance, have shown much potential in this regard. Although early successful attempts were conducted as far back as the 1930s–40s, these were generally used to demonstrate differences in the type and density of vessel inclusions (Titterington 1935, cited in Berg 2008: 1177) or individual defects in the production of individual vessels (McEwan 1997, cited in Berg 2008: 1177). It was Rye (1977; 1981: 61–2) who effectively brought this technique to mainstream archaeological attention. An outline of its utility for understanding forming techniques was explicitly addressed by Carr (1990), and more recently by Pierret (2019).

Rye (1977: 206; 1981: 51–3) recognised that the application of pressure to soft clay causes inclusions and voids to take up particular orientation patterns. These patterns vary depending on the nature of the pressure exerted on the clay matrix and are therefore largely determined by the primary forming technique (Fig. 4.3). Not only is it possible to identify sharply differentiated techniques, such as slab-building and

[15] Coils are created by rolling clay on a flat surface or between the hands to create a rope-like shape (Velde and Druc 1999: 164).

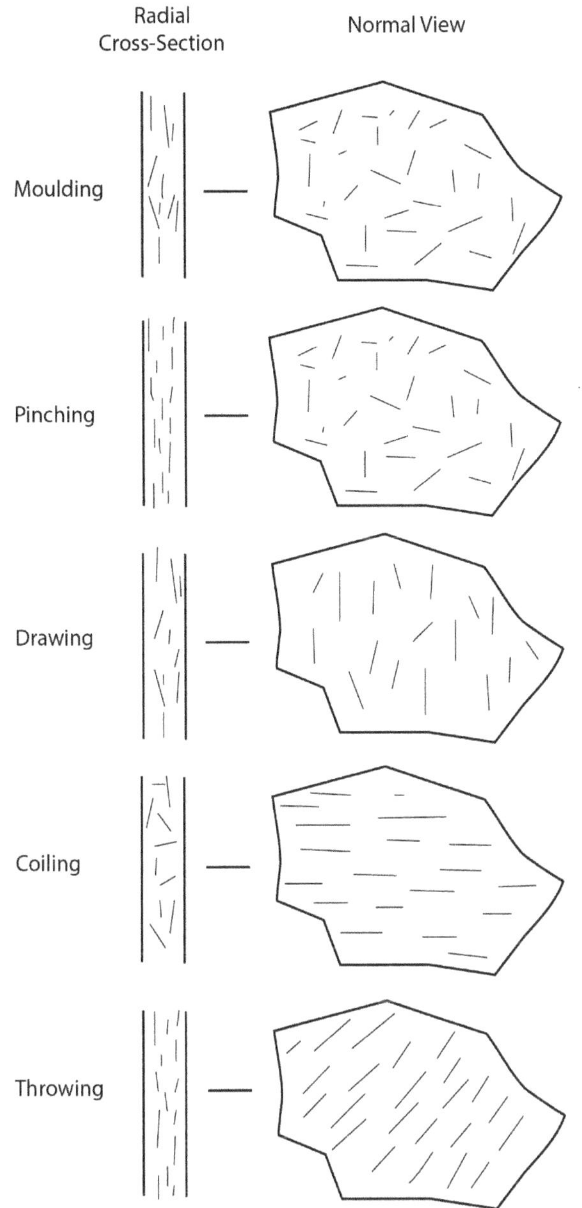

FIG. 4.3. Generalised patterns of inclusion orientation determined according to primary forming technique (after Berg 2008: 1178, fig. 1).

wheel-throwing, but also more subtle differences between wheel-throwing and most methods of wheel-coiling (see Berg 2008; 1180–1; Berg 2011; Henrickson 1991).

Patterns of inclusion orientation are generally fixed during primary forming. Therefore, while their visibility, macro- and microscopically, may be masked somewhat by secondary forming and finishing techniques, such as scraping, burnishing, painting, or slipping, they are never obliterated entirely (after Berg 2008: 1181–5). Secondary forming techniques, on the other hand, such as turning or beating, can usually be identified much more successfully through visual analysis (Berg and Ambers 2012). Roux (2019: 180–5) asserts that reliable identification of primary forming techniques cannot be gathered solely from inclusion and pore orientation, identified in X-ray analysis, but should as far as possible be analysed in conjunction with microscopic and macroscopic data of vessels profiles and radial cross-sections (Berg 2008). Accordingly, Roux outlines a number of key macroscopic traits that can help to separate wheel-coiled vessels from their wheel-thrown counterparts.

Vessel surfaces

- Differences in wall thickness along the horizontal plane; consistent wall thickness is typical of throwing, while uneven walls are typical of wheel-coiling, as they mark the differential thickness of the original coils.
- Differences in wall thickness along the radial plane; walls becoming gradually thinner higher up the vessel are generally thrown, whereas vessels that vary, and occasionally become thicker at points higher up the vessel, are indicative of wheel-coiling, where a thicker coil was placed above a thinner coil;
- Curvilinear concentric fissures located on key compression zones, thus marking coil joins, are typical features of wheel-coiling;
- Horizontal fractures along coil joins also indicate wheel-coiling.

Radial cross-sections

- Long horizontal or oblique fissures indicating coil joins;
- Fine fissures subparallel to the extension of the vessel walls;
- Random-parallel orientation of inclusions, as a result of the differential pressures involved in wheel-coiling e.g. differential sequences of coiling, drawing, and pinching (Methods 1–4: see Roux 2019: 86, fig. 2.37).

4.2.2 Forming the Tell Khaiber Assemblage

A sample of thirty-one Tell Khaiber vessels from several different shape categories were selected for X-ray photographs.[16] These were analysed and interpreted with the guidance of Dr. Ina Berg at the University of Manchester. Several distinct forming techniques are attested, alone and in combination, in the manufacture of the different shape families present in the Tell Khaiber assemblage.

All vessels, other than cooking pots (Family 80) and some infrequent trays and basins (Family 20), show clear evidence for the use of RKE at some point in the production process, either in primary forming or finishing. Significantly, however, no vessels yield definitive signatures for wheel-throwing. Instead, the majority of Tell Khaiber's vessels were wheel-

[16] X-rays were performed at a local clinic in Nasiriyah, using a Collimator: Lighting Supply 24V 100W; Focus 1000m; Radiation Field (Max) 432×432mm; Total Filtration >2.5mm A1. TRIUP International Corp. The X-ray clinic could not provide the original digital images for further modification or enhancement, but supplied the images as printed X-ray film. The images presented here are photographs of these films on a light box.

coiled, a technique employed either in building the entire vessel rough-out, or for specific sections of composite vessels, where wheel-coiling was combined with other techniques. The entire Tell Khaiber assemblage can be split into five broadly defined Forming Groups (A–E) (see Fig. 4.21).

Forming Group A: Bowls (Families 5 and 10), Small Hole-Mouth (Family 75), and Small Vessel Stands (Type 85.1)

Bowls demonstrate many of the usual signatures associated with the application of RKE:

- Ridging and rilling patterns on the interior and exterior surfaces, which are representative of the manual pressures applied when shaping and/or finishing the vessel on the wheel.
- The 'slurry effect' (after Rye 1981: 75), which is a typical consequence of the water added during wheel production to help maintain the clay's plasticity; this smudging is usually distributed irregularly across both the inner and outer surfaces of vessels.
- Concentric spirals on the exterior base, the signature left when vessels are removed from the rotating wheel-head using a taut implement such as a string (Rye 1981: 80, fig. 63). Occasionally the bases of bowls also yield the fingerprints of the potters who lifted them from the wheel.

Van As and Jacobs (2014: 88) have taken these macroscopic signatures to suggest that second millennium vessels (bowls, cups, and goblets) from Tell ed-Der were thrown off the hump, one after another in quick succession. Yet, as numerous ceramicists have noted in recent years, these visual signatures are not definitive of wheel-throwing. They only demonstrate that the wheel was used at some point during forming and/or finishing.

Instead, bowls from Tell Khaiber show a number of features consistent with wheel-coiling (Fig. 4.5):

- A horizontal-oblique orientation of inclusions and pores.
- Asymmetries in rim thickness, when examined from the top down, a diagnostic feature of the differential thickness of the original coil.
- Evidence of curvilinear concentric fissures, indicative of coil joins running horizontally or obliquely around the vessel.
- The decentralised position of the base in relation to the vessel walls; such imperfect centring would have made it impossible to throw the vessel on the wheel.

It is difficult to state definitively whether Tell Khaiber's bowls were built through separate coiled segments or through coil spiralling. However, the asymmetrical orientation of the ridging, visible macroscopically on the surfaces of the vessels, but more clearly visible in the X-ray images (Fig. 4.5), strongly suggests the routine use of coil spiralling. It is likely that the potter wound a coiled spiral to form the rough-out of the vessel walls, before using RKE to join, thin, and shape the vessel's preform; this would conform to wheel-coiling Method 3 (after Roux 2019: 84–6).

FIG. 4.4. Macroscopic signatures of wheel-production on bowls: a) fine rilling and surface smudging (p3064-445); b) fine concentric circles on base (p3080-79); c) regular surface undulations and ridging (p9018-33); d) concentric circles on irregularly shaped base (p3054-399). Not to scale.

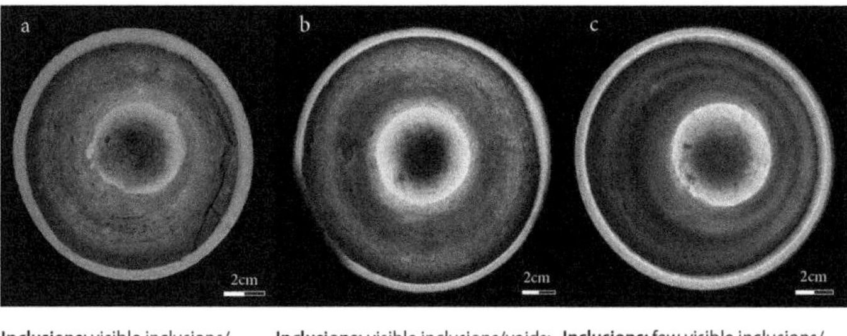

Inclusions: visible inclusions/voids; horizontal-oblique orientation.
Shape: imperfect centering; spiralling ridge pattern; uneven rim thickness.
Coil Seams: curvilinear concentric fissures.

Inclusions: visible inclusions/voids; horizontal-oblique orientation.
Shape: regular concentric ridge pattern; uneven rim thickness.
Coil Seams: curvilinear concentric fissures.

Inclusions: few visible inclusions/voids; horizontal-oblique orientation.
Shape: pronounced imperfect centering; irregular spiralling ridge pattern; uneven rim thickness.
Coil Seams: curvilinear concentric fissures.

FIG. 4.5. X-ray images of Type 5.1 bowls showing inclusions and shape evidence consistent with wheel-coiling: a) p3064-276; b) p3064-653; c) p3099-13.

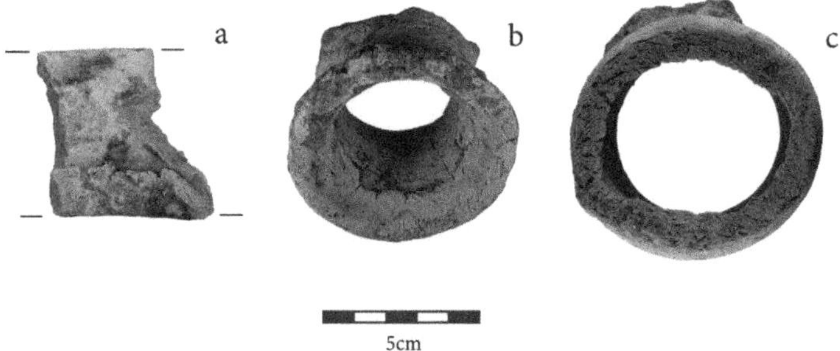

FIG. 4.6. Evidence for rough folding of the base and irregular ovoid shape of some small pot stands: a) p6166-19; b) p5022-16; c) p5016-1.

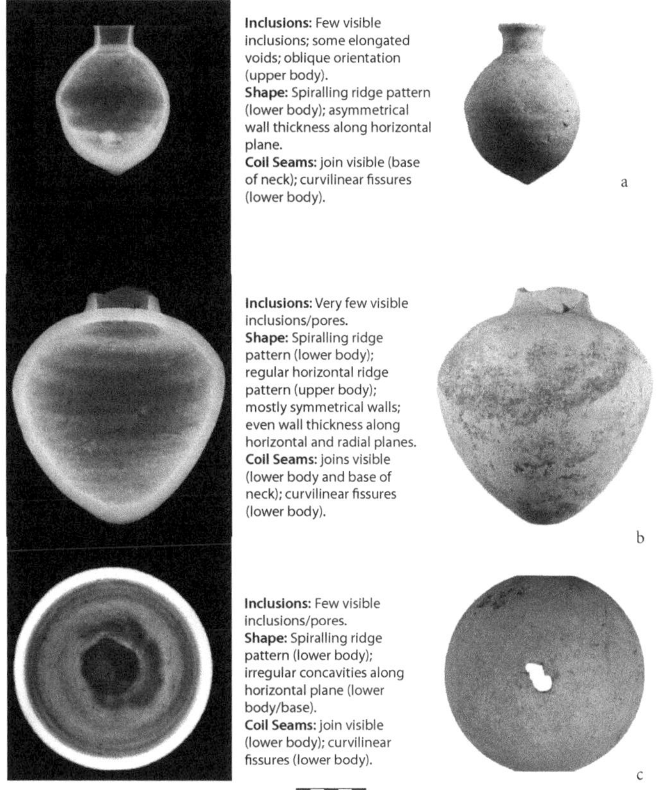

Inclusions: Few visible inclusions; some elongated voids; oblique orientation (upper body).
Shape: Spiralling ridge pattern (lower body); asymmetrical wall thickness along horizontal plane.
Coil Seams: join visible (base of neck); curvilinear fissures (lower body).
a
Inclusions: Very few visible inclusions/pores.
Shape: Spiralling ridge pattern (lower body); regular horizontal ridge pattern (upper body); mostly symmetrical walls; even wall thickness along horizontal and radial planes.
Coil Seams: joins visible (lower body and base of neck); curvilinear fissures (lower body).
b
Inclusions: Few visible inclusions/pores.
Shape: Spiralling ridge pattern (lower body); irregular concavities along horizontal plane (lower body/base).
Coil Seams: join visible (lower body); curvilinear fissures (lower body).
c

FIG. 4.7. X-ray images of bottles: a) p3124-18; b) p8032-37; c) p8083-6.

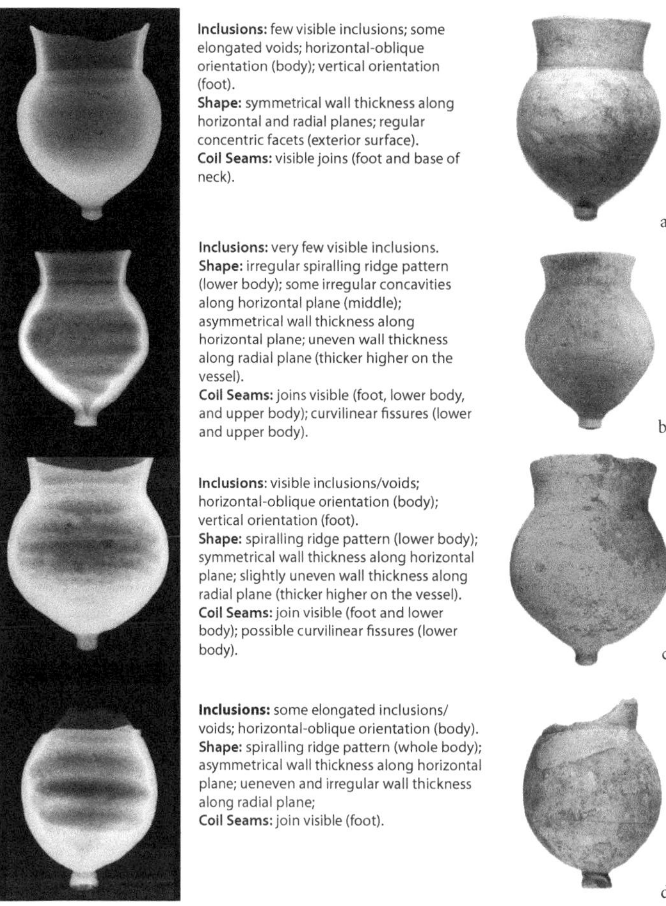

Inclusions: few visible inclusions; some elongated voids; horizontal-oblique orientation (body); vertical orientation (foot).
Shape: symmetrical wall thickness along horizontal and radial planes; regular concentric facets (exterior surface).
Coil Seams: visible joins (foot and base of neck).
a
Inclusions: very few visible inclusions.
Shape: irregular spiralling ridge pattern (lower body); some irregular concavities along horizontal plane (middle); asymmetrical wall thickness along horizontal plane; uneven wall thickness along radial plane (thicker higher on the vessel).
Coil Seams: joins visible (foot, lower body, and upper body); curvilinear fissures (lower and upper body).
b
Inclusions: visible inclusions/voids; horizontal-oblique orientation (body); vertical orientation (foot).
Shape: spiralling ridge pattern (lower body); symmetrical wall thickness along horizontal plane; slightly uneven wall thickness along radial plane (thicker higher on the vessel).
Coil Seams: join visible (foot and lower body); possible curvilinear fissures (lower body).
c
Inclusions: some elongated inclusions/voids; horizontal-oblique orientation (body).
Shape: spiralling ridge pattern (whole body); asymmetrical wall thickness along horizontal plane; ueneven and irregular wall thickness along radial plane;
Coil Seams: join visible (foot).
d
5cm

FIG. 4.8. X-ray images of narrow footed cups. a) p1085-17; b) p9020-41; c) p6127-1; d) p3102-2.

Two other vessel families fit within this general forming group. Small hole mouth vessels (Family 75), for instance, are the only other vessel types to routinely demonstrate string-cut bases, which suggests that the lower bodies were formed by the same means as bowls. The upper bodies, on the other hand, show evidence of coil segments being added to the base, before being joined, shaped, and thinned using RKE, in a similar manner to many bottles, cups, and jugs (see Fig. 4.8–9). While no X-rays were performed on small pot stands (Type 85.1), macroscopic analysis appears to show that they too were wheel-coiled. While showing surface evidence of RKE (e.g. fine rilling and smudging), this is often coupled with faintly perceptible horizontal-obliquely oriented ridging, which was probably also the result of a single spiralled coil. The general lack of vessel symmetry in profile (Fig. 4.6c), and the frequent occurrence of bases folded roughly inwards (Fig. 4.6 a–b), provides further evidence for wheel-coiling.

Forming Group B: Bottles (Family 45), Cups (Family 50), Jugs (Family 55), and Small Beakers (Family 35)

The first step in producing Tell Khaiber's cups, jugs, and bottles broadly mirrored the manufacture of bowls, in that the potter wound a coiled spiral of clay to form the lower body. This coil was then joined, thinned, and shaped using RKE. Again, this can be observed in the irregular horizontal-oblique orientation of the ridging on the interior surface, which assumes an asymmetrical alignment across opposite walls of the vessels (Fig. 4.8–10). This forming technique usually reached the lower body or the middle of the vessel, but may occasionally have been applied to the entire body of cups, up to the base of the neck (e.g Fig. 4.8d).

During this first forming phase, it appears that the potter left a small hole in the base of the vessel, ready for the foot to be attached at a later stage. In vessels where there is no discernible foot, such as round bottomed bottles (Family 45) and cups (Type 50.6), no hole was left; instead, the spiralled coil of clay was closed during this initial forming stage, sometimes by manually pressing and pinching (e.g. Fig. 4.7c).

Just below the midpoint of most bottles, cups, and jugs, the coil spiralling technique was replaced by the building of the upper body, probably by using separate coiled segments. These segments were placed one on top of another, before being joined, thinned, and shaped by applying RKE in combination with manual pressures (Roux and Courty 1998: fig.2). The wheel-coiled segment technique can be recognised by the horizontal alignment of coil ridges and the relative symmetry of wall thickness along the horizontal plane. A further indication of coiled segments is the differentiation in wall thickness of vessels on the radial plane, in that the thickness occasionally increases higher up the vessel (Fig. 4.8 and 4.10); this is typical of the building of vessels with separate coils, where the coil above can be slightly thicker than the one placed below. It is, however, inconsistent with wheel-

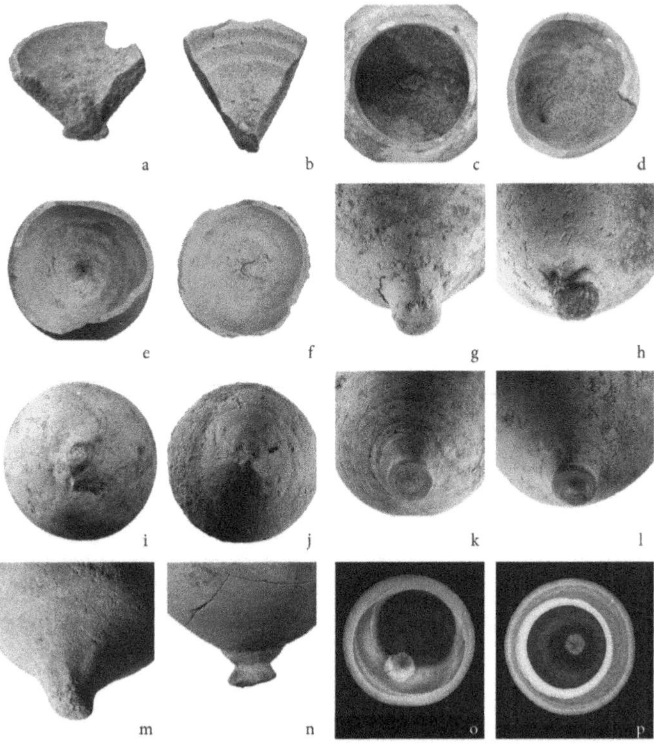

FIG. 4.9. Technical signatures of unstable footed cups, showing interior (a-f), exterior (g-n), and X-ray images (o-p). Not to scale.

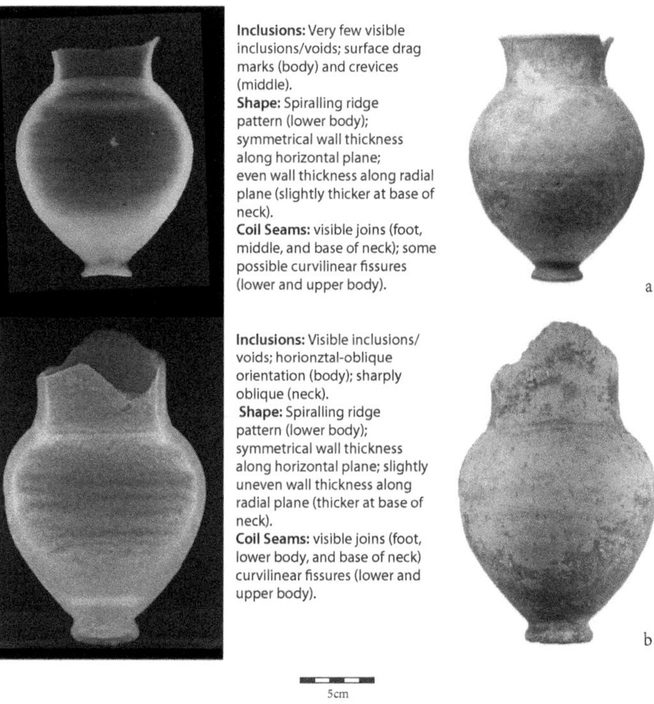
Inclusions: Very few visible inclusions/voids; surface drag marks (body) and crevices (middle).
Shape: Spiralling ridge pattern (lower body); symmetrical wall thickness along horizontal plane; even wall thickness along radial plane (slightly thicker at base of neck).
Coil Seams: visible joins (foot, middle, and base of neck); some possible curvilinear fissures (lower and upper body).
a
Inclusions: Visible inclusions/voids; horionztal-oblique orientation (body); sharply oblique (neck).
Shape: Spiralling ridge pattern (lower body); symmetrical wall thickness along horizontal plane; slightly uneven wall thickness along radial plane (thicker at base of neck).
Coil Seams: visible joins (foot, lower body, and base of neck) curvilinear fissures (lower and upper body).
b
5cm

FIG. 4.10. X-ray images of a stable footed cup (a: p3064-226) and a jug (b: p6124-19).

throwing, where thrown walls usually become gradually thinner higher up the vessel. In some cases, the separation between coils, or between the lower and upper body, can be identified by horizontal curvilinear fissures (e.g. Fig. 4.7–10). Occasionally, use of pinching and drawing to combine the lower and upper bodies of cups is also identifiable by irregular vertically oriented concavities, visible only in the X-ray imagery (e.g. Fig. 4.8b).

The direction of pores and inclusions subtly varies between vessels, as well as at different points of the same vessel. The sequential wheel-coiling process outlined here generally leaves a horizontal-oblique orientation of inclusions/pores (see Fig. 4.8). This is consistent with the original alignment of inclusions parallel to the placed coil, coupled with the exertion of various manual pressures used with RKE to consolidate joins, and to thin and shape the vessel (after Roux 2019: 185). The necks and rims of vessels were applied as extra coiled segments in much the same way as the upper bodies; the relative neatness of the neck and rim, with little evidence of interior ridging, reflects the increased attention paid by the potter to finishing these elements. The resulting smoothness of the interior neck, for instance, is better suited to the controlled pouring of liquids, which was of course the primary intended use of cups and jugs. The increased manual pressures applied during joining and finishing the neck and rim resulted in a more pronounced oblique pattern of inclusions and voids; this might even conform to Method 4, where the neck/rim consists of one thrown coil (Roux 2019: 84–6).

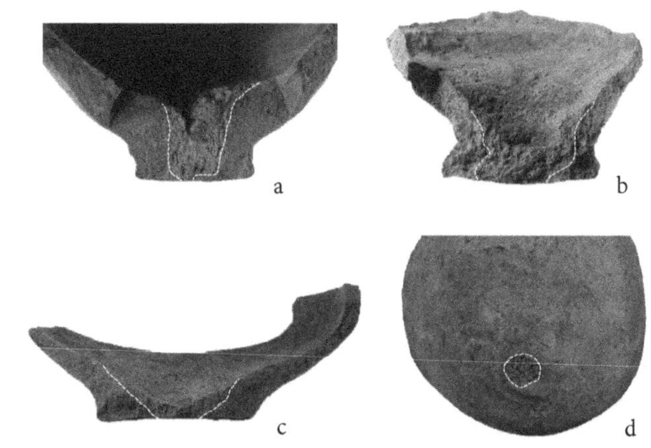

FIG. 4.11. A selection of vessels demonstrating base techniques incorporating the addition of a chaffy clay tenon, marked by the white dashed line: a–b) jugs (p1137-5 and p3084-55); c) bowl (p5057-2); d) cup with broken foot (p1166-28).

5cm

FIG. 4.12. Pronounced angular body shape of some cups, marking the points of joins: a) p3084-33; b) p3088-31; c) p9020-106.

The final stage of producing the vessel rough-out or preform for a cup or jug was the production of the foot. This process appears to have taken place once the body of the vessel had dried to a leather-hard consistency. At this point, the potter could invert the vessel onto its rim in order to attach and shape the foot. It is this part of the vessel that demonstrates the most diversity in shape, the fundamental difference being the separation between the production of stable (Types 50.1–3 and Family 55) and unstable feet (Types 50.4–5).

The feet of unstable footed cups consisted of a stumped coil of clay, which was manually applied to the hole left at the bottom of the lower body. This stump was then twisted and drawn to join and shape. This process is also suggested by the spiralling orientation of pores around the feet of several cups (e.g. Fig. 4.9o–p) as well as their vertical orientation in the foot itself (Fig. 4.8). It also left one of two traces on the interior base: either a small excess of clay poking through the interior base into which the foot had been pressed (Fig. 4.9a–c), or a narrow hole leading into the foot (Fig. 4.9d–f). The place where the foot/base joins the lower body is sometimes indicated by a pronounced curvilinear crack or fissure directly above the foot (e.g. Fig 4.9i) or a sharp turn in the orientation of the vessel's profile; it is also sometimes accompanied by neat rilling, indicating where the join has been tidied using RKE (e.g. Fig. 4.9k–l, and n). Once the attachment is completed, the attention paid to reshaping and finishing the foot varies markedly. Usually, RKE is used to trim and finish the foot, leaving it neat and well-defined with a fine rilling pattern (Fig. 4.9k–l); occasionally, however, the foot is left as a rough stump, exhibiting only the manual twisting and drawing pressures of its formation (Fig. 4.9g–j, and m).

Stable feet were produced in a similar fashion to unstable variants, through application of a separate coil of clay to the lower body while the vessel was inverted on the wheel. For these broader feet, however, this coil of clay was often wrapped around a tenon of chaffy clay, which was added by potters as a preventative measure to help stop the total mass of wet clay from cracking during subsequent drying and firing. This strategy, which has been discussed extensively elsewhere (Glatz and Casana 2016: 141–3; van As and Jacobs 1987: 42–51; 2014: 81), was not restricted to cups and jugs, but was occasionally also used on bowls and beakers (Fig. 4.11).

The composite sequence of production outlined above incorporates several forming techniques and discrete stages. The main separations between the different stages of vessel formation generally occur in specific locations: directly above the foot, at the midpoint, and at the base of the neck. While some vessels do show surface evidence for coil seams at these points (e.g. Fig. 4.10a), in most vessels these seams are well merged and, without supporting X-ray evidence, are suggested only by occasional sharp changes in wall direction (Fig. 4.12). Nevertheless, the points of coil seams are also the location of significant compression zones for these vessels, that is the areas subjected to maximal stress during production and use (after Roux 2019: 179–88). It is therefore no surprise that these areas mark the most frequent points of vessel breakage amongst Tell Khaiber's bottles, cups, and jugs.

Forming Group C: Jars (Family 70), Large Beakers (Family 35), and Large Vessel Stands (Type 85.2)

Due to issues of preservation, it was not possible to produce X-rays of any complete jar profiles; the lower sections of these vessels in particular tend to fragment readily. Macroscopic evidence suggests that the lower bodies of jars were produced differently from the rest of the assemblage, with no definitive evidence for the use of RKE. Running concentrically around the horizontal axis of the interior of these vessels are regular concavities, which are consistent with manual pressures applied regularly to the interior surface (Fig. 4.13e and 4.14d). The exterior surface, on the other hand, is smooth and does not show the same scraping/smoothing signatures as bottles, cups, and jugs. These manual pinching and drawing processes are reflected in the random orientation of inclusions visible on lower jar bodies (Fig. 4.13b–e).

It is therefore likely that the lower body of jars also started as a coiled spiral, but was then pressed by the potter into a concave mould to join the coils and shape the body (Rye 1981: 81). This mould may have been a re-used jar base, or, more likely, a shallow plastered pit, such as those found in the pottery workshop at Tell Sabi Abyad (Duistermaat 2008: 359–63, figs. V.11–12). The common indented dimple on the interior base of jars (Fig. 4.13f) suggests that the bases were closed through pressing down the coil from the interior. The

FIG. 4.13. Interior surface signatures for the main sections of jars: a) p5016-3; b) p6111-63; c) p8013-13; d) p6111-68; e) p1159-1; f) p3085-283.

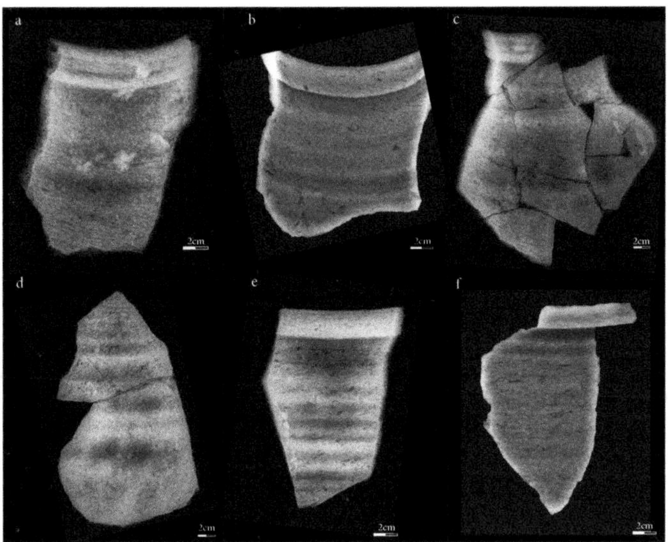

FIG. 4.14. X-ray images of jar rims and upper bodies (a: p6141-1; b: p8083-1; c: p8013-14), jar middle to upper (d: p6111-63), and the upper bodies of large beakers (e: p8008-114; f: p8082-42).

reduced wall thickness thus created at this position formed an inherent point of weakness common to jars, with many vessels broken at this point.

Above the lower body, the production technique changed. The regular concavities noted for the lower body typically give way to a horizontally oriented ridging pattern, which runs irregularly along the radial plane of the vessel (Fig. 4.13b–d). It appears therefore that Tell Khaiber's potters built the upper profiles of jars using individual coiled segments, which were joined, thinned, and shaped in turn using RKE (van As and Jacobs 2014: 88); the same technique was used for larger cylindrical beakers (Fig. 4.14e–f). Indeed, the extensive horizontal or oblique patterning of inclusions and voids on the upper bodies, which become more sharply oblique at the neck and rim, are common to both these vessel types. This further demonstrates the marked preference by mid-second millennium potters for using RKE to shape vessels along the horizontal axis, rather than harnessing its rotary force to lift vessel walls.

Once the wall of a jar or large beaker had been built, the thickened rim band, typical of these vessels, was formed from an extra coil of clay. These rim bands were subsequently finished, using RKE to finish the several common types of these Families, which are differentiated only by the number of grooves on the rim (e.g. Types 70.2 and 70.3). The point at which the rim band was attached and joined to the body can occasionally be identified by the overlapping excess of clay on the interior (Fig. 4.13a).

Finally, it seems that large vessel stands (Type 85.2) were produced using similar techniques to those for jars. Individual coiled segments were laid one on top of another, before being pinched to join. This is evidenced by regular well-defined concavities along the horizontal plane of some examples (Fig. 4.15). Many vessels were then brought to their final shape, smoothed, and finished using RKE.

FIG. 4.15. Interior surface of Type 85.2 pot stand fragment (p6136-90), demonstrating regular concavities along the horizontal plane.

Forming Group D: Pithoi (Families 25 and 30)

Pithoi were mostly coil built. The base was formed in the same manner as a regular jar base, as can be observed macroscopically from the typical impressed dimple (Fig. 4.16a). The upper bodies of pithoi were built of thick coiled segments, which were seemingly joined together without RKE, by extensive drawing of the coils. This manual drawing is identifiable by the sharply oblique orientation of inclusions and pores visible in X-rays (Fig. 4.17). The fine horizontal rilling that is present on the surfaces of pithoi demonstrates that extensive final surface smoothing took place using RKE, perhaps with the vessel inverted on the wheel. These finishing processes subsequently obliterated much of the surface evidence for coiling and drawing. The regular ribs attached to the exterior surfaces of pithoi were probably positioned at prominent joins between large coils, a common technique used to buttress the key compression zones of such large vessels.

The final part in the production process was the manufacture of base additions. For regular pithoi (Family 25), the vessel body was upturned and a ring base, shaped separately of a large coil of clay (Fig. 2.12), was attached to the exterior base; this ring base was often produced of a clay matrix with more chaff than the rest of the vessel, meaning that the join is clearly visible. For pithoi with pierced bases (Family 30), on the other hand, a separate coil of clay was attached to the centre of the exterior base, which was then pierced with a narrow hole to form the protruding 'bunghole' shape that defines this family (Fig. 2.14).

Pithoi are the only vessels in the Tell Khaiber assemblage that out of necessity may have been produced in the immediate vicinity of the Fortified Building. Some of these vessels are extremely large and cumbersome, and occasionally have rim diameters wider than some of the door openings in the building. It would therefore have made little sense to move them over extended distances.

Forming Group E: Cookpots (Family 80)

Cookpots were entirely handmade. Indeed, the high density and large size of mineral inclusions in these vessels (Fabric G) would have reduced vessel plasticity in a manner incompatible

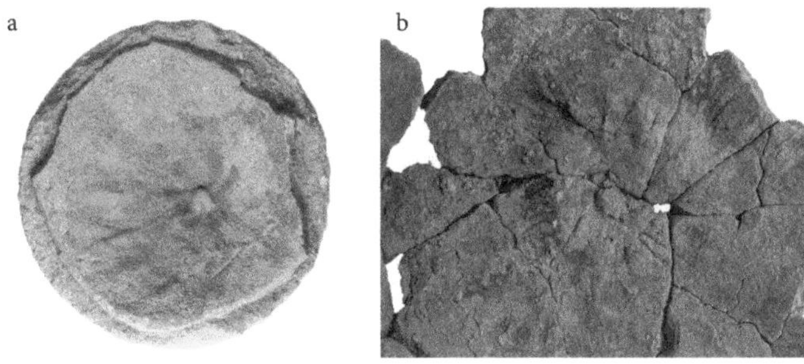

FIG. 4.16. Views of interior bases of a pithos (a: p6122-1) and a cookpot (b: p5063-1), showing characteristic spiralling dimples. Not to scale.

FIG. 4.17. X-ray image of the neck and rim of a pithos (p3125-1).

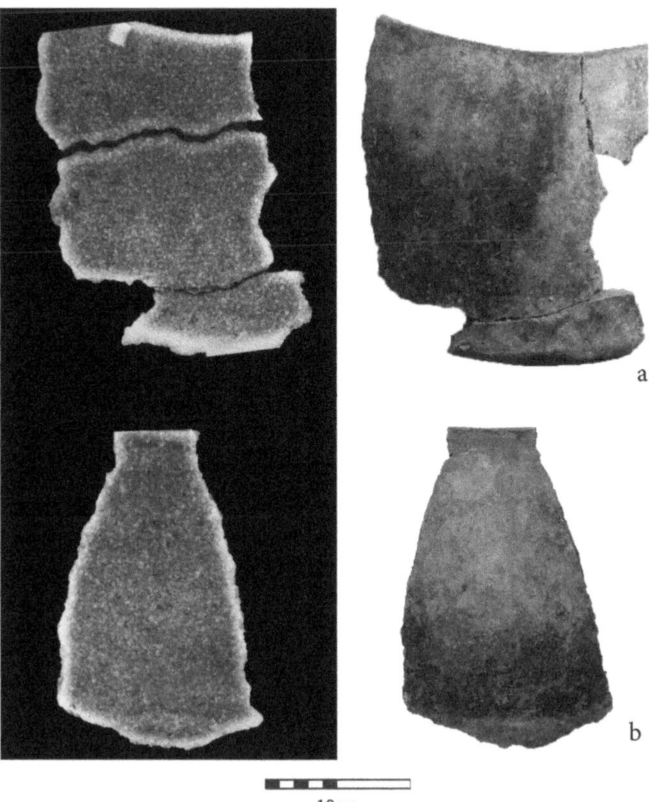

FIG. 4.18. X-ray images of cookpot profiles: a) p1079-51; b) p9018-87.

with wheel production (after Rye 1981: 61). Cookpot bases demonstrate the typical dimple base (Fig. 4.16b), present also in jar and pithos bases, so again indicate production by coiling and pressing the lower body into a mould, before building the walls. The oblique coil seams used to build the walls are perceptible in the X-ray images and often form points of vessel breakage (e.g. Fig. 4.18a). Joins between the coils were consolidated and the walls were thinned using the paddle and anvil technique. This is demonstrated by regular localised casts resulting in differential wall thickness along the horizontal and vertical planes of the interior surface (Rye 1981: 84–5, fig. 70f).

Ad Hoc Production: Basins/Trays (Family 20)

A less well-defined forming group is composed of unique handmade vessels. These are a mixed group of vessels that vary morphologically, but were generally produced by coiled segments, which were manually pinched and drawn to join.

4.2.3 Surface Treatments and Decoration at Tell Khaiber

Treatment or decoration of a vessel's surface has the capacity to alter the aesthetic of the vessel, thus enabling the communication of specific meanings or social identities (e.g. Bowser 2000; Gosselain 2000; Hegmon 1992; Hegmon and Kulow 2005). However, post-forming treatments may also be used to confer specific use-related properties (Rice 1987: 231; Rye 1981: 24).

Several techniques of surface modification can be identified in the Tell Khaiber assemblage. As already touched upon, vessels of all sizes were routinely turned. This process involved the use of a knife or other sharp tool, which was held against the surface of a vessel as it rotated on the wheel. The pressure exerted worked with RKE to remove excess clay, thus thinning the vessel walls and adding finesse to the final shape (Rye 1981: 62–3). Scraping and turning is most effectively conducted when the clay is almost leather hard. These secondary treatments can obliterate surface evidence for primary forming techniques, since they often remove any evidence of fingerprints that can be picked up through visual or X-ray analysis. Many cups show evidence for extensive trimming and scraping with a smooth-edged tool. This presents visually as numerous angular and pronounced facets, sometimes 5–10mm thick, running along the horizontal plane of the vessel's exterior surface (Fig. 4.19b), or as fine striations around the base (Fig. 4.9k–l). Sometimes grit drag marks are also visible along the vessel's surface (Rye 1981: 86–7).

Smoothing of vessel surfaces with wet hands or a wet cloth was also common and can be recognised by a fine rilling pattern, where the potter's fingerprints left regular, fine casts. This is most clearly visible on the surfaces of bowls (Family 5) and some cups (Family 50). Smoothing is also evidenced by smudged patches on the exterior surface (Fig. 4.19a), clearly discernible on the exterior of cookpots (Family 80). More discretely, smoothing is present as a light layer of self-slip, that is a thin coating of clay, the same colour as or a shade lighter than, the clay body. It occurs when the surface is formed,

FIG. 4.19. Examples of surface treatments: surface smudging on cookpot exterior (a: 9018-87); surface scraping on cup exterior (b: p1085-17); red-pink slip on bowl exterior (c: p4067-16); and pink-purple slip on cup interior (d: p9018-83). Not to scale.

smoothed, and manipulated with wet hands (Rye 1981: 57) and is therefore common with many smaller vessels (Forming Groups A–B), where water was continuously added to the surface during wheel-based production. Since self-slip is usually the inadvertent result of various forming and finishing processes, it should be distinguished from the practice of deliberate slipping, where a vessel is purposely coated with a liquid suspension of clay to enhance its visual appearance or to ensure impermeability (Rye 1981: 57). Deliberate slipping is rare in the Tell Khaiber assemblage and is demonstrated only by a small number of bowls, cups and bottles (Fig. 4.19c–d). Burnishing, the process by which a shiny, smooth texture is obtained by rubbing the leather-hard surface of a vessel with a small blunt object, is also rare, apart from on squat, round bottomed bottles (Type 45.2).

Many vessels also exhibit concentric incised or impressed lines or bands running around the upper body or the base of the neck. While impressed bands were most likely the work of the potters' fingers, incised lines and toothcomb decoration could only have been achieved with the use of a sharp tool (Rye 1981: 90–2). Both decorative techniques must have been accomplished using RKE, with either finger or tool held stationary against the vessel surface while it turned on the wheel. When this technique was used on overly wet clay, the effect is smudged, whereas on dry clay the effect is comparatively rough. The variation in the neatness of execution within the Tell Khaiber assemblage suggests that these decorative techniques were regularly produced on both wet and dry, even leather-hard, clays (Fig. 4.20).

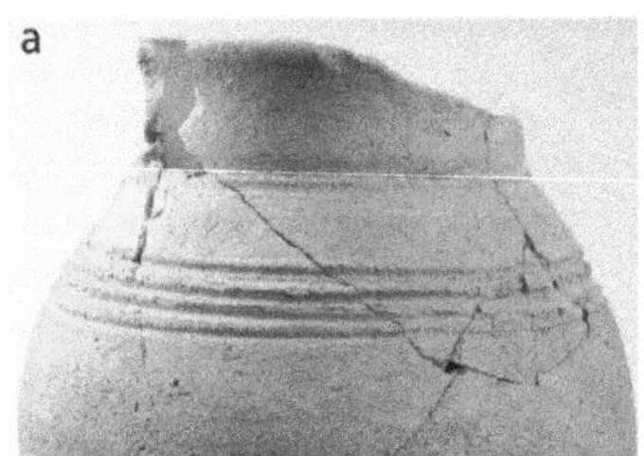

FIG. 4.20. Incised and impressed concentric line decoration around the shoulder of cup and jug (a: p9020-112; b: p1153-1), and impressed and wavy band decoration on a large beaker (c: p5022-66).

4.2.4 Quality Control

It is important when discussing forming and finishing techniques to consider the issue of vessel standardisation. Standardisation refers to how tightly Sealand potters conformed to specific shape types. Rice (1981) considers the process of standardisation to emerge via the interplay of two key factors: an increasingly narrow concept of what constitutes an acceptable vessel—the intentional—alongside the increasing skill of the potter in achieving that concept—the mechanical.

Here, I will discuss briefly the intentional aspects of standardisation, as this is important to understanding the framework of value production that structured Sealand period pottery manufacture.[17] To do this, I will employ a method known as the envelope system (Orton et al. 1993: 158–9). The envelope system is achieved by reducing illustrated examples of a specific pottery vessel type to a common size and overlaying them. This creates a composite picture of similarity and difference of shape, with the shaded area—or envelope—in between encompassing all individual shape variants. This permits the ceramicist to unpack the key attributes of the potter's 'mental template' (after Deetz 1967: 45–7; see also Rye 1981: 59), or 'ideal vessel form' (Glatz 2015: 17) more effectively. Envelopes are presented here for Tell Khaiber's two most common vessel Families: bowls and cups (Fig. 4.22).

It is immediately clear that each individual example conforms tightly to a specific shape type. The 25 complete carinated bowls (Fig. 4.22a) share several distinctive attributes: a flat to slightly indented base, flaring outwards directly into a shallow, straight-sided body, with a sharp curve

[17] For a more detailed analysis of both the intentional and mechanical aspects of standardisation in the Tell Khaiber assemblage, see Calderbank 2020a.

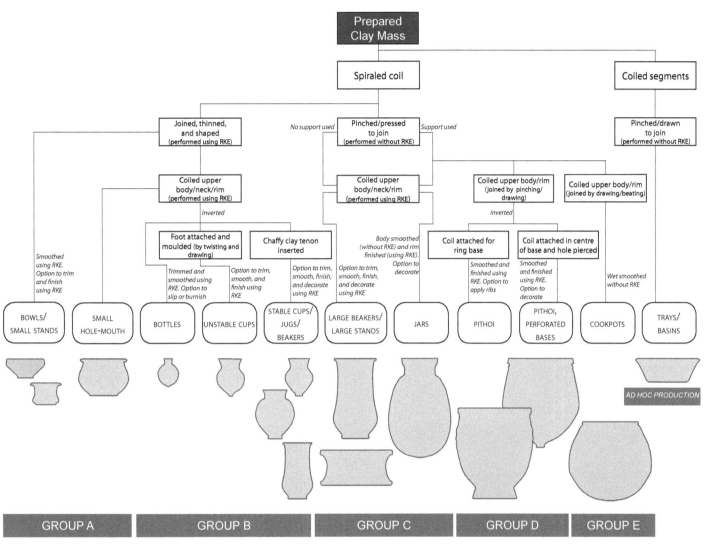

FIG. 4.21. A technical tree illustrating the primary and secondary forming choices generally made when building the different vessel families in the Tell Khaiber assemblage.

or carination close to an almost vertically oriented, rounded rim. These attributes all combine to form part of a clearly defined mental template. Despite these shared attributes, we also see a degree of difference between individual vessels, particularly in the width of the base, the orientation of the body, and the sharpness and direction of the curve or carination. This pattern is repeated in the envelope system for curved bowls (Fig. 4.22b). Again, the shared attributes—a flat base, giving directly into a shallow, rounded body, with a simple rounded rim—are clear for each individual vessel. Yet, there is also a degree of slippage or differentiation in the execution of each individual vessel.

Cups at Tell Khaiber are separated into two main categories: stable and unstable. These two cup categories show a slightly different pattern of standardisation. As with bowls, there was clearly a sharply defined mental template in the potters' minds when manufacturing these vessels; each must demonstrate a short foot, a round body shape, and a short, clearly defined neck with a slightly everted, rounded rim. Each of the 26 stable footed cup profiles shares these features (Fig. 4.22d), as do the 40 unstable footed examples (Fig. 4.22e). Yet, as a whole, unstable footed cups show a

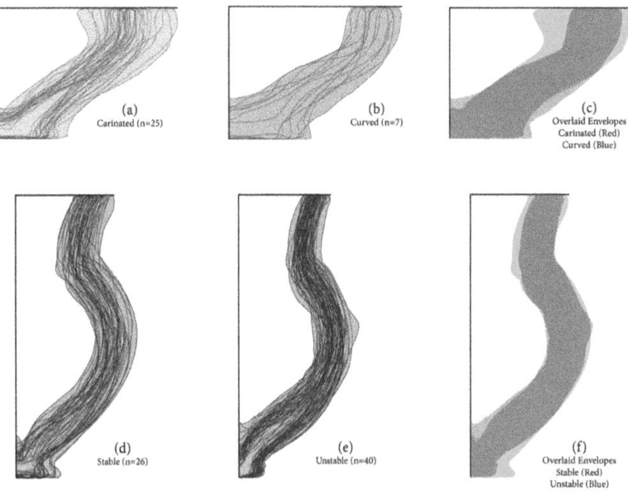

FIG. 4.22. Envelope systems for common bowls (a–c) and cups (d–f).

higher level of standardisation than stable footed variants, as demonstrated by the tighter envelope.

This is not to say, of course, that such cups were invariably produced to a rigid standard. Several acutely lopsided or misformed cups (Fig. 4.23) and ones with extensive cracking at the base (e.g. Fig. 4.9i), as well as lopsided bowls, sometimes with very rough bases, were present in the Tell Khaiber assemblage. Such misformed vessels would have been common in pottery workshops. In the Late Bronze Age workshop at Tell Sabi Abyad, for instance, a number of unfired vessel fragments, or 'cast offs,' were identified (Duistermaat 2007). However, since the Fortified Building at Tell Khaiber existed at a distance from the production context of its ceramics, the presence of these misformed vessels speaks to the fact that, although a mental template was desired, its implementation was not always strictly adhered to. In order to arrive at Tell Khaiber, these lopsided vessels would presumably have passed some level of formal or informal quality checks not only by the relevant pottery workshop(s) themselves, but also by the administrators stationed at Tell Khaiber. It appears that, to each of these respective actors, if these vessels were judged to be functional, they were also deemed acceptable for circulation and use.

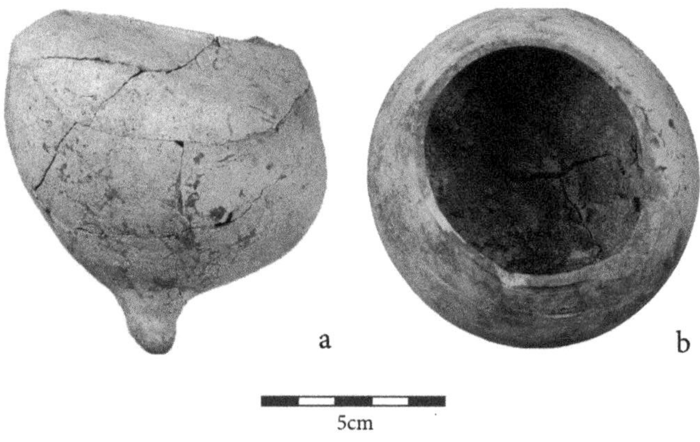

FIG. 4.23. An acutely asymmetrical cup with a rough shaped foot (a: p8083-23), and a misshapen vessel with a severe crack on the interior base (b: p8083-44).

4.3 Drying and Firing

4.3.1 Background and Methods

With the entire manufacturing process dependent on the success of the drying and firing procedure, it is no wonder that these elements are often, to judge from ethnographic parallels, shrouded in ritual and metaphor (Barley 1994; Gosselain 1999: 209–11, 215–7). As Vandiver (1991: 362) describes it, 'the process of transformation during forming and firing seems to have had the appeal of a somewhat magic process in which clay, made plastic by water, is formed into magic shapes and then undergoes mutation by fire to rocklike hardness.' Mesopotamian creation narratives (see Foster 1991; 2010: 142 for references) tell us of clay people and animals that were set in the sun to dry, while others were baked in 'kiln-wombs.' Yet, comparatively little is written about the technicalities of this process.

A single Old Babylonian administrative record from Sippar-Ammanum (Edzard 1970: No. 198, ll. 89–141) can be related directly to the technical firing of vessels. This text lists 10 oven fillings, accounting for 130–140 vessels in total (Sallaberger 1996: 17). Since the type of vessels fired cannot be reliably identified, however, the size and nature of the kiln itself cannot be accurately reconstructed. Nevertheless, the average of 13–14 vessels per firing does suggest small-scale potting and firing activities at Tell ed-Der.

Further indirect references in texts might speak to the type of fuel that was commonly used by Mesopotamian potters in stoking their fires. In an economic document from Ur III Umma, for instance, a potter is listed as a recipient of a substantial amount of waste straw (140 bales, each ca. 30kg) from the sheepfold (Umma 76, obv. 1–4, transl. Sallaberger 1996: 17). Another Umma text refers to ten bundles of straw to be sent to the pottery workshop (MVN 14, 440, transl. Sallaberger 1996: 18). Finally, in various other documents, Inim-Šara, named elsewhere as a supplier of pottery vessels, acts as supervisor of a pottery workshop; in this role he receives supplies of straw, split branches of Euphrates cotton, and gatherings of shrubs (Sallaberger 1996: 18). It is not made clear if in any of these cases this plant material was used as firing fuel or as tempering material (see §4.1), but the quantities would certainly support its use as fuel.

Another form of fuel, suggested by van As and Jacobs (2014: 91–2), is crude oil. Certainly oil products were extremely common in second millennium Mesopotamia (Forbes 1964, cited in van As and Jacobs 2014: 91); bitumen, as we have seen, was a common surface additive to many larger vessels. It is conceivable therefore that potters may have used crude oil or lumps of bitumen as fuel for their firings, as is common practice amongst modern Iraqi potters (Van As and Jacobs 2014: 91–2). However, these fuel sources would have been difficult to obtain relative to farm waste in the form of brushwood, shrubs, and waste straw; bitumen, for instance, was relatively valuable and required specialist labour to collect. Furthermore, agricultural waste would have released less dense smoke and fewer noxious gases. These features may have made these sources of fuel far more suitable for second millennium potters, thus explaining their frequent attestations in the texts.

Although the exact nature of kilns is difficult to identify from the written sources, numerous pyrotechnic installations have been identified in the second millennium archaeological record. These include several large updraft kilns at Tell Zubeidi (Boehmer and Dämmer 1985: 28–31), eight kilns at Tell Kasaran (Quarantelli 1985: 69), one at Tell Asmar (Frankfort et al. 1940: 9, fig. 2), several from Tell Deylam (Armstrong and Gasche 2014: 8), three from Failaka (Kjaerum and Højlund 2013: 97), and several very well preserved kilns with chimneys from Umm al-Hafriyat

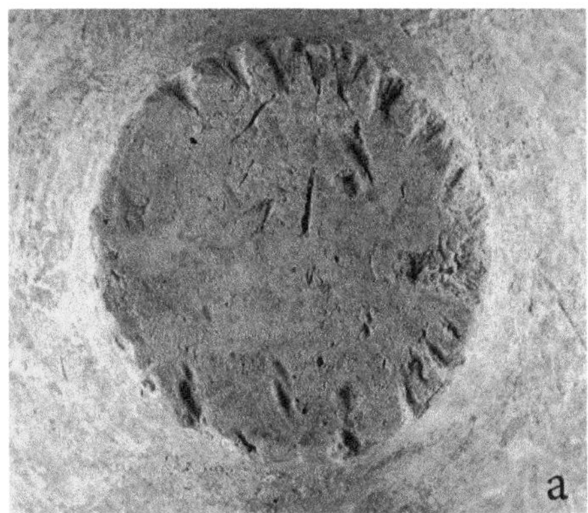

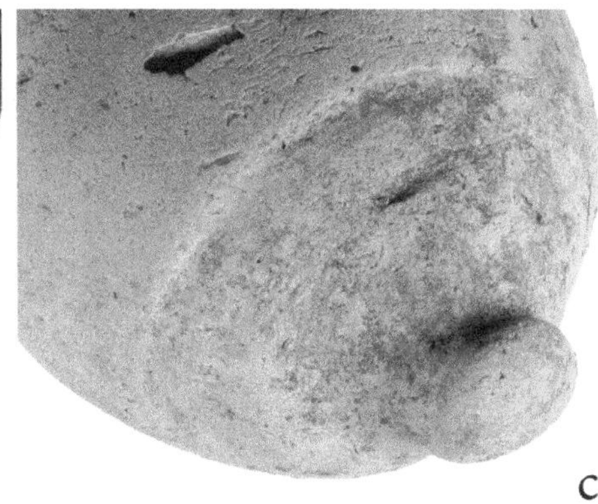

FIG. 4.24. Possible reed impression on the base of a bowl (a: p3099-13) and deep impressed 'contact lines' around lower third of two unstable footed cups (b: p5022-62; c: p9018-36). Not to scale.

(Vandiver pers. comm., 1989, cited in Moorey 1994: 157). A well preserved 'beehive' type updraft kiln has also recently been found at the Kassite period site of Khani Masi (Glatz et al. 2019: 455–6). Updraft kilns are two-level structures, with the upper chamber holding the stacked vessels directly above a lower fire chamber. A series of intersecting flues transfer the heat from the lower into the upper chamber, while a permanent or temporary roof sealed the contents from the outside air. The lower chamber was usually accessible from the side so that fuel could be added to alter the kiln's temperature. Air holes in the kiln walls or roof could be left open or sealed to increase or decrease air flow, therefore altering the firing atmosphere (Sinopoli 1991: 32–3).

4.3.2 Drying and Firing of the Tell Khaiber Assemblage

Since no kilns are associated with second millennium occupation at Tell Khaiber, evidence for the relevant drying and firing procedures must be sought amongst the vessels themselves.

Drying processes are rather ephemeral, and consequently leave little observable evidence (van As and Jacobs 2014: 89). It is unlikely that vessels were left to dry in intensive sunlight, since drying out too quickly would have risked the formation of cracks (van As and Jacobs 1992: 538). Any vessels that developed catastrophic cracks would have been discarded and would therefore not have entered the archaeological record at Tell Khaiber. To counteract such cracks, vessels underwent specific base treatments during forming (see Fig. 4.11) and were probably left to dry gradually in a shaded area. Some vessels, such as unstable footed cups, may have been set in pot stands to dry. A suggestion of this comes with the occasional occurrence of deep circular impressions, or 'contact lines' (after Rye 1981: 63), imprinted around the lower third of cups (Fig. 4.24a–b). Additionally, the irregular impressions around the base of some bowls may also have been caused by placing these vessels on reed matting to dry (Fig. 4.24c).

Without extensive testing of small clay briquettes or test sherds exposed to different firing conditions (Velde and Druc 1999: 252), the best indication of both firing technique and approximate temperature is through examination of vessel colour, both of the surface and the core (Rice 1987: 343–5). Subtle changes in colour can be attributed to innumerable variables. These include, but are not limited to: the chemical composition of clays, the nature of inclusions, the size of a vessel, the thickness of its respective walls, and even the position of a vessel within an individual kiln firing (van As and Jacobs 2014: 83). While general differences in colour are usually determined by firing temperature, the consistency of colour throughout a clay matrix is largely the result of firing atmosphere.

At Tell Khaiber, pottery colours were recorded by visual analysis.[18] Estimates of firing temperature could then be made based upon results of firing tests conducted on Middle Assyrian ceramics from Tell Sheikh Hamad (Schneider 2006: 395) and Tell Sabi Abyad (Duistermaat 2008), in the Khabur region of modern Syria. Due to similarities in geological conditions, these results were considered to also be representative for Tell Khaiber's clays (Table 4.1).[19] These firing estimates should not be deemed precise, but should be considered to provide solid approximations.

For recording bulk sherds, a coarse separation was made in the Tell Khaiber database between green and buff categories (Table 4.2). While high-fired pottery takes on a typical olive or dark green appearance, buff wares, encompassing a range of brown, red, orange, and cream colours, all conform to medium-low firing temperatures. Illustrated sherds were provided with more detailed colour descriptions and were classified according to ten different colour categories: white, cream, yellow, orange, red, buff, brown, grey, black, and green (see Plates). These colours are part of a spectrum, which allows for more refined interpretations.

The lowest temperatures were reserved for cooking vessels (Family 80); these were often fired below 700°C, and often in a reducing atmosphere. Other lower fired sherds (ca. 700–800°C) took on a brown/red/pink hue, while orange/buff/yellow wares

[18] Since the same person (the author) recorded the Tell Khaiber pottery each season, visual examination was considered accurate enough not to warrant the significant increase in time needed to record colour using a Munsell Colour Chart.

[19] The association between firing temperature and colour was further supported by a visit to a potter's workshop in Nasiriyah in 2015, where local alluvial clays, collected from a riverine source close to Ur and Tell Khaiber, and heated to various temperatures, followed a very similar colour pattern to those identified in the Khabur region.

Core \ Surface	Brown/Deep red	Dark brown/Grey/ Black	Pink/Orange/Buff	Buff/Cream/Green(ish)	Dark green, occasionally cracked and warped
Core same as surface	Oxidising, low temperature	Reducing, medium temperature	Oxidising, medium temperature	Oxidising, high temperature	Very high/over-fired
Dark (Black/Grey/Brown)	Incompletely oxidising, low temperature and/ or shorter firing period	Reducing, medium temperature	Incompletely oxidising, medium temperature	Incompletely oxidising, higher temperature	Very high/over-fired
Other (Red/Orange/Buff)	Oxidising, low or varying temperature and/or shorter firing period	Reducing in later stages of firing, medium temperature	Oxidising, medium or varying temperature	Oxidising, higher or varying temperature	
Approx. firing temperature	700–800 °C	700–950 °C	800–950 °C	950–1100 °C	>1100 °C

TABLE 4.1. Estimates of firing temperature/technique based on the colour of vessel surfaces and cores (based on Duistermaat 2008: 45, table II.2).

were fired at regular temperatures of approximately 800–950°C. As mentioned above, sherds fired at high temperatures (ca. 950–1000°C) were frequently green to olive green in colour, becoming darker as the temperature rose. Some of the especially high-fired wares (ca. >1000°C) demonstrate a distinct grey-black core, and were on the borderline of becoming vitrified, warped, and unusable; such sherds, termed wasters, were the result of failed firings. These heavily warped second millennium shapes are absent from the Tell Khaiber assemblage, but vessels yielding colours consistent with each of the other temperature classes are common.

Most Tell Khaiber vessels were almost certainly kiln fired, judging by the general consistency of colour between the surfaces and the core. This indicates that vessels were usually fired under well controlled, completely oxidising conditions (Rye 1981: 25). In most vessels, the core tends to be a shade darker than the surface, and in some larger vessels with thicker walls there are significant irregularities in the colour of the core compared to the colour of the surface. This may be attributed to the period of firing perhaps being insufficient for the temperature to penetrate the vessel walls evenly. Only cooking wares, with dark, clearly defined cores seem to have been routinely and deliberately fired under incompletely oxidising conditions. Since incomplete oxidisation occurs when vessels are fired at relatively low temperatures and for short periods (Rice 1987: 88), this pattern amongst cooking wares should perhaps be considered as an inadvertent by-product rather than a deliberate functional or aesthetic decision.

Table 4.2 shows that approximately 67% of all vessels recorded were fired under low–medium temperature conditions, thus providing vessels with a range of lighter colours. Just 33% of vessels were fired at high temperatures. It is therefore clear that the temperature of firing was associated with the specific category of vessel. Curiously, it appears that larger vessels were fired at higher temperatures than smaller vessels: 63% of pithoi (Family 25) and 49% of jars (Family 70), for instance, display the characteristic green colour of high-temperature firing. A possibility for this trend is that larger vessels, being the heaviest, were placed lower in the kiln, closer to the heat source, and were therefore exposed to the highest kiln temperatures. Perhaps smaller vessels were occasionally also stacked inside larger vessels. In these contexts, the higher firing patterns of larger vessels may well have been the inadvertent product of stacking patterns. However, this pattern could also be interpreted as deliberate. Since low-firing can render larger vessels brittle and unsuitable for their context of use, high-firing may have been adopted as an economic safety mechanism. It is also possible that these vessels were high-fired to promote particular use-related attributes, such as impermeability. This may also have been the case for bottles (Family 45), which show a similar frequency of high-firing.

On the other hand, the dominance of high-firing in the small sample of goblets in the assemblage may well have a techno-chronological explanation, as these vessels only appear in the mixed deposits which postdate the primary Tell Khaiber sequence (§3.1.3).

Family		Sherd Count	Green	Buff
40	Goblets	21	85.7%	14.3%
25	Pithoi	379	63.1%	36.9%
70	Jars	1262	49.2%	50.8%
45	Bottles	19	47.4%	52.6%
30	Pithoi (perforated bases)	20	45%	55%
20	Trays/Basins	32	43.8%	56.2%
55	Jugs	239	41.4%	58.6%
50	Cups	882	30.1%	69.9%
35	Beakers	131	28.2%	71.8%
85	Pot stands	163	22.1%	77.9%
10	Bowls with shaped elements	175	21.7%	78.3%
75	Small hole-mouth vessels	32	15.6%	84.4%
5	Bowls	1021	11%	89%
80	Large hole-mouth vessels	204	6.4%	93.6%
Total		**4913**	**33.1%**	**66.9%**

TABLE 4.2. Generalised firing patterns for Tell Khaiber's vessel families, organised according to the relative frequency of green, high-fired wares.

Smaller vessels, such as bowls (Families 5 and 10), cups (Family 50), and vessel stands (Family 85), were usually fired at low–medium temperatures (70–90%). Two reasons may account for this predominance in low-fired wares. The first might be economic, in that, as the most common vessel types, it would have been economically advantageous to fire at lower temperatures and for a shorter period, thereby utilising less fuel. Another reason, however, may have been the desired semipermeability of these vessels to encourage surface evaporation, thus keeping liquid contents cool (Skibo et al. 1989: 129–31).

Hole-mouth vessels (Families 75 and 80), both small and large, also show a heavy dependency on low-fired wares (84–94%). The difference in firing practice with these vessels is further emphasized by the high frequency of incompletely oxidised cores, often of a grey-black colour, in contrast to the usual deep brown surface colour. Since low-fired vessels are generally far more resistant to thermal stresses (Frink and Harry 2008), low firing of hole-mouth vessels should certainly be seen as a deliberate use-related choice suited to their role as cooking wares.

4.4 Identifying Techno-Groups at Tell Khaiber

Although the absence of any archaeologically identifiable production facilities in the immediate vicinity of Tell Khaiber renders this analysis of Sealand period pottery production incomplete, it is certainly not without significant merit. Drawing on a range of textual, ethnographic, archaeological, and archaeometric evidence has generated significant insights into the key stages of the *chaîne opératoire*. This multifaceted analysis has demonstrated that the vessel types that cluster together in terms of fabric composition (§4.1.2) are the same that group together in the execution of specific forming techniques (§4.2.2), and, to a large extent, in firing temperature and atmosphere too (§4.3.2). Accordingly, this suggests the presence of four broadly discrete yet occasionally overlapping Techno-Groups that account for the majority of Tell Khaiber's vessel assemblage.

Techno-Group 1

Types: Bowls, Small Cylindrical Beakers, Bottles, Cups, Jugs, Small Hole-mouth, and Small Vessel Stands (Families 5, 10, 35, 45, 50, 55, 75 and Type 85.1).
Clay Preparation: Fabrics A, B, C, D, E, and H.
Forming Technique: Wheel-coiled.
Firing Technique: Low-medium fired under completely oxidising conditions.

Techno-Group 2

Types: Large Cylindrical Beakers, Jars, and Large Vessel Stands (Families 35, 70, and Types 85.2–3).
Clay Preparation: Fabrics E, F, and H.
Forming Technique. Use of a mould/wheel-coiled.
Firing Technique. Often high-fired, usually under completely oxidising conditions.

Techno-Group 3

Types: Pithoi and Pithoi with Perforated Bases (Families 25 and 30).
Clay Preparation: Fabric F.
Forming Technique: Use of a mould/coiled.
Firing Technique: Often high-fired, usually under completely oxidising conditions.

Techno-Group 4

Types: Large Hole-Mouth (Family 80).
Clay Preparation: Fabrics F and G.
Forming Technique: Use of mould/coiled/paddle and anvil.
Firing Technique: Low-fired, usually under incompletely oxidising conditions.

5. Patterns of Use and Discard

I will now trace the various contextual relationships that Tell Khaiber's vessels entered into once they left the workshop. To achieve this, I will address the limited evidence available for vessel circulation, before establishing the use-contexts of different vessels and how these use-contexts may have been distributed across Tell Khaiber's Fortified Building and associated structures.

5.1 Arrival of Vessels at Tell Khaiber

To judge from the vessel fabrics, the overwhelming majority of the pots excavated must have been produced locally to Tell Khaiber (§4.1.2). Nevertheless, there is little evidence for the mechanisms by which these vessels reached the Fortified Building. Tell Khaiber's archive provides two numerical accounts (1096.55 and 3064.65) listing ten pottery vessel types received by Tell Khaiber's administrative apparatus (fig. 5.1). These vessels, in alphabetical order, are:

dannitu

Likely a localised reproduction of the more common Old Babylonian term *dannu*, which has etymological links to the word for 'strong' or 'mighty' (CDA D 56).
Total number imported: 10 (1096.55 o5).
Vessel identification: it is likely that this vessel should be associated with pithoi (Family 25).[20]

kabkaru

A type of container (CDA K 140); this term has only been encountered in later textual sources from the first millennium (Steinkeller 1991: 3-4).
Total number imported: 9 (3064.65 o3).
Vessel identification: judging by the relative count of this vessel type and the position of ***kabkaru*** in 1096.55, directly above ***kallu*** (Family 5 bowls, see below), it is plausible that these should be associated with larger, grooved bowls (Family 10).

kallu

A small bowl (CAD K 83; CDA K 142); a term commonly used throughout the second millennium BCE (Sallaberger 1996: 82).
Total number imported: 40 (3064.65 o4).
Vessel identification: it is almost certain that these should be associated with Tell Khaiber's bowls, and, perhaps more specifically, with smaller bowls (Family 5).

kalparu

A term unique to the Tell Khaiber archive.
Total number imported: 180 (60 in 1096.55 o2; 120 in 3064.65 o5).
Vessel identification: imported in similar frequency to the ***kaptukkû*** (see below) and may have carried out a similar function: a jar (Family 70)?

kaptukkû

A 'two-***sūtu*** container' (CDA K 148; Sallaberger 1996: 84), which is roughly equal to 20 litres.
Total number imported: 110 (30 in 1096.55 o1; 80 in 3064.65 o2).
Vessel identification: judging by the high number of these vessels and by the intended vessel capacity, which matches up very well with six Family 70 vessels,[21] these are almost certainly jars (Family 70) of a specific size.

katagallu

A term unique to the Tell Khaiber archive.
Total number imported: 10 (3064.65 o8).
Vessel identification: judging by the relative number of vessels and the position of the ***katagallu*** in 1096.55, between two cup types (***laḫannu*** and ***lurmu***, see below), these vessels might tentatively be associated with Tell Khaiber's small bottles (Family 45).

[20] Text-object vessel identifications should not be considered as fixed and immutable, but as fluid. The vessel identifications proposed here are based on a detailed relational text-object analysis (Calderbank 2021), most of which is not examined further in this volume.

[21] n=6; Range: 17–20.16L: Avg. 18.6L.

1096.55

Obv.

30 ^{dug}*kap-tu-[uk-ku]*	30 2-*sūtu* containers
1 ŠU ^{dug}*kal-<<is>>-pa-rum*	60 *kalparum*-vessels
20 ^{dug}*us-su*	20 duck-shaped containers
10 ^{dug}*ku-uk-ku-bu*	10 drinking-horns
10 ^{dug}*dan-ni-tu*	10 large vessels
1 ŠU ^{dug}*lu-ur-mu-ú*	60 drinking cups

Rev.

20 ^{dug}x x x x	20 ....-vessels
(1 line blank)	
⸢^{iti}AB.È U$_4$ 6?-KAM⸣	Ṭebetu (month XI), day 6

3064.65

Obv.

ma-ḫi-ir [...] ŠA MA [...]	Received [...] ... [...]
1.20$^{!}$ ^{dug}*kap-⸢tu⸣-[uk-ku]*	80 2-*sūtu* containers
9 ^{dug}*kab-ka-⸢rum⸣* [(...)]	9 *kabkarum*-containers
40 ^{dug}*ka-al-⸢lu$^{?}$⸣* [(...)]	40 *kallu*-bowls
2 ŠU ^{dug}*kal-pa-rum-⸢ma⸣* [...]	120 *kalparum*
⸢*me*⸣*-at* ^{dug}*us-su*	100 duck-shaped containers
20 ^{dug}*ku-uk-ku-bu*	20 drinking-horns
10 ^{dug}*ka-ta-ga-al-lu*	10 *katagallu*-vessels

Rev.

⸢*me*⸣*-at* ^{dug}⸢*la*⸣*-ḫa-nu*	100 *laḫannu*-flasks
TA 2 ITI	for 2 months
DA ^{iti}APIN.DU$_8$.A	from/to Arahsamnu (month VIII)
ma-ḫi-ir	received

FIG. 5.1. Two numerical accounts from Tell Khaiber listing the receipt of pottery vessels (Translation by E. Robson: <http://build-oracc.museum.upenn.edu/urap/corpus>).

kukkubu

A vessel used for drinking, sometimes translated as a 'rhyton' (CDA K 165) or a bottle (Sallaberger 1996: 84).

Total number imported: 30 (10 in 1096.55 o4; 20 in 3064.65 o7).

Vessel identification: the relative frequency of *kukkubu* (30) compared with *laḫannu* and *lurmu* cup types (n=160, see below) matches well with the relative percentages of jugs (4.1%) compared to cups (14.5%) in the bulk sherd data (Ratio of 1 jug to approx. 4 cups); this, alongside the traditional association between *kukkubu* and drinking contexts (Sallaberger 1996: 84) suggests that they should be associated with jugs (Family 55).

laḫannu

A drinking vessel, sometimes translated as a bottle or flask (CDA L 175); commonly used throughout the second millennium BCE (Sallaberger 1996: 84, pl. 2.4–6).

Total number imported: 100 (3064.65 r1).

Vessel identification: these are likely to be common cups (Family 50); it is, however, difficult to identify the difference between the *laḫannu* and the *lurmu* (see below).

lurmu

An 'ostrich-egg vessel' (CDA L 185).

Total number imported: 60 (1096.55 o6).

Vessel identification: these are likely to be common cups (Family 50). One might expect these 'ostrich-egg' ceramic vessels to be comparatively finely-made ceramic skeuomorphs, but such fine-wares are not present in the Tell Khaiber assemblage; it is therefore difficult to identify the perhaps subtle differences between *lurmu* and the *laḫannu* vessels (see above).

ussu

A ceramic term unique to the Tell Khaiber archive; the term shares its etymology with the Akkadian word for duck or duck-weight (*ūsu*, CAD U 282), perhaps in reference to the typical shape of the corresponding vessel or ceramic object; alternatively this might be a localised reproduction of a word used for cracked pot (*nussu*, CAD N/2 352) found in vessel list Ḫḫ X, line 100 (Civil 1996: 138).

Total number imported: 120 (20 in 1096.55 o3; 100 in 3064.65 o6).

Vessel identification: no commonly occurring pottery vessel types at Tell Khaiber show morphological similarities to a duck, meaning a reliable association cannot be suggested based on shape. Instead, the etymological association might have been functionally determined; perforated pot discs, for instance, would most likely have been used as net sinkers used to catch fish or wild water fowl, including ducks. It was potentially this functional association that established their identity as pottery 'ducks' or 'duck-weights'. The relatively large number of *ussu* listed in the numerical accounts aligns well with the common archaeological occurrence of perforated pot discs (e.g. in Room 600; §5.3.2).

Significant details are lacking from these numerical accounts. For instance, it is not stated where these vessels were brought in from, or whether they arrived empty or containing associated goods. I would suggest the former, because if these vessels were filled, the contents would most likely have taken precedence in the text, as is the case for documents in the contemporary CUSAS 9 archive (Dalley 2009); for example, a '1 *kaptukkû*-vessel of ghee' (CUSAS 9-104).

It is also clear that the pottery types listed do not cover the entire repertoire of vessel types present in the excavated

<table>
<tr><th>Food Processing</th><th>Cooking</th><th>Brewing</th><th>Storage (Bulk)</th><th>Storage (Special)</th><th>Measuring</th><th>Serving and Eating</th><th>Serving and Drinking</th><th>'Ritual'</th></tr>
<tr><td>20s</td><td>75.1-3</td><td colspan="2">25s</td><td>45s</td><td>35s</td><td>5s</td><td>50s</td><td>N/A</td></tr>
<tr><td>90.2</td><td>80s</td><td>30s</td><td>70s</td><td>75.4</td><td>90.3</td><td>10s</td><td>55s</td><td></td></tr>
<tr><td>90.6</td><td>90.9</td><td>85.3</td><td>85.2</td><td></td><td></td><td></td><td>85.1</td><td></td></tr>
<tr><td>90.8</td><td></td><td></td><td colspan="2">90.1</td><td></td><td></td><td>90.7</td><td></td></tr>
</table>

TABLE 5.1. Families/Types subdivided according to probable use-context.

assemblage. They do, however, appear to represent many of the most common forms, especially cups, jugs, and jars, for which a regular flow of imports would have been essential for the smooth operation of daily routines within the building. These vessels appear to have been brought in to Tell Khaiber periodically and in bulk, with these two receipts dating to *Arahsamnu* (October–November) and *Ṭebetu* (December–January). Since these months cover a period of intensive sowing activity across Mesopotamia (LaPlaca and Powell 1990), it might suggest a functional connection between the most numerous of vessels accounted for, jars (*kalparu* and *kaptukkû*), and significant seed storage.

It must also be noted here that there are numerous examples of vessel re-use at Tell Khaiber (Family 95). This indicates that the necessary vessels needed to fulfil specific tasks were not always ready-to-hand, but needed to be ordered from elsewhere. Consequently, the inhabitants of Tell Khaiber occasionally had to make do with modifying other vessels in times of need.

5.2 Vessel Distributions: Methodological Outline

Distributive analyses of material culture can prove informative in assessing the organisation of activities and the relationships between people at an individual site. In turn, understanding these behaviours is fundamental to understanding the functioning of society and economy at a broader scale (Allison 2009). However, such detailed spatial approaches are notably rare in Mesopotamian contexts.[22] While not all archaeological contexts are suited to distributive artefact analyses (see Sinopoli 2013: 85 for a discussion), these methods have proven particularly useful in rigidly planned and spatially bounded archaeological contexts, such as Roman forts (Allison 2006). As such, the Fortified Building at Tell Khaiber, as a closed architectural system, is perfectly suited to such a study. The Fortified Building's scale and structured plan, with clearly delineated spaces, as well as restricted and controllable points of access, mean that the excavated pottery relates entirely to the use and disposal patterns that took place within the building. Discrete assemblages can therefore be reliably associated with the activities that occurred within, or at least near to, each specific room or area.

Once vessels arrived at Tell Khaiber, their circulation within the settlement was largely contingent on their intended use. A fully integrated analysis of the uses of Tell Khaiber's different vessel families, drawing upon material, lexical, historical, and ethnographic evidence is presented in detail elsewhere (Calderbank 2021).[23] For the purposes of this volume, it is sufficient to say that the central use-contexts in which second-millennium pottery vessels operated were:

- Processing of food and drink
- Cooking
- Beer brewing
- Storage (Bulk)
- Storage (Special)
- Measuring
- Serving and Eating
- Serving and Drinking
- 'Ritual'

It is possible, with reference to fabric, shape, and volume, to determine which of Tell Khaiber's vessel families and types would have been best suited to fulfilling these intended uses, and thus map their spatial distribution across the site using GIS analysis of complete vessels alongside bulk sherd data drawn from Appendix A. Table 5.1 shows the most likely intended uses of each individual vessel type. The only ambiguous vessels in this regard are pithoi (Family 25) and lids (Type 90.1). While pithoi could have been used both in brewing or bulk storage, lids could have been used both for bulk and for special storage. Since these respective vessel types straddle two categories, their statistics are added to the relevant statistical counts of both use-contexts.

The subdivisions in Table 5.1 are used in conjunction with the area statistics in Appendix A to provide frequency counts for each use-context in each chronological phase and spatial area of the site. In the results presented here, these use-context counts are always converted to relative percentages. Relative percentages allow for ease of reference across different areas of the site where the sherd counts, determined by sample size, might vary. Percentages also

[22] Exceptions include Franke's (1987) and Stone's (1987) analyses of Old Babylonian urban dwellings at Nippur, and, farther afield, Marchetti and Nigro's (1995–6) analysis of Early Bronze Age ceramics from a public building at Ebla and Jamieson's (2000) discussion of room use and vessel function in an elite house at Iron Age Tell Ahmar, Syria.

[23] For a similar analysis of the Old Babylonian pottery from Tell Ed-Der, see Sallaberger (1996: pls.1–6), and for Mesopotamian ceramics more generally, see Ellison (1984a; 1984b) and Potts (1999: 138–63). For an in-depth discussion of pottery function more generally, see Skibo (2012).

Use-Context Phase	Food Processing	Cooking	Brewing	Storage (Bulk)	Storage (Special)	Measuring	Serving and Eating	Serving and Drinking
1 (n= 148)	-	2.0%	8.8%	37.1%	0.7%	1.4%	23.0%	27.0%
2.1 (n= 1080)	0.7%	3.7%	6.9%	29.5%	0.4%	2.6%	29.6%	26.7%
2.2 (n= 2117)	0.7%	4.4%	8.7%	34.5%	0.4%	3.0%	23.7%	24.6%
2.3 (n= 469)	0.9%	5.5%	8.5%	37.5%	1.3%	2.8%	21.3%	22.2%
MT (n= 936)	0.6%	3.9%	3.6%	28.9%	0.4%	4.8%	25.9%	31.9%
MSu (n= 1000)	0.9%	3.6%	11.8%	39.3%	0.9%	1.7%	11.1%	30.7%
EH (n= 303)	0.3%	1.7%	5.6%	34.7%	0.3%	2.0%	17.5%	38.0%
Total (n= 6251)	**0.7%**	**3.8%**	**8.0%**	**34.2%**	**0.5%**	**2.9%**	**22.2%**	**27.7%**

TABLE 5.2. Relative percentages of different use-contexts by phase, based on vessel subdivisions in Table 5.1.

compensate somewhat for the skewing effects of differential vessel breakage, of large pithoi and jars compared with cups and bowls, for instance, or even small bottles, which are rarely encountered in a fragmentary state.

The breakdown of percentage distributions of vessels according to use-context and phase is provided in Table 5.2 and Fig. 5.2. These statistics demonstrate only subtle differences between Phases 1–2.3, which strongly suggests that the general activities taking place throughout the building's primary use-life remained consistent. Consequently, the statistics for the different chronological phases are generally conflated in the following analysis. This allows us to emphasise spatial differentiation. Accordingly, a detailed pattern of bulk sherd distributions according to the specific areas of the Fortified Building and Eastern Houses is presented in Table 5.3.

This bulk statistical data is reinforced throughout this Chapter by GIS data for individual complete vessels. In order to demonstrate direct associations between different vessel types as excavated, some architectural plans are presented. These contain stylised images of different vessel types, which are positioned according to GIS data gathered for these complete vessels. For the precise location of the Rooms and Areas discussed throughout this Chapter, the reader should consult the comprehensive architectural plan of the Fortified Building (Fig. 1.2) or the illustrated relative distributions (Fig. 5.3). Together, these sources of bulk sherd statistics and GIS data permits a detailed reconstruction of the activities that took place across the site and the ways in which people may have moved through and engaged with the different excavated spaces.

Nevertheless, before we begin this assessment, the limitations of excavation must be acknowledged. The analysis presented in this Chapter works only with those areas of the site that have been subjected to rigorous excavation and recording. Since this comprises approximately 10% of the total area of the Fortified Building, our interpretations can only represent a small, albeit still significant, portion of the whole.

5.3 Vessel Distributions: Results and Discussion

5.3.1 Fortified Building: Northern Unit

As one entered the Fortified Building through the single, narrow entrance in the northeast wall, one came upon Room 152, set slightly off the central passage (Area 125). In this small room, pithoi with perforated bases (e.g. p8082-42) were common, which contributes to the strong evidence for beer brewing (15.8%). Concurrently, this room also demonstrated clear evidence for both bulk (43.9%) and special storage (2.3%), the latter in the shape of a burnished bottle (p8083-6), which perhaps originally contained beer flavourings. Alongside these were a high percentage of measuring vessels (5.9%), alongside three complete cups (p8083-17, 23, and 44).

Room 156, located down a narrow passage directly east of the main entrance, in the northeast corner of the building, demonstrated the only *in situ* evidence for beer brewing (31.3%). An installation was encountered (Fig. 5.4), consisting of a largely complete pithos with a perforated base (p6165-45), lying upturned alongside a closed pot stand (p6165-44), which held a cup (p6165-43) inside. Directly

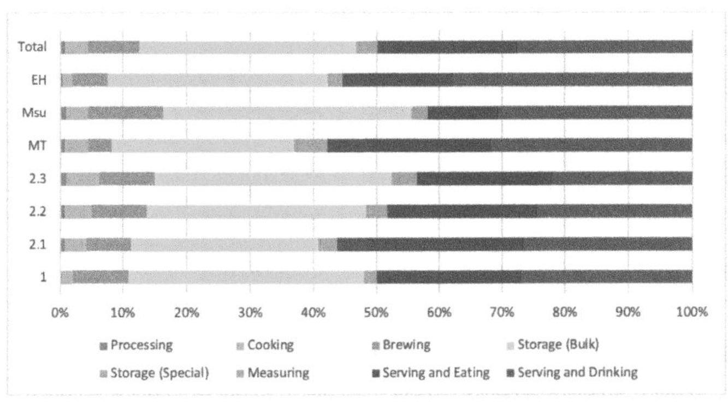

FIG. 5.2. Relative percentages of different use-contexts by phase, based on Table 5.2.

Area	Food Processing	Cooking	Brewing	Storage (Bulk)	Storage (Special)	Measuring	Serving and Eating	Serving and Drinking
Total (n= 6251)	0.7%	3.8%	8.1%	34.2%	0.5%	2.9%	22.2%	27.7%
Northern Unit								
Rm. 152 (n=171)	0.6%	-	15.8%	43.9%	2.3%	5.9%	7.6%	24%
Rm. 156 (n=48)	2.1%	2.1%	31.3%	39.6%	-	-	2.1%	22.9%
Rm. 101 (n=556)	0.7%	5%	4.9%	25.4%	-	2.5%	41.7%	19.8%
Rms. 140-142 (n=311)	0.6%	3.5%	9%	34.7%	1.3%	4.8%	11.3%	34.7%
Southern Unit								
Area 315 (n=736)	0.4%	3.4%	9.5%	39%	-	2.0%	14%	31.7%
Vaults (n=59)	-	1.7%	15.3%	42.4%	1.7%	1.7%	18.6%	18.6%
Admin. Suite (n=398)	-	2%	5.8%	28.1%	0.3%	2.5%	45.5%	15.8%
Rm. 314 (n=361)	0.3%	3.6%	5.8%	25.8%	0.8%	3%	33.2%	27.4%
Rms. 600-601 (n=524)	1.2%	5.5%	7.4%	38%	0.2%	3.4%	16.8%	27.5%
Rm. 316 (n=320)	1.3%	5.9%	8.8%	36.9%	1.6%	2.5%	24.4%	18.8%
Towers								
Tower 124 (n=115)	1.7%	4.4%	-	30.4%	0.9%	7.8%	38.3%	16.5%
Tower 302 (n=50)	-	4%	-	40%	-	6%	16%	34%
Tower 304 (n=574)	0.7%	4%	3.8%	30.1%	-	4.9%	25.3%	31.2%
Tower 616 (n=197)	0.5%	3.1%	6.1%	21.3%	1.5%	2.5%	22.8%	42.1%
Eastern Houses								
House 1 (n=160)	-	-	5.6%	33.1%	0.6%	2.5%	18.8%	39.4%
House 2 (n=64)	-	1.6%	4.7%	35.9%	-	1.6%	14.1%	42.2%
House 3 (n=51)	2%	5.9%	5.9%	35.3%	-	2%	17.7%	31.4%

TABLE 5.3. Relative percentages of use-contexts in the different excavated areas of the Fortified Building. High relative percentages (>10% above total stratified building assemblage) are highlighted in brown. For a graphic representation of these statistics, see Fig. 5.3.

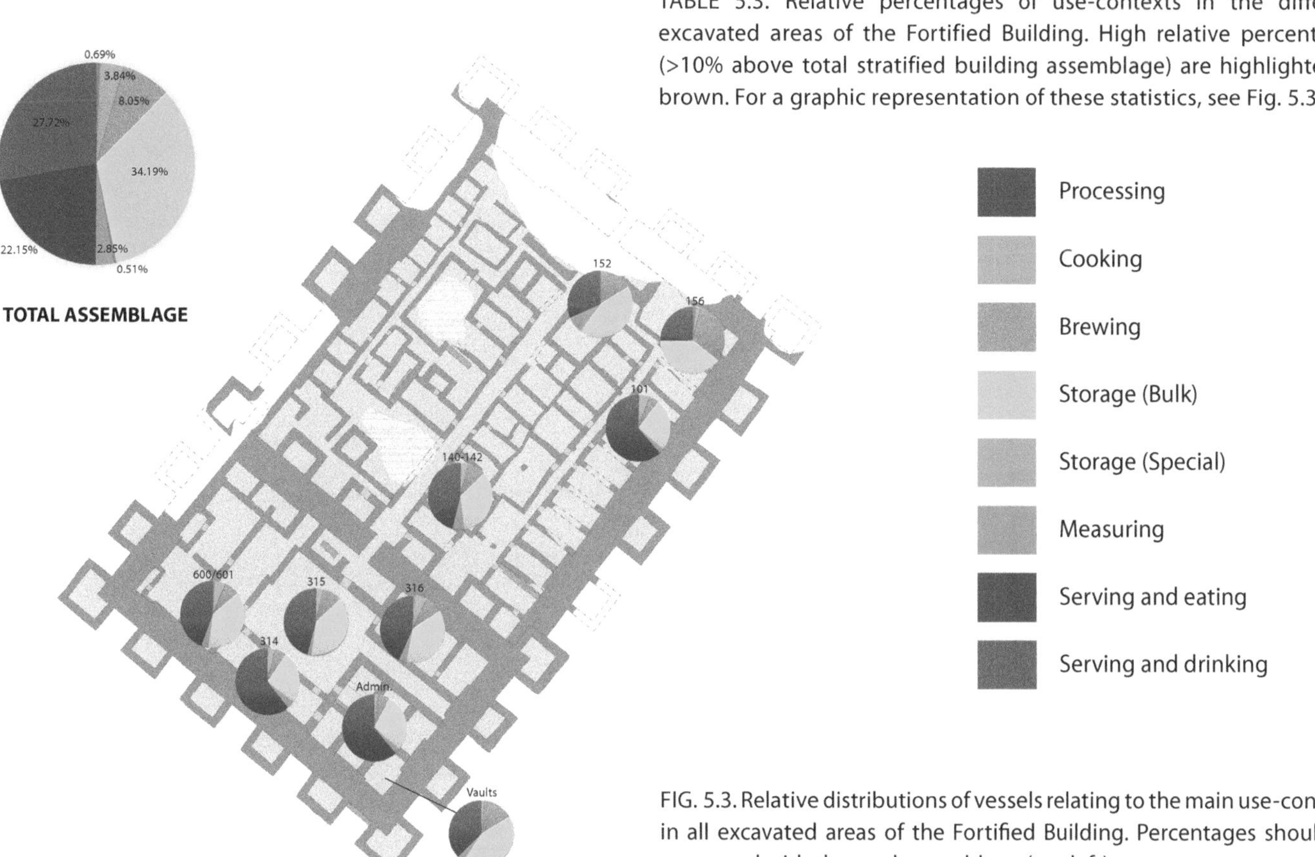

FIG. 5.3. Relative distributions of vessels relating to the main use-contexts in all excavated areas of the Fortified Building. Percentages should be compared with the total assemblage (top left).

FIG. 5.4. Beer installation in Room 156.

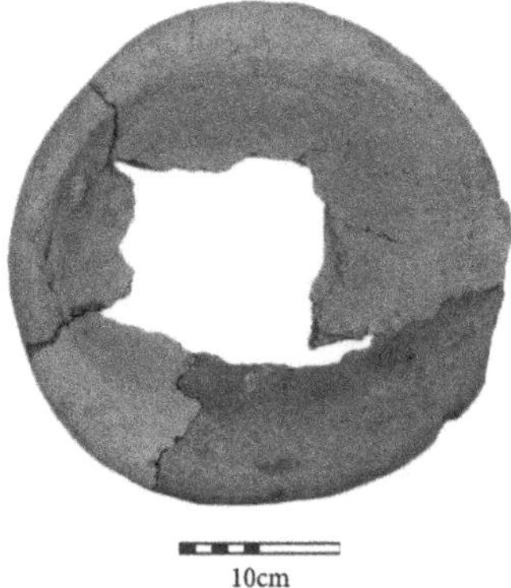

FIG. 5.5. Grinding basin found in the south corner of Room 101, showing extensive wear on the interior surface.

alongside lay another complete cup (p6165-38). The vessels comprising this installation are commonly found together both archaeologically and textually in ancient Mesopotamia (Gates 1988; Zarnkow et al. 2006). Although serving and drinking vessels yield low relative percentages in the assemblage of Room 152 and the surface scraped deposits of Room 156, they are very well represented in comparison with serving and eating vessels, which are conspicuously rare in both rooms.

Further along the tightly controlled eastern passage (Area 110) leading to the eastern wing of the building, are Rooms 99–110, a group of standardised rectangular rooms. Of these, only Room 101 was subjected to vertical excavation. This room contained all of the basic equipment needed for rudimentary domestic occupation: a roughly manufactured basin demonstrating extensive wear on the interior (p1080-14) was present, perhaps for processing grain (Fig. 5.5); in the northwest corner of the room was a series of consecutive *tannurs* for baking bread, the lowest of which contained a small cup (p1085-16),[24] probably used to remove ashy deposits; finally, there was a concentration of animal bones and a heavily sooted cookpot (p1079-51) sitting beside the *tannur*. Indeed, cooking wares composed 5% of the bulk sherds in Room 101. This evidence, in combination, illustrates that baking and other forms of cooking were carried out by the room's occupants.

Room 101 also contains an extremely high percentage of serving and consumption vessels. Best represented are eating vessels, which constitute 41.7% of the room's total assemblage. However, numerous complete cups and jugs were also found directly associated with the room's earliest occupation surface (Figs. 5.6–7); these were generally grouped against the southeast wall of the room, indicating further spatial subdivisions at play. It is clear, therefore, that food was not only produced on site but was also regularly consumed there, while drinks may well have been supplied

FIG. 5.6. Vessels sat on earliest floor (context 1080) in south corner of Room 101. Photo facing south.

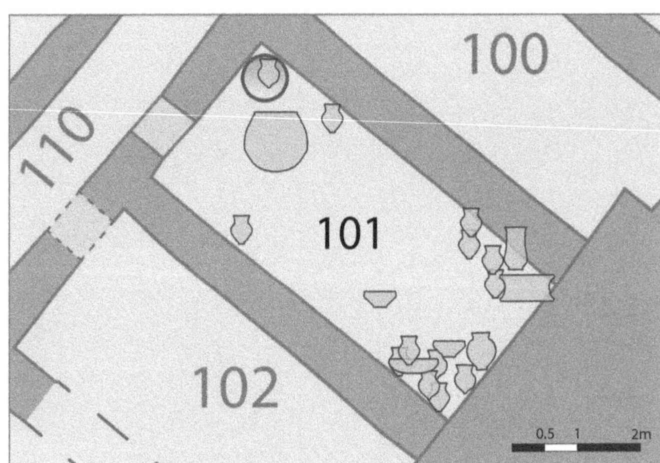

FIG. 5.7. Room 101. Distribution of vessels.

by the brewing facilities located nearby (Rooms 152 and 156). Together, this material suggests a consistent domestic function throughout Room 101's occupational history, albeit quite an impoverished one. Although they were not fully excavated, identical functions can be inferred for the rest of the rooms along the east wing of the northern unit (Rooms 99–109), since surface scraping

[24] Similar contextual associations between cups and *tannurs* and between cups and large pithoi are common across the site, suggesting a common use of these vessels as dippers.

FIG. 5.8. Group of vessels in the south corner of Room 142. Photo facing south.

FIG. 5.9. Fragmentary cylindrical vessel (p5022-66).

revealed standardised layouts and an associated *tannur* beside most doorways. The ceramic evidence therefore reinforces the interpretation of these rooms as purpose-built accommodation for small groups of people, possibly military personnel connected with the defensive aspect of the Fortified Building (Shepperson, forthcoming).

Following the building's central passage (Area 125) southwest from the main entrance, one reached a self-contained suite of rooms set off to the east (Rooms 140–2). This area was intermittently involved in beer brewing (9%), which took place in both the earliest deposits encountered (Room 141: context 5060) and the latest (Room 142; context 5029), as demonstrated by the presence of several pithoi with bunghole bases (e.g. p5060-10 and 5029-1).

The main room (Room 142) is a long and rectangular space which was covered with carefully laid reed matting (Fig. 5.10). It appears, on first impressions, to have been a suitable place for group feasting, where people may have sat in rows on the floor with food spread out in between, as is common in the marshes of southern Iraq today. While the particularly high percentage of serving and drinking vessels (34.7%) supports this interpretation, the scarcity of bowls (11.3%) casts some doubt; unless, that is, the bowls

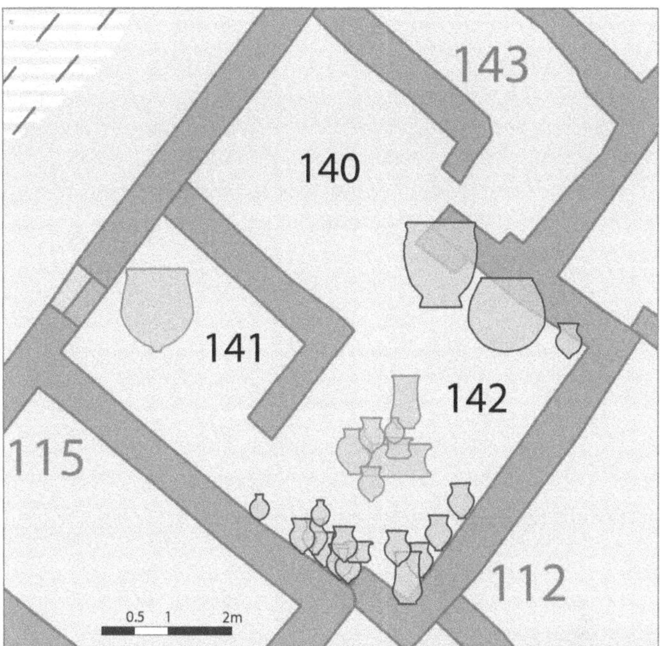

FIG. 5.10. Rooms 140–2. *Above*: distribution of vessels, with Phase 2.3 vessels outlined in orange. *Below*: phytolith-rich remnants of reed matting covering Room 142. Photo facing northeast.

were stored elsewhere and were brought into the room only intermittently. A group of fourteen cups and jugs, as well as three pot stands, were found grouped in the southeast corner of Room 142 (Fig. 5.8 and 5.10). Alongside were two small bottles for special liquid storage (p5045-1 and p5045-10), as well as several measuring vessels (4.8%), including two elaborately decorated examples bearing a complex series of wavy bands and incised ridges (p5022-65 and p5022-66). One of these vessels also demonstrates a unique notched rim shape and a series of holes cut beneath the rim band (Fig. 5.9); it may be that this elaborate vessel was once suspended from the ceiling, with a lid secured to protect the contents. This assemblage supports the suggestion that elaborate communal drinking activities may have taken place in Room 142.

5.3.2 Fortified Building: Southern Unit

Access to the southern unit of the building was tightly controlled. The narrow passageway opens almost directly onto a large courtyard (Area 315), separated only by possible small guardrooms (unexcavated Rooms 617 and 619). Area 315 may have been used for bulk storage (39%),[25] perhaps of goods brought into the building for consumption or onward dispatch. Drinking activities (31.7%) also took place here, but judging by the isolation of individual cups, this appears to have occurred rather informally. Given the size of the area, and the shade provided intermittently by a centrally situated tree, the courtyard would have formed a suitable place for people to congregate.

To the southeast of the courtyard, the vaults of Level 1 provide little information on their original use. This is because the material accumulated represents deliberate packing for the laying of the Level 2 architecture, which contains a large concentration of bulk storage types (42.4%), alongside some peculiar complete vessels deposited in the corners of specific vaults (see §5.4.2). The administrative suite of Level 2, on the other hand, provides an assemblage dominated by serving and consumption vessels, particularly those related to eating (45.5%). In some instances, these bowls were found on their side or upside down, perhaps indicating that they were originally set on a shelf or table and subsequently collapsed into the rooms. Considering the context of these bowls alongside numerous tablets, it is also possible that they were (re)used as receptacles for holding temporary markers while tracking administrative tasks.

Drinking vessels, on the other hand, are encountered much more infrequently in these administrative rooms (15.8%). Not only were they found in relative isolation, unlike in Room 142, they are also more individualistic in style compared to the rest of the Tell Khaiber assemblage: a tall cup (p3064-226) found in Room 300 and a unique beaker (p1096-456) found in Room 309 (Fig. 5.12). These vessels may have belonged to specific individuals, or were perhaps used for particular serving practices, such as for the consumption of certain types of drink.

The administrative suite was also used for the bulk storage of more valuable goods, such as bitumen. This is demonstrated by two jars (p3064-565 and p3064-678) which were surrounded by bitumen lumps and interspersed with the tablets deposited in Room 300. Jar p3064-678 bore a pot mark, while another sherd with a similar mark (p1096-493) was encountered in an adjacent room (Room 317) (§5.4.3). This mixture of administrative practices, bulk storage, and everyday commensal activities initially appears curious. It is conceivable that the build-up of occupation deposits in this part of the building demonstrates a conflation of different short-term phases of differential room use. It may also be that the jars containing bitumen collapsed

FIG. 5.11. Isolated bowl (p3064-445) found on its side in the administrative suite.

FIG. 5.12. Unique drinking vessel shapes from the administrative suite: a) p3064-226; b) p1096-456.

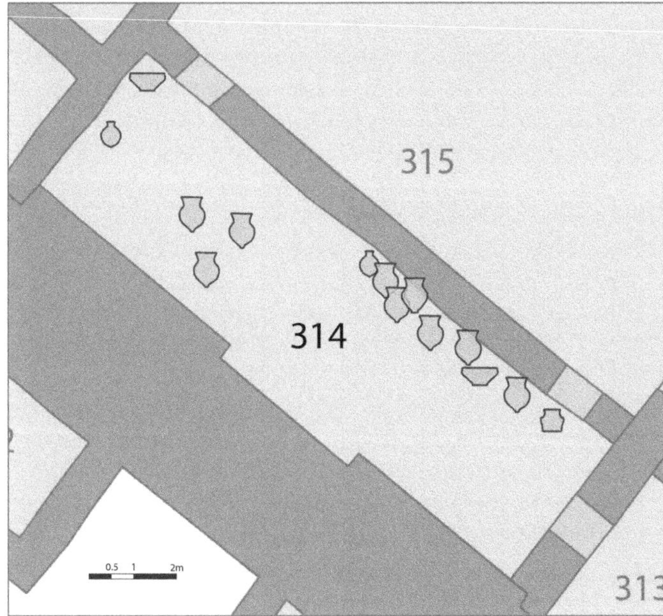

FIG. 5.13. Room 314. Distribution of vessels.

[25] The high number of pithos sherds associated with bulk storage has also skewed the relative percentages for beer brewing in Area 315 (9.5%) and the vaults (15.3%). The absence of pithoi with perforated bases, however, suggests that brewing activities did not take place in these areas.

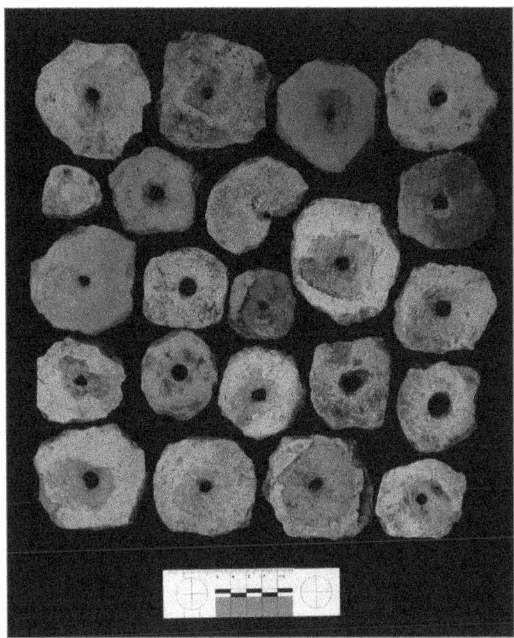

FIG. 5.14. Assemblage of pot discs in Room 600 (context 6036).

FIG. 5.15. Fragmented grinding vessel (p8021-11) in Room 316.

FIG. 5.16. Fragmented cooking pot base (p8013-12) in Room 316.

into these rooms from an upper storey. More likely, however, is that the stored bitumen played a functional role in administrative upkeep, to seal the lids of jars or other containers after sorting and inspection, while the bowls were similarly used for short-term administrative organisation.

Room 314, accessed from the southwest side of the courtyard, shows strong evidence for serving and consumption activities (Total: 60.7%), with a number of complete bowls and cups (contexts 1139, 1142, and 1166). The profile of a larger stone bowl (1166:8) adds further evidence for the performance of more conspicuous consumption of food and/or drink in this area. Alongside this were three types of special storage vessels: a small bottle with a rounded base (p1166-58), a larger, globular bottle with a button base (p1142-8), and a squat hole-mouth vessel (p1167-6). Significantly, these were also found alongside a small, skilfully manufactured stone vessel (1166:33) in the southeast doorway leading to the courtyard. This is a clear indication for the storage of more valuable goods in Room 314.

To the northwest of the courtyard, Rooms 600/601 show a range of activities, including food processing (1.2%), cooking (5.5%), storage of both bulk (38%) and more valuable goods (0.2%), as well as measuring (3.4%). The only clues as to the nature of what may have been stored and processed comes from the presence of a group of nineteen perforated pot discs found in Room 600 (Fig. 5.14), which were chipped from re-used jar sherds. Since these perforated discs may well have functioned as net sinkers for fishing or for catching water fowl, the jars in these rooms could well have been used for the storage of dried or salted fish, or perhaps the derivative fermented sauce (Akk. *siqqum*, see Reynolds 2007: 180).

Room 316, accessed to the northeast of the courtyard, was a spacious kitchen. The pottery assemblage shows evidence for the following activities, either in the bulk statistics or in the contextual data.

Food Processing (1.3%)

For the most part, it appears that coarse quern stones, flint blades, and rubbing tools were used for processing food in Room 316. Nevertheless, there is also a large fragment of an expertly manufactured basin (p8021-11). Although missing its legs, this basin has a very large circumference (>600mm) and a shallow interior depth. Its surface is embedded with large angular grit inclusions (Fig. 5.15), rendering it suitable for rubbing or grating foodstuffs of various kinds effectively. Its size also meant that it could potentially have been used by several people simultaneously.

Cooking (5.9%)

Cooking wares are particularly common in the bulk sherd data, as well as in the complete vessel assemblage. Examples include a small hole-mouth vessel with a flat base (p8013-10), as well as a heavily used and burnt lower portion of a large hole-mouth cooking vessel (Fig. 5.16), all found in the latest episodes of activity in Room 316. A collection of bones was found in the base of the latter vessel, indicating its possible use to grill or fry meat.

FIG. 5.17. Possible fragment of a bread mould (p8008-11) in Room 316.

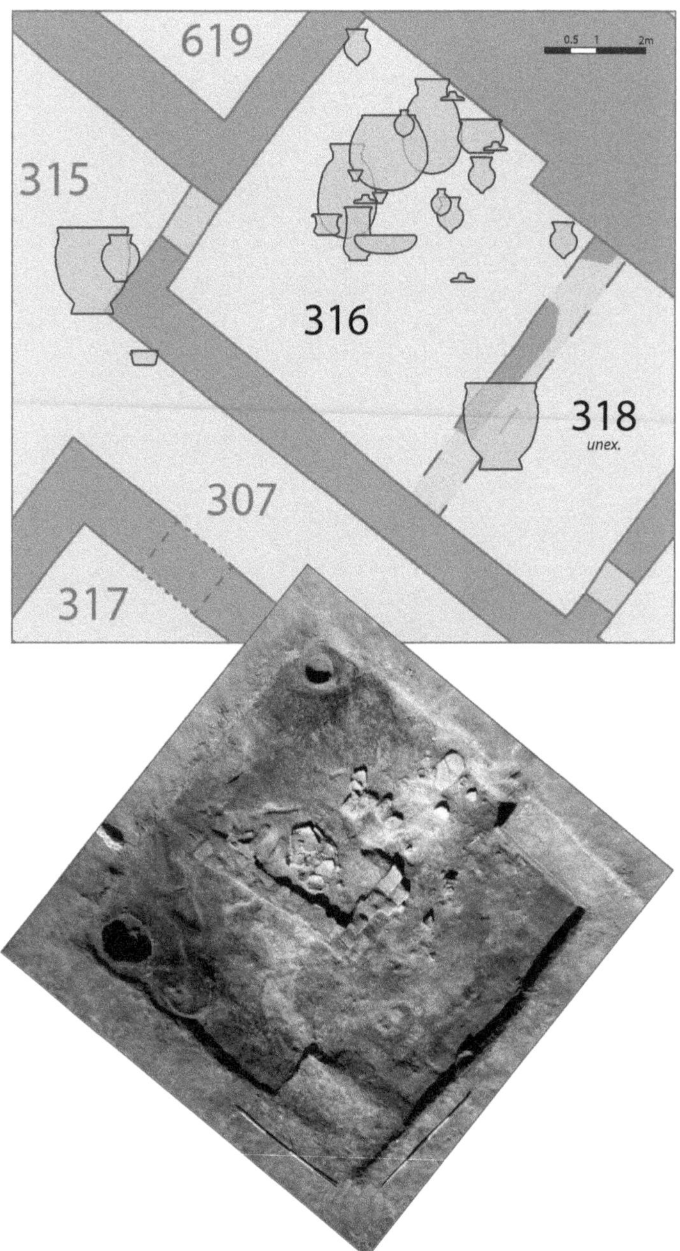

FIG. 5.18. Room 316. *Above*: distribution of vessels. *Below*: aerial view during excavation.

Bread preparation was also a common activity in Room 316, with numerous *tannurs* present both within the room itself, as well as directly outside its entrance, in the adjacent courtyard. A unique coarse ceramic object bearing regular concave grooves set within a circular border, was also found (Fig. 5.17). This resembles a fragment of an elaborate bread mould, similar to those found at Old Babylonian Mari (Margueron 2004: 515–6), where the dough would have been pressed into the indented design, before a second ceramic piece was sealed on top. The perforations visible in the top of the object may have been used to join and secure both parts of the bread mould during baking.

Bulk Storage (36.9%)

Two broken jars (p8013-13/14) were found in the centre of Room 316, surrounded by a dense concentration of fish bones. Presumably then, these vessels were originally used to hold dried or salted fish or *siqqum* sauce. A complete pithos (p8058-6) was also present, *in situ*, located on the other side of a dividing wall, separating Room 316 from Room 318 to the southeast. This vessel bore decomposed remnants of fabric directly beneath the rim band, indicating the original position of a fastening to close the vessel (Fig. 2.10a). This suggests that the rooms to the southeast of Room 316 (Rooms 318 and 303), which remain largely unexcavated, may at least in part have operated as a kind of pantry dedicated to storing foodstuffs.

Special Storage (1.6%)

A small bottle (p8013-1) and a larger, globular bottle (p8032-37) with a heavily burnished finish were found in the centre of Room 316. It is likely that these vessels contained more valuable oils or spices used for cooking.

Measuring (2.5%)

Several measuring vessels were found alongside various cooking and processing implements in Room 316: a larger fragmentary vessel (p8008-114) with several sets of incised lines on the exterior (p8008-114), a smaller vessel, broken above a set of incised lines around the middle of the body (p8016-8), and a small conical vessel (p8021-1). In this context, these vessels may have been used for measuring liquids, various flavourings, or spices.

Serving and Consumption (Eating: 24.4%; Drinking: 18.8%)

The varied and often unique vessels in Room 316 represent elaborate cooking and baking activities. These are attested on a scale unmatched elsewhere in the Fortified Building, much greater than in the modest food preparation recognised in Room 101. This level of specialist food preparation must have been conducted, or at least overseen, by the cooks (*nuhatimmu*) mentioned in Tell Khaiber's texts.[26] Yet the scarcity of complete serving and consumption vessels, particularly the lack of bowls, suggests that, despite extensive preparation, food was not consumed in this room. Instead, it was probably prepared for those people living and working elsewhere in the southern unit, perhaps in Room 314, Area 315, and the administrative suite.

5.3.3 Fortified Building - Towers

All of the towers show a consistent pattern of serving and consumption vessels. Drinking vessels dominate in Towers 302, 304, and 616 (31.2–42.1%) and eating bowls are extremely frequent in Tower 124 (38.3%). In Tower 304, a total of over thirty drinking cups and jugs were found, alongside four small pot stands and three measuring vessels of different sizes, while in Tower 616, twenty-one complete cups and jugs were found alongside one small pot stand. Occasionally, the assemblages were also composed of different, functionally associated, vessel types, such as a pithos, a cup, a cooking vessel, and a jar, which were encountered together in Tower 304 (Fig. 5.19). The tower material appears to represent episodes of discrete discard, perhaps associated with specific events. Many of the deposited vessels were well-used and exhibited extensive wear around both the bases and the rims. The extremely dense concentration in which these ceramics were found (see Fig. 5.20) precludes any practical use of the tower rooms. Rather, the towers were probably used as convenient spaces for the periodic discard of sometimes functionally associated materials.

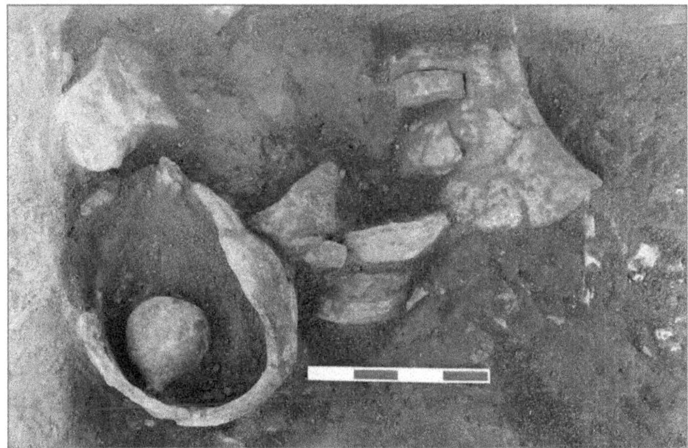

FIG. 5.19. A fragmentary pithos (unrecorded), containing cup (p3054-21), alongside an upturned jar (p3054-402) and cookpot (p3054-393) in Tower 304.

FIG. 5.20. Oblique view of Tower 302 after surface scraping, showing the density of material accumulated against the southeast face of the main perimeter wall. Photo facing north.

5.3.4 Eastern Houses

Each house demonstrates a high relative percentage of drinking among the activities attested (House 1: 39.4%; House 2: 42.2%; House 3: 31.4%), which is particularly significant when compared to the low frequencies of eating vessels (House 1: 18.8%; House 2: 14.1%; House 3: 17.7%). In the surface-scraped material, several cups (p4034-28 and p4034-29) were found alongside a large jug (p4034-11). Numerous complete cups were also found in House 1,[27] including a small cup found nestled inside the neck of a small jug, thus further strengthening the functional association between the two vessel families. Two distinctive tall cups with funnel necks were also found in House 2 (p4006-2 and p4084-1) alongside more typical cup shapes (p4084-53 and p4084-54). Bulk sherd distributions can help to tease out subtleties in the functions

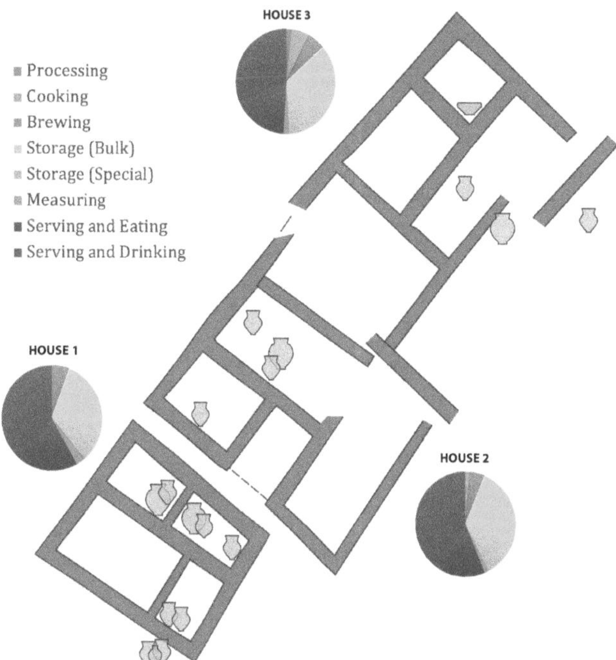

FIG. 5.21. Eastern houses with complete vessel distributions, alongside relative percentages of vessels relating to the main use-contexts.

[26] At least three different cooks are named: *Sippitum* (3064.49 r35 and 3064.53 r29), *Ea-šarrum* (1124.2 o14), and a fragmentary name (3064.57 r20).

[27] House 1 cups: p4010-8, p4053-14, p4056-10/11, p4062-46, and p4067-23/24.

of the different Houses. House 3, for instance, was used for food-processing (2%) and cooking (5.9%) activities, and perhaps also some small-scale food consumption (e.g. bowl p4066-19). House 2 was mainly used for serving and drinking (42.2%). House 1, on the other hand, seems to have been used for special storage (0.6%) and serving and drinking (39.4%). Bulk storage was remarkably consistent across all three houses (33.1–35.9%). Rather than distinct bounded units, we might perhaps envisage these houses as part of a relational complex of spaces, with each 'House' serving a series of separate yet complementary functions.

5.4 Functional Considerations

5.4.1 Eating and Drinking Cultures

There is a recurrent pattern in the Tell Khaiber assemblage whereby drinking vessels were regularly found together in groups (e.g. Rooms 101, 142, 314, Towers 304 and 616, and the Eastern Houses). Bowls, on the other hand, were usually encountered in isolation. This suggests a difference in eating and drinking cultures at play across the site. While drinking appears to have been a communal and occasionally rather elaborate activity, eating seems to have taken place under more solitary circumstances. This trend probably relates to the offering of drinks as a socially appropriate gesture or an accepted form of Mesopotamian hospitality (Michalowski 1994).

The shape of specific pottery vessels influences the bodily gestures possible during use (Whalen 2014) and could therefore impact significantly upon commensal contexts. The use of common vessel shapes has the effect of making people feel at ease, while uncommon vessel shapes, and the unusual bodily gestures they demand, may have the effect of making the user feel uneasy, thus destabilising social order. There is little doubt that the vessels used for everyday drinking activities at Tell Khaiber were cups (Family 50). Yet these cups were produced in two primary types: stable (Types 50.1–3) and unstable (Types 50.4–6). Although, visually, the differences between the two are minimal, they would have had a significant impact on the ways these vessels could have been handled and used.

Two potential reasons for this difference come to mind, one of which was underpinned by practical concerns and one that was determined by social gestures. On the practical side, unstable cups would have been associated with small cylindrical pot stands, and at events where cups were filled regularly, probably from Tell Khaiber's jugs (Family 55), the use of these pot stands would have added increased stability (more so than a normal stable foot), thus preventing vessels from tipping and spilling. Alternatively, the narrow feet of the unstable cups could also have helped when setting these cups into soft ground. A social consideration would be that a cup with an unstable foot required all contents to be consumed before the vessel was set down. This may have suited customary serving, toasting, and drinking traditions,

Area	Sherd Count	Stable Cups (Types 50.1-3)	Unstable Cups (Types 50.4-6)
	FORTIFIED BUILDING		
Total	817	32.0%	68.0%
SOUTHERN UNIT			
Vaults	8	37.5%	62.5%
Area 315	141	28.4%	71.6%
Admin. Suite	45	37.8%	62.2%
Rm. 314	64	18.8%	81.2%
Rms. 600/601	104	23.1%	76.9%
Rm. 316	33	24.2%	75.8%
NORTHERN UNIT			
Rm. 152	27	25.9%	74.1%
Rm. 156	9	11.1%	88.9%
Rm. 101	84	44.0%	56.0%
Rms. 140-142	79	34.2%	65.8%
TOWERS			
124	17	41.2%	58.8%
302	16	50.0%	50.0%
304	130	36.2%	63.8%
616	60	38.3%	61.7%
	EASTERN HOUSES		
Total	**79**	**69.6%**	**30.4%**
House 1	48	66.7%	33.3%
House 2	20	85.0%	15.0%
House 3	11	54.5%	45.5%

TABLE 5.4. Relative distributions of stable and unstable footed cup types across the excavated areas of the Fortified Building and Eastern Houses.

which were perhaps associated with the specific beer types attested in the contemporary CUSAS 9 archive.[28] The frequent archaeological presence of both stable and unstable cups might suggest two different drinking traditions performed simultaneously in the same commensal contexts at Tell Khaiber; it is this division that might be reflected in the respective vessel names for cups, the *laḫannu* and *lurmu* (see §5.1).

The relative frequencies of these two categories of cups might help to tease out some tentative explanations for these differences at Tell Khaiber (Table 5.4). Indeed, it is immediately clear that while stable feet are prevalent in the Eastern Houses, unstable variants are dominant across the Fortified Building. This broad separation, as was discussed in §3.14, acts as a subtle chronological indicator. However, it may also be a product of the different activities taking place in both parts of the site. Although some areas of the Fortified Building (vaults and Room 156) have too small a sample size to draw significant conclusions, Area 315 and Rooms 314,

[28] These types of beer are listed and discussed by Boivin (2018: 164–6).

FIG. 5.22. Vessels set in the corners of vaults. Vault 1 (p3098-9), left, and Vault 3 (p3124-18), right. Photos facing southeast.

600/601, 316, and 152 in particular show a strong emphasis on the use of unstable cups. There are, however, areas where the balance is more even. The administrative suite, for instance, demonstrates a relatively high percentage of stable footed types (37.8%). Moreover, Room 101 in the northern unit yields a relatively even percentage of the two vessel categories, which is notably out of character with the rest of the Fortified Building assemblage other than in the towers.

It is possible that the areas with the most regular daily comings and goings, congregations and subsequent dispersals, were the areas in which unstable footed cups were most common. The regular movement through these areas may have been the result either of specific labour activities (e.g. Area 315 and Room 316) or of a regular influx of guests (e.g. Rooms 142 and 314) who had to be greeted with appropriate acts of hospitality. On the other hand, the more restricted, domestic spaces recognised in §5.3, such as Room 101 and the Eastern Houses, may have seen less movement in and out, and thus less need for unstable variants and the social gestures that these vessels entailed.

5.4.2 'Ritual' Depositions

Ritual activities and performances suffused Mesopotamian life. Pottery vessels were used for offerings and libations to deities, for communing with dead ancestors (the *kispu*), and even for commonplace aspects of friendship or business, which were secured through actions such as the consumption of liquids or the smashing of a pot (Michalowski 1994). However, the foods and drinks consumed and the equipment used in these ritual performances appear to have mirrored those of more everyday activities (e.g. Ristvet 2015).

The separation of commensal and ritual behaviour is particularly difficult to disentangle. We might for instance expect a vessel used for public ceremonies or libations to be more elaborately decorated, exaggerated in shape, or perhaps even inscribed with votive text (e.g. Eidem 1987: 179–80). But these are absent at Tell Khaiber. Vessels such as goblets (Family 45), with tall ostentatious necks, do not enter the Tell Khaiber assemblage until the Kassite period (§3.1.3).

In the Sealand period, ritual behaviour seems to have involved ordinary vessels, the same as those used in everyday commensal performances. Presumably, these vessels and their contents were occasionally framed and animated by different meanings, dependent on their context of use or deposition. Bringing these common material elements together in novel configurations would have created meaningful connections with potentially transformative consequences (Harris 2017: 132). These performances may conform to what van Gennep (1960: 12–13) described as the 'pivoting of the sacred,' where the lines between ordinary and extraordinary, physical and metaphysical, were blurred.

Nevertheless, these elements are particularly hard to determine statistically, and can only occasionally be identified contextually. The fills of several of Tell Khaiber's vaults at the end of Level 1, for instance, demonstrate a curious material pattern. Vaults 1, 2, and 3, each contained a single intact vessel (Fig. 5.22).[29] There appears to have been no functional reason to discard these vessels, as they were still fully serviceable. It is more likely that their structured deposition represents a ritual foundation deposit intended to safeguard architectural renovations, as was common practice in Mesopotamian society (Ellis 1968).

A similar example of ritual deposition may be observed in a pit cut into the latest deposits of Room 142. This pit contained a cache of cups, jugs, pot stands, and measuring vessels, which were taken out of circulation and partially covered by a large bitumen-painted pithos sherd (Fig. 5.23). Instead of a foundation deposit, however, their stratigraphic association with the latest secure phase of the building's use (Phase 2.3) might mark this event as a closing deposit.

The most easily identifiable form of ritual activity involving pots, however, were burials. A common practice for adult burials of the Kassite period was to lay the body, often in a crouched position, inside two large pots laid rim-to-rim (Sternitzke 2017: 365–9). Such burials are only attested in the intrusive upper mixed deposits at Tell Khaiber, following the cessation of primary occupation in the Fortified Building. While the adult jar burials at Tell Khaiber were composed of two large pithoi (Family 25), infants were placed in single jars (Family 70), of which the neck was sometimes broken and a

[29] Vault 1: jug p3098-99; Vault 2: cup p3102-2; and Vault 3: bottle p3124-18.

bowl (Family 5) placed over the opening (Fig. 5.24). Similar forms of infant burial, while common in the Kassite period (Sternitzke 2017: 368–9), are also well attested in other periods across the Near East (e.g. Streit 2016).

Burying people in pottery vessels was a practical measure, serving to contain the decomposing body, and thus worked to limit the odour of decomposition and to deter potential predators and vermin. However, the practice must have held a spiritual component too, helping to protect the living from rogue ancestral spirits, as a potent metaphor for the containment of impurities (Sallaberger 1996: 84–93), and also to protect the deceased as they transitioned to a new state of being.

Pots were not only used to contain the dead, but also to sustain their spirit. During the second millennium, for instance, goods deposited directly alongside the deceased often consisted of a single commensal vessel—a cup, goblet, or bowl—held to the lips (Woolley 1976: 38). At Tell Khaiber, however, grave goods were almost always absent, apart from in one double-pithos burial inside House 1 of the Eastern Houses, which held a female interred with a jug (p4041-1), two bronze pins and a beautiful necklace of precious stones.

5.4.3 Pot marks

Pot marks have been found on five jar sherds. Two body sherds, one of which derives from a bitumen covered jar (Fig. 5.25a), were found in the administrative suite, while another, with a similar design, was found in Room 142 (Fig. 5.25b). An almost complete jar with an oblique hourglass design on the shoulder was found in the mixed surface-scraped deposits, close to a large body sherd bearing a comparable, although unfortunately fragmented, triangular motif on the upper body (Fig. 5.25c–d).

Since these markings appear to have been made post-firing, it is unlikely that they were designed to record the output of different stages of labour (e.g. Glatz 2012). Neither were they attempts at any known cuneiform sign, markers of vessel volume (Postgate, N. 2016, pers. comm.), or stylised renderings of familiar religious or royal iconography (e.g. Laursen 2016). It is unclear what exactly the pot marks do signify. They might have been a way of communicating intended destinations and recipients, markers of receipt, or even indicators of the commodity held within. It is also possible that they functioned as apotropaic devices designed to safeguard the vessels and their contents.

A further tantalising possibility arises with reference to four tablets in the CUSAS 9 archive that bear linear inscriptions on their edges (Dalley 2009: 15 and pl. CLXXV). Hamidović (2014) has raised the possibility that these represent an early form of alphabetic script in Mesopotamia, having strong parallels with proto-Canaanite alphabetical scripts (see also Koller 2018). He then draws parallels between these designs and a sample of motifs encountered on mid-second millennium pottery from Qala'at al-Bahrain and Failaka Island (Periods 3B–4B: 1600–1300) (Højlund 1987: 170; Laursen 2016: 6). These parallels he considers indicative of Mesopotamian–Arabian trade contacts during the Sealand period (see also Boivin 2018: 116). The linear motifs from Tell Khaiber demonstrate clear stylistic similarities with these contemporary marks from Failaka Island, and with some of the linear markings on the CUSAS 9 tablets. Under these circumstances, it may be significant that two of Tell Khaiber's five examples were found in the administrative suite, contextually associated with the tablet archive.

FIG. 5.23. A cache of drinking and measuring vessels in the upper, Phase 2.3 deposits of Room 142 (context 5016). Partially covered by a large painted pithos sherd (p5018-1).

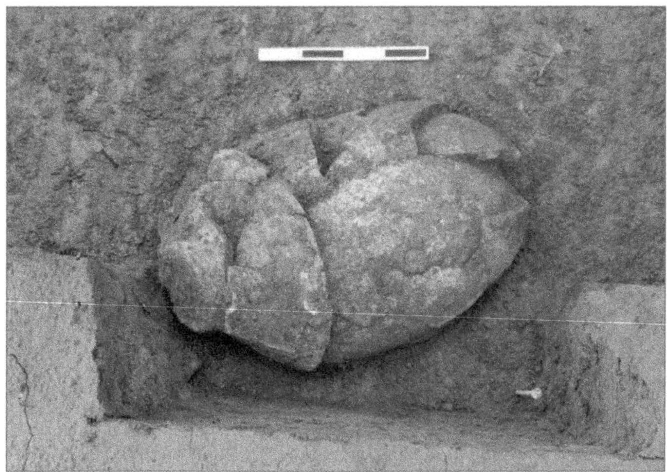

FIG. 5.24. Infant jar burial (vessels p1097-1 and p1098-1).

FIG. 5.25. Post-firing pot marks etched into the exterior surfaces of jars: a) p3064-678; b) p5047-12; b); c) p6111-68; d) p6111-63.

6. Pottery and Sealand Society

6.1 Typology and Chronology

The pottery assemblage from Tell Khaiber represents the only securely stratified material that can be reliably associated with the First Sealand Dynasty. The typology is based on analysis of 9,328 diagnostic sherds and approximately 400 complete or nearly complete vessel profiles. These are separated into 18 vessel shape *families*, which in turn are composed of 77 constituent *types*. Overall, this represents a limited shape repertoire of plain, typically undecorated vessels. The most chronologically diagnostic vessel types for the Sealand period are carinated bowls (Type 5.1), carinated bowls with grooves beneath the rim (Types 10.1–2), round-bodied cups with squat necks and with stable or unstable feet (Types 50.1–6), and jars with grooved rim bands (Types 70.2–3). The rest of the vessel types are more ambiguous and hold longer currencies in the second millennium ceramic record (Armstrong and Gasche 2014).

The corpus shows only minor stylistic development through the primary occupation period (Phases 1–2.3). This, alongside detailed stylistic comparisons with the stratified assemblages from the Gulf (§3.3.4) and the limited architectural changes between the different phases of the site (see Moon ed., fothcoming), is consistent with a short period of primary occupation, spanning perhaps 50–100 years. A small selection of Kassite period wares were also present in the mixed surface-scraped deposits, which are representative of secondary ephemeral use of the site after the Fortified Building had been abandoned (§3.1.3).

The Tell Khaiber typology now stands as a comprehensive comparative corpus which can be used to recognise, and in some instances reanalyse, contemporary material from across the immediate region. Currently, the primary Sealand period assemblage does not demonstrate any clear chronological overlaps with securely stratified assemblages anywhere else in the Mesopotamian heartland. Although the closest parallels in Babylonia derive from the late 17th century house of Ur-Utu at Tell ed-Der (Gasche 1989), as well as some of the earliest Kassite period vessels from both Tell ed-Der and Nippur, the Tell Khaiber assemblage as a whole does not yield any neat transitional or 'hybrid' types that bridge the gap between these two periods.

A few unstratified vessels do, however, provide an indication for continuity of occupation in or around the traditional Mesopotamian cities during the Sealand period (§3.2). These include selected vessels from Uruk, and several cups, one from a grave at Ur and further examples from soundings carried out by Sir Leonard Woolley at Umm Faisit, in the immediate vicinity of Ur (Woolley 1976). Likewise, a recent reassessment of the ceramic material from Babylon shows some evidence for vessels comparable with typical Sealand types (Sternitizke 2016a), which might lend support to the emerging hypothesis that occupation continued almost uninterrupted at the Babylonian state capital.

The pottery tradition that existed during the Late Old Babylonian period patently did not break down under the social and political strains placed on it by the degradation of the central Babylonian state. Neither, however, did it maintain the essential continuity implied by Ayoub (1982) and, more recently, by Armstrong and Gasche (2014). Rather, levels of continuity and change were specific to different vessel families. Large storage vessels, for instance, express a good deal of conservatism and interregional consistency, while other vessel types, particularly those used in serving, eating, and drinking, showed a higher degree of chronological and regional variability. Goblets, which were the most common vessels of the Old Babylonian period, appear to have dropped out of circulation entirely during the period of the First Sealand Dynasty, emerging again only in deposits associated with the Kassite period. It is unlikely that this absence can be explained away as a quirk of the Tell Khaiber assemblage, since a similar absence exists in contemporary assemblages in the Gulf, at Failaka Island and Qala'at al-Bahrain. Perhaps the networks governing goblet production and use shared a more intimate connection with state infrastructure during the Old Babylonian and Kassite periods, and these networks either could not have been, or deliberately were not, maintained during the period of Sealand control.

As a consequence of the fragmentary comparative record, this volume cannot offer decisive resolution to the persistent issue of the second millennium Mesopotamian chronology (see Pruzsinszky 2009). It does, however, call into question the archaeological validity of the Low Chronology, which places the Fall of Babylon at 1499 BCE (Cole 2014; Gasche et al. 1998). This shortened chronology rests on the assertion that 'the similarities in form between the [pottery] shapes belonging to the end of our early second-millennium sequence and those we date to the beginning of the 14th century do not allow for the intervention of so great a span of time' (Gasche et al. 1998: 1). This argument places significant emphasis on preconceived ideas regarding the speed of ceramic change, which is an inherently unstable and subjective metric. Furthermore, too much credence is placed on material from the contentious Susa sequence as a plug in the developmental gap. The pottery from Susa demonstrates almost no similarities with the Sealand assemblage from Tell Khaiber (§3.3.1), despite the extensive relationships that apparently existed between the Sealand and Elam during this period (Boivin 2018: 104–7). Likewise, followers of the Low Chronology have paid comparatively little attention to the archaeological evidence at hand from the Gulf. Højlund (1987; 1989) has long been of the opinion that the pottery from Failaka Island (Periods 3A–B) and Qala'at al-Bahrain (Period IIIa) slots into this mid-second millennium gap, and that this pottery must have been the result of extensive contacts between the people of northern and central Gulf and the Sealand inhabitants of southern Iraq, all of whom were occupants of the extended Gulf littoral zone of the Middle–Late Bronze Age (Jotheri 2016: 170–6). The material from Tell Khaiber provides categorical support for Højlund's Sealand hypothesis.

6.2 Sealand Culture and Politics in Babylonia and Beyond

Although the precise calendrical dates of Tell Khaiber's primary occupational sequence cannot be stated with certainty (see Moon ed., fothcoming), the pottery assemblage, in combination with relevant historical and archaeological evidence from Babylonia and the Gulf, does permit some tentative conclusions. The following narrative presents a general positioning of Tell Khaiber's occupation within the framework of historical events and processes that defined the mid-second millennium. This historical position will no doubt become better aligned and refined as supplementary contemporary evidence emerges in future.

The dating of Tell Khaiber's textual archive to the reign of the eighth Sealand king Ayadaragalama places occupation not only generations after the cessation of Babylonian control in southern Mesopotamia, but also in a period following the prolonged skirmishes between the Old Babylonian and Sealand kings. While Gulkišar's famous clashes with the last Babylonian king Samsuditana ostensibly gained the Sealand Dynasty significant territory, this territory may well have been consolidated under the sovereignty of the following kings Pešgaldaramaš and Ayadaragalama (Boivin 2018: 20–60). At this point, the dynasty may have exercised control as far north as Nippur,[30] with the Fortified Building at Tell Khaiber constructed as a means of subjugating and administering just a part of this burgeoning territory.

Although stratified archaeological evidence is entirely lacking from all major Mesopotamian cities during this period, selective ceramic parallels do raise the potential of continued occupation, at least on a small scale, at some southern cities, particularly at Ur and Uruk (§1.3.1). Ceramic and textual evidence also suggest that Babylon maintained some degree of habitation throughout the mid-second millennium (Sternitzke 2016a; 2016b), although it is unlikely that the Sealand Dynasty's territorial control ever stretched this far north (for debate, see Boivin 2018: 117–21). Several Sealand vessel types are even present on the northern periphery of Babylonia, at Tell Yelkhi in the Hamrin and even Tell Bderi in the Syrian Jazirah (§3.3.2–3). Since these Sealand vessels appear to have been folded into otherwise dominant local ceramic traditions, they might suggest the development of long-distance trading networks along the Diyala and Khabur rivers.

This ceramic evidence, alongside the continuities evident in the Sealand scribal tradition (Dalley 2009; Robson 2017), are clearly inconsistent with the traditional narrative of wholesale state collapse in southern Babylonia (e.g. Charpin 1986; 1988). Yet it seems unlikely, from the archaeological record as it currently stands, that the southern cities maintained the scale of occupation and continuity in religious practices interpreted by Dalley (2009: 4–10) based on the CUSAS 9 archive; these textual claims to continuity may perhaps have been part of the incipient Sealand state's 'discourse of desire' (Richardson 2012: 4), projected as a strategy by which to consolidate and expand its power (after Richardson 2017).

The Sealand period was evidently one of extensive transformation. As Gasche (1989: 139) posited, and Al-Hamdani (2015) has recently echoed, it is likely that in the wake of urban failure across Mesopotamia, the small non-urban sites, such as Tell Khaiber and potentially also Umm Faisit, hold vast untapped information relating to the Sealand period. There is an uncertainty as to whether previously unknown larger communal centres may also have formed significant nodes in these shifting socioeconomic networks. One potential candidate for such a site is Dehaila, a ca. 60ha site pinpointed by Al-Hamdani (2015: 168–74), from surface survey, as a potential Sealand period capital. An excavation team led by the Russian Academy of Sciences, Moscow, has recently initiated test excavations at Dehaila (Jankowski-Diakonoff et al. 2020); the results of this work may well provide valuable contributions to the Sealand debate over the coming years.

[30] The CUSAS 9 archive demonstrates the significance of the Nippur pantheon (Boivin 2018: 234–5).

Dates	Events / Synchronisms	Evidence (Babylonia)	Sources	Events/ Synchronisms (Dilmun)	Evidence (Gulf)		Sources	Tell Khaiber
ca. 1740	Rim-Sin II rebellion	Abandonment / deurbanisation of southern and central cities	Boivin (2018: 86–91); Goetze (1964: 97)	Period of "efflorescence"	Royal Mounds of A'ali	Failaka (Period 2B and Phase 5); Qala'at al-Bahrain (Period IIc)	Højlund (1987: 117–18; 2016: 255–6; 2019); Højlund and Andersen (1994; 1997); Laursen (2017: 381–4)	
ca. 1732–1690	Establishment of First Sealand Dynasty; Samsuiluna and Abi-ešuh fail to capture Iluma-ilu		Boivin (2018: 91–104); Brinkman (2017); van Koppen (2017)	Degradation and collapse of royal authority		"Enigmatic Pottery" at Qala'at al-Bahrain (Post-IIc)	Højlund (2019); Højlund and Andersen (1994; 1997); Laursen (2017: 384–7)	
ca. 1690-1640	"A Fragile equilibrium". Continued skirmishes between Babylonian and Sealand kings, particularly between Samsuditana and Gulkišar (ca. 1600)	Abandonment / deurbanisation of northern cities	Boivin (2018: 112–21); Brinkman (2017); Horsnell (1999); van Koppen (2017); Zomer (2021)	Brief post-collapse period			Laursen (2017: 388)	
ca. 1640–1580		No securely stratified evidence		Restoration of kingship / Dilmun "Renaissance"	Un-named King of Dilmun, Al Maqsha Royal Mound; Failaka (Period 3A)		Højlund (1987: 119–24; 2016: 256–7; 2019); Højlund and Andersen (1994; 1997); Laursen (2017: 389–90)	
	Fall of Babylon (1595)		Oates (1979: 84)					
ca. 1580–1500	Kassite consolidation of northern plains; Sealand consolidation of south		Boivin (2018: 115–7); Brinkman (2017); van Koppen (2017)		Failaka (Period 3B and Phase 6); Qala'at al-Bahrain (Period IIIa)			Approximate period of primary occupation (Phases 1–2.3)
ca. 1460				Sealand conquest and loss of independence	Eagamil year name on tablet from Qala'at al-Bahrain (Period IIIb1); Failaka (Phase 7)		Cavigneaux and André-Salvini (forthcoming); Højlund (2016: 257–8); Laursen (2017: 390)	
ca. 1460–1450	Kassite conquest of Sealand under Ulam-Burariaš; Eagamil flees to Elam; Agum III ultimately quashes Sealand resistance		Boivin (2018: 108–11, 121–3); Grayson (1975); van Koppen (2017)	Kassite conquest	Agum III year name on tablet from Qala'at al-Bahrain (Period IIIb1); Failaka (Phase 7)		André-Salvini and Lombard (1997: 167); Laursen (2017: 390); Olijdam (1997: 199–203)	Short hiatus
ca. 1450–1150	Kassite control and consolidation in north and south	Re-occupation of major cities	Brinkman (1976); Clayden (1989; 2020)	Kassite control and consolidation	Kassite kings and governors listed in tablets from Qala'at al-Bahrain (Period IIIb1); Failaka (Periods 4A–B and Phases 7–8)		André-Salvini (2000); Højlund (1987: 124–9; 2016: 257–60; 2019); Højlund and Andersen (1994; 1997); Laursen (2017: fig.513)	Episodes of building re-use (Mixed Phases)

TABLE 6.1. Significant historical events discussed in the text and their relevant sources of archaeological and textual evidence, alongside a tentative positioning of Tell Khaiber's occupational sequence.

The end of Tell Khaiber's primary period of occupation is more difficult to pin down relative to historical events. Site disuse and abandonment may well have aligned with mounting tensions during the mid-15th century BCE, when Ulam-buriaš, the Kassite king resident at Babylon, struck south to occupy parts of the southern plains, and Eagamil, the last king of the Sealand, fled to Elam (Grayson 1975). Yet, it is possible that the Sealand Dynasty was already on a downwards trend, with social and economic pressures whittling away Sealand power and political legitimacy during the first half of the 15th century. The downsizing of operations and ultimate abandonment of Tell Khaiber's Fortified Building, seemingly with no evidence of violent conflict, is perhaps a symptom of this general infrastructural degradation in the decades prior to Ulam-Buriaš' military successes and Agum III's decisive conquest.

It is worth making an excursus here to address in more detail the significant connections demonstrated between Tell Khaiber and sites in the Gulf. The ups and downs of Dilmunite society appear to have been intimately tied to the fortunes of southern Babylonia during the volatile centuries of the mid-second millennium. As such, these connections help to buttress our chronological and cultural understanding of Tell Khaiber and its ceramics.

The Old Babylonian period was a time of so-called 'efflorescence' in the Gulf (Laursen 2017: 381–4). Local Dilmunite royal authority, with its roots in the thriving trading system mediating between Babylonia and the lands to the east such as Oman and the Indus, was well established (Laursen and Steinkeller 2017; Oppenheim 1954). The capital of Dilmun, Qala'at al-Bahrain, continued to thrive for some time despite the wider context of southern Mesopotamian rebellions against Babylonian rule, with several large public buildings erected in Period IIc (ca. 1740 BCE). In fact, the associated Royal Mounds of A'ali, which had long been the resting place of the Dilmun kings, reached a peak in quality and economic wealth at a time contemporary with the weakening of Babylonian power under Samsuiluna (Laursen 2017: 381). Then rather abruptly, according to the archaeological record (ca. 1720–1690 calibrated BCE), Qala'at al-Bahrain suffered a period of sweeping depopulation, with a layer of drift sand accumulating on the floors of its temples and public buildings. Meanwhile, Failaka Island, which had in Period 2B/Phases 2–5 (ca. 1800–1700 BCE) seen a simultaneous investment in public architecture in the form of an industrial 'palace' and specialist workshops, shows a similarly sudden occupational break (Højlund and Abu-Laban 2016: 255–6). By 1690 BCE the abandonment of the Royal Mounds of A'ali had marked the end of the ruling dynasty (Laursen 2017: 384) as Dilmunite society too fell victim to 'world recession' (after Crawford 1996).

Armstrong (2017) has recently suggested that, following this collapse in Dilmunite society, the extensive ceramic similarities between Mesopotamia and the Gulf began to re-emerge only in the middle-to-late 15th century as a direct consequence of Kassite imperial expansion into Dilmun. The evidence assessed in this volume and elsewhere (Højlund 2016; Laursen 2017) forces us to set these cultural connections back significantly.

Following an unspecified period of occupational hiatus after the Dilmunite collapse, Failaka Island shows small-scale reoccupation in Period 3A/Phase 5 (ca. 1650 BCE). Once resettled, the composition of the material assemblages altered significantly, with Mesopotamian style pottery dominating and easing out local Barbar wares (§3.3.4). Architecturally, this period is marked only by the construction of several small houses, as well as rather ephemeral re-use of the site's industrial 'palace' (Højlund and Abu-Laban 2016: 256–7). It is in Period 3B/Phase 6 (ca. 1600–1500 BCE) that Failaka Island shows genuine rejuvenation, with the resumption of large-scale storage practices in the industrial 'palace,' in addition to the construction of new public buildings and a concomitant influx in figurative styles of both a Mesopotamian and a local Dilmun tradition on stamp seals and stone vessels (Højlund 2016: 257).

In line with these developments on Failaka is an ostensible 'renaissance' of local, perhaps royal authority on Bahrain (Laursen 2017: 389). The Al-Maqsha Royal Mound, located one kilometre from Qala'at al-Bahrain, and thus removed from the traditional A'ali Mound burial mound complex, has recently supplied a Bayesian calibrated age of 1644–1583 BCE (68.2% confidence) for its construction (Laursen 2017: 374, fig. 508). The Al-Maqsha burial mound is also considered to have been broadly contemporary not only with the onset of Period 3B/Phase 6 on Failaka Island, but also with the reinstitution of urban life at Qala'at al-Bahrain, Period IIIa. Period IIIa demonstrates the extensive re-use of those palatial warehouses and storerooms used in Periods IIb–c (Højlund 2019: 161–2; Højlund and Andersen 1997: 50–68), with tablets indicating the renewed scale and complexity of the administrative tasks taking place therein (Cavigneaux and André-Salvini, forthcoming).

The most significant stylistic parallels between these Gulf assemblages and the Tell Khaiber assemblage aligns with this period of Dilmunite 'renaissance' (ca. 1600–1500 BCE). These similarities were shared in other elements of culture and iconography too. During the 16th century, inscriptions on Dilmun style seals found at Failaka and Qala'at al-Bahrain, for instance, illustrate the renewed primacy in the ideology of the god Inzak/Anzak, the traditional patron god of Dilmun (Laursen 2017: 389; Marchesi 2017: 425–37). This should be considered alongside the frequency of personal names containing the name Anzak in both the Tell Khaiber and CUSAS 9 archives. Indeed, the fact that Anzak was linked to otherwise Akkadian names in the Sealand archives indicates the extent to which this deity was integrated into Sealand society during the reign of Ayadaragalama in the mid-16th century (Dalley 2013: 181–2), a clear indication of the alignment of Sealand and Dilmunite ideologies. Intriguing too is the small sample of pot marks found at Tell Khaiber and at Failaka, which may potentially indicate the unofficial use of a shared alphabetic script, as also exemplified by several tablets of the CUSAS 9 archive (§5.4.3).

These sources of evidence challenge the common perception that the Mesopotamian heartland formed an inalienable core of shared beliefs, cultural practices, and material traditions. Mesopotamia and Dilmun already shared significant connections at the top of society during the early second millennium: Dilmunite kings were of Amorite descent, its administrative elite used cuneiform tablets, and its royal funerary customs and other cultic activity reflected those of Mesopotamia (Laursen and Steinkeller 2017; Laursen 2017). Nevertheless, significant cultural reconfiguration occurred during the mid-second millennium, which drew the people of the Sealand and inhabitants of the Gulf into ever tighter social and economic relationships on various social scales, as demonstrated by the production and consumption of shared pottery wares (see also Calderbank 2020b). It has been suggested that these closely forged ties were the direct consequence of organised political unification, or annexation on behalf of an expansionist Sealand state (Boivin 2018: 122; Crawford 1996; Dalley 2013: 182). There is no doubt that direct control of Dilmun would have proven economically beneficial, enabling the Sealanders to reignite the lucrative trade routes of the early second millennium. Pots, however, do not mean political sovereignty. Rather than direct political control, networks of soft diplomacy based upon shared everyday routines and cultural beliefs may have proven sufficient for tapping into these economic opportunities.

Consequently, while the above evidence could be considered to represent a political merger between the Sealand Dynasty and Dilmunite hierarchy in approximately 1600 BCE, following the reign of the un-named king buried in the Al-Maqsha royal tomb, Laursen (2017: 389–90) is firmly of the opinion that Dilmun continued to operate as an independent polity, under local sovereignty, until approximately 1500 BCE, and only then did it relinquish its political independence to Sealand rulers (see also Højlund 1989). A single year name associated with the final Sealand king Eagamil (ca. 1460 BCE) is the only positive evidence for direct Sealand governance of Qala'at al-Bahrain (Cavigneaux and André-Salvini, forthcoming). This was soon followed by a tablet bearing Kassite King Agum III's title, as the First Sealand Dynasty's fall in southern Mesopotamia precipitated an attendant political change in Dilmun (Laursen 2017: 390 and fig. 513).

6.3 The Pottery Economy at Tell Khaiber

The previous two sections have used Tell Khaiber's pottery assemblage to inform larger-scale chronological issues, or the historical *longue durée*. Nevertheless, it is clear that the unique interpretive potential of ancient ceramic assemblages lies in the unparalleled information that they can provide about small-scale material engagements. Particularly relevant are the ways in which pottery vessels were integrated into Sealand people's everyday social and economic routines, and the means by which *chaîne opératoire* analyses articulate aspects of production and use.

Chapter 4 demonstrated the complexity of Sealand period vessel production. Using textual and material analysis, in combination with X-ray analysis of a sample of vessels of different shape families, it was possible to demonstrate a level of complexity to Bronze Age Mesopotamian pottery manufacture that has rarely been credited (see also Romano and Zingale 2019). Significantly, this analysis challenges the traditional view that second millennium vessels were mostly wheel-*thrown*. Instead, Sealand period potters made extensive use of the wheel-coiling technique, utilising the rotative kinetic energy (RKE) of the turning wheel not to lift vessel walls vertically, but to join and thin coils and to shape vessels along the horizontal axis.

Together, through detailed analysis of clay preparation, forming technique, and firing procedures, it was possible to designate four Techno-Groups to which the majority of the Tell Khaiber assemblage conformed (§4.4). It is difficult to pinpoint exactly what these respective Techno-Groups represent; they may reflect accepted technological traditions or 'ways of doing' (after Roux 2016: 2), which were specific to different vessel categories and were recognised and practised by all individual potters servicing Tell Khaiber, or they may represent the output of different workshops or individual potters, specialising in the production of certain vessel families. Regardless, the apparent similarity of most vessel shapes and associated production techniques with those identified amongst Old Babylonian assemblages (Bürger 2011; van As and Jacobs 2014) suggests a consistency in potting networks through time. This is significant, as it means extensive communication between Babylonian potters operating within integrated communities of practice (Berg 2015; Wenger 1998). It was these craft networks that enabled the successful dissemination of distinct plain ware potting traditions spatially and temporally during the mid-second millennium, in the face of large-scale political change.

It is currently unclear how exactly the potters servicing Tell Khaiber were connected to the site's administrative apparatus. Of over 150 individuals, including 25 professions, listed in the Tell Khaiber tablet archive (Robson 2017: 33), there is no mention of a potter (Akk. *pahāru*) directly associated with the Fortified Building. Neither is there any archaeological evidence for contemporary production facilities in the excavated or surveyed area of the site. Rather, specific vessel types were brought into the building only periodically (§5.1). This supports the hypothesis that most vessels were produced locally, yet at a distance from the Fortified Building, physically and perhaps also economically.

The Tell Khaiber pottery assemblage demonstrates a clear intention for pots with a standardised appearance, albeit with some diversity in the execution of individual vessels (§4.2.4). While Pfälzner (1995: 260–2) considers standardised Mitanni and Middle Assyrian ceramics to have been the direct result of state-controlled mass-production (see also Blackman et al. 1993), Wattenmaker (1998a; 1998b) has argued that such styles were driven by a desire of Mesopotamian populations, from all sections of society, to conform to an urban identity. In the context of a seemingly laconic administrative apparatus at Tell Khaiber, with little evidence for rigid hierarchy or intervention in craft activity (Robson 2017), it is highly unlikely that the standardised appearance of Tell Khaiber's vessels was driven by centralised political forces, either in terms of will or capacity (for similar arguments, see Steinkeller 1996). Instead, it is far more likely that dislocated communities of craft practice and their rigid ways of doing were to a significant degree responsible for the standardised appearance of Tell Khaiber's vessels (Calderbank 2020a).

Of course, levels of similarity and difference in the production of specific vessel shapes, and consequently the entire assemblage, would also have been framed by the intended uses of vessels and the impact on consumers. Thus, when the administrators of Tell Khaiber requested 80 *kaptukkû* and 100 *laḫannu* vessels (3064.65), for instance, each party involved in this economic flow—producers, recipients, and consumers—needed to be clear which vessel shape was expected and potters needed to produce vessels with profiles, volumes, and specific shape attributes loosely conforming to the appropriate standard (§4.2.4). This standard was primarily driven by functionality. Pots, it seems, were deliberately designed to be stylistically and functionally unobtrusive, thus permitting the smooth operation of everyday routines across Tell Khaiber.

This volume assesses pottery function in terms of common vessel use-contexts during the mid-second millennium BCE (Chapter 5). Tell Khaiber's vessels were used for cooking, beer brewing, measuring, food-processing, storage of bulk and special goods, serving and consumption of food and drink, and ritual activity. High resolution analysis of the spatial distributions of these vessel types, using bulk sherd statistics (Appendix A) and GIS data for complete vessels, reveals not only the multifunctional and multifaceted nature of pottery engagements, but also the ways in which these activities were curated and distributed across the different spaces of the Fortified Building. The formal and informal divisions between these activities helps to determine distinct functional sub-assemblages that were restricted to specific areas of the site. Together, these discrete material configurations reinforce the sense of communal integration of a partially-resident set of administrators, labourers, and craftspersons, for example the cooks and brewers present in the tablet archive (Robson 2017; Robson, forthcoming).

There is no recognisable 'fine-ware' tradition at Tell Khaiber, despite the production of tablet clays demonstrating that the skill and knowledge to produce vessels with fine matrices was culturally and technologically understood (Robson, forthcoming). Furthermore, there is little evidence that certain pottery styles or fabric types were restricted to certain areas of the building. Instead, once vessels entered the Fortified Building, they were distributed equally in accordance with the tasks for which they were required. The Tell Khaiber pottery assemblage, as a whole, is therefore consistent with the broader interpretation of the site as a functional, administrative centre. The total assemblage is dominated by a limited set of activities, with a particular material emphasis on those vessels associated with bulk storage and communal drinking. Other uses, such as food-processing, cooking, brewing, measuring, and special storage appear to have formed subsidiary roles, and were generally restricted to specific areas of the site (§5.3). What is more, the relative percentages of these functional types remain broadly consistent throughout the phases of Tell Khaiber's primary occupation (Phases 1–2.3), thus indicating functional consistency in the use of the Fortified Building. It is only in the later, mixed deposits that a range of other, more ritually oriented depositions—burials and pits containing vessel caches (§5.4.2)—assumed increased significance.

Although stylistically distinct, the main vessels constituting the Sealand assemblage at Tell Khaiber demonstrate a broad continuity with the main vessel types of the Old Babylonian period. This continuity in material style is no doubt related to continuity in certain foodways. If this is the case, however, the absence of certain other frequent Old Babylonian types at Tell Khaiber must also be noted. While the lack of large deep bowls and flat trays and platters (Armstrong and Gasche 2014: pls. 1–9) suggests changing concepts around the communal sharing of food (pls. 25–30), the absence of the ubiquitous Old Babylonian goblet (pls. 57–9) might indicate a relative lack of, or at least variation in, performative acts of drinking at Tell Khaiber. The relative absence of such communal and special-purpose vessels at Tell Khaiber might tentatively be attributed to the reduced population of Sealand period communities in southern Mesopotamia, which led to an associated downsizing of everyday meals involving a more limited number of participants.[31] Nevertheless, one-off feasts and communal gatherings might be inferred from the large number of drinking vessels disposed of in the building's unoccupied towers (§5.3.3).

These absences in vessel types might also be explained as a product of the unique functional identity of Tell Khaiber. Currently, this site represents only a snapshot of pottery engagements in the Sealand period. Different sets of Sealand vessels, intended for some of the more performative ceremonial functions encountered in the CUSAS 9 archive (Dalley 2009: 59–112), for instance, may well be found at contemporary sites: from the associated 'palace' referred to in Tell Khaiber's archive (Robson 2017: 33),[32] from the numerous 'special purpose sites' identified by Al-Hamdani's (2015: 164–8) survey, or from the potentially contemporaneous urban centre of Dehaila (Jankowski-Diakonoff et al. 2020). Only then can we assess whether the social and economic relationships in which Tell Khaiber's assemblage was embedded should be considered as broadly representational or as more distinctive.

6.4 Mesopotamian Pottery Studies

At the point of writing, Mesopotamian pottery analyses of the early historical periods are at an important juncture. A number of large-scale survey and excavation projects have returned to the south of Iraq after a long hiatus. These projects are generating enormous quantities of securely stratified material and are mobilising this data to address new and progressive research questions.

It is imperative that Mesopotamian pottery studies are attentive to the complex contextual ways in which ancient craft traditions were (re)produced from the ground up. Accordingly, future research should operate a holistic approach, which integrates multiple sources of evidence—material, scientific, and textual—in combination (e.g. Duistermaat 2017), and that we seek to address issues extending beyond passive typology building. Pottery, as the most abundant form of material culture used by all levels of ancient societies, held a unique capacity to move between different social strata, mediating relationships along the way. Pollock (2015) has captured this interpretive scalability effectively in her use of the historical paradigm of *Alltagsgeschichte*,[33] where archaeological understandings of small-scale material engagements—of pottery production, circulation, and use, for instance—provide a way of

[31] Twiss (2017) has noted similar small-scale commensal activities punctuated by one-off feasts at Tell Sakhariya, a site located 6km east of Ur which has been identified with ancient Gaeš (Zimansky and Stone 2016). Tell Sakhariya is said to have been visited intermittently during the centuries of the mid-second millennium, although the ceramics from the site are not yet published.

[32] Potentially associated with the Sealand period palatial site of Kār-Šamaš (Boivin 2015). Location currently unknown.

[33] Loosely translated as 'history of the everyday' (Pollock 2015: 10).

unravelling the intricate webs by which ordinary people's mundane acts constituted broader networks and, ultimately, influenced the mechanics of politics and society.

Studies of second millennium Mesopotamia have tended to focus on sweeping sociopolitical upheaval on the one hand (e.g. van de Mieroop 2004: 122–5), while emphasising continuity and stability of a Babylonian pottery tradition on the other (after Armstrong and Gasche 2014). Yet, this apparent dissonance between historical and material evidence is rarely addressed head-on.[34] Pottery evidence from the literate periods is largely used to buttress the historical narrative, and rarely to tell alternative stories of craft continuity, resilience, and resistance. It is misleading to assume a long-term view of the second millennium pottery tradition as isolated, passive, and enduring. Instead, it has proven productive in this volume to consider the Tell Khaiber assemblage as historically emergent, with vessels drawing their producers and consumers into specific types of craft practices, commensal activities, and social relationships that connected people from across the extended littoral regions of southern Mesopotamia and the Gulf. Pottery vessels assumed a mediating role in the ongoing negotiations between technological tradition, sociopolitical change, and a more informal reconfiguration of cultural and economic networks during the First Dynasty of the Sealand.

[34] For a broader critique on the disciplinary separation between archaeological and historical analyses in Ancient Near Eastern studies, see Gates 2005.

Appendix A: Bulk Diagnostic Sherd Distributions

Data in the following tables are separated according to room/area. Within tables, counts of each vessel type are organised according to context and associated phase within that room/area. Total counts and relative percentages are also provided for each entire room/area. Contexts highlighted in brown indicate discrete floors and surfaces. The data for the entire Tell Khaiber assemblage is provided at the start of the appendix and can be used as a comparative benchmark for each room/area.

TOTAL ASSEMBLAGE		
	Total	
FAMILY	#	%
5	15	0.16
5.1	799	8.57
5.2	452	4.85
5.3	7	0.08
5.4	27	0.29
5.5	12	0.13
	1312	14.07
10	11	0.12
10.1	133	1.43
10.2	107	1.15
10.3	13	0.14
10.4	6	0.06
	270	2.89
15	1	0.01
15.1	493	5.29
15.2	50	0.54
	544	5.83
20	4	0.04
20.1	41	0.44
20.2	2	0.02
	47	0.50
25	19	0.20
25.1	279	2.99
25.2	51	0.55
25.3	40	0.43
25.4	111	1.19
25.5	103	1.10
	603	6.46
30	0	0.00
30.1	2	0.02
30.2	21	0.23
30.3	3	0.03
	26	0.28
35	9	0.10
35.1	6	0.06
35.2	117	1.25
35.3	13	0.14
35.4	19	0.20
35.5	28	0.30
	192	2.06
40	1	0.01
40.1	19	0.20
40.2	42	0.45
40.3	5	0.05
	67	0.72
45	2	0.02
45.1	14	0.15
45.2	5	0.05
45.3	2	0.02
45.4	1	0.01
	24	0.26
50	33	0.35
50.1	289	3.10
50.2	175	1.88
50.3	112	1.20
50.4	205	2.20
50.5	598	6.41
50.6	17	0.18
50.7	5	0.05
	1434	15.37

TOTAL ASSEMBLAGE		
	Total	
FAMILY	#	%
55	4	0.04
55.1	263	2.82
55.2	137	1.47
55.3	8	0.09
	412	4.42
60	8	0.09
60.1	1156	12.39
60.2	10	0.11
60.3	8	0.09
60.4	3	0.03
	1185	12.70
65	7	0.08
65.1	552	5.92
65.2	173	1.85
65.3	10	0.11
65.4	15	0.16
	757	8.12
70	27	0.29
70.1	152	1.63
70.2	696	7.46
70.3	853	9.14
70.4	33	0.35
70.5	86	0.92
70.6	9	0.10
70.7	4	0.04
70.8	2	0.02
	1862	19.96
75	2	0.02
75.1	30	0.32
75.2	7	0.08
75.3	3	0.03
75.4	4	0.04
	46	0.49
80	22	0.24
80.1	130	1.39
80.2	74	0.79
80.3	2	0.02
	228	2.44
85	5	0.05
85.1	160	1.72
85.2	97	1.04
85.3	10	0.11
	272	2.92
90	1	0.01
90.1	7	0.08
90.2	3	0.03
90.3	3	0.03
90.4	4	0.04
90.5	1	0.01
90.6	1	0.01
90.7	2	0.02
90.8	2	0.02
90.9	1	0.01
	25	0.27
95	1	0.01
95.1	8	0.09
95.2	3	0.03
95.3	7	0.08
95.4	3	0.03
	22	0.24
Total	9328	100

VAULTS 1–6													
	PHASE 1											Total	
FAMILY	3057	3059	3098	3099	3102	3104	3106	3124	3125	3128	3101	#	%
5												0	0.00
5.1	2			1			1		3			7	9.72
5.2	1			1				1				3	4.17
5.3												0	0.00
5.4												0	0.00
5.5												0	0.00
	3	0	0	2	0	0	1	1	3	0	0	10	13.89
10												0	0.00
10.1												0	0.00
10.2		1										1	1.39
10.3												0	0.00
10.4												0	0.00
	0	1	0	0	0	0	0	0	0	0	0	1	1.39
15												0	0.00
15.1				2								2	2.78
15.2												0	0.00
	0	0	0	2	0	0	0	0	0	0	0	2	2.78
20												0	0.00
20.1												0	0.00
20.2												0	0.00
	0	0	0	0	0	0	0	0	0	0	0	0	0.00
25				1					1			2	2.78
25.1				1		1			1	2		5	6.94
25.2												0	0.00
25.3									1			1	1.39
25.4												0	0.00
25.5										1		1	1.39
	0	0	0	2	0	1	0	0	3	3	0	9	12.50
30												0	0.00
30.1												0	0.00
30.2												0	0.00
30.3												0	0.00
	0	0	0	0	0	0	0	0	0	0	0	0	0.00
35												0	0.00
35.1												0	0.00
35.2												0	0.00
35.3												0	0.00
35.4												0	0.00
35.5		1										1	1.39
	0	1	0	0	0	0	0	0	0	0	0	1	1.39
40												0	0.00
40.1												0	0.00
40.2												0	0.00
40.3												0	0.00
	0	0	0	0	0	0	0	0	0	0	0	0	0.00
45												0	0.00
45.1								1				1	1.39
45.2												0	0.00
45.3												0	0.00
45.4												0	0.00
	0	0	0	0	0	0	0	1	0	0	0	1	1.39
50									1			1	1.39
50.1								1				1	1.39
50.2					1							1	1.39
50.3		1										1	1.39
50.4												0	0.00
50.5							1	1	1	1		4	5.56
50.6				1								1	1.39
50.7												0	0.00
	0	1	0	1	1	0	1	2	2	1	0	9	12.50

VAULTS 1–6													
	PHASE 1											Total	
FAMILY	3057	3059	3098	3099	3102	3104	3106	3124	3125	3128	3101	#	%
55												0	0.00
55.1			1					1				2	2.78
55.2												0	0.00
55.3												0	0.00
	0	0	1	0	0	0	0	1	0	0	0	2	2.78
60												0	0.00
60.1	2		1					4	2		1	10	13.89
60.2												0	0.00
60.3												0	0.00
60.4												0	0.00
	2	0	1	0	0	0	0	4	2	0	1	10	13.89
65												0	0.00
65.1				2								2	2.78
65.2				2			1	2	2	2		9	12.50
65.3												0	0.00
65.4												0	0.00
	0	0	0	4	0	0	1	2	2	2	0	11	15.28
70												0	0.00
70.1												0	0.00
70.2			1			2		1	2			6	8.33
70.3					1			4	1			6	8.33
70.4												0	0.00
70.5									1			1	1.39
70.6												0	0.00
70.7												0	0.00
70.8												0	0.00
	0	0	1	0	1	2	0	5	4	0	0	13	18.06
75												0	0.00
75.1												0	0.00
75.2												0	0.00
75.3												0	0.00
75.4												0	0.00
	0	0	0	0	0	0	0	0	0	0	0	0	0.00
80									1			1	1.39
80.1												0	0.00
80.2												0	0.00
80.3												0	0.00
	0	0	0	0	0	0	0	0	1	0	0	1	1.39
85												0	0.00
85.1												0	0.00
85.2						1				1		2	2.78
85.3												0	0.00
	0	0	0	0	0	1	0	0	0	1	0	2	2.78
90												0	0.00
90.1												0	0.00
90.2												0	0.00
90.3												0	0.00
90.4												0	0.00
90.5												0	0.00
90.6												0	0.00
90.7												0	0.00
90.8												0	0.00
90.9												0	0.00
	0	0	0	0	0	0	0	0	0	0	0	0	0.00
95												0	0.00
95.1												0	0.00
95.2												0	0.00
95.3												0	0.00
95.4												0	0.00
	0	0	0	0	0	0	0	0	0	0	0	0	0.00
Total	5	3	3	11	2	4	3	16	17	7	1	72	100

AREA 315																																	
	PHASE 1								PHASE 2.1						PHASE 2.2																	Total	
FAMILY	1168	1169	1175	1164	1174	3200	3202	3201	3182	3185	3187	3183	3194	3179	3177	3176	3169	3171	3166	3168	3163	3158	3160	3154	3151	3149	3146	3144	3142	3147	3131	#	%
5																																0	0.00
5.1	3		1		3	1	1	1		6	5			2	1	13	2			2	2	15	7	1	4			1		1		72	8.26
5.2										1						2											1					4	0.46
5.3																																0	0.00
5.4																																0	0.00
5.5																																0	0.00
	3	0	1	0	3	1	1	1	0	7	5	0	0	2	1	15	2	0	0	2	2	15	7	1	4	0	1	1	0	1	0	76	8.72
10																																0	0.00
10.1		2			7			1		3						3	1				1	1		1								20	2.29
10.2	2	1								1					1		1						1									7	0.80
10.3																																0	0.00
10.4																																0	0.00
	2	3	0	0	7	0	0	1	0	4	0	0	0	0	1	3	2	0	0	0	1	1	1	1	0	0	0	0	0	0	0	27	3.10
15																																0	0.00
15.1	3	1	1		1	3				13	2			2	8	13	1			5	2	9	3	1	3		1				2	74	8.49
15.2																				1												1	0.11
	3	1	1	0	1	3	0	0	0	13	2	0	0	2	8	13	1	0	0	6	2	9	3	1	3	0	1	0	0	0	2	75	8.60
20																																0	0.00
20.1																1				1				1								3	0.34
20.2																																0	0.00
	0	0	0	0	0	0	0	0	0	0	0	0	0	0	0	1	0	0	0	1	0	0	0	1	0	0	0	0	0	0	0	3	0.34
25																																0	0.00
25.1	1		1					1		3					2	9	2			3	3	2	1		1						2	31	3.56
25.2										1					1	1				1	1		2	2	1							10	1.15
25.3											1																					1	0.11
25.4					1					2						3				2	1	1	1									11	1.26
25.5										2						3				4	1	1										11	1.26
	1	0	1	0	1	0	0	1	0	8	1	0	0	0	3	16	2	0	0	10	6	4	4	2	2	0	0	0	0	0	2	64	7.34
30																																0	0.00
30.1																																0	0.00
30.2																1	1			1	1			1								5	0.57
30.3																																0	0.00
	0	0	0	0	0	0	0	0	0	0	0	0	0	0	0	1	1	0	0	1	1	0	0	1	0	0	0	0	0	0	0	5	0.57
35																																0	0.00
35.1															1	1							1									3	0.34
35.2					1					3						3						1	1		2							11	1.26
35.3																				1												1	0.11
35.4																																0	0.00
35.5																																0	0.00
	0	0	0	0	1	0	0	0	0	3	0	0	0	0	1	4	0	0	0	1	0	1	2	0	2	0	0	0	0	0	0	15	1.72
40																																0	0.00
40.1																																0	0.00
40.2																																0	0.00
40.3																																0	0.00
	0	0	0	0	0	0	0	0	0	0	0	0	0	0	0	0	0	0	0	0	0	0	0	0	0	0	0	0	0	0	0	0	0.00
45																																0	0.00
45.1																																0	0.00
45.2																																0	0.00
45.3																																0	0.00
45.4																																0	0.00
	0	0	0	0	0	0	0	0	0	0	0	0	0	0	0	0	0	0	0	0	0	0	0	0	0	0	0	0	0	0	0	0	0.00
50		1								1				1	1													1			1	6	0.69
50.1	2	1	1			1		1		8							4			3	5			1							1	28	3.21
50.2	1														1	1						2										5	0.57
50.3					1															1	4								1			7	0.80
50.4		1								1		1				2				5	2	7	2	2	1	1	1					26	2.98
50.5	1		3		4	2			1	9	4	1	3	2	3	17	2					4	4	3	2		1			2	4	72	8.26
50.6															1	1									1							3	0.34
50.7																																0	0.00
	4	3	4	0	5	3	0	1	1	19	4	2	3	3	6	21	6	0	0	9	11	13	6	6	4	1	2	1	1	2	6	147	16.86

AREA 315																																	
	PHASE 1								PHASE 2.1						PHASE 2.2																	Total	
FAMILY	1168	1169	1175	1164	1174	3200	3202	3201	3182	3185	3187	3183	3194	3179	3177	3176	3169	3171	3166	3168	3163	3158	3160	3154	3151	3149	3146	3144	3142	3147	3131	#	%
55																																0	0.00
55.1			1		4					6					4	11	1			3	4	5	1		1	1						42	4.82
55.2			2					1	1	3				1		3				5	2	4										22	2.52
55.3																																0	0.00
	0	0	3	0	4	0	0	1	1	9	0	0	0	1	4	14	1	0	0	8	6	9	1	0	1	1	0	0	0	0	0	64	7.34
60																																0	0.00
60.1	2	3	1		3	1			1	9	3				3	11	1	1			2	12	5	2	2	1		3				66	7.57
60.2																																0	0.00
60.3																																0	0.00
60.4																																0	0.00
	2	3	1	0	3	1	0	0	1	9	3	0	0	0	3	11	1	1	0	0	2	12	5	2	2	1	0	3	0	0	0	66	7.57
65										1						1																2	0.23
65.1			1		2	2	1			7	2			1	2	7	2				1	3	3	1	4	1	2				2	44	5.05
65.2				1	1	1		1		1		1												1								7	0.80
65.3																							1									1	0.11
65.4																																0	0.00
	0	0	1	1	3	3	1	1	0	9	2	1	0	1	2	8	2	0	0	0	1	3	4	2	4	1	2	0	0	0	2	54	6.19
70																				1				1			1					3	0.34
70.1																3				4	2	2		1		1						13	1.49
70.2	1	2	2		6	2	1	1		9	1			1	1	17	2			7	12	9	6	1	5	2		1				89	10.21
70.3	2	1	2		1	1		1	2	15	4		1		6	16	3	1		7	6	11	4	2	2	1	3	1		2	2	97	11.12
70.4																																0	0.00
70.5					1					3						1			1			3	1									10	1.15
70.6	1																															1	0.11
70.7																																0	0.00
70.8																																0	0.00
	4	3	4	0	8	3	1	2	2	27	5	0	1	1	7	37	5	1	1	19	20	25	11	5	7	4	4	2	0	2	2	213	24.43
75																																0	0.00
75.1																1																1	0.11
75.2																														1		1	0.11
75.3																																0	0.00
75.4																																0	0.00
	0	0	0	0	0	0	0	0	0	0	0	0	0	0	0	1	0	0	0	0	0	0	0	0	0	0	0	0	0	1	0	2	0.23
80																1									1							2	0.23
80.1						1				2						1				1		2	2		1							10	1.15
80.2						1				1						2				1	1	3			1							10	1.15
80.3																																0	0.00
	0	0	0	0	0	2	0	0	0	3	0	0	0	0	0	4	0	0	0	2	1	5	2	0	3	0	0	0	0	0	0	22	2.52
85																																0	0.00
85.1		1							2	1		1	1			1					1	5	1	1	5	1	1					22	2.52
85.2		1			1											4	1					1	2									10	1.15
85.3																															1	1	0.11
	0	2	0	0	1	0	0	0	2	1	0	1	1	0	0	5	1	0	0	0	1	6	3	1	5	1	1	0	0	0	1	33	3.78
90																																0	0.00
90.1																																0	0.00
90.2																																0	0.00
90.3																																0	0.00
90.4																																0	0.00
90.5																																0	0.00
90.6																																0	0.00
90.7																																0	0.00
90.8																																0	0.00
90.9										1																						1	0.11
	0	0	0	0	0	0	0	0	0	1	0	0	0	0	0	0	0	0	0	0	0	0	0	0	0	0	0	0	0	0	0	1	0.11
95																																0	0.00
95.1										1													1									2	0.23
95.2																																0	0.00
95.3										1													1									2	0.23
95.4																1																1	0.11
	0	0	0	0	0	0	0	0	0	2	0	0	0	0	0	1	0	0	0	0	0	0	2	0	0	0	0	0	0	0	0	5	0.57
Total	19	15	16	1	37	16	3	8	7	115	22	4	5	10	36	155	24	2	1	59	54	103	51	23	37	9	11	7	1	6	15	872	100

ADMINISTRATIVE SUITE																				
	PHASE 2.1				PHASE 2.2														Total	
FAMILY	3122	3066	3096	3123	3056	3065	3064	3080	3119	3116	1112	1114	1096	1124	1157	1159	1163	1164	#	%
5	1																		1	0.19
5.1		1		2	1	1	34	18	5	1	2		16	1	17		4		103	19.54
5.2	1				1	2	25	4				3	7				1		44	8.35
5.3															1				1	0.19
5.4													1	1					2	0.38
5.5																			0	0.00
	2	1	0	2	2	3	59	22	5	1	2	3	24	2	18	0	5	0	151	28.65
10				1			1						1						3	0.57
10.1									2		1	1	4		3		2		13	2.47
10.2	1	1					3	1							3		4		13	2.47
10.3													1						1	0.19
10.4																			0	0.00
	1	1	0	1	0	0	4	1	2	0	1	1	6	0	6	0	6	0	30	5.69
15																			0	0.00
15.1	3			2	2		2	3	1			1			1				15	2.85
15.2															2				2	0.38
	3	0	0	2	2	0	2	3	1	0	0	1	0	0	3	0	0	0	17	3.23
20																			0	0.00
20.1																			0	0.00
20.2																			0	0.00
	0	0	0	0	0	0	0	0	0	0	0	0	0	0	0	0	0	0	0	0.00
25																			0	0.00
25.1	1		3		1		1					1	3						10	1.90
25.2				1	1	3						1							6	1.14
25.3																	2		2	0.38
25.4																			0	0.00
25.5					1		2					2							5	0.95
	1	0	3	1	3	3	3	0	0	0	0	4	3	0	0	0	2	0	23	4.36
30																			0	0.00
30.1																			0	0.00
30.2																			0	0.00
30.3																			0	0.00
	0	0	0	0	0	0	0	0	0	0	0	0	0	0	0	0	0	0	0	0.00
35									1										1	0.19
35.1							1						1						2	0.38
35.2												2	1		2		1		6	1.14
35.3									1										1	0.19
35.4																			0	0.00
35.5																			0	0.00
	0	0	0	0	0	0	1	0	2	0	0	2	2	0	2	0	1	0	10	1.90
40																			0	0.00
40.1																			0	0.00
40.2																			0	0.00
40.3																			0	0.00
	0	0	0	0	0	0	0	0	0	0	0	0	0	0	0	0	0	0	0	0.00
45																			0	0.00
45.1																			0	0.00
45.2																			0	0.00
45.3																			0	0.00
45.4																			0	0.00
	0	0	0	0	0	0	0	0	0	0	0	0	0	0	0	0	0	0	0	0.00
50			1						1			1							3	0.57
50.1						1	4		2						1				8	1.52
50.2							3	1	2			1							7	1.33
50.3												1					1		2	0.38
50.4							3					2	1		3				9	1.71
50.5					2	1	5	1	5				1	1	1		1		18	3.42
50.6													1						1	0.19
50.7																			0	0.00
	0	0	1	0	2	2	15	2	10	0	0	5	3	1	5	0	2	0	48	9.11

ADMINISTRATIVE SUITE																				
	PHASE 2.1				PHASE 2.2														Total	
FAMILY	3122	3066	3096	3123	3056	3065	3064	3080	3119	3116	1112	1114	1096	1124	1157	1159	1163	1164	#	%
55																			0	0.00
55.1	1						1		2										4	0.76
55.2	1								1						4				6	1.14
55.3																			0	0.00
	2	0	0	0	0	0	1	0	3	0	0	0	0	0	4	0	0	0	10	1.90
60																			0	0.00
60.1		2	1	1	1	2	35	14	10		1	7	20	1	7		1		103	19.54
60.2																			0	0.00
60.3																			0	0.00
60.4																			0	0.00
	0	2	1	1	1	2	35	14	10	0	1	7	20	1	7	0	1	0	103	19.54
65	1																		1	0.19
65.1	1		1	4			4	1	2			3	1						17	3.23
65.2	3	1		2			2		2				1				1	1	13	2.47
65.3							1												1	0.19
65.4				1															1	0.19
	5	1	1	7	0	0	7	1	4	0	0	3	2	0	0	0	1	1	33	6.26
70							1					1							2	0.38
70.1							1	1			1		2		1				6	1.14
70.2	1		1	1	3	1	2	4	3		1	5	6		2	1	1		32	6.07
70.3	3		1	1	1		7	5	1			2	4	1	2				28	5.31
70.4																			0	0.00
70.5	1							2	6			1	1						11	2.09
70.6												1	1						2	0.38
70.7																			0	0.00
70.8																			0	0.00
	5	0	2	2	4	1	11	12	10	0	2	10	14	1	5	1	1	0	81	15.37
75																			0	0.00
75.1															1				1	0.19
75.2																			0	0.00
75.3							1												1	0.19
75.4																			0	0.00
	0	0	0	0	0	0	1	0	0	0	0	0	0	0	1	0	0	0	2	0.38
80																			0	0.00
80.1				1															1	0.19
80.2	1			1			1						1		1				5	0.95
80.3																			0	0.00
	1	0	0	2	0	0	1	0	0	0	0	0	1	0	1	0	0	0	6	1.14
85																			0	0.00
85.1												3	1		1				5	0.95
85.2	3	1									1		2						7	1.33
85.3																			0	0.00
	3	1	0	0	0	0	0	0	0	0	1	3	3	0	1	0	0	0	12	2.28
90																			0	0.00
90.1															1				1	0.19
90.2																			0	0.00
90.3																			0	0.00
90.4																			0	0.00
90.5																			0	0.00
90.6																			0	0.00
90.7																			0	0.00
90.8																			0	0.00
90.9																			0	0.00
	0	0	0	0	0	0	0	0	0	0	0	0	0	0	1	0	0	0	1	0.19
95																			0	0.00
95.1																			0	0.00
95.2																			0	0.00
95.3																			0	0.00
95.4																			0	0.00
	0	0	0	0	0	0	0	0	0	0	0	0	0	0	0	0	0	0	0	0.00
Total	23	6	8	18	14	11	140	55	47	1	7	39	78	5	54	1	19	1	527	100

ROOM 314							
	PHASE 2.1		PHASE 2.2			Total	
FAMILY	1142	1166	1138	1139	1167	#	%
5	2		1			3	0.62
5.1	24	32		25	4	85	17.56
5.2	1			5		6	1.24
5.3						0	0.00
5.4						0	0.00
5.5						0	0.00
	27	32	1	30	4	94	19.42
10						0	0.00
10.1	2	2		3	1	8	1.65
10.2	3	11		3		17	3.51
10.3	1					1	0.21
10.4						0	0.00
	6	13	0	6	1	26	5.37
15						0	0.00
15.1	5	14	2	8		29	5.99
15.2				1	1	2	0.41
	5	14	2	9	1	31	6.40
20		1				1	0.21
20.1						0	0.00
20.2						0	0.00
	0	1	0	0	0	1	0.21
25						0	0.00
25.1	2	7				9	1.86
25.2		1		1		2	0.41
25.3	1	2				3	0.62
25.4	2			1		3	0.62
25.5		1	1	1		3	0.62
	5	11	1	3	0	20	4.13
30						0	0.00
30.1						0	0.00
30.2		1				1	0.21
30.3						0	0.00
	0	1	0	0	0	1	0.21
35	1					1	0.21
35.1						0	0.00
35.2	1	3		1	2	7	1.45
35.3		2				2	0.41
35.4						0	0.00
35.5				1		1	0.21
	2	5	0	2	2	11	2.27
40						0	0.00
40.1						0	0.00
40.2						0	0.00
40.3						0	0.00
	0	0	0	0	0	0	0.00
45						0	0.00
45.1		1				1	0.21
45.2						0	0.00
45.3	1					1	0.21
45.4						0	0.00
	1	1	0	0	0	2	0.41
50	1	1				2	0.41
50.1		6		1		7	1.45
50.2	1	2				3	0.62
50.3		2				2	0.41
50.4	2	7		4	1	14	2.89
50.5	8	18	2	10		38	7.85
50.6						0	0.00
50.7						0	0.00
	12	36	2	15	1	66	13.64

ROOM 314							
	PHASE 2.1		PHASE 2.2			Total	
FAMILY	1142	1166	1138	1139	1167	#	%
55		1				1	0.21
55.1	4	7		4		15	3.10
55.2		3				3	0.62
55.3						0	0.00
	4	11	0	4	0	19	3.93
60						0	0.00
60.1	24	23	3	26	6	82	16.94
60.2		1		1		2	0.41
60.3						0	0.00
60.4						0	0.00
	24	24	3	27	6	84	17.36
65						0	0.00
65.1	7	4		10	1	22	4.55
65.2		4		1		5	1.03
65.3						0	0.00
65.4		1				1	0.21
	7	9	0	11	1	28	5.79
70	1					1	0.21
70.1		7				7	1.45
70.2	8	12	1	8	1	30	6.20
70.3	5	11	1	9		26	5.37
70.4						0	0.00
70.5		1				1	0.21
70.6						0	0.00
70.7						0	0.00
70.8						0	0.00
	14	31	2	17	1	65	13.43
75						0	0.00
75.1		1				1	0.21
75.2		1				1	0.21
75.3						0	0.00
75.4					1	1	0.21
	0	2	0	0	1	3	0.62
80		1		1	1	3	0.62
80.1		1		3	1	5	1.03
80.2		1		2		3	0.62
80.3						0	0.00
	0	3	0	6	2	11	2.27
85						0	0.00
85.1	3	9	1	1		14	2.89
85.2	1	4		3		8	1.65
85.3						0	0.00
	4	13	1	4	0	22	4.55
90						0	0.00
90.1						0	0.00
90.2						0	0.00
90.3						0	0.00
90.4						0	0.00
90.5						0	0.00
90.6						0	0.00
90.7						0	0.00
90.8						0	0.00
90.9						0	0.00
	0	0	0	0	0	0	0.00
95						0	0.00
95.1						0	0.00
95.2						0	0.00
95.3						0	0.00
95.4						0	0.00
	0	0	0	0	0	0	0.00
Total	111	207	12	134	20	484	100

ROOMS 600 & 601												
	600		601	600				601				
	PHASE 2.1			PHASE 2.2							Total	
FAMILY	6042	6059	6058	6035	6038	6036	6040	6041	6057	6060	#	%
5											0	0.00
5.1	4	1	5			7	1	21			39	5.92
5.2	2	5	10	1		1	4	19			42	6.37
5.3											0	0.00
5.4											0	0.00
5.5											0	0.00
	6	6	15	1	0	8	5	40	0	0	81	12.29
10											0	0.00
10.1						1		1			2	0.30
10.2		2	1					2			5	0.76
10.3											0	0.00
10.4											0	0.00
	0	2	1	0	0	1	0	3	0	0	7	1.06
15											0	0.00
15.1		5	7	2	1	5	1	10			31	4.70
15.2											0	0.00
	0	5	7	2	1	5	1	10	0	0	31	4.70
20											0	0.00
20.1	2	1				2	1				6	0.91
20.2											0	0.00
	2	1	0	0	0	2	1	0	0	0	6	0.91
25											0	0.00
25.1		2	4			2		9		1	18	2.73
25.2			1					5			6	0.91
25.3											0	0.00
25.4			1			1		4			6	0.91
25.5			3			1		5			9	1.37
	0	2	9	0	0	4	0	23	0	1	39	5.92
30											0	0.00
30.1											0	0.00
30.2											0	0.00
30.3											0	0.00
	0	0	0	0	0	0	0	0	0	0	0	0.00
35											0	0.00
35.1											0	0.00
35.2			3	1		1	1	9			15	2.28
35.3											0	0.00
35.4											0	0.00
35.5			2					1			3	0.46
	0	0	5	1	0	1	1	10	0	0	18	2.73
40											0	0.00
40.1											0	0.00
40.2											0	0.00
40.3											0	0.00
	0	**0**	**0**	**0**	**0**	**0**	**0**	**0**	**0**	**0**	**0**	**0.00**
45											0	0.00
45.1		1									1	0.15
45.2											0	0.00
45.3											0	0.00
45.4											0	0.00
	0	1	0	0	0	0	0	0	0	0	1	0.15
50											0	0.00
50.1		2	4	1		5		5			17	2.58
50.2	1		2	1		1					5	0.76
50.3								2			2	0.30
50.4		2	3	1		2	1	13			22	3.34
50.5	1	2	20	2	1	4	2	25			57	8.65
50.6						1					1	0.15
50.7											0	0.00
	2	6	29	5	1	13	3	45	0	0	104	15.78

ROOMS 600 & 601												
	600		601	600				601				
	PHASE 2.1			PHASE 2.2							Total	
FAMILY	6042	6059	6058	6035	6038	6036	6040	6041	6057	6060	#	%
55											0	0.00
55.1		1	10			2	1	9		2	25	3.79
55.2											0	0.00
55.3											0	0.00
	0	1	10	0	0	2	1	9	0	2	25	3.79
60											0	0.00
60.1	8	7	18			10	2	23	1		69	10.47
60.2							1				1	0.15
60.3		1	1				1			1	4	0.61
60.4											0	0.00
	8	8	19	0	0	10	4	23	1	1	74	11.23
65											0	0.00
65.1		1	8			3	2	43			57	8.65
65.2		2	1					8			11	1.67
65.3											0	0.00
65.4											0	0.00
	0	3	9	0	0	3	2	51	0	0	68	10.32
70											0	0.00
70.1		3	2	2				6			13	1.97
70.2	3	2	7	6	2	4	2	31			57	8.65
70.3		1	17	5		8	2	37		1	71	10.77
70.4			1			1		2			4	0.61
70.5			1			2		3		1	7	1.06
70.6											0	0.00
70.7											0	0.00
70.8											0	0.00
	3	6	28	13	2	15	4	79	0	2	152	23.07
75											0	0.00
75.1						1		2			3	0.46
75.2											0	0.00
75.3											0	0.00
75.4											0	0.00
	0	0	0	0	0	1	0	2	0	0	3	0.46
80								1			1	0.15
80.1			2			1	1	7			11	1.67
80.2			3			1	1	9			14	2.12
80.3											0	0.00
	0	0	5	0	0	2	2	17	0	0	26	3.95
85											0	0.00
85.1		4	4					7			15	2.28
85.2	1	2	1					4			8	1.21
85.3											0	0.00
	1	6	5	0	0	0	0	11	0	0	23	3.49
90											0	0.00
90.1											0	0.00
90.2											0	0.00
90.3											0	0.00
90.4		1									1	0.15
90.5											0	0.00
90.6											0	0.00
90.7											0	0.00
90.8											0	0.00
90.9											0	0.00
	0	1	0	0	0	0	0	0	0	0	1	0.15
95											0	0.00
95.1											0	0.00
95.2											0	0.00
95.3											0	0.00
95.4											0	0.00
	0	0	0	0	0	0	0	0	0	0	0	0.00
Total	22	48	142	22	4	67	24	323	1	6	659	100

ROOM 316																											
FAMILY	PHASE 2.2		PHASE 2.3																							Total	
	8058	8065	8000	8012	8006	8010	8064	8008	8013	8016	8017	8018	8021	8020	8031	8032	8051	8055	8053	8056	8022	8028	8033	8038	8060	#	%
5	1	1						1													1		2			6	1.42
5.1	1		1	1			1	12		2		6	1	4		5	2		2	3			10		3	54	12.80
5.2								3				1				3										7	1.66
5.3																											0.00
5.4																										0	0.00
5.5																										0	0.00
	2	1	1	1	0	0	1	16	0	2	0	7	1	4	0	8	2	0	2	3	1	0	12	0	3	67	15.88
10								1						1												2	0.47
10.1				1				3		1						1										6	1.42
10.2								2																		2	0.47
10.3																										0	0.00
10.4																										0	0.00
	0	0	0	1	0	0	0	6	0	1	0	0	0	1	0	1	0	0	0	0	0	0	0	0	0	10	2.37
15																										0	0.00
15.1		1					1	3				3							1	1	1		1		1	13	3.08
15.2																										0	0.00
	0	1	0	0	0	0	1	3	0	0	0	3	0	0	0	0	0	0	1	1	1	0	1	0	1	13	3.08
20							1																			1	0.24
20.1			1																							1	0.24
20.2																										0	0.00
	0	0	1	0	0	0	1	0	0	0	0	0	0	0	0	0	0	0	0	0	0	0	0	0	0	2	0.47
25												1								1						2	0.47
25.1								1	2	1		1				1			1	1			1			9	2.13
25.2																										0	0.00
25.3							2	1				1		1												5	1.18
25.4	2	1					1							1		1										6	1.42
25.5			1			1	1	2																		5	1.18
	2	1	1	0	0	1	4	4	2	1	0	3	0	2	0	2	0	0	1	2	0	0	1	0	0	27	6.40
30																										0	0.00
30.1																										0	0.00
30.2																										0	0.00
30.3																										0	0.00
	0	0	0	0	0	0	0	0	0	0	0	0	0	0	0	0	0	0	0	0	0	0	0	0	0	0	0.00
35																										0	0.00
35.1																										0	0.00
35.2							1	2		1										1						5	1.18
35.3																										0	0.00
35.4								1																		1	0.24
35.5										1																1	0.24
	0	0	0	0	0	0	1	3	0	2	0	0	0	0	0	0	0	0	0	1	0	0	0	0	0	7	1.66
40																										0	0.00
40.1																										0	0.00
40.2																										0	0.00
40.3																										0	0.00
	0	**0**	**0**	**0**	**0**	**0**	**0**	**0**	**0**	**0**	**0**	**0**	**0**	**0**	**0**	**0**	**0**	**0**	**0**	**0**	**0**	**0**	**0**	**0**	**0**	**0**	**0.00**
45																										0	0.00
45.1																										0	0.00
45.2																1										1	0.24
45.3																										0	0.00
45.4																										0	0.00
	0	0	0	0	0	0	0	0	0	0	0	0	0	0	0	1	0	0	0	0	0	0	0	0	0	1	0.24
50								1								1							1			3	0.71
50.1			1					2	1	1									1							6	1.42
50.2								1																		1	0.24
50.3																					1					1	0.24
50.4							2	3	1																1	7	1.66
50.5	1		1				1	3		1		1	1	1						1	3		1		2	17	4.03
50.6																										0	0.00
50.7																										0	0.00
	1	0	2	0	0	0	3	10	2	2	0	1	1	1	0	1	0	0	1	1	4	0	2	0	3	35	8.29

ROOM 316																											
	PHASE 2.2		PHASE 2.3																							Total	
FAMILY	8058	8065	8000	8012	8006	8010	8064	8008	8013	8016	8017	8018	8021	8020	8031	8032	8051	8055	8053	8056	8022	8028	8033	8038	8060	#	%
55								1																		1	0.24
55.1								3				2		1		1				2		1	2		1	13	3.08
55.2															1											1	0.24
55.3																										0	0.00
	0	0	0	0	0	0	0	4	0	0	0	2	0	1	1	1	0	0	0	2	0	1	2	0	1	15	3.55
60																										0	0.00
60.1					1		2	9		5	1	7	1	11	1	13	1	1	6	3	7	1			7	77	18.25
60.2																										0	0.00
60.3																										0	0.00
60.4																										0	0.00
	0	0	0	0	1	0	2	9	0	5	1	7	1	11	1	13	1	1	6	3	7	1	0	0	7	77	18.25
65																										0	0.00
65.1		2	3					14	2		1	1	2	3		1							9		2	40	9.48
65.2							1	2																		3	0.71
65.3		1																								1	0.24
65.4																										0	0.00
	0	3	3	0	0	0	1	16	2	0	1	1	2	3	0	1	0	0	0	0	0	0	9	0	2	44	10.43
70							1												2				3		1	7	1.66
70.1							1													1				1	1	4	0.95
70.2		1	2				1	7	1			2		2		2			1	2	2		1		2	26	6.16
70.3	1	2	1	1			4	8	1	1		4	2	2		3		1	2	4	2			1	1	41	9.72
70.4																										0	0.00
70.5									1	2		1				1									1	6	1.42
70.6																										0	0.00
70.7																										0	0.00
70.8																										0	0.00
	1	3	3	1	0	0	7	15	3	3	0	7	2	4	0	6	0	1	5	7	4	0	4	2	6	84	19.91
75																										0	0.00
75.1														2							1				1	4	0.95
75.2									1																	1	0.24
75.3																										0	0.00
75.4				1																						1	0.24
	0	0	0	1	0	0	0	0	1	0	0	0	0	2	0	0	0	0	0	0	1	0	0	0	1	6	1.42
80								1								1			1	1						4	0.95
80.1													1	1					1						1	4	0.95
80.2										1	1			1						1			1			5	1.18
80.3									1																	1	0.24
	0	0	0	0	0	0	0	1	1	1	1	0	1	2	0	1	0	0	2	2	0	0	1	0	1	14	3.32
85																										0	0.00
85.1		1						2		2		1		1		2										9	2.13
85.2								3																		3	0.71
85.3																										0	0.00
	0	1	0	0	0	0	0	5	0	2	0	1	0	1	0	2	0	0	0	0	0	0	0	0	0	12	2.84
90																										0	0.00
90.1								1	2																	3	0.71
90.2																					1					1	0.24
90.3													1													1	0.24
90.4																										0	0.00
90.5																										0	0.00
90.6																										0	0.00
90.7																										0	0.00
90.8													1													1	0.24
90.9																										0	0.00
	0	0	0	0	0	0	0	1	2	0	0	0	2	0	0	0	0	0	0	0	1	0	0	0	0	6	1.42
95																										0	0.00
95.1																										0	0.00
95.2									1																	1	0.24
95.3																	1									1	0.24
95.4																										0	0.00
	0	0	0	0	0	0	0	0	1	0	0	0	0	0	0	0	1	0	0	0	0	0	0	0	0	2	0.47
Total	6	10	11	4	1	1	21	93	14	19	3	32	10	32	2	37	4	2	18	22	19	2	32	2	25	422	100

ROOM 152								
FAMILY	PHASE 2.1	PHASE 2.2					Total	
	8084	8079	8080	8081	8082	8083	#	%
5	1						1	0.71
5.1			1	1	3	2	7	4.96
5.2		1					1	0.71
5.3							0	0.00
5.4							0	0.00
5.5							0	0.00
	1	1	1	1	3	2	9	6.38
10							0	0.00
10.1				1		1	2	1.42
10.2				1		1	2	1.42
10.3							0	0.00
10.4							0	0.00
	0	0	0	2	0	2	4	2.84
15							0	0.00
15.1	2	1			3	2	8	5.67
15.2		1					1	0.71
	2	2	0	0	3	2	9	6.38
20							0	0.00
20.1				1			1	0.71
20.2							0	0.00
	0	0	0	1	0	0	1	0.71
25							0	0.00
25.1	1	1			1		3	2.13
25.2					2		2	1.42
25.3					1	2	3	2.13
25.4	1	1		2	9		13	9.22
25.5					1	1	2	1.42
	2	2	0	2	14	3	23	16.31
30							0	0.00
30.1							0	0.00
30.2	1				2	1	4	2.84
30.3							0	0.00
	1	0	0	0	2	1	4	2.84
35							0	0.00
35.1							0	0.00
35.2					1	3	4	2.84
35.3					1	1	2	1.42
35.4		1					1	0.71
35.5						3	3	2.13
	0	1	0	0	2	7	10	7.09
40							0	0.00
40.1							0	0.00
40.2							0	0.00
40.3							0	0.00
	0	**0**	**0**	**0**	**0**	**0**	**0**	**0.00**
45		1					1	0.71
45.1							0	0.00
45.2						1	1	0.71
45.3							0	0.00
45.4							0	0.00
	0	1	0	0	0	1	2	1.42
50					1		1	0.71
50.1	1	1			1	2	5	3.55
50.2							0	0.00
50.3				1	1		2	1.42
50.4	1	1			1	3	6	4.26
50.5	7	3		1		3	14	9.93
50.6							0	0.00
50.7							0	0.00
	9	5	0	2	4	8	28	19.86

ROOM 152								
FAMILY	PHASE 2.1	PHASE 2.2					Total	
	8084	8079	8080	8081	8082	8083	#	%
55							0	0.00
55.1	3	1		1	1	1	7	4.96
55.2		1				1	2	1.42
55.3							0	0.00
	3	2	0	1	1	2	9	6.38
60							0	0.00
60.1	2	1			1	2	6	4.26
60.2							0	0.00
60.3							0	0.00
60.4							0	0.00
	2	1	0	0	1	2	6	4.26
65					1		1	0.71
65.1	2	3		4	2	2	13	9.22
65.2		1					1	0.71
65.3							0	0.00
65.4							0	0.00
	2	4	0	4	3	2	15	10.64
70					1		1	0.71
70.1		1			2	1	4	2.84
70.2	5	1		5	3	2	16	11.35
70.3	9	7		5	4	3	28	19.86
70.4							0	0.00
70.5						2	2	1.42
70.6							0	0.00
70.7							0	0.00
70.8							0	0.00
	14	9	0	10	10	8	51	36.17
75		1					1	0.71
75.1							0	0.00
75.2							0	0.00
75.3							0	0.00
75.4	1					1	2	1.42
	1	1	0	0	0	1	3	2.13
80							0	0.00
80.1							0	0.00
80.2							0	0.00
80.3							0	0.00
	0	0	0	0	0	0	0	0.00
85							0	0.00
85.1					1	3	4	2.84
85.2					1		1	0.71
85.3							0	0.00
	0	0	0	0	2	3	5	3.55
90							0	0.00
90.1							0	0.00
90.2							0	0.00
90.3							0	0.00
90.4							0	0.00
90.5							0	0.00
90.6							0	0.00
90.7							0	0.00
90.8							0	0.00
90.9							0	0.00
	0	0	0	0	0	0	0	0.00
95							0	0.00
95.1							0	0.00
95.2							0	0.00
95.3							0	0.00
95.4						1	1	0.71
	0	0	0	0	0	1	1	0.71
Total	37	29	1	23	45	45	180	100

ROOM 156		
FAMILY	PHASE 2.2	
	6165	%
5	0	0.00
5.1	1	2.22
5.2	0	0.00
5.3	0	0.00
5.4	0	0.00
5.5	0	0.00
	1	2.22
10	0	0.00
10.1	0	0.00
10.2	0	0.00
10.3	0	0.00
10.4	0	0.00
	0	0.00
15	0	0.00
15.1	0	0.00
15.2	0	0.00
	0	0.00
20	0	0.00
20.1	1	2.22
20.2	0	0.00
	1	2.22
25	0	0.00
25.1	6	13.33
25.2	0	0.00
25.3	0	0.00
25.4	3	6.67
25.5	1	2.22
	10	22.22
30	0	0.00
30.1	0	0.00
30.2	3	6.67
30.3	0	0.00
	3	6.67
35	0	0.00
35.1	0	0.00
35.2	0	0.00
35.3	0	0.00
35.4	0	0.00
35.5	0	0.00
	0	0.00
40	0	0.00
40.1	0	0.00
40.2	0	0.00
40.3	0	0.00
	0	**0.00**
45	0	0.00
45.1	0	0.00
45.2	0	0.00
45.3	0	0.00
45.4	0	0.00
	0	0.00
50	0	0.00
50.1	0	0.00
50.2	0	0.00
50.3	1	2.22
50.4	1	2.22
50.5	7	15.56
50.6	0	0.00
50.7	0	0.00
	9	20.00

ROOM 156		
FAMILY	PHASE 2.2	
	6165	%
55	0	0.00
55.1	1	2.22
55.2	1	2.22
55.3	0	0.00
	2	4.44
60	0	0.00
60.1	4	8.89
60.2	0	0.00
60.3	0	0.00
60.4	0	0.00
	4	8.89
65	0	0.00
65.1	1	2.22
65.2	0	0.00
65.3	0	0.00
65.4	0	0.00
	1	2.22
70	0	0.00
70.1	0	0.00
70.2	0	0.00
70.3	6	13.33
70.4	1	2.22
70.5	0	0.00
70.6	0	0.00
70.7	0	0.00
70.8	0	0.00
	7	15.56
75	0	0.00
75.1	0	0.00
75.2	0	0.00
75.3	0	0.00
75.4	0	0.00
	0	0.00
80	0	0.00
80.1	1	2.22
80.2	0	0.00
80.3	0	0.00
	1	2.22
85	0	0.00
85.1	2	4.44
85.2	2	4.44
85.3	2	4.44
	6	13.33
90	0	0.00
90.1	0	0.00
90.2	0	0.00
90.3	0	0.00
90.4	0	0.00
90.5	0	0.00
90.6	0	0.00
90.7	0	0.00
90.8	0	0.00
90.9	0	0.00
	0	0.00
95	0	0.00
95.1	0	0.00
95.2	0	0.00
95.3	0	0.00
95.4	0	0.00
	0	0.00
Total	45	100

ROOM 101

	PHASE 2.1				PHASE 2.2								Total	
FAMILY	1079	1085	1080	1088	1059	1058	1068	1072	1076	1075	1073	1077	#	%
5	1												1	0.12
5.1	60		2	1	2		8		1		4	1	79	9.48
5.2	94	7	2	4	2		9	1		1	10	5	135	16.21
5.3													0	0.00
5.4	1												1	0.12
5.5													0	0.00
	156	7	4	5	4	0	17	1	1	1	14	6	216	25.93
10													0	0.00
10.1	7										3		10	1.20
10.2	3			1							1		5	0.60
10.3													0	0.00
10.4	1												1	0.12
	11	0	0	1	0	0	0	0	0	0	4	0	16	1.92
15													0	0.00
15.1	49						5				5		59	7.08
15.2													0	0.00
	49	0	0	0	0	0	5	0	0	0	5	0	59	7.08
20													0	0.00
20.1	2												2	0.24
20.2							1						1	0.12
	2	0	0	0	0	0	1	0	0	0	0	0	3	0.36
25													0	0.00
25.1	8	1			1		1						11	1.32
25.2	2		1										3	0.36
25.3													0	0.00
25.4	5						1						6	0.72
25.5	4						1						5	0.60
	19	1	1	0	1	0	3	0	0	0	0	0	25	3.00
30													0	0.00
30.1													0	0.00
30.2													0	0.00
30.3													0	0.00
	0	0	0	0	0	0	0	0	0	0	0	0	0	0.00
35	1												1	0.12
35.1													0	0.00
35.2	11											1	12	1.44
35.3													0	0.00
35.4													0	0.00
35.5			1										1	0.12
	12	0	1	0	0	0	0	0	0	0	0	1	14	1.68
40													0	0.00
40.1													0	0.00
40.2													0	0.00
40.3													0	0.00
	0	0	0	0	0	0	0	0	0	0	0	0	0	0.00
45													0	0.00
45.1													0	0.00
45.2													0	0.00
45.3													0	0.00
45.4													0	0.00
	0	0	0	0	0	0	0	0	0	0	0	0	0	0.00
50													0	0.00
50.1	18		7	1		1					2		29	3.48
50.2	3	1	1						1				6	0.72
50.3	1						1						2	0.24
50.4	3	1	2		1		1		2			2	12	1.44
50.5	25		2		1		1			1	3	2	35	4.20
50.6													0	0.00
50.7													0	0.00
	50	2	12	1	2	1	3	0	3	1	5	4	84	10.08

ROOM 101

	PHASE 2.1				PHASE 2.2								Total	
FAMILY	1079	1085	1080	1088	1059	1058	1068	1072	1076	1075	1073	1077	#	%
55													0	0.00
55.1	13										1		14	1.68
55.2	1												1	0.12
55.3													0	0.00
	14	0	0	0	0	0	0	0	0	0	1	0	15	1.80
60													0	0.00
60.1	124	2	1	2	2	3	21	1		2	16	8	182	21.85
60.2							1						1	0.12
60.3	2												2	0.24
60.4													0	0.00
	126	2	1	2	2	3	22	1	0	2	16	8	185	22.21
65													0	0.00
65.1	43		2	1							3		49	5.88
65.2	4				1								5	0.60
65.3													0	0.00
65.4	1												1	0.12
	48	0	2	1	1	0	0	0	0	0	3	0	55	6.60
70		1											1	0.12
70.1	5						1						6	0.72
70.2	24	2			2	1	2			2	1	1	35	4.20
70.3	51			1	3		2				4	2	63	7.56
70.4	2						1						3	0.36
70.5	3										1		4	0.48
70.6													0	0.00
70.7			1										1	0.12
70.8													0	0.00
	85	3	1	1	5	1	6	0	0	2	6	3	113	13.57
75													0	0.00
75.1	5										1		6	0.72
75.2	1												1	0.12
75.3													0	0.00
75.4													0	0.00
	6	0	0	0	0	0	0	0	0	0	1	0	7	0.84
80													0	0.00
80.1	14			1		1					1		17	2.04
80.2	1						1				1		3	0.36
80.3	1												1	0.12
	16	0	0	1	0	1	1	0	0	0	2	0	21	2.52
85													0	0.00
85.1	8						1					2	11	1.32
85.2	3												3	0.36
85.3	2												2	0.24
	13	0	0	0	0	0	1	0	0	0	0	2	16	1.92
90													0	0.00
90.1													0	0.00
90.2													0	0.00
90.3													0	0.00
90.4											2		2	0.24
90.5													0	0.00
90.6													0	0.00
90.7													0	0.00
90.8			1										1	0.12
90.9													0	0.00
	0	0	1	0	0	0	0	0	0	0	2	0	3	0.36
95													0	0.00
95.1													0	0.00
95.2	1												1	0.12
95.3													0	0.00
95.4													0	0.00
	1	0	0	0	0	0	0	0	0	0	0	0	1	0.12
Total	608	15	23	12	15	6	59	2	4	6	59	24	833	100

ROOMS 140–142																											
	PHASE 2.1					PHASE 2.2															PHASE 2.3					Total	
FAMILY	5054	5056	5057	5060	5065	5022	5008	5017	5033	5035	5044	5040	5045	5047	5048	5050	5062	5063	5053	5019	5014	5018	5016	5029	5007	#	%
5																										0	0.00
5.1				1		2	13	3		2		4					2								5	32	8.74
5.2																										0	0.00
5.3																										0	0.00
5.4																										0	0.00
5.5																										0	0.00
	0	0	0	1	0	2	13	3	0	2	0	4	0	0	0	0	2	0	0	0	0	0	0	0	5	32	8.74
10																										0	0.00
10.1							1																			1	0.27
10.2							1									1										2	0.55
10.3																										0	0.00
10.4																										0	0.00
	0	0	0	0	0	0	2	0	0	0	0	0	0	0	0	1	0	0	0	0	0	0	0	0	0	3	0.82
15																										0	0.00
15.1			1				3	3				2				1									1	11	3.01
15.2							1																1		1	3	0.82
	0	0	1	0	0	0	4	3	0	0	0	2	0	0	0	1	0	0	0	0	0	0	1	0	2	14	3.83
20																										0	0.00
20.1												1														1	0.27
20.2								1																		1	0.27
	0	0	0	0	0	0	0	1	0	0	0	1	0	0	0	0	0	0	0	0	0	0	0	0	0	2	0.55
25												1														1	0.27
25.1				2			1						1	2		3						1			3	13	3.55
25.2																										0	0.00
25.3																1										1	0.27
25.4	1		1			1	1									2									2	8	2.19
25.5							1																			1	0.27
	1	0	1	2	0	1	3	0	0	0	0	1	1	2	0	6	0	0	0	0	0	1	0	0	5	24	6.56
30																										0	0.00
30.1																										0	0.00
30.2				2																				1	1	4	1.09
30.3																										0	0.00
	0	0	0	2	0	0	0	0	0	0	0	0	0	0	0	0	0	0	0	0	0	0	0	1	1	4	1.09
35						1		1																		2	0.55
35.1																										0	0.00
35.2								1																		1	0.27
35.3																									1	1	0.27
35.4								5															1		1	7	1.91
35.5						1								1		1							1			4	1.09
	0	0	0	0	0	2	0	7	0	0	0	0	0	1	0	1	0	0	0	0	0	0	2	0	2	15	4.10
40																										0	0.00
40.1																										0	0.00
40.2																										0	0.00
40.3																										0	0.00
	0	0	0	0	0	0	0	0	0	0	0	0	0	0	0	0	0	0	0	0	0	0	0	0	0	0	0.00
45						1																				1	0.27
45.1													2													2	0.55
45.2																							1			1	0.27
45.3																										0	0.00
45.4																										0	0.00
	0	0	0	0	0	1	0	0	0	0	0	0	2	0	0	0	0	0	0	0	0	0	1	0	0	4	1.09
50																							1			1	0.27
50.1						5	1					2	1												3	12	3.28
50.2						4	1			1													1			7	1.91
50.3						3	1	1		2									1							8	2.19
50.4			1	2		4	4	3		3			1			1									2	21	5.74
50.5	1			1		11	2	5		1	1	1	2	3									1		2	31	8.47
50.6																										0	0.00
50.7																										0	0.00
	1	0	1	3	0	27	9	9	0	7	1	3	4	3	0	1	0	0	1	0	0	0	3	0	7	80	21.86

ROOMS 140–142																											
FAMILY	PHASE 2.1					PHASE 2.2															PHASE 2.3					Total	
	5054	5056	5057	5060	5065	5022	5008	5017	5033	5035	5044	5040	5045	5047	5048	5050	5062	5063	5053	5019	5014	5018	5016	5029	5007	#	%
55																										0	0.00
55.1		1				4	2									1										8	2.19
55.2								1								2							1			4	1.09
55.3																										0	0.00
	0	1	0	0	0	4	2	1	0	0	0	0	0	0	0	3	0	0	0	0	0	0	1	0	0	12	3.28
60																										0	0.00
60.1						9	2	11	1	4		2	2		1						1		1		1	35	9.56
60.2																										0	0.00
60.3																										0	0.00
60.4																										0	0.00
	0	0	0	0	0	9	2	11	1	4	0	2	2	0	1	0	0	0	0	0	1	0	1	0	1	35	9.56
65									1																1	2	0.55
65.1	1	1					2	5	1	1			1			1				1					3	17	4.64
65.2							2						1	1						1						5	1.37
65.3																									2	2	0.55
65.4																										0	0.00
	1	1	0	0	0	0	4	5	2	1	0	0	2	1	0	1	0	0	0	2	0	0	0	0	6	26	7.10
70																										0	0.00
70.1						1	1	3		1													1		3	10	2.73
70.2				1	1	3	6	2		1	1	2	1	2	1	2									5	28	7.65
70.3				1		6	4	8	2	3		4		1									1		3	33	9.02
70.4										1																1	0.27
70.5						2				2						1										5	1.37
70.6														1												1	0.27
70.7																										0	0.00
70.8																										0	0.00
	0	0	0	2	1	12	11	13	2	8	1	6	1	4	1	3	0	0	0	0	0	0	2	0	11	78	21.31
75																										0	0.00
75.1						1						1														2	0.55
75.2																										0	0.00
75.3																										0	0.00
75.4																										0	0.00
	0	0	0	0	0	1	0	0	0	0	0	1	0	0	0	0	0	0	0	0	0	0	0	0	0	2	0.55
80																1										1	0.27
80.1							1							1		1		1							1	5	1.37
80.2						1				1						1										3	0.82
80.3																										0	0.00
	0	0	0	0	0	1	1	0	0	1	0	0	0	1	0	3	0	1	0	0	0	0	0	0	1	9	2.46
85																										0	0.00
85.1	1					7	1			3						1					1		1		1	16	4.37
85.2		1						1								1							1		2	6	1.64
85.3																										0	0.00
	1	1	0	0	0	7	1	1	0	3	0	0	0	0	0	2	0	0	0	0	1	0	2	0	3	22	6.01
90																										0	0.00
90.1																										0	0.00
90.2																										0	0.00
90.3																										0	0.00
90.4																										0	0.00
90.5																										0	0.00
90.6																										0	0.00
90.7																										0	0.00
90.8																										0	0.00
90.9																										0	0.00
	0	0	0	0	0	0	0	0	0	0	0	0	0	0	0	0	0	0	0	0	0	0	0	0	0	0	0.00
95										1																1	0.27
95.1						1																				1	0.27
95.2																							1			1	0.27
95.3																				1						1	0.27
95.4																										0	0.00
	0	0	0	0	0	1	0	0	0	1	0	0	0	0	0	0	0	0	0	1	0	0	1	0	0	4	1.09
Total	4	3	3	10	1	68	52	54	5	27	2	20	12	12	2	22	2	1	1	3	2	1	14	1	44	366	100

EASTERN PASSAGE (AREA 110)						
	PHASE 2.2				Total	
FAMILY	1056	1089	1091	1092	#	%
5					0	0.00
5.1			7	6	13	10.16
5.2			11	5	16	12.50
5.3					0	0.00
5.4			1		1	0.78
5.5					0	0.00
	0	0	19	11	30	23.44
10					0	0.00
10.1			1		1	0.78
10.2				1	1	0.78
10.3					0	0.00
10.4					0	0.00
	0	0	1	1	2	1.56
15					0	0.00
15.1			2	3	5	3.91
15.2			1		1	0.78
	0	0	3	3	6	4.69
20					0	0.00
20.1		1	1		2	1.56
20.2					0	0.00
	0	1	1	0	2	1.56
25					0	0.00
25.1			4		4	3.13
25.2					0	0.00
25.3					0	0.00
25.4			2		2	1.56
25.5			3	1	4	3.13
	0	0	9	1	10	7.81
30					0	0.00
30.1					0	0.00
30.2					0	0.00
30.3					0	0.00
	0	0	0	0	0	0.00
35					0	0.00
35.1					0	0.00
35.2				2	2	1.56
35.3					0	0.00
35.4					0	0.00
35.5				1	1	0.78
	0	0	0	3	3	2.34
40					0	0.00
40.1					0	0.00
40.2					0	0.00
40.3					0	0.00
	0	0	0	0	0	0.00
45					0	0.00
45.1					0	0.00
45.2					0	0.00
45.3					0	0.00
45.4					0	0.00
	0	0	0	0	0	0.00
50					0	0.00
50.1			2	1	3	2.34
50.2			1		1	0.78
50.3			1		1	0.78
50.4			3		3	2.34
50.5			2	4	6	4.69
50.6					0	0.00
50.7					0	0.00
	0	0	9	5	14	10.94

EASTERN PASSAGE (AREA 110)						
	PHASE 2.2				Total	
FAMILY	1056	1089	1091	1092	#	%
55					0	0.00
55.1	1			1	2	1.56
55.2					0	0.00
55.3					0	0.00
	1	0	0	1	2	1.56
60					0	0.00
60.1	1	1	10	4	16	12.50
60.2					0	0.00
60.3					0	0.00
60.4					0	0.00
	1	1	10	4	16	12.50
65					0	0.00
65.1		2	3	1	6	4.69
65.2			4	3	7	5.47
65.3					0	0.00
65.4			1		1	0.78
	0	2	8	4	14	10.94
70					0	0.00
70.1			1		1	0.78
70.2			6	2	8	6.25
70.3			1	4	5	3.91
70.4					0	0.00
70.5				1	1	0.78
70.6					0	0.00
70.7					0	0.00
70.8					0	0.00
	0	0	8	7	15	11.72
75					0	0.00
75.1			1	3	4	3.13
75.2					0	0.00
75.3					0	0.00
75.4					0	0.00
	0	0	1	3	4	3.13
80					0	0.00
80.1		1	3	4	8	6.25
80.2			1	1	2	1.56
80.3					0	0.00
	0	1	4	5	10	7.81
85					0	0.00
85.1					0	0.00
85.2					0	0.00
85.3					0	0.00
	0	0	0	0	0	0.00
90					0	0.00
90.1					0	0.00
90.2					0	0.00
90.3					0	0.00
90.4					0	0.00
90.5					0	0.00
90.6					0	0.00
90.7					0	0.00
90.8					0	0.00
90.9					0	0.00
	0	0	0	0	0	0.00
95					0	0.00
95.1					0	0.00
95.2					0	0.00
95.3					0	0.00
95.4					0	0.00
	0	0	0	0	0	0.00
Total	2	5	73	48	128	100

CENTRAL PASSAGE (AREA 125)								
	PHASE 2.3						Total	
FAMILY	8072	8073	8074	8075	8076	8077	#	%
5					1		1	0.75
5.1			2	1	5		8	6.02
5.2							0	0.00
5.3		1					1	0.75
5.4							0	0.00
5.5							0	0.00
	0	1	2	1	6	0	10	7.52
10							0	0.00
10.1		1	3		1		5	3.76
10.2		2			3		5	3.76
10.3							0	0.00
10.4							0	0.00
	0	3	3	0	4	0	10	7.52
15							0	0.00
15.1	2	3	1	4	1		11	8.27
15.2			2				2	1.50
	2	3	3	4	1	0	13	9.77
20							0	0.00
20.1							0	0.00
20.2							0	0.00
	0	0	0	0	0	0	0	0.00
25							0	0.00
25.1					1		1	0.75
25.2					1		1	0.75
25.3	1						1	0.75
25.4	1			1			2	1.50
25.5							0	0.00
	2	0	0	1	2	0	5	3.76
30							0	0.00
30.1							0	0.00
30.2				1	1		2	1.50
30.3							0	0.00
	0	0	0	1	1	0	2	1.50
35							0	0.00
35.1							0	0.00
35.2							0	0.00
35.3							0	0.00
35.4							0	0.00
35.5					1		1	0.75
	0	0	0	0	1	0	1	0.75
40							0	0.00
40.1							0	0.00
40.2							0	0.00
40.3							0	0.00
	0	0	0	0	0	0	0	0.00
45							0	0.00
45.1							0	0.00
45.2							0	0.00
45.3							0	0.00
45.4							0	0.00
	0	0	0	0	0	0	0	0.00
50					1		1	0.75
50.1	3	1		2	3		9	6.77
50.2	2	2	1		1		6	4.51
50.3				1			1	0.75
50.4							0	0.00
50.5		2	1	3	2	1	9	6.77
50.6							0	0.00
50.7							0	0.00
	5	5	2	6	7	1	26	19.55

CENTRAL PASSAGE (AREA 125)								
	PHASE 2.3						Total	
FAMILY	8072	8073	8074	8075	8076	8077	#	%
55							0	0.00
55.1	1		1		1		3	2.26
55.2				1			1	0.75
55.3							0	0.00
	1	0	1	1	1	0	4	3.01
60							0	0.00
60.1		4	1	1	5		11	8.27
60.2							0	0.00
60.3							0	0.00
60.4							0	0.00
	0	4	1	1	5	0	11	8.27
65							0	0.00
65.1	1	1		1			3	2.26
65.2		1					1	0.75
65.3							0	0.00
65.4							0	0.00
	1	2	0	1	0	0	4	3.01
70							0	0.00
70.1					1		1	0.75
70.2		1	1	2	4	2	10	7.52
70.3	3	9	6	5	2		25	18.80
70.4							0	0.00
70.5				1			1	0.75
70.6							0	0.00
70.7							0	0.00
70.8							0	0.00
	3	10	7	8	7	2	37	27.82
75							0	0.00
75.1							0	0.00
75.2			1				1	0.75
75.3					1		1	0.75
75.4							0	0.00
	0	0	1	0	1	0	2	1.50
80							0	0.00
80.1			1		1		2	1.50
80.2			1		1		2	1.50
80.3							0	0.00
	0	0	2	0	2	0	4	3.01
85							0	0.00
85.1		1			1		2	1.50
85.2				1			1	0.75
85.3							0	0.00
	0	1	0	1	1	0	3	2.26
90							0	0.00
90.1							0	0.00
90.2							0	0.00
90.3							0	0.00
90.4							0	0.00
90.5							0	0.00
90.6							0	0.00
90.7							0	0.00
90.8							0	0.00
90.9							0	0.00
	0	0	0	0	0	0	0	0.00
95							0	0.00
95.1			1				1	0.75
95.2							0	0.00
95.3							0	0.00
95.4							0	0.00
	0	0	1	0	0	0	1	0.75
Total	14	29	23	25	39	3	133	100

JOINING PASSSAGE (AREAS 131 & 619)									
	PHASE 2.3							Total	
FAMILY	1126	1129	1133	1132	1131	1136	1137	#	%
5								0	0.00
5.1	5	5		4		8	10	32	21.05
5.2							1	1	0.66
5.3								0	0.00
5.4								0	0.00
5.5								0	0.00
	5	5	0	4	0	8	11	33	21.71
10				1			1	2	1.32
10.1		2		1				3	1.97
10.2	1						1	2	1.32
10.3								0	0.00
10.4				1				1	0.66
	1	2	0	3	0	0	2	8	5.26
15								0	0.00
15.1	5	1				2	1	9	5.92
15.2								0	0.00
	5	1	0	0	0	2	1	9	5.92
20								0	0.00
20.1								0	0.00
20.2								0	0.00
	0	0	0	0	0	0	0	0	0.00
25	2		1					3	1.97
25.1				1			1	2	1.32
25.2								0	0.00
25.3								0	0.00
25.4		1					1	2	1.32
25.5								0	0.00
	2	1	1	1	0	0	2	7	4.61
30								0	0.00
30.1								0	0.00
30.2								0	0.00
30.3								0	0.00
	0	0	0	0	0	0	0	0	0.00
35								0	0.00
35.1								0	0.00
35.2							2	2	1.32
35.3								0	0.00
35.4								0	0.00
35.5								0	0.00
	0	0	0	0	0	0	2	2	1.32
40								0	0.00
40.1								0	0.00
40.2								0	0.00
40.3								0	0.00
	0	0	0	0	0	0	0	0	0.00
45								0	0.00
45.1								0	0.00
45.2								0	0.00
45.3								0	0.00
45.4								0	0.00
	0	0	0	0	0	0	0	0	0.00
50								0	0.00
50.1		1						1	0.66
50.2	1	1					1	3	1.97
50.3								0	0.00
50.4		2				2		4	2.63
50.5		1				1	4	6	3.95
50.6								0	0.00
50.7								0	0.00
	1	5	0	0	0	3	5	14	9.21

JOINING PASSSAGE (AREAS 131 & 619)									
	PHASE 2.3							Total	
FAMILY	1126	1129	1133	1132	1131	1136	1137	#	%
55								0	0.00
55.1		1		1		2		4	2.63
55.2								0	0.00
55.3							1	1	0.66
	0	1	0	1	0	2	1	5	3.29
60								0	0.00
60.1		3		1		3	16	23	15.13
60.2								0	0.00
60.3								0	0.00
60.4								0	0.00
	0	3	0	1	0	3	16	23	15.13
65								0	0.00
65.1	3	1				1	3	8	5.26
65.2				1				1	0.66
65.3								0	0.00
65.4								0	0.00
	3	1	0	1	0	1	3	9	5.92
70				1			1	2	1.32
70.1	1				1			2	1.32
70.2	1	1		3			4	9	5.92
70.3	3	2		2		1	8	16	10.53
70.4								0	0.00
70.5							1	1	0.66
70.6								0	0.00
70.7								0	0.00
70.8								0	0.00
	5	3	0	6	1	1	14	30	19.74
75								0	0.00
75.1							2	2	1.32
75.2								0	0.00
75.3								0	0.00
75.4								0	0.00
	0	0	0	0	0	0	2	2	1.32
80	1	1				1		3	1.97
80.1	1					1		2	1.32
80.2						1		1	0.66
80.3								0	0.00
	2	1	0	0	0	3	0	6	3.95
85								0	0.00
85.1				1		1	1	3	1.97
85.2								0	0.00
85.3								0	0.00
	0	0	0	1	0	1	1	3	1.97
90								0	0.00
90.1								0	0.00
90.2					1			1	0.66
90.3								0	0.00
90.4								0	0.00
90.5								0	0.00
90.6								0	0.00
90.7								0	0.00
90.8								0	0.00
90.9								0	0.00
	0	0	0	0	1	0	0	1	0.66
95								0	0.00
95.1								0	0.00
95.2								0	0.00
95.3								0	0.00
95.4								0	0.00
	0	0	0	0	0	0	0	0	0.00
Total	24	23	1	18	2	24	60	152	100

	SURFACE SCRAPE																														
	MIXED PHASES																														
FAMILY	1126	1138	3131	6061	6062	6065	6066	6067	6068	6070	6072	6076	6077	6078	6082	6083	6085	6087	6088	6089	6090	6091	6096	6111	6116	6118	6122	6124	6125	6126	6127	6135
5		1																														
5.1	5							1	4		1			2			1					7	6	4	2	2				1		1
5.2					2				3				1		1							3				1						
5.3																																
5.4										1									1	1					2							
5.5																			1													
	5	1	0	0	2	0	0	1	7	1	1	0	1	2	1	0	1	0	2	1	0	10	6	4	4	3	0	0	0	1	0	1
10										1														1								
10.1					2	1																	2		1			2				
10.2	1																						4									
10.3																																
10.4																	1									1						
	1	0	0	0	2	1	0	0	0	1	0	0	0	0	0	0	1	0	0	0	0	0	6	1	1	1	0	2	0	0	0	0
15																																
15.1	5	2	2						1	2				1			1		2				4	1	2	4		3		4		
15.2										1														1								1
	5	2	2	0	0	0	0	0	1	3	0	0	0	1	0	0	1	0	2	0	0	0	4	2	2	4	0	3	0	4	0	1
20																									1							
20.1					1		1		1	1																						
20.2																																
	0	0	0	0	1	0	1	0	1	1	0	0	0	0	0	0	0	0	0	0	0	0	0	0	1	0	0	0	0	0	0	0
25	2																						2		1							1
25.1			2	3	6			4		1	1		2	2								6	1	3	4	2			1	1		
25.2																						1	2									
25.3										1										1												
25.4																							1	1		1		1				
25.5		1					1		2		1			3		1	1					2	1	2		1		1				
	2	1	2	3	6	0	1	4	2	2	2	0	2	5	0	1	1	0	0	1	0	9	7	6	5	4	0	2	1	1	0	1
30																																
30.1																																
30.2																						1										
30.3																																
	0	0	0	0	0	0	0	0	0	0	0	0	0	0	0	0	0	0	0	0	0	1	0	0	0	0	0	0	0	0	0	0
35																																
35.1																																
35.2					2								1	1								1	4							1		
35.3																																
35.4																																
35.5																																
	0	0	0	0	2	0	0	0	0	0	0	0	1	1	0	0	0	0	0	0	0	1	4	0	0	0	0	0	0	1	0	0
40																																
40.1																																
40.2																			2													
40.3																			1													
	0	0	0	0	0	0	0	0	0	0	0	0	0	0	0	0	0	0	3	0	0	0	0	0	0	0	0	0	0	0	0	0
45																																
45.1																						1								1		
45.2																																
45.3																																
45.4																																
	0	0	0	0	0	0	0	0	0	0	0	0	0	0	0	0	0	0	0	0	0	1	0	0	0	0	0	0	0	1	0	0
50			1																			1	1	1				1		2		
50.1			1		1	1		1	5	4	2			6					1			4	5	2	4	4		8		1		
50.2	1					1		1		1												1	2	2	2			1		1		
50.3					1			1	1	5									3				1									1
50.4													1	1								1	2	2	1						1	
50.5		2	4		1	1		1	6					3		1	1					3	12	4	2	2		4		3		
50.6																						1	1									
50.7																																
	1	2	6	0	3	3	0	4	12	10	2	0	1	10	0	1	1	0	4	0	0	11	24	11	9	6	0	14	0	7	1	1

6136	6145	6153	6156	6157	6158	6159	6162	6163	6164	6166	6167	6169	6175	6176	6178	6181	6183	6184	Total #	Total %
																			1	0.08
8								3	1	2					1				52	4.17
																			11	0.88
																			0	0.00
										2			3				1		11	0.88
													1	2	3	1	4		12	0.96
8	0	0	0	0	0	0	0	3	1	4	0	0	4	2	4	1	5	0	87	6.97
													1						3	0.24
4							1												13	1.04
																			5	0.40
																			0	0.00
									1										3	0.24
4	0	0	0	0	0	0	1	0	1	0	0	0	1	0	0	0	0	0	24	1.92
																			0	0.00
7							1	4	2		1								49	3.93
										3	3		9	2	3	2			25	2.00
7	0	0	0	0	0	0	1	4	2	3	4	0	9	2	3	2	0	0	74	5.93
																			1	0.08
1								1											6	0.48
																			0	0.00
1	0	0	0	0	0	0	0	1	0	0	0	0	0	0	0	0	0	0	7	0.56
1											2								9	0.72
3							4	2	1	1	4								54	4.33
1							1	1		1									7	0.56
								1		1			4		3		2	1	14	1.12
								1			1								6	0.48
								1					2				1		21	1.68
5	0	0	0	0	0	0	5	6	1	3	7	0	6	0	3	0	3	1	111	8.89
																			0	0.00
1								1											2	0.16
1																			2	0.16
																			0	0.00
2	0	0	0	0	0	0	0	1	0	0	0	0	0	0	0	0	0	0	4	0.32
															1				1	0.08
																			0	0.00
						1	1												12	0.96
																			0	0.00
										1									1	0.08
								1					1						2	0.16
0	0	0	0	0	0	1	1	1	0	1	0	0	1	0	1	0	0	0	16	1.28
											1								1	0.08
										1			5		4		7		17	1.36
2											2		3	3	2		2	13	29	2.32
											1				1			1	4	0.32
2	0	0	0	0	0	0	0	0	0	1	4	0	8	3	7	0	9	14	51	4.09
										1									1	0.08
							1			1	1								5	0.40
																			0	0.00
																			0	0.00
													1						1	0.08
0	0	0	0	0	0	0	1	0	0	2	1	0	1	0	0	0	0	0	7	0.56
1										1			2		1				12	0.96
1							3	1		3	1		1					2	62	4.97
4						1	1	7	2	2									30	2.40
1								1											15	1.20
2								2		1	1							1	16	1.28
18							1	8	2	2	3		1		1				86	6.89
										2									4	0.32
															5				5	0.40
27	0	0	0	0	0	1	5	19	4	11	5	0	4	0	7	0	0	3	230	18.43

SURFACE SCRAPE (cont'd.)																																
	MIXED PHASES																															
FAMILY	1126	1138	3131	6061	6062	6065	6066	6067	6068	6070	6072	6076	6077	6078	6082	6083	6085	6087	6088	6089	6090	6091	6096	6111	6116	6118	6122	6124	6125	6126	6127	6135
55																						2										
55.1				1	2								1									5	3	2	1	1				1		
55.2					1				1	1							1		1	1			1	1		1				1		
55.3									1																	1		1				
	0	0	0	1	3	0	0	0	2	1	0	0	1	0	0	0	1	0	1	1	0	7	4	3	1	3	0	1	0	2	0	0
60																																
60.1		3		1	1				4					2				1	5	1		3		5		3				1	1	
60.2									1																							
60.3																																
60.4																							1									
	0	3	0	1	1	0	0	0	5	0	0	0	0	2	0	0	0	1	5	1	0	3	1	5	0	3	0	0	0	1	1	0
65																																
65.1	3		2		9	1	1	4	7	7	8		2	15			2			1		12	10	4	7	6		1		3		
65.2					5			1	1		1	1		2	1							2	7		1			2				
65.3																								1						1		
65.4										1																						
	3	0	2	0	14	1	1	5	8	8	9	1	2	17	1	0	2	0	0	1	0	14	17	5	8	6	0	3	0	4	0	0
70																				1		2						1		1		
70.1	1							1		2		1		1		1						1	1		1					2		
70.2	1	1		1	2			3		1	3		1	4			1		1	1		10	12	7	2			2		2		
70.3	3	1	2	1	7				2		4	1		1	1	1	3		1	1	1	12	8	9	7	5		7		11		
70.4								1											4													
70.5					1					1												1	3	1						1		
70.6																								1						1	1	
70.7																								1				1				
70.8																																
	5	2	2	2	10	0	0	5	2	4	7	2	1	6	1	2	4	0	6	3	1	26	24	19	10	5	0	11	0	18	1	0
75								1																								
75.1														1																		
75.2																								1								
75.3																																
75.4																																
	0	0	0	0	0	0	0	1	0	0	0	0	0	1	0	0	0	0	0	0	0	0	0	1	0	0	0	0	0	0	0	0
80	1																								1							
80.1	1				1			1						1									3		1	1		1				
80.2								1			1											2	1	3	1	1						
80.3																																
	2	0	0	0	1	0	0	2	0	0	1	0	0	1	0	0	0	0	0	0	0	2	4	3	3	2	0	1	0	0	0	0
85																																
85.1		1				1			1		1												4		1	1						1
85.2								2														1		2		2				1		
85.3			1																						1							
	0	1	1	0	0	1	0	2	1	0	1	0	0	0	0	0	0	0	0	0	0	1	4	2	2	3	0	0	0	1	0	1
90																																
90.1																							1									
90.2																																
90.3																							1									
90.4																																
90.5																																
90.6																																
90.7																																
90.8																																
90.9																																
	0	0	0	0	0	0	0	0	0	0	0	0	0	0	0	0	0	0	0	0	0	0	2	0	0	0	0	0	0	0	0	0
95																																
95.1																																
95.2																																
95.3																								1								
95.4																											1					
	0	0	0	0	0	0	0	0	0	0	0	0	0	0	0	0	0	0	0	0	0	0	0	1	0	0	1	0	0	0	0	0
Total	24	12	15	7	45	6	3	24	41	31	23	3	9	46	3	4	12	1	23	8	1	86	107	63	46	40	1	37	1	41	3	5

6136	6145	6153	6156	6157	6158	6159	6162	6163	6164	6166	6167	6169	6175	6176	6178	6181	6183	6184	Total #	Total %
																			2	0.16
4								5	2	6	1		2						37	2.96
2							1	1	1		1	1							17	1.36
																			3	0.24
6	0	0	0	0	0	0	1	6	3	6	2	1	2	0	0	0	0	0	59	4.73
																			0	0.00
13		2		1	2	2		3		1	1						1		57	4.57
1								1											3	0.24
																			0	0.00
																			1	0.08
14	0	2	0	1	2	2	0	4	0	1	1	0	0	0	0	0	1	0	61	4.89
1																			1	0.08
14							1	2	2	1	4		4		1				134	10.74
2	1					1	1												29	2.32
											1								3	0.24
1											1								3	0.24
18	1	0	0	0	0	1	2	2	2	1	6	0	4	0	1	0	0	0	170	13.62
										1	1								7	0.56
		1						1	1		1		8		1		1		26	2.08
8						1	1	5	4	1					3		1	1	80	6.41
10						2	3	7	5	2	5				1				124	9.94
									1						2			1	9	0.72
2													1						11	0.88
																			3	0.24
																			2	0.16
									1										1	0.08
20	0	1	0	0	0	3	4	13	12	4	7	0	9	0	7	0	2	2	263	21.07
																			1	0.08
																			1	0.08
																			1	0.08
																			0	0.00
																			0	0.00
0	0	0	0	0	0	0	0	0	0	0	0	0	0	0	0	0	0	0	3	0.24
1	1				1														5	0.40
1							1		1		1		1						15	1.20
2				1				1											14	1.12
																			0	0.00
4	1	0	0	1	1	0	1	1	1	0	1	0	1	0	0	0	0	0	34	2.72
																			0	0.00
2			1			1	1		1	1									18	1.44
3							2	1		1			2						17	1.36
										1									3	0.24
5	0	0	1	0	0	1	3	1	1	3	0	0	2	0	0	0	0	0	38	3.04
																			0	0.00
																		1	2	0.16
			1																1	0.08
																			1	0.08
																			0	0.00
																			0	0.00
								1											1	0.08
																			0	0.00
																			0	0.00
																			0	0.00
0	0	0	1	0	0	0	0	1	0	0	0	0	0	0	0	0	0	1	5	0.40
																			0	0.00
										1									1	0.08
																			0	0.00
1																			2	0.16
																			1	0.08
1	0	0	0	0	0	0	0	0	0	1	0	0	0	0	0	0	0	0	4	0.32
124	2	3	2	2	3	9	25	63	28	41	38	1	52	7	33	3	20	21	1248	100

TOWER 124				
	MIXED		Total	
FAMILY	1005	1094	#	%
5			0	0.00
5.1		9	9	5.17
5.2	3	21	24	13.79
5.3			0	0.00
5.4	1	1	2	1.15
5.5			0	0.00
	4	31	35	20.11
10			0	0.00
10.1	1	4	5	2.87
10.2	3	1	4	2.30
10.3			0	0.00
10.4			0	0.00
	4	5	9	5.17
15			0	0.00
15.1	2	8	10	5.75
15.2			0	0.00
	2	8	10	5.75
20			0	0.00
20.1		2	2	1.15
20.2			0	0.00
	0	2	2	1.15
25			0	0.00
25.1			0	0.00
25.2			0	0.00
25.3			0	0.00
25.4			0	0.00
25.5			0	0.00
	0	0	0	0.00
30			0	0.00
30.1			0	0.00
30.2			0	0.00
30.3			0	0.00
	0	0	0	0.00
35			0	0.00
35.1			0	0.00
35.2	5	2	7	4.02
35.3			0	0.00
35.4			0	0.00
35.5		2	2	1.15
	5	4	9	5.17
40			0	0.00
40.1			0	0.00
40.2			0	0.00
40.3			0	0.00
	0	0	0	0.00
45			0	0.00
45.1	1		1	0.57
45.2			0	0.00
45.3			0	0.00
45.4			0	0.00
	1	0	1	0.57
50			0	0.00
50.1	4	1	5	2.87
50.2		2	2	1.15
50.3			0	0.00
50.4	1		1	0.57
50.5	4	5	9	5.17
50.6			0	0.00
50.7			0	0.00
	9	8	17	9.77

TOWER 124				
	MIXED		Total	
FAMILY	1005	1094	#	%
55			0	0.00
55.1			0	0.00
55.2			0	0.00
55.3			0	0.00
	0	0	0	0.00
60			0	0.00
60.1		33	33	18.97
60.2			0	0.00
60.3		1	1	0.57
60.4			0	0.00
	0	34	34	19.54
65			0	0.00
65.1		8	8	4.60
65.2		3	3	1.72
65.3			0	0.00
65.4	2		2	1.15
	2	11	13	7.47
70			0	0.00
70.1	1	2	3	1.72
70.2	8	6	14	8.05
70.3	9	4	13	7.47
70.4	2		2	1.15
70.5		1	1	0.57
70.6			0	0.00
70.7			0	0.00
70.8		1	1	0.57
	20	14	34	19.54
75			0	0.00
75.1		1	1	0.57
75.2			0	0.00
75.3			0	0.00
75.4			0	0.00
	0	1	1	0.57
80			0	0.00
80.1		3	3	1.72
80.2	1		1	0.57
80.3			0	0.00
	1	3	4	2.30
85		1	1	0.57
85.1	1	1	2	1.15
85.2	1		1	0.57
85.3			0	0.00
	2	2	4	2.30
90			0	0.00
90.1			0	0.00
90.2			0	0.00
90.3			0	0.00
90.4			0	0.00
90.5			0	0.00
90.6			0	0.00
90.7			0	0.00
90.8			0	0.00
90.9			0	0.00
	0	0	0	0.00
95			0	0.00
95.1			0	0.00
95.2		1	1	0.57
95.3			0	0.00
95.4			0	0.00
	0	1	1	0.57
Total	50	124	174	100

TOWER 302				
	MIXED		Total	
FAMILY	1005	1094	#	%
5			0	0.00
5.1		2	2	2.99
5.2		6	6	8.96
5.3			0	0.00
5.4			0	0.00
5.5			0	0.00
	0	8	8	11.94
10			0	0.00
10.1			0	0.00
10.2			0	0.00
10.3			0	0.00
10.4			0	0.00
	0	0	0	0.00
15			0	0.00
15.1		3	3	4.48
15.2			0	0.00
	0	3	3	4.48
20			0	0.00
20.1			0	0.00
20.2			0	0.00
	0	0	0	0.00
25			0	0.00
25.1			0	0.00
25.2			0	0.00
25.3			0	0.00
25.4			0	0.00
25.5			0	0.00
	0	0	0	0.00
30			0	0.00
30.1			0	0.00
30.2			0	0.00
30.3			0	0.00
	0	0	0	0.00
35			0	0.00
35.1			0	0.00
35.2		1	1	1.49
35.3		1	1	1.49
35.4		1	1	1.49
35.5			0	0.00
	0	3	3	4.48
40			0	0.00
40.1			0	0.00
40.2			0	0.00
40.3			0	0.00
	0	0	0	0.00
45			0	0.00
45.1			0	0.00
45.2			0	0.00
45.3			0	0.00
45.4			0	0.00
	0	0	0	0.00
50			0	0.00
50.1		5	5	7.46
50.2			0	0.00
50.3	1	2	3	4.48
50.4		2	2	2.99
50.5		6	6	8.96
50.6			0	0.00
50.7			0	0.00
	1	15	16	23.88

TOWER 302				
	MIXED		Total	
FAMILY	1005	1094	#	%
55			0	0.00
55.1			0	0.00
55.2			0	0.00
55.3			0	0.00
	0	0	0	0.00
60			0	0.00
60.1		6	6	8.96
60.2			0	0.00
60.3			0	0.00
60.4			0	0.00
	0	6	6	8.96
65			0	0.00
65.1		1	1	1.49
65.2		6	6	8.96
65.3		1	1	1.49
65.4			0	0.00
	0	8	8	11.94
70			0	0.00
70.1		1	1	1.49
70.2		10	10	14.93
70.3		8	8	11.94
70.4			0	0.00
70.5			0	0.00
70.6			0	0.00
70.7			0	0.00
70.8			0	0.00
	0	19	19	28.36
75			0	0.00
75.1			0	0.00
75.2			0	0.00
75.3			0	0.00
75.4			0	0.00
	0	0	0	0.00
80			0	0.00
80.1		1	1	1.49
80.2		1	1	1.49
80.3			0	0.00
	0	2	2	2.99
85			0	0.00
85.1		1	1	1.49
85.2		1	1	1.49
85.3			0	0.00
	0	2	2	2.99
90			0	0.00
90.1			0	0.00
90.2			0	0.00
90.3			0	0.00
90.4			0	0.00
90.5			0	0.00
90.6			0	0.00
90.7			0	0.00
90.8			0	0.00
90.9			0	0.00
	0	0	0	0.00
95			0	0.00
95.1			0	0.00
95.2			0	0.00
95.3			0	0.00
95.4			0	0.00
	0	0	0	0.00
Total	1	66	67	100

TOWER 304									
FAMILY	MIXED							Total	
	3054	3083	3084	3085	3087	3088	3089	#	%
5								0	0.00
5.1	23	1	6	31	2	10		73	9.07
5.2	17		1	22		6		46	5.71
5.3								0	0.00
5.4				1				1	0.12
5.5								0	0.00
	40	1	7	54	2	16	0	120	14.91
10								0	0.00
10.1	8			1		2		11	1.37
10.2	2			4		2		8	0.99
10.3	1				1	3	1	6	0.75
10.4								0	0.00
	11	0	0	5	1	7	1	25	3.11
15								0	0.00
15.1	10		1	18		14		43	5.34
15.2	3			1				4	0.50
	13	0	1	19	0	14	0	47	5.84
20								0	0.00
20.1	3			1				4	0.50
20.2								0	0.00
	3	0	0	1	0	0	0	4	0.50
25								0	0.00
25.1	8	1		1		2		12	1.49
25.2				1				1	0.12
25.3	1							1	0.12
25.4								0	0.00
25.5	3		1	2		2		8	0.99
	12	1	1	4	0	4	0	22	2.73
30								0	0.00
30.1								0	0.00
30.2								0	0.00
30.3								0	0.00
	0	0	0	0	0	0	0	0	0.00
35				1				1	0.12
35.1								0	0.00
35.2	6			3		3	1	13	1.61
35.3						2		2	0.25
35.4				4		3		7	0.87
35.5	2			1	1	1		5	0.62
	8	0	0	9	1	9	1	28	3.48
40								0	0.00
40.1								0	0.00
40.2	1							1	0.12
40.3								0	0.00
	1	0	0	0	0	0	0	1	0.12
45								0	0.00
45.1								0	0.00
45.2								0	0.00
45.3								0	0.00
45.4								0	0.00
	0	0	0	0	0	0	0	0	0.00
50								0	0.00
50.1	16		3	2		1		22	2.73
50.2	8	1		6	1	2		18	2.24
50.3	1			2		3	1	7	0.87
50.4	8			3		1		12	1.49
50.5	28	1	5	19		16		69	8.57
50.6	1			1				2	0.25
50.7								0	0.00
	62	2	8	33	1	23	1	130	16.15

TOWER 304									
FAMILY	MIXED							Total	
	3054	3083	3084	3085	3087	3088	3089	#	%
55								0	0.00
55.1	17		1	1	1	1		21	2.61
55.2	1			2		4		7	0.87
55.3								0	0.00
	18	0	1	3	1	5	0	28	3.48
60								0	0.00
60.1	60	7	5	44	2	9		127	15.78
60.2						1		1	0.12
60.3				1				1	0.12
60.4								0	0.00
	60	7	5	45	2	10	0	129	16.02
65								0	0.00
65.1	18	1		16		13	1	49	6.09
65.2	4		1	5		11		21	2.61
65.3								0	0.00
65.4						2		2	0.25
	22	1	1	21	0	26	1	72	8.94
70			1					1	0.12
70.1	3			1		2		6	0.75
70.2	14	1	1	12	1	13		42	5.22
70.3	39		4	23	1	17	2	86	10.68
70.4								0	0.00
70.5	1			1		11		13	1.61
70.6								0	0.00
70.7								0	0.00
70.8								0	0.00
	57	1	6	37	2	43	2	148	18.39
75								0	0.00
75.1	2							2	0.25
75.2								0	0.00
75.3				1				1	0.12
75.4								0	0.00
	2	0	0	1	0	0	0	3	0.37
80						1		1	0.12
80.1	5			8		5		18	2.24
80.2						1		1	0.12
80.3								0	0.00
	5	0	0	8	0	7	0	20	2.48
85	1							1	0.12
85.1	14		2	4	1			21	2.61
85.2	3							3	0.37
85.3								0	0.00
	18	0	2	4	1	0	0	25	3.11
90								0	0.00
90.1								0	0.00
90.2								0	0.00
90.3								0	0.00
90.4				1				1	0.12
90.5				1				1	0.12
90.6								0	0.00
90.7								0	0.00
90.8								0	0.00
90.9								0	0.00
	0	0	0	2	0	0	0	2	0.25
95	1					1		2	0.25
95.1								0	0.00
95.2								0	0.00
95.3								0	0.00
95.4								0	0.00
	1	0	0	0	0	1	0	2	0.25
Total	332	13	32	246	11	165	6	805	100

TOWER 616								
	MIXED						Total	
FAMILY	9017	9018	9020	9022	9023	9025	#	%
5			1				1	0.42
5.1	1	14	12	1		1	29	12.08
5.2				1			1	0.42
5.3							0	0.00
5.4							0	0.00
5.5							0	0.00
	1	14	13	2	0	1	31	12.92
10							0	0.00
10.1			5		1		6	2.50
10.2	2		5				7	2.92
10.3							0	0.00
10.4			1				1	0.42
	2	0	11	0	1	0	14	5.83
15				1			1	0.42
15.1	1	5	7				13	5.42
15.2	2						2	0.83
	3	5	7	1	0	0	16	6.67
20							0	0.00
20.1							0	0.00
20.2							0	0.00
	0	0	0	0	0	0	0	0.00
25		1					1	0.42
25.1		2		1			3	1.25
25.2							0	0.00
25.3		1					1	0.42
25.4		1	1				2	0.83
25.5	1	1					2	0.83
	1	6	1	1	0	0	9	3.75
30							0	0.00
30.1							0	0.00
30.2			1				1	0.42
30.3							0	0.00
	0	0	1	0	0	0	1	0.42
35							0	0.00
35.1							0	0.00
35.2		1	2				3	1.25
35.3		1					1	0.42
35.4			1				1	0.42
35.5							0	0.00
	0	2	3	0	0	0	5	2.08
40							0	0.00
40.1							0	0.00
40.2							0	0.00
40.3							0	0.00
	0	0	0	0	0	0	0	0.00
45							0	0.00
45.1							0	0.00
45.2		1	1				2	0.83
45.3							0	0.00
45.4							0	0.00
	0	1	1	0	0	0	2	0.83
50		1	1				2	0.83
50.1	2	4	6	2			14	5.83
50.2		1	4				5	2.08
50.3		1	1		2		4	1.67
50.4			1				1	0.42
50.5	1	11	23		1		36	15.00
50.6							0	0.00
50.7							0	0.00
	3	18	36	2	3	0	62	25.83

TOWER 616								
	MIXED						Total	
FAMILY	9017	9018	9020	9022	9023	9025	#	%
55							0	0.00
55.1		3	4				7	2.92
55.2		5	6		1		12	5.00
55.3							0	0.00
	0	8	10	0	1	0	19	7.92
60							0	0.00
60.1		10	6	1			17	7.08
60.2							0	0.00
60.3							0	0.00
60.4							0	0.00
	0	10	6	1	0	0	17	7.08
65							0	0.00
65.1	4	4	4				12	5.00
65.2	1	1	4				6	2.50
65.3							0	0.00
65.4		1					1	0.42
	5	6	8	0	0	0	19	7.92
70			1				1	0.42
70.1	1		1				2	0.83
70.2	1	3	1				5	2.08
70.3	2	9	8		1		20	8.33
70.4							0	0.00
70.5			3				3	1.25
70.6							0	0.00
70.7							0	0.00
70.8							0	0.00
	4	12	14	0	1	0	31	12.92
75							0	0.00
75.1							0	0.00
75.2							0	0.00
75.3							0	0.00
75.4							0	0.00
	0	0	0	0	0	0	0	0.00
80	1						1	0.42
80.1	1	2	1				4	1.67
80.2		1					1	0.42
80.3							0	0.00
	2	3	1	0	0	0	6	2.50
85							0	0.00
85.1		1			1		2	0.83
85.2		1					1	0.42
85.3		1	1				2	0.83
	0	3	1	0	1	0	5	2.08
90							0	0.00
90.1			1				1	0.42
90.2							0	0.00
90.3							0	0.00
90.4							0	0.00
90.5							0	0.00
90.6			1				1	0.42
90.7							0	0.00
90.8							0	0.00
90.9							0	0.00
	0	0	2	0	0	0	2	0.83
95		1					1	0.42
95.1							0	0.00
95.2							0	0.00
95.3							0	0.00
95.4							0	0.00
	0	1	0	0	0	0	1	0.42
Total	21	89	115	7	7	1	240	100

SOUNDING NE OF FORTIFIED BUILDING						
	MIXED				Total	
FAMILY	5000	5001	5003	5006	#	%
5					0	0.00
5.1	1	5	2	1	9	6.12
5.2					0	0.00
5.3		3	1		4	2.72
5.4					0	0.00
5.5					0	0.00
	1	8	3	1	13	8.84
10		1			1	0.68
10.1	2		1		3	2.04
10.2					0	0.00
10.3					0	0.00
10.4					0	0.00
	2	1	1	0	4	2.72
15					0	0.00
15.1	4	8	5		17	11.56
15.2		2	1	2	5	3.40
	4	10	6	2	22	14.97
20		1			1	0.68
20.1			1		1	0.68
20.2					0	0.00
	0	1	1	0	2	1.36
25		2			2	1.36
25.1	1	3			4	2.72
25.2		1			1	0.68
25.3		1	1		2	1.36
25.4	1	2			3	2.04
25.5		1	1		2	1.36
	2	10	2	0	14	9.52
30					0	0.00
30.1					0	0.00
30.2					0	0.00
30.3					0	0.00
	0	0	0	0	0	0.00
35					0	0.00
35.1					0	0.00
35.2					0	0.00
35.3					0	0.00
35.4					0	0.00
35.5					0	0.00
	0	0	0	0	0	0.00
40					0	0.00
40.1					0	0.00
40.2					0	0.00
40.3					0	0.00
	0	0	0	0	0	0.00
45					0	0.00
45.1					0	0.00
45.2					0	0.00
45.3					0	0.00
45.4					0	0.00
	0	0	0	0	0	0.00
50					0	0.00
50.1			1		1	0.68
50.2		12	1		13	8.84
50.3		7	2		9	6.12
50.4					0	0.00
50.5	1				1	0.68
50.6					0	0.00
50.7					0	0.00
	1	19	4	0	24	16.33

SOUNDING NE OF FORTIFIED BUILDING						
	MIXED				Total	
FAMILY	5000	5001	5003	5006	#	%
55					0	0.00
55.1			1		1	0.68
55.2		4			4	2.72
55.3		4			4	2.72
	0	8	1	0	9	6.12
60					0	0.00
60.1		6	1		7	4.76
60.2					0	0.00
60.3					0	0.00
60.4					0	0.00
	0	6	1	0	7	4.76
65					0	0.00
65.1		3	1		4	2.72
65.2					0	0.00
65.3					0	0.00
65.4					0	0.00
	0	3	1	0	4	2.72
70			1		1	0.68
70.1			2		2	1.36
70.2	8	13	5	1	27	18.37
70.3	1	3	1		5	3.40
70.4					0	0.00
70.5			1		1	0.68
70.6					0	0.00
70.7					0	0.00
70.8					0	0.00
	9	16	10	1	36	24.49
75					0	0.00
75.1					0	0.00
75.2					0	0.00
75.3					0	0.00
75.4					0	0.00
	0	0	0	0	0	0.00
80					0	0.00
80.1					0	0.00
80.2					0	0.00
80.3					0	0.00
	0	0	0	0	0	0.00
85					0	0.00
85.1					0	0.00
85.2		8	3		11	7.48
85.3					0	0.00
	0	8	3	0	11	7.48
90					0	0.00
90.1					0	0.00
90.2					0	0.00
90.3		1			1	0.68
90.4					0	0.00
90.5					0	0.00
90.6					0	0.00
90.7					0	0.00
90.8					0	0.00
90.9					0	0.00
	0	1	0	0	1	0.68
95					0	0.00
95.1					0	0.00
95.2					0	0.00
95.3					0	0.00
95.4					0	0.00
	0	0	0	0	0	0.00
Total	19	91	33	4	147	100

BAKED BRICK CHAMBER						
	MIXED				Total	
FAMILY	9005	9007	9008	9009	#	%
5					0	0.00
5.1					0	0.00
5.2					0	0.00
5.3					0	0.00
5.4					0	0.00
5.5					0	0.00
	0	0	0	0	0	0.00
10					0	0.00
10.1					0	0.00
10.2			1		1	3.45
10.3					0	0.00
10.4					0	0.00
	0	0	1	0	1	3.45
15					0	0.00
15.1					0	0.00
15.2					0	0.00
	0	0	0	0	0	0.00
20					0	0.00
20.1					0	0.00
20.2					0	0.00
	0	0	0	0	0	0.00
25					0	0.00
25.1	2				2	6.90
25.2					0	0.00
25.3					0	0.00
25.4					0	0.00
25.5					0	0.00
	2	0	0	0	2	6.90
30					0	0.00
30.1					0	0.00
30.2					0	0.00
30.3					0	0.00
	0	0	0	0	0	0.00
35	1				1	3.45
35.1					0	0.00
35.2					0	0.00
35.3					0	0.00
35.4					0	0.00
35.5					0	0.00
	1	0	0	0	1	3.45
40					0	0.00
40.1					0	0.00
40.2				4	4	13.79
40.3					0	0.00
	0	0	0	4	4	13.79
45					0	0.00
45.1					0	0.00
45.2					0	0.00
45.3					0	0.00
45.4					0	0.00
	0	0	0	0	0	0.00
50					0	0.00
50.1	1				1	3.45
50.2			1		1	3.45
50.3	2	1	3		6	20.69
50.4					0	0.00
50.5					0	0.00
50.6					0	0.00
50.7					0	0.00
	3	1	4	0	8	27.59

BAKED BRICK CHAMBER						
	MIXED				Total	
FAMILY	9005	9007	9008	9009	#	%
55					0	0.00
55.1					0	0.00
55.2			1	1	2	6.90
55.3					0	0.00
	0	0	1	1	2	6.90
60					0	0.00
60.1					0	0.00
60.2					0	0.00
60.3					0	0.00
60.4					0	0.00
	0	0	0	0	0	0.00
65					0	0.00
65.1					0	0.00
65.2					0	0.00
65.3					0	0.00
65.4					0	0.00
	0	0	0	0	0	0.00
70					0	0.00
70.1	1				1	3.45
70.2		1	5	1	7	24.14
70.3			1		1	3.45
70.4					0	0.00
70.5					0	0.00
70.6					0	0.00
70.7					0	0.00
70.8					0	0.00
	1	1	6	1	9	31.03
75					0	0.00
75.1					0	0.00
75.2					0	0.00
75.3					0	0.00
75.4					0	0.00
	0	0	0	0	0	0.00
80					0	0.00
80.1					0	0.00
80.2					0	0.00
80.3					0	0.00
	0	0	0	0	0	0.00
85					0	0.00
85.1			2		2	6.90
85.2					0	0.00
85.3					0	0.00
	0	0	2	0	2	6.90
90					0	0.00
90.1					0	0.00
90.2					0	0.00
90.3					0	0.00
90.4					0	0.00
90.5					0	0.00
90.6					0	0.00
90.7					0	0.00
90.8					0	0.00
90.9					0	0.00
	0	0	0	0	0	0.00
95					0	0.00
95.1					0	0.00
95.2					0	0.00
95.3					0	0.00
95.4					0	0.00
	0	0	0	0	0	0.00
Total	7	2	14	6	29	100

INTRUSIVE BURIALS																	
	MIXED															Total	
FAMILY	1097	1098	1143	1151	1153	3034	3091	4038	4041	6092	6093	6141	6170	8006	8029	#	%
5																0	0.00
5.1		1					1		1							3	6.12
5.2								1								1	2.04
5.3															1	1	2.04
5.4																0	0.00
5.5																0	0.00
	0	1	0	0	0	0	1	1	1	0	0	0	0	0	1	5	10.20
10																0	0.00
10.1								1								1	2.04
10.2																0	0.00
10.3																0	0.00
10.4																0	0.00
	0	0	0	0	0	0	0	1	0	0	0	0	0	0	0	1	2.04
15																0	0.00
15.1																0	0.00
15.2																0	0.00
	0	0	0	0	0	0	0	0	0	0	0	0	0	0	0	0	0.00
20																0	0.00
20.1																0	0.00
20.2																0	0.00
	0	0	0	0	0	0	0	0	0	0	0	0	0	0	0	0	0.00
25																0	0.00
25.1								2	1	1	1					5	10.20
25.2																0	0.00
25.3																0	0.00
25.4															1	1	2.04
25.5													1			1	2.04
	0	0	0	0	0	0	0	2	1	1	1	0	1	0	1	7	14.29
30																0	0.00
30.1																0	0.00
30.2																0	0.00
30.3																0	0.00
	0	0	0	0	0	0	0	0	0	0	0	0	0	0	0	0	0.00
35																0	0.00
35.1																0	0.00
35.2																0	0.00
35.3																0	0.00
35.4																0	0.00
35.5																0	0.00
	0	0	0	0	0	0	0	0	0	0	0	0	0	0	0	0	0.00
40																0	0.00
40.1																0	0.00
40.2																0	0.00
40.3																0	0.00
	0	0	0	0	0	0	0	0	0	0	0	0	0	0	0	0	0.00
45																0	0.00
45.1																0	0.00
45.2																0	0.00
45.3																0	0.00
45.4																0	0.00
	0	0	0	0	0	0	0	0	0	0	0	0	0	0	0	0	0.00
50																0	0.00
50.1									1							1	2.04
50.2									2							2	4.08
50.3						1		1	1							3	6.12
50.4																0	0.00
50.5									1						1	2	4.08
50.6																0	0.00
50.7																0	0.00
	0	0	0	0	0	1	0	1	5	0	0	0	0	0	1	8	16.33

INTRUSIVE BURIALS																	
	MIXED															Total	
FAMILY	1097	1098	1143	1151	1153	3034	3091	4038	4041	6092	6093	6141	6170	8006	8029	#	%
55																0	0.00
55.1					1		1									2	4.08
55.2								1	2							3	6.12
55.3																0	0.00
	0	0	0	0	1	0	1	1	2	0	0	0	0	0	0	5	10.20
60																0	0.00
60.1								10						1	1	12	24.49
60.2																0	0.00
60.3																0	0.00
60.4																0	0.00
	0	0	0	0	0	0	0	10	0	0	0	0	0	1	1	12	24.49
65																0	0.00
65.1			1													1	2.04
65.2																0	0.00
65.3																0	0.00
65.4																0	0.00
	0	0	1	0	0	0	0	0	0	0	0	0	0	0	0	1	2.04
70																0	0.00
70.1									1							1	2.04
70.2				1				1	2							4	8.16
70.3							1		1			1				3	6.12
70.4																0	0.00
70.5																0	0.00
70.6																0	0.00
70.7	1															1	2.04
70.8																0	0.00
	1	0	0	1	0	0	1	1	4	0	0	1	0	0	0	9	18.37
75																0	0.00
75.1																0	0.00
75.2																0	0.00
75.3																0	0.00
75.4																0	0.00
	0	0	0	0	0	0	0	0	0	0	0	0	0	0	0	0	0.00
80																0	0.00
80.1																0	0.00
80.2																0	0.00
80.3																0	0.00
	0	0	0	0	0	0	0	0	0	0	0	0	0	0	0	0	0.00
85																0	0.00
85.1								1								1	2.04
85.2																0	0.00
85.3																0	0.00
	0	0	0	0	0	0	0	1	0	0	0	0	0	0	0	1	2.04
90																0	0.00
90.1																0	0.00
90.2																0	0.00
90.3																0	0.00
90.4																0	0.00
90.5																0	0.00
90.6																0	0.00
90.7																0	0.00
90.8																0	0.00
90.9																0	0.00
	0	0	0	0	0	0	0	0	0	0	0	0	0	0	0	0	0.00
95																0	0.00
95.1																0	0.00
95.2																0	0.00
95.3																0	0.00
95.4																0	0.00
	0	0	0	0	0	0	0	0	0	0	0	0	0	0	0	0	0.00
Total	1	1	1	1	1	1	3	18	13	1	1	1	1	1	4	49	100

HOUSE 1															
	412			405			404		409			410		Total	
FAMILY	4051	4052	4070	4053	4054	4069	4055	4067	4056	4058	4060	4010	4062	#	%
5														0	0.00
5.1	3		1			2	1	4		3			3	17	7.49
5.2	5		1	1		1	1						1	10	4.41
5.3														0	0.00
5.4	1													1	0.44
5.5														0	0.00
	9	0	2	1	0	3	2	4	0	3	0	0	4	28	12.33
10														0	0.00
10.1								2						2	0.88
10.2														0	0.00
10.3														0	0.00
10.4														0	0.00
	0	0	0	0	0	0	0	2	0	0	0	0	0	2	0.88
15														0	0.00
15.1	3	2				2	2		1	1				11	4.85
15.2														0	0.00
	3	2	0	0	0	2	2	0	1	1	0	0	0	11	4.85
20														0	0.00
20.1														0	0.00
20.2														0	0.00
	0	0	0	0	0	0	0	0	0	0	0	0	0	0	0.00
25														0	0.00
25.1	1		2	2									2	7	3.08
25.2														0	0.00
25.3														0	0.00
25.4													1	1	0.44
25.5								1						1	0.44
	1	0	2	2	0	0	0	1	0	0	0	0	3	9	3.96
30														0	0.00
30.1														0	0.00
30.2														0	0.00
30.3														0	0.00
	0	0	0	0	0	0	0	0	0	0	0	0	0	0	0.00
35														0	0.00
35.1														0	0.00
35.2			2										1	3	1.32
35.3														0	0.00
35.4														0	0.00
35.5							1							1	0.44
	0	0	2	0	0	0	1	0	0	0	0	0	1	4	1.76
40														0	0.00
40.1														0	0.00
40.2	1													1	0.44
40.3														0	0.00
	1	0	0	0	0	0	0	0	0	0	0	0	0	1	0.44
45														0	0.00
45.1														0	0.00
45.2														0	0.00
45.3														0	0.00
45.4														0	0.00
	0	0	0	0	0	0	0	0	0	0	0	0	0	0	0.00
50														0	0.00
50.1	2		2		1	1	1						2	9	3.96
50.2	2		1	1		3	1		2				6	16	7.05
50.3	1											1	5	7	3.08
50.4	1						1	2				1		5	2.20
50.5	2		2				2	1		1			2	10	4.41
50.6								1						1	0.44
50.7														0	0.00
	8	0	5	1	1	4	5	4	2	1	0	2	15	48	21.15

HOUSE 1															
	412			405			404		409			410		Total	
FAMILY	4051	4052	4070	4053	4054	4069	4055	4067	4056	4058	4060	4010	4062	#	%
55														0	0.00
55.1	4	1	1		1		1	1					2	11	4.85
55.2	2			1										3	1.32
55.3														0	0.00
	6	1	1	1	1	0	1	1	0	0	0	0	2	14	6.17
60														0	0.00
60.1	28	1	1	1	4	2	6	6	1	1	1	2	8	62	27.31
60.2										1				1	0.44
60.3														0	0.00
60.4														0	0.00
	28	1	1	1	4	2	6	6	1	2	1	2	8	63	27.75
65														0	0.00
65.1													1	1	0.44
65.2									1					1	0.44
65.3														0	0.00
65.4														0	0.00
	0	0	0	0	0	0	0	0	1	0	0	0	1	2	0.88
70														0	0.00
70.1	1													1	0.44
70.2	6	2	3	4	1	1	2	2				1	7	29	12.78
70.3	5	2	2					4					1	14	6.17
70.4														0	0.00
70.5														0	0.00
70.6														0	0.00
70.7														0	0.00
70.8														0	0.00
	12	4	5	4	1	1	2	6	0	0	0	1	8	44	19.38
75														0	0.00
75.1														0	0.00
75.2														0	0.00
75.3														0	0.00
75.4														0	0.00
	0	0	0	0	0	0	0	0	0	0	0	0	0	0	0.00
80														0	0.00
80.1														0	0.00
80.2														0	0.00
80.3														0	0.00
	0	0	0	0	0	0	0	0	0	0	0	0	0	0	0.00
85														0	0.00
85.1											1			1	0.44
85.2														0	0.00
85.3														0	0.00
	0	0	0	0	0	0	0	0	0	0	1	0	0	1	0.44
90														0	0.00
90.1														0	0.00
90.2														0	0.00
90.3														0	0.00
90.4														0	0.00
90.5														0	0.00
90.6														0	0.00
90.7														0	0.00
90.8														0	0.00
90.9														0	0.00
	0	0	0	0	0	0	0	0	0	0	0	0	0	0	0.00
95														0	0.00
95.1														0	0.00
95.2														0	0.00
95.3														0	0.00
95.4														0	0.00
	0	0	0	0	0	0	0	0	0	0	0	0	0	0	0.00
Total	68	8	18	10	7	12	19	24	5	7	2	5	42	227	100

HOUSE 2					
FAMILY	400	401	402	Total	
	4006	4084	4074	#	%
5				0	0.00
5.1	3			3	3.61
5.2	2		1	3	3.61
5.3				0	0.00
5.4	1			1	1.20
5.5				0	0.00
	6	0	1	7	8.43
10				0	0.00
10.1				0	0.00
10.2	1			1	1.20
10.3	1			1	1.20
10.4				0	0.00
	2	0	0	2	2.41
15				0	0.00
15.1				0	0.00
15.2				0	0.00
	0	0	0	0	0.00
20				0	0.00
20.1				0	0.00
20.2				0	0.00
	0	0	0	0	0.00
25				0	0.00
25.1	1			1	1.20
25.2				0	0.00
25.3				0	0.00
25.4	1			1	1.20
25.5	1			1	1.20
	3	0	0	3	3.61
30				0	0.00
30.1				0	0.00
30.2				0	0.00
30.3				0	0.00
	0	0	0	0	0.00
35				0	0.00
35.1				0	0.00
35.2		1		1	1.20
35.3				0	0.00
35.4				0	0.00
35.5				0	0.00
	0	1	0	1	1.20
40				0	0.00
40.1				0	0.00
40.2				0	0.00
40.3				0	0.00
	0	**0**	**0**	**0**	**0.00**
45				0	0.00
45.1				0	0.00
45.2				0	0.00
45.3				0	0.00
45.4				0	0.00
	0	0	0	0	0.00
50				0	0.00
50.1	3	1		4	4.82
50.2	5	4	1	10	12.05
50.3	3			3	3.61
50.4		2		2	2.41
50.5	1			1	1.20
50.6				0	0.00
50.7				0	0.00
	12	7	1	20	24.10

HOUSE 2					
FAMILY	400	401	402	Total	
	4006	4084	4074	#	%
55				0	0.00
55.1	3		1	4	4.82
55.2	1			1	1.20
55.3				0	0.00
	4	0	1	5	6.02
60				0	0.00
60.1	10	7	3	20	24.10
60.2				0	0.00
60.3				0	0.00
60.4				0	0.00
	10	7	3	20	24.10
65				0	0.00
65.1	1	1		2	2.41
65.2				0	0.00
65.3				0	0.00
65.4				0	0.00
	1	1	0	2	2.41
70				0	0.00
70.1	1	1		2	2.41
70.2	5	4		9	10.84
70.3	3	3	2	8	9.64
70.4				0	0.00
70.5				0	0.00
70.6				0	0.00
70.7				0	0.00
70.8				0	0.00
	9	8	2	19	22.89
75				0	0.00
75.1				0	0.00
75.2				0	0.00
75.3				0	0.00
75.4				0	0.00
	0	0	0	0	0.00
80				0	0.00
80.1				0	0.00
80.2		1		1	1.20
80.3				0	0.00
	0	1	0	1	1.20
85				0	0.00
85.1	1	1		2	2.41
85.2	1			1	1.20
85.3				0	0.00
	2	1	0	3	3.61
90				0	0.00
90.1				0	0.00
90.2				0	0.00
90.3				0	0.00
90.4				0	0.00
90.5				0	0.00
90.6				0	0.00
90.7				0	0.00
90.8				0	0.00
90.9				0	0.00
	0	0	0	0	0.00
95				0	0.00
95.1				0	0.00
95.2				0	0.00
95.3				0	0.00
95.4				0	0.00
	0	0	0	0	0.00
Total	49	26	8	83	100

HOUSE 3							
	414	413			408	Total	
FAMILY	4085	4049	4065	4050	4037	#	%
5						0	0.00
5.1	1		1			2	2.90
5.2	2	1	2		2	7	10.14
5.3						0	0.00
5.4						0	0.00
5.5						0	0.00
	3	1	3	0	2	9	13.04
10						0	0.00
10.1						0	0.00
10.2						0	0.00
10.3						0	0.00
10.4						0	0.00
	0	0	0	0	0	0	0.00
15						0	0.00
15.1			1			1	1.45
15.2						0	0.00
	0	0	1	0	0	1	1.45
20						0	0.00
20.1			1			1	1.45
20.2						0	0.00
	0	0	1	0	0	1	1.45
25						0	0.00
25.1					1	1	1.45
25.2						0	0.00
25.3						0	0.00
25.4				1		1	1.45
25.5	1					1	1.45
	1	0	0	1	1	3	4.35
30						0	0.00
30.1						0	0.00
30.2						0	0.00
30.3						0	0.00
	0	0	0	0	0	0	0.00
35						0	0.00
35.1						0	0.00
35.2			1			1	1.45
35.3						0	0.00
35.4						0	0.00
35.5						0	0.00
	0	0	1	0	0	1	1.45
40						0	0.00
40.1						0	0.00
40.2						0	0.00
40.3						0	0.00
	0	0	0	0	0	0	0.00
45						0	0.00
45.1						0	0.00
45.2						0	0.00
45.3						0	0.00
45.4						0	0.00
	0	0	0	0	0	0	0.00
50						0	0.00
50.1			1	2		3	4.35
50.2			1	1		2	2.90
50.3				1		1	1.45
50.4			1	1		2	2.90
50.5			1		2	3	4.35
50.6						0	0.00
50.7						0	0.00
	0	0	4	5	2	11	15.94

HOUSE 3							
	414	413			408	Total	
FAMILY	4085	4049	4065	4050	4037	#	%
55						0	0.00
55.1					1	1	1.45
55.2	1				1	2	2.90
55.3						0	0.00
	1	0	0	0	2	3	4.35
60						0	0.00
60.1	2	7	4	1	6	20	28.99
60.2						0	0.00
60.3						0	0.00
60.4						0	0.00
	2	7	4	1	6	20	28.99
65						0	0.00
65.1						0	0.00
65.2						0	0.00
65.3						0	0.00
65.4						0	0.00
	0	0	0	0	0	0	0.00
70						0	0.00
70.1						0	0.00
70.2	1	1	5		1	8	11.59
70.3		1	2	1	3	7	10.14
70.4						0	0.00
70.5						0	0.00
70.6						0	0.00
70.7						0	0.00
70.8						0	0.00
	1	2	7	1	4	15	21.74
75						0	0.00
75.1						0	0.00
75.2						0	0.00
75.3						0	0.00
75.4						0	0.00
	0	0	0	0	0	0	0.00
80						0	0.00
80.1			1		1	2	2.90
80.2					1	1	1.45
80.3						0	0.00
	0	0	1	0	2	3	4.35
85						0	0.00
85.1			2			2	2.90
85.2						0	0.00
85.3						0	0.00
	0	0	2	0	0	2	2.90
90						0	0.00
90.1						0	0.00
90.2						0	0.00
90.3						0	0.00
90.4						0	0.00
90.5						0	0.00
90.6						0	0.00
90.7						0	0.00
90.8						0	0.00
90.9						0	0.00
	0	0	0	0	0	0	0.00
95						0	0.00
95.1						0	0.00
95.2						0	0.00
95.3						0	0.00
95.4						0	0.00
	0	0	0	0	0	0	0.00
Total	8	10	24	8	19	69	100

Appendix B: Concordance of Numbers used for Pottery

Each complete vessel and diagnostic sherd has its own unique *Pottery Number*. A selection of these, usually complete or almost complete vessels, also received an *Object Number*, by which they were entered in the Object Catalogue for Tell Khaiber, with one or more individual photographs, along with non-pottery finds. Some of these were then selected by the SBAH staff working with us to be sent to the Iraq Museum at the end of each season, and each of these (or sometimes a group) has a *TK1 Number*, by which it is identified in the separate Arabic language catalogue for the site, and at the museum. A selection made from the latter (again, individual or groups) has been given Iraq Museum (*IM*) numbers, for which we do not have a record.

Sherd No.	Object No.	TK1 No.
p0.1	0:7	
p0.98	0:20	
p1005.3	1005:3	TK1 43
p1005.66	1005:2	TK1 3
p1005.7	1005:7	TK1 1
p1005.71	1005:29	
p1005.8	1005:8	TK1 2
p1010.14	1010:14	
p1010.48	1010:13	
p1037.27	1037:3	
p1039:105	1039:8	TK1 75
p1068.36	1068:19	TK1 124
p1073.78	1073:12	TK1 150
p1073.79	1073:10	TK1 152
p1073.80	1073:23	TKI 265
p1074.31	1074:3	TK1 153
p1078.1	1078:3	TK1 176
p1078.66	1078:2	TK1 199
p1078.76	1078:11	TK1 322
p1079.112	1079:7	
p1079.142	1079:19	TK1 206
p1079.222	1079:30	TK1 303
p1079.223	1079:8	TK1 303

Sherd No.	Object No.	TK1 No.
p1079.224	1079:42	
p1079.227	1079:11	
p1079.462	1079:76	
p1079.51	1079:60	
p1079.769	1079:83	TK1 320
p1080.11	1080:1	TK1 247
p1080.12	1080:5	TK1 254
p1080.13	1080:11	TK1 301
p1080.14	1080:3	
p1080.15	1080:9	TK1 301
p1080.16	1080:10	TK1 301
p1080.17	1080:15	TK1 301
p1080.18	1080:16	TK1 301
p1080.20	1080:14	
p1080.21	1080:2	
p1080.22	1080:13	
p1080.28	1080:17	
p1080.7	1080:4	TK1 203
p1085.17	1085:3	TK1 321
p1092.47	1092:3	TK1 385
p1094.192	1094:18	TK1 387
p1094.194	1094:21	
p1096.456	1096:33	TK1 515

Sherd No.	Object No.	TK1 No.
p1097.1	1097:1	TK1 505
p1098.1	1098:1	TK1 497
p1137.35	1137:1	TK1 605
p1137.4	1137:5	
p1139.108	1139:6	
p1139.110	1139:22	TK1 626
p1139.126	1139:28	TK1 605
p1139.78	1139:5	TK1 605
p1139.89	1139:21	
p1142.18	1142:4	TK1 605
p1142.50	1142:3	
p1142.8	1142:2	TK1 605
p1157.215	1157:1	
p1157.54	1157:8	TK1 663
p1159.1	1159:1	
p1163.12	1163:2	
p1166.117	1166:25	
p1166.118	1166:29	
p1166.119	1166:27	
p1166.203	1166:1	
p1166.204	1166:24	
p1166.205	1166:43	TK1 704
p1166.68	1166:11	TK1 697

Sherd No.	Object No.	TK1 No.
p1166.69	1166:18	
p1166.70	1166:12	
p1166.71	1166:23	TK1 690
p1167.6	1167:3	TK1 688
p2.3	2:3	TK1 41
p2000.4	2000:4	TK1 42
p3001.1	3001:1	
p3002.2	3002:2	TK1 40
p3006.12	3006:12	TK1 36
p3009.1	3009:1	TK1 4
p3009.17	3009:17	TK1 39
p3015.2	3015:2	TK1 34
p3025.1	3025:16	
p3025.2	3025:3	TK1 71
p3025.3	3025:20	TK1 72
p3025.82	3025:35	
p3054.21	3054:27	TK1 251
p3054.22	3054:23	TK1 253
p3054.249	3054:20	TK1 310
p3054.267	3054:48	TK1 441
p3054.3	3054:22	TK1 249
p3054.341	3054:47	TK1 440
p3054.342	3054:56	TK1 441
p3054.396	3054:53	TK1 441
p3054.397	3054:46	TK1 441
p3054.399	3054:69	TK1 438
p3054.4	3054:6	TK1 250
p3054.400	3054:51	
p3054.401	3054:52	TK1 441
p3054.402	3054:71	
p3054.403	3054:65	TK1 502
p3054.405	3054:55	TK1 509
p3054.49	3054:31	TK1 258
p3054.5	3054:28	TK1 248
p3054.50	3054:5	
p3054.51	3054:21	TK1 310
p3054.52	3054:24	TK1 310
p3058.14	3058:2	TK1 148
p3058.15	3058:3	
p3064.1	3064:1	TK1 125
p3064.226	3064:61	TK1 319
p3064.276	3064:91	TK1 317
p3064.445	3064:103	TK1 317
p3064.489	3064:105	TK1 319
p3064.564	3064:99	TK1 319
p3064.565	3064:112	TK1 511

Sherd No.	Object No.	TK1 No.
p3064.577	3064:109	TK1 380
p3064.653	3064:126	TK1 514
p3064.677	3064:134	
p3064.678	3064:130	
p3075.1	3075:1	
p3075.2	3075:2	
p3079.10	3079:3	TK1 386
p3079.9	3079:2	TK1 386
p3080.4	3080:8	TK1 383
p3080.79	3080:30	
p3084.15	3084:3	TK1 384
p3084.16	3084:12	TK1 384
p3084.33	3084:11	TK1 384
p3084.34	3084:15	TK1 500
p3084.35	3084:4	TK1 508
p3084.37	3084:19	
p3084.4	3084:2	TK1 384
p3085.121	3085:40	
p3085.122	3085:1	TK1 437
p3085.123	3085:12	TK1 437
p3085.124	3085:11	TK1 437
p3085.125	3085:26	TK1 437
p3085.126	3085:22	TK1 437
p3085.127	3085:31	TK1 437
p3085.129	3085:50	TK1 437
p3085.130	3085:21	TK1 437
p3085.23	3085:10	TK1 388
p3085.281	3085:55	
p3085.283	3085:6	
p3085.336	3085:29	
p3087.14	3087:1	TK1 439
p3087.15	3087:4	TK1 498
p3088.181	3088:16	TK1 504
p3088.182	3088:20	
p3088.183	3088:6	
p3088.31	3088:14	TK1 512
p3091.1	3091:2	TK1 514
p3091.2	3091:3	
p3091.3	3091:1	
p3098.9	3098:1	TK1 514
p3099.13	3099:2	TK1 514
p3102.2	3102:2	TK1 516
p3119.18	3119:2	
p3119.55	3119:5	
p3124.12	3124:3	TK1 606
p3154.23	3154:2	

Sherd No.	Object No.	TK1 No.
p3159.1	3159:2	
p3159.8	3159:8	
p3159.9	3159:7	
p3168.1	3168:1	
p3168.25	3168:6	
p3168.59	3168:7	
p3176.154	3176:21	
p3185.108	3185:16	
p3185.30	3185:1	
p3185.78	3185:11	
p3185.82	3185:10	TK1 681
p3186.20	3186:3	
p3189.3	3189:3	
p4006.12	4006:12	TK1 204
p4010.7	4010:4	TK1 76
p4010.8	4010:3	
p4011.1	4011:2	
p4021.12	4021:3	TK1 73
p4021.13	4021:2	TK1 79
p4021.14	4021:1	TK1 77
p4034.28	4034:1	TK1 74
p4034.29	4034:6	TK1 127
p4034.31	4034:2	TK1 120
p4036.20	4036:10	
p4038.1	4038:2	
p4038.2	4038:3	
p4041.1	4041:1	TK1 70
p4043.8	4043:1	TK1 126
p4053.14	4053:2	TK1 154
p4056.10	4056:1	TK1 200
p4056.11	4056:2	TK1 207
p4062.26	4062:2	TK1 201
p4066.19	4066:3	TK1 205
p4067.23	4067:2	TK1 198
p4067.24	4067:1	TK1 208
p4084.1	4084:1	TK1 202
p4084.53	4084:7	TK1 259
p4084.54	4084:6	
p4085.1	4085:5	TK1 302
p5007.4	5007:6	
p5007.42	5007:2	
p5008.22	5008:6	
p5016.1	5016:6	
p5016.11	5016:4	
p5016.12	5016:8	
p5016.2	5016:5	

Sherd No.	Object No.	TK1 No.
p5016.3	5016:7	
p5016.8	5016:1	
p5016.9	5016:3	
p5018.1	5018:1	
p5019.2	5019:1	
p5022.11	5022:1	
p5022.12	5022:9	
p5022.13	5022:8	
p5022.40	5022:4	
p5022.54	5022:26	
p5022.55	5022:25	
p5022.56	5022:20	
p5022.57	5022:16	
p5022.58	5022:22	
p5022.59	5022:18	
p5022.60	5022:19	
p5022.61	5022:21	
p5022.62	5022:17	
p5022.63	5022:24	
p5022.64	5022:23	
p5022.65	5022:15	
p5022.66	5022:27	
p5024.1	5024:1	TK1 702
p5029.1	5029:1	
p5040.20	5040:4	
p5045.1	5045:1	TK1 703
p5045.10	5045:4	TK1 682
p5045.9	5045:3	TK1 698
p5053.1	5053:2	
p5060.1	5060:1	
p5063.1	5063:1	
p6036.10	6036:6	TK1 121
p6036.11	6036:4	TK1 122
p6036.116	6036:42	
p6036.117	6036:13	TK1 149
p6036.118	6036:11	TK1 151
p6036.119	6036:16	
p6036.123	6036:7	
p6042.32	6042:5	
p6042.40	6042:4	TK1 311
p6049.1	6049:1	TK1 123
p6059.174	6059:17	
p6059.27	6059:13	TK1 256
p6059.28	6059:6	TK1 252
p6059.6	6059:14	TK1 257
p6059.7	6059:16	TK1 255

Sherd No.	Object No.	TK1 No.
p6060.3	6060:2	
p6062.3	6062:2	TK1 323
p6065.1	6065:1	TK1 324
p6068.1	6068:2	TK1 318
p6068.41	6068:6	TK1 499
p6068.42	6068:5	TK1 318
p6068.43	6068:4	TK1 318
p6068.44	6068:3	TK1 318
p6068.45	6068:1	TK1 382
p6068.46	6068:9	
p6070.40	6070:5	
p6078.27	6078:7	TK1 381
p6078.79	6078:9	TK1 381
p6088.14	6088:3	TK1 501
p6091.1	6091:5	TK1 517
p6092.1	6092:1	
p6093.1	6093:1	
p6111.68	6111:7	
p6111.69	6111:16	
p6111.70	6111:16	
p6111.71	6111:19	
p6116.67	6116:7	
p6118.43	6118:9	TK1 607
p6122.1	6122:1	
p6124.19	6124:2	TK1 518
p6124.27	6124:3	TK1 518
p6125.1	6125:1	
p6126.1	6126:1	
p6126.46	6126:5	TK1 518
p6126.47	6126:7	TK1 518
p6127.2	6127:1	TK1 518
p6136.127	6136:10	TK1 607
p6136.132	6136:11	TK1 607
p6136.89	6136:7	TK1 607
p6136.90	6136:2	
p6141.1	6141:1	
p6156.5	6156:1	TK1 626
p6156.7	6156:3	
p6161.6	6161:1	
p6163.33	6163:9	
p6163.34	6163:8	
p6163.54	6163:13	
p6163.64	6163:5	
p6165.27	6165:8	
p6165.38	6165:3	
p6165.43	6165:7	

Sherd No.	Object No.	TK1 No.
p6165.44	6165:2	TK1 707
p6166.1	6166:1	
p6166.21	6166:4	
p6166.22	6166:3	
p6166.41	6166:6	
p6175.40	6175:8	
p6178.33	6178:3	
p6178.34	6178:1	
p6178.35	6178:4	
p7006.1	7006:5	
p7006.2	7006:7	
p7006.67	7006:6	TK1 379
p7011.1	7011:1	
p7011.44	7011:4	TK1 389
p7046.1	7046:1	TK1 397
p8008.9	8008:1	TK1 519
p8013.1	8013:14	TK1 519
p8013.10	8013:15	
p8013.11	8013:11	
p8013.12	8013:22	
p8013.13	8013:17	
p8013.14	8013:19	
p8013.2	8013:16	TK1 519
p8013.7	8013:21	
p8013.9	8013:10	TK1 626
p8016.7	8016:3	TK1 519
p8016.8	8016:4	TK1 519
p8018.24	8018:2	TK1 626
p8021.1	8021:1	TK1 519
p8021.11	8021:5	
p8029.3	8029:3	
p8029.4	8029:4	
p8032.19	8032:3	TK1 608
p8032.37	8032:5	
p8032.37	8032:6	TK1 608
p8047.2	8047:1	
p8051.4	8051:1	
p8058.6	8058:3	
p8074.13	8074:2	
p8075.25	8075:2	
p8082.1	8082:1	
p8082.16	8082:2	
p8083.1	8083:15	
p8083.16	8083:3	
p8083.17	8083:7	TK1 699
p8083.22	8083:6	

Sherd No.	Object No.	TK1 No.
p8083.23	8083:8	
p8083.45	8083:12	
p8083.46	8083:2	
p8083.6	8083:4	
p9001.10	9001:12	
p9001.11	9001:8	
p9001.12	9001:19	TK1 694
p9001.13	9001:18	
p9001.14	9001:15	
p9001.15	9001:9	TK1 693
p9001.16	9001:5	
p9001.17	9001:6	
p9001.18	9001:16	
p9001.6	9001:10	TK1 683
p9001.7	9001:14	
p9001.8	9001:7	
p9001.9	9001:13	
p9002.1	9002:10	TK1 696
p9002.19	9002:3	
p9002.4	9002:5	TK1 695
p9002.5	9002:4	
p9002.7	9002:9	
p9002.8	9002:1	TK1 684
p9002.9	9002:2	
p9018.34	9018:15	
p9018.35	9018:16	
p9018.36	9018:7	TK1 685
p9018.37	9018:30	
p9018.38	9018:23	TK1 705
p9018.39	9018:27	TK1 733
p9018.40	9018:24	
p9018.82	9018:26	TK1 700
p9018.87	9018:33	
p9018.88	9018:4	
p9018.89	9018:32	
p9020.1	9020:5	
p9020.105	9020:27	TK1 734
p9020.106	9020:6	
p9020.107	9020:15	TK1 686
p9020.111	9020:29	
p9020.112	9020:7	TK1 692
p9020.113	9020:31	
p9020.114	9020:2	
p9020.115	9020:36	
p9020.2	9020:12	TK1 689
p9020.39	9020:4	TK1 691
p9020.40	9020:17	
p9020.41	9020:21	TK1 706
p9020.42	9020:22	
p9020.43	9020:34	
p9020.87	9020:28	TK1 687
p9022.7	9022:1	
p9023.5	9023:7	
p9023.6	9023:9	
p9023.7	9023:8	

Bibliography

Adams, R, McC. 1981. *Heartland of Cities: Surveys of Ancient Settlement and Land Use on the Central Floodplain of the Euphrates.* Chicago: University of Chicago Press.

Adams, W. V., and Adams, E. W. 1991. *Archaeological Typology and Practical Reality: A Dialectical Approach to Artifact Classification and Sorting.* Cambridge: Cambridge University Press.

Adams, R, McC., and Nissen, H. J. 1972. *The Uruk Countryside: The Natural Setting of Urban Societies.* Chicago: University of Chicago Press.

Allison, P. M. 2006. Mapping for Gender. Interpreting Artefact Distribution Inside 1st- and 2nd- century A.D. forts in Roman Germany. *Archaeological Dialogues,* 13(1): 1–20.

Allison, P. M. 2009. Understanding Pompeian Households Practices Through Their Material Culture. *FACTA: A Journal of Roman Material Culture Studies,* 3: 11–33.

Al-Hamdani, A. 2015. Shadow States: The Archaeology of Power in the Marshes of Southern Mesopotamia. Ph.D. thesis, Stony Brook University.

Andre-Salvini, B. 2000. The Cuneiform Tablets of Qal'at al-Bahrain. In Crawford, H., and Rice, M. (eds.), *Traces of Paradise. The Archaeology of Bahrain 2500 BC–300 AD.* London: The Dilmun Committee, London, 112–4.

André-Salvini, B., and Lombard, P. 1997. La découverte épigraphique de 1995 à Qal'at al-Bahrein: un Jalon pour la chronologie de la phase Dilmoun Moyen dans le Golfe arabe. *Proceedings of the Seminar for Arabian Studies,* 27: 165–70.

Armstrong, J, A. 1992. West of Edin: Tell al-Deylam and the Babylonian City of Dilbat. *Biblical Archaeologist,* 55: 219–26.

Armstrong, J, A. 1993. Pottery. In Zettler, R. L. (ed.), *Nippur III: Kassite Buildings in Area WC-1.* Chicago: The Chicago University Press, 67–80.

Armstrong, J, A. 2001. Late Old Babylonian Pottery from Area B at Tell ed-Deylam (Dilbat). In Breniquet, C., and Kepinski, C (eds.), *Etudes Mésopotamiennes: Recueil de textes offert à Jean-Louis Huot.* Paris, 1–20.

Armstrong, J, A. 2017. Babylonian Pottery in the Kassite Period. In Bartelmus, A., and Sternitzke, K. (eds.), *Karduniaš. Babyonia Under the Kassites. Vol. II. The Proceedings of the Symposium Held in Munich, 30 June to 2 July 2011.* Berlin: de Gruyter, 437–78.

Armstrong, J. A., and Brandt, M. C. 1994. Ancient Dunes at Nippur. In Gasche, H. (ed.), *Cinquante-deux réflexions sur le Proche-orient ancien offertes en hommage à Léon De Meyer.* MHEM 2. Leuven: Peeters, 255–63.

Armstrong, J. A., and Gasche, H. 2014. *Mesopotamian Pottery: a guide to the Babylonian tradition in the second millennium B.C.* MHEM II, VI. University of Ghent and the Oriental Institute of the University of Chicago.

Ayoub, S. 1982. *Die Keramik in Mesopotamien und in den Nachbargebieten.* Munich: Mäander.

Barley, N. 1994. *Smashing Pots: Feats of Clay from Africa.* London: British Museum Press.

Berg, I. 2007. Meaning in the Making: the potter's wheel at Phylakopi, Melos (Greece). *Journal of Anthropological Archaeology,* 26: 234–52.

Berg, I. 2008. Looking Through Pots: recent advances in ceramics X-radiography. *Journal of Archaeological Science,* 35: 1177–88.

Berg, I. 2011. Exploring the Chaîne Opératoire of Ceramics through X-radiography. In Scarcella, S. (ed.), *Archaeological Ceramics: A Review of Current Research.* British Archaeological Reports 2193. Oxford: Archaeopress, 57–63.

Berg, I. 2013. The Potter's Wheel in Mycenaean Greece: a re-assessment. In Graziadjo, G., Guglielmino, R., Lenuzza, V., and Vitale, S. (eds.), Φιλική Συναυλία: *Studies in Mediterranean Archaeology for Mario Benzi.* British Archaeological Reports 2460. Oxford: Archaeopress, 113–21.

Berg, I. 2015. Potting Skill and Learning Networks in Bronze Age Crete. In Gauß, W. Klebinder-Gauß, G. von Rueden, C (eds.), *The Transmission of Technical Knowledge in the Production of Ancient Mediterranean Pottery: Proceedings of the International Conference at the Austrian Archaeological Institute at Athens 23rd–25th November 2012.* Österreichisches Archäologisches Institut Sonderschriften Band 54, 17–34.

Berg, I. 2020. The Potter's Wheel. In Smith, C. (ed.), *Encyclopaedia of Global Archaeology. 2nd ed.* Springer, 1–13.

Berg, I., and Ambers, J. 2012. Identifying Forming Techniques in Knossian Bronze Age pottery: The Potential of X-Radiography. In Andreadaki-Vlazaki, M. M. (ed.), Πεπραγμένα Ι› Διεθνούς Κρητολογικού Συνεδρίου. Vol. A' 3. Chania: Φιλολογικός Σύλλογος "Ο Χρυσόστομος, 367–80.

Bergamini, G. 2002–3. *Introduzione.* In Bergamini, G., Gabutti, A., and Valtz, E. (eds.), La ceramic di Tell Yelkhi. *Mesopotamia*, 37–38: 5–20.

Black, J. A. 1991. *Sumerian Grammar in Babylonian Theory.* Biblical Institute Press.

Black, J., George, A., and Postgate, N. 2000. *A Concise Dictionary of Akkadian. 2nd printing. SANTAG Vol. 5.* Wiesebaden: Harrasowitz Verlag.

Blackman, M. J., Stein, G, J., and Vandiver, P. B. 1993. The Standardization Hypothesis and Ceramic Mass Production: Technological, Compositional, and Metric Indexes of Craft Specialization at Tell Leilan, Syria. *American Antiquity,* 58(1): 60–80.

Boehmer, R. M., and Dämmer, H. W. 1985. *Tell Imlihiye, Tell Zubeidi, Tell Abbas.* Baghdader Forschungen, 7. Mainz am Rhein: von Zabern.

Boivin, O. 2015. Kār-Šamaš as a South-Western Palace Town of the Sealand I Kingdom. *Nouvelles Assyriologiques Brèves et Utilitaires,* 4(97): 162–4.

Boivin, O. 2018. *The First Dynasty of the Sealand in Mesopotamia.* SANER, 20. Berlin: De Gruyter.

Bowser, B. 2000. From Pottery to Politics: An Ethnoarchaological Study of Political Factionalism, Ethnicity, and Domestic Pottery Style in the Ecuadorian Amazon. *Journal of Archaeological Method and Theory,* 7(3): 219–48

Brinkman, J. A. 1976. *Materials and studies for Kassite history, Volume I.* Chicago: University of Chicago Press.

Brinkman, J. A. 2017. Babylonia Under the Kassites: Some Aspects for Consideration. In Bartelmus, A., and Sternitzke, K. (eds.), *Karduniaš. Babyonia Under the Kassites. Vol. 1. The Proceedings of the Symposium Held in Munich, 30 June to 2 July 2011.* Berlin: De Gruyter, 1–44.

Bronitsky, G., and Hamer, R. 1986. Experiments in Ceramic Technology: The Effects of Various Tempering Materials on Impact and Thermal-Shock Resistance. *American Antiquity,* 51(1): 89–101.

Bürger, U. 2011. Some Remarks on "Old Babylonian" Pottery. In Miglus, P. A., and Mühl, S. (eds.), *Between the Cultures. The Central Tigris Region From the 3rd to the 1st Millennium BC. Conference at Heidelberg, January 22nd–24th, 2009.* Heidelberg: Heidelberger Orientverlag, 157–64.

Calderbank, D. 2018. Moulding Clay to Model Sealand Society: Pottery Production and Function at Tell Khaiber, Southern Iraq. Ph.D. thesis, University of Manchester.

Calderbank, D. 2020a. Gulf Connections at Tell Khaiber. Interpreting Standardised Pottery Styles in the Sealand Period. In Otto, A., Herles, M., and Kaniuth, K. (eds.), *Proceedings of the 11th International Congress on the Archaeology of the Ancient Near East,* München, Volume 2. Wiesebaden: Harassowitz, 31–42.

Calderbank, D. 2020b. Dispersed Communities of Practice During the First Dynasty of the Sealand: The Pottery from Tell Khaiber, Southern Iraq. In Paulus, S., and Clayden, T. (eds.), *Babylonia Under the Sealand and Kassite Dynasties.* SANER. Berlin: De Gruyter, 57–86.

Calderbank, D. 2021. What's in a Vessel's Name? A Relational Text-Object Approach to the Uses of Mesopotamian Pottery. *American Journal of Archaeology,* 125(1): 29–64.

Calderbank, D. in prep. 'The Early Pottery from Tell Khaiber'.

Calderbank, D., and Moon, J. 2017. A Ceramic Assemblage of the Early Literate Periods from Sumer. In Heffron, Y., Stone, A., and Worthington, M (eds.), *At the Dawn of History. Ancient Near Eastern Studies in Honour of J. N. Postgate. Volume 1.* Indiana: Eisenbrauns, 73–84.

Campbell, S., Calderbank, D., Moon, J., and Killick, R. 2017. A Kassite Settlement in southern Babylonia: Investigations at Tell Khaiber 2. *Sumer,* 63: 93–108.

Campbell, S., Moon, J., Killick, R., Calderbank, D., Robson, E., Shepperson, M., and Slater, F. 2017. Tell Khaiber: An Administrative Centre of the Sealand Period. *Iraq,* 79: 21–46.

Carr, C. 1990. Advances in Ceramic Radiography and Analysis: Applications and Potentials. *Journal of Archaeological Science,* 17: 13–34.

Cavigneaux, A., and André-Salvini, B. forthcoming. Cuneiform Tablets from Qal'at. Dilmun and the Sealand at the Dawn of the Kassite Era. In Lombard. P., and Al-Sindi, Kh. (eds.), *Twenty Years of Bahrain Archaeology, 1986–2006.* Actes de colloque international de Manama, 9–12 décembre 2007. Bahrain: Ministry of Culture.

Charpin, D. 1986. *Le Clerge d'Ur au siecle d'Hammurabi.* Geneva: Librairie Droz.

Charpin, D. 1988. Le Repli des Cultes Sumeriens en Babylonie du Nord. *Nouvelles Assyriologiques Brèves et Utilitaires,* 22(2).

Charpin, D. 1990. A Contribution to the Geography and History of the Kingdom of Kahat. In Eichler, S., Wäfler, M., and Warburton, D. (eds.), *Tell al-Hamidiya 2.* Fribourg, 67–85.

Choleva, M. 2012. The First Wheelmade Pottery at Lerna: wheel-thrown or wheel-fashioned? *Hersperia,* 81: 343–81.

Civil, M. 1996. *HAR-ra = hubullu: Tablet X dug = karpatu.* Published with Sallaberger, W. *Der_Babylonische Töpfer und seine Gefässe.* In DeMeyer L. and Gasche H. (eds.). MHEM 2/3. Ghent: University of Ghent, 129–63.

Clayden, T. 1989. *Aspects of the Early History of the Kassites and the Archaeology of the Kassite Period in Iraq (c.1600–1150 BC).* Oxford: Oxford University Press.

Clayden, T. 2020. Ur in the Kassite Period. In Clayden, T., and Paulus, S. (eds.), *Babylonia Under the Sealand and Kassite Dynasties.* SANER. Berlin: De Gruyter, 88–124.

Cole, S. W. 2014. Chronology Revisited. In Armstrong, J. A. and Gasche, H. (eds.), *Mesopotamian Pottery: a guide to the Babylonian tradition in the second millennium B.C.* MHEM II, VI. University of Ghent and the Oriental Institute of the University of Chicago, 3–5.

Courty, M. A., and Roux, V. 1995. Identification of Wheel Throwing on the Basis of Ceramic Surface Features and Microfabrics. *Journal of Archaeological Science,* 22: 17–50.

Crawford, H. 1996. Dilmun, Victim of World Recession. *Proceedings of the Seminar for Arabian Studies,* 26: 13–22.

Dalley, S. 1989. *Myths from Mesopotamia: Creation, the Flood, Gilgamesh, and Others.* Oxford: Oxford University Press.

Dalley, S. 2009. *Babylonian Tablets from the First Sealand Dynasty in the Schøyen Collection.* CUSAS 9; Bethesda: CDL Press.

Dalley, S. 2013. Gods from north-eastern and north-western Arabia in cuneiform texts from the First Sealand Dynasty, and a cuneiform inscription from Tell en-Nasbeh, c.1500 BC. *Arabian Archaeology and Epigraphy,* 25: 177–85.

Deetz, J. 1967. *Invitation to Archaeology.* Garden City: Natural History Press.

Deschesne, O. 1996. Le bitumen dans l'antiquité*. In Connan, J., and Deschesne, O. (eds.), Le bitume* á *Suse. Collection du Musée du Louvre.* Paris: Elf Aquitaine, 18–46.

Dougherty, R. P. 1932. *The Sealand of Ancient Arabia.* Connecticut: Yale University Press.

Duistermaat, K. 2007. Not Fit for Firing: Unfired Vessel Fragments from Late Bronze Age Tell Sabi Abyad, Syria, and Their Value for the Study of Pottery Technology. *Leiden Journal of Pottery Studies,* 23: 21–40.

Duistermaat, K. 2008. *The Pots and Potters of Assyria: Technology and Organisation of Production, Ceramic Sequence, and Vessels Function at Late Bronze Age Tell Sabi Abyad, Syria.* Leiden: Brepols.

Duistermaat, K. 2017. The Organization of Pottery Production: Toward a Relational Approach. In Hunt, A. (ed.), *The Oxford Handbook of Ceramic Analysis.* Oxford: Oxford University press, 114–47.

Edzard, D. O. 1970. *Altbabylonische Rechts- und Wirtschaftsurkunden aus Tell ed-Der im Iraq Museum, Baghdad.* München: Verlag der Bayerischen Akademie der Wissenschaften.

Eidem, J. 1987. The Inscribed Pottery. In Højlund, F. (ed.), *Failaka / Dilmun: The Second Millennium Settlements. Volume 2: The Bronze Age Pottery.* JASP, 17(2). Aarhus: Jutland Archaeological Society, 179–80.

Ellis, R. S. 1958. *Foundation Deposits in Ancient Mesopotamia.* New Haven: Yale University Press.

Ellison, R. 1984a. The Uses of Pottery. *Iraq,* 46(1): 63–8.

Ellison, R. 1984b. Methods of Food Preparation in Mesopotamia (c.3000–600 BC). *Journal of the Economic and Social History of the Orient,* 27(1): 89–98.

Ericson, J. E., and Stickel, E. G. 1973. A Proposed Classification System for Ceramics. *World Archaeology,* 4(3): 357–67.

Forbes, R. J. 1964. *Studies in Ancient Technology 1. Bitumen and Petroleum in Antiquity. The Origin of Alchemy. Water Supply.* Leiden: Brill.

Foster, K. P. 1991. Ceramic Imagery in Ancient Near Eastern Literature. In Vandiver, P. B., Druzik, J, Wheeler, G. S. (eds.), *Materials Issues in Art and Archaeology II: Symposium Held April 17–21, 1990, San Francisco, California, USA.* Pittsburgh, 389–413.

Foster, K. P. 2010. Well-Tempered Words: Ceramic Metaphors in Mesopotamian Literature. In Melville, S. C., and Slotsky, A. L (eds.), *Opening the Tablet Box: Near Eastern Studies in Honour of Benjamin R. Foster.* Culture and Ancient History of the Ancient Near East, 42. Leiden: Brill, 141–54.

Franke, J. A. 1987. Artifact Patterning and Functional Variability in the Urban Dwelling: Old Babylonian Nippur, Iraq. Ph.D. thesis, University of Chicago.

Frankfort, R., Lloyd, S., Jacobsen, T. 1940. *The Gimilsin Temple and the Palace of the Rulers at Tell Asmar.* Oriental Institute Publications, 43. Chicago: University of Chicago Press.

Frink, L., and Harry, K. G. 2008. The Beauty of the "Ugly" Eskimo Cooking Pots. *American Antiquity,* 73(1): 103–20.

Gasche, H. 1973. *La poterie élamite du deuxième millénaire a.C.* Leiden: Brill.

Gasche, H. 1989. *La Babylonie au 17e siècle avant notre* ère*: approche archéologique, problèmes et perspectives.* MHEM 1. Ghent: University of Ghent Press.

Gasche, H., Armstrong, J. A., Cole, S. W., and Gurzadyan, V. G. 1998. *Dating the Fall of Babylon: A Reappraisal of Second-Millennium Chronology.* MHEM II, IV. University of Ghent and the Oriental Institute of the University of Chicago.

Gates, M.-H. 1988. Dialogues between Ancient Near Eastern Texts and the Archaeological Record: Test Cases from Bronze Age Syria. *Bulletin of the American School of Oriental Research,* 270: 63–91.

Gates, M.-H. 2005. Archaeology and the Ancient Near East: Methods and Limitations. In Snell, D. C. (ed.), *A Companion to the Ancient Near East.* London: Blackwell, 63–78.

Gentili, P. 2012. Some Notes Between Yelkhi and 'Dating'. *Mesopotamia,* 47: 103–12.

Ghirshman, R. 1964. Suse. Campagne de fouilles 1962–1963. Rapport préliminaire. *Arts Asiatiques,* 10: 3–20.

Ghirshman, R. 1967. Suse. Campagne de l'hiver 1965–1966. Rapport préliminaire. *Arts Arsiatiques,* 15: 3–27.

Glatz, C. 2012. Bearing the Marks of Control? Reassessing Pot Marks in Late Bronze Age Anatolia. *Journal of Archaeology,* 116(1): 5–38.

Glatz, C. 2015. Introduction: Plain and Simple? Another Look at Plain Pottery Traditions in Early Complex Societies. In Glatz, C (ed.), Plain *Pottery Traditions of the Eastern Mediterranean and Near East: Production, Use, and Social Significance.* California: West Coast Press, 13–37.

Glatz, C., and Casana, J. 2016. Of Highland-Lowland Borderlands: Local Societies and Foreign Power in the Zagros-Mesopotamian Interface. *Journal of Anthropological Archaeology,* 44: 127–47.

Glatz, C., Casana, J., Bendrey, R., Beysal, E., Calderbank, D., Chelazzi, F., Del Bravo, F., Erskine, N., Hald, M., Jacoby Laugier, E., Jensen, E., Perruchini, E. 2019. Babylonian Encounters in the Upper Diyala Valley: Contextualizing the Results of Regional Survey and the 2016–17 Excavations at Khani Masi. *American Journal of Archaeology,* 123(3): 439–71.

Goetze, A. 1964. The Kassite and Near Eastern Chronology. *Journal of Cuneiform Studies,* 18(4): 97–101.

Gosselain, O. P. 1992. Bonfire of the Enquiries. Pottery Firing Temperatures in Archaeology: What For? *Journal of Archaeological Science,* 19: 243–59.

Gosselain, O. P. 1999. In Pots We Trust: The Processing of Clay and Symbols in Sub-Saharan Africa. *Journal of Material Culture,* 4(2): 205–30.

Gosselain, O. P. 2000. Materializing Identities: An African Perspective. *Journal of Archaeological Method and Theory,* 7(3): 187–217.

Grayson, A. K. 1975. *Assyrian and Babylonian Chronicles. Texts from Cuneiform Sources 5.* Locust Valley, NY: J.J. Augustin.

Hamidović, D. 2014. Alphabetical Inscriptions from the Sealand. *Mesopotamica,* 1: 137–55.

Harris, O. J. T. 2017. Assemblages and Scale in Archaeology. *Cambridge Archaeological Journal,* 27(1): 127–39.

Hegmon, M. 1992. Archaeological Research on Style. *Annual Review of Anthropology,* 21: 517–36.

Hegmon, M., and Kulow, S. 2005. Painting as Agency, Style as Structure: Innovations in Mimbres Pottery Designs from Southwest New Mexico. *Journal of Archaeological Method and Theory,* 12(4): 313–34.

Henrickson, R. C. 1991. Wheelmade or Wheel-finished? Interpretation of 'wheelmarks' on pottery. In Vandiver, P. B., Druzik, G. S., and Wheeler, G. S. (eds.), *Materials Issues in Art and Archaeology II.* Materials Research Society. Pittsburgh, 523–41.

Herbert, J. H., and Smith, S. M. 2010. *Identifying Grog in Archaeological Pottery.* Paper submitted at the First Annual Conference, Reconstructive/Experimental Archaeology. Gastonia: North Carolina, 1–17.

Hodder, I. 2012. *Entangled: An Archaeology of the Relationships Between Humans and Things.* Oxford: Wiley-Blackwell.

Horsnell, M. J. A. 1999. *The Year-Names of the First Dynasty of Babylon.* Ontario: McMaster University Press.

Højlund, F. 1987. *Failaka/Dilmun: The Second Millennium Settlements. Volume 2: The Bronze Age Pottery.* JASP, 17(2) Aarhus: Jutland Archaeological Society.

Højlund, F. 1989. Dilmun and the Sealand. In De Meyer, L. and Gasche, H. (eds.), *NAPR 2.* Ghent: University of Ghent Press, 9–14.

Højlund, F. 2007. *The Burial Mounds of Bahrain. Social complexity in Early Dilmun.* JASP, 58. Aarhus: Jutland Archaeological Society.

Højlund, F. 2019. *Qala'at al-Bahrain Volume 3. The Western and Southern City Walls and Other Excavations.* JASP, 30(3). Aarhus: Jutland Archaeological Society.

Højlund, F., and Abu-Laban, A. 2016. *Tell F6. Excavations on Failaka Island: Kuwaiti-Danish Excavations 2008–2012.* JASP, 92. Aarhus: Jutland Archaeological Society.

Højlund, F., and Andersen, H. H. 1994. *Qala'at al-Bahrain Volume 1. The Northern City Wall and the Islamic Fortress.* JASP, 30(1). Aarhus: Jutland Archaeological Society.

Højlund, F., and Andersen, H. H. 1997. *Qala'at al-Bahrain Volume 2. The Central Monumental Buildings.* JASP, 30(2). Aarhus: Jutland Archaeological Society.

Højlund, F. in prep. *Tell F3. Excavations on Failaka Island: Kuwaiti-Danish Excavations 2012–2017.* JASP. Aarhus: Jutland Archaeological Society.

Hunger, H. 2009. How uncertain is the Mesopotamian chronology? In Warburton, A. (ed.), *Time's Up! Dating the Minoan Eruption of Santorini.* Athens: Danish Institute in Athens, 145–52.

Jamieson, A.S. 2000. Identifying Room Use and Vessel Function: A Case-Study of Iron Age Pottery from Building C2 at Tell Ahmar, North Syria. In Bunners, G. (ed.), *Essays on Syria in the Iron Age.* Ancient Near Eastern Studies 7. Louvain: Peeters.

Jankowski-Diakonoff, A., Calderbank, D., Jotheri, J., Novikov, V. 2020. Results of the Test Season of the Iraqi-Russian Expedition at Tell Dehaila-1 (in Russian). *Oriens,* 5.

Jotheri, J. H. A. 2016. Holocene Avulsion History of the Euphrates and Tigris Rivers in the Mesopotamian Floodplain. Ph.D. thesis, Durham University.

Kaniuth, K. 2017. Isin in the Kassite Period. In Bartelmus, A., and Sternitzke, K. (eds.) *Karduniaš. Babylonia Under the Kassites, Vol. II. The Proceedings of the Symposium Held in Munich 30 June to 2 July 2011.* Berlin: De Gruyter, 492-507.

Kjaerum, P., and Højlund, F. 2013. Failaka/Dilmun: The Second Millennium Settlements. Vol. 3, The Bronze Age Architecture. JASP, 17(3). Aarhus: Jutland Archaeological Society.

Kempton, W. 1981. *The Folk Classification of Ceramics: A Study of Cognitive Prototypes.* New York: Academic Press.

Koller, A. 2018. The Diffusion of the Alphabet in the Second Millennium BCE: On the Movements of Scribal Ideas from Egypt to the Levant, Mesopotamia, and Yemen. *Journal of Ancient Egyptian Interconnections*, 20: 1–14.

Kepinski-Lecomte, C. (ed.), 1992. *Haradum 1. Une ville nouvelle sur le Moyen-Euphrate (XVIIIe-XVIIe siècles av. J.-C.).* Paris: Éditions Recherche sur les Civilisations.

Knappett, C., and Hilditch, J. 2015. Colonial Cups? The Minoan Plain Handleless Cup as Icon and Index. In Glatz, C (ed.), *Plain Pottery Traditions of the Eastern Mediterranean and Near East: Production, Use, and Social Significance. California: West Coast Press*, 91–114.

LaPlaca, P. J. and Powell, M. A. 1990. The Agricultural Cycle and the Calendar at Pre-Sargonic Girsu. *Bulletin on Sumerian Agriculture*, 5: 75–104.

Laursen, S, T. 2016. Symbols of Dilmun's Royal House–A Primitive System of Communication Adopted from the Late Indus World? *Arabian Archaeology and Epigraphy*, 27: 2–18.

Laursen, S. T. 2017. *The Royal Mounds of A'ali in Bahrain. The Emergence of Kingship in Early Dilmun*. JASP, 100. Aarhus: Jutland Archaeological Society.

Laursen, S. T., and Steinkeller, P. (eds.), 2017. *Babylonia, the Gulf Region and the Indus: Archaeological and Textual Evidence for Contact in the Third and Early Second Millennium BC.* Indiana: Eisenbrauns.

Lemonnier, P. 1983. L'étude des systèmes techniques, une urgence en technologie culturelle. *Techniques and Culture*, 1: 11–34.

Lemonnier, P. 1993. *Elements for an Anthropology of Technology. Anthropological Papers no. 88.* Ann Arbor: Museum of Anthropology, University of Michigan.

Manning, S. W., Grigs, C. B., Lorentzen, B., Barjamovic, G., Bronk Ramsey, C., Kromer, B., and Wild, E. M. 2016. Integrated Tree-Ring-Radiocarbon High-Resolution Timeframe to Resolve the Earlier Second Millennium BCE Mesopotamian Chronology. *PLoS One*, 11(7): 1–27.

Marchesi, G. 2017. Appendix 5: Inscriptions from the Royal Mounds of A'Ali (Bahrain) and Related Texts. In Laursen, S. T. (ed.), *The Royal Mounds of A'ali in Bahrain. The Emergence of Kingship in Early Dilmun*. JASP, 100. Aarhus: Jutland Archaeological Society, 425–38.

Marchetti, N., and L. Nigro. 1995–1996. Handicraft Production, Secondary Food Transformation and Storage in the Public Building P4 at EB IVA Ebla. *Berytus* 42: 8–36.

Margueron, J.-C. 2004. *Mari: Métropole de l'Euphrate, au IIIe et au début du IIe millénaire av JC.* Paris: Picard.

McCown, D. E., and Haines, R. C. 1967. *Nippur I: Temple of Enlil, Scribal Quarter, and Soundings*. Oriental Institute Publications, 78. Chicago: University of Chicago Press.

McEwan, C. 1997. Whistling vessels from pre-Hispanic Peru. In Freestone, I., Gaimster, D. (eds.), *Pottery in the Making: World Ceramic Traditions.* London: British Museum Press, London, 176–81.

Metab, A. 1989–1990. Excavations at Tell Muhammad (Arabic). *Sumer*, 46: 127–59.

Metab, A., and Hamza, H. A. 2003–2004. Excavations at Tell Muhammad (Season 8, 1999). *Sumer*, 52: 358–84.

Michalowski, P. 1994. The Drinking Gods: Alcohol in Mesopotamian Ritual and Mythology. In Milano, L. (ed.), *Drinking in Ancient Societies: History and Culture of Drinks in the Ancient Near East. Papers of a Symposium helfd in Rome, May 17–19, 1990.* Winona Lake: Eisenbrauns, 27–44.

Miller, D. 1985. *Artefacts as Categories: A Study of Ceramic Variability in Central India.* Cambridge: Cambridge University Press.

Moon, J. (ed.), forthcoming, *Tell Khaiber.*

Moorey, P. R. S. 1994. *Ancient Mesopotamian Materials and Industries: The Archaeological Evidence*. Oxford: Clarendon Press.

Oates, J. 1979. *Babylon*. London: Thames and Hudson Ltd.

Ochsenschlager, E. L. 1981. The Mendes–Al-Hiba System of Pottery Classification. In Arnold, D. (ed.), *Studien zur altägyptischen Keramik*. Mainz am Rhine: Philipp von Zabern, 79–84.

Olijdam, J. 1997. Nippur and Dilmun in the Second Half of the Fourteenth Century BC: A Re-Evaluation of the Ili-ip-pasara Letters. *Proceedings of the Seminar for Arabian Studies*, 217: 199–203.

Oppenheim, A. L. 1954. The Seafaring Merchants of Ur. *Journal of the American Oriental Society*, 74(1): 6–7.

Orton, C., and Hughes, M. 2013. *Pottery in Archaeology: Second Edition*. Cambridge: Cambridge University Press.

Orton, C, Tyres, P., and Vince, A. 1993. *Pottery in Archaeology*. Cambridge: Cambridge University Press.

Oselini, V. 2018. The Cultural Influence of Mesopotamian States in the Upper and Middle Course of the Diyala River During the Mid-2nd Millennium BC. In Horejs et al. (eds.), *Proceedings of the 10th International Congress on the Archaeology of the Ancient Near East, 25–29th April, 2016, Vienna*. Wiesebaden: Harassowitz, 391–404.

Peña, J. P. 2007. *Roman Pottery in the Archaeological Record*. Cambridge: Cambridge University Press.

Peterson, J. 2019. *The Literary Sumerian of Old Babylonian Ur: UET 6/1–3 in Transliteration and Translation with Select Commentary*. CDLP 17.

Pfälzner, P. 1990. Tell Bderi. The Development of a Bronze Age Town. In Kerner, S. (ed.), *The Near East in Antiquity.* Amman: Al Kutba Publishers, 63–79.

Pfälzner, P. 1995. *Mittanische und mittelassyrische Keramik. Eine chronologische, funktionale und produktionsökonomische Analyse.* Berichte Der Ausgrabung Tall Šeh Hamad / Dur-Katlimmu 3. Berlin: Dietrich Reimer Verlag.

Pfälzner, P. 2007. The Late Bronze Age Ceramic Traditions of the Syrian Jazirah. In al-Maqdissī, M., Matoïan, V., and Nicolle, C. (eds.), *Céramique de l'âge du bronze en Syrie, 2, L'Euphrate et la région de Jézireh. Beyrouth. Bibliothèque archéologique et historique.* Beyrouth:

Institut Français d'Archéologie du Proche-Orient, 231–91.

Pierret, A. 2019. Application of X-Radiography to the Identification of Fashioning Techniques. In Roux, V. (ed.), *Ceramics and Society: A Technological Approach to Archaeological Assemblages*. Springer, 192–5.

Pollock, S. (ed.), 2015. *Between Feasts and Daily Meals: Towards and Archaeology of Commensal Spaces.* Berlin: Topoi.

Pons, N. 1989. La poterie et les tombes du chantier F. In De Meyer, L. and Gasche, H. (eds.), *NAPR 3*. Ghent: University of Ghent Press, 19–36.

Potts, D. T. 1999. *Mesopotamian Civilization. The Material Foundations*. London: Athlone Press.

Powell, M. A. 1987–1990. Masse und Gewichte. *Reallexikon der Assyriologie*, 7: 457–517.

Pruzsinszky, R. 2009. *Mesopotamian Chronology of the 2nd Millennium B.C. An Introduction to the Textual Evidence and Related Chronological Issues.* Wien: Verlag der Österreichischen Akademie der Wissenschaften.

Quarantelli, E. 1985. *The Land Between the Two Rivers: Twenty Years of Italian Archaeology in the Middle East–The Treasures of Mesopotamia.* Turin: Il Quadrante.

Quinn, P. 2013. *Ceramic Petrography. The Interpretation of Archaeological Pottery and Related Artefacts in Thin Section*. Oxford: Archaeopress.

Reynolds, F. 2007. Food and Drink in Babylonia. In Leick, G. (ed.), *The Babylonian World.* London: Routledge, 171–84.

Rice, P. M. 1981. Evolution of Specialized Pottery Production: A Trial Model. *Current Anthropology*, 22(3): 219–40.

Rice, P. M. 1987. *Pottery Analysis. A Sourcebook*. Chicago: University of Chicago Press.

Riemer, H. 1997. Form und Funktion. Zur systematischen Aufnahme und vergleichenden Analyse prähistorischer Gefäßkeramik. *Archäologische Informationen*, 20: 117–31.

Richardson, S. 2002. The Collapse of a Complex State: A Reappraisal of the End of the First Dynasty of Babylon, 1683–1597 B.C. Ph.D. thesis, Columbia University.

Richardson, S. 2005. Trouble in the Countryside *Ana Tarṣi* Samsuditana: Militarism, Kassites, and the Fall of Babylon I. In van Soldt (ed.), *Ethnicity in Ancient Mesopotamia.* Leiden: Institut néerlandais du Proche-Orient, 273–89.

Richardson, S. 2012. Early Mesopotamia: The Presumptive State. *The Past and Present Society*, 215: 3–49.

Richardson, S. 2017. Before Things Worked: A "Low-Power" Model of Early Mesopotamia. In Ando, C., and Richardson, S (eds.), *Ancient States and Infrastructural Power: Europe, Asia, and America.* Philadelphia: University of Pennsylvania Press, 17–62.

Ristvet, L. 2015. *Ritual, Performance, and Politics in the Ancient Near East.* Cambridge: Cambridge University Press.

Roaf, M. 2012. The fall of Babylon in 1499 NC or 1595 MC. *Akkadica*, 133: 147–74.

Robson, E. 2017. The Archive. In Campbell, S., Moon, J., Killick, R., Robson, E., Calderbank, D., Shepperson, M., and Slater, F: (2017) Tell Khaiber: an administrative centre of the Sealand Dynasty period. *Iraq*, 78: 28–34.

Robson, E. forthcoming. 'The Cuneiform Tablets'. In Moon, J. (ed.), *Tell Khaiber.*

Romano, L., and Zingale, M. 2019. Area 1 Pottery–Part 1. A Preliminary Assessment on Typology, Technology and Use. In Romano, L., and D'Agostino, F. (eds.), *Abu Tbeirah Excavations I. Area 1. Last Phase and Building A–Phase 1.* Rome: Sapienza Università Editrice, 323–70.

Roux, V. 2016. Ceramic Manufacture: the Chaîne Opératoire Approach. In Hunt, A. M. W. (ed.), *The Oxford Handbook of Archaeological Ceramic Analysis.* Oxford: Oxford University Press, 101–13.

Roux, V. 2019. *Ceramics and Society: A Technological Approach to Archaeological Assemblages.* Springer.

Roux, V., and Corbetta, D. 1989. *The Potter's Wheel: Craft Specialization and Technical Competence.* New Dehli: Oxford and IBH Publishing Co.

Roux, V., and Courty, M. 1998. Identification of Wheel-Fashioning Methods: Technological Analysis of 4th–3rd Millennium BC Oriental Ceramics. *Journal of Archaeological Science*, 25: 747–63.

Rye, O. S. 1977. Pottery Manufacturing Techniques: X-ray Studies. *Archaeometry*, 19: 205–11.

Rye, O. S. 1981. *Pottery Technology. Principles and Reconstruction.* Washington: Taraxacum.

Sallaberger, W. 1996. *Der Babylonische Töpfer und seine Gefässe.* MHEM III. Ghent: University of Ghent.

Schneider, G. 2006. Mineralogisch-chemische Untersuchungen der mittel- und neuassyrische Keramik von Tall Šēh Hamad. In Kreppner F. J. (ed.), *Die Keramik des "Roten Hauses" von Tall Šēh Hamad/Dūr-Katlimmu.* Berichte der Ausgrabung Tall Šēh Hamad/Dūr-Katlimmu 7, Wiesbaden: Harrasowitz, 391–420.

Sheppreson, M. forthcoming. 'The Organization, Form and Function of the Fortified Building'. In Moon, J. (ed.), *Tell Khaiber.*

Sinopoli, C. M. 1991. *Approaches to Archaeological Ceramics.* New York: Plenum Press.

Skibo, J. M. 2012. *Understanding Pottery Function.* New York: Springer.

Skibo, J. M., Schiffer, M. B., and Reid, K. C. 1989. Organic-Tempered Pottery: An Experimental Study. *American Antiquity*, 54(1): 122–46.

Steinkeller, P. 1991. The Container *kabkūru*. *Nouvelles Assyriologiques Brèves et Utilitaires*, 1991(1): 3–4.

Steinkeller, P. 1996. The Organization of Crafts in Third Millennium Babylonia: The Case of Potters. *Altorientalische Forschungen*, 23(2): 232–53.

Steponaitis, V. P. 1984. Technological Studies of Prehistoric Pottery from Alabama: Physical Properties and Vessel

Function. In van der Leeuw, S. E., and Pritchard, A. C. (eds.), *The Many Dimensions of Pottery*. Amsterdam: Amsterdam University Press, 79–121.

Sternizke, K. 2016a. Babylon im 2. Jahrtausend vor Christus. Die archäologischen Befunde der altbabylonischen und kassitischen Zeit aus den Deutschen Grabungen von 1899–1917. Ph.D. thesis, Universität Bern.

Sternitzke, K. 2016b. Der Kontext der altbabylonischen Archive aus Babylon. *Mitteilungen der Deutschen Orient-Gesellschaft zu Berlin*, 148: 179–97.

Sternitzke, K. 2017. Bestattungen in der Kassiten- un Isin II-Zeit. In Bartelmus, A., and Sternitzke, K. (eds.), *Karduniaš. Babylonia Under the Kassites, Vol. II. The Proceedings of the Symposium Held in Munich 30 June to 2 July 2011*. Berlin: De Gruyter, 351–420.

Stone, E, C. 1977. Economic crisis and social upheaval in Old Babylonian Nippur. In Cuyler Young, T., and Levine, L. D. (eds.), *Mountains and Lowlands: Essays on the Archaeology of Greater Mesopotamia. Bibliothecha Mesopotamica 7*. Malibu: Undena Publications, 267–89.

Stone, E, C. 1987. *Nippur Neighborhoods*. Studies in Ancient Oriental Civilization 44. Chicago: University of Chicago Press.

Streit, K. 2016. Protohistoric Infant Jar Burials of the Southern Levant in Context: Tracing Cultural Influences in the Late Sixth and Fifth Millennia BCE. In Ganor, S., Kriemerman, I., Streit, K., Mumcuoglu, M. (eds.), *From Sha'ar Hagolan to Shaaraim: Essays in Honor of Prof. Yosef Garfinkel*. Jerusalem: Israel Exploration Society, 171–86.

Tite, M. S. 1999. Pottery Production, Distribution, and Consumption: The Contribution of the Physical Sciences. *Journal of Archaeological Method and Theory*, 6(3): 181–233.

Titterington, P. F. 1935. Certain Bluff Mounds of Western Jersey County, Illinois. *American Antiquity*, 1: 6–46.

Twiss, K. C. 2017. Animals of the Sealands: Ceremonial Activities in the Southern Mesopotamian "Dark Age". *Iraq*, 79: 257–67.

Ur, J. 2013. Patterns of Settlement in Sumer and Akkad. In Crawford, H. (ed.), *The Sumerian World*. London: Routledge, 131–55.

Valtz, E. 2002–2003. La Ceramica Dei Livelli II e I. In Bergamini, G., Gabutti, A., and Valtz, E. (eds.), La ceramic di Tell Yelkhi. *Mesopotamia*, 37–38: 265–320.

van As, A., and Jacobs, L. 1987. Second Millenium B.C. Goblet Bases from Tell ed-Deir: The Relationship Between Form and Technique. In van As, A. (ed.), *A Knapsack Full of Pottery: Archaeo-Ceramological Miscellanea dedicated to H. J. Franken on the Occasion of his Seventieth Birthday. July 4, 1987*. Newsletter of the Department of Pottery Technology 5. Leiden, 39–53.

van As, A., and Jacobs, L. 1992. The Work of the Potter in Ancient Mesopotamia During the Second Millennium B.C. In Vandiver P. B. (ed.), *Materials Issues in Art and Archaeology III. Materials Research Society 267*. Pittsburgh: Materials Research Society, 529–44.

van As, A., and Jacobs, L. 2014. The Babylonian Potter: Environment, Clay and Techniques. In Armstrong, J. A., and Gasche, H: (eds.), *Mesopotamian Pottery: a guide to the Babylonian tradition in the second millennium B.C.* Chicago: University of Chicago Press, 75–83.

van de Mieroop, M. 2004. *A History of the Ancient Near East, ca. 3000–323 BC. 3rd ed.* Oxford: Blackwells.

van Ess, M. 1988. Keramik von der Akkad- bis zum Ende der altbabylonischen Zeit aus den Planquadraten N XV und XVI und aus dem Sînkasid-Palast in Uruk-Warka. *Baghdader Mitteilungen*, 19: 321–442.

van Ess, M. 2014. Characteristics of Middle Babylonian Pottery Production as Mirrored on Old Babylonian Pottery–Continuity or Change? In Luciani, M and Hausleiter, A. (eds.), *Recent Trends in the Study of Late Bronze Age Ceramics in Syro-Mesopotamia and Neighbouring Regions: Proceedings of the International Workshop in Berlin, 2–5 November 2006*. Orient Archäologie, 32. Marburg: Verlag Marie Leidorf, 333–83.

van Gennep, A. 1960. *The Rites of Passage*. London: Routledge.

van Koppen, F. 2010. The Old to Middle Babylonian Transition: History and Chronology of the Mesopotamian Dark Age. *Ägypten und Levante*, 20: 453–63.

van Koppen, F. 2017. The Early Kassite Period. In Bartelmus, A., and Sternitzke, K. (eds.), *Karduniaš. Babyonia Under the Kassites. Vol. 1. The Proceedings of the Symposium Held in Munich, 30 June to 2 July 2011*. Berlin: De Gruyter, 45–92.

van Lerberghe, K., and Voet, G. 2009. *A Late Old Babylonian Temple Archive from Dūr-Abiešuḫ*, CUSAS, 8. Bethesda: CDL Press.

Vandiver, P. B. 1991. The Cultural Uses of Ceramics. In Vandiver, P. B., Druzik, J., and Wheeler, G. S. (eds.), *Materials Issues in Art and Archaeology II*. Pittsburgh: The Materials Research Society.

Velde, B., and Druc, I. C. 1999. *Archaeological Ceramic Materials: Origins and Utilization*. Berlin: Springer.

Wattenmaker, P. 1998a. *Household and State in Upper Mesopotamia: Specialized Economy and the Social Uses of Goods in an Early Complex Society*. Washington: Smithsonian Institution Press.

Wattenmaker, P. 1998b. Craft Production and Social Identity in Northwest Mesopotamia. In Costin, C., and Wright, R. (eds.), *Craft and Social Identity*. Archaeological Papers of the American Anthropological Association, 8. Arlington: American Anthropological Association, 47–55.

Wenger, E. 1998. *Communities of Practice: Learning, Meaning, and Identity*. Cambridge: Cambridge University Press.

Whalen, J. 2014. Feasting and Shared Drinking Practices in the Early Bronze Age II–III (2650–2000 BC) of North-central and Western Anatolia. Ph.D. thesis, University of Edinburgh.

Woolley, L. 1954. *Ur of the Chaldees. A Record of Seven years of Excavation*. London: Pelican.

Woolley, L. 1965. *Ur Excavations Vol. VIII. The Kassite Period and the Period of the Assyrian Kings*. London: British Museum.

Woolley, L. and Mallowan, M. 1976. *Ur Excavations Vol. VII: The Old Babylonian Period*. London: British Museum.

Wright, H. T. 1981. The Southern Margins of Sumer: An Archaeological Survey of the Areas of Eridu and Ur. In Adams, R. M: *Heartland of Cities*. Chicago: University of Chicago Press, 295–338.

Yoffee, N. 2014. The Age of Opportunity: Social and Political Transitions in Mid-Second Millennium BC Mesopotamia. In Cancik-Kirschbaum, E., Brisch, N., and Eidem, J. (eds.), *Constituent, Confederate, and Conquered Space: The Emergence of the Mitanni State*. Berlin: De Gruyter, 259–64.

Zarins, J. 1989. Eastern Saudi Arabia and External Relations: Selected Ceramic, Steatite, and Textual Evidence: 3500–1900 BC. In Frifelt, K., and Sorensen, P. (eds.), *South Asian Archaeology 1985*. London: Curzon Press, 74–103.

Zarnkow, M., Spieleder, E., Back, W., Sacher, B., Otto, A., and Einwag, B. 2006. Interdisziplinäre Untersuchungen zum altorientalischen Bierbrauen in der Siedlung von Tall Bazi/Nordsyrien vor rund 3200 Jahren. *Technikgeschichte*, 73(1): 3–26.

Zarnkow, M., Otto, A., and Einwag, B. 2011. Interdisciplinary Investigations into the Brewing Technology of the Ancient Near East and the Potential of the Cold Mashing Process. In Schiefenhövel, W. and Macbeth, H. (eds.) *Liquid Bread: Beer and Brewing in Cross-Cultural Perspective*. Oxford: Berghahn, 47-54.

Zettler, R. L. 1992. *The Ur III Temple of Inanna at Nippur: the operation and organization of urban religious institutions in Mesopotamia in the late third millennium B.C.* Berlin: Reimer.

Zimansky, P., and Stone, E. 2016. Tell Sakhariya and Gaeš. In Kaelin O., Stucky, R., and Jamieson, A. (eds.), *Proceedings of the 9th International Congress on the Archaeology of the Ancient Near East, 9–13 June 2014, Basel. Vol. 3*. Wiesbaden: Harrassowitz, 57–66.

Zomer, E. 2021. Enmity against Samsu-ditāna. In De Graef, K. and Goddeeris, A. (eds.) *Law and (Dis)Order in the Ancient Near East. Proceedings of the 59th Rencontre Assyriologique International Held at Ghent, Belgium, 15-19 July 2013*. Pennsylvania: Penn University Press, 324–32.

Pottery Plates

PLATE 1

#	Pottery Number	Rim Di. (mm)	Base Di. (mm)	Volume (L)	Surface/ Fabric Colour	Fabric Type	Room/ Area	Phase	Surface Treatment/ Decoration	Notes
1	p3099-13	122	46	0.25	Cream	D	Vaults	1	Impressed groove beneath rim.	Plugged base.
2	p3064-445	125	50	0.28	Pink	A	Admin.	2.2	Impressed groove beneath rim.	
3	p3064-276	128	43	0.26	Pink-cream/ Pink	D	Admin.	2.2		
4	p3091-1	158	50	0.56	Pink/ Dark pink	F	Burial	Mixed		Plugged base.
5	p3088-138	130	57	0.38	White-cream/ Pale pink	A	304	Mixed		
6	p3080-4	125	48	0.29	Pink-white/ Pink	C	Admin.	2.2		
7	p1139-89	147	57	0.39	White-cream/ Pink	D	314	2.2		Plugged base.
8	p1142-50	156	55	0.49	Cream/ Pale brown	A	314	2.1		Plugged base.
9	p6037-24	110	47	0.31	Cream-brown/ Cream	F	-	-		
10	p3080-79	119	40	0.24	Pink/ Pink-brown	A	Admin.	2.2		
11	p1166-205	136	49	0.28	White-cream/ White-grey	F	314	2.1	Traces of pink slip (?) on surfaces.	
12	p3064-653	168	58	0.59	Cream/ Pink	E	Admin.	2.2		Filled-in base.
13	p3087-15	177	58	0.58	Yellow-cream/ Cream	A	304	Mixed		Filled-in base.
14	p5007-4	126	39	0.27	Yellow-cream/ Cream	E	140–2	2.3		

FAMILY 5

Type 5.1

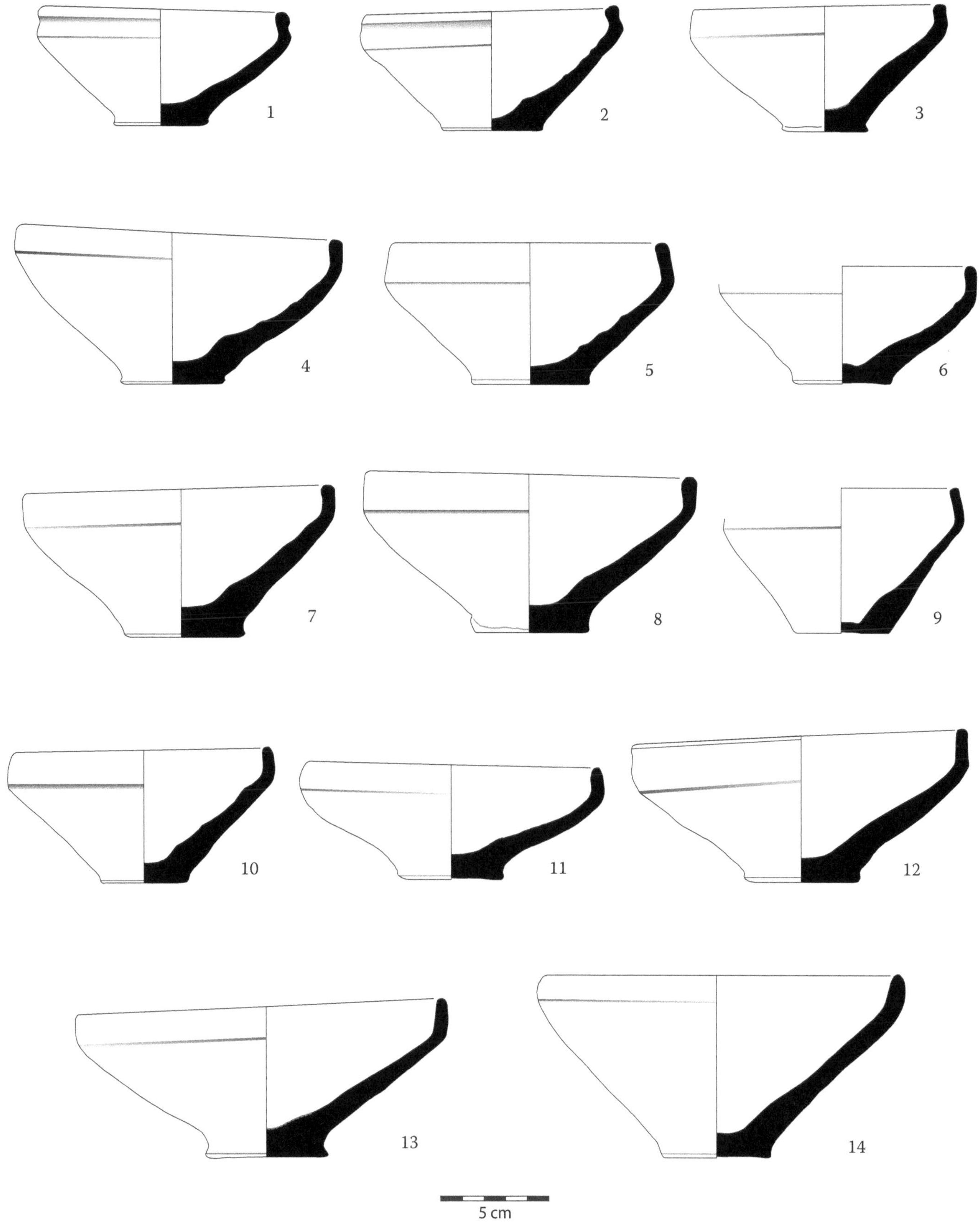

PLATE 2

#	Pottery Number	Rim Di. (mm)	Base Di. (mm)	Volume (L)	Surface/ Fabric Colour	Fabric Type	Room/ Area	Phase	Surface Treatment/ Decoration	Notes
15	p1080-10	218	73	1.54	White-cream/ Pink	B	101	2.1		Plugged/filled-in base. Thumbprint on ext. base.
16	p1098-1	234	96	1.85	Cream-white/ Cream-pale brown	F/E	Burial	Mixed		
17	p1010-12	182	52	0.85	Pink/ Pink	A	-	-		
18	p6068-41	157	52	0.57	Cream-pink/ Pink	A	Mixed	Mixed		Filled-in base.
19	p4066-19	112	52	0.23	Cream-brown/ Pale brown	D	-	Houses		
20	p4085-1	118	51	0.24	Green/ Pale orange	C	House 3	Houses		Filled-in base.
21	p6078-27	120	damaged	0.24	Cream/ Cream	D	Surface	Mixed		Filled-in base.
22	p1080-6	156	51	0.45	Cream/ Pale orange	B	101	2.1		
23	p9020-113	160	65	0.37	Pale pink/ Pink	E	616	Mixed		Bitumen coated interior, dripping over breaks and down exterior.
24	p3084-34	168	61	0.66	Green-yellow/ Cream	H	304	Mixed		Filled-in base.
25	p1039-66	126	47	0.26	Green/ Pink	A	-	-		
26	p3080-97	150	55	0.4	Pale brown/ Red-brown	E	Admin.	2.2	Impressed groove beneath rim.	Filled-in base.
27	p6042-9	155	48	0.40	Green/ Pale orange-brown	D	600	2.1		
28	p3066-28	130	35	0.31	Yellow/ Pale green-yellow	E	Admin.	2.1		

Type 5.1 *cont'd.*

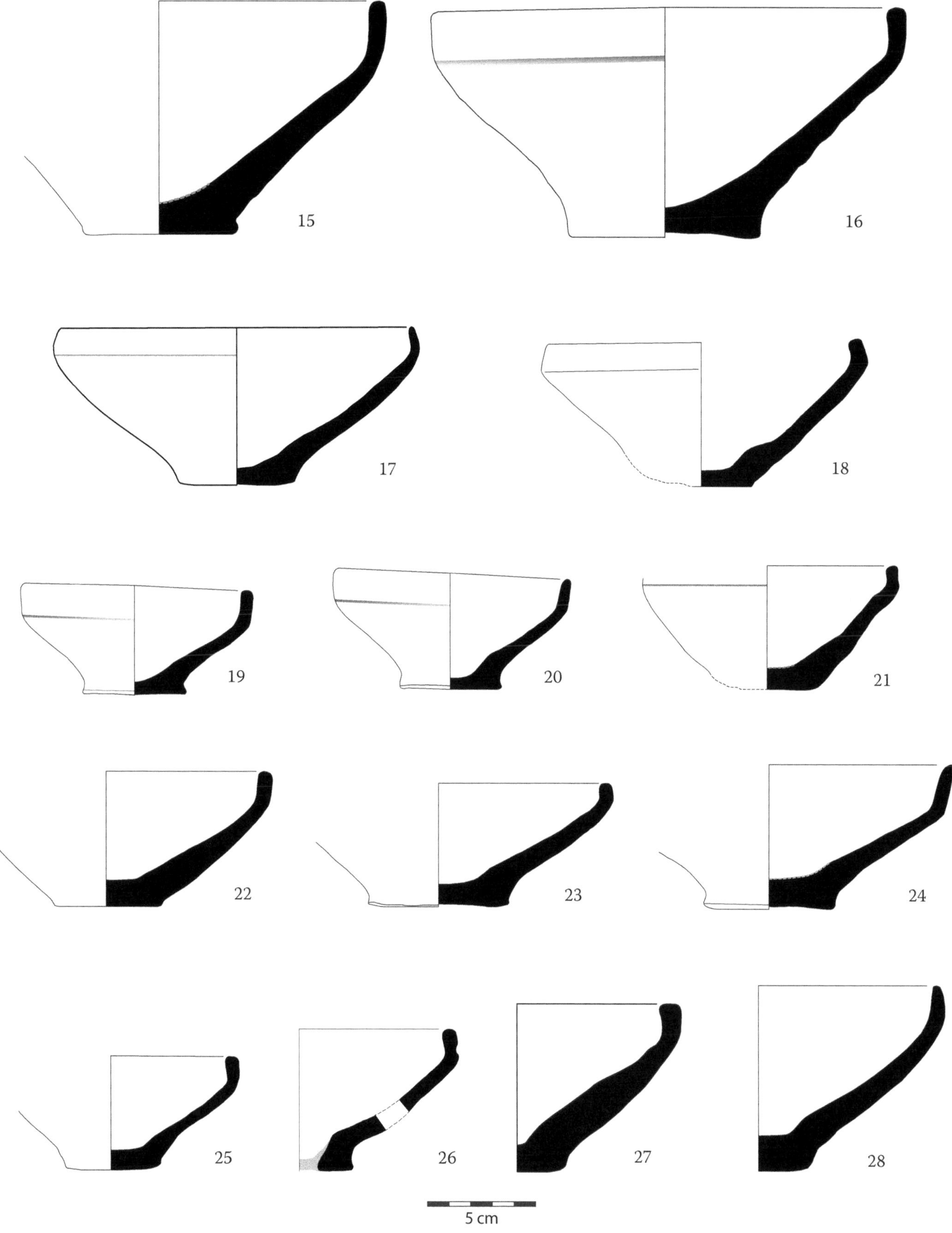

PLATE 3

#	Pottery Number	Rim Di. (mm)	Base Di. (mm)	Volume (L)	Surface/ Fabric Colour	Fabric Type	Room/ Area	Phase	Surface Treatment/ Decoration	Notes
29	p1157-1	110	48	0.18	Pink-pale orange/Orange	A/E	Admin.	2.2		
30	p9020-111	146	60	0.38	White-cream/ Grey	H	616	Mixed	Traces of pink slip (?) on surfaces.	
31	p4034-20	112	58	0.23	Cream/ Pink	F	-	Houses		
32	p3025-15	92	48	0.20	Pink/ Red-orange	D	302	Mixed		
33	p9018-89	155	53	0.48	White-pink/ Orange	E	616	Mixed		
34	p9018-33	180	65	0.96	Green-yellow/ Orange-brown	E	616	Mixed		

#	Pottery Number	Rim Di. (mm)	Base Di. (mm)	Volume (L)	Surface/ Fabric Colour	Fabric Type	Room/ Area	Phase	Surface Treatment/ Decoration	Notes
1	p1139-126	107	48	0.11	Green-yellow/ Grey-green	H	314	2.2		
2	p1094-25	120	60	0.19	Pale green/ Pale cream	A	124	Mixed		Plugged base.
3	p3054-399	122	45	0.16	Green/ Green	H	304	Mixed	Impressed groove beneath rim.	Filled-in base.
4	p5008-22	110	55	0.15	Pale green/Pale pink	D	140–2	2.2		Sandy filled-in base. Irregular string-cut base.
5	p1139-28	116	48	0.17	Cream/ Pink	D	314	2.2		Filled-in base.
6	p6058-82	100	40	0.12	Yellow-cream/ Pink	D	601	2.1		
7	p6163-54	135	52	0.31	Pink/ Pink	E	Surface	Mixed		
8	p1010-48	94	51	0.13	Cream-pink/ Pink	A	-	-	Ridge beneath rim (manufacturing mark).	Filled-in base. Roughly shaped.
9	p8076-39	85	-	0.07	White-cream/ Pale pink	D	125	2.3		

Type 5.1 *cont'd.*

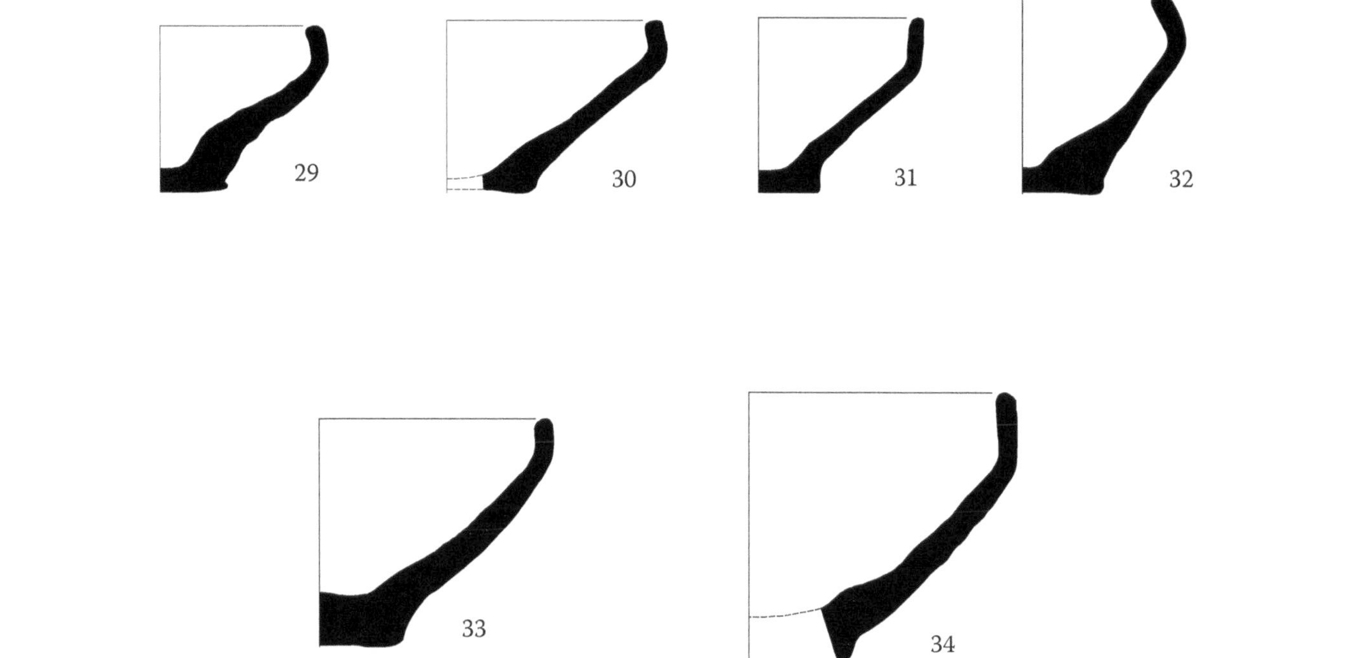

Type 5.2

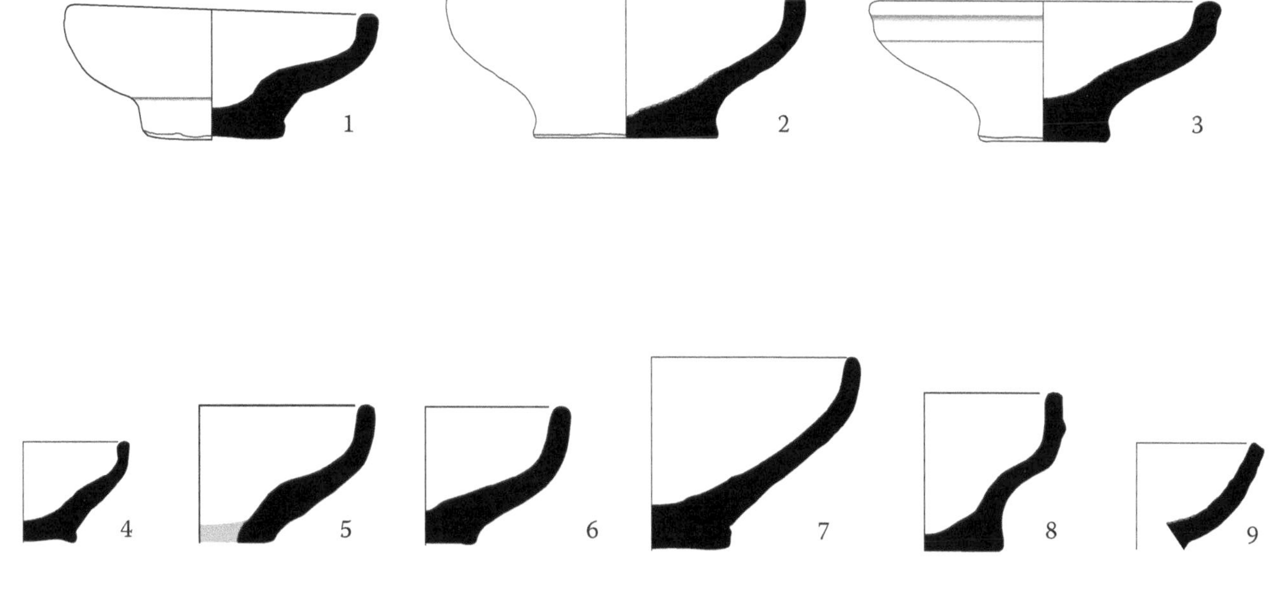

5 cm

PLATE 4

#	Pottery Number	Rim Di. (mm)	Base Di. (mm)	Volume (L)	Surface/ Fabric Colour	Fabric Type	Room/ Area	Phase	Surface Treatment/ Decoration	Notes
1	p8029-3	175	60	1.18	Pale green/ Pale pink	D	Burial	Mixed	Slipped?	

#	Pottery Number	Rim Di. (mm)	Base Di. (mm)	Volume (L)	Surface/ Fabric Colour	Fabric Type	Room/ Area	Phase	Surface Treatment/ Decoration	Notes
1	p6088-14	135	49	0.21	Green-brown/ Pink	F	Surface	Mixed		Filled-in base.
2	p5001-17	150	-	-	Yellow-cream/ Cream	E	Sounding	Mixed		
3	p6089-5	190	-	-	Pink/ Dark pink	D	Surface	Mixed		
4	p1036-20	180	-	-	Cream/ Cream	F	-	-		

#	Pottery Number	Rim Di. (mm)	Base Di. (mm)	Volume (L)	Surface/ Fabric Colour	Fabric Type	Room/ Area	Phase	Surface Treatment/ Decoration	Notes
1	p6175-22	170	57	0.31	Yellow/ Pale green	H	Surface	Mixed		

Type 5.3

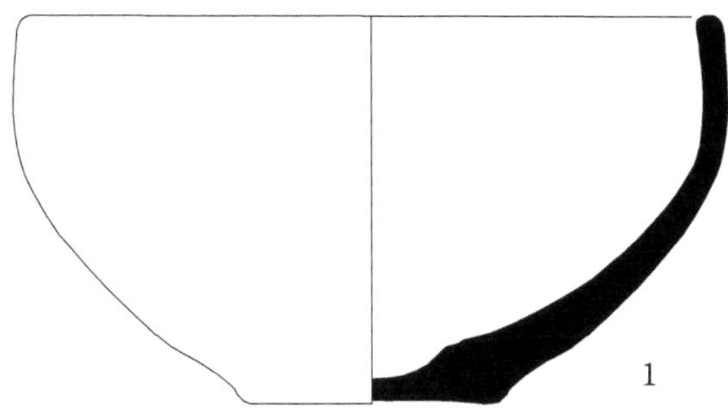

Type 5.4

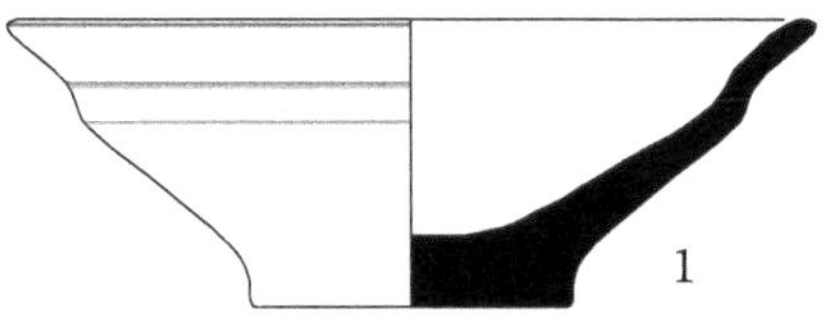

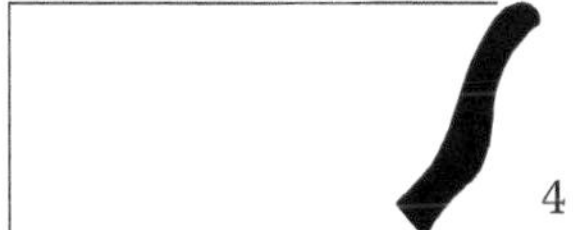

Type 5.5

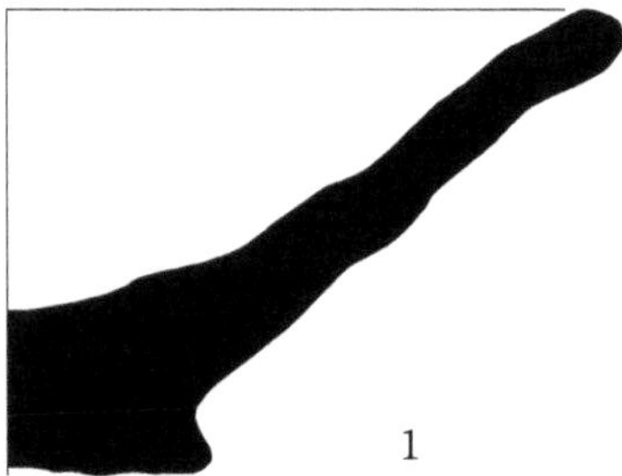

5 cm

PLATE 5

#	Pottery Number	Rim Di. (mm)	Base Di. (mm)	Volume (L)	Surface/ Fabric Colour	Fabric Type	Room/ Area	Phase	Surface Treatment/ Decoration	Notes
1	p1096-307	220	-	-	Cream-yellow/ Cream-grey	D	Admin.	2.2	3 impressed bands beneath rim.	
2	p1096-472	230	-	-	Yellow-cream/ Pale orange	D	Admin.	2.2	2 impressed bands beneath rim.	
3	p1096-489	250	-	-	Cream/ Pale brown	E	Admin.	2.2	2 impressed bands beneath rim.	
4	p6036-111	220	-	-	Cream/ Pink	E	600	-	2 impressed bands beneath rim.	
5	p8008-55	240	-	-	Pink-red/ Orange	E	316	2.3	3 impressed bands beneath rim.	
6	p3176-36	280	-	-	Cream/ Pale brown	E	315	2.2	5 impressed bands beneath rim.	
7	p1079-577	330	-	-	Cream-yellow/ Orange-brown	D	101	2.1	2 impressed bands beneath rim.	
8	p1094-24	240	-	-	Pink/ Pink-orange	D	124	Mixed	2 impressed bands beneath rim.	
9	p6116-38	260	-	-	Cream/ Grey-brown	A	Surface	Mixed	3 impressed bands beneath rim.	Sooting on interior.
10	p3024-44	360	-	-	Red-brown	D	-	-	2 impressed bands beneath rim.	

#	Pottery Number	Rim Di. (mm)	Base Di. (mm)	Volume (L)	Surface/ Fabric Colour	Fabric Type	Room/ Area	Phase	Surface Treatment/ Decoration	Notes
1	p3024-9	300	-	-	Cream/ Cream	F	-	-	3 impressed bands beneath rim.	
2	p1126-26	160	-	-	Cream/ Pink	E with "grog"?	131/619	2.2	2 impressed bands beneath rim.	
3	p1139-90	250	-	-	Pink/ Dull pink	E	314	2.2	3 impressed bands beneath rim.	
4	p1142-15	290	-	-	Cream-pink/ Pink	E	314	2.1	4 impressed bands beneath rim.	
5	p9020-38	260	-	-	Pale green/ Pink	E	616	Mixed	3 impressed bands beneath rim.	
6	p3064-667	270	-	-	Yellow-green/ Yellow-green	F	Admin.	2.2	4 impressed bands beneath rim.	
7	p3039-10	220	-	-	Cream/ Pink	F	-	-	3 impressed bands beneath rim.	
8	p6096-72		-	-	Pale green/ Pink	E	Surface	Mixed	2 impressed bands beneath rim.	
9	p3088-184	300	-	-	White-cream/ Grey-green	F	304	Mixed	3 impressed bands beneath rim.	
10	p1139-51	220	-	-	Cream/ Pale pink	E	314	2.2	2 impressed bands beneath rim.	

FAMILY 10

Type 10.1

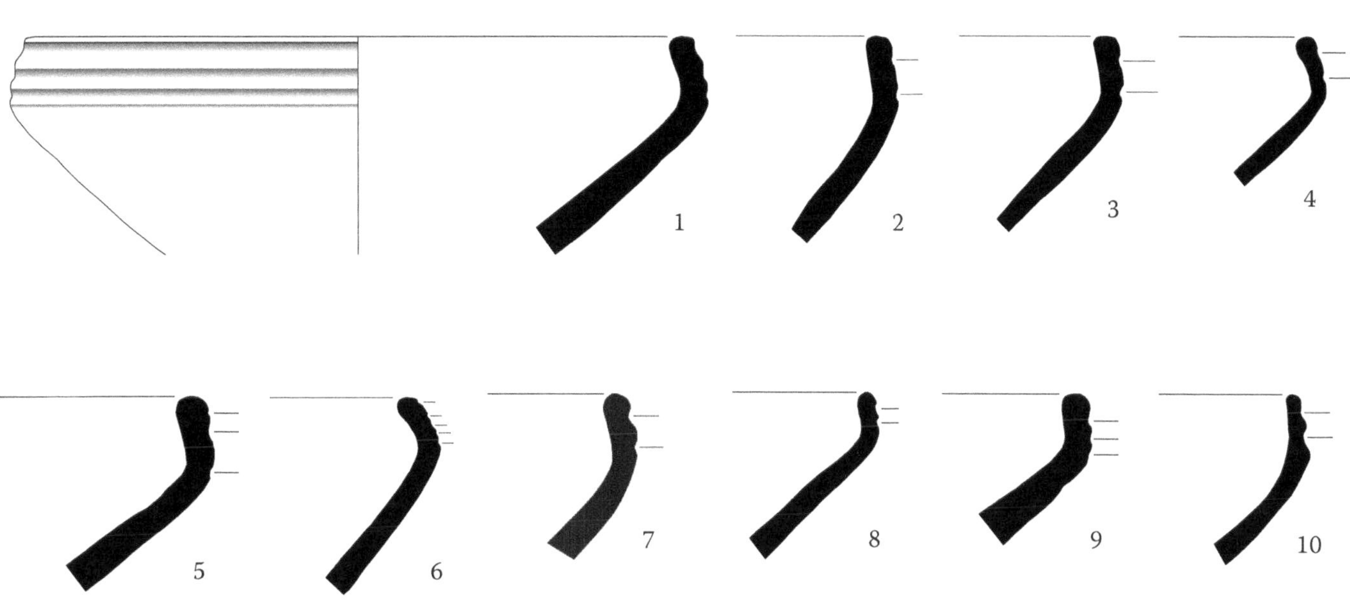

Type 10.2

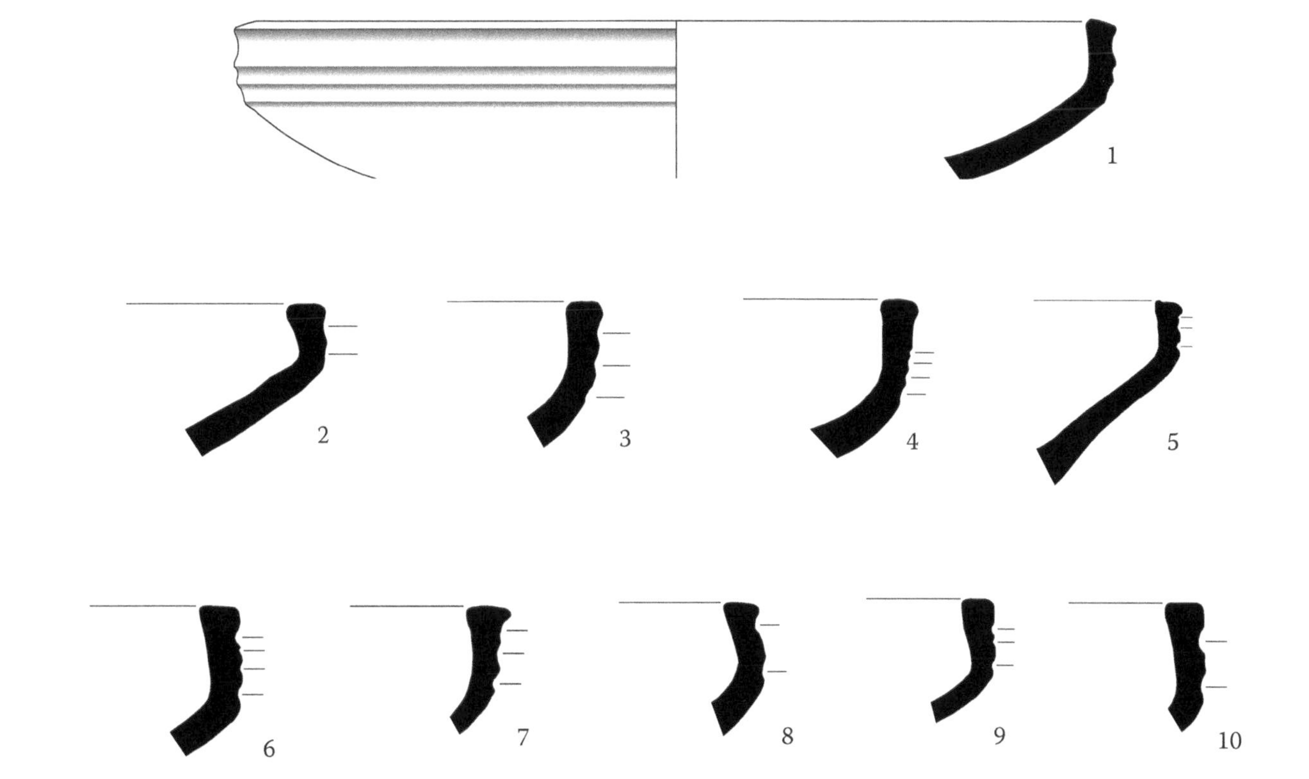

5 cm

PLATE 6

#	Pottery Number	Rim Di. (mm)	Base Di. (mm)	Volume (L)	Surface/ Fabric Colour	Fabric Type	Room/ Area	Phase	Surface Treatment/ Decoration	Notes
1	p3088-45	270	-	-	Pale pink-cream/ Pink	E	304	Mixed		
2	p1142-48	220	-	-	Cream/ Pale brown	F	314	2.1		
3	p3089-5	260	-	-	Pink/ Pale Brown	C/E	304	Mixed		
4	p3088-175	250	-	-	Cream-yellow/ Cream-yellow	E	304	Mixed		
5	p4006-5	230	-	-	White/ Dull pink	E	House 2	Houses		
6	p6175-39	360	-	-	Yellow-green/ Yellow-green	H	Surface	Mixed	Ridged band with incised crescents.	

#	Pottery Number	Rim Di. (mm)	Base Di. (mm)	Volume (L)	Surface/ Fabric Colour	Fabric Type	Room/ Area	Phase	Surface Treatment/ Decoration	Notes
1	p1079-789	130	-	-	Cream/ Pink-cream	A	101	2.1	5 impressed/incised bands beneath rim.	
2	p1132-22	200	-	-	Dull pink/ Red-brown	F	131/619	2.2	2 impressed bands beneath rim.	
3	p6085-12	260	-	-	Cream-yellow/ Pink	E	Surface	Mixed	2 impressed/incised bands beneath rim.	
4	p6118-42	300	-	-	Cream/ Pink	E	Surface	Mixed	5 impressed/incised bands beneath rim.	

Type 10.3

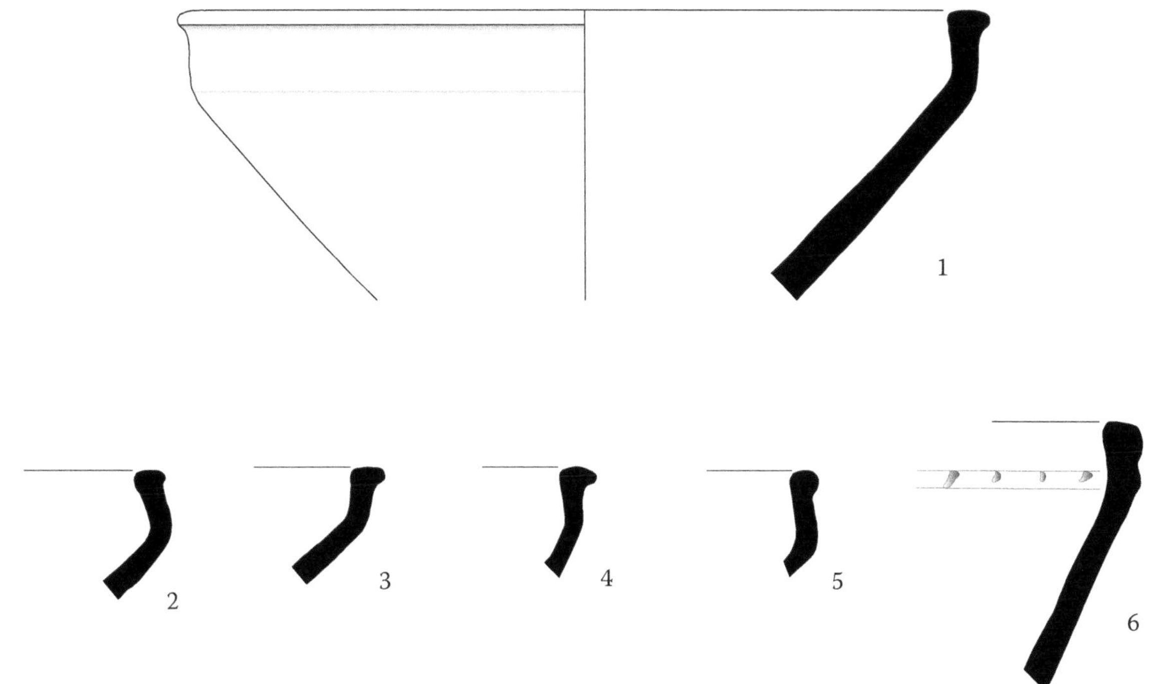

Type 10.4

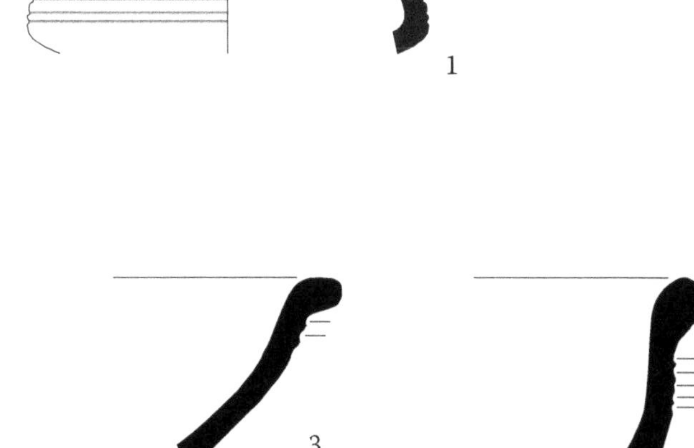

5 cm

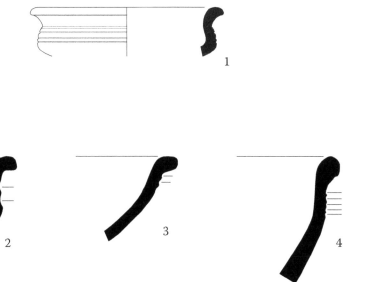

PLATE 7

#	Pottery Number	Rim Di. (mm)	Base Di. (mm)	Volume (L)	Surface/ Fabric Colour	Fabric Type	Room/ Area	Phase	Surface Treatment/ Decoration	Notes
1	p3099-12	-	60	-	Pink/ Grey	E	Vaults	1		
2	p3119-51	-	65	-	Pink-cream/ Brown	D	Admin.	2.2		Filled-in base.
3	p1166-201	-	60	-	Yellow-cream/ Pale pink	E	314	2.1		
4	p3054-391	-	55	-	Pink/ Pale brown	E	304	Mixed		Plugged base.

#	Pottery Number	Rim Di. (mm)	Base Di. (mm)	Volume (L)	Surface/ Fabric Colour	Fabric Type	Room/ Area	Phase	Surface Treatment/ Decoration	Notes
1	p3054-329	-	55	-	Cream/ Pink	A	304	Mixed		Filled-in base. Lopsided vessel.
2	p3054-332	-	50	-	Green/ Pink	D	304	Mixed	Slipped?	
3	p1139-41	-	35	-	Cream/ Pale pink	D	314	2.2		
4	p1091-394	-	40	-	Cream-white/ Pink	E	110	2.2		
5	p3085-163	-	50	-	Cream/ Pink	D	304	Mixed		
6	p9022-5	-	55	-	White/ Pale orange	D	616	Mixed	Neat, finished base.	

FAMILY 15

Type 15.1

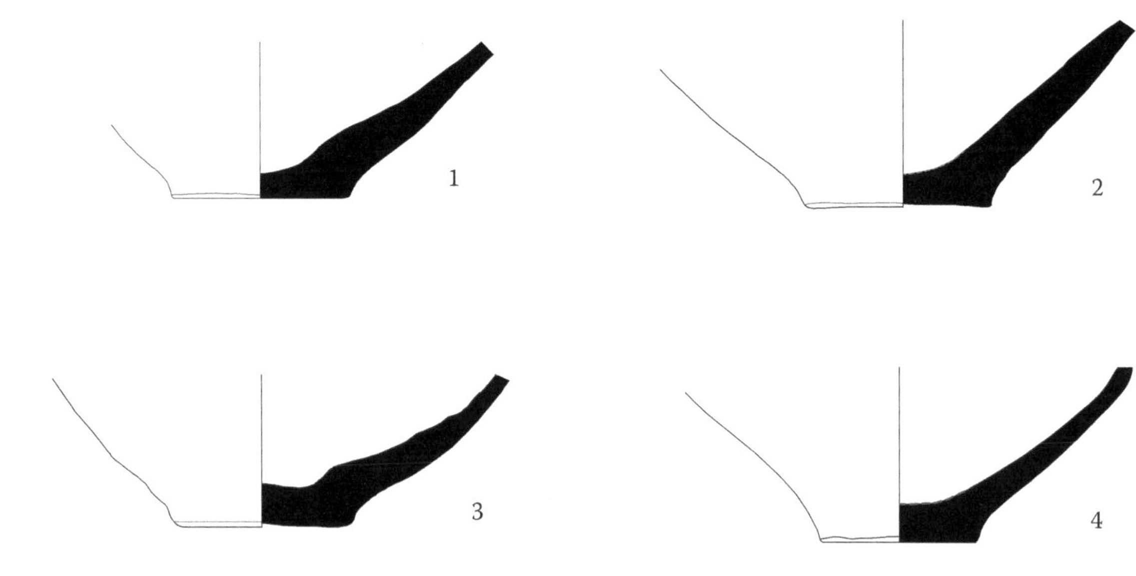

Type 15.2

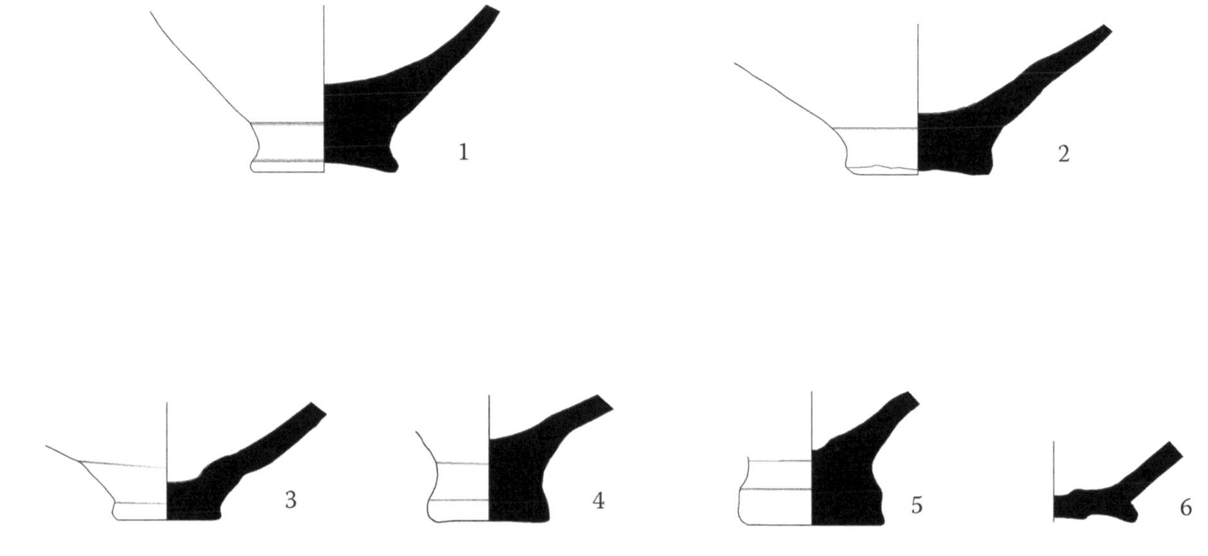

5 cm

PLATE 8

#	Pottery Number	Rim Di. (mm)	Base Di. (mm)	Volume (L)	Surface/ Fabric Colour	Fabric Type	Room/ Area	Phase	Surface Treatment/ Decoration	Notes
1	p3085-280	Irregular	Irregular	-	Green-yellow/ Grey (base) Pink (walls)	F/E	304	Mixed		
2	p6036-70	380	-	-	Red-orange/ Grey-black	F	600	2.2	Impressed band around rim.	
3	p6037-22	500+	-	-	Cream-brown/ Brown	H	-	-	Impressed band beneath rim.	
4	p6040-30	500+	-	-	Green/ Green	F	600	2.2	Impressed band beneath rim.	
5	p3176-6	Imperceptible	Imperceptible	-	Cream-yellow/ Pink-red	F	315	2.2		Heavy finger-print impressions on interior surface.
6	p1079-599	Irregular	Irregular	-	Brown-red/ Pink	F	101	2.1		
7	p8081-12	330	300	-	Pale Green/ Cream-grey	F	152	2.2		Roughly made.
8	p5040-8	400	-	-	Pale green/ Pink-red	F	140–2	2.1		
9	p1094-67	ca. 400 Irregular	-	-	Green/ Green	E	124	Mixed		
10	p3054-334	370	200	ca. 2.7	Pink-red/ Brown-red	F	304	Mixed		
11	p6068-13	500+	-	-	Cream-brown/ Pink-brown	F	Surface	Mixed		
12	p3054-167	350	-	-	Cream/ Orange-red	F	304	Mixed	Impressed band beneath rim.	

FAMILY 20

Type 20.1

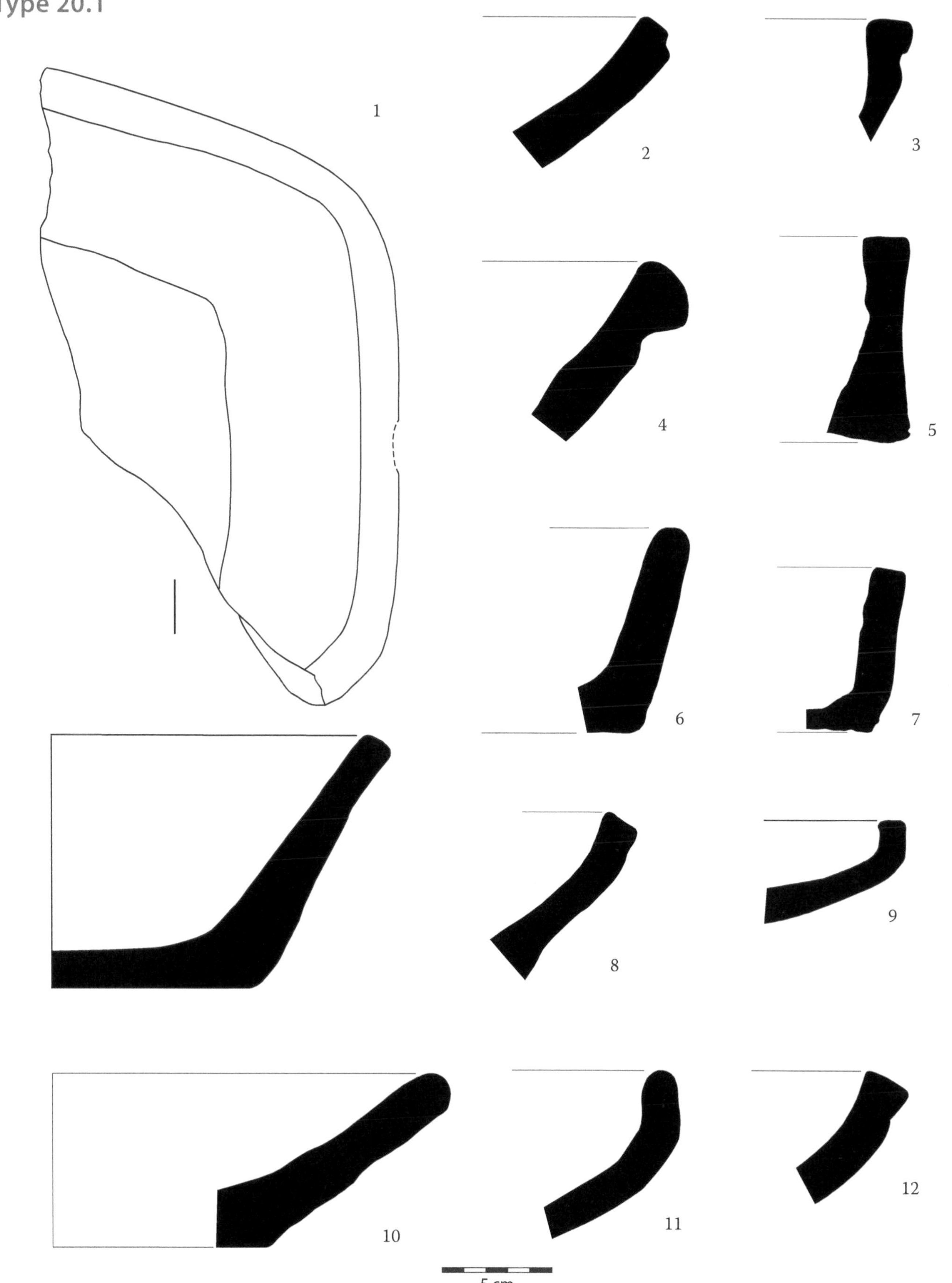

PLATE 9

#	Pottery Number	Rim Di. (mm)	Base Di. (mm)	Volume (L)	Surface/ Fabric Colour	Fabric Type	Room/ Area	Phase	Surface Treatment/ Decoration	Notes
13	p6062-36	360	-	-	Cream-brown/ Cream	F	Surface	Mixed		
14	p1094-160	430	360	ca. 2.8	Cream-brown/ Grey-brown	F	124	Mixed		
15	p3024-20	230	220	ca. 1.7	Green/ Green	F	-	-		
16	p3024-63	320	300	ca. 1.3	Green-yellow/ Green	F	-	-		

#	Pottery Number	Rim Di. (mm)	Base Di. (mm)	Volume (L)	Surface/ Fabric Colour	Fabric Type	Room/ Area	Phase	Surface Treatment/ Decoration	Notes
1	p1068-36	230	260	1.9	Green-brown/ Green-brown	F	101	2.2		

Type 20.1 *cont'd.*

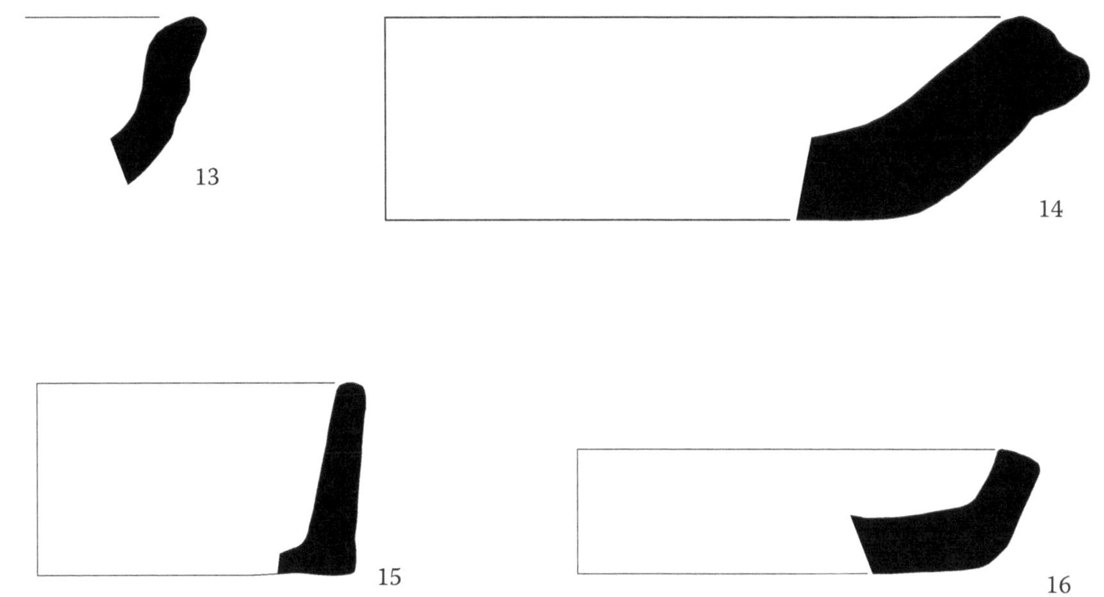

Type 20.2

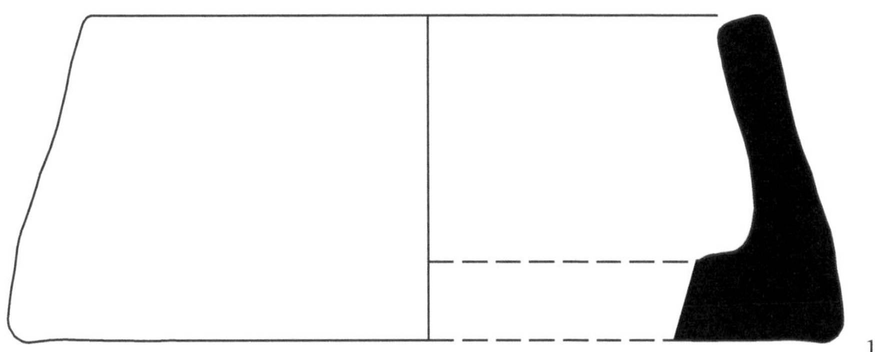

5 cm

PLATE 10

#	Pottery Number	Rim Di. (mm)	Base Di. (mm)	Volume (L)	Surface/ Fabric Colour	Fabric Type	Room/ Area	Phase	Surface Treatment/ Decoration	Notes
1	p4038-1	620	370	164	Green-grey/ Green	F	Burial	Mixed	5 applied bands on upper body.	Pot burial.
2	p3056-8	480	-	-	Cream/ Pink	F	Admin.	2.2	2 grooved bands beneath rim.	
3	p1142-77	500+	-	-	Yellow-green/ Green	F	314	2.1	2 grooved bands beneath rim.	
4	p3158-33	480	-	-	Green-yellow/ Green-yellow	F	315	2.2		Bitumen stained ext.
5	p8013-3	480	-	-	Green-yellow/ Green	F	316	2.3	2 grooved bands beneath rim.	
6	p4034-33	400	-	-	Pale green/ Green	F	-	Houses	1 applied band beneath rim.	
7	p5018-1	-	-	-	Pale green/Grey	F	140–2	2.3		Bitumen coated/stained interior and exterior surface. Thick between ridges.

FAMILY 25

Type 25.1

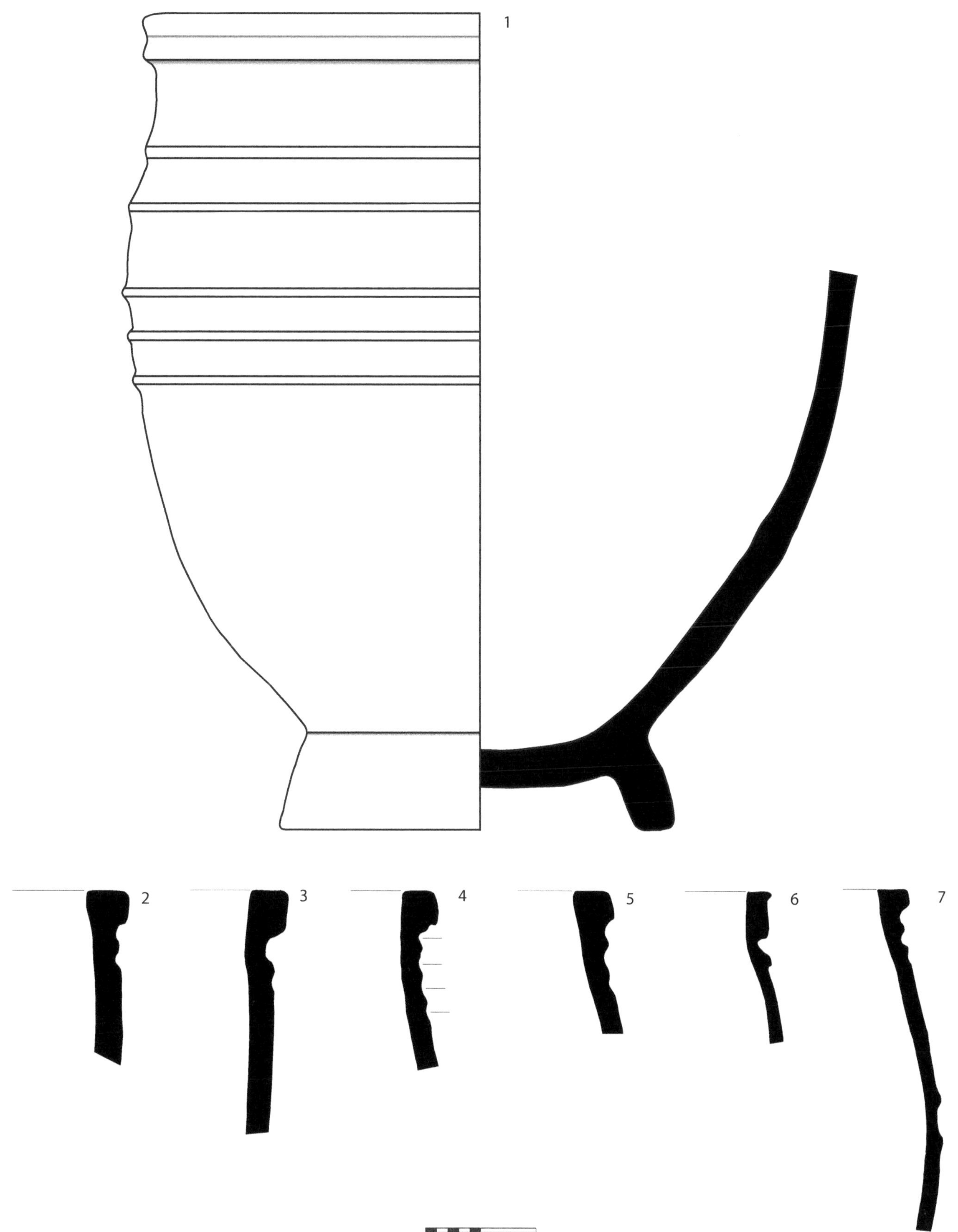

PLATE 11

#	Pottery Number	Rim Di. (mm)	Base Di. (mm)	Volume (L)	Surface/ Fabric Colour	Fabric Type	Room/ Area	Phase	Surface Treatment/ Decoration	Notes
8	p3083-15	560	-	-	Pink-red/ Black-grey	E	304	Mixed	2 grooved bands beneath rim.	
9	p6116-40	390	-	-	Green-yellow/ Pink	F	Surface	Mixed	Grooved band beneath rim.	
10	p6126-3	430	-	-	Yellow-green/ Grey-green	F	Surface	Mixed	2 grooved bands beneath rim.	
11	p6163-42	520	-	-	Green/ Green	F	Surface	Mixed	Incised crescent band beneath rim.	Bitumen coated interior/ bitumen stained exterior.
12	p6125-1	570	370	118.4	Green/ Green	F	Surface	Mixed	1 deep groove beneath rim. 4+ applied bands on body. Bitumen coated interior and exterior; 10cm thick on exterior, exhibiting rope impressions.	
13	p3075-2	540	325	77.6	-	-	Burial	Mixed	3 applied bands on body.	Pot burial.
14	p3075-1	620	-	151.9	-	-	Burial	Mixed	3 applied bands on upper body.	Pot burial.

Type 25.1 *cont'd.*

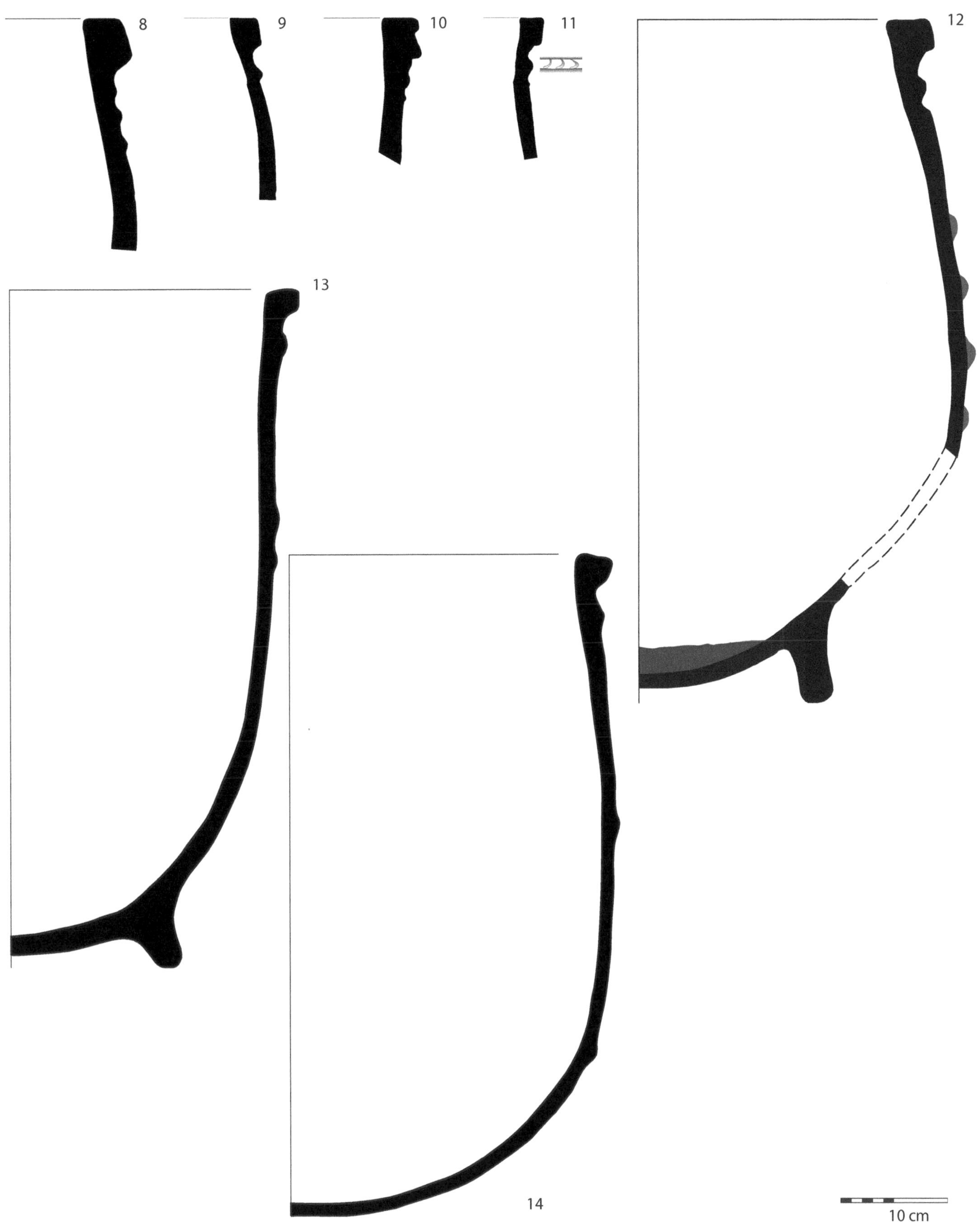

PLATE 12

#	Pottery Number	Rim Di. (mm)	Base Di. (mm)	Volume (L)	Surface/ Fabric Colour	Fabric Type	Room/ Area	Phase	Surface Treatment/ Decoration	Notes
15	p6092-1	770	320	144	Green/ Grey-pink	F	Burial	Mixed	2 applied bands on body. Bitumen coated interior and exterior.	Pot burial.
16	p6093-1	825	475	228.1	Green/ Green	F	Burial	Mixed	3 applied bands on body.	Pot burial.

Type 25.1 *cont'd.*

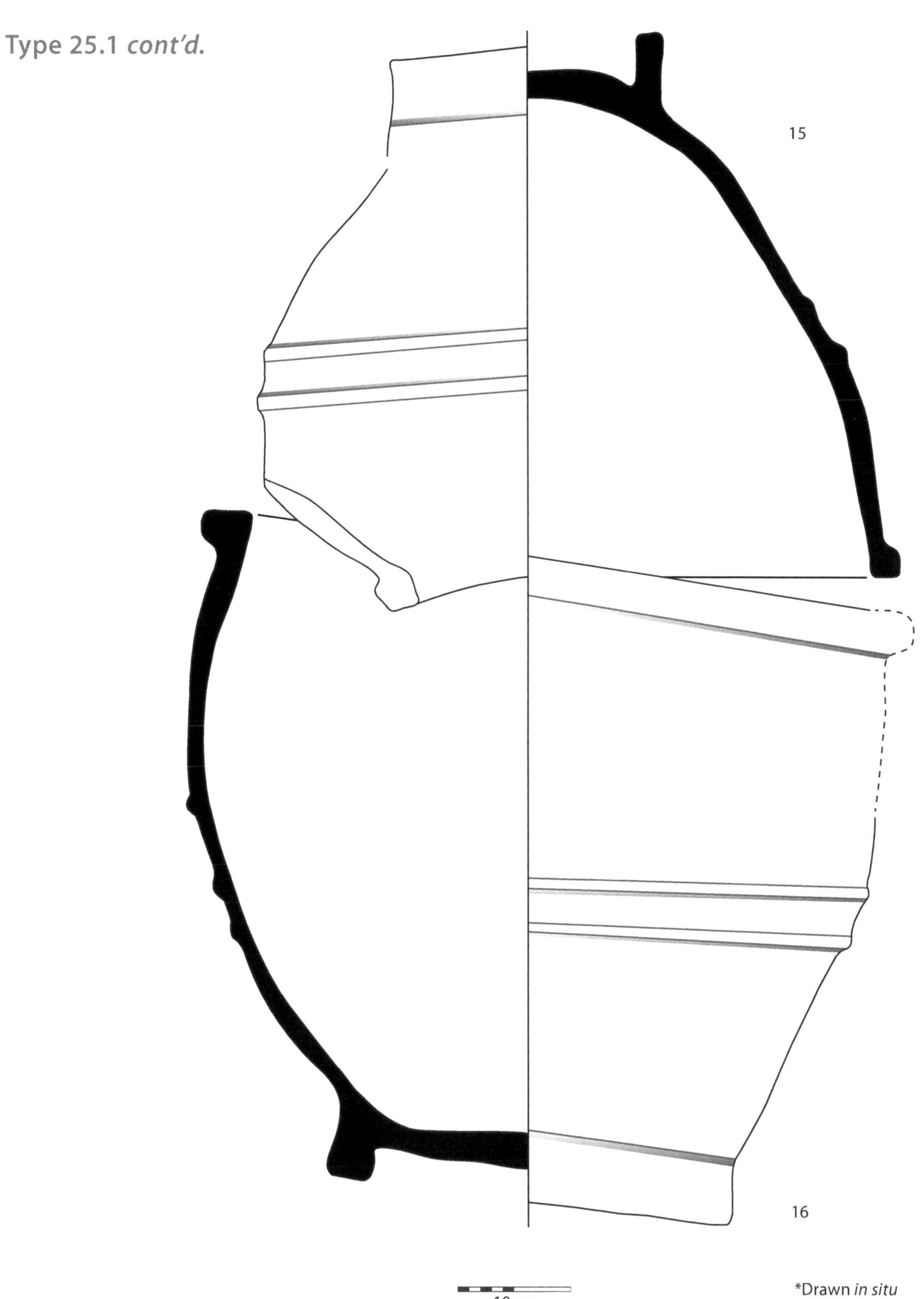

*Drawn *in situ*

PLATE 13

#	Pottery Number	Rim Di. (mm)	Base Di. (mm)	Volume (L)	Surface/ Fabric Colour	Fabric Type	Room/ Area	Phase	Surface Treatment/ Decoration	Notes
1	p1039-27	380	-	-	Green/ Green	F	-	-	2+ grooved bands beneath rim.	
2	p3154-18	450	-	-	Dark green/ Green	F	315	2.2	1 grooved band beneath rim.	
3	p6051-33	340	-	-	Red-orange/ Red-orange	F	-	-	1+ grooved band beneath rim.	
4	p3079-7	440	-	-	Green-yellow/ Cream-green	F	-	-	1 grooved band beneath rim.	
5	p9018-80	270	-	-	Yellow/ Grey	F	616	Mixed	Ridges beneath rim and around body.	

#	Pottery Number	Rim Di. (mm)	Base Di. (mm)	Volume (L)	Surface/ Fabric Colour	Fabric Type	Room/ Area	Phase	Surface Treatment/ Decoration	Notes
1	p3125-15	500+	-	-	Green/ Green-grey	F	302	1	4 grooved bands beneath rim.	
2	p1078-78	-	-	-	Bright green/ Green-brown	H	-	-	Multiple grooved bands.	
3	p5040-20	230	-	-	Green/ Green	F	140–2	2.2	3 ridges and grooves on upper body.	High-fired. Slightly warped.
4	p6007-64	-	-	-	Green/ Green	F overfired	-	-		Warped.
5	p1163-11	380	-	-	Green/ Green	F	Admin.	2.2		

Type 25.2

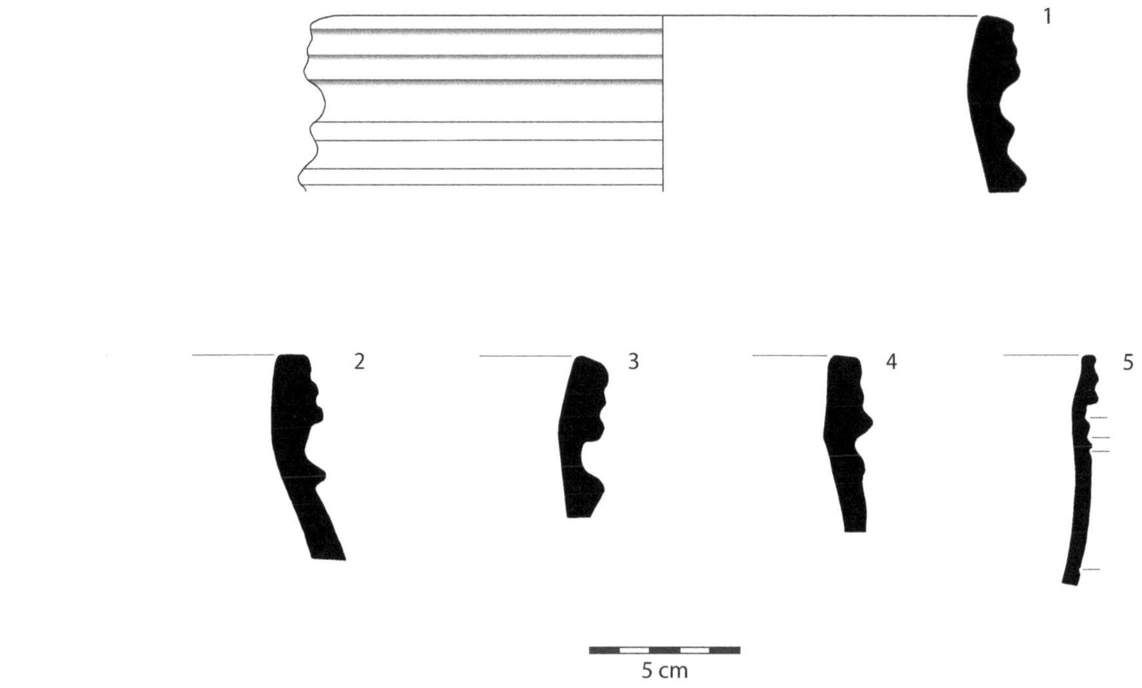

Type 25.3

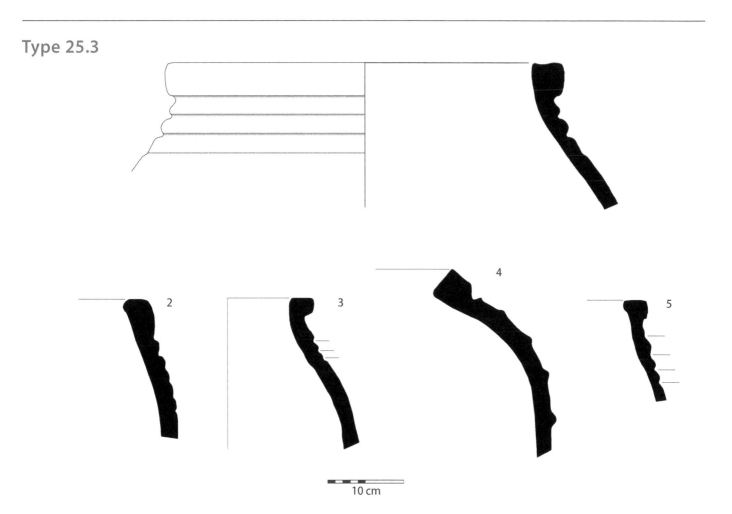

PLATE 14

#	Pottery Number	Rim Di. (mm)	Base Di. (mm)	Volume (L)	Surface/ Fabric Colour	Fabric Type	Room/ Area	Phase	Surface Treatment/ Decoration	Notes
6	p8008-57	270	-	-	Green/ Green	F	316	2.3	Multiple grooved bands beneath rim.	Large shell incl.
7	p8020-5	220	-	-	Green/ Green	F	316	2.3	Multiple grooved bands beneath rim.	
8	p8083-39	350	-	-	Yellow/ Green	F	152	2.2		Bitumen coated interior.
9	p8083-38	240	-	-	Pale green/ Grey-green	F	152	2.2	Incised crescent decoration.	
10	p1079-250	200	-	-	Cream-pink/ Red-pink	F	101	2.1	2 grooved bands beneath rim.	
11	p3054-386	380	-	-	Green-yellow/ Grey	F	304	Mixed	Multiple grooved bands.	

#	Pottery Number	Rim Di. (mm)	Base Di. (mm)	Volume (L)	Surface/ Fabric Colour	Fabric Type	Room/ Area	Phase	Surface Treatment/ Decoration	Notes
1	p6096-118	300	-	-	Green/ Grey	F	Surface	Mixed	4 grooved bands beneath rim.	
2	p1139-13	400	-	-	Green/ Green	E	314	2.2	1 grooved band beneath rim. 2 incised lines on upper body.	
3	p1079-343	290	-	-	Cream/ Pink	F	101	2.1	3 grooved bands beneath rim.	
4	p1079-765	290	-	-	White/ Pale brown	F	101	2.1	3 grooved bands beneath rim.	
5	p8058-1	290	-	-	Green/ Green-brown	F	316	2.2	2 grooved bands beneath rim.	
6	p8058-6	290	-	-	Green/ Green-brown	F	316	2.2	1 relief band beneath rim. Bitumen coated interior and exterior surfaces; 5cm thick beneath rim, exhibiting rope impressions.	
7	p6111-69	320	-	-	Cream/ Pink	E	Surface	Mixed	2 grooved bands beneath rim.	
8	p6096-8	280	-	-	Green/ Black	Over-fired	Surface	Mixed	Rim band merges with body. 2 grooved bands.	
9	p1077-5	190	-	-	Green-yellow/ Cream-brown	F	101	2.2	2 grooved bands beneath rim.	

Type 25.3 *cont'd.*

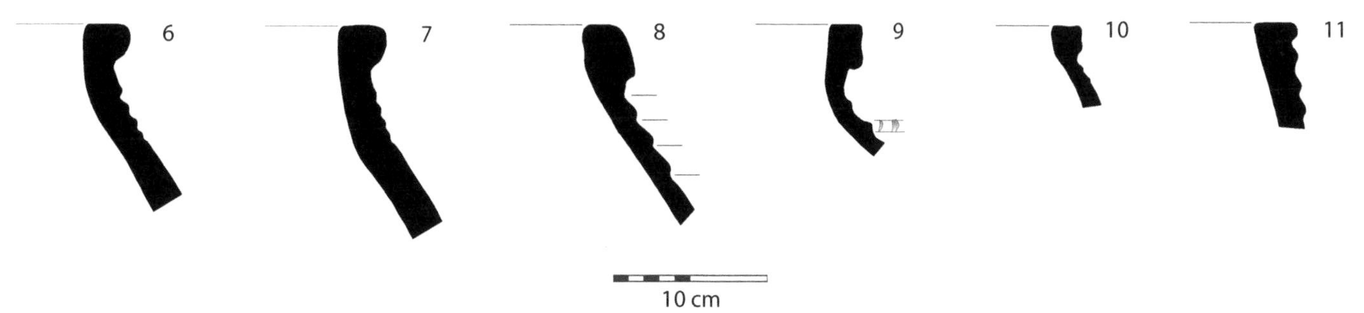

Type 25.4

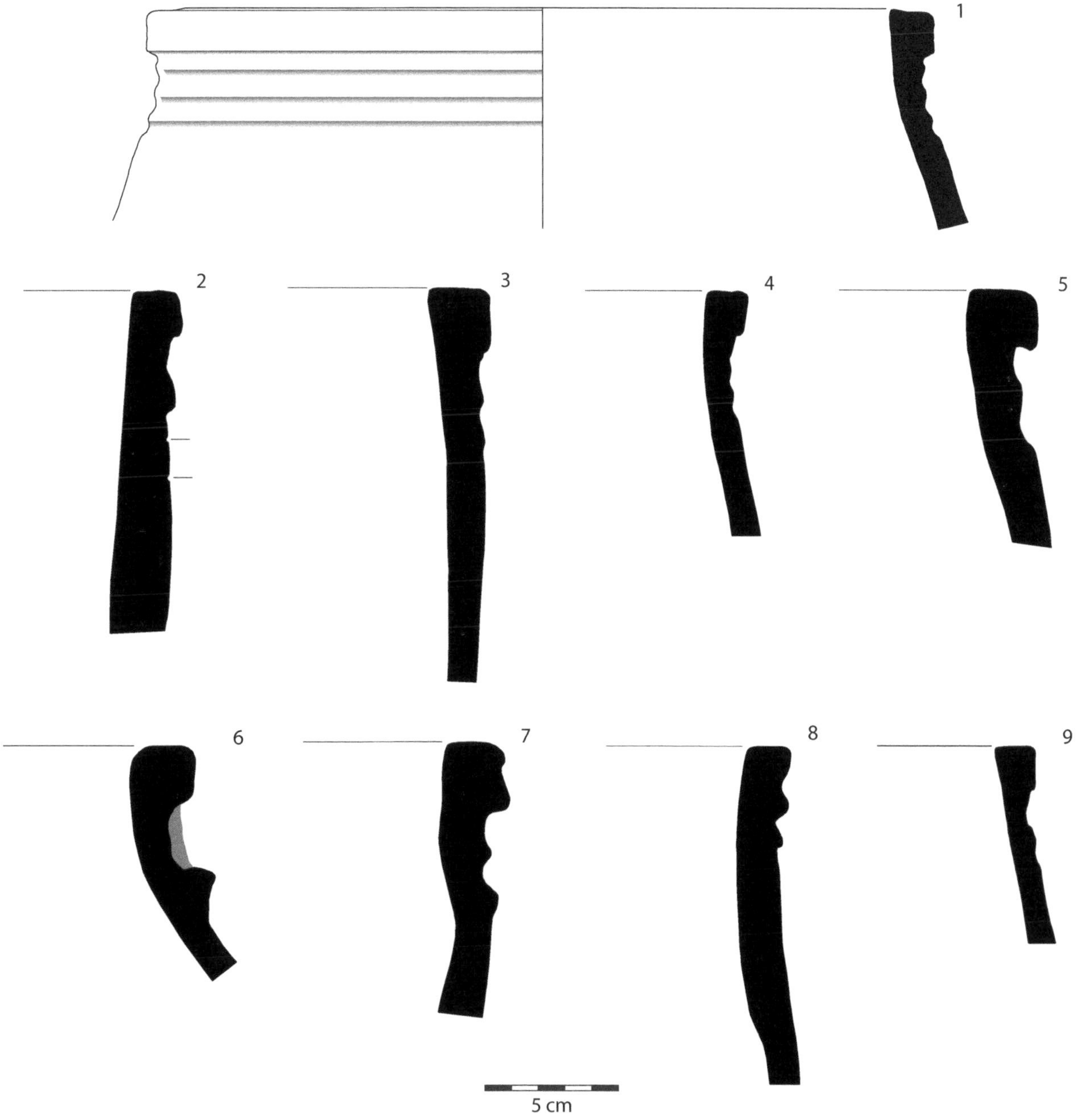

1

2 3 4 5

6 7 8 9

5 cm

PLATE 15

#	Pottery Number	Rim Di. (mm)	Base Di. (mm)	Volume (L)	Surface/ Fabric Colour	Fabric Type	Room/ Area	Phase	Surface Treatment/ Decoration	Notes
1	p4022-14	-	450	-	Green/ Green	F	-	Houses		
2	p4006-48	-	260	-	Green/ Green	F	House 2	Houses		
3	p3168-25	-	170	-	Pale orange/ Orange	F	315	2.2		
4	p6085-10	-	350	-	Green-yellow/ Orange-red	F	Surface	Mixed		Black stained (burnt?) interior surface.
5	p8010-1	-	360	-	Green/ Green	F	316	2.3		
6	p6111-26	-	340	-	Grey/ Red	F	Surface	Mixed		
7	p3151-39	-	160	-	Green/ Pale green	F	315	2.2		
8	p3085-267	-	360	-	Cream-yellow/ Pink	F	304	Mixed		

Type 25.5

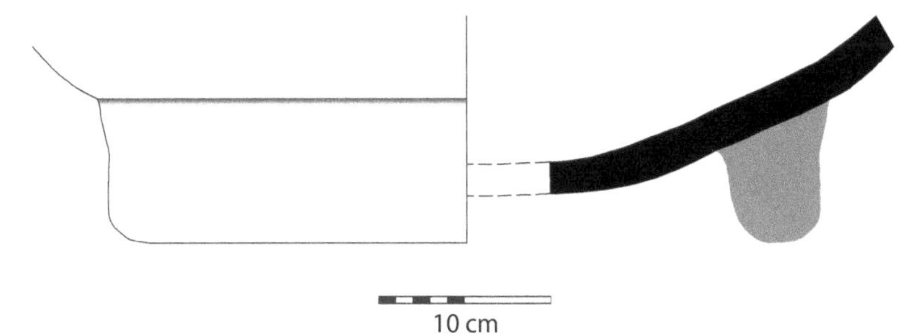

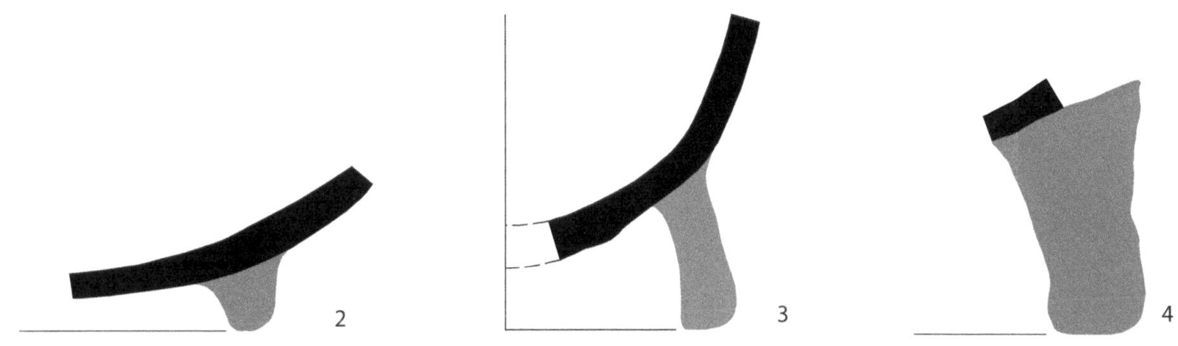

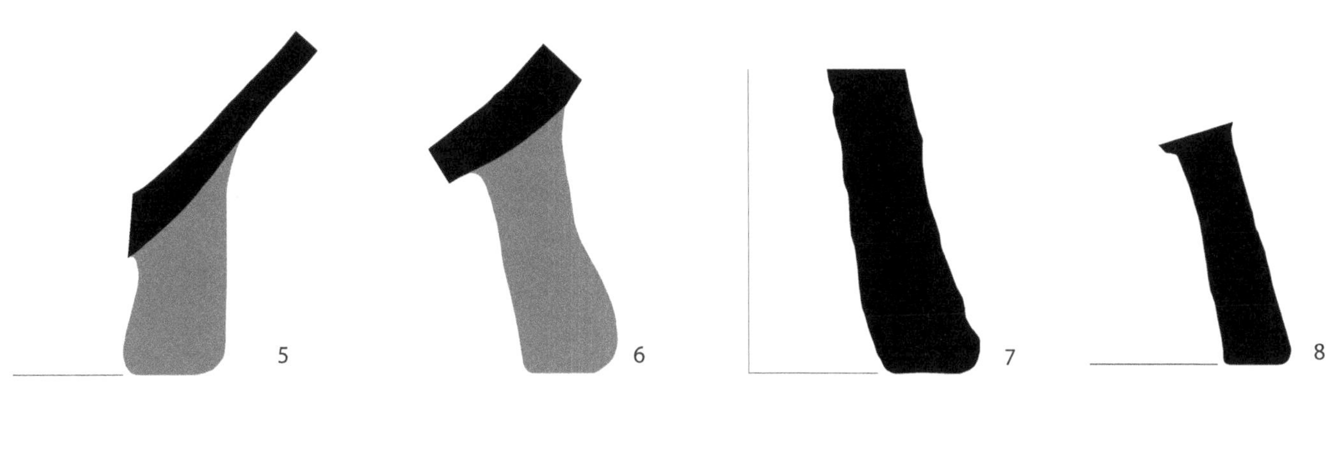

PLATE 16

#	Pottery Number	Rim Di. (mm)	Base Di. (mm)	Volume (L)	Surface/ Fabric Colour	Fabric Type	Room/ Area	Phase	Surface Treatment/ Decoration	Notes
1	p5029-1	430	55 (14)	23.84 to bottom third; 46.7 including middle third; 60.64 up to bottom of rim band.	Green-yellow/ Pink-red	F	140–2	2.3	Slipped (?) interior and exterior surfaces. Incised crescents beneath rim. Alternating impressed bands and wavy bands on entire body.	
2	p5060-10	330	58 (21)	2.92 bottom half; 15.28 to bottom of rim band.	White-pink/ Pink	F	140–2	2.1	Impressed bands around upper body, middle section, and just above base.	
3	p8082-42	270	45 (13)	3.20 bottom third; 6.68 to middle third; 10.32 to below rim band.	Pale green/ Pink	F	152	2.2	Alternating impressed bands and half-wavy bands on entire body.	
4	p6136-88	400	-	-	Green-brown/ Green-brown	F	Surface	Mixed	2 grooved beneath rim. Fingernail impressions at rim. Impressed bands on body, with lightly impressed wavy decoration in between.	
5	p1171-45	350	-	-	Pale green/ Green	F	-	-	Multiple sets of impressed bands around body.	
6	p8082-43	230	-	-	White/ Grey-green	F	152	2.2	Impressed band beneath rim, and 2 around body.	

Type 35.1

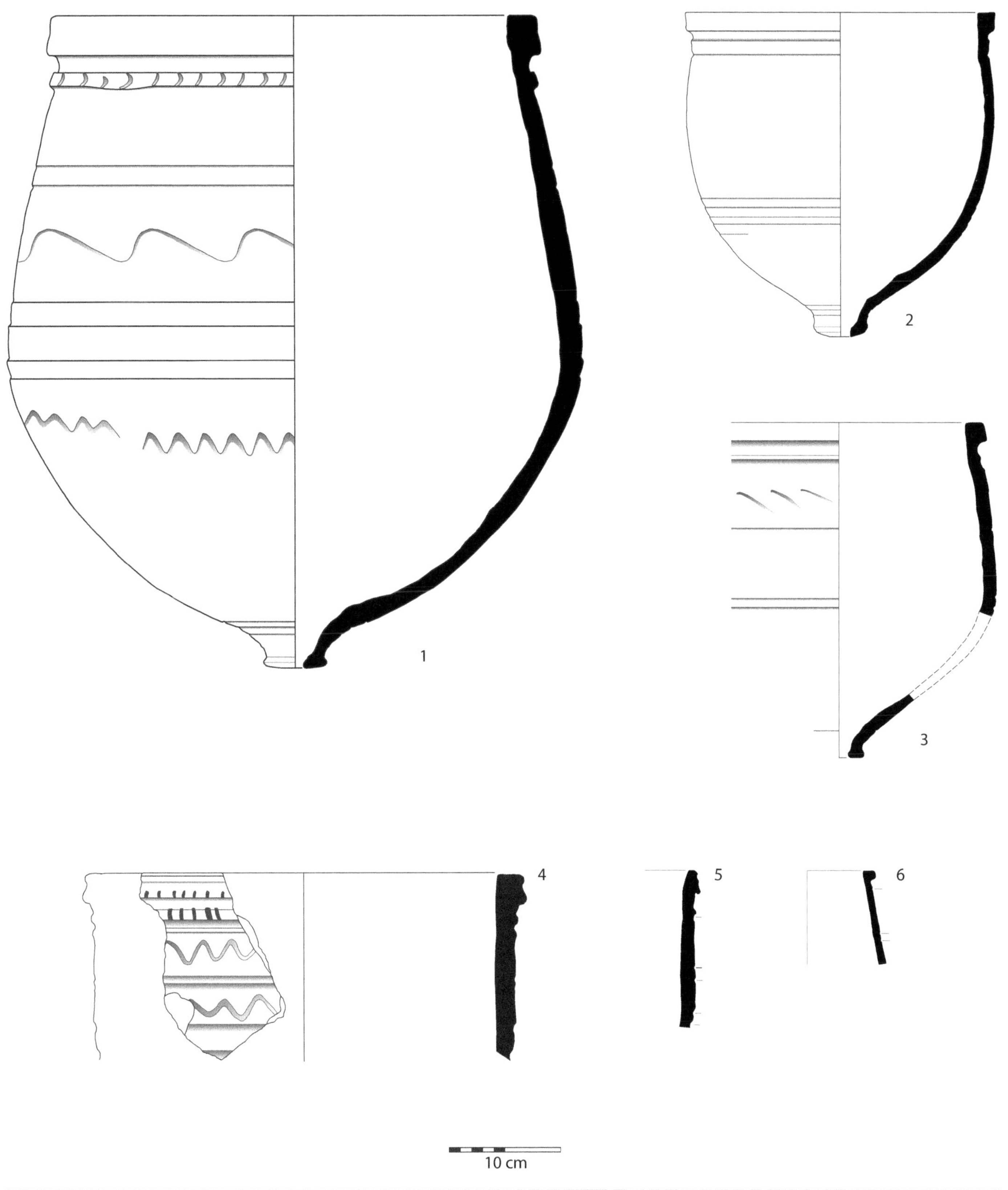

PLATE 17

#	Pottery Number	Rim Di. (mm)	Base Di. (mm)	Volume (L)	Surface/ Fabric Colour	Fabric Type	Room/ Area	Phase	Surface Treatment/ Decoration	Notes
1	p6165-45	-	85 (16)	30+	Yellow/ Pink-orange	F	156	2.2	Bitumen coated interior. Bitumen coating around exterior base, and ca. 9cm up the exterior body.	
2	p5060-1	-	110 (28)	-	Cream - yellow/Pale brown	F	140–2	2.1	Bitumen coated interior. Bitumen coated exterior base and part-way up body.	
3	p3033-51	-	85 (30)	-	Cream/ Pink	F	-	-		Deliberate base perforation?
4	p3176-55	-	60 (25)	-	Pale pink/ White-cream	C/E	315	2.2		
5	p6165-19	-	45 (30)	-	Green/ Green	H	156	2.2		
6	p1166-17	-	50 (22)	-	Cream-Brown/ Pink-brown	F	314	2.1		
7	p3163-51	-	50 (25)	-	Cream-yellow/ Cream-yellow	F	315	2.2		
8	p8076-8	-	70 (25)	-	Yellow-cream/ Cream	F	125	2.3		
9	p6091-93	-	50 (20)	-	Pale green/ Pale green	H	Surface	Mixed	2 incised bands around lower body.	
10	p6136-23	-	50 (25)	-	Green-brown/ Brown	H	Surface	Mixed	5 incised bands around lower body.	
11	p8075-25	-	77 (25)	-	Cream-pink/ White-cream	F	125	2.3	Irregularly incised relief band above base.	

Type 30.2

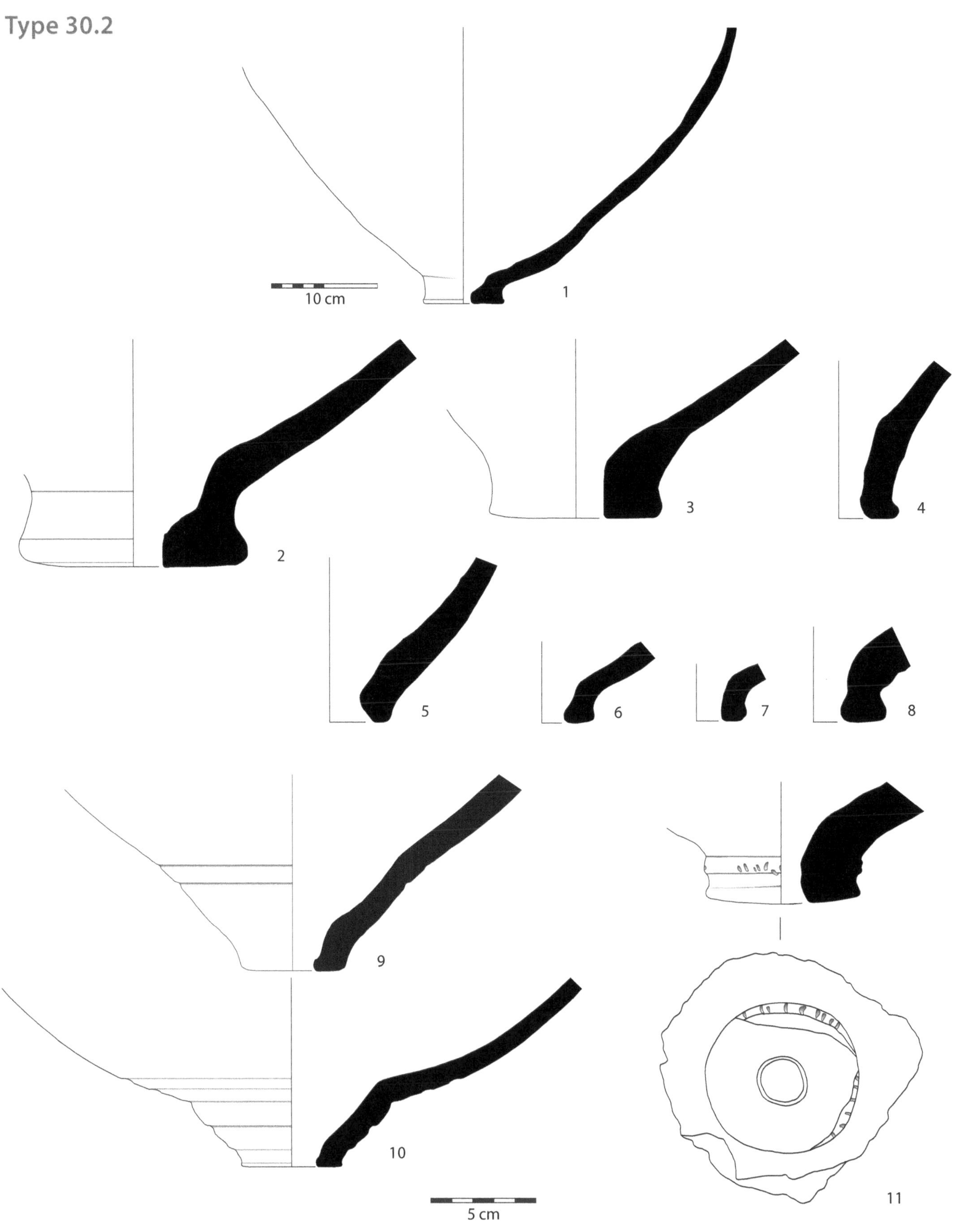

PLATE 18

#	Pottery Number	Rim Di. (mm)	Base Di. (mm)	Volume (L)	Surface/ Fabric Colour	Fabric Type	Room/ Area	Phase	Surface Treatment/ Decoration	Notes
1	p1114-26	-	-	-	Green/ Green	F	Admin.	2.2	Multiple impressed bands, a relief band with fingernail incisions, and a lightly impressed wavy band. Decoration just above base.	
2	p6126-31	-	-	-	Green/ Green	F	Surface	Mixed	Multiple impressed bands, fingernail incisions, and wavy impressed band around shoulder.	
3	p8083-5	-	-	-	Pale green/ Pink	F	152	2.2	Three sets of impressed bands up body. Two potter's marks (?).	

Type 30.3

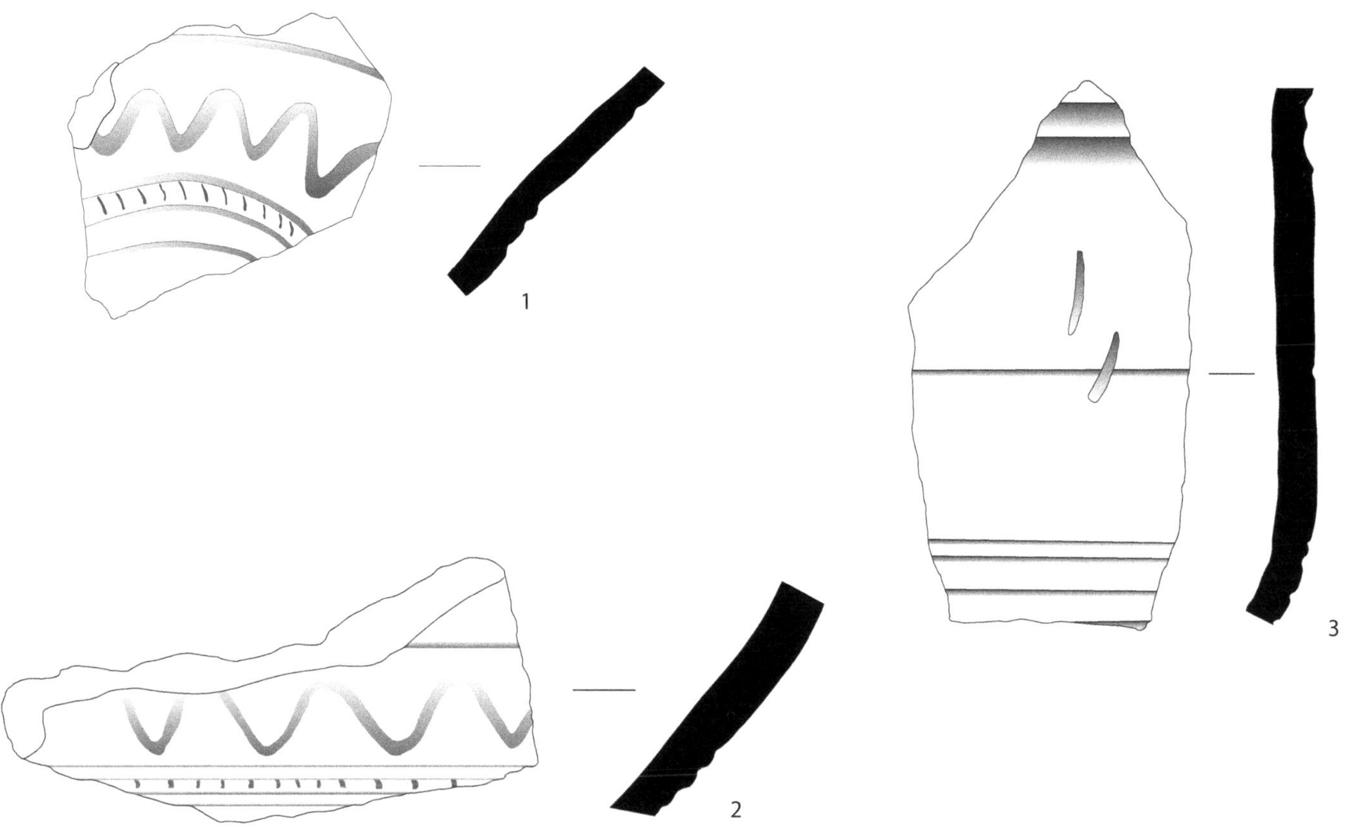

5 cm

PLATE 19

#	Pottery Number	Rim Di. (mm)	Base Di. (mm)	Volume (L)	Surface/ Fabric Colour	Fabric Type	Room/ Area	Phase	Surface Treatment/ Decoration	Notes
1	p1096-456	100	62	0.55	Pale orange-brown/ Orange-brown	A	Admin.	2.2		
2	p3064-227	85	-	-	Pale pink/ Pink	A	Admin.	2.2	3 incised lines beneath rim; 3 incised lines on body.	
3	p3058-4	140	-	-	Pale green/ Pale pink	A	-	-	3 incised lines on upper body.	Filled-in base.

#	Pottery Number	Rim Di. (mm)	Base Di. (mm)	Volume (L)	Surface/ Fabric Colour	Fabric Type	Room/ Area	Phase	Surface Treatment/ Decoration	Notes
1	p3088-182	125	80	Lower Quarter: 0.46 2nd Quarter: 0.34 3rd Quarter: 0.32 Upper Quarter: 0.30 Total: 1.42	Green/ Black	Over-fired	304	Mixed	6 incised bands on lower body; 6 in the middle; 5 on the upper body.	Plugged base.
2	p5022-65	115	57	0.46 to bottom section; 0.66 to 2nd section; 0.93 to 3rd section; 1.13 to bottom of rim band.	Pale orange/ Orange	A	140–2	2.2	Slipped exterior. Alternate impressed bands, small linear incisions, and wavy bands.	
3	p1139-125	110		Lower: 0.1 Total: 0.43	Dark cream/ Cream	A	314	2.2	Impressed band on lower body.	
4	p1114-38	140	-	-	Cream/ Pink	A	Admin.	2.2	Impressed band beneath rim; impressed band at midpoint.	
5	p6041-354	140	-	-	Pale pink/ Pink	E	601	2.2	2 impressed bands on upper body.	

FAMILY 35

Type 35.1

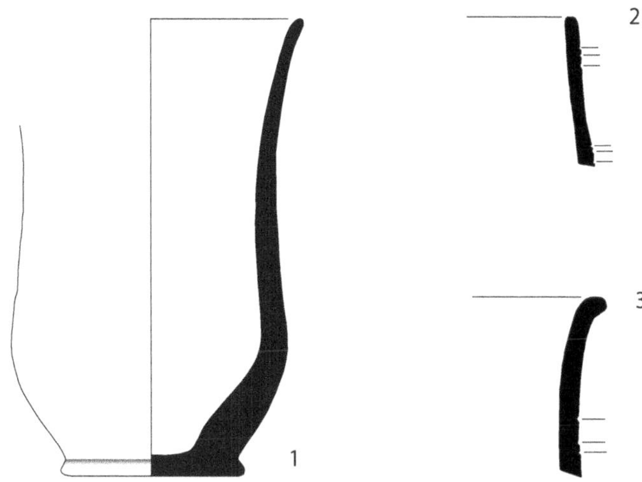

Type 35.2

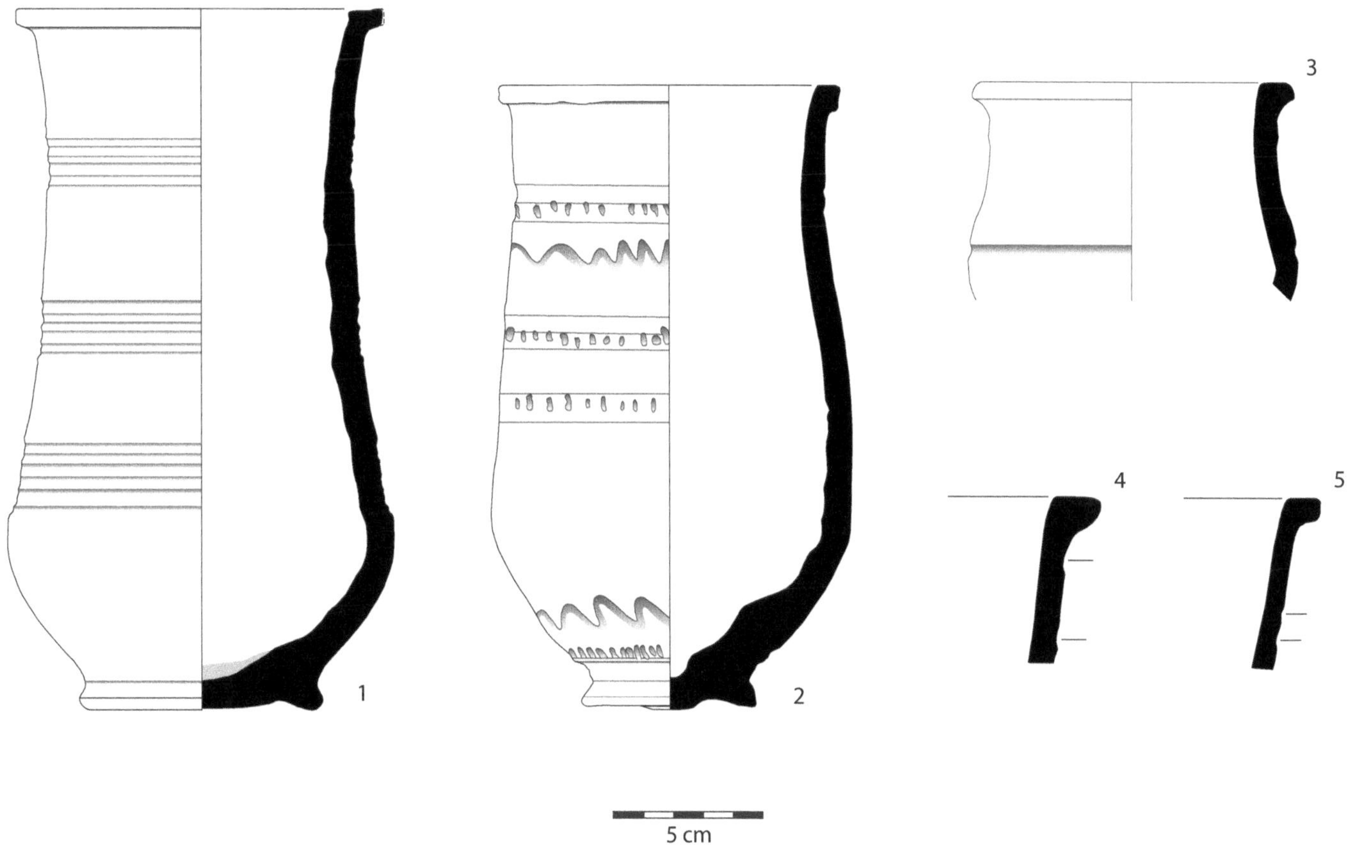

3

4 5

1 2

5 cm

PLATE 20

#	Pottery Number	Rim Di. (mm)	Base Di. (mm)	Volume (L)	Surface/ Fabric Colour	Fabric Type	Room/ Area	Phase	Surface Treatment/ Decoration	Notes
6	p8008-114	140	-	Middle section: 0.54 Middle to upper: 0.52	Pale orange-pink/ Dark pink	E	316	2.3	2 incised bands beneath rim; 2 in the middle.	
7	p1094-246	170	-	-	Cream/ Cream-pale brown	D	124	Mixed	Impressed band beneath rim; 1 in the middle.	
8	p6096-93	160	-	-	Cream/ Pink-pale orange	E	Surface	Mixed	5 impressed bands on upper body.	
9	p6096-41	170	-	-	Pale green/ Pale cream	F	Surface	Mixed	Pink wash? One impressed band on upper body.	
10	5022-66	220	-	Middle section; 1.44 Upper section: 1.6	Pale green/ Cream	F	140–2	2.2	Two sets of impressed and wavy bands around body.	4 pierced repair (?) holes directly beneath rim.
11	p3054-325	-	-	-	Green/ Green	F	304	Mixed	2 impressed bands on upper body.	
12	p3085-165	160	-	-	Yellow-green/ Pale green	E	304	Mixed	3 impressed bands on body.	
13	p3025-74	150	-	-	Green-yellow/ Pale pink	D	302	Mixed		
14	p6091-76	180	-	-	Yellow-pale brown/ Pale brown	E	Surface	Mixed	2 impressed bands on upper body.	

#	Pottery Number	Rim Di. (mm)	Base Di. (mm)	Volume (L)	Surface/ Fabric Colour	Fabric Type	Room/ Area	Phase	Surface Treatment/ Decoration	Notes
1	p4036-20	-	-	Lower: 0.1 To middle: 0.49	Pale pink/ Pink	D	-	Houses	3 incised bands on lower body; 4 incised bands on middle of body.	
2	p3088-137	-	-	-	White-cream/ Pink-cream	A	304	Mixed	Impressed band on lower body; 6 incised lines in middle of body; 6 incised lines on upper(?) body.	
3	p3088-136	-	-	-	Cream-yellow/ Pink-cream	D	304	Mixed	Impressed band on lower body; 9 incised lines in middle of body; 6 incised lines on upper(?) body.	
4	p3025-83	-	-	-	Pink/ Orange-red	A	302	Mixed	2 incised bands on middle of body; 2 incised bands on upper body.	
5	p3119-54	-	-	-	White-cream/ Pale pink	A – with "grog"?	Admin.	2.2	3 incised bands on lower body; 4 incised bands on middle of body.	

Type 35.2 *cont'd.*

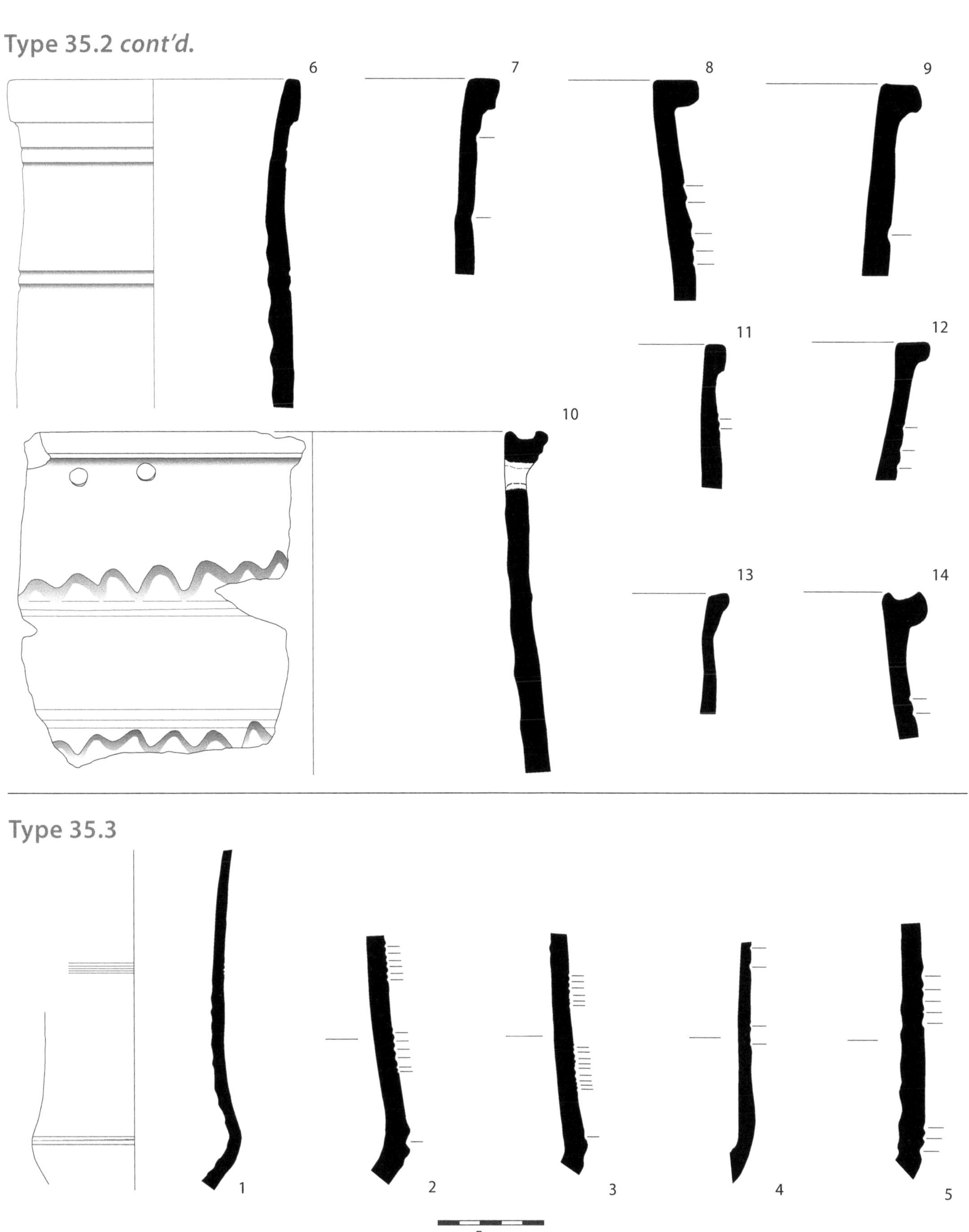

PLATE 21

#	Pottery Number	Rim Di. (mm)	Base Di. (mm)	Volume (L)	Surface/ Fabric Colour	Fabric Type	Room/ Area	Phase	Surface Treatment/ Decoration	Notes
1	p3085-281	-	65	Lower: 0.08 To middle: 0.45	Cream-white/ Pale orange	E	304	Mixed	2 impressed bands on lower body; 5 incised bands on middle.	Filled-in base.
2	p3025-80	-	60		Pale pink/ Red	A	302	Mixed		
3	p3088-135	-	100	Lower: 0.24	Cream-yellow/ Pink-cream	D	304	Mixed	Slipped? Impressed band on lower body.	
4	p8008-26	-	100	-	Dull green/ Orange	D	316	2.3		

#	Pottery Number	Rim Di. (mm)	Base Di. (mm)	Volume (L)	Surface/ Fabric Colour	Fabric Type	Room/ Area	Phase	Surface Treatment/ Decoration	Notes
1	p6058-104	-	65	Lower: 0.06	Cream-yellow/ Brown-green	E	601	2.1	Impressed band on lower body.	
2	p8016-8	-	39	Lower: 0.09	Green/ Green	A	316	2.3	2 incised lines on lower body.	
3	p3085-125	-	47	Lower: 0.09	Green-yellow/ Pale green	D	304	Mixed	2 impressed bands on lower body.	
4	p8074-17	-	40	0.05 to impressed bands around body.	Pink/ Pale pink	E	125	2.3	2 impressed bands.	
5	p3054-394	-	45	Lower: 0.07	Green/ Pale green	D	304	Mixed	Impressed band on lower body.	
6	p8083-41	-	93	0.92 to impressed bands around body.	Pale pink/ Pink	E/F	152	2.2	2 lightly impressed bands around body.	
7	p6166-40	-	40	0.12 to impressed bands around body.	Yellow-cream/ Pink	E	Surface	Mixed	2 impressed bands around body.	
8	p3059-16	-	35	Lower 0.02	White/ Pale orange	A	Vaults	1	Impressed band on lower body.	
9	p8083-40	-	50	0.1 to impressed bands around body.	Dark green/ Green	B	152	2.2	2+ incised bands around body.	
10	p3054-328	-	40	-	Cream/ Cream-pale pink	D	304	Mixed		Filled-in base.
11	p5017-55	-	63	-	Orange/ Pink-brown	C/E	140–2	2.2		
12	p5017-41	-	85	-	Pink/ Orange	C	140–2	2.2		
13	p8083-21	-	72	0.26 to impressed bands around body.	White/ Pink	D	152	2.2	Slipped (?) exterior. Impressed band at base; 2+ impressed bands around body.	
14	p1080-20	-	65	-	Pink/ Pink	C	101	2.1		

Type 35.4

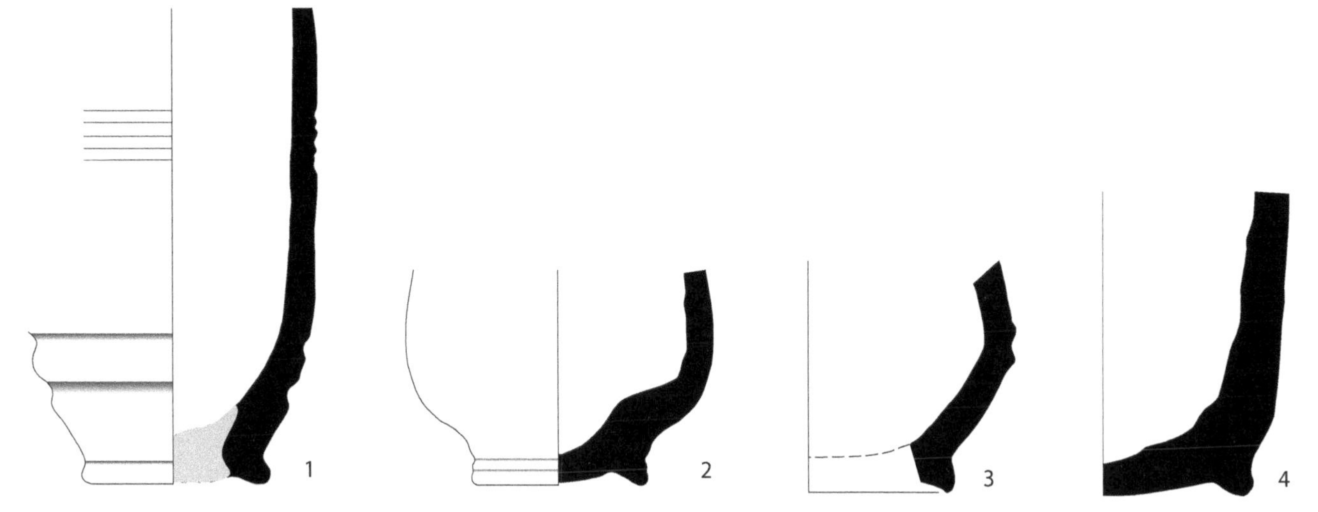

Type 35.5

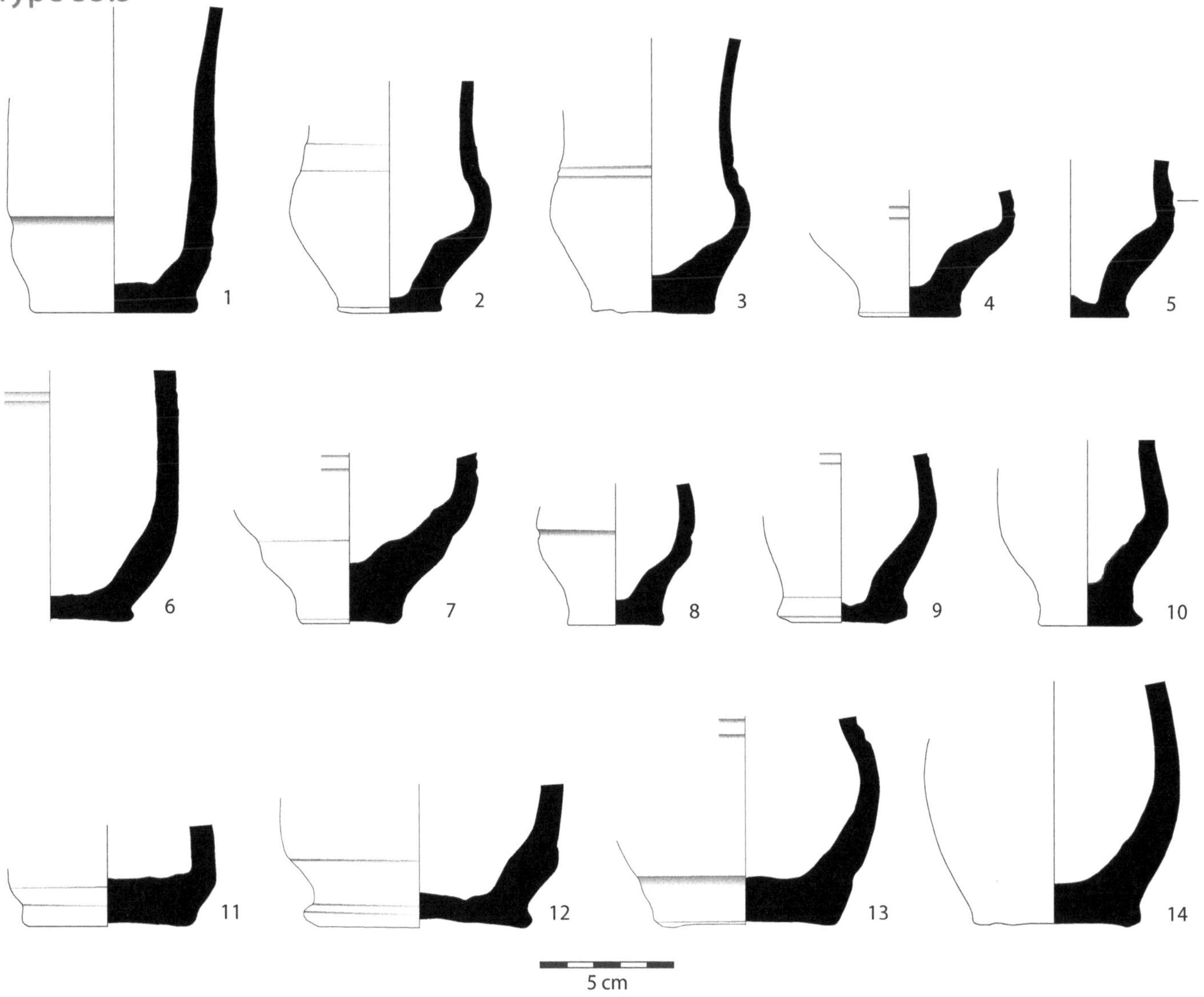

1 2 3 4 5

6 7 8 9 10

11 12 13 14

5 cm

PLATE 22

#	Pottery Number	Rim Di. (mm)	Base Di. (mm)	Volume (L)	Surface/ Fabric Colour	Fabric Type	Room/ Area	Phase	Surface Treatment/ Decoration	Notes
15	p3087-11	-	100	-	Green/ Cream	E	304	Mixed		
16	p1094-191	-	80	-	Cream-brown/ Pale brown	E	124	Mixed		Plugged base.
17	p6163-25	-	80	-	Yellow-cream/ orange	F	Surface	Mixed		
18	p1094-194	-	127	Lower: 1.05	Green/ Green	F	124	Mixed	5 impressed bands on body.	
19	p5008-43	-	105	-	Pale brown/ Pale brown	E	140–2	2.2		Bitumen coated interior around base. Finger impression at exterior base.
20	p5016-12	-	95	0.9 to lines in the middle of the body.	Green/ Grey-green	E/H	140–2	2.3	2 impressed bands around body.	
21	p5016-7	-	85	0.87 to bands around body.	Pink/ Pale brown	E	140–2	2.3	Incised line around lower body; 3 impressed bands around body.	

Type 35.5 *cont'd.*

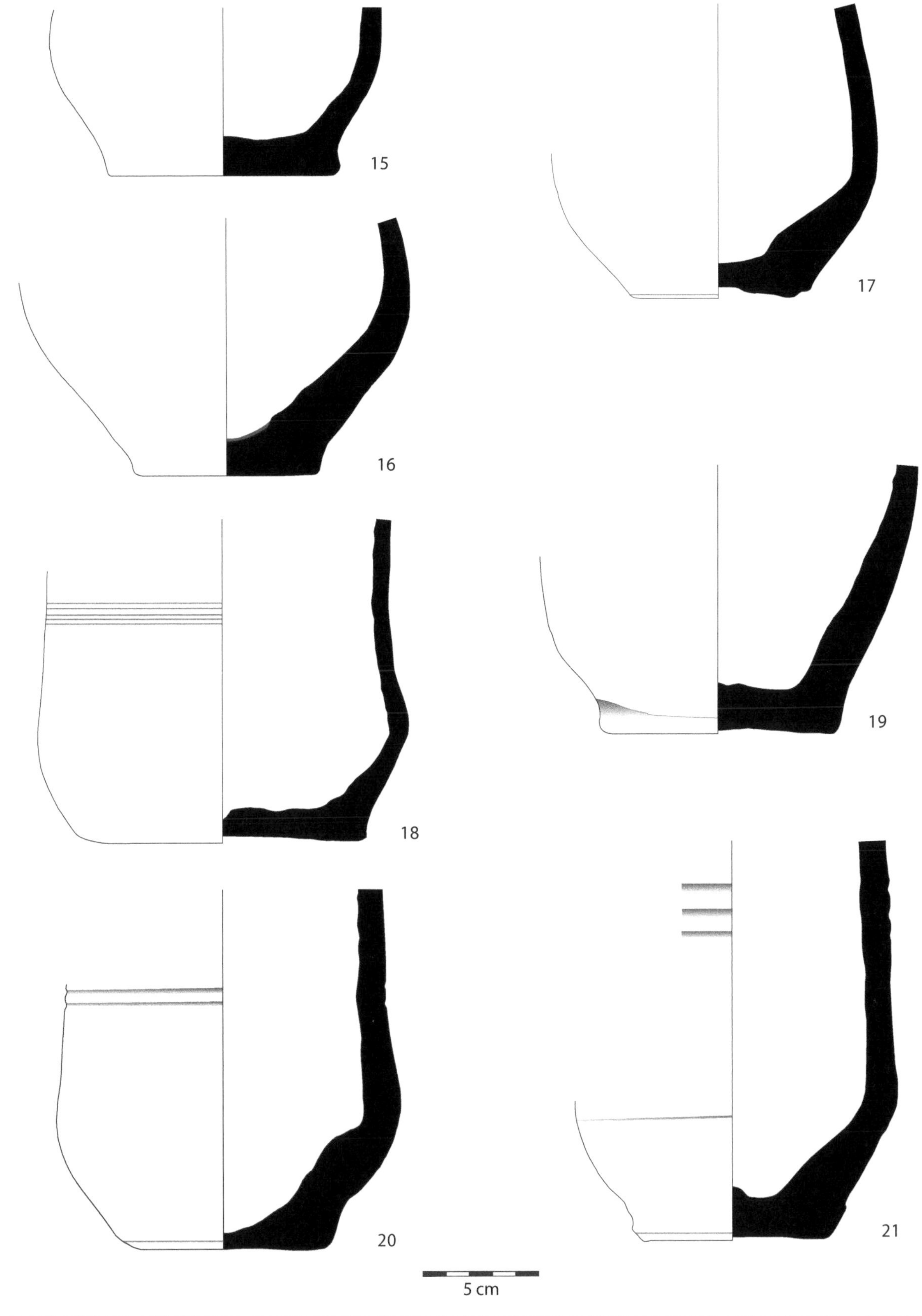

PLATE 23

#	Pottery Number	Rim Di. (mm)	Base Di. (mm)	Volume (L)	Surface/ Fabric Colour	Fabric Type	Room/ Area	Phase	Surface Treatment/ Decoration	Notes
1	p0-1	-	70	-	Green/ Green-grey	F	-	-		
2	p6183-20	-	62	-	Green/ Green	F	Surface	Mixed		
3	p6183-7	-	65	-	Green/ Orange	F	Surface	Mixed		
4	p1078-73	-	70	-	Pale green/ Orange-brown	F	-	-		
5	p6183-18	70	-	-	Pale green/ Grey-green	H	Surface	Mixed		
6	p6175-52	-	-	-	Green/ Green	H	Surface	Mixed		
7	p6178-31	-	-	-	Pale green/ Orange	F	Surface	Mixed		
8	p6166-34	-	-	-	Yellow-green/ Yellow-green	H	Surface	Mixed		
9	p6175-19	-	-	-	Green/ Green	H	Surface	Mixed		

FAMILY 40

Type 40.1

PLATE 24

#	Pottery Number	Rim Di. (mm)	Base Di. (mm)	Volume (L)	Surface/ Fabric Colour	Fabric Type	Room/ Area	Phase	Surface Treatment/ Decoration	Notes
1	p2000-4	42	37	0.21	-	-	-	-		
2	p3002-2	72	21	0.36	-	-	-	-		
3	p5001-18	-	38	-	Pale green/ Grey-green	D	Sounding	Mixed		Filled-in base.
4	p4051-119	-	45	-	Cream-brown/ Pale brown	E	House 1	Houses	Red washed exterior?	
5	p6175-26	-	50	-	Pale green/ Pale brown	D	Surface	Mixed		
6	p6088-12	-	55	-	Green/ Grey	H	Surface	Mixed		
7	p9008-12	-	40	-	Pale pink/ Pink	C - shell incl.	616	Mixed		
8	p6136-54	-	50	-	Grey-green/ Pink	H	Surface	Mixed		Filled-in base.
9	p4000-13	-	45	-	Green/ Green	F	-	Houses		
10	p1103-11	-	45	-	Pale green/ Pale orange	H	-	-		
11	p9009-2	-	60	-	Dark green	Overfired	Sounding	Mixed		Filled-in base.
12	p6088-15	-	65	-	Green/ Green-grey	H	Surface	Mixed		Filled-in base.

Type 40.2

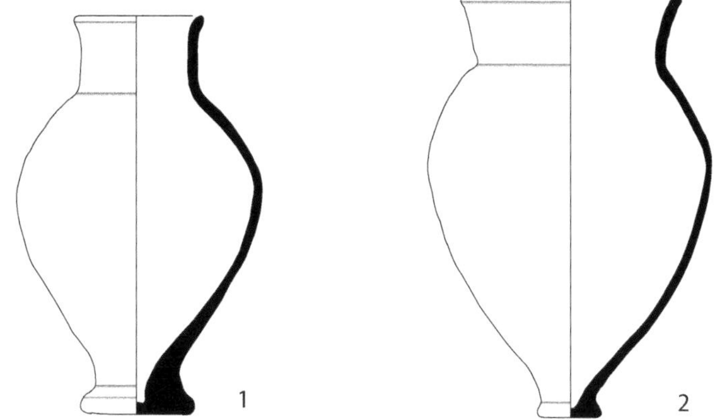

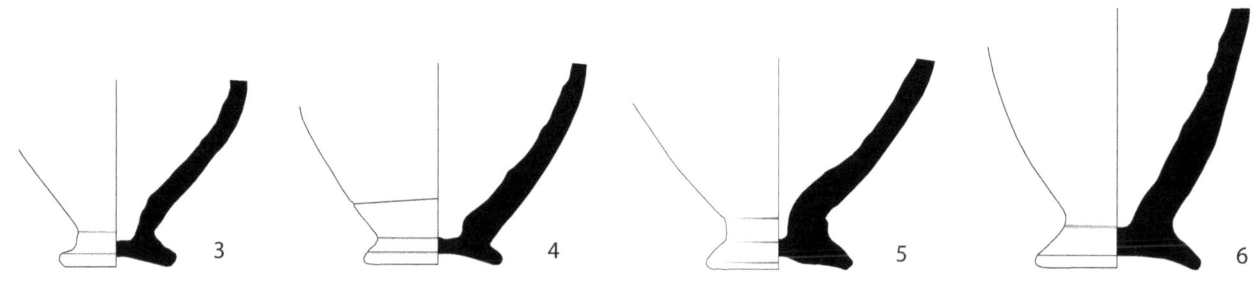

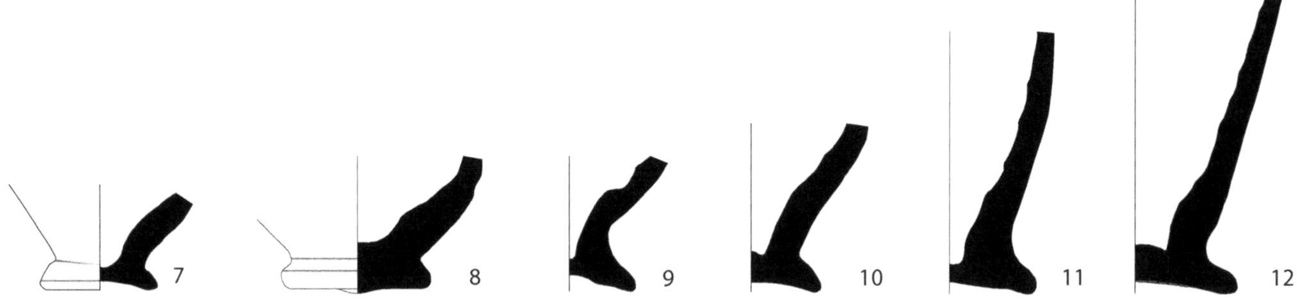

5 cm

PLATE 25

#	Pottery Number	Rim Di. (mm)	Base Di. (mm)	Volume (L)	Surface/ Fabric Colour	Fabric Type	Room/ Area	Phase	Surface Treatment/ Decoration	Notes
1	p6178-34	-	35	0.27 to base of neck; ca. 0.5 to top of neck.	Pink-brown/ Orange	E	Surface	Mixed		
2	p6088-1	-	35		Green/ Green	H	Surface	Mixed		

Type 40.3

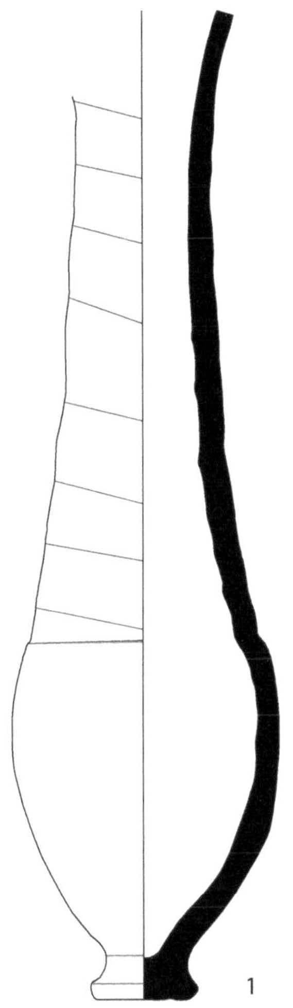

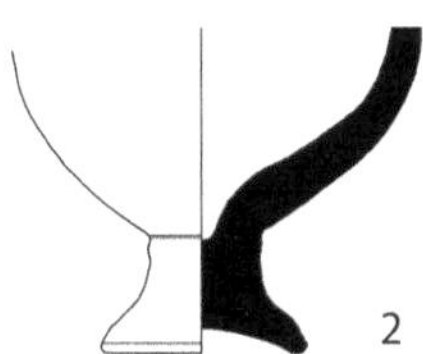

5 cm

PLATE 26

#	Pottery Number	Rim Di. (mm)	Base Di. (mm)	Volume (L)	Surface/ Fabric Colour	Fabric Type	Room/ Area	Phase	Surface Treatment/ Decoration	Notes
1	p3124-18	37	5	0.24	White-cream	-	-	1		
2	p1005-66	37	0	0.21	-	-	-	-		
3	p6059-27	40	0	0.13	Pale brown/ Cream-brown	A	600	2.1		
4	p9020-105	40	0	0.1	White/ Pale orange	D	616	Mixed		
5	p6091-1	48	15	0.06	Pale green-yellow/ Pale green	H	Surface	Mixed		
6	p5045-1	48	3	0.06	Pale pink/ Pink	B	140–2	2.2	Scraping marks around body. Slipped (?) exterior.	
7	p4021-14	35	10	0.06	Cream/ Pink	E	-	Houses	.	
8	p1078-1	50	10	0.1	Green-yellow/ Green-yellow	A	-	-		
9	p6166-1	50	5	0.06	Yellow-green/ Yellow-green	D	Surface	Mixed	Scraping marks around body. Slipped (?) exterior.	
10	p5045-10	48	14	0.04	Pale green/Grey-green	D	140–2	2.2		Chipped/smoothed rim.
11	p1039-104	45	15	0.08	Cream/ Pink	E	-	-		
12	p6126-1	-	5	0.12	Green-yellow/ Pink	A	Surface	Mixed		
13	p8013-1	-	15	0.1	Green/ Green	A	316	2.3		Sooting in concentric ring around body. Base worn/ smoothed.
14	p1166-68	-	12	0.05	Yellow-green/ Pale green	D	314	2.1	Rough, hand-moulded base.	
15	p6162-18	-	14	0.05	Pale green/ Pale green	H	Surface	Mixed		

Type 45.1

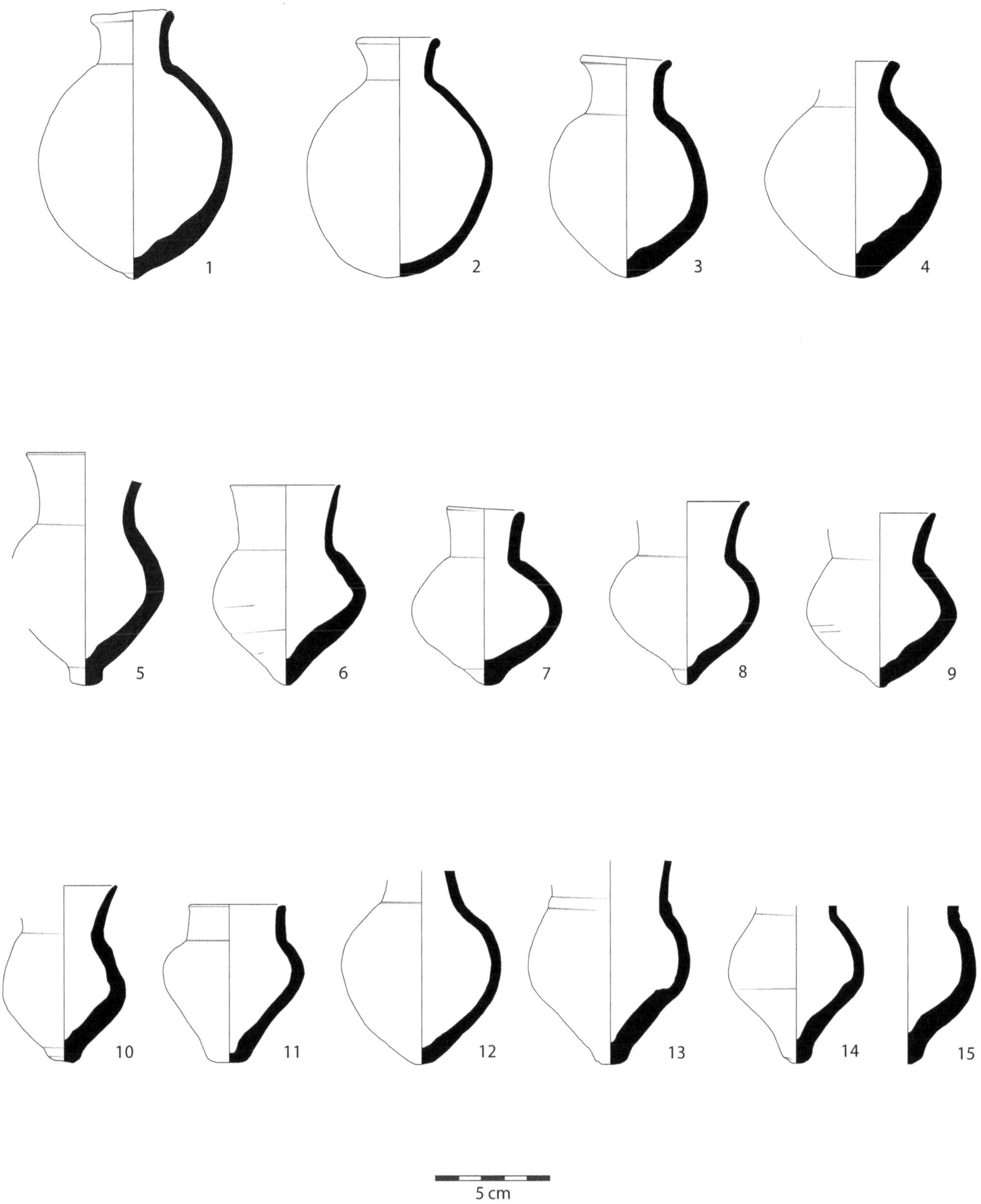

1 2 3 4

5 6 7 8 9

10 11 12 13 14 15

PLATE 27

#	Pottery Number	Rim Di. (mm)	Base Di. (mm)	Volume (L)	Surface/ Fabric Colour	Fabric Type	Room/ Area	Phase	Surface Treatment/ Decoration	Notes
1	p8032-37	-	0	0.52	White with pink patches/ Pink	G Import?	316	2.3	Heavily burnished exterior surface.	
2	p8083-6	-	-	0.88	Pale green/ Orange-pink	A	152	2.2	Slipped (?) exterior.	Neat breaks around base of neck and base. Perhaps deliberate for reuse?
3	p5016-3	-	0	-	Black/ Grey-black	C Import?	140–2	2.3	Heavily burnished exterior.	

#	Pottery Number	Rim Di. (mm)	Base Di. (mm)	Volume (L)	Surface/ Fabric Colour	Fabric Type	Room/ Area	Phase	Surface Treatment/ Decoration	Notes
1	p1142-8	54	18	0.59	Pale orange/ Pink-orange	C	314	2.1	Slipped exterior surface?	
2	p9018-38	43	9	0.13	Pale pink	C	616	Mixed	Calcite permeating exterior surface.	Heavily chipped/smoothed around rim.

#	Pottery Number	Rim Di. (mm)	Base Di. (mm)	Volume (L)	Surface/ Fabric Colour	Fabric Type	Room/ Area	Phase	Surface Treatment/ Decoration	Notes
1	p6175-40	-	16	0.07	Yellow-green/ Brown	D	Surface	Mixed		

Type 45.2

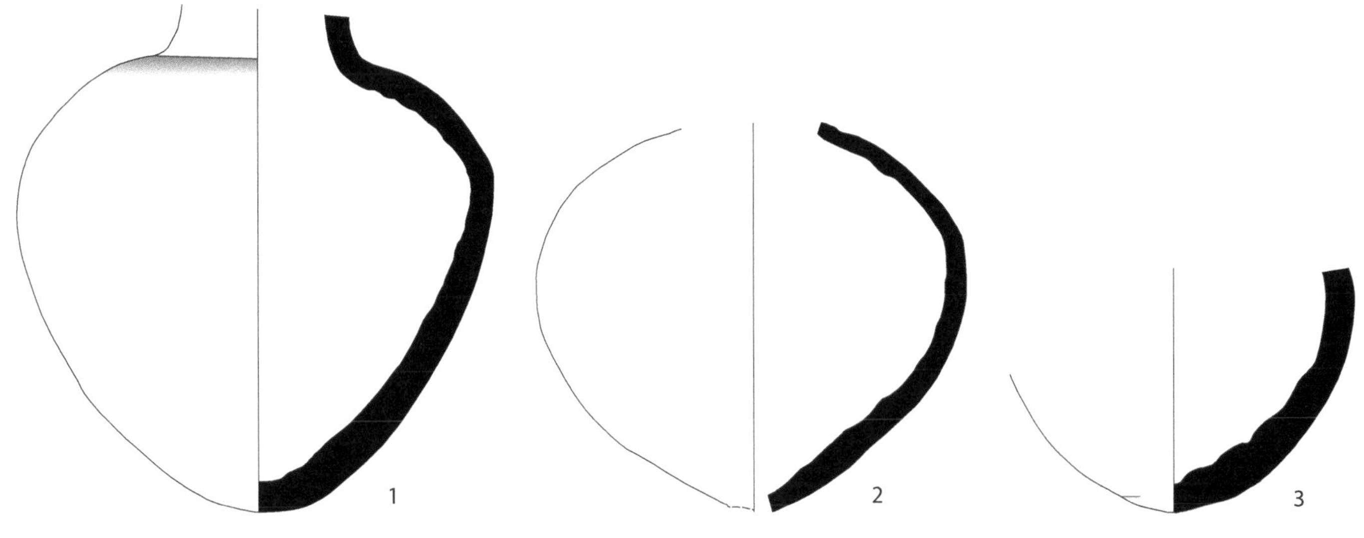

Type 45.3

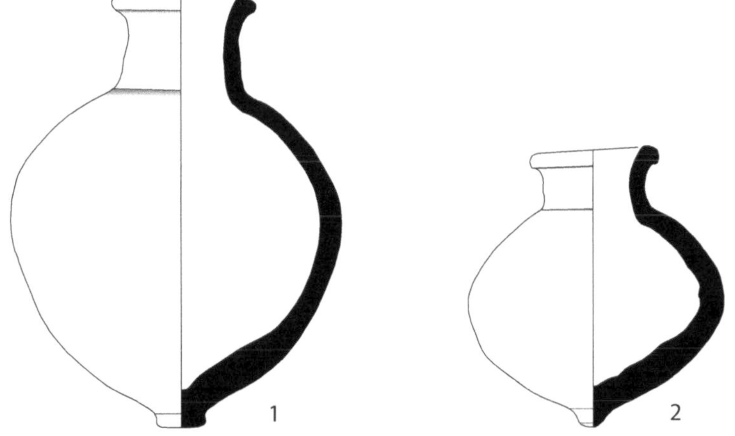

Type 45.4

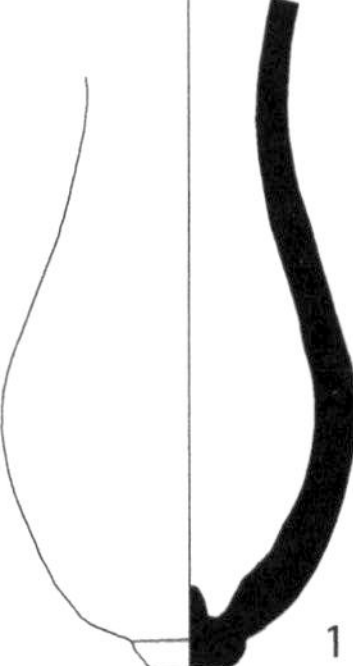

5 cm

PLATE 28

#	Pottery Number	Rim Di. (mm)	Base Di. (mm)	Volume (L)	Surface/ Fabric Colour	Fabric Type	Room/ Area	Phase	Surface Treatment/ Decoration	Notes
1	p3054-5	85	40	0.84	Green/ Green	D	304	Mixed	Incised band around shoulder.	
2	p3084-15	82	36	0.49	Green/ Pale green	A	304	Mixed		Worn base.
3	p6136-127	80	23	0.3	Green/ Pale pink	A	Surface	Mixed	Lightly incised band around shoulder.	
4	p5045-9	70	22	0.2	Cream-yellow/ Cream-yellow	A	140–2	2.2		
5	p6124-27	82	23	0.28	Pale green/ Pale green	D	Surface	Mixed		
6	p3054-4	78	17	0.46	Pale green/ Orange-pink	A	304	Mixed		
7	p9022-7	68	25	0.26	Pale pink/ Pink-brown	B	616	Mixed	Well defined neck.	Smoothed base.
8	p9020-39	74	20	0.22	Cream/ Pale orange	E	616	Mixed	Slipped (?) exterior.	Sooted exterior. Sooting over base and rim.
9	p3015-2	74	23	0.34	-		-	-		
10	p3006-12	72	19	0.24	-		-	-		
11	p5022-13	-	34	0.59	Cream/ Pale orange	D	140–2	2.2	Deformities and surface scraping around lower and middle third of vessel. Clearly defined ridge at the base of the neck.	
12	p8018-24	-	19	0.43	Grey-green/ Pink-orange	D	316	2.3	3 incised lines around shoulder.	

FAMILY 50

Type 50.1

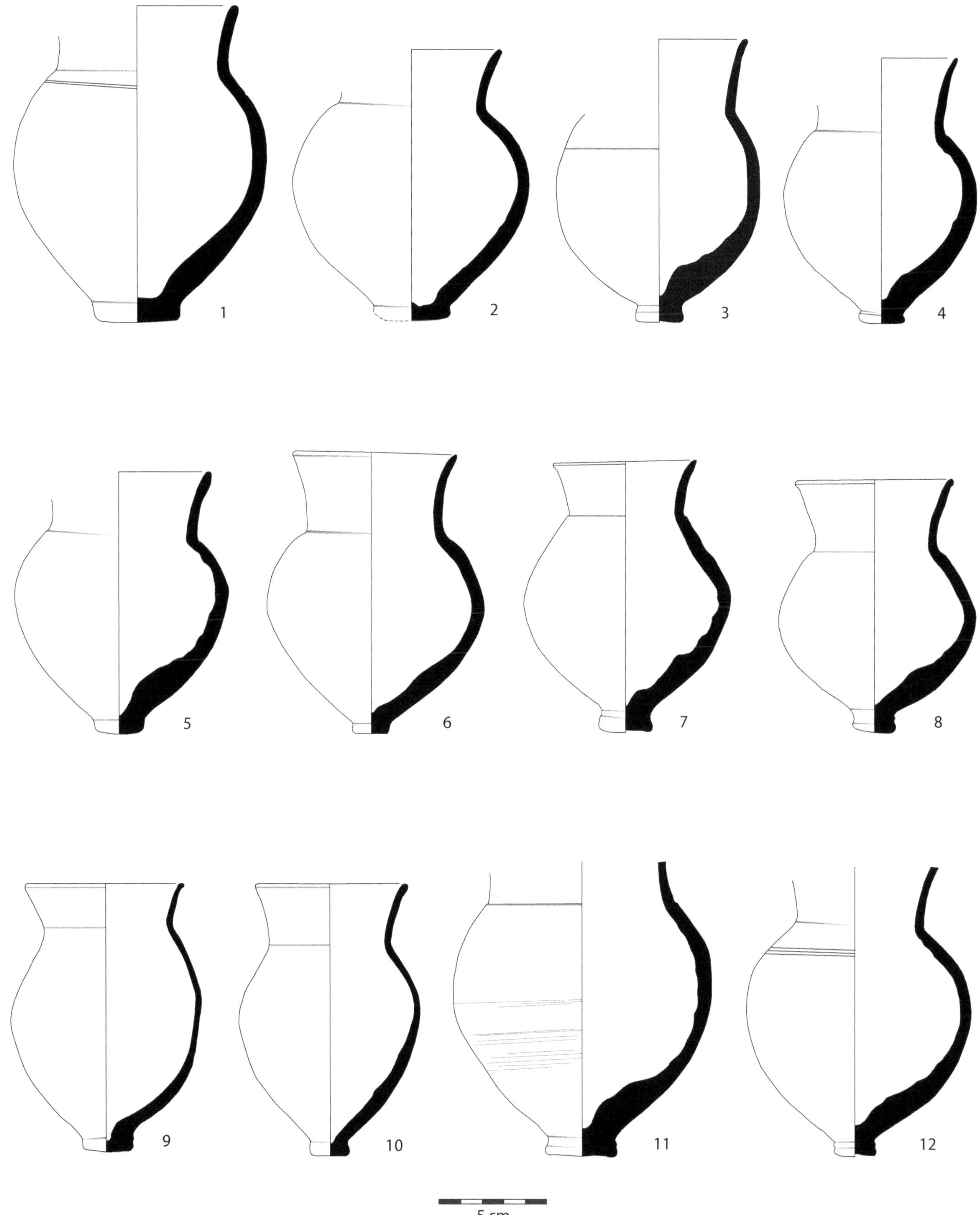

PLATE 29

#	Pottery Number	Rim Di. (mm)	Base Di. (mm)	Volume (L)	Surface/ Fabric Colour	Fabric Type	Room/ Area	Phase	Surface Treatment/ Decoration	Notes
13	p9018-35	-	38	0.45	Yellow-green/ Pale green	E	616	Mixed		Filled-in base.
14	p6126-46	-	39	0.53	Pale green/ Dull cream	H	Surface	Mixed	Scraping on lower exterior.	
15	p1005-3	-	26	0.44	-		-	Mixed		
16	p6163-33	-	42	0.42	Pale green/ Pale orange	B	Surface	Mixed		
17	p1080-16	-	30	0.2	White/ Pink	E	101	2.1		
18	p1079-769	-	25	0.44	Pale pink/ Pink-orange	E	101	2.1		
19	p6068-44	-	22	0.25	Green-yellow/ Pink-grey	A	Surface	Mixed		
20	p1080-15	-	19	0.35	White/ Pink	E	101	2.1		
21	p3119-18	-	26	0.18	Yellow-grey/ Cream	A	Admin.	2.2		
22	p1005-7	70	32	0.35	-	-	-	Mixed		

Type 50.1 *cont'd.*

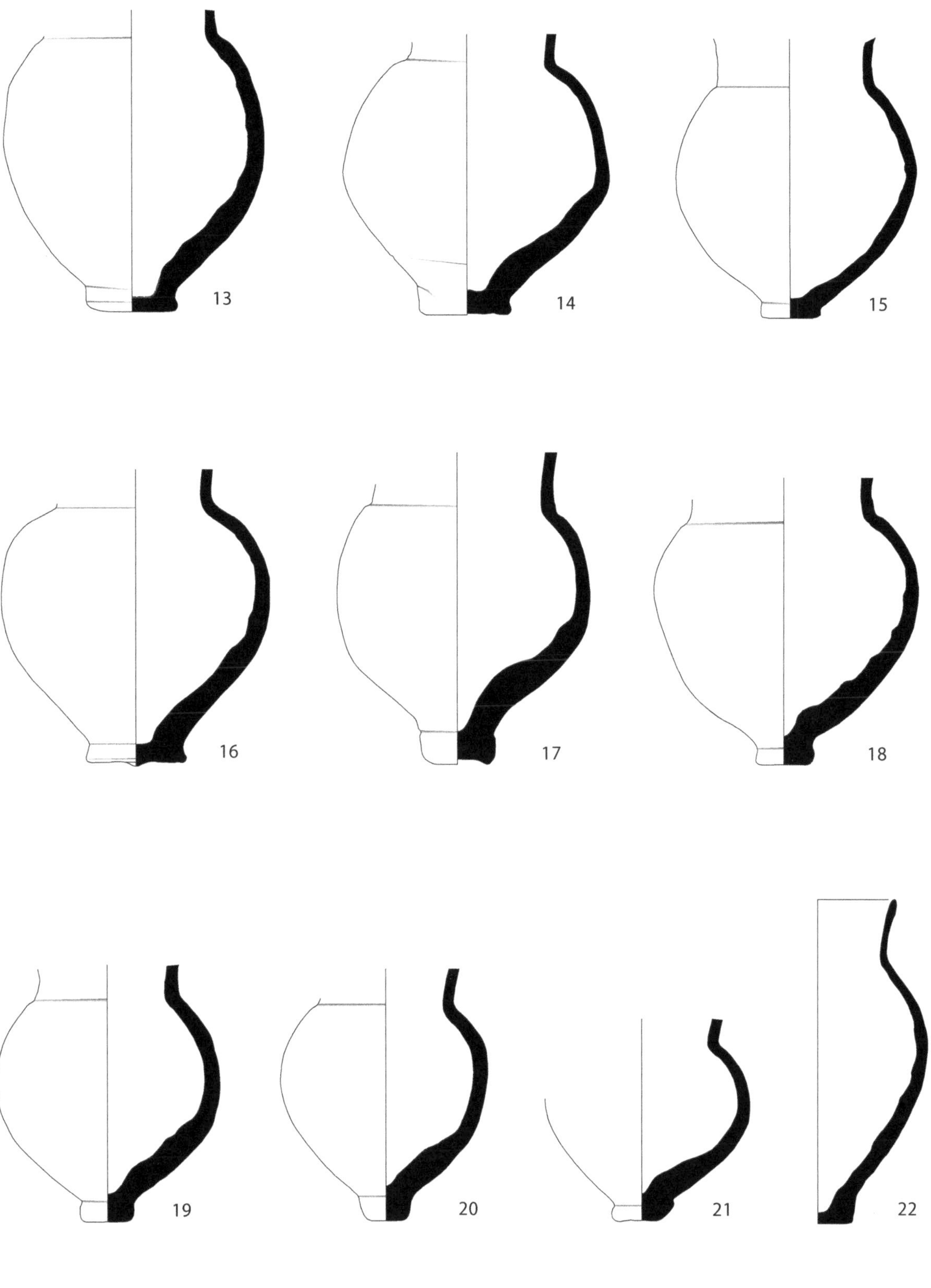

PLATE 30

#	Pottery Number	Rim Di. (mm)	Base Di. (mm)	Volume (L)	Surface/ Fabric Colour	Fabric Type	Room/ Area	Phase	Surface Treatment/ Decoration	Notes
23	p3054-249	-	45	0.82	White/ Pink-brown	E	304	Mixed		
24	p6166-2	-	42	0.54	-	-	Surface	Mixed		Chipped base.
25	p6068-46	-	23	0.55	Cream-yellow/ Pink	A	Surface	Mixed		
26	p4084-54	-	43	0.4	Pink-red/ Orange-red	C	House 2	Houses	3 impressed grooves around shoulder.	
27	p3085-130	-	44	0.47	Pale green/ Cream-white	A	304	Mixed	2 grooved bands around base.	Plugged base.
28	p3054-400	-	36	0.46	Red-brown/ Red-brown	E	304	Mixed		Filled-in base.
29	p4034-28	-	27	0.22	Pale green/ Pale green	D	-	Houses		
30	p3159-9	-	27	0.54	Green/ Green	D	-	-	Roughly formed base.	
31	p1080-22	-	20	0.4	Pink/ Pink	E	101	2.1		
32	p8032-19	-	25	0.56	White/ Pale pink	A	316	2.3	Lightly incised band around shoulder.	Sooting on exterior. Worn base with some bitumen(?).
33	p3025-2	-	12	0.32	Green/ Pink	E	302	Mixed	2 incised bands at base of neck.	
34	p9020-104	-	24	0.14	Cream-yellow/ Cream	E	616	Mixed		Chipped/smoothed base.
35	p3054-401	-	22	0.26	Orange-brown/ Orange-brown	C	304	Mixed	Purple-pink slipped(?) exterior.	
36	p6165-43	-	19	0.26	Grey-orange/ Grey-orange	B	156	2.2	Deep incised band part way around lower third of vessel body.	
37	p1037-27	-	21	-	Cream/ Pink	E	-	-		

#	Pottery Number	Rim Di. (mm)	Base Di. (mm)	Volume (L)	Surface/ Fabric Colour	Fabric Type	Room/ Area	Phase	Surface Treatment/ Decoration	Notes
1	p3064-226	78	35	0.72	Pink-orange/ Pink	A	Admin.	2.2		Plugged base.
2	p1078-66	78	29	0.53	Green-grey/ Pale orange	D	-	-	Evidence of scraping on exterior.	
3	p3064-577	72	25	0.31	Cream-white/ Cream-pale brown	A	Admin.	2.2		
4	p9018-82	72	26	0.23	Yellow/ Pale brown	B	616	Mixed		Worn base.

Type 50.1 *cont'd.*

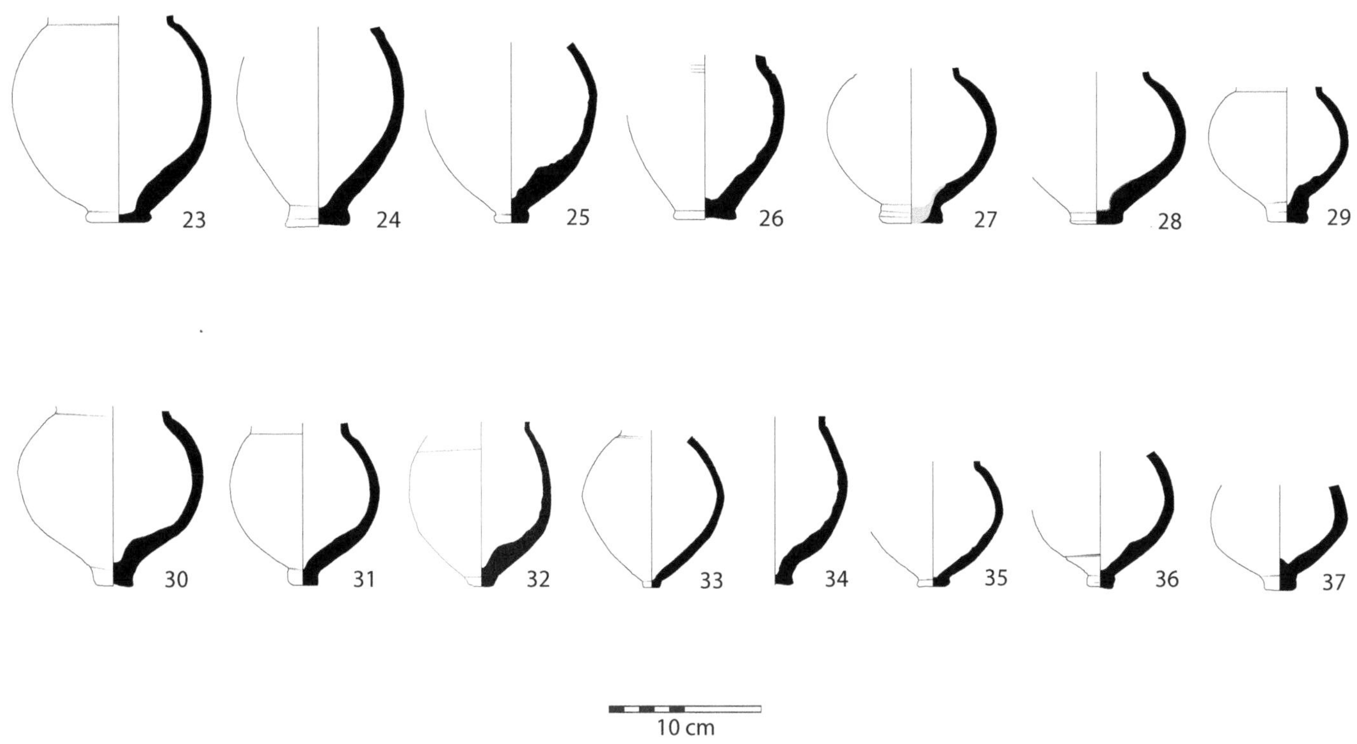

Type 50.2

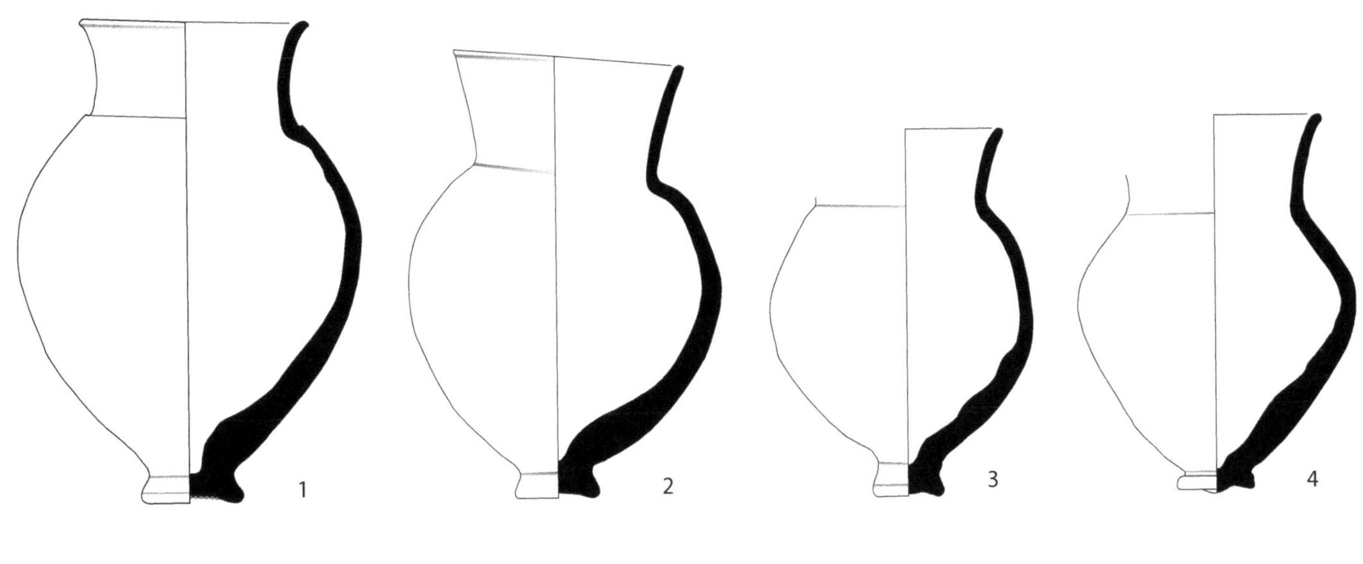

PLATE 31

#	Pottery Number	Rim Di. (mm)	Base Di. (mm)	Volume (L)	Surface/ Fabric Colour	Fabric Type	Room/ Area	Phase	Surface Treatment/ Decoration	Notes
5	p4021-13	70	40	0.43	Pale green/ Pale green	D	-	Houses	Evidence of scraping on exterior.	
6	p4084-53	66	31	0.88	Green/ Pale orange	C	House 2	Houses		
7	p9020-2	78	23	0.23	Cream/ Orange	B	616	Mixed	Slipped (?) exterior.	
8	p4053-14	62	37	0.43	Green-yellow/ Green-yellow	A	House 1	Houses		
9	p9020-107	68	32	0.27	White-cream/ Pale orange	D	616	Mixed	Lightly impressed band around shoulder.	Chipped/worn base.
10	p4034-29	52	16	0.22	Pale green/ Pale green	D	-	Houses	Evidence of scraping on lower exterior.	Worn base.
11	p4084-1	75	20	0.58	Green/ Yellow-green	D	House 2	Houses		
12	p4006-2	78	30	0.4	Pale pink/ Pink	C/E	House 2	Houses		
13	p5022-60	-	25	0.54	Yellow-cream/ Grey-green	H	140–2	2.2		Chipped/worn base.
14	p5053-1	-	28	0.5	Pale green/ Pale brown	E	140–2	2.2	Incised band around shoulder.	Heavily smoothed base.
15	p6166-41	-	25	0.47	Red-orange/ Brown	E	Surface	Mixed	Scraping marks around lower third of body.	

Type 50.2 *cont'd.*

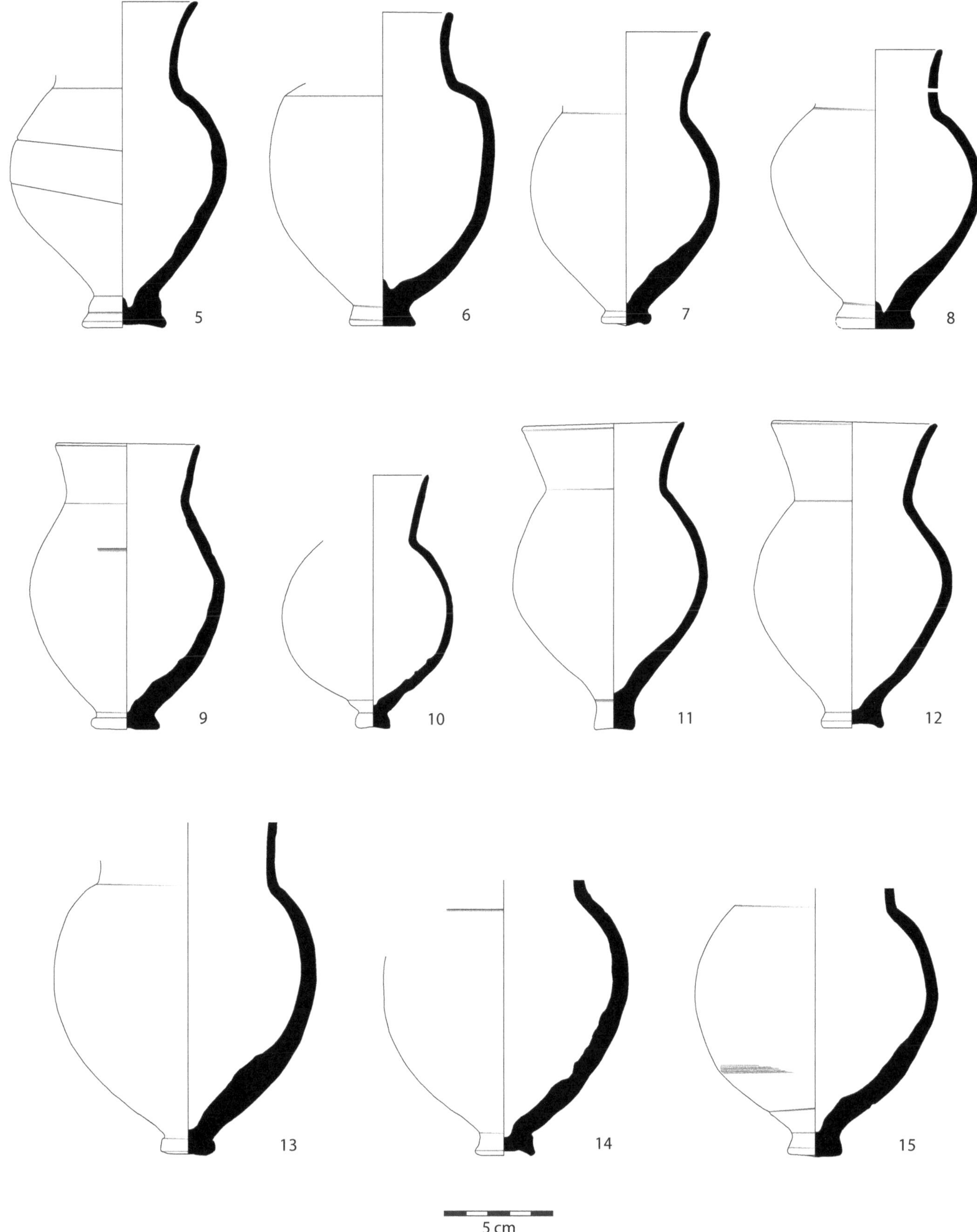

PLATE 32

#	Pottery Number	Rim Di. (mm)	Base Di. (mm)	Volume (L)	Surface/ Fabric Colour	Fabric Type	Room/ Area	Phase	Surface Treatment/ Decoration	Notes
16	p3054-51	-	24	0.55	White/ Pink	C	304	Mixed		
17	p1080-18	-	20	0.3	White/ Pink	E	101	2.1		
18	p1080-13	-	21	0.22	White/ Orange-pink	E	101	2.1		
19	p3025-3	-	19	0.24	Cream/ Pale green	D	302	Mixed		
20	p3102-2	-	19	0.21	Pale pink/ Pink	A	Vaults	1	Evidence of scraping on exterior.	
21	p3085-23	-	20	0.22	Cream/ Pale pink	C	304	Mixed		Bitumen coated interior. Bitumen stained exterior.
22	p4056-10	-	41	0.4	Pink/ Red-orange	D	House 1	Houses	Incised grooved band around shoulder.	
23	p3085-122	-	38	0.37	Pale pink/ Pink	A	304	Mixed		Filled-in base.
24	p4056-11	-	27	0.41	Green/ Brown	A	House 1	Houses		
25	p6036-119	-	50	-	Green/ Green	D	600	2.2		
26	p5022-54	-	26	-	Cream/ Pink	E	140–2	2.2	Scraping marks around lower third of vessel.	
27	p5022-55	-	29	-	Pale green/ Grey-green	E	140–2	2.2		

Type 50.2 *cont'd.*

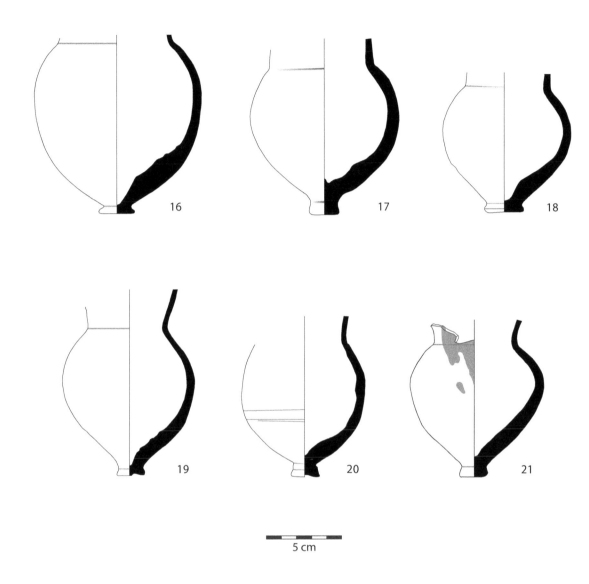

16 17 18

19 20 21

5 cm

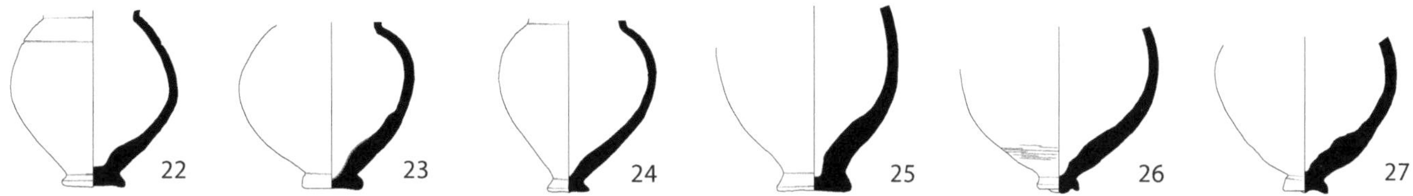

10 cm

PLATE 33

#	Pottery Number	Rim Di. (mm)	Base Di. (mm)	Volume (L)	Surface/ Fabric Colour	Fabric Type	Room/ Area	Phase	Surface Treatment/ Decoration	Notes
1	p5022-63	80	29	0.4	Yellow/ Pale pink	A	140–2	2.2		
2	p4062-46	74	45	0.45	-	-	House 1	Houses		
3	p4021-12	64	34	0.3	Cream/Pale orange	E	-	Houses		
4	p9020-112	80	36	0.66	White-pale brown/Brown	B	616	Mixed	Slipped (?) exterior. 4 deep incised bands around shoulder; 2 impressed bands at base of neck.	
5	p6049-1	-	35	0.46	Pale green/ Pink-orange	A	-	-	Evidence of scraping on lower exterior.	
6	p3054-21	-	34	0.4	Cream-brown/ Orange-red	E	304	Mixed	Grooved band at base of neck.	
7	p4043-8	-	50	0.31	Dull cream/ Pink	A	-	Houses		
8	p5001-92	-	37	0.19	Pale orange/ Pale orange	A	Sounding	Mixed		Filled-in base.
9	p9023-6	-	36	-	Pink/ Pink	D	616	Mixed		Bitumen stained interior and exterior; bitumen over breaks. Associated with vessel p9023-7.

Type 50.3

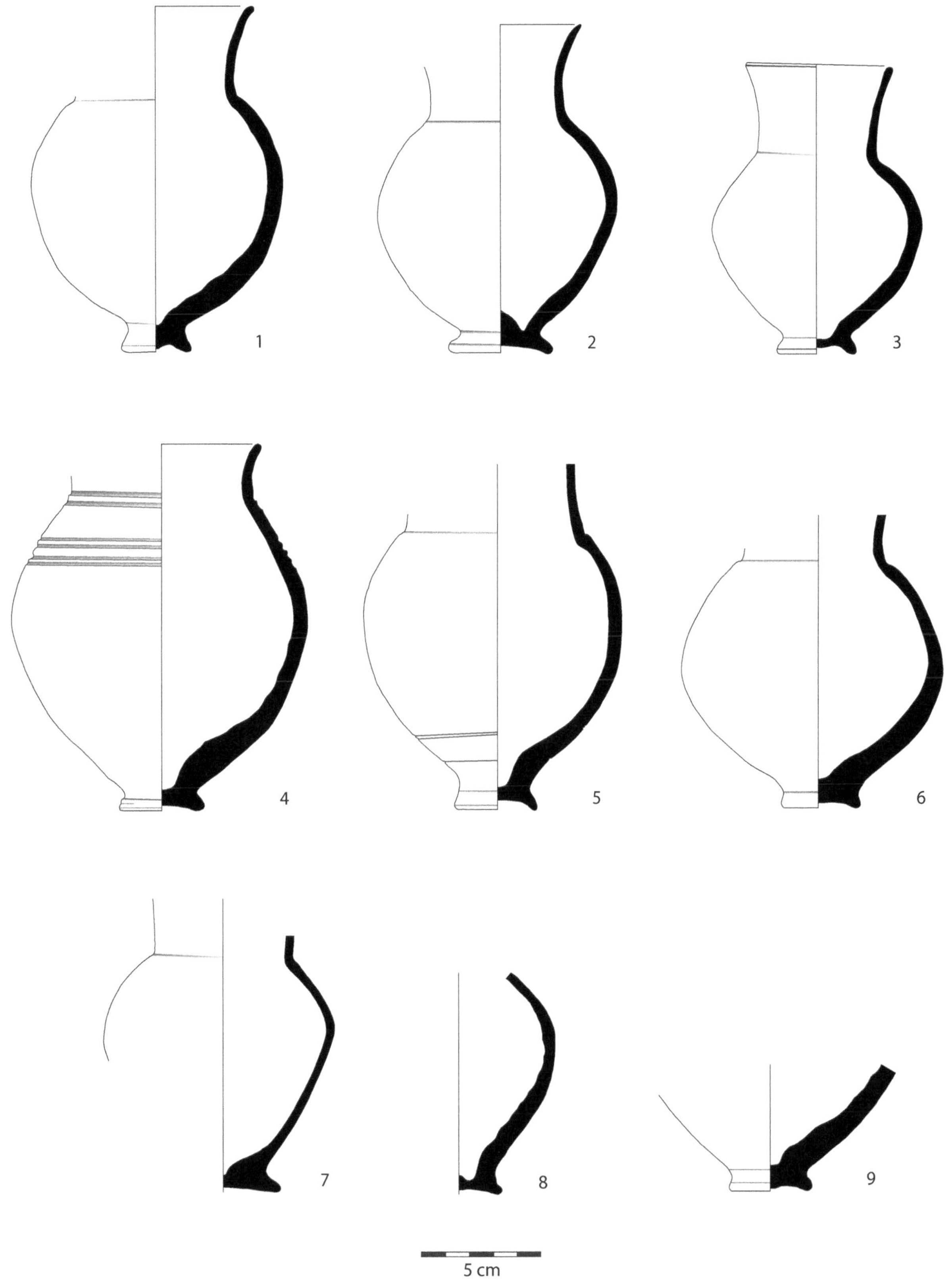

PLATE 34

#	Pottery Number	Rim Di. (mm)	Base Di. (mm)	Volume (L)	Surface/ Fabric Colour	Fabric Type	Room/ Area	Phase	Surface Treatment/ Decoration	Notes
1	p9018-39	73	17	0.25	Cream-yellow/ Pale orange	E	616	Mixed		Smoothed base.
2	p6036-117	77	12	0.35	Green-yellow/ Green-yellow	A	600	2.2		
3	p3064-1	75	17	0.35	Pale green/ Orange	A	Admin.	2.2	3 incised bands around base of neck.	
4	p1074-31	70	18	0.32	Pale green/ Pale orange	A	-	-		
5	p5022-11	79	12	0.42	Pink/ Dark pink	D	140–2	2.2	Deformation on body.	
6	p3054-22	76	16	0.57	Green/ Green	D	304	Mixed	Evidence of scraping on exterior.	
7	p6127-1	85	14	0.41	Pale green	D	Surface	Mixed		Chipped rim and worn base.
8	p1085-17	80	14	0.35	White-pale pink	A	101	2.1	Evidence of scraping on exterior.	
9	p3159-1	70	13	0.25	Pale green/ Orange	A	-	-	Indentation on lower body.	
10	p5007-42	68	11	0.18	Pale green/ Pale green	H	140–2	2.3	Slipped (?) exterior.	
11	p8013-2	68	12	0.2	Green/ Cream	A	316	2.3		
12	p4067-24	-	9	0.24	Pale pink/ Orange	A	House 1	Houses		

Type 50.4

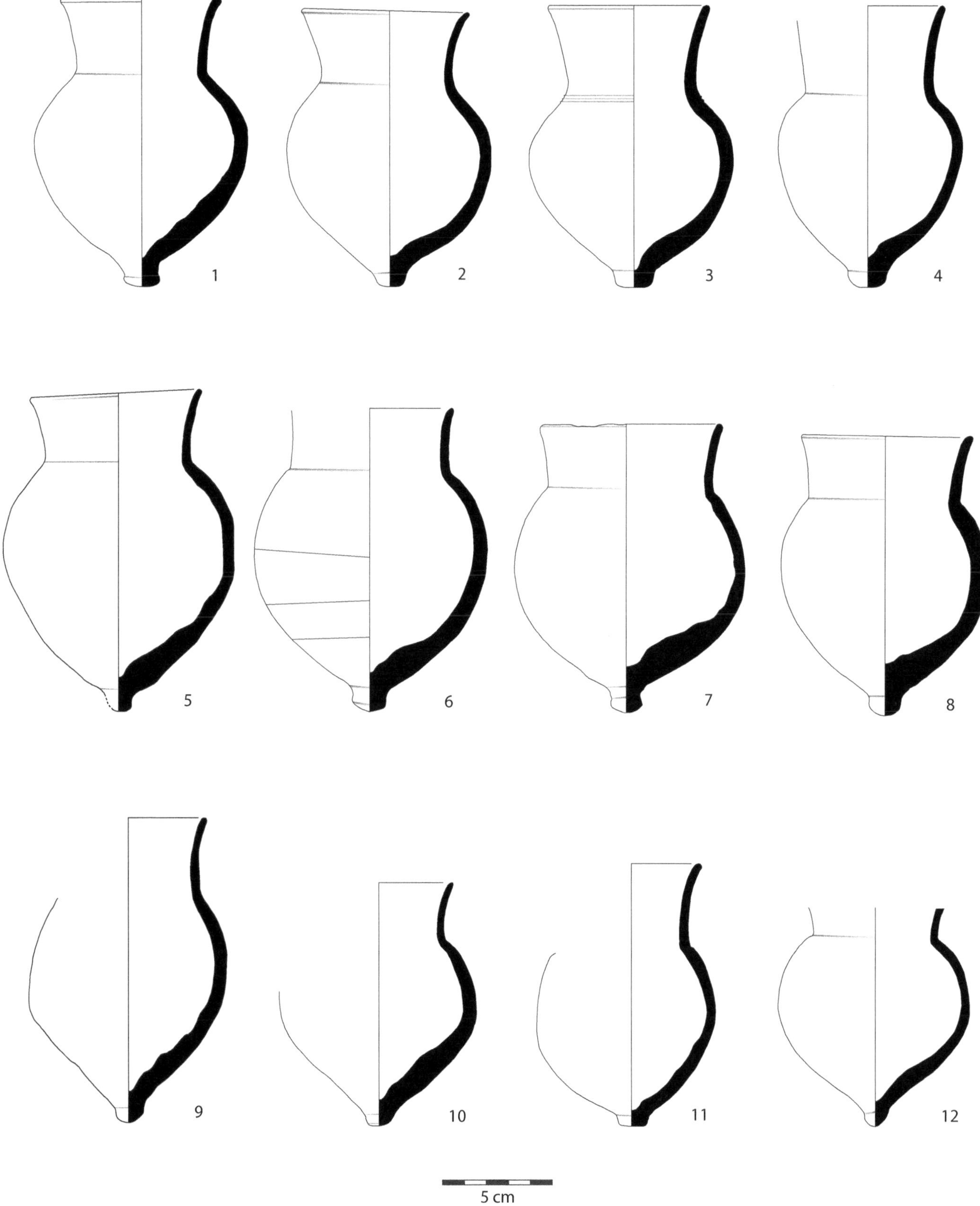

PLATE 35

#	Pottery Number	Rim Di. (mm)	Base Di. (mm)	Volume (L)	Surface/ Fabric Colour	Fabric Type	Room/ Area	Phase	Surface Treatment/ Decoration	Notes
13	p5022-62	-	18	0.38	Yellow-cream/ Yellow-cream	E	140–2	2.2	2 irregular tooth-combed decoration at base of neck. Deep scraping marks on lower third of vessel.	
14	p1080-11	-	17	0.41	Pale green/ Cream	C	101	2.1		
15	p2-3	-	15	0.32	-	-	-	-		
16	p6136-89	-	19	0.27	Pale brown/ Red	E	Surface	Mixed	Pinched base, left rough and unfinished. Later patching?	
17	p3185-30	-	11	0.18	White/ Cream	D	315	2.1		
18	p3064-489	-	13	0.19	Pale pink/ Pink	A	Admin.	2.2		
19	p6136-56	-	12	0.21	Green-yellow/ Cream	H	Surface	Mixed		
20	p1166-69	-	13	0.2	Dark pink/ Dark pink	C	314	2.1		
21	p5022-12	-	16	0.48	Green/ Grey	E	140–2	2.2	Scraping marks around bottom third. Incised line around shoulder.	
22	p1166-203	-	17	0.38	White/ Pale pink	A	314	2.1	2 impressed ridges at base of neck; 2 tooth-combed incisions around shoulder. Slipped (?) exterior. Deep purple slipped interior.	
23	p3154-23	-	13	0.29	Pale green/ Pale pink	A	315	2.2	Ridges at base of neck.	Base heavily chipped/worn.
24	p1139-110	-	12	0.2	Yellow-cream/ Pink	A	314	2.2	Pronounced ridges at base of neck.	Base heavily worn.
25	p1080-28	-	20	0.45	Pale green/ Green-grey	D	101	2.1		
26	p3079-9	-	16	0.28	Orange/ Pink	C/D	-	-		
27	p8082-1	-	15	0.28	Pale orange/ Orange	D	316	2.2	Slipped (?) exterior.	
28	p9020-115	-	21	0.22	Pale pink/ Pale brown	E	616	Mixed		Rough, chipped base.
29	p9023-5	-	15	0.29	Cream/ Cream-pale brown	D	616	Mixed		Heavily chipped base.
30	p5022-56	-	20	-	Pale orange/ Brown	E	140–2	2.2		
31	p3085-45	-	15	-	Pale green/ Grey	A	304	Mixed		
32	p3088-44	-	15	-	Pale pink/ Pale brown	E	304	Mixed		

Type 50.4 *cont'd.*

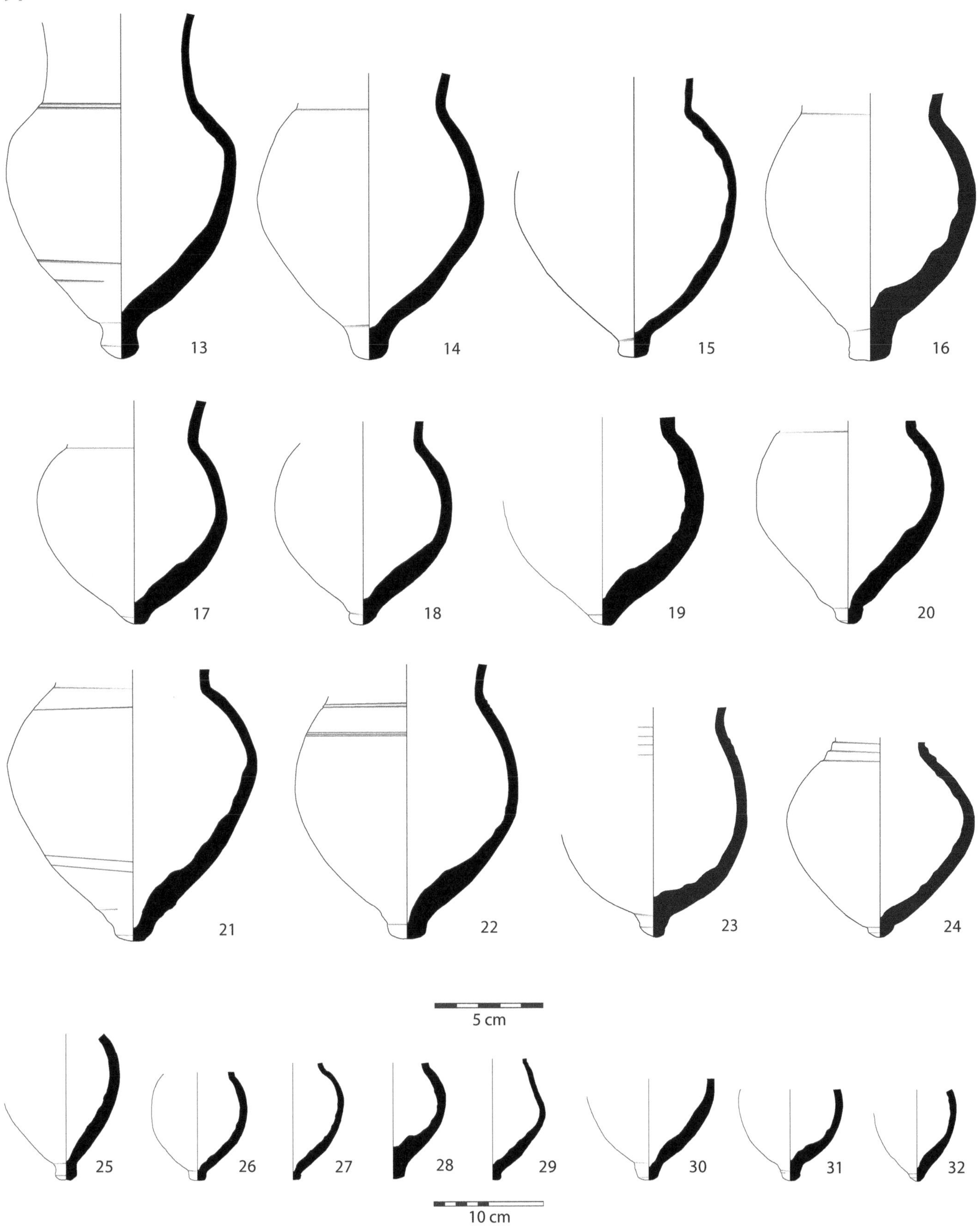

PLATE 36

#	Pottery Number	Rim Di. (mm)	Base Di. (mm)	Volume (L)	Surface/ Fabric Colour	Fabric Type	Room/ Area	Phase	Surface Treatment/ Decoration	Notes
1	p1079-142	75	22	0.33	Pale pink/ Pink-orange	C	101	2.1		
2	p1079-222	77	20	0.36	Pale green/ Pink	D	101	2.1		
3	p3185-108	80	19	0.25	White/ Pink	E	315	2.1		Chipped/smoothed rim and base.
4	p1073-78	73	19	0.28	Pale green/ Green-grey	A	101	2.2		
5	p3064-564	73	21	0.33	Cream-white/ Cream-white	A	Admin.	2.2		
6	p1073-79	76	21	0.29	Cream-pink/ Orange	C	101	2.2		
7	p1092-57	80	20	0.36	White/ Pale pink-cream	A	110	2.2		Deep gouge in exterior surface.
8	p3064-661	70	20	0.23	Pink/ Pink	A	Admin.	2.2		Worn/smoothed base.
9	p1080-12	85	25	0.56	Pale green/ Pale green	D	101	2.1		
10	p5022-59	70	13	0.4	Yellow-green/ Yellow-green	B	140–2	2.2		
11	p1142-18	72	18	0.21	Green/ Pale brown	E	314	2.1		Worn/chipped base.
12	p1166-204	60	20	0.2	White/ Pink	A	314	2.1		Heavily chipped and smoothed rim and base. Discoloured wear band around middle of body.

Type 50.5

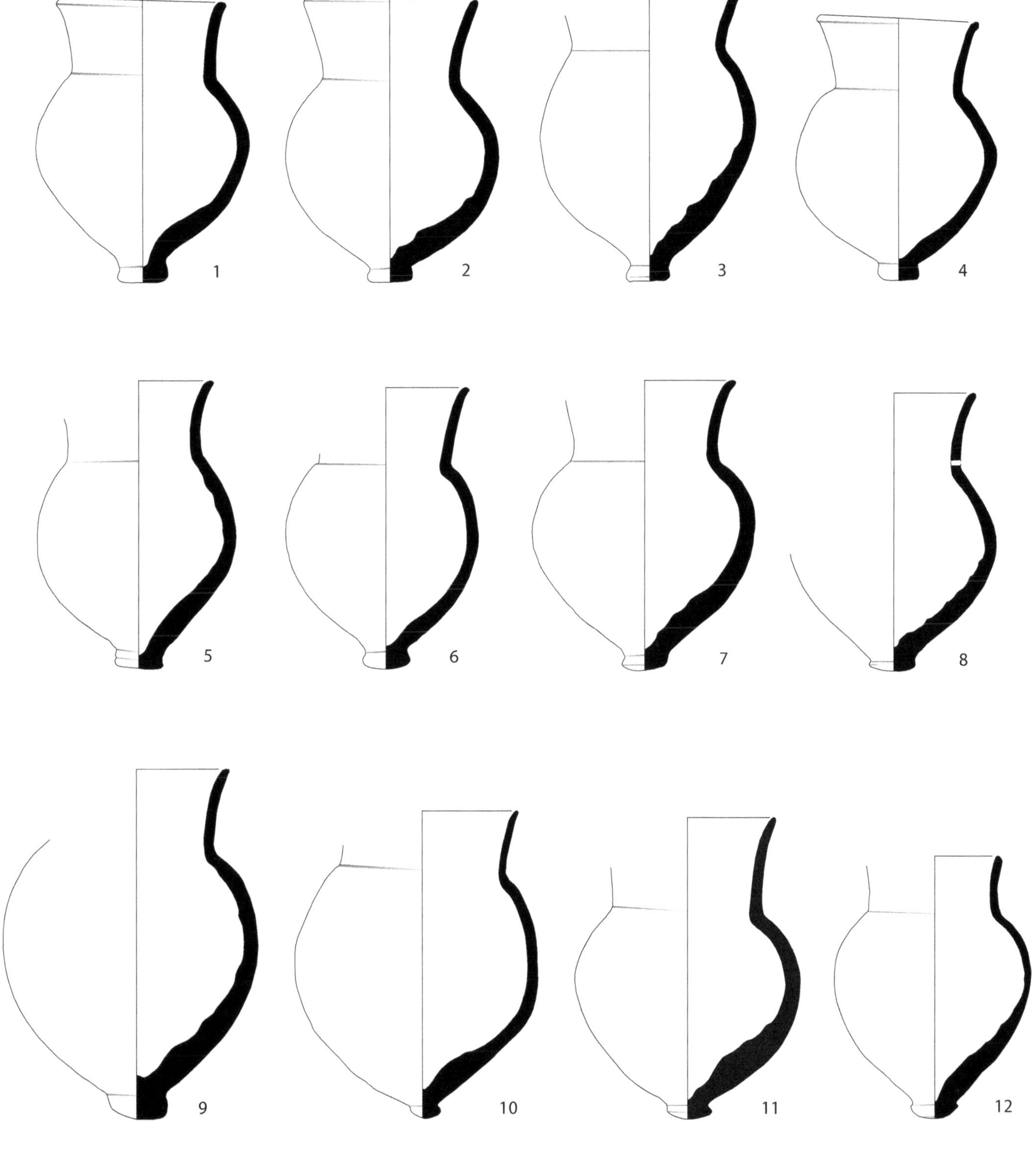

PLATE 37

#	Pottery Number	Rim Di. (mm)	Base Di. (mm)	Volume (L)	Surface/ Fabric Colour	Fabric Type	Room/ Area	Phase	Surface Treatment/ Decoration	Notes
13	p3085-126	76	22	0.6	Pale green/ Green	D	304	Mixed		
14	p5016-8	80	25	0.49	Pale green/ Pink	E	140–2	2.1	Slipped (?) exterior.	
15	p3054-52	84	13	0.51	Pale green-grey/ Pale green	D	304	Mixed		
16	p1166-71	78	20	0.21	Yellow-green/ Cream	D	314	2.1	Gouges in exterior surface.	Worn base.
17	p3054-3	80	22	0.46	Cream-brown/ Pink	B	304	Mixed		
18	p3054-397	74	17	0.34	Yellow-green/ Cream	A	304	Mixed		
19	p3084-4	77	20	0.41	Pink-red/ Brown-red	C	304	Mixed		
20	p3085-123	73	20	0.42	Pale pink/ Pink-orange	A	304	Mixed		
21	p6163-64	75	17	0.46	Yellow-cream/ Pale orange	D	Surface	Mixed	Slipped (?) exterior.	
22	p8083-17	80	20	0.27	Pale pink/ Pink	E	152	2.2	Impressed band at base of neck.	
23	p6165-38	75	20	0.34	Cream-yellow/ Pale brown	C/E	156	2.2		
24	p8029-4	82	16	0.27	White/ White	A	Burial	Mixed		Chipped/smoothed base. Sinuous neck/rim shape.

Type 50.5 *cont'd.*

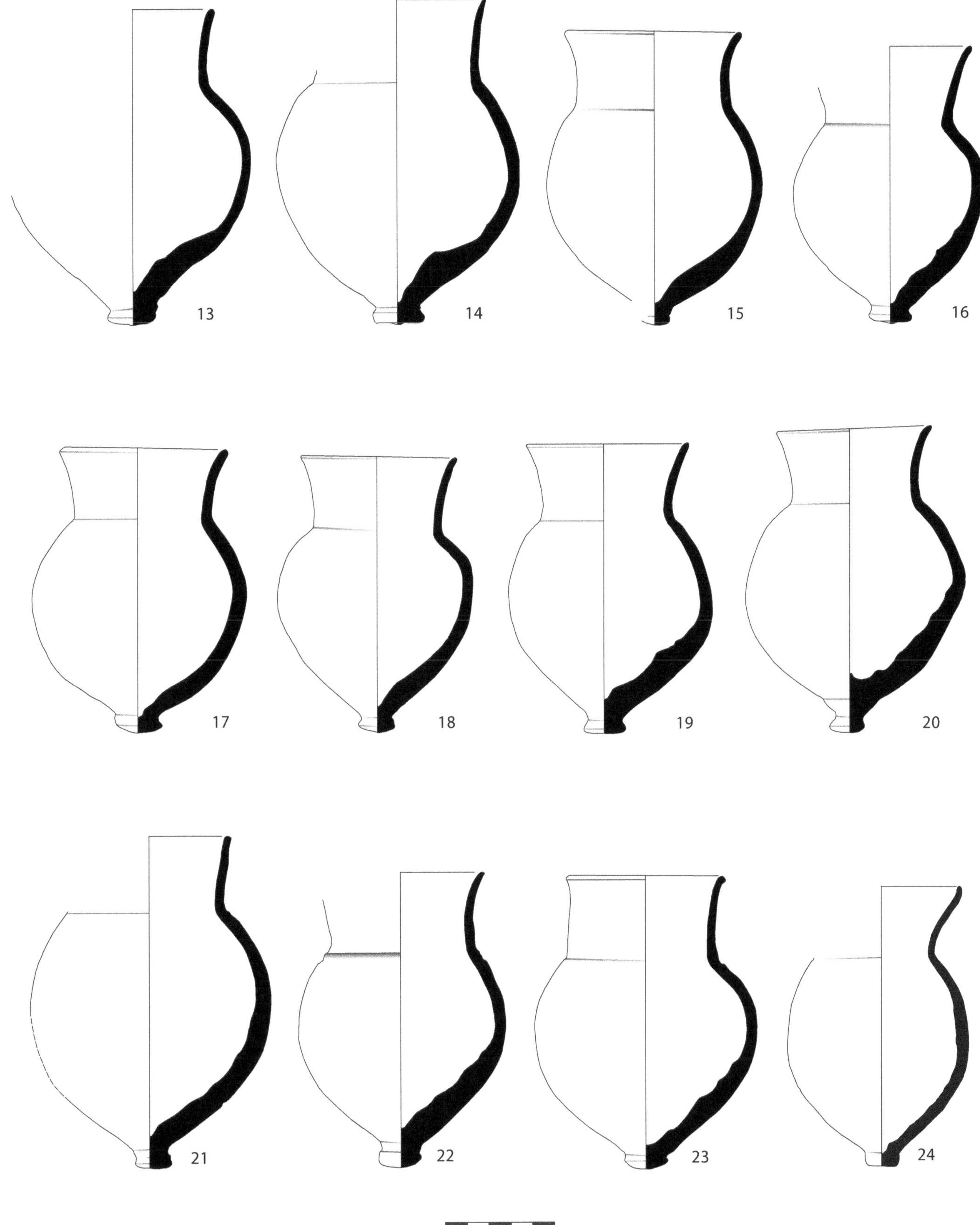

PLATE 38

#	Pottery Number	Rim Di. (mm)	Base Di. (mm)	Volume (L)	Surface/ Fabric Colour	Fabric Type	Room/ Area	Phase	Surface Treatment/ Decoration	Notes
25	p9020-106	74	25	0.25	White-cream/ White-cream	D	616	Mixed	Impressed band at base of neck.	Chipped/smoothed base.
26	p9020-87	70	18	0.21	Pale green/ Pale orange	E	616	Mixed	Slipped (?) exterior.	
27	p9018-36	80	18	0.19	Cream/ Cream-brown	A	616	Mixed	Deep ridges around lower third of vessel.	Smoothed around middle of vessel due to use.
28	p6126-47	78	25	0.24	Pink/ Pink	C/E	Surface	Mixed	Evidence for scraping on lower exterior.	
29	p6136-132	80	19	0.39	Yellow-green	A	Surface	Mixed	2 impressed bands on shoulder, and 1 lightly incised line beneath.	Chipped/worn rim.
30	p5022-61	80	22	0.36	Cream/ Pink	A	140–2	2.2	2-3 tooth-combed decoration at base of neck.	
31	p6036-118	72	20	0.3	Green-yellow/ Green-yellow	A	600	2.2	2 ridged lines around shoulder.	
32	p9020-41	62	16	0.18	Brown-pink	E	616	Mixed		
33	p1166-117	-	22	0.19	Yellow-green/ Yellow-green	A/B	314	2.1		Worn base.
34	p1166-119	-	24	0.25	White/ Pale pink	D	314	2.1		Bitumen coated interior; large pieces in base; bitumen staining on exterior and over breaks.
35	p5022-40	-	23	0.34	Yellow/ Pale orange	E	140–2	2.2	Scraping marks on upper third of body.	

Type 50.5 *cont'd.*

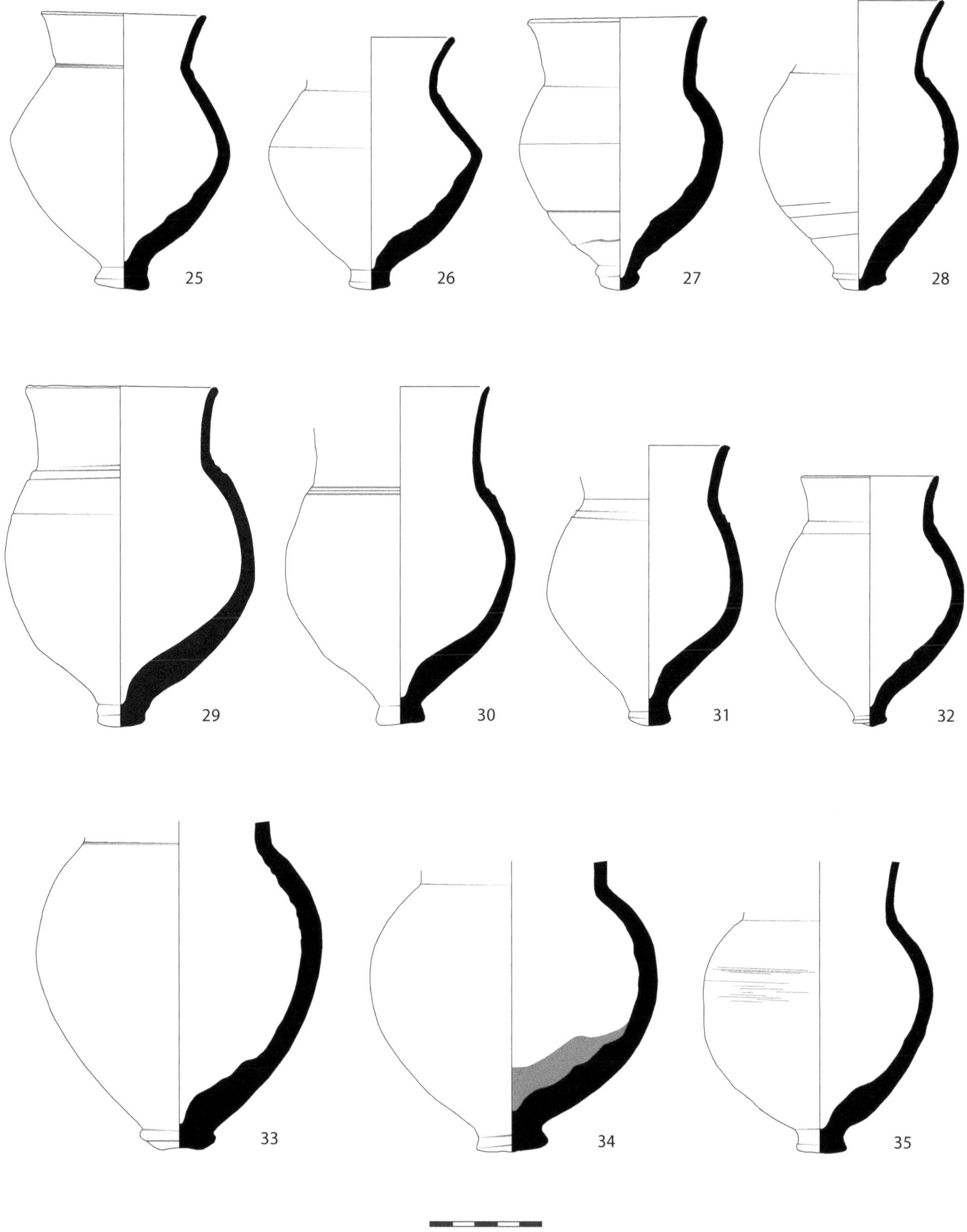

PLATE 39

#	Pottery Number	Rim Di. (mm)	Base Di. (mm)	Volume (L)	Surface/ Fabric Colour	Fabric Type	Room/ Area	Phase	Surface Treatment/ Decoration	Notes
36	p3185-78	-	19	0.23	White/ Grey	B	315	2.1		
37	p1139-108	-	21	0.26	White-cream/ Cream-pink	D	314	2.2		Worn base.
38	p1080-17	-	23	0.21	White/ Pink	D	101	2.1		
39	p3085-129	-	19	0.21	Pale pink/ Pink-brown	E	304	Mixed		
40	p9018-37	-	18	0.26	Yellow-green/ Pale orange	D	616	Mixed		Worn base.
41	p9018-40	-	18	0.22	Pale green/ Grey-green	E	616	Mixed		Worn/smoothed base.
42	p6068-45	-	18	0.2	Cream-yellow/ Cream-brown	A	Surface	Mixed		
43	p9018-34	-	18	0.27	Yellow/ Pale brown	D	616	Mixed		Worn/ smoothed base.
44	p1079-212	-	17	0.21	White-pale green/ Pink	D	101	2.1		
45	p1079-223	-	18	0.2	White-pale green/ Pink	D	101	2.1		
46	p9020-1	-	18	0.23	Grey-green/ Pale orange	D with shell	616	Mixed	Slipped (?) exterior.	Worn base.
47	p6062-3	-	19	0.25	Orange-brown/ Orange-brown	D	Surface	Mixed		
48	p3084-16	-	14	0.22	Cream-pale green/ Cream	D	304	Mixed	Evidence of scraping on exterior surface.	
49	p3054-342	-	19	0.16	Cream-pink/ Orange-red	A	304	Mixed	Evidence of scraping on exterior surface.	
50	p3054-396	-	13	0.22	Pale green/ Pink	D	304	Mixed	Slipped(?) exterior.	
51	p3088-31	-	21	0.18	Cream/ Pale pink	A	304	Mixed	Slipped (?) exterior.	Deformed body; fingerprints.

Type 50.5 *cont'd.*

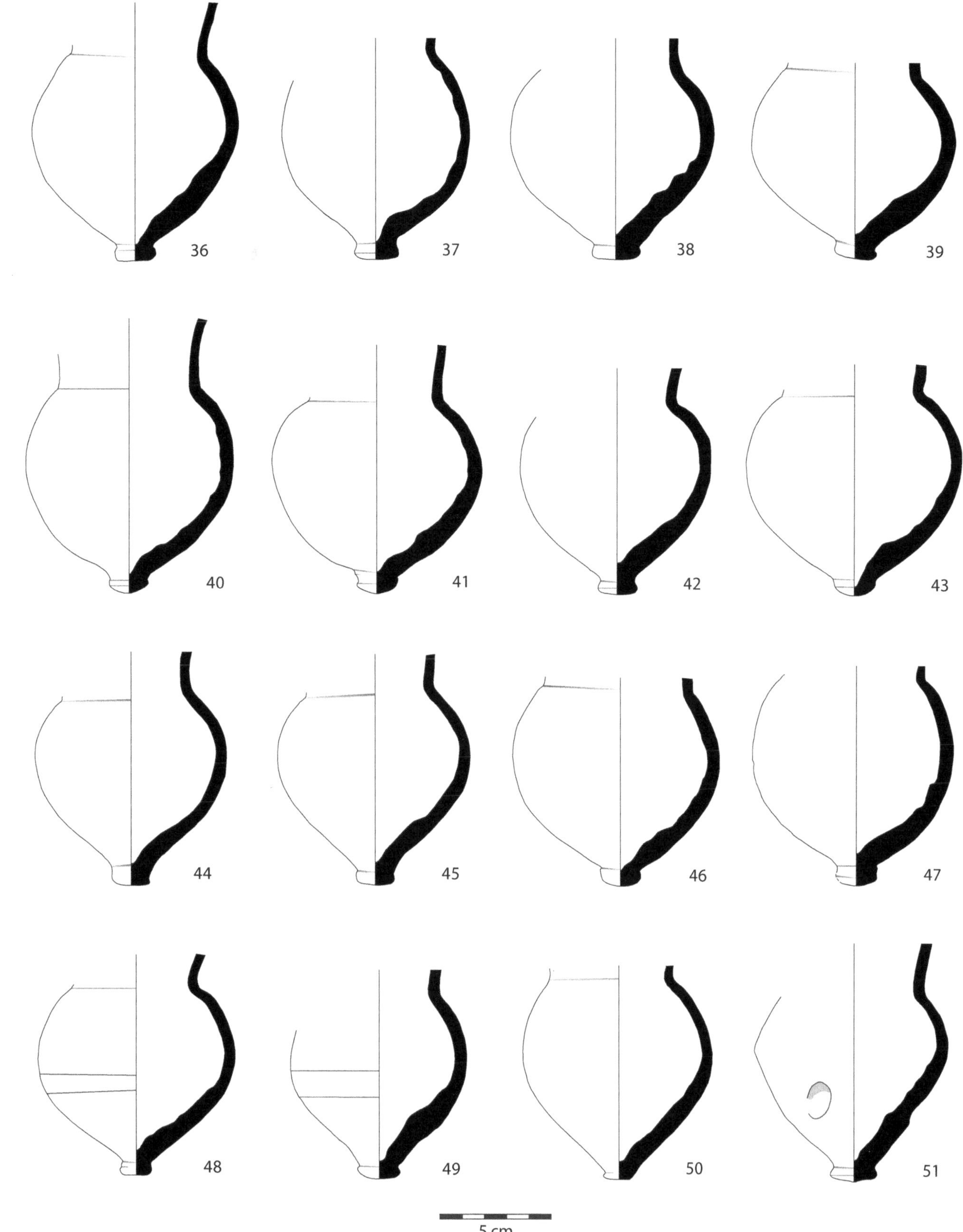

PLATE 40

#	Pottery Number	Rim Di. (mm)	Base Di. (mm)	Volume (L)	Surface/ Fabric Colour	Fabric Type	Room/ Area	Phase	Surface Treatment/ Decoration	Notes
52	p3084-33	-	21	0.25	Pale green/ Cream	D	304	Mixed		Chipped base.
53	p1139-78	-	18	0.19	Cream-pale brown/ Pale brown	D	314	2.2		
54	p5022-64	-	19	0.2	Green/ Pale green	D	140–2	2.2	2 deep scraping marks around lower third of vessel. Well defined neck.	
55	p6036-11	-	14	0.38	Cream-brown/ Brown	A	600	2.2	Incised band around shoulder.	
56	p6078-79	-	16	0.27	Green/ Cream-brown	A	Surface	Mixed	2/3 light ridged lines around shoulder.	
57	p3054-267	-	20	0.25	Pale pink/ Pink-brown	E	304	Mixed	Base is an irregular, ovoid shape.	
58	p1166-70	-	18	0.14	Cream-yellow/ Pale pink	E	314	2.1		Worn base.
59	p3088-183	-	25		White-pale pink/ Cream-pink	E	304	Mixed		Worn/smoothed base.
60	p6068-42	-	22		Pink/ Orange-red	C	Surface	Mixed		
61	p9020-42	-	24	0.31	Pale green/ Pale orange	B	616	Mixed	Slipped (?) exterior.	
62	p8083-23	-	12	0.2	White/ White-grey	A/D	152	2.2	Heavily deformed body shape. Roughly shaped base.	
63	p8083-44	-	16	0.29	Pale green/ Pale green	D	152	2.2	Base very roughly formed. Base cracked on interior.	

Type 50.5 *cont'd.*

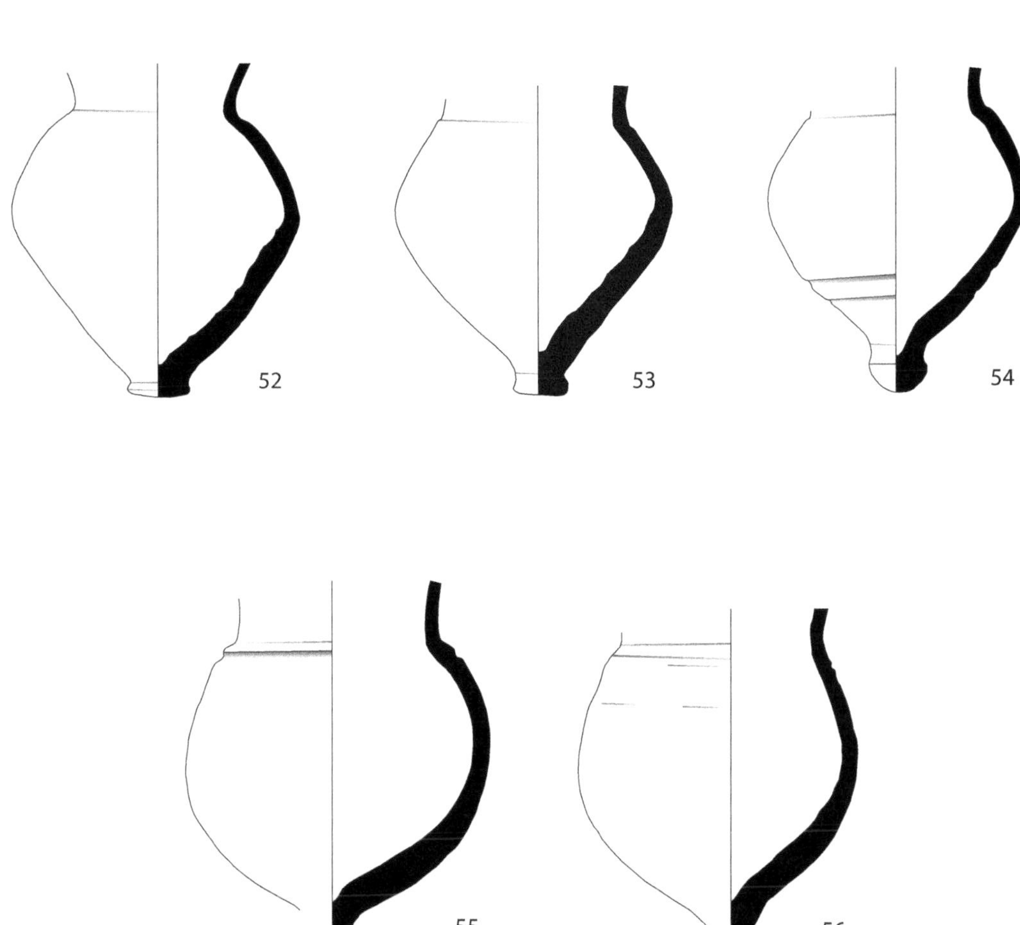

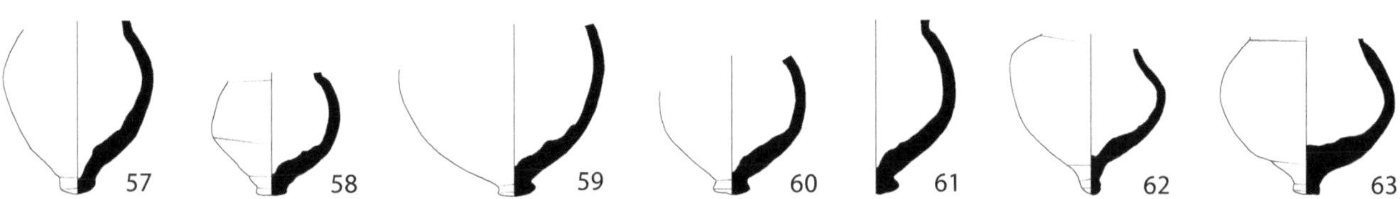

PLATE 41

#	Pottery Number	Rim Di. (mm)	Base Di. (mm)	Volume (L)	Surface/ Fabric Colour	Fabric Type	Room/ Area	Phase	Surface Treatment/ Decoration	Notes
1	p3085-124	-	3	0.29	Cream/ Dull cream	A	304	Mixed		
2	p3054-202	-	5	-	Pale green/ Pale orange	D	304	Mixed	Evidence of scraping around exterior base.	
3	p3186-18	-	5	-	White/ Pink	C	-	-		
4	p3177-35	-	5	-	Brown/ Pink	E	315	2.2		
5	p3151-19	-	4	-	Cream/ Pink	D	315	2.2		
6	p6166-32	-	2	-	Pink/ Pale pink	C	Surface	Mixed		

#	Pottery Number	Rim Di. (mm)	Base Di. (mm)	Volume (L)	Surface/ Fabric Colour	Fabric Type	Room/ Area	Phase	Surface Treatment/ Decoration	Notes
1	p6175-21	-	24	-	Grey-orange/ Cream-orange	D	Surface	Mixed		
2	p6175-53	-	28	-	Yellow-green/ Grey-green	D	Surface	Mixed		
3	p6178-25	-	23	-	Pale green/Grey-green	H	Surface	Mixed		

Type 50.6

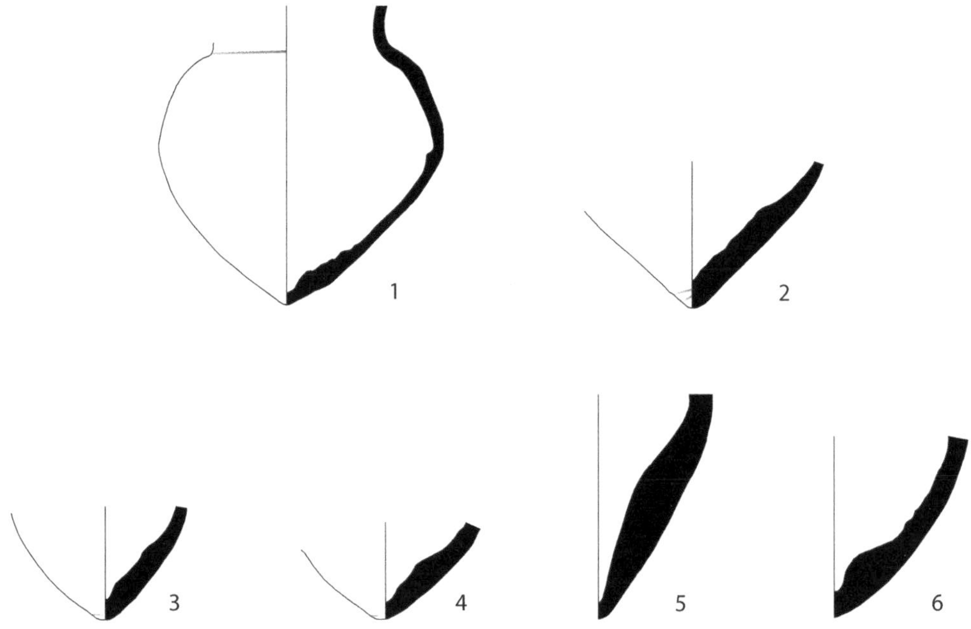

Type 50.7

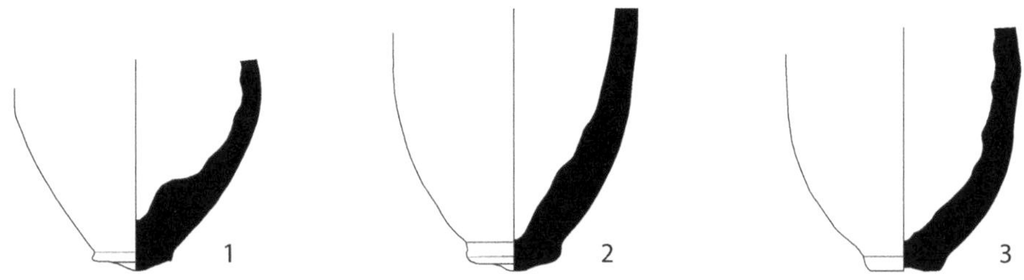

5 cm

PLATE 42

#	Pottery Number	Rim Di. (mm)	Base Di. (mm)	Volume (L)	Surface/ Fabric Colour	Fabric Type	Room/ Area	Phase	Surface Treatment/ Decoration	Notes
1	p3058-14	115	79	3.17	Green/ Red-brown	F	-	-	Slipped(?) exterior. 2 incised lines at base of neck.	
2	p1153-1	110	81	2.85	Yellow-cream/ Cream	E	Burial	Mixed	2 deeply incised bands around shoulder.	
3	p1080-7	84	38	0.96	Pale green/ Pale green	D	101	2.1	Impressed band around shoulder.	
4	p3085-127		44	0.47	Pale green/ Cream-white	A	304	Mixed	2 grooved bands around base.	Plugged base.
5	p6042-40	85	35	0.88	Pale green/ Pale orange	C	600	2.1		

Type 55.1

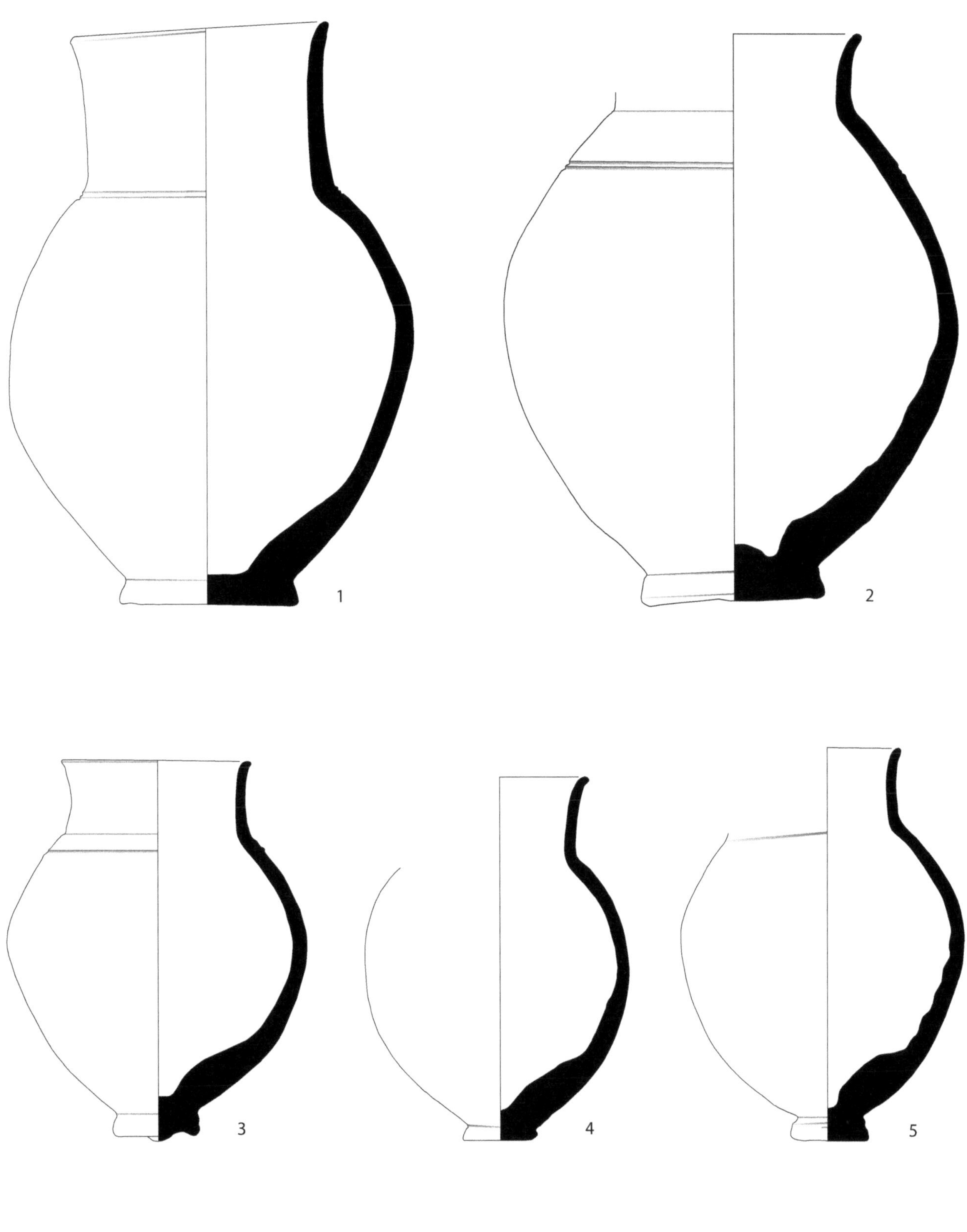

PLATE 43

#	Pottery Number	Rim Di. (mm)	Base Di. (mm)	Volume (L)	Surface/ Fabric Colour	Fabric Type	Room/ Area	Phase	Surface Treatment/ Decoration	Notes
6	p4041-1	80	47	0.96	Pale green	A	Burial	Houses	Ridged band around body. Evidence of scraping?	
7	p3054-405	82	48	0.86	Cream-pale green/ Pink	A	304	Mixed		
8	p1010-14		53	1.18	-	-	-	-		
9	p3084-35	89	51	1.03	Yellow-green/ White-cream	A	304	Mixed	2 impressed bands around shoulder.	Plugged base.
10	p3119-55	-	56	1.02	White-pale green/ White	A	Admin.	2.2	4 incised bands around shoulder. 2 impressed bands at base of neck.	Plugged base.
11	p3087-14	-	43	0.75	Pale green/ Dull cream	A	304	Mixed	Ridged band around shoulder.	Patches of sooting. Plugged(?) base.
12	p4067-23	-	48	0.83	Green/ Green	D	House 1	Houses	Incised groove around shoulder.	
13	p6005-13	-	55	-	Green/ Green	D	-	-		Deliberately perforated(?) or plugged base.
14	p1091-216	-	45	-	Pale pink/ Pink	E	110	2.2		Filled-in(?) base.

Type 55.1 *cont'd.*

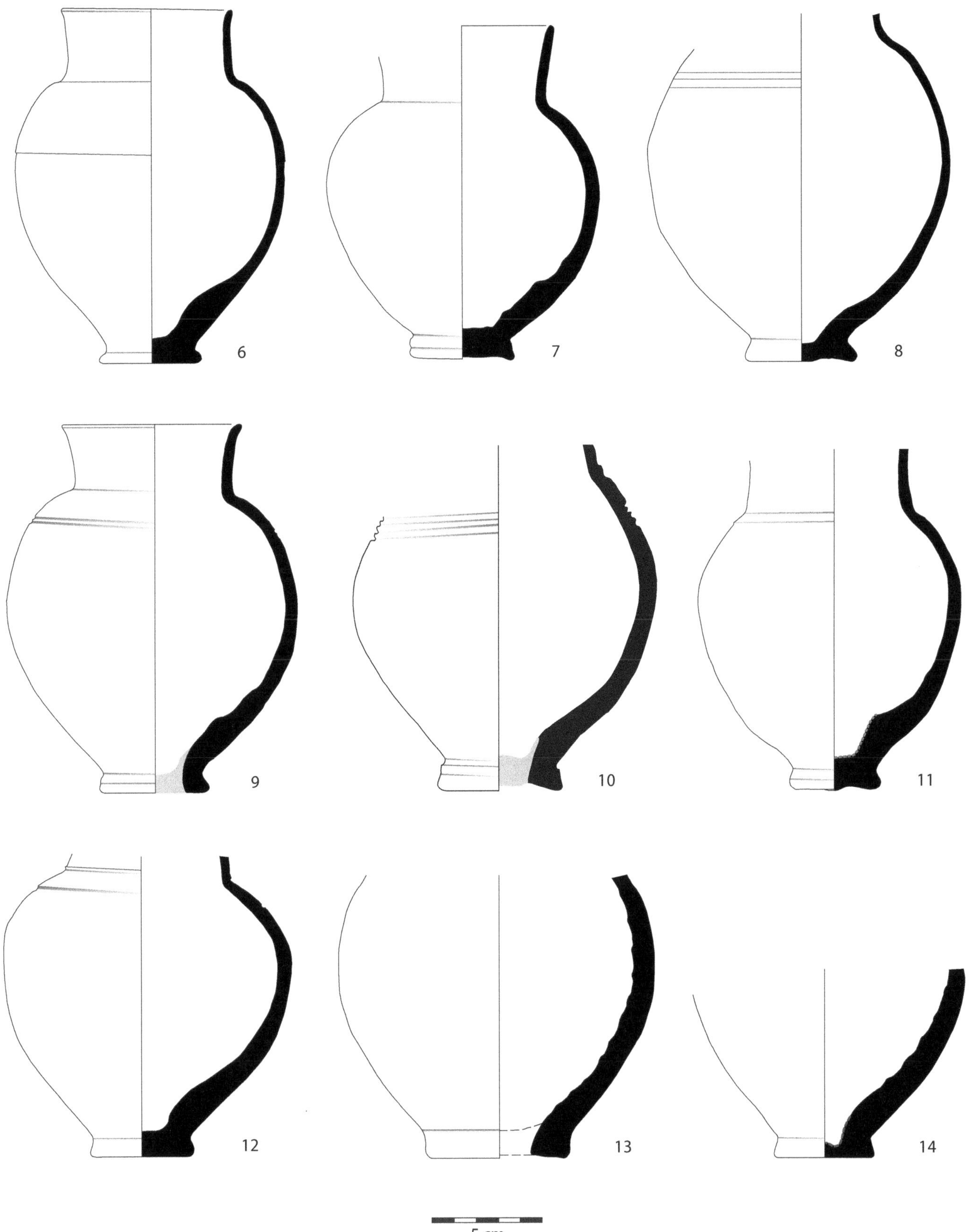

PLATE 44

#	Pottery Number	Rim Di. (mm)	Base Di. (mm)	Volume (L)	Surface/ Fabric Colour	Fabric Type	Room/ Area	Phase	Surface Treatment/ Decoration	Notes
15	p3168-59	-	73	3.15	Cream/ Pink	B	315	2.2	3 incised bands around shoulder.	
16	p3091-2	-	75	-	Pink/ Pink	C	Burial	Mixed		Plugged base.
17	p8083-46	-	62	1.26	White/ Cream	F	152	2.2	Lightly impressed band at base of neck.	Filled-in base.
18	p5022-39	-	55	-	Pale green/ Cream	E	140–2	2.2		Filled-in base.
19	p1079-97	-	60	-	White-cream/ Pale brown	A	101	2.1		
20	p3054-246	-	70	-	Pale green/ Orange-grey	F	304	Mixed		

Type 55.1 *cont'd.*

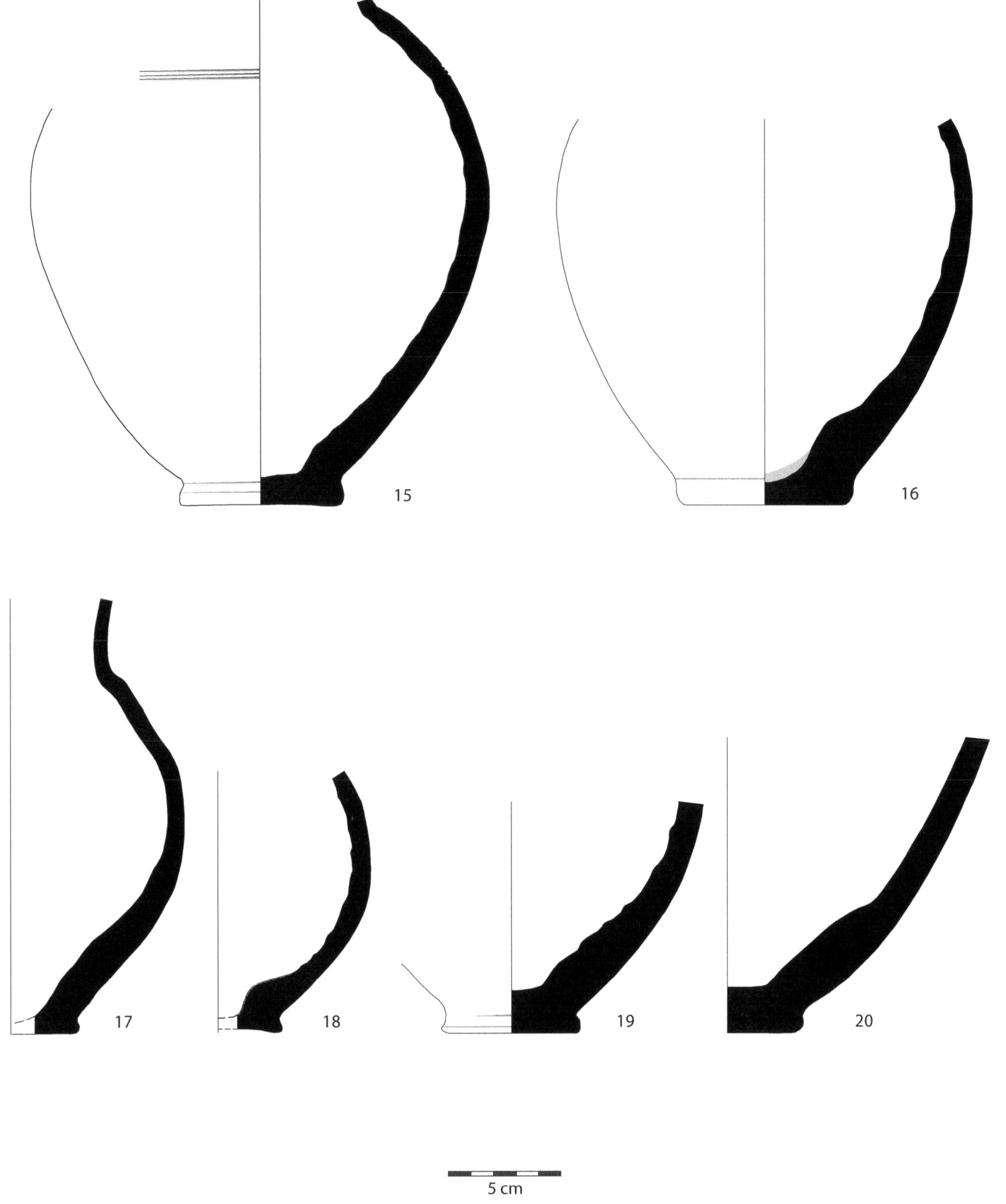

PLATE 45

#	Pottery Number	Rim Di. (mm)	Base Di. (mm)	Volume (L)	Surface/ Fabric Colour	Fabric Type	Room/ Area	Phase	Surface Treatment/ Decoration	Notes
1	p4034-31	92	72	1.98	Green/ Green	F	-	Houses		
2	p4011-1	84	66	1.77	Cream-white/ Cream	D	-	Houses		
3	p3009-17	65	46	0.82	-	-	-	-		
4	p9023-7	-	63	1.68	Pale green/ Green	F	616	Mixed		Filled-in base. Bitumen coated interior, and over breaks. Associated with p9023-6.
5	p5016-11	-	74	-	Pale orange/ Pale brown	E	140–2	2.3	Slipped (?) exterior.	
6	p3098-9	-	39	-	Cream/ Cream	A	Vaults	1		Plugged base.
7	p6111-25	-	55	-	Green/ Orange	H	Surface	Mixed		
8	p3124-17	-	50	-	Pink-cream/ Pink-brown	A	Vaults	1		Plugged(?) base.
9	p3088-48	-	55	-	Green/ Cream	A	304	Mixed	Bitumen coated interior.	Filled-in(?) base.
10	p1079-462	-	55	-	Yellow-cream/ Cream-brown	E	101	2.1		Plugged base.

Type 55.2

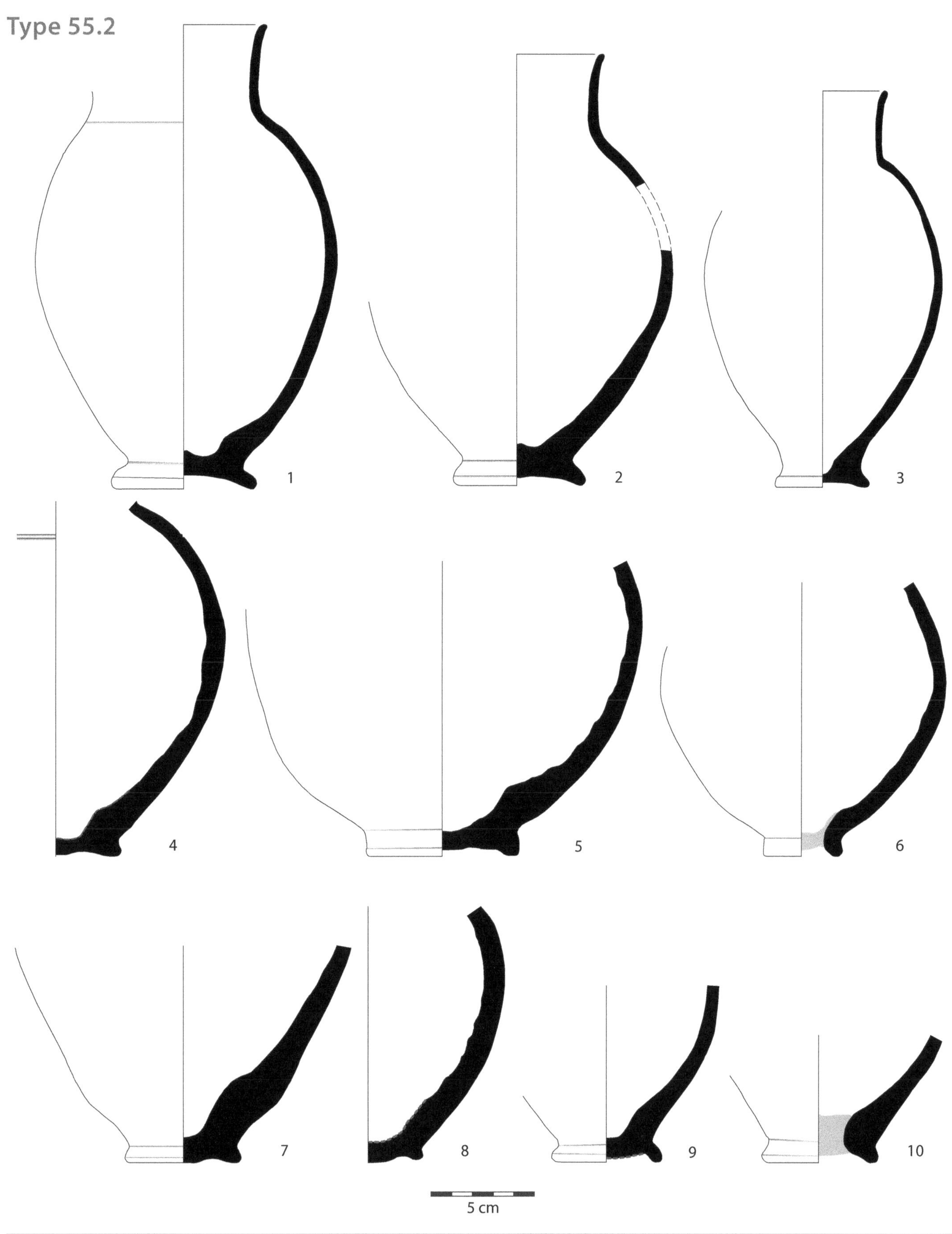

PLATE 46

#	Pottery Number	Rim Di. (mm)	Base Di. (mm)	Volume (L)	Surface/ Fabric Colour	Fabric Type	Room/ Area	Phase	Surface Treatment/ Decoration	Notes
1	p1137-35	100	44	0.86	Green/ Cream-pale green	A	131/619	2.2	2 impressed bands around base of neck. Incised line around shoulder.	Plugged(?) base.
2	p6068-43	108	51	0.9	Green-yellow/ Green-yellow	A	Surface	Mixed		Plugged(?) base.
3	p6124-19	90	44	0.78	Pink-brown/ Pink-brown	A	Surface	Mixed	2 impressed bands around base of neck.	
4	p6118-43	90	40	0.42	Pale orange/ Pink	A	Surface	Mixed	2 impressed bands around base of neck.	

Type 55.3

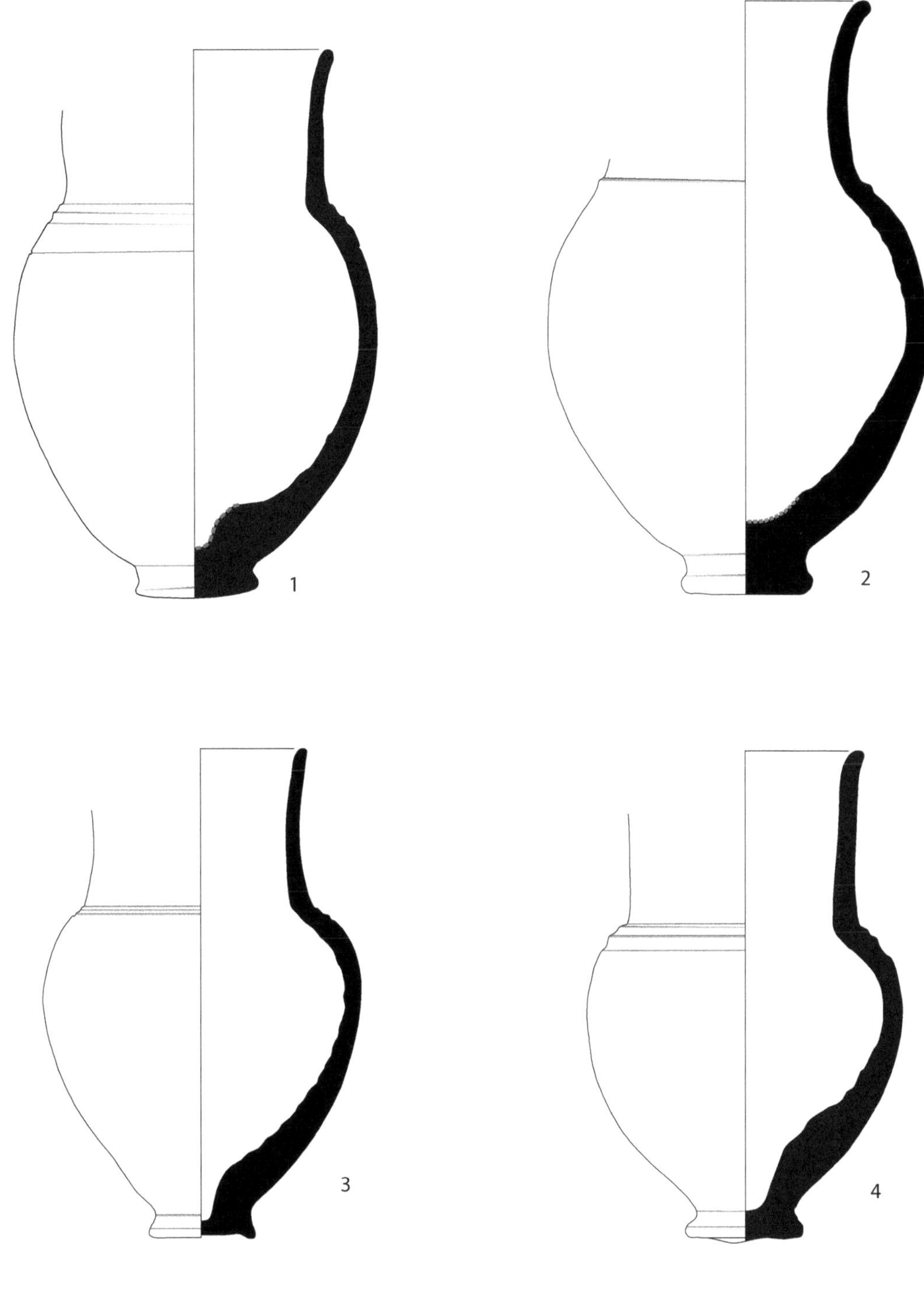

PLATE 47

#	Pottery Number	Rim Di. (mm)	Base Di. (mm)	Volume (L)	Surface/ Fabric Colour	Fabric Type	Room/ Area	Phase	Surface Treatment/ Decoration	Notes
1	p4058-8	80	-	-	Pink-cream/ Pink-orange	A	House 1	Houses		
2	p4010-8	75	-	-	Green/ Green	D	House 1	Houses	Evidence of scraping on body.	
3	p3025-82	65	-	-	Pink/ Pink-orange	A	302	Mixed		
4	p3065-9	80	-	-	Cream/ Cream-grey	E	Admin.	2.2	Incised line around shoulder.	
5	p3151-40	95	-	-	Cream-pale green/ Pale brown	E	315	2.2	Incised line around base of neck.	
6	p9022-6	80	-	-	Pale orange/ Pink	F	616	Mixed	3 incised bands around shoulder.	
7	p3001-1	114	-	-	Green/ Green	over-fired	-	-	4 incised lines around base of neck. 5 incised lines around shoulder.	
8	p6036-116	80	-	-	Pale green/ Green	D	600	2.2	4 ridges around base of neck/upper shoulder. 2 incised bands around shoulder.	

#	Pottery Number	Rim Di. (mm)	Base Di. (mm)	Volume (L)	Surface/ Fabric Colour	Fabric Type	Room/ Area	Phase	Surface Treatment/ Decoration	Notes
1	p6040-48	90	-	-	Green/ Grey	D	600	2.2		
2	p4021-5	100	-	-	Cream/ Pink	E	-	Houses		
3	p6068-3	90	-	-	Green-yellow/ Green-yellow	A	Surface	Mixed		

FAMILY 60

Type 60.1

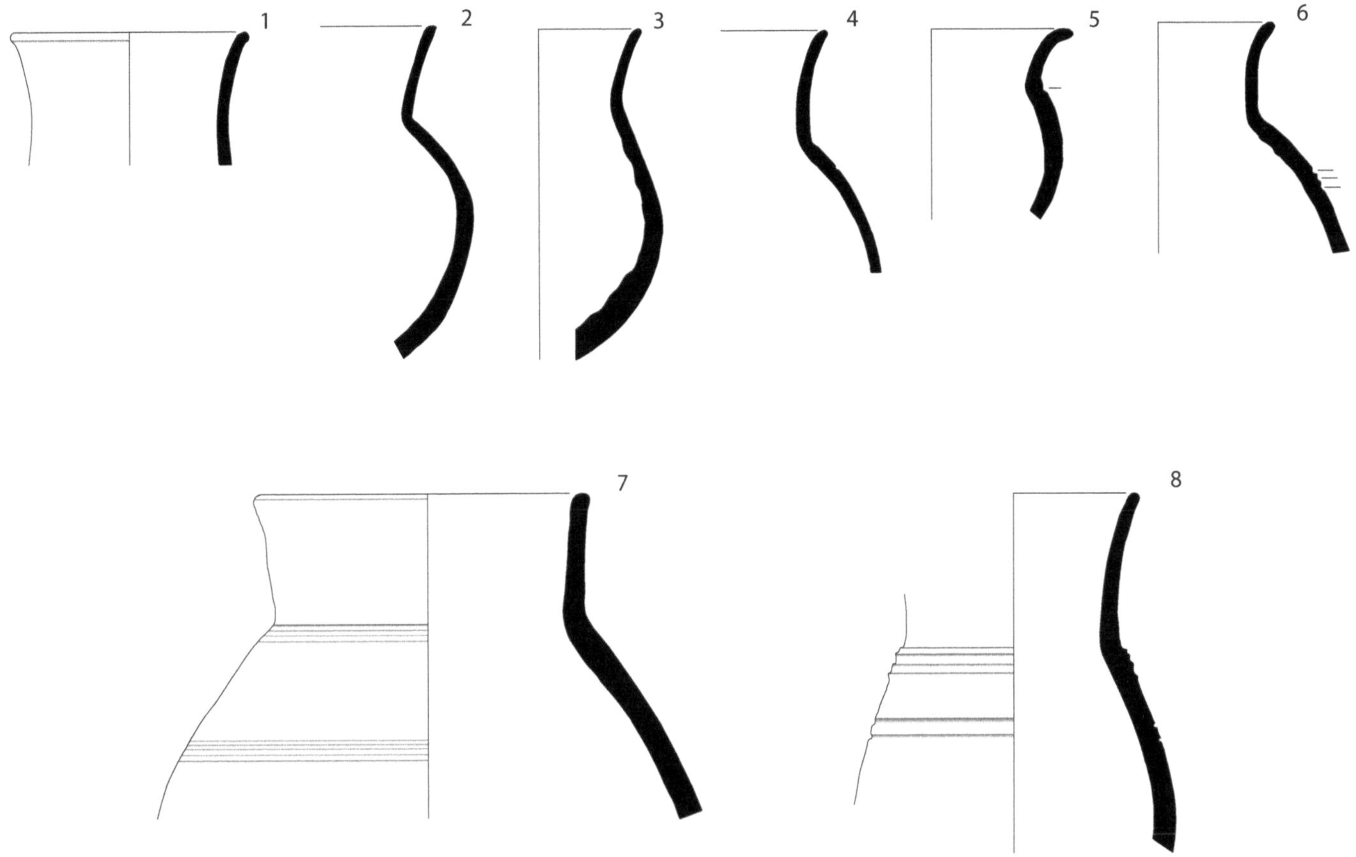

Type 60.2

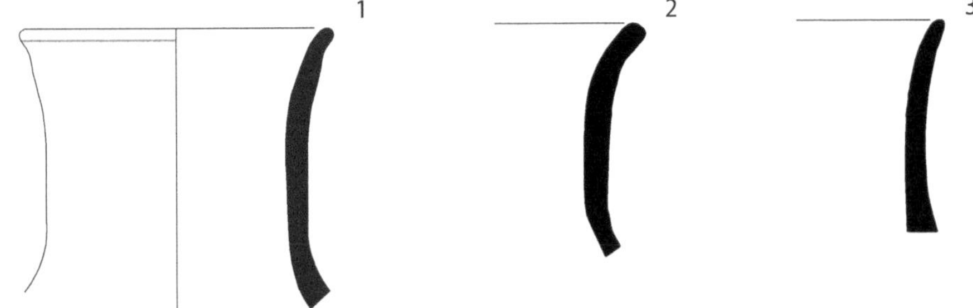

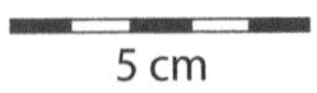

5 cm

PLATE 48

#	Pottery Number	Rim Di. (mm)	Base Di. (mm)	Volume (L)	Surface/ Fabric Colour	Fabric Type	Room/ Area	Phase	Surface Treatment/ Decoration	Notes
1	p1094-132	105	-	-	Cream-pale pink/ Orange	E	124	Mixed	Ridged bands around neck.	
2	p1079-792	110	-	-	Cream/ Pale pink	A	101	2.1	Ridged bands around neck.	
3	p6060-2	110	-	-	Dark orange/ Orange-pink	C	601	2.2	Ridged bands around neck.	
4	p3085-83	120	-	-	Green/ Pale green	D	304	Mixed	Ridged bands around neck.	

#	Pottery Number	Rim Di. (mm)	Base Di. (mm)	Volume (L)	Surface/ Fabric Colour	Fabric Type	Room/ Area	Phase	Surface Treatment/ Decoration	Notes
1	p6178-33	125	-	-	White/ Pink	F	Surface	Mixed	Complex series of incised and impressed decoration on rim and up whole body.	
2	p1055-4	110	-	-	Cream/ Cream-brown	C/D	-	-		
3	p6096-119	100	-	-	Cream/ Brown	C	Surface	Mixed		

Type 60.3

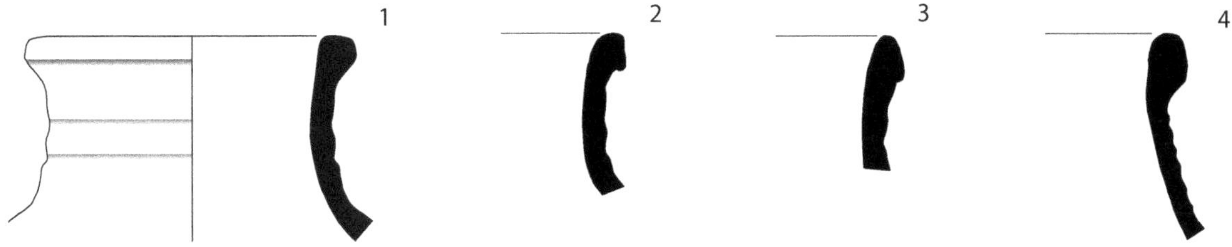

Type 60.4

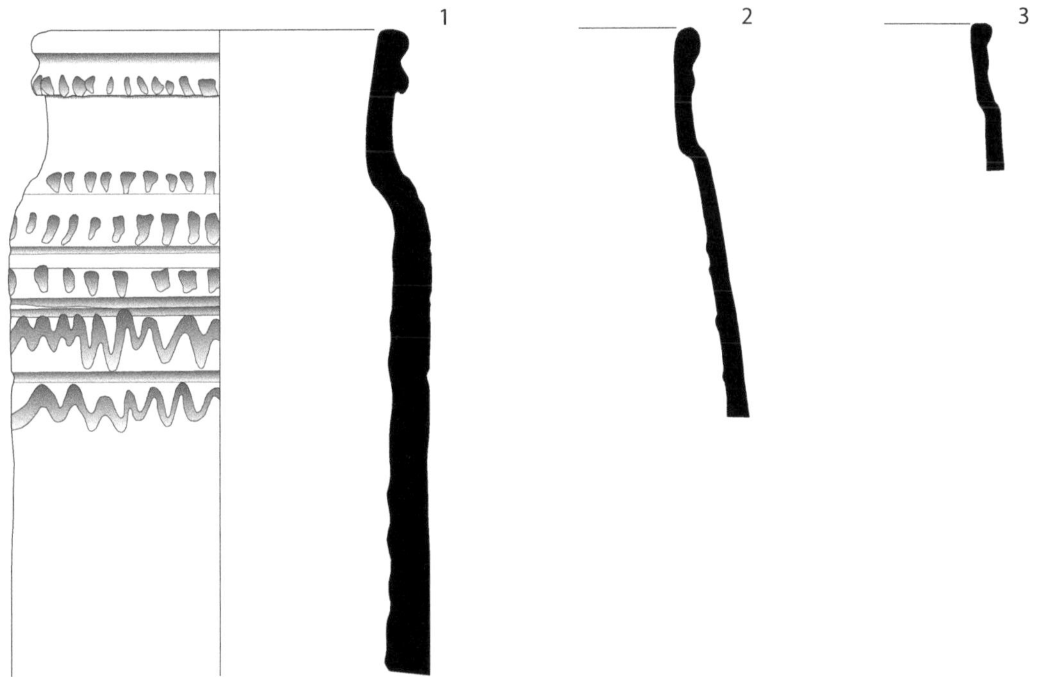

5 cm

PLATE 49

#	Pottery Number	Rim Di. (mm)	Base Di. (mm)	Volume (L)	Surface/ Fabric Colour	Fabric Type	Room/ Area	Phase	Surface Treatment/ Decoration	Notes
1	p3088-47	-	110	-	Pink/ Black core	E	304	Mixed		String-cut base.
2	p1010-29	-	100	-	Pink/ Pink	-	-	-		String-cut base.
3	p6118-24	-	90	-	Cream/ Brown-pink	E	Surface	Mixed		String-cut base. Plugged base?
4	p3083-14	-	90	-	Cream/ Pink-red	D	304	Mixed		String-cut base. Plugged base?
5	p6058-31	-	57	-	Cream/ Pale orange	D, with shell	601	2.1		
6	p6111-46	-	90	-	Pink/ Pink-brown	E	Surface	Mixed		Plugged?
7	p3123-15	-	85	-	Pink-orange/ Pink	E	Admin.	2.1		String-cut base.
8	p8020-16	-	90	-	Green/ Pale green-grey	H	316	2.3		Plugged base?
9	p3088-159	-	90	-	Pale green/ Cream	D	304	Mixed		Plugged base?
10	p3054-395	-	125	-	Pink-red/ Red-brown	E	304	Mixed		String-cut base. Plugged base?
11	p6136-19	-	65	-	Pale orange/ Dark orange	C	Surface	Mixed		String-cut base. Plugged base?

FAMILY 65

Type 65.1

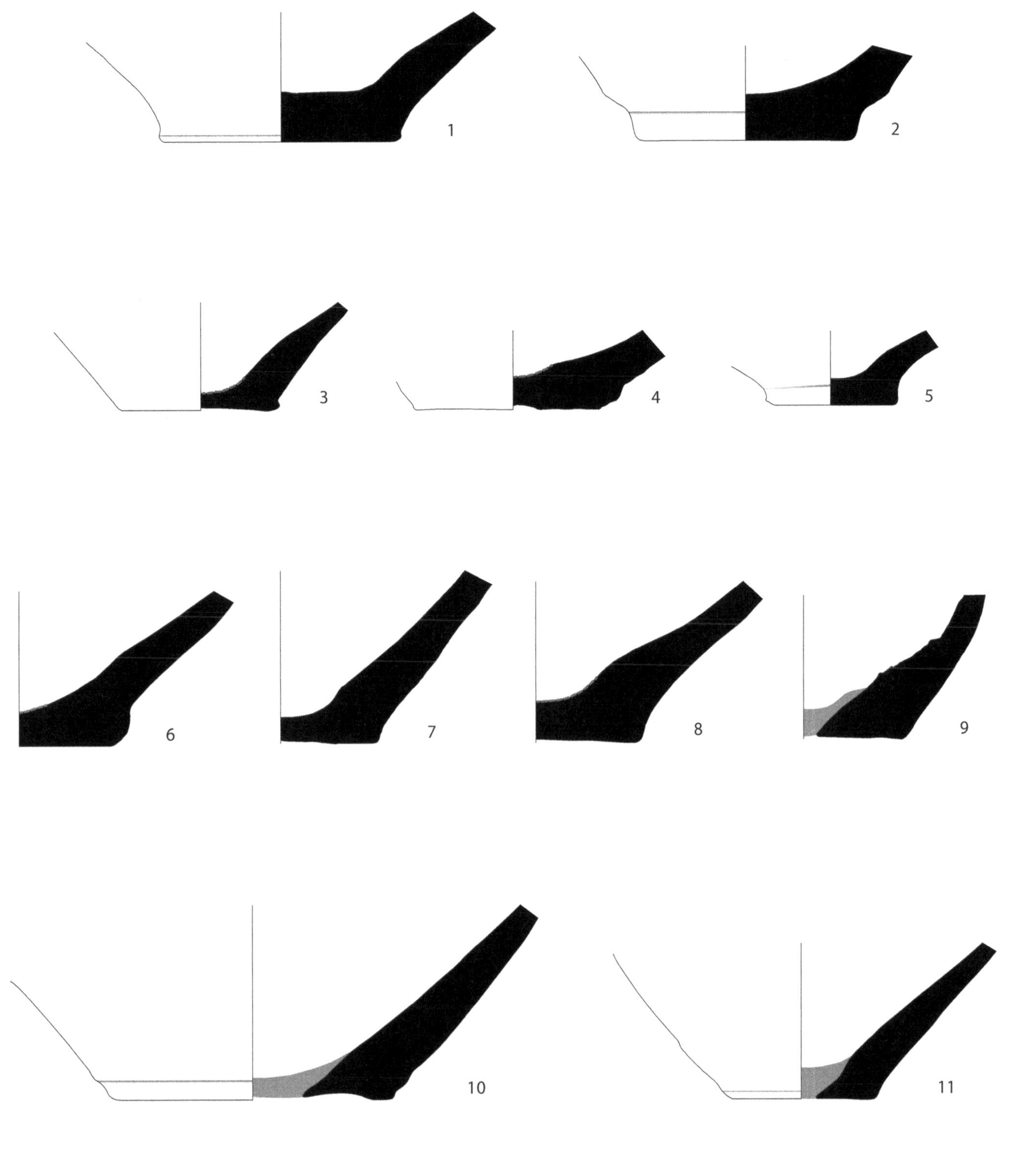

PLATE 50

#	Pottery Number	Rim Di. (mm)	Base Di. (mm)	Volume (L)	Surface/ Fabric Colour	Fabric Type	Room/ Area	Phase	Surface Treatment/ Decoration	Notes
1	p3054-50	-	70	-	Pale brown/ Pale brown	F	304	Mixed		
2	p3088-46	-	100	-	Cream/ Pink	E	304	Mixed		Plugged base?
3	p1080-21	-	90	-	Cream/ Cream	F	101	2.1		
4	p3125-11	-	100	-	Cream/ Pale brown	D	302	Mixed		
5	p6096-43	-	85	-	Brown/ Brown-pink	F	Surface	Mixed		Plugged base.
6	p3025-23	-	110	-	Pale green-yellow/ Pale brown	F	302	Mixed		

#	Pottery Number	Rim Di. (mm)	Base Di. (mm)	Volume (L)	Surface/ Fabric Colour	Fabric Type	Room/ Area	Phase	Surface Treatment/ Decoration	Notes
1	p6111-10	-	170	-	Green/ Green-brown	F	Surface	Mixed		String-cut base.
2	p3064-677	-	240	-	White/ Grey	F	Admin.	2.2		Plugged base?
3	p8065-10	-	170	-	Cream-pink/ Orange-brown	B	316	2.2		String-cut base.
4	p6126-30	-	95	-	Cream/ Cream	D	Surface	Mixed	Pink wash(?) exterior.	Plugged base.

Type 65.2

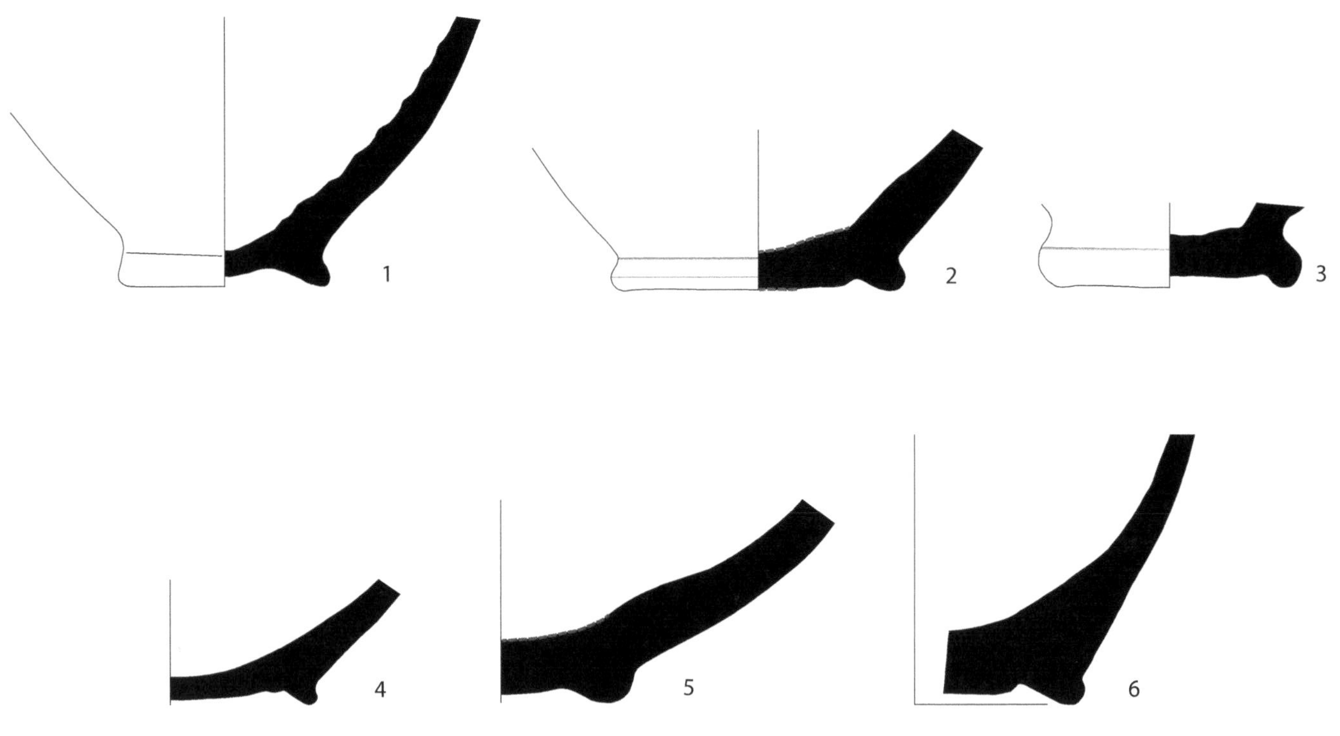

Type 65.3

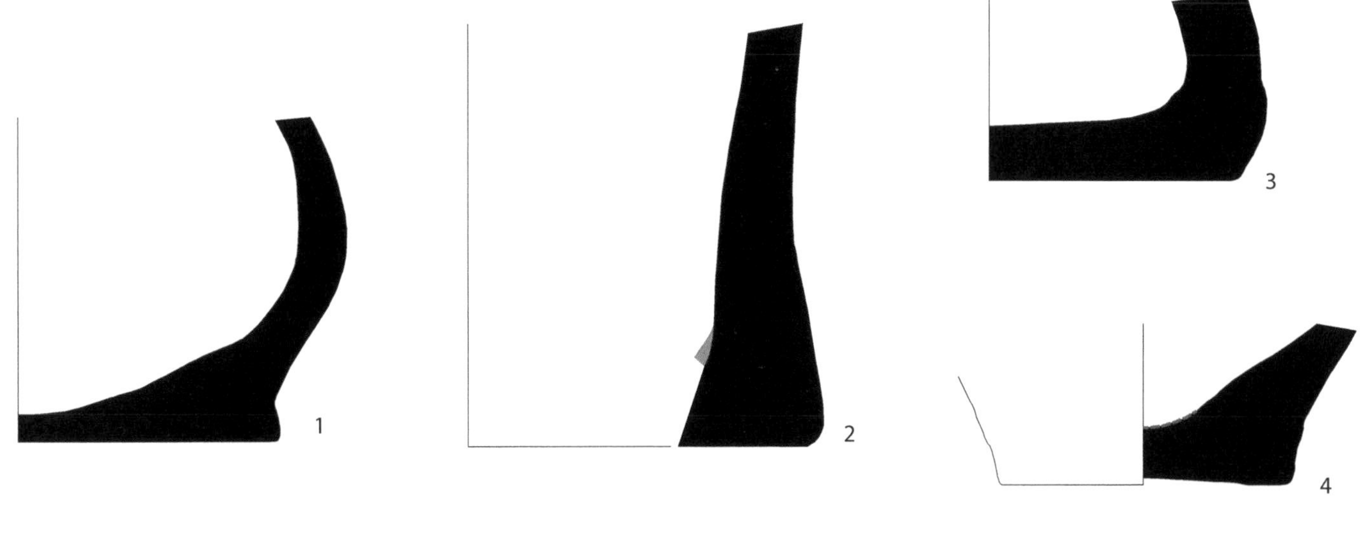

5 cm

PLATE 51

#	Pottery Number	Rim Di. (mm)	Base Di. (mm)	Volume (L)	Surface/ Fabric Colour	Fabric Type	Room/ Area	Phase	Surface Treatment/ Decoration	Notes
1	p9018-81	-	50	-	Red-orange/ Brown	D	616	Mixed		
2	p3088-98	-	50	-	Red-pink/ Pink-brown	C	304	Mixed		
3	p3088-23	-	45	-	Red-pink/ Brown-red	B	304	Mixed		
4	p1091-395	-	45	-	Cream/ White	-	110	2.2		
5	p3123-14	-	45	-	Green/ Green	-	Admin.	2.1		Finger impressions on exterior.
6	p6136-101	-	50	-	Pale green/ Pink	D	Surface	Mixed		String-cut base. Sooted interior.
7	p6070-24	-	40	-	Red-orange/ Red-orange	F	Surface	Mixed		

Type 65.4

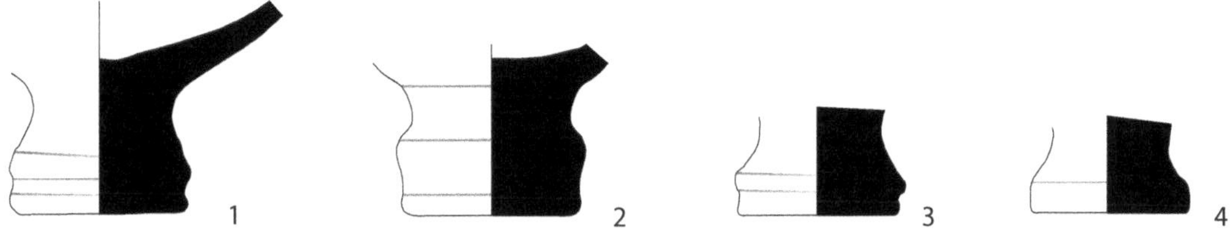

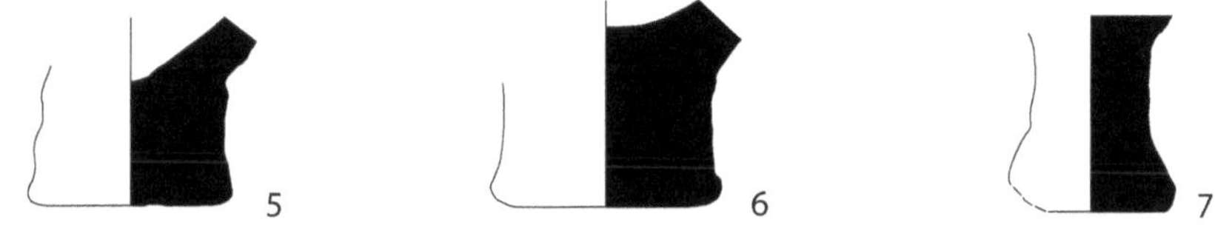

PLATE 52

#	Pottery Number	Rim Di. (mm)	Base Di. (mm)	Volume (L)	Surface/ Fabric Colour	Fabric Type	Room/ Area	Phase	Surface Treatment/ Decoration	Notes
1	p8013-13	160	-	-	Yellow-brown/ Pale green-grey	H	316	2.3	Incised band around shoulder.	
2	p3025-25	180	-	-	Yellow-brown/ Green-yellow	F	302	Mixed	2 incised bands around shoulder.	
3	p1079-491	190	-	-	Cream-white/ Pink-orange	B/G	101	2.1	Incised band around shoulder.	
4	p6037-9	150	-	-	Cream/ Cream-brown	F	-	-		

FAMILY 70

Type 70.1

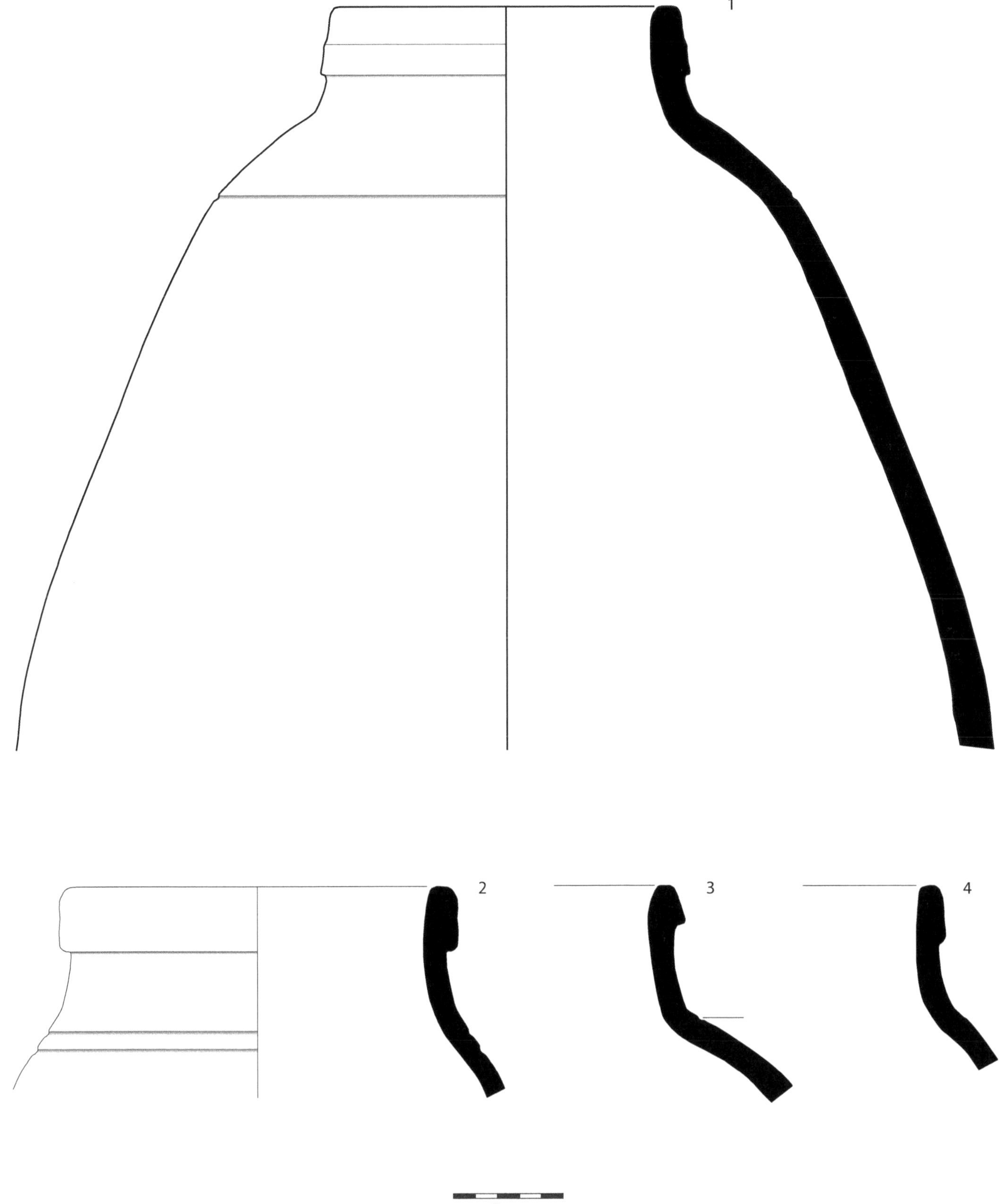

PLATE 53

#	Pottery Number	Rim Di. (mm)	Base Di. (mm)	Volume (L)	Surface/ Fabric Colour	Fabric Type	Room/ Area	Phase	Surface Treatment/ Decoration	Notes
5	p8083-1	145	-	-	Cream-yellow/ Cream	D	152	2.2	Lightly impressed band around shoulder.	
6	p3088-171	150	-	-	Green/ Green-grey	F	304	Mixed	2+ incised bands around shoulder.	
7	p3088-171	150	-	-	Green/ Green-grey	F	304	Mixed	2+ incised bands around shoulder.	

#	Pottery Number	Rim Di. (mm)	Base Di. (mm)	Volume (L)	Surface/ Fabric Colour	Fabric Type	Room/ Area	Phase	Surface Treatment/ Decoration	Notes
1	p3088-128	180	-	-	Pale green/ Cream	D	304	Mixed		
2	p1159-1	180	-	19.98	Pale green/ Grey-white	F	Admin.	2.2	Impressed band around shoulder.	
3	p3088-129	150	-	-	Cream-white/ Cream	F	304	Mixed	2 incised bands around shoulder.	
4	p6111-48	150	-	-	Green/ Green	F	Surface	Mixed	Incised band around shoulder.	Bitumen stained exterior.

Type 70.1 *cont'd.*

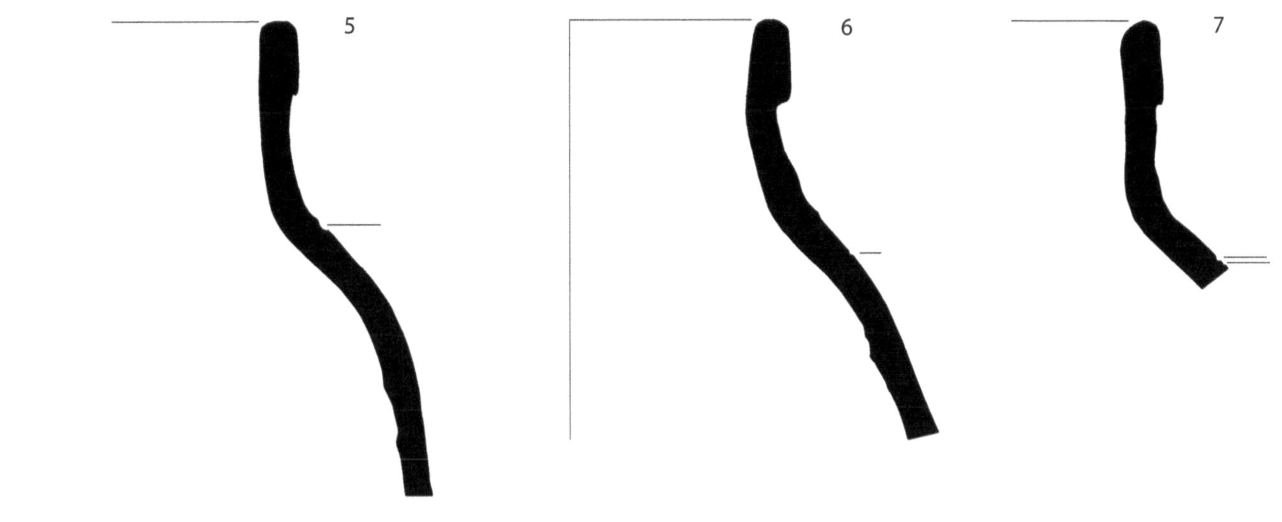

Type 70.2

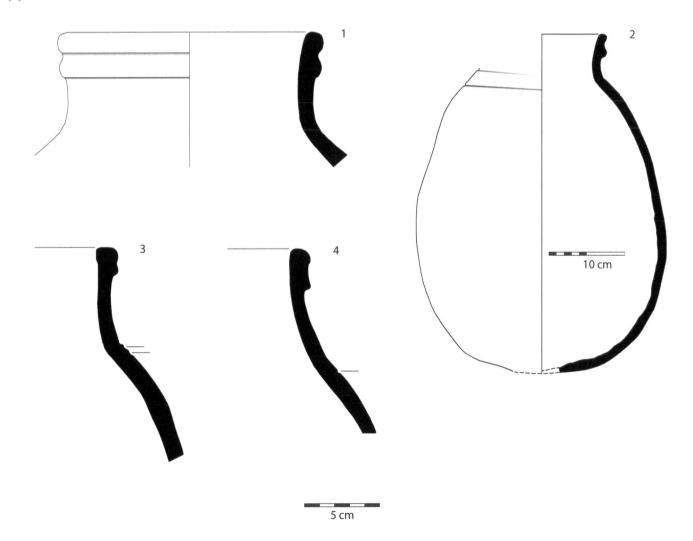

1
2
10 cm
3
4

5 cm

PLATE 54

#	Pottery Number	Rim Di. (mm)	Base Di. (mm)	Volume (L)	Surface/ Fabric Colour	Fabric Type	Room/ Area	Phase	Surface Treatment/ Decoration	Notes
5	p6111-68	140	0	17.08	Pale green/ Grey-pink	F	Surface	Mixed	Incised markings on upper body. Incised band around shoulder.	
6	p6022-5	300	-	-	Green/ Green	F	-	-	2 incised bands around shoulder.	
7	p3085-85	140	-	-	Pale green/ Pale green	D	304	Mixed		
8	p1085-23	140	-	-	White-cream/ Cream	F	101	2.1		
9	p3154-17	165	-	-	Green/ Grey-green	F	315	2.2		
10	p4054-4	150	-	-	White-cream/ Cream-pink	F	House 1	Houses	Incised band around shoulder.	

Type 70.2 *cont'd.*

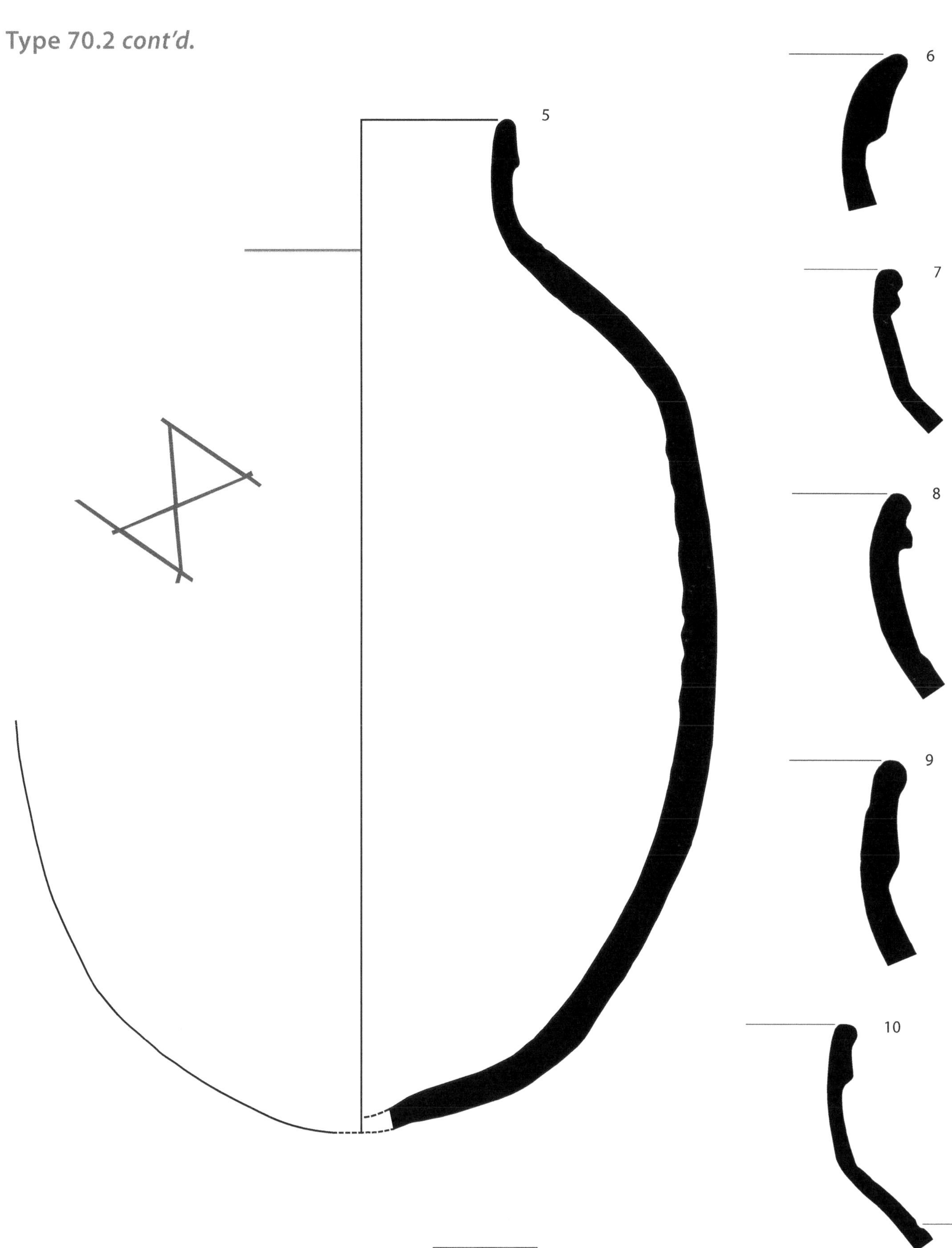

PLATE 55

#	Pottery Number	Rim Di. (mm)	Base Di. (mm)	Volume (L)	Surface/ Fabric Colour	Fabric Type	Room/ Area	Phase	Surface Treatment/ Decoration	Notes
11	p4053-17	170	-	-	Red-orange/ Red-orange	F	House 1	Houses	Multiple ridges beneath rim.	
12	p6022-5	300	-	-	Green/ Green	F	-	-	2 incised bands around shoulder.	
13	p8083-16	160	-	-	Grey-green/ Grey-brown	F	152	2.2	3 lightly impressed bands around shoulder.	

#	Pottery Number	Rim Di. (mm)	Base Di. (mm)	Volume (L)	Surface/ Fabric Colour	Fabric Type	Room/ Area	Phase	Surface Treatment/ Decoration	Notes
1	p6036-123	156	-	-	Cream-pale green/ Pale green	F	600	2.2	3 incised bands around shoulder.	
2	p6060-3	165	-	-	Green-brown/ Brown-grey	F	601	2.2	2 incised bands around shoulder.	

Type 70.2 *cont'd.*

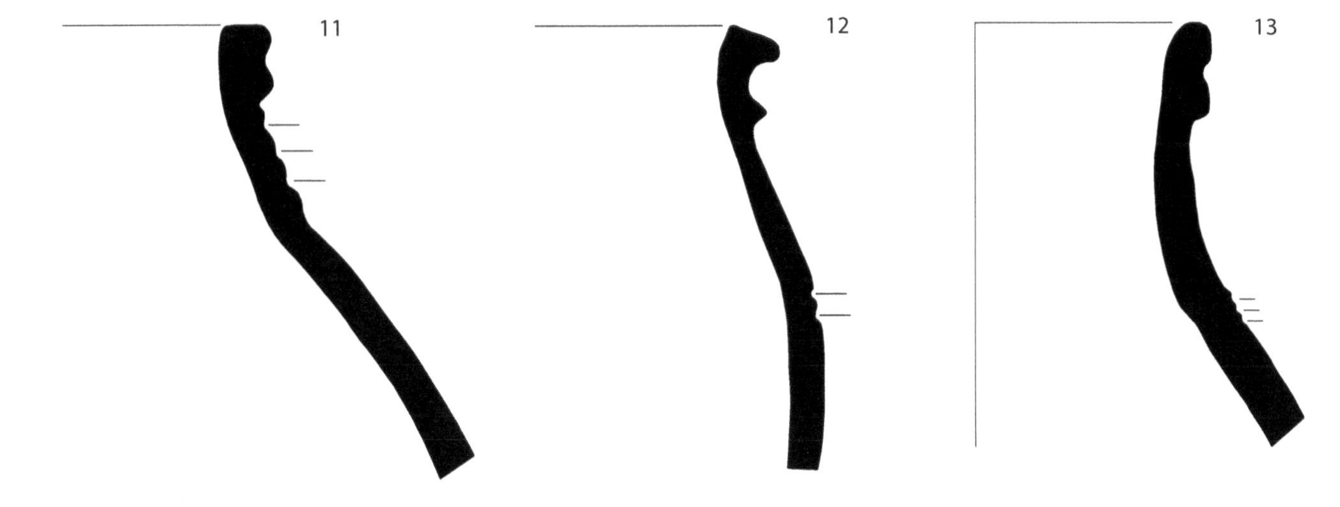

Type 70.3

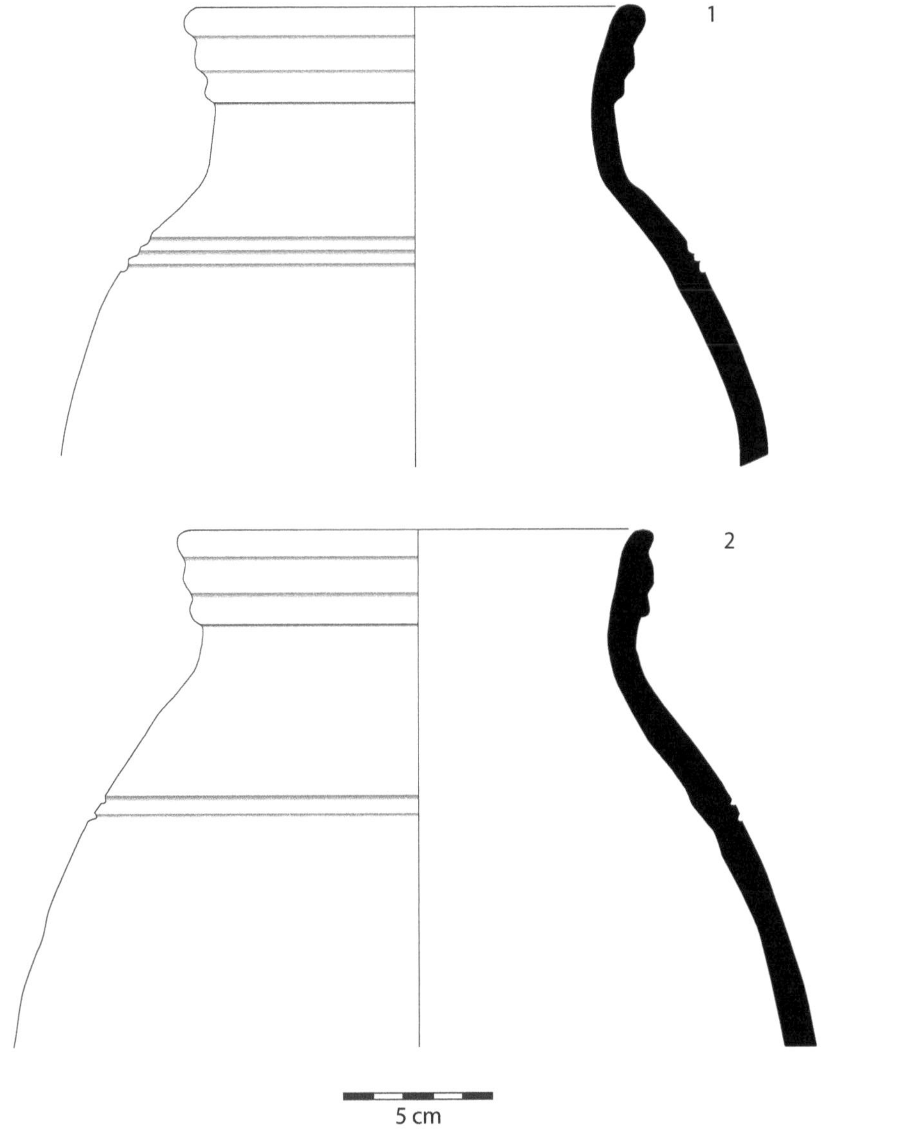

PLATE 56

#	Pottery Number	Rim Di. (mm)	Base Di. (mm)	Volume (L)	Surface/ Fabric Colour	Fabric Type	Room/ Area	Phase	Surface Treatment/ Decoration	Notes
3	p3091-3	165	0	19.66	Pale green-cream/ Grey	F	Burial	Mixed	2 incised bands around shoulder.	
4	p6141-1	160	0	20.16	Green/ Green	F	Burial	Mixed	Ridged band around base of neck.	
5	p8013-14	155-175 irregular	-	-	Green-grey/ Green-grey	F	316	2.3	Irregular oval orifice. 1 thick impressed band around shoulder.	
6	p3064-565	156	-	ca. 17.5	Pale green/ Pale green-grey	F	Admin.	2.2	Ridged band around base of neck. 2 incised bands around shoulder.	
7	p3054-402	148	-	-	Green/ green-brown	D	304	Mixed	Red-purple wash(?). 1 or 2 incised bands around shoulder.	
8	p3084-37	150	-	-	Green/ Cream	D	304	Mixed	2 incised bands around shoulder.	

Type 70.3 *cont'd.*

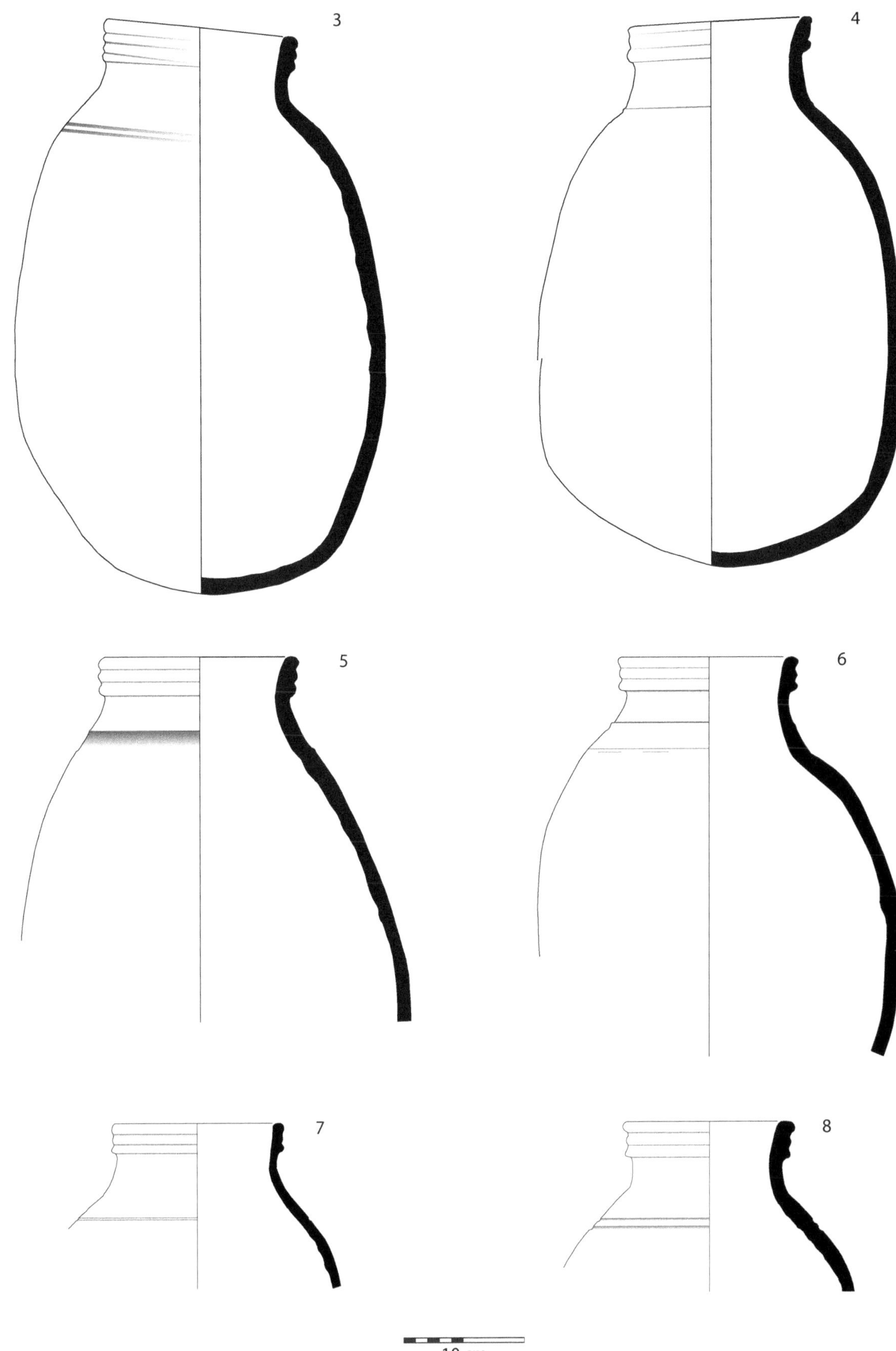

PLATE 57

#	Pottery Number	Rim Di. (mm)	Base Di. (mm)	Volume (L)	Surface/ Fabric Colour	Fabric Type	Room/ Area	Phase	Surface Treatment/ Decoration	Notes
9	p3054-201	170	-	-	Green/ Green	F	304	Mixed	Incised band around shoulder.	
10	p3055-10	160	-	-	Green/ Green	F	-	-	Incised band around shoulder.	
11	p8047-1	135	-	-	Dark green/ Dark green	H	-	-	3 incised bands around shoulder.	Infant burial.
12	p1092-30	160	-	-	Green/ Green	F	110	2.2	5 incised bands around shoulder.	
13	p3025-48	130	-	-	Green/ Green	F	302	Mixed		
14	p3085-47	115	-	-	Cream/ Cream-grey	F	304	Mixed	2 incised bands around shoulder.	
15	p3085-169	160	-	-	Pale brown-green/ Pink-brown	D	304	Mixed	2 incised bands around shoulder.	
16	p3088-127	190	-	-	Orange-pink/ Pale brown	C/F	304	Mixed		
17	p3088-49	170	-	-	Pink/ Pink	D	304	Mixed	Incised band around shoulder.	
18	p3056-70		-	-	Grey-black/ Red-black	F	Admin.	2.2	Multiple ridges beneath rim.	
19	p3085-260	180	-	-	Green/ Green-grey	H	304	Mixed	Incised band around shoulder. Incised band lower down body.	
20	p3025-13	130	-	-	Green/ Green	F	302	Mixed	3 incised grooves around shoulder.	
21	p3084-24	180	-	-	Red-pink/ Brown-red	C	304	Mixed		
22	p4037-3	160	-	-	Cream/ Pale brown	F	House 3	Houses		
23	p6083-3	200	-	-	Green/ Green	H	Surface	Mixed		
24	p1079-436	170	-	-	Green/ Green	F	101	2.1		

Type 70.3 *cont'd.*

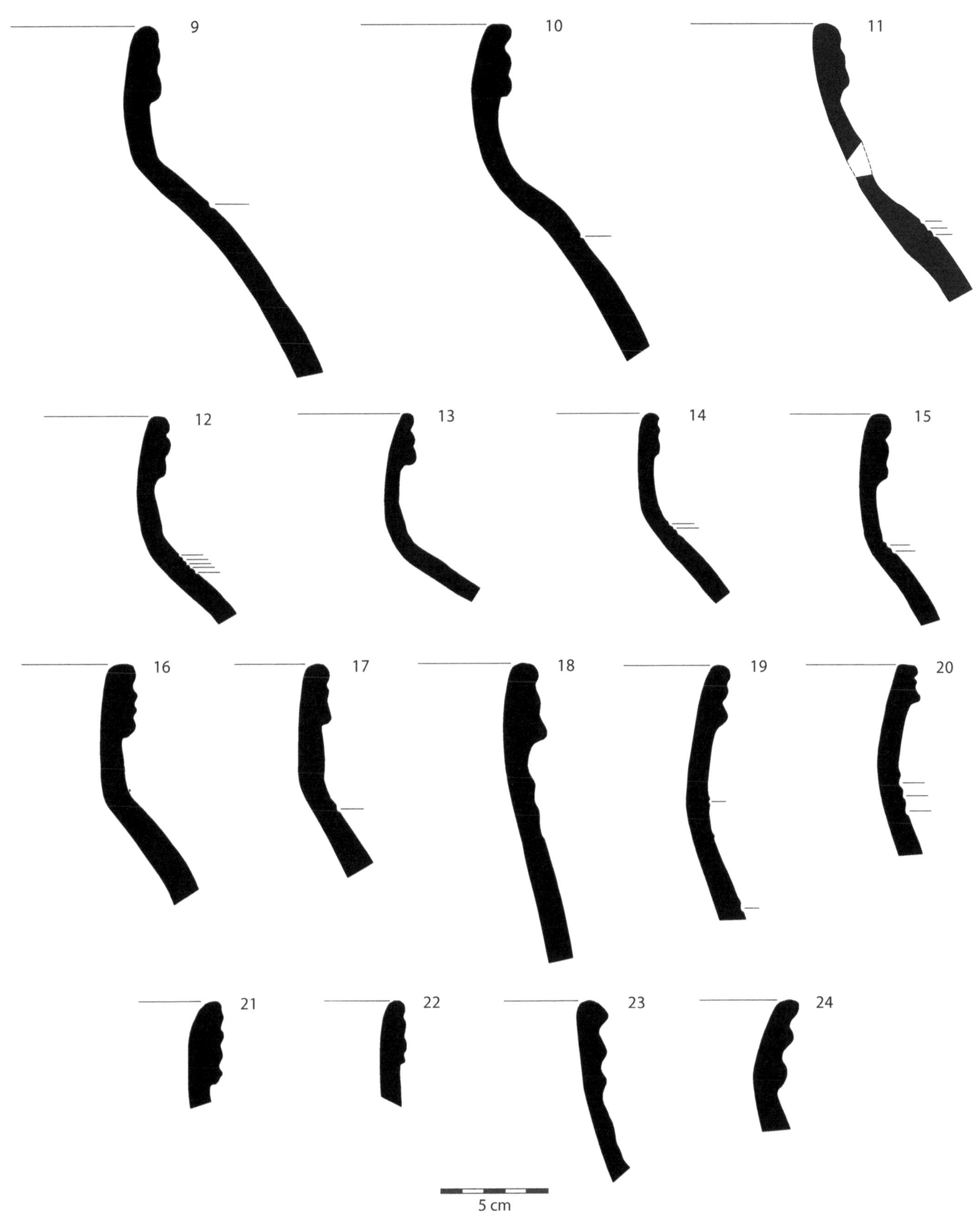

PLATE 58

#	Pottery Number	Rim Di. (mm)	Base Di. (mm)	Volume (L)	Surface/ Fabric Colour	Fabric Type	Room/ Area	Phase	Surface Treatment/ Decoration	Notes
1	p4003-17	190	-	-	Pale green/ Pale brown	F	-	Houses		
2	p6041-230	180	-	-	Pale orange/ Pink-grey	D	601	2.2		
3	p1068-95	150	-	-	Grey/ Red-brown	C	101	2.2		
4	p3064-4	170	-	-	Pale green/ Grey	F	Admin.	2.2		
5	p1033-11	150	-	-	Green/ Green	F	-	-		

#	Pottery Number	Rim Di. (mm)	Base Di. (mm)	Volume (L)	Surface/ Fabric Colour	Fabric Type	Room/ Area	Phase	Surface Treatment/ Decoration	Notes
1	p3085-283	142	0	9.33	White-pale green/ Pink	F	304	Mixed	Incised band around shoulder.	
2	p1034-9	170	-	-	Green/ Green	F	-	-		
3	p6036-120	150	-	-	Pale green/ Cream	F	600	2.2		
4	p3122-22	170	-	-	Pale pink/ Pink	D	Admin.	2.1		
5	p6060-4	160	-	-	Green/ Brown	F	601	2.2		
6	p3054-323	140	-	-	Green/ Grey-pink	D	304	Mixed		
7	p6126-28	170	-	-	Green-yellow/ Pale brown	D	Surface	Mixed		

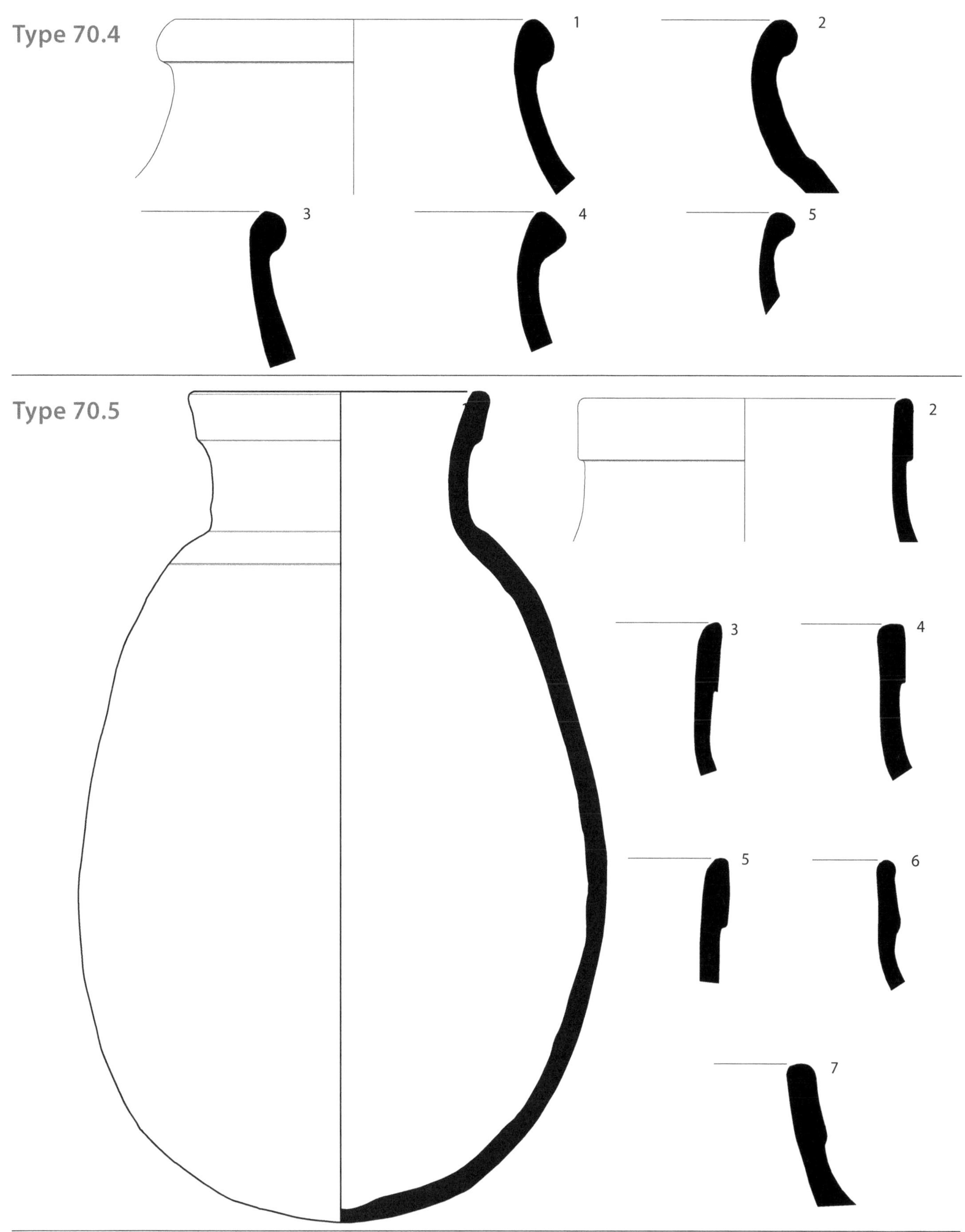

Type 70.4
1
2
3
4
5
Type 70.5
2
3
4
5
6
7
5 cm

PLATE 59

#	Pottery Number	Rim Di. (mm)	Base Di. (mm)	Volume (L)	Surface/ Fabric Colour	Fabric Type	Room/ Area	Phase	Surface Treatment/ Decoration	Notes
1	p6070-21	110	-	-	Green-brown/ Cream	H	Surface	Mixed	Fingernail incisions rim band.	
2	p6126-37	140	-	-	Pale green/ Pink	F	Surface	Mixed	Fingernail incisions on rim band.	
3	p3064-678	ca. 210		ca. 17	Pale brown/ Cream	B	Admin.	2.2	Incised markings on body.	Top of rim broken. Bitumen coated int./ext. Covers breaks. Lumps of bitumen alongside.
4	p6111-63	-	-	-	Green-brown/ Green	F	Surface	Mixed	Incised markings on body. 1 or 2 incised bands around shoulder.	
5	p1096-493	-	-	-	Yellow-green/ Grey-green	F	Admin.	2.2	Incised markings. Sooting on exterior surface.	
6	p5047-12	-	-	-	Pale green/ Cream	F	140–2	2.2	Incised markings on exterior surface.	

Type 70.6

PLATE 60

#	Pottery Number	Rim Di. (mm)	Base Di. (mm)	Volume (L)	Surface/ Fabric Colour	Fabric Type	Room/ Area	Phase	Surface Treatment/ Decoration	Notes
7	p6166-21	95	-	-	Pale green/ Pale pink	E	Surface	Mixed	Pink-red patches on exterior surface. Elaborate cross-hatched decoration on exterior body.	
8	p6127-3	-	-	-	Pale pink/ Pink-orange	F	Surface	Mixed	Ridged band with fingernail incisions around base of neck.	

#	Pottery Number	Rim Di. (mm)	Base Di. (mm)	Volume (L)	Surface/ Fabric Colour	Fabric Type	Room/ Area	Phase	Surface Treatment/ Decoration	Notes
1	p1097-1	-	0	9.91	Green/ Green	H	Burial	Mixed	Incised band around shoulder.	
2	p6124-25	-	0	-	Grey/ Pale brown	D	Surface	Mixed		Worn/ smoothed interior and exterior. Reuse?
3	p6111-70	-	0	-	Cream/ Pink-brown	F	Surface	Mixed		

Type 70.6 *cont'd.*

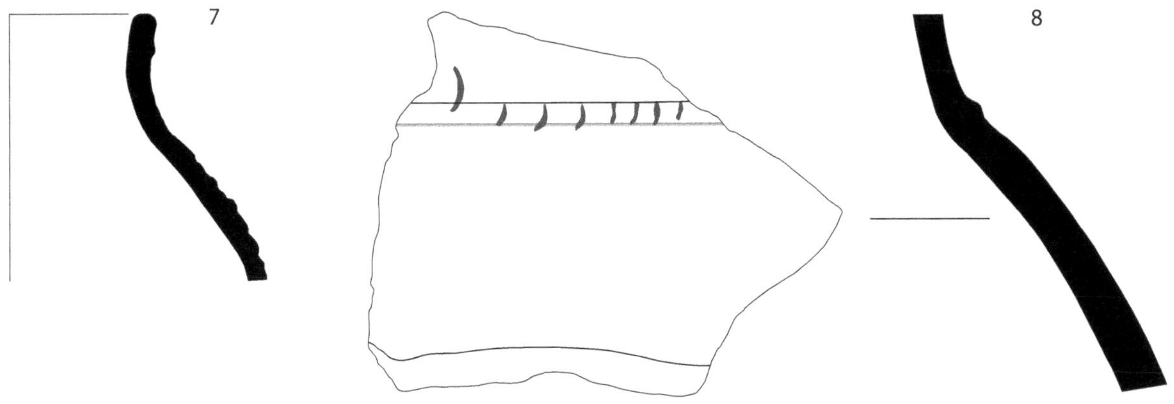

Type 70.7

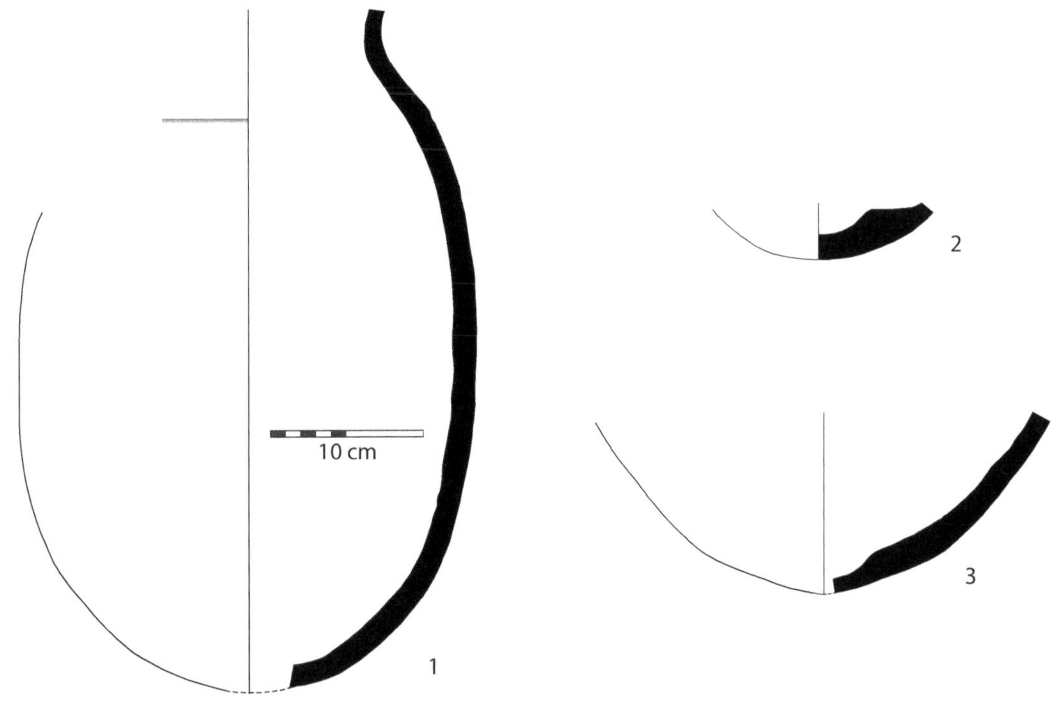

5 cm

PLATE 61

#	Pottery Number	Rim Di. (mm)	Base Di. (mm)	Volume (L)	Surface/ Fabric Colour	Fabric Type	Room/ Area	Phase	Surface Treatment/ Decoration	Notes
1	p1094-193	350	380 irregular	-	Cream/ Pink-grey	F	124	Mixed		Vessel height unknown.

Type 70.8

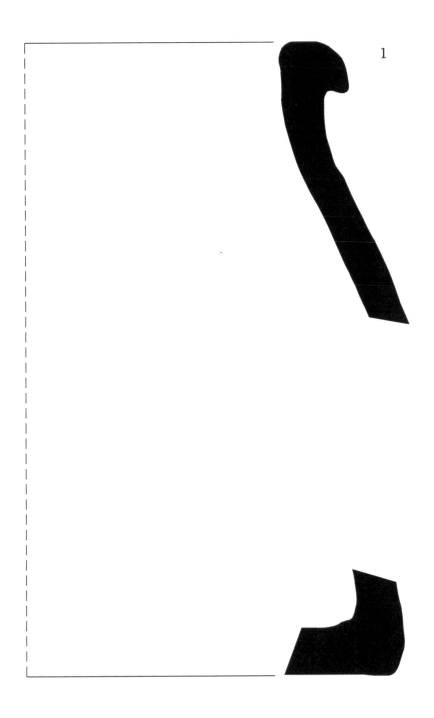

PLATE 62

#	Pottery Number	Rim Di. (mm)	Base Di. (mm)	Volume (L)	Surface/ Fabric Colour	Fabric Type	Room/ Area	Phase	Surface Treatment/ Decoration	Notes
1	p1092-27	120	-	-	Cream-brown/ Cream-brown	A	110	2.2	Impressed band beneath rim.	
2	p4008-12	120	-	-	Cream/ Grey	D	-	Houses		
3	p1039-69	100	-	-	Cream/ Orange	F	-	-		
4	p1079-134	85	-	-	White/ Pink-orange	D	101	2.1	Light ridge beneath rim.	
5	p5022-36	75	-	-	White/ Pale pink	E	140–2	2.2		
6	p1091-546	80	-	-	Cream/ Yellow	F	110	2.2	Incised band beneath rim.	
7	p6067-26	130	-	-	Cream-brown/ Yellow-brown	F	Surface	Mixed		
8	p6041-105	70	-	-	Pink/ Green-grey	F	601	2.2	Lug applied to rim.	

#	Pottery Number	Rim Di. (mm)	Base Di. (mm)	Volume (L)	Surface/ Fabric Colour	Fabric Type	Room/ Area	Phase	Surface Treatment/ Decoration	Notes
1	p8013-10	138	72	0.76	White-cream/ Pale brown	F	316	2.3		String-cut base. Plugged. Very chaffy fabric.
2	p1079-698	110	-	-	Pale green/ Pale green	H	101	2.1		
3	p1079-608	100	-	-	Pale green/ Pale green	H	101	2.1		
4	p3147-6	80	-	-	Cream/ Yellow	F	315	2.2	Incised band beneath rim.	
5	p4026-3	130	-	-	Yellow/ Yellow-grey	F	-	Houses		
6	p6111-24	80	-	-	Green/ Pale green	A	Surface	Mixed		Sooted exterior.

FAMILY 75

Type 75.1

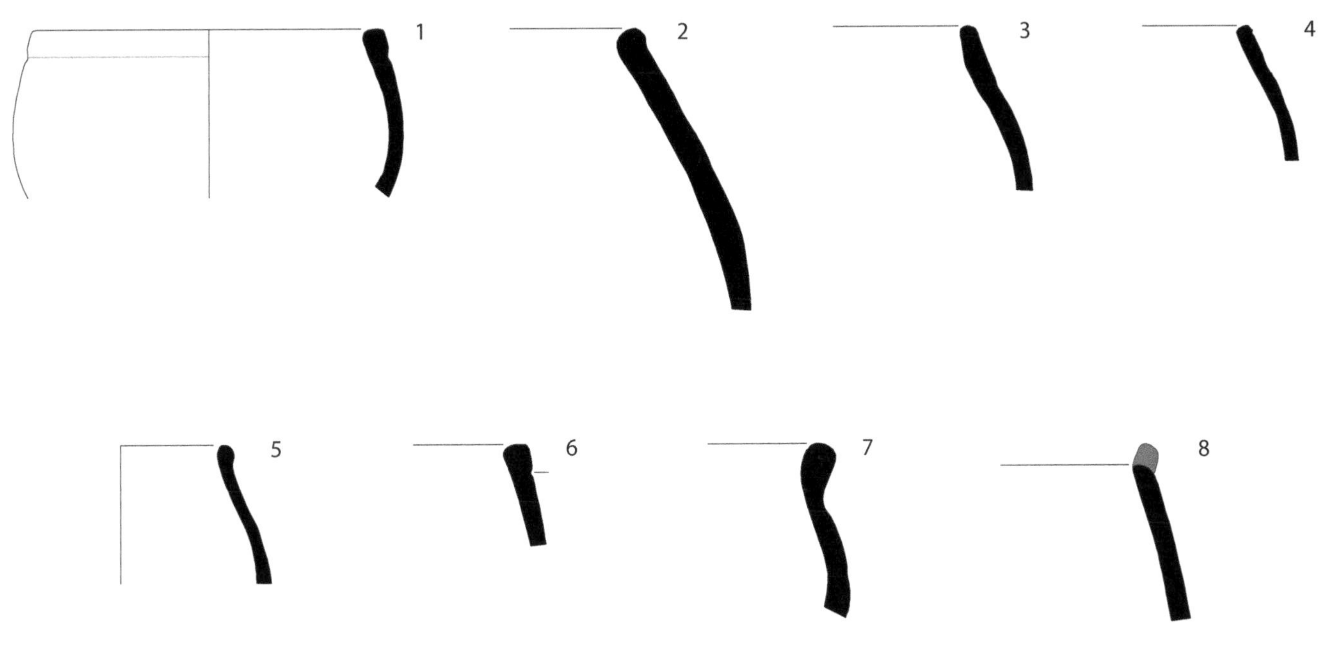

Type 75.2

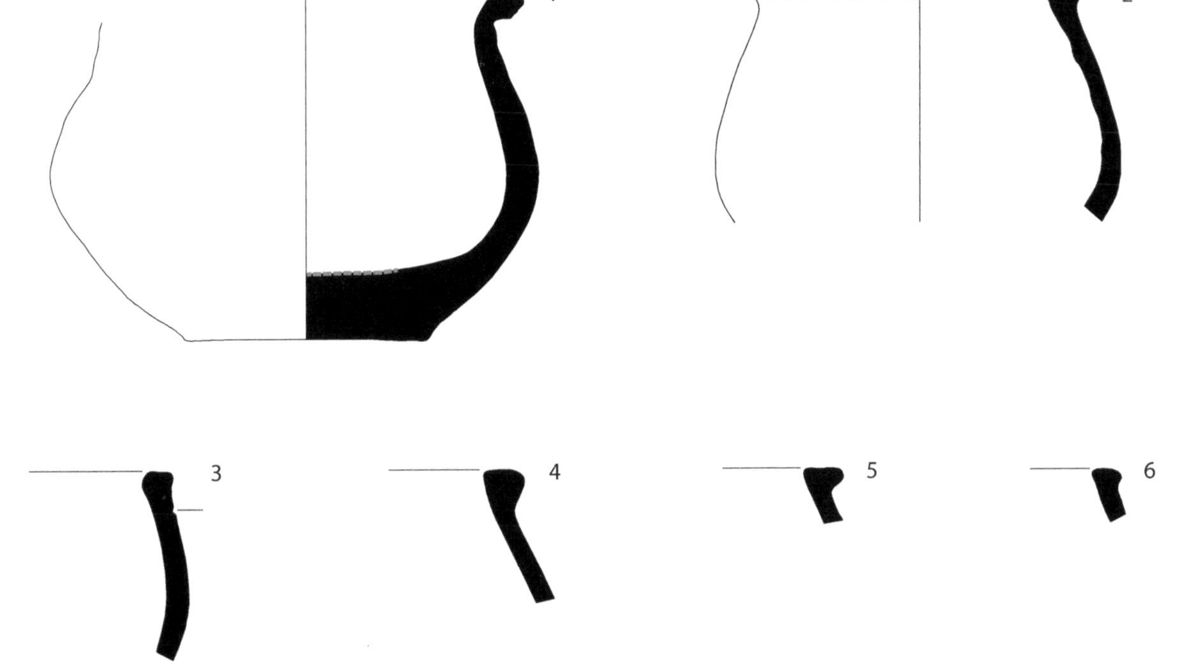

5 cm

PLATE 63

#	Pottery Number	Rim Di. (mm)	Base Di. (mm)	Volume (L)	Surface/ Fabric Colour	Fabric Type	Room/ Area	Phase	Surface Treatment/ Decoration	Notes
1	p3085-265	95	-	-	Pink-cream/ Pink-cream	A	304	Mixed		
2	p3064-657	60	-	-	White-pale pink/ Pink	A	Admin.	2.2		
3	p8076-38	80	-	-	White-cream/ Cream	A	125	2.3		

#	Pottery Number	Rim Di. (mm)	Base Di. (mm)	Volume (L)	Surface/ Fabric Colour	Fabric Type	Room/ Area	Phase	Surface Treatment/ Decoration	Notes
1	p1167-6	61	64	0.09	Green/ Pink	B/F	314	2.2	Slipped (?) exterior.	String-cut base. Heavily chipped rim. Worn base.
2	p8083-22	75	42	0.1	Pale green/ Grey-green	D	152	2.2	4 deep incised lines around neck.	String-cut base.
3	p8012-4	110	-	-	Pink/ Pink	F	316	2.3	3 incised lines around base of neck.	
4	p8084-36	105	-	-	Cream/ Orange	E	152	2.1	4 incised lines around neck.	

Type 75.3

Type 75.4

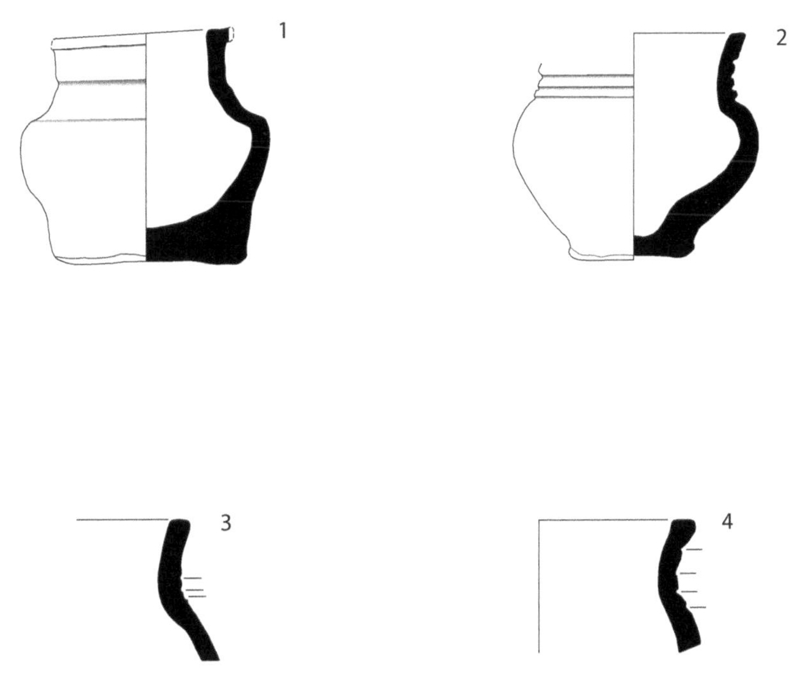

5 cm

PLATE 64

#	Pottery Number	Rim Di. (mm)	Base Di. (mm)	Volume (L)	Surface/ Fabric Colour	Fabric Type	Room/ Area	Phase	Surface Treatment/ Decoration	Notes
1	p1079-51	230	-	ca. 15	Cream-grey/ Pink-brown	G	101	2.1	Applied lug at rim.	
2	p9018-87	230	-	9.93+	Green-yellow/ Blue-black	G	616	Mixed		Band of soot directly above carination of the body.
3	p6078-44	-	-	-	Yellow-green/ Brown	G	Surface	Mixed		
4	p6162-17	190	-	-	Pale green/ Orange-pink	E	Surface	Mixed	Slipped (?) interior and exterior surfaces.	
5	p1088-1	340	-	-	Grey/ Pink-grey	G	101	2.1		
6	p1092-28	270	-	-	Black/ Dark grey	G	110	2.2		
7	p3088-173	160	-	-	Cream/ Dark pink	G	304	Mixed		

FAMILY 80

Type 80.1

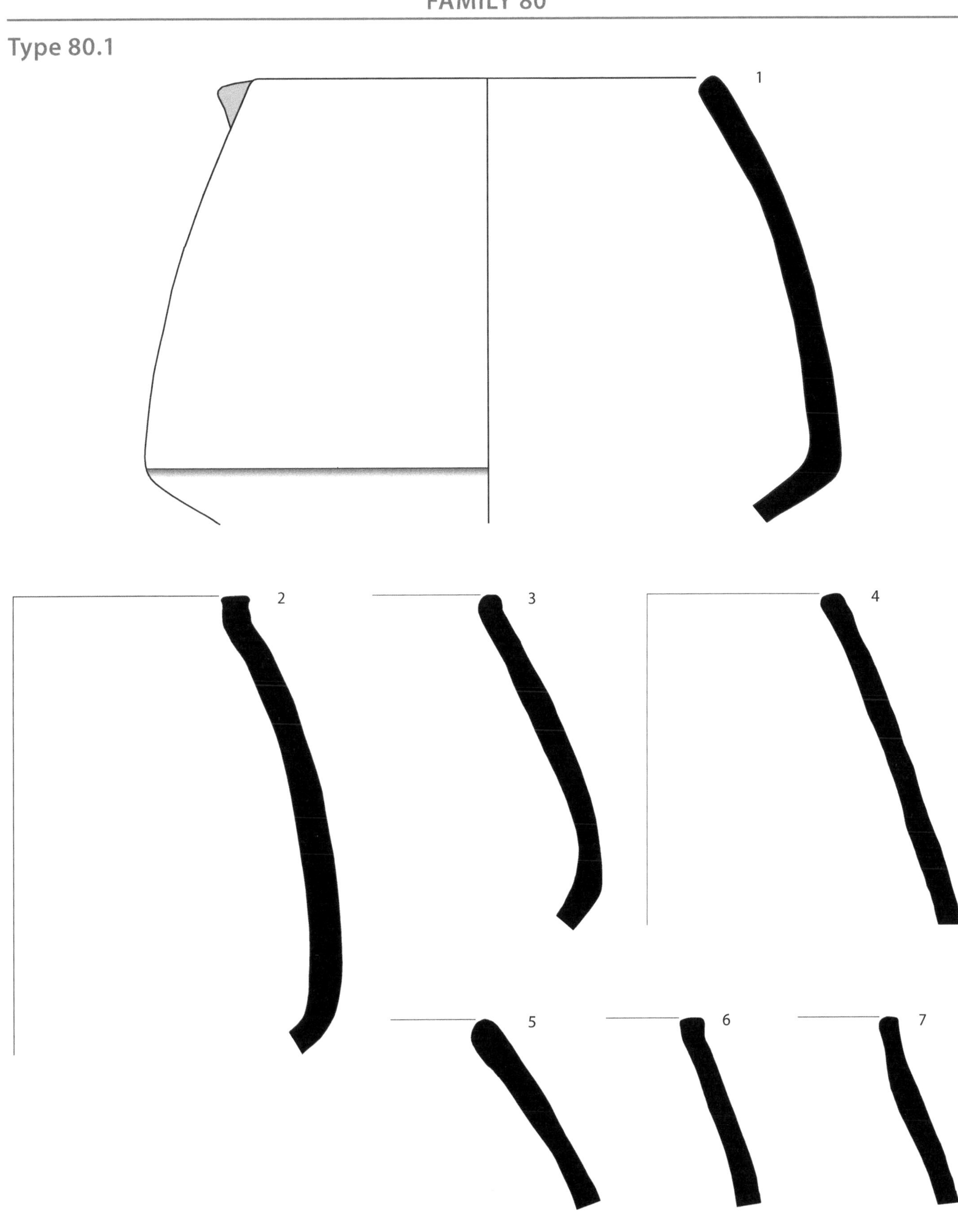

PLATE 65

#	Pottery Number	Rim Di. (mm)	Base Di. (mm)	Volume (L)	Surface/ Fabric Colour	Fabric Type	Room/ Area	Phase	Surface Treatment/ Decoration	Notes
8	p1136-15	230	-	-	Grey-black/ Grey-black	G	131/619	2.2		Burnt exterior.
9	p3088-100	180	-	-	Pink/ Pink with black core	G	304	Mixed	Applied lug at rim.	
10	p3085-278	240	-	-	Orange/ Brown	G	304	Mixed	Applied lug at rim.	
11	p1091-491	190	-	-	Cream/ Brown	G	110	2.2	Applied lug at rim.	
12	p6041-103	240	-	-	Brown-black/ Orange-brown	G, with shell	601	2.2	Applied lug at rim.	
13	p3044-6	300	-	-	Dark grey/ Grey	G	-	-	Applied lug at rim.	
14	p8060-25	-	-	-	White/ Cream-pale pink	G	316	2.3	Applied lug beneath rim.	

#	Pottery Number	Rim Di. (mm)	Base Di. (mm)	Volume (L)	Surface/ Fabric Colour	Fabric Type	Room/ Area	Phase	Surface Treatment/ Decoration	Notes
1	p5063-1	235	22	16.51	Pink-orange/ Orange-brown	G	140–2	2.2	Slipped exterior. Applied lug at rim.	Irregular sooting patterns on exterior body.

Type 80.1 *cont'd.*

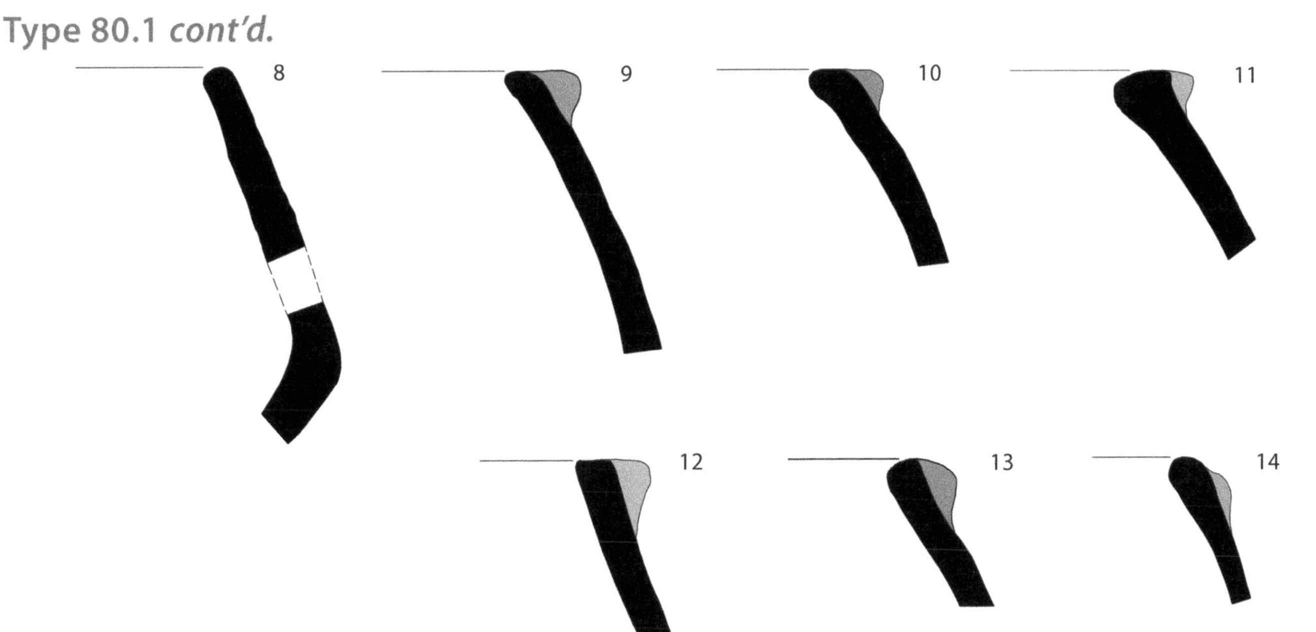

Type 80.2

1

5 cm

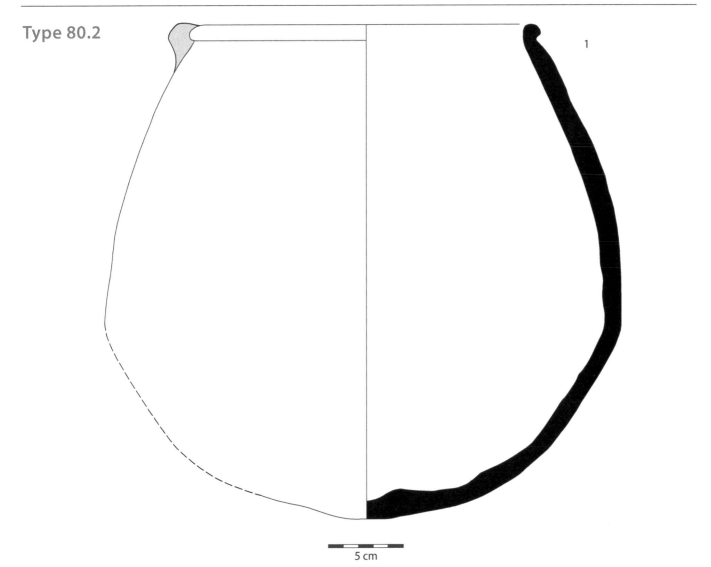

PLATE 66

#	Pottery Number	Rim Di. (mm)	Base Di. (mm)	Volume (L)	Surface/ Fabric Colour	Fabric Type	Room/ Area	Phase	Surface Treatment/ Decoration	Notes
2	p6041-446	270	-	-	Pink/ Pink-orange	F	601	2.2		
3	p3025-38	200	-	-	Green-yellow/ Cream-grey	F	302	Mixed		
4	p6091-34	190	-	-	Orange-brown/ Orange-red	G	Surface	Mixed		
5	p3039-24	240	-	-	Green/ Pink	F	-	-		
6	p1157-20	240	-	-	Pale pink/ Orange	G	Admin.	2.2		
7	p6157-1	200	-	-	Red-orange/ Pale brown	G	Surface	Mixed		
8	p6116-39	240	-	-	Pale green/ Pink	D	Surface	Mixed		
9	p6041-102	180	-	-	Cream/ Dark orange	G	601	2.2		
10	p3054-393	210	-	-	Cream/ Orange	G	304	Mixed	Plum wash(?) exterior. Applied lug at rim.	
11	p8076-40	210	-	-	Pale green/ Grey	G, lots of voids	125	2.3	Applied lug at rim.	
12	p6136-129	200	-	-	Pale orange/ Blue-black	F/G	Surface	Mixed	.	Sooted rim.
13	p6111-23	150	-	-	Dark orange/ Orange	G	Surface	Mixed		Sooted around rim.
14	p6041-194	200	-	-	Black-brown/ Grey-brown	G	Burial	Mixed		
15	p3064-675	170	-	-	Cream/ Grey	D	Admin.	2.2	2 impressed bands around shoulder.	
16	p1079-460	150	-	-	Cream-brown/ Brown	F	101	2.1		
17	p1166-67	200	-	-	White/ Pale brown	C/E	314	2.1	4+ incised bands around shoulder.	
18	p3088-85	170	-	-	Cream-pale orange/ Pale orange	G	304	Mixed	4 incised bands around shoulder.	

Type 80.2 *cont'd.*

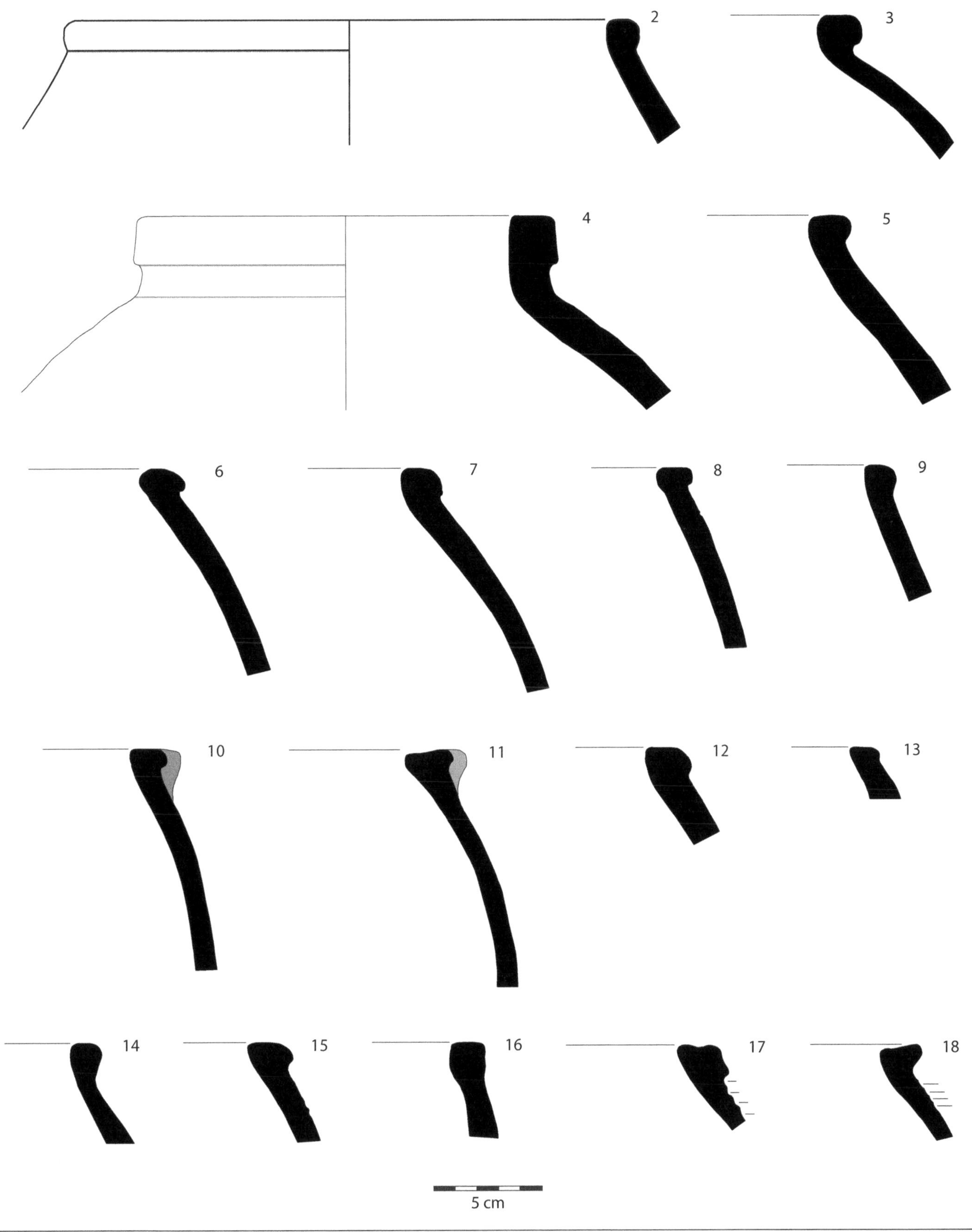

PLATE 67

#	Pottery Number	Rim Di. (mm)	Base Di. (mm)	Volume (L)	Surface/ Fabric Colour	Fabric Type	Room/ Area	Phase	Surface Treatment/ Decoration	Notes
1	p8013-12	-	-	-	Pale orange/ Grey-black	G	316	2.3		Sooted exterior. Charred interior.
2	p1079-463	-	-	-	Pale pink/ Pink-grey	G	101	2.1		Sooting/bitumen staining on exterior carination.

Type 80.3

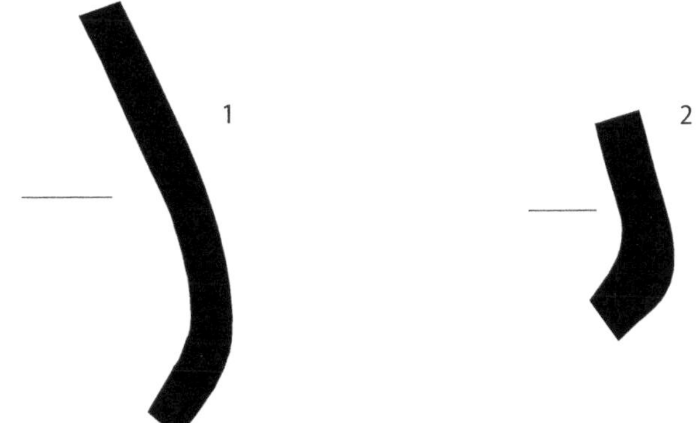

5 cm

PLATE 68

#	Pottery Number	Rim Di. (mm)	Base Di. (mm)	Volume (L)	Surface/ Fabric Colour	Fabric Type	Room/ Area	Phase	Surface Treatment/ Decoration	Notes
1	p8016-7	105	75	-	Pink/ Pink	E	316	2.3	Incised line. Evidence of scraping on exterior.	
2	p6059-6	95	70	-	Pink-brown/ Red	E	600	2.1		
3	p6059-28	85	80	-	Green/ Pink-orange	D	600	2.1	Evidence of scraping on exterior.	
4	p3058-15	110	90	-	Pale green/ Dark orange	F	-	-		
5	p9023-1	83	72	-	Pale green/grey-green	E	616	Mixed		
6	p3054-341	100	85	-	Pale brown-pink/ Orange-red	E	304	Mixed		
7	p3054-403	102	80	-	Orange-cream/ Dark brown	A	304	Mixed		
8	p5022-58	105	71 irregular	-	Cream-grey/ Yellow-cream	E	140–2	2.2	Rough base.	
9	p3054-49	90	90	-	Pale green/ Green-brown	D	304	Mixed		
10	p6065-1	90	90	-	Pale brown/ Pink-brown	A	Surface	Mixed		
11	p6059-7	80	70	-	Cream-pale brown/ Cream-pale brown	D	600	2.1		
12	p1096-378	104	155	-	Yellow-cream/ Cream	F	Admin.	2.2		
13	p1005-71	100	85	-	Pale green/ Green-grey	F, with shell	124	Mixed		
14	p5016-1	100	72 Irregular	-	Pale pink/ Pink	F	140–2	2.3		
15	p3054-333	125	110	-	Cream-yellow/ Pink-brown	E	304	Mixed		
16	p3054-392	100	80	-	Cream-pale brown/ Pink-orange	A	304	Mixed		
17	p3084-32	115	105	-	Cream-yellow/ Pale green	D	304	Mixed		

FAMILY 85

Type 85.1

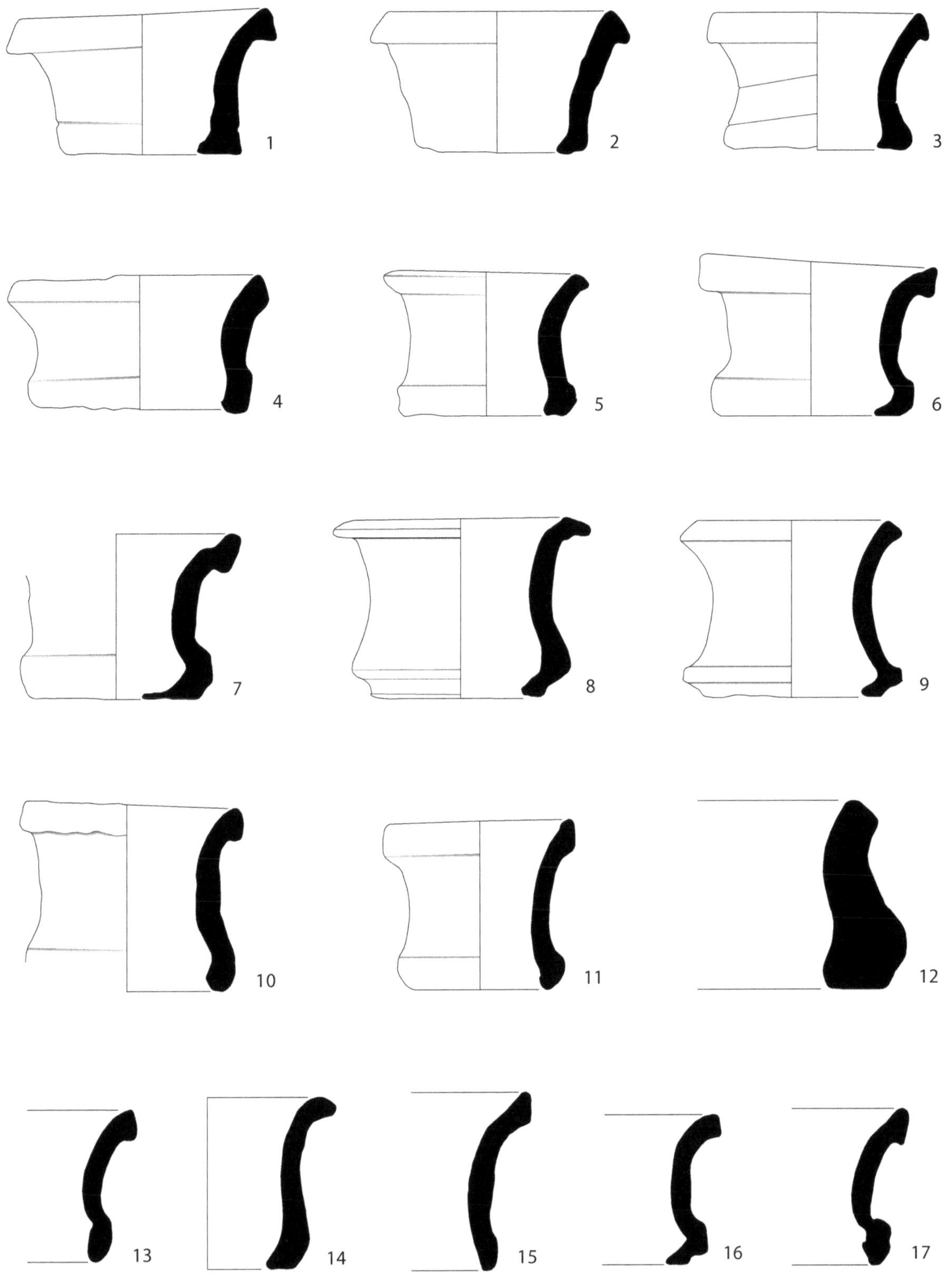

PLATE 69

#	Pottery Number	Rim Di. (mm)	Base Di. (mm)	Volume (L)	Surface/ Fabric Colour	Fabric Type	Room/ Area	Phase	Surface Treatment/ Decoration	Notes
18	p3087-9	100	95	-	Pink-brown/ Orange-pink	D	304	Mixed		
19	p1078-46	100	85	-	Green-yellow/ Orange	D	-	-		
20	p3085-269	120	90	-	Pink-cream/ Pale orange	E	304	Mixed		
21	p3085-121	100	85	-	Cream-yellow/ Cream	A	304	Mixed		
22	p8008-24	110	70	-	White-pale pink/ Pale orange	D	316	2.3	Incised line around body, above base.	
23	p6041-232	90	75	-	Pink/ Orange	F	601	2.2		
24	p3149-5	105	75	-	Pale orange/ Pale orange	C	315	2.2		
25	p6096-42	105	75	-	Pale pink/ Dark brown	E	Surface	Mixed		
26	p1079-277	110	80	-	White-pale pink/ Pale brown	F	101	2.1		
27	p3054-79	120	80	-	Cream/ Orange-brown	F	304	Mixed	Ridged band around body, above base.	
28	p6096-9	100	70	-	Yellow-pink/ Pale orange	E	Surface	Mixed	Incised line around body, above base.	

#	Pottery Number	Rim Di. (mm)	Base Di. (mm)	Volume (L)	Surface/ Fabric Colour	Fabric Type	Room/ Area	Phase	Surface Treatment/ Decoration	Notes
1	p6042-32	254	246	-	Yellow-green/ Red-brown	F	600	2.1		
2	p3009-1	165	158	-	-	-	-	-		
3	p6136-90	240	226	-	Red-pink/ Black	F	Surface	Mixed	Finger impressions on interior surface.	
4	p5001-15	190	210	-	Green/ Grey-green	F, with shell	Sounding	Mixed	Fingerprints on interior surface.	
5	p6058-92	260	210	-	Cream/ Grey	F	601	2.1		

Type 85.1 *cont'd.*

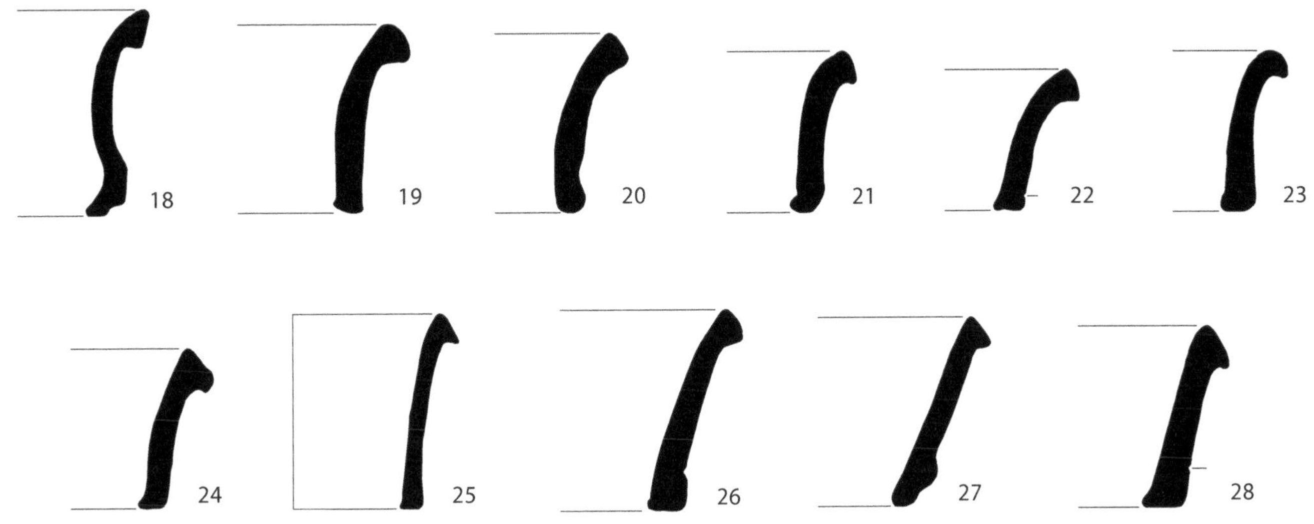

Type 85.2

1
2
3
4
5

5 cm

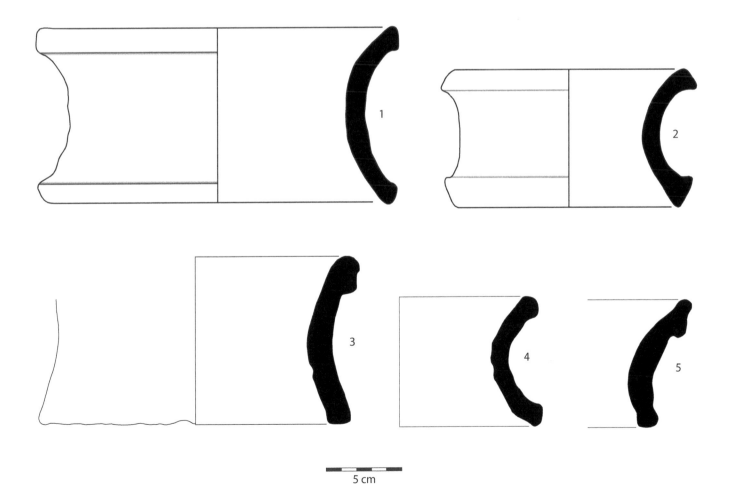

PLATE 70

#	Pottery Number	Rim Di. (mm)	Base Di. (mm)	Volume (L)	Surface/ Fabric Colour	Fabric Type	Room/ Area	Phase	Surface Treatment/ Decoration	Notes
6	p5016-9	250 warped	215	-	Dark green/ Dark green	H, overfired	140–2	2.3	2 impressed bands around body.	
7	p3025-1	260	240	-	Red-brown/ Dark brown	F	302	Mixed		
8	p1079-224	260	240	-	White-grey/ Grey	F	101	2.1		

#	Pottery Number	Rim Di. (mm)	Base Di. (mm)	Volume (L)	Surface/ Fabric Colour	Fabric Type	Room/ Area	Phase	Surface Treatment/ Decoration	Notes
1	p6116-57	290	190	-	Dark green/ Dark green	F	Surface	Mixed		
2	p6165-18	240	175	-	Pale orange/ Red-orange	F	156	2.2		S-cut base.
3	p1079-210	110	85	-	Cream-pink/ Pink	F	101	2.1		
4	p5024-1	96	82	0.11	Cream-pale orange	E	140–2	2.2		
5	p1079-210	110	85	-	Cream-pink/ Pink	F	101	2.1		

Type 85.2 *cont'd.*

Type 85.3

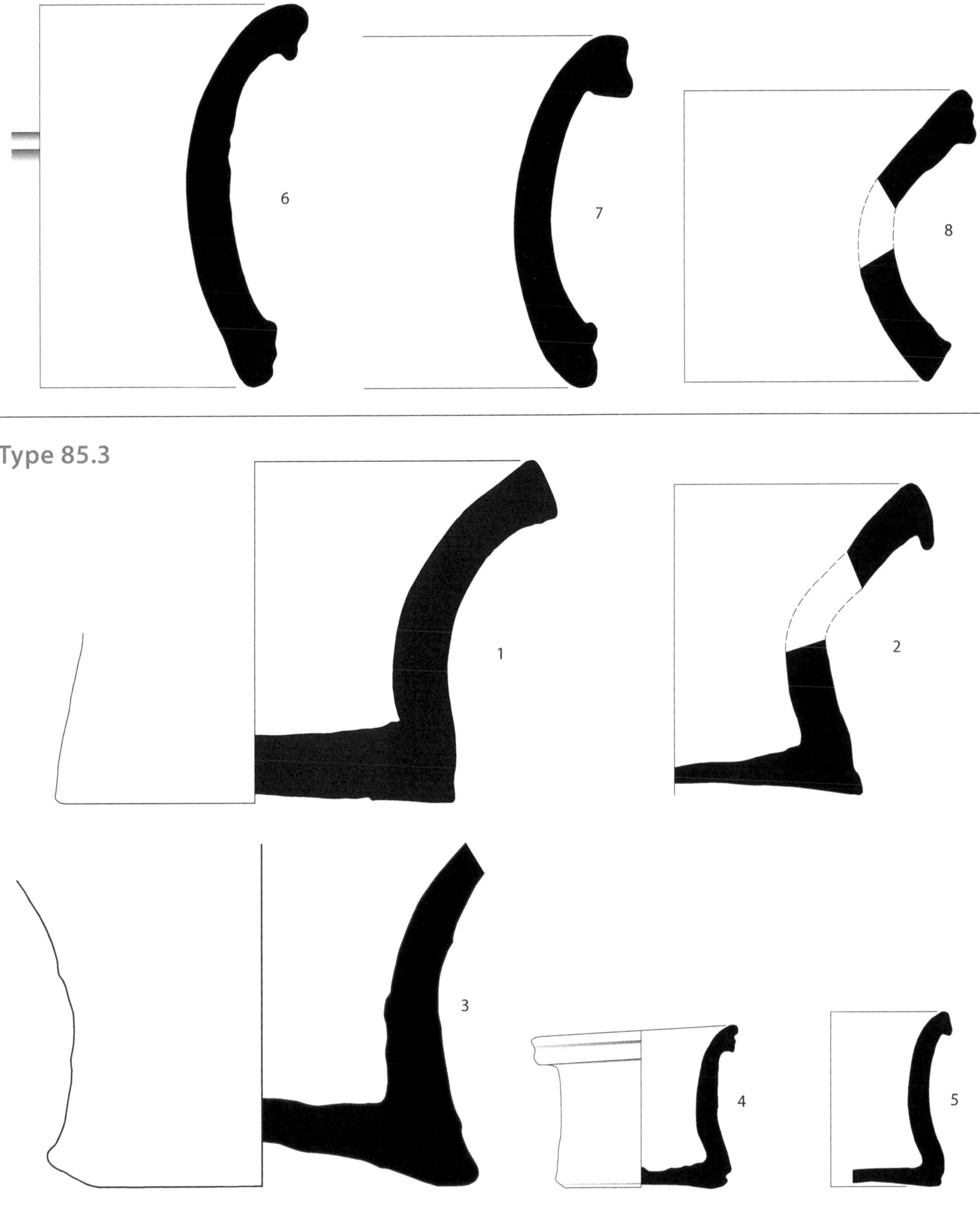

PLATE 71

#	Pottery Number	Rim Di. (mm)	Base Di. (mm)	Volume (L)	Surface/ Fabric Colour	Fabric Type	Room/ Area	Phase	Surface Treatment/ Decoration	Notes
6	p6165-44	265	185	1.11	Yellow-green	F	156	2.2	Finger impressions on exterior near base and on bottom of vessel.	S-cut base.
7	p9020-114	275	185	2.09	Yellow-green/ Grey-green	F	616	Mixed	5 large applied lugs arranged irregularly directly beneath rim.	

Type 85.3 *cont'd.*

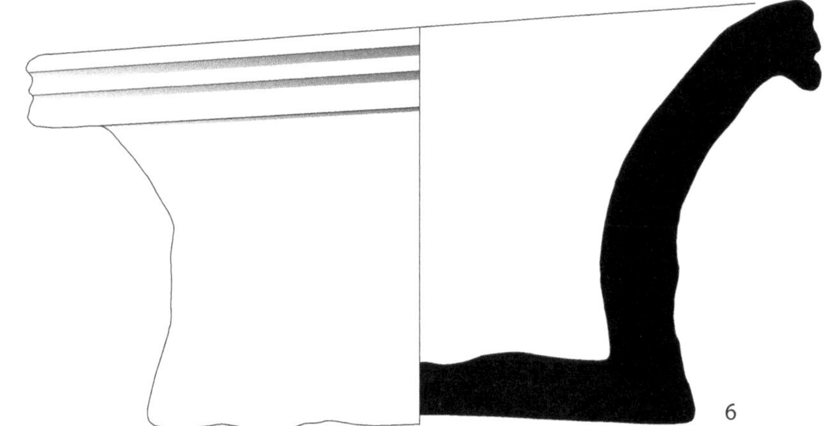

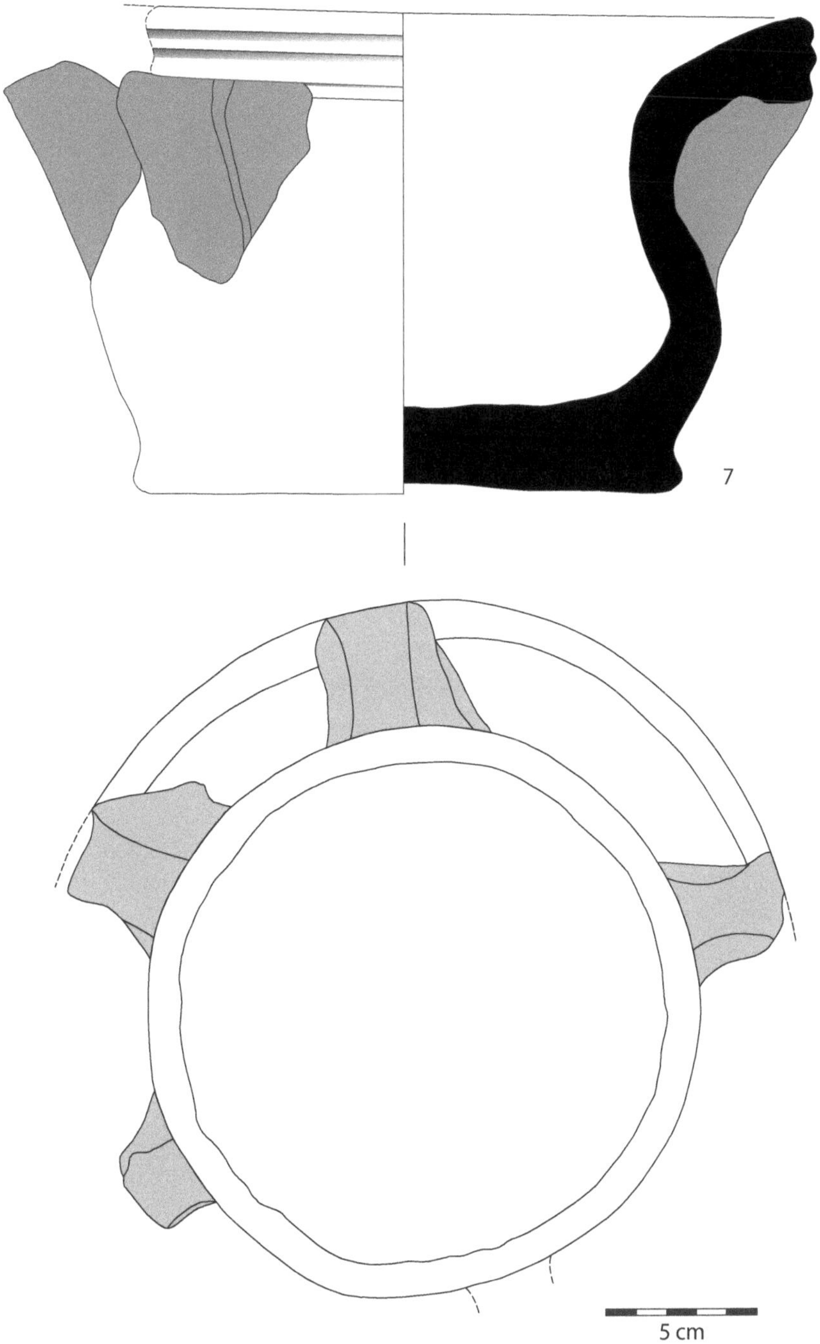

7

5 cm

PLATE 72

#	Pottery Number	Rim Di. (mm)	Base Di. (mm)	Volume (L)	Surface/ Fabric Colour	Fabric Type	Room/ Area	Phase	Surface Treatment/ Decoration	Notes
1	p8008-9	34	123	-	Pale green-yellow/ Pink	F	316	2.3		Worn handle. Chipped around circumference.
2	p6184-22	22	78	-	White-cream/ Pale brown	E	Surface	Mixed		
3	p1157-54	25	61	-	Orange-pink/ Red-orange	D	Admin.	2.2	Slipped (?) surfaces.	Chipped/worn on top.
4	p9020-46	5	46	-	Green	D	616	Mixed		Discolouration around base due to heavy use.
5	p8013-9	35 Irregular	70 Irregular	-	Dark brown	-	316	2.3		Very low fired.
6	p8013-11	5	47	-	Cream/ Grey	F	316	2.3		Worn and chipped around circumference.
7	p6096-21	35	-	-	Green/ Green	F	Surface	Mixed		

#	Pottery Number	Rim Di. (mm)	Base Di. (mm)	Volume (L)	Surface/ Fabric Colour	Fabric Type	Room/ Area	Phase	Surface Treatment/ Decoration	Notes
1	p8022-4	-	-	-	Pale green/ Grey	A	316	2.3	3+ holes through body.	
2	p1131-2	130	20	0.24	Dark grey-green/ Green	A	131/619	2.2	Perforated base.	
3	p6156-5	77	15	0.04	Orange-pink/ Pink	A	Surface	Mixed	2 holes through body. Perforated base.	

FAMILY 90

Type 90.1

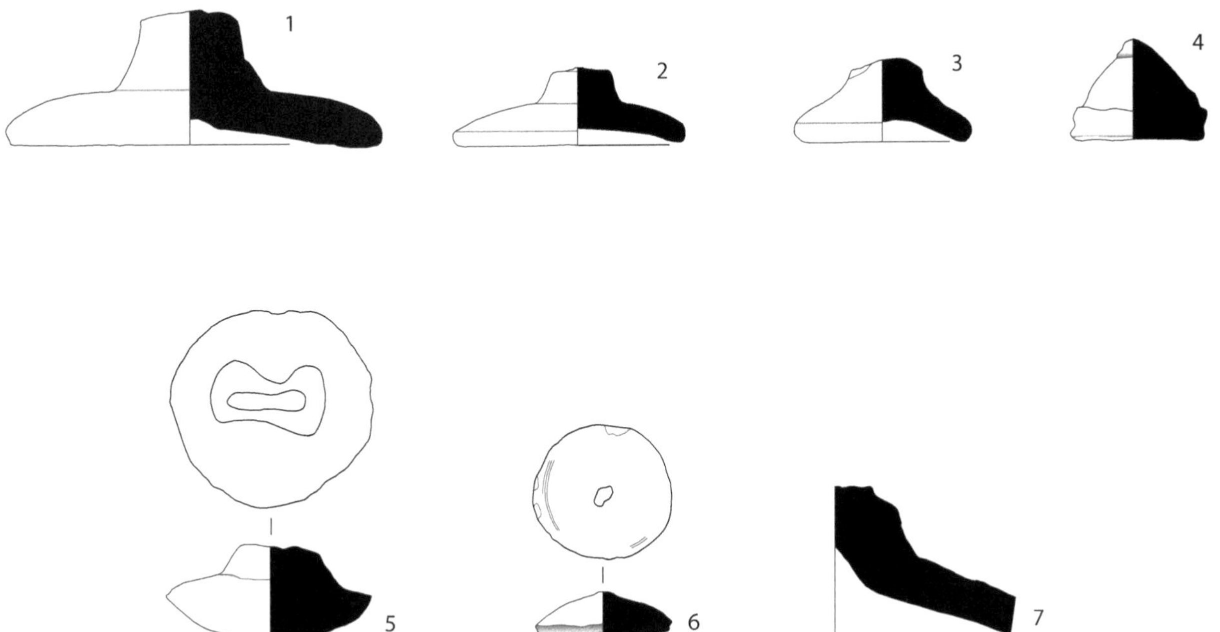

Type 90.2

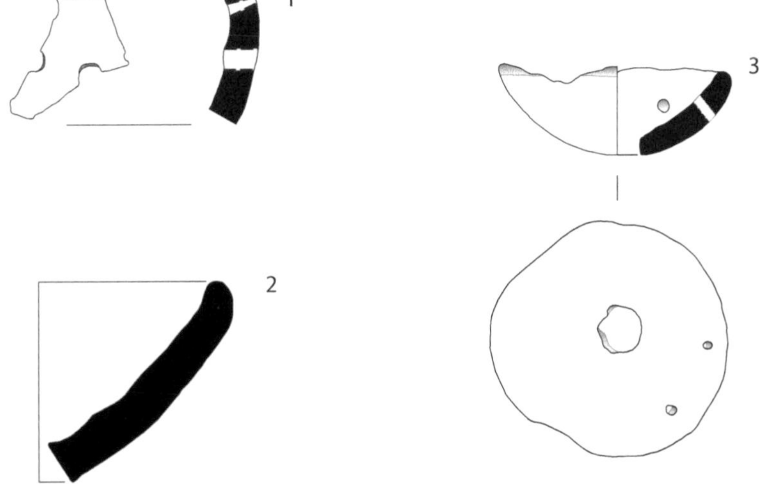

5 cm

PLATE 73

#	Pottery Number	Rim Di. (mm)	Base Di. (mm)	Volume (L)	Surface/ Fabric Colour	Fabric Type	Room/ Area	Phase	Surface Treatment/ Decoration	Notes
1	p8021-1	56	30	0.03	Pale orange/ Pale orange	C	316	2.3		
2	p5001-53	79	31	0.06	Yellow-cream/ Pale brown	B	Sounding	Mixed	Roughly shaped/ unfinished base.	
3	p6096-46	-	18	-	Pale orange/ Pale orange	C	Surface	Mixed		

#	Pottery Number	Rim Di. (mm)	Base Di. (mm)	Volume (L)	Surface/ Fabric Colour	Fabric Type	Room/ Area	Phase	Surface Treatment/ Decoration	Notes
1	p6059-74	30	30	-	Pink/ Grey	-	600	2.1		Very low fired.
2	p1073-80	-	0	-	Dark brown	-	101	2.2		Very low fired.
3	p3085-279	-	0	-	Pink-orange/ Grey	-	304	Mixed		Very low fired.

#	Pottery Number	Rim Di. (mm)	Base Di. (mm)	Volume (L)	Surface/ Fabric Colour	Fabric Type	Room/ Area	Phase	Surface Treatment/ Decoration	Notes
1	p3085-279	-	68	-	Pink/ Pink-orange	B	304	Mixed	2 perforations aligned on either side of body.	Bitumen coated interior. Bitumen stained exterior.

Type 90.3

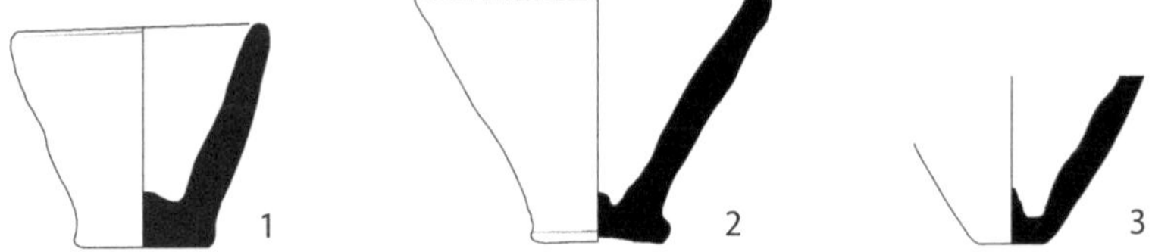

Type 90.4

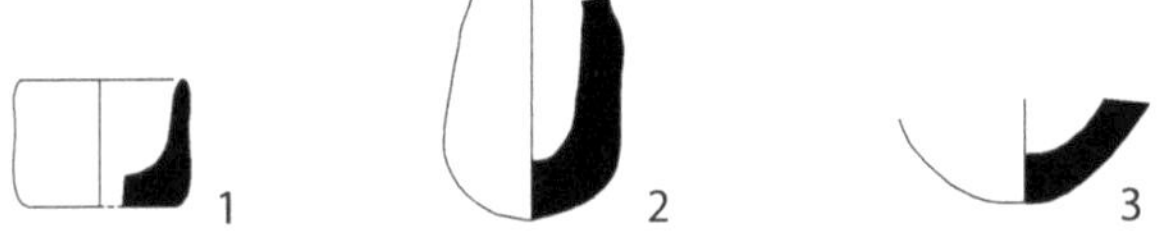

Type 90.5

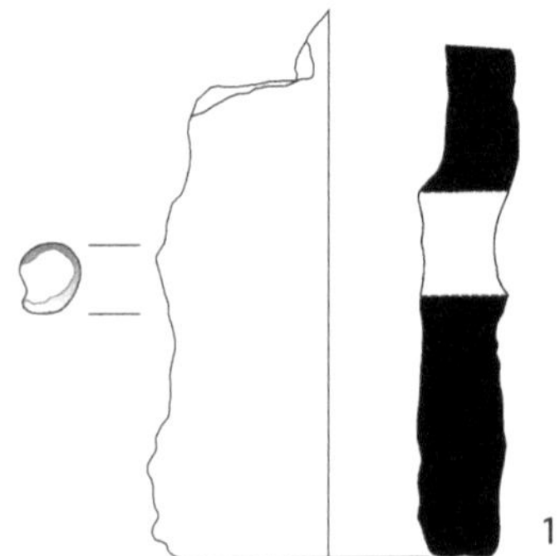

5 cm

PLATE 74

#	Pottery Number	Rim Di. (mm)	Base Di. (mm)	Volume (L)	Surface/ Fabric Colour	Fabric Type	Room/ Area	Phase	Surface Treatment/ Decoration	Notes
1	p6163-34	-	112 (33)	0.28+	Red/ Red	B	Surface	Mixed	Perforated base worn around interior.	Deliberately broken part way up?

#	Pottery Number	Rim Di. (mm)	Base Di. (mm)	Volume (L)	Surface/ Fabric Colour	Fabric Type	Room/ Area	Phase	Surface Treatment/ Decoration	Notes
1	p9020-43	-	47	0.44	Green/ Pale brown	F	616	Mixed	Relief band at base of neck.	String-cut base.
2	p1078-76	-	77	0.36	Pale green/ Pale green	F	-	-		String-cut base.

Type 90.6

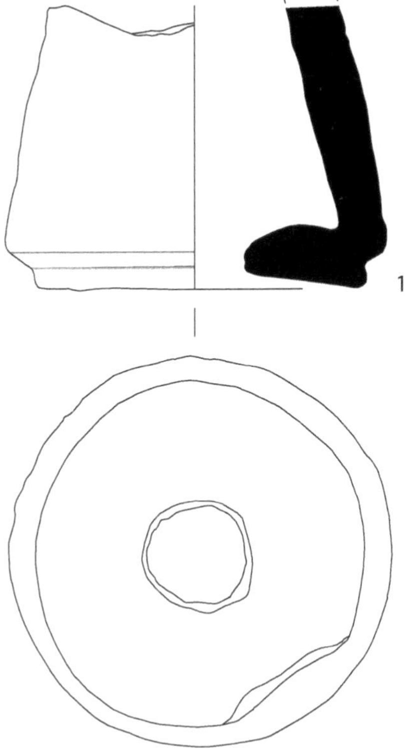

Type 90.7

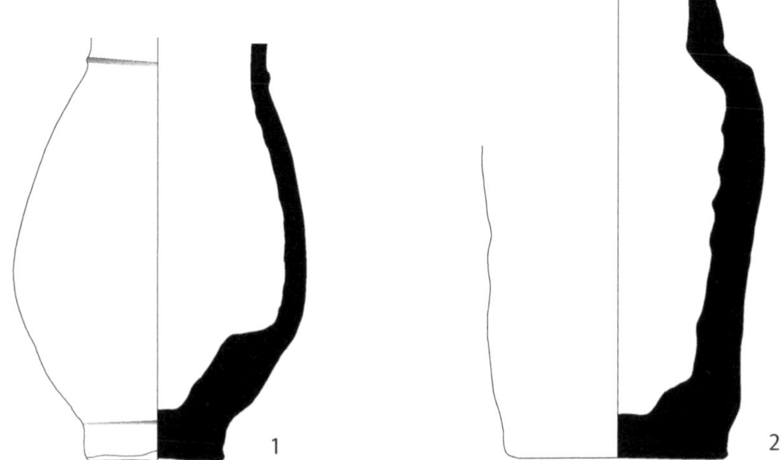

PLATE 75

#	Pottery Number	Rim Di. (mm)	Base Di. (mm)	Volume (L)	Surface/ Fabric Colour	Fabric Type	Room/ Area	Phase	Surface Treatment/ Decoration	Notes
1	p8021-11	600+	600+	-	Cream/ Pink	F	316	2.3	Large grits embedded in interior surface.	Ring base broken.
2	p1080-14	310	-	1.95	Dark green/ Dark green	F, overfired	101	2.1	Very heavily worn/ ground on interior. Centre broken.	Broken pedestal base.

#	Pottery Number	Rim Di. (mm)	Base Di. (mm)	Volume (L)	Surface/ Fabric Colour	Fabric Type	Room/ Area	Phase	Surface Treatment/ Decoration	Notes
1	p3185-115	150	-	-	Black-grey/ Dark blue	A	315	2.1	Heavily burnished surfaces.	Broken tripod (?) base.

Type 90.8

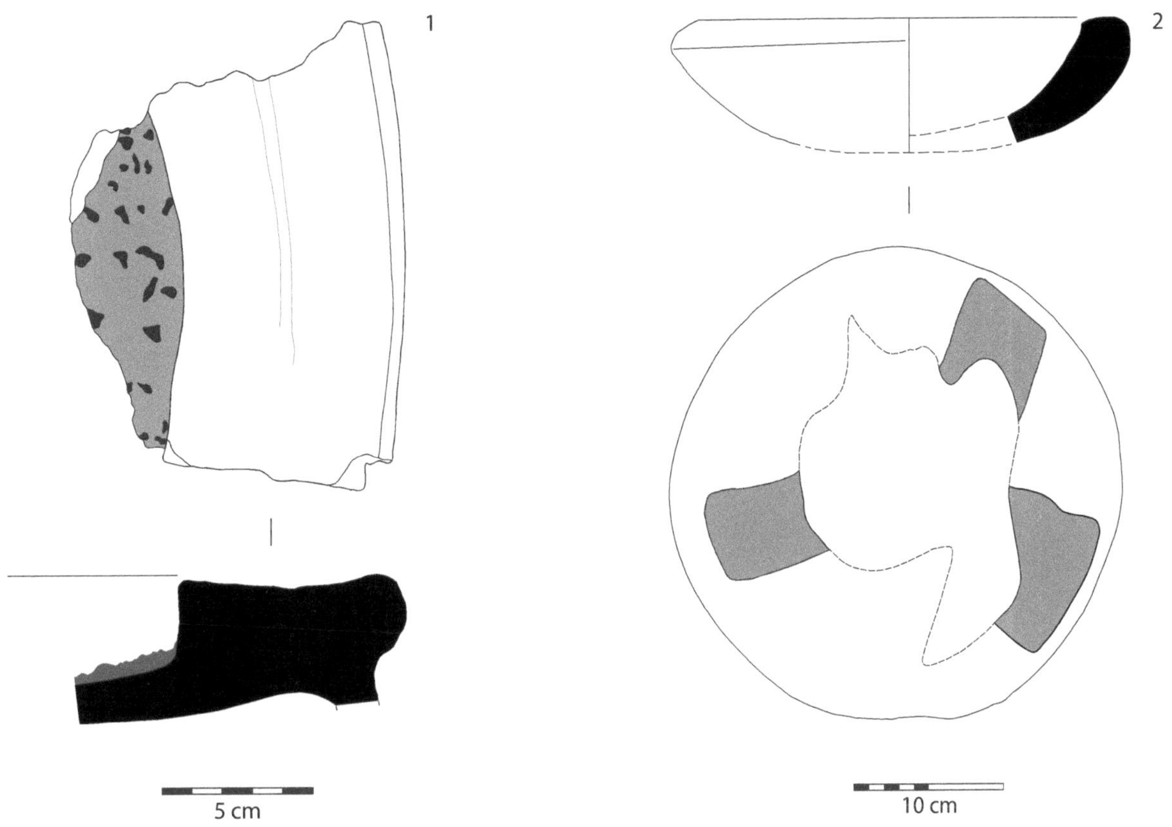

Type 90.9

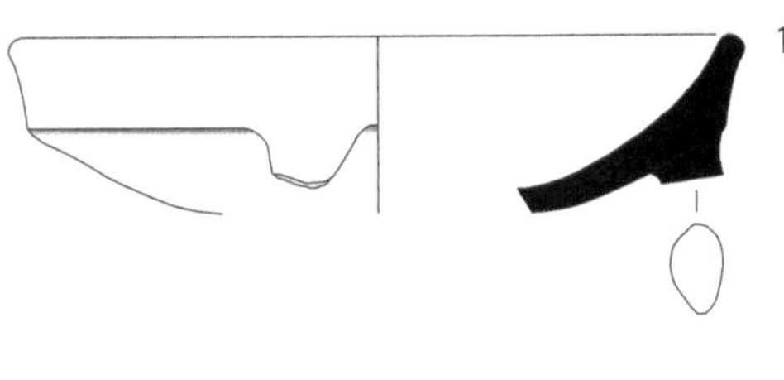

PLATE 76

#	Pottery Number	Rim Di. (mm)	Base Di. (mm)	Volume (L)	Surface/ Fabric Colour	Fabric Type	Room/ Area	Phase	Surface Treatment/ Decoration	Notes
1	p5022-37	55	110	0.04	Cream-yellow/ Pale brown	D	140–2	2.2		Smoothed around top.
2	p6166-20	49	92	0.02	Green/ Green	H	Surface	Mixed		
3	p3054-404	23	73	-	Pale green	-	304	Mixed		
4	p8074-13	11	67	-	White/ Pink-orange	C	125	2.3		
5	p3088-181	25	76	-	Orange-pale pink/ Pink	A	304	Mixed		Wear on exterior base and lower body.
6	p3186-20	52	44	-	White/ Pink	B	-	-		
7	p9018-88	44	-	-	Grey-yellow	F	616	Mixed		String-cut on top.

#	Pottery Number	Rim Di. (mm)	Base Di. (mm)	Volume (L)	Surface/ Fabric Colour	Fabric Type	Room/ Area	Phase	Surface Treatment/ Decoration	Notes
1	p1094-192	-	24	0.18	White-pale pink/ Pink	A	124	Mixed		Heavy wear on base. Smoothing on upper body.
2	p8013-7	-	90	-	Cream/ Pale orange	E	316	2.3		Burnt patches on interior. String-cut base; plugged and worn through.
3	p1079-494	-	40	-	White-grey/ Cream-grey	D	101	2.1		Heavy wear at base.

FAMILY 95

Type 95.1

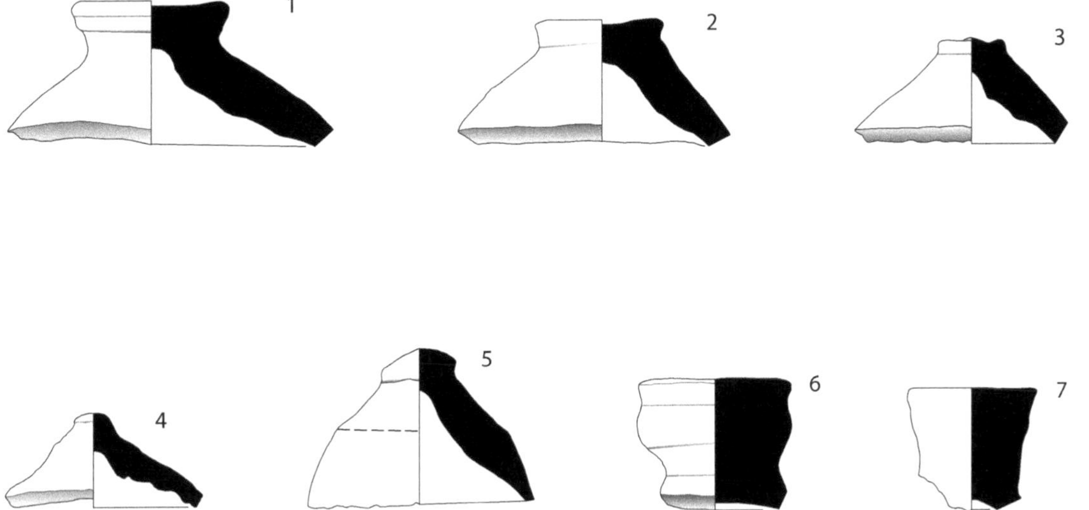

Type 95.2

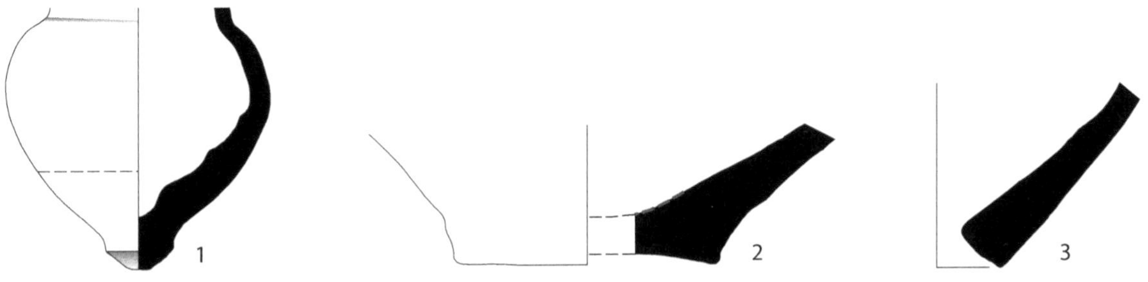

5 cm

PLATE 77

#	Pottery Number	Rim Di. (mm)	Base Di. (mm)	Volume (L)	Surface/ Fabric Colour	Fabric Type	Room/ Area	Phase	Surface Treatment/ Decoration	Notes
1	p5019-2	266	154	3.06	Pink-orange/ Red-brown	F	140–2	2.2	Scraping marks on lower body.	
2	p6111-71	140	63	0.35	Pale green/ Pink	F	Surface	Mixed		Filled-in base.
3	p6136-136	106	52	0.12	Green/ Pale brown	H	Surface	Mixed		Filled-in base.
4	p5016-2	112	22	0.21	Pale green/ Pale brown	E	140–2	2.3	Scraping marks on lower body.	
5	p3189-3	76	59	0.02	Pale green/ Grey-green	F	-	-	Very neatly chipped.	S-cut base.
6	p8051-4	58	41	0.01	White/ Pink	E	316	2.3		Filled-in base.
7	p3160-23	61	37	0.01	Cream-yellow/ Pale brown	D	315	2.2		Worn interior base.
8	p3185-82	58	28	0.04	Pale orange/ Pink	-	315	2.1		

#	Pottery Number	Rim Di. (mm)	Base Di. (mm)	Volume (L)	Surface/ Fabric Colour	Fabric Type	Room/ Area	Phase	Surface Treatment/ Decoration	Notes
1	p8083-45	80	90	-	Pale pink/ Pink	D	152	2.2	Slipped (?) exterior. Incised relief band around top of pedestal.	Chipped base.
2	p3176-154	135	120	-	Green/ Green	D	315	2.2	Incised relief band around top of pedestal.	
3	p6122-1	222	224	-	Green/ Green-brown	F	Surface	Mixed		Worn circular groove near centre of interior base.

Type 95.3

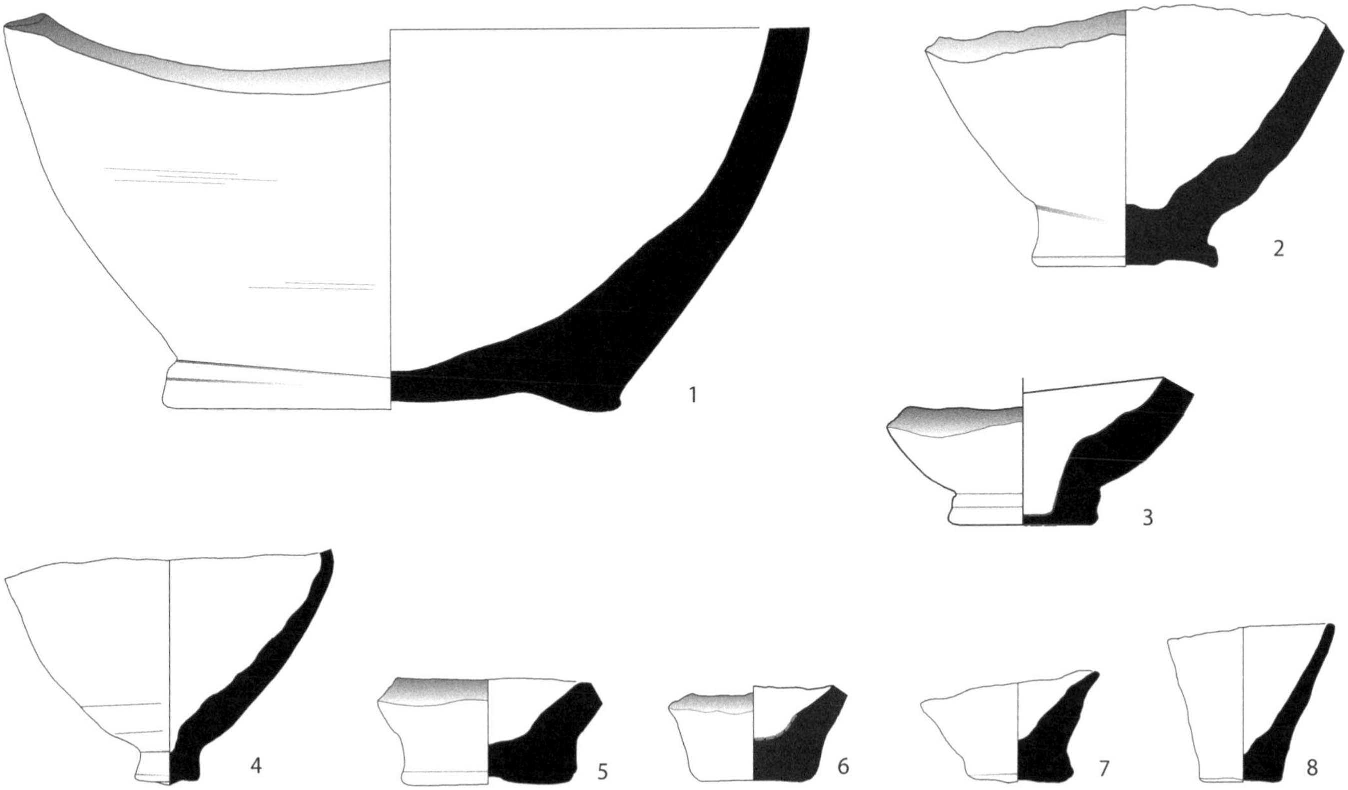

1 2 3 4 5 6 7 8

Type 95.4

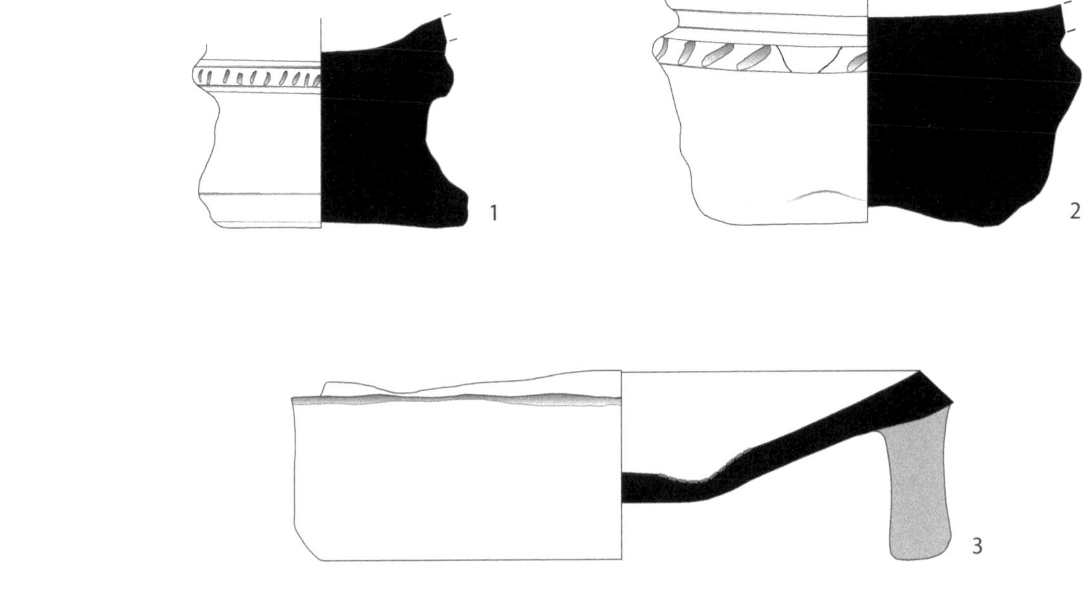

5 cm

Arabic Summary

مدينة نيبور. هذا وربما كان للبناء المُحصَّن دوراً في إخضاع هذه المنطقة والسيطرة عليها . من المؤكد أنه كانتْ فترة القطر البحري فترةَ تحوُّل واسع النطاق ، وسيوضِّحُ العمل المستقبلي في مواقع أخرى خاصية هذا الفترة .

تتعارضُ الأدلة الخزفية جنبًا إلى جنب مع الاستمرارية التي شوهدت في الطريقة التقليدية لِكُتّاب فترة القطر البحري (Dalley 2009 ؛ Robson 2017) بشكلٍ واضحٍ مع السرد التقليدي لإنهيار الدولة بأكملها في جنوب بابِل (على سبيل المثالِ 1989 ؛ Charpin 1986) . ومن الواضِح أنَّه كانتْ هناك عِلاقة وثيقة مع جزيرة فيلكا وحضارة ديلمون في البحرين ، حيثُ تمَّ مُؤخراً تحديدُ تلِ دفن ملكي معزول يُدعى (المقشة) والذي يرجعُ تأريخه إلى هذه الفترة (Laursen 2017: 374). قد لا يُمثِّلُ هذا الأمرإندماجًا سياسيًا ، ولكنه يُمثِلُ علاقة اقتصادية ودبلوماسية مُعتدِلة . هذا ويوضِّحُ الجدول 6.1 موقعًا مبدئياً لتلِّ خيبر في سياقٍ تأريخي أوسع .

لا يمكن أن يخبرنا الفُخار عن السياسة ، لكن تُعتبرُ دراسته جيدة لفهمِ الارتباطات المادية على نطاق صغير. هذا وقد تمكَّنا من توضيحِ طرق الإنتاج ومجموعة الأشكال المخزونة لموقِع تل خيبر. لا نعرف بالضبط كيف ارتبط صانعو الخزف بالإستيطان – إذْ أنَّهم لم يكونوا من بين ال 25 مهنة المذكورة في الأرشيف ، لكننا نعلمُ أنهم أنتجوا أوانيًا نموذجية للإستخدامِ هناك . هذا وعندما أمر مديرو موقِع تل خيبر ب 80 "kaptukkû" و 100 "lahannu" فإنَّهم كانوا يعرفون نوع الأواني التي يريدونها ، كما كان صانعو الخزف يعرفون ماذا يصنعون .

هذا وأنَّ جميعَ الأشكال ليستْ بارِزة ولا برّاقة ، وإنما هي مُخصَّصة للإستخدام اليومي . كما إننا بحاجة إلى المزيد من مواقع فترة القطر البحري للتنقيب عنها ودراستها قبل أن نتمكَّن من فهم الاختلافات الصغيرة عن التجميع النموذجي البابلي القديم ، وكذلك ما إذا كانت مُستمَدة من الدور الخاص لتل خيبر كمُستوطَنةٍ .

بدأ إستكشافُ جنوب العراق من الناحية الأثرية مرة أخرى بعد فترة إنقطاعٍ طويلة ، وهذا هو وقت التغيير لدراسات الخزف . كما تمَّ إستخدامُ الفخار من الفترات التأريخية لدعم السرد التأريخي بطريقة غير فعّالة ، ولكن بدلاً من ذلك يمكنُ لِلفخارِ أن يروي قصصًا بديلة عن استمرارية مهنة الحرف اليدوية ومرونتها وصلابتها . هذا وقد نظرنا في هذا المُجلَّد إلى عملية تجميعَ الفخارمن موقِع تل خيبر وللطريقة التي يربُط بها المُنتجين والمُستهلكين في الممارسات الحرفية والأنشطة التبادلية ، كما أننا عرضنا كيف يلعبُ الفخار دوره في العلاقات الاجتماعية والسياسية والثقافية والاقتصادية التي تمتَّدُ في جميع أنحاء جنوب بلاد ما بين النهرين وفي الخليج في عهد سُلالة القطر البحري الأولى .

المكانة العالية . كما كانتْ الغرفة 316 في فترة إسستيطانها الأخيرة على الأقل عبارةً عن مطبخٍ به العديد من الأغراض للطحن والقياس والتخزين والطهي . هذا وتمَّ العثورُ على أعدادٍ كبيرةٍ من الأواني في الأبراج والتي يبدو أنها إستُخدِمَتْ للتخلُّص من القُمامة والأشياء المكسورة بما في ذلك الفُخار. كما كان للبيوت الشرقية أكواباً كثيرةً للشُرب ، لكن كان عدد أوعية الأكل قليل .ومنَ المُمكِنِ أنَّ تكون الأنواعَ المختلفة من الأكواب التي وجدناها مُخصَّصة لأنواعٍ مُختلِفة من أنشطةِ الشُربِ .

لا يوجد هنالك دليل على الأوعية الفُخارية المُصمَّمة خصيصًا لأنشطة الطقوس ، لذلك من الممكن أن تكون قد إستُخدِمتْ نفس الأوعية المُستَخدَمة يوميًا . إحتوى كل قبو في الوحدة الجنوبية على وِعاء فخاري واحد والتي ربما تكون مرتبطة بالطقوسِ الخاصة بإنهاء عملية البناء . هذا وقد تكون الحفرة الموجودة في الغرفة 142 والتي تحتوي على مخبأ للأوعية شيئًا مشابهًا . كانتْ الأوعية الفخارية تُستخدَم أحيانًا للدفن ، أما المدافن ذات حاويات التخزين المزدوجة فكانتْ تُستَخدمُ للبالغين ، بينما يتُّم دفنُ الأطفالِ في جرَّةٍ واحدةٍ .

الفُخار ومُجتمعُ سُلالة القطر البحري

تعتبرُ مجموعة تل خيبر الفخارية حاليًا هي المجموعة الوحيدة ذات الطبقية الآمنة والمُرتبِطة بشكلٍ موثوق مع سلالة القطر البحري الأولى . إنَّ أكثرَ الأشكال التي يتم تشخيصها حسب الترتيب الزمني هي أنواع الوعاء المُسنَّن 5.1 ، 1.10-2 و أنواع الأكواب المُستديرة 1.50-6 وأنواعُ الجِرار 2.70-3 . هذا وتَمَّ العثور على جميع الأشكال الأخرى أيضًا في فترات سابقة ولاحقة في أماكن أُخرى . لا توجد سوى تغييرات طفيفة في الشكل أثناء فترة الإستيطان الأولي (المراحل 3.2-1) والتي تُطابِق التغييرات

الطفيفة في الهندسة المعمارية ، لذلك فإننا نقترحُ فترة زمنية ربما تتراوح من 50 إلى 100 عام لمراحِلِ الاستيطان التي تمَّ تنقيبها . كما يُشيرُ عددٌ صغيرٌ من أنواع الفترة الكيشية في الرواسبِ المُكشوطة من السطح إلى وجودِ إستخدامٍ ثانوي للموقِع سريعِ الزوال بعد خروج المبنى المُحصَّن عن نِطاق الإستخدام .هذا وربما تزامنتْ نهاية مستوطنة تل خيبر مع فترة التوتر السياسي المُتصاعد في منتصف القرن الخامس عشر عندما ضرب الملك الكيشي ألوم بورياش في بابل جنوب البلاد وهرب آخر ملوك سُلالة القطر البحري إيكاميل إلى بِلاد عِيلام .

تُعتبرُ المقارنات الخزفية الطبقية ذات مشاكِل كبيرة ، لكن قد توحي أوجه التشابه مع المواد الخزفية من تل الدير في القرن السابع عشر وأوروك وأور وبابل بأن بابل في نهاية المطاف لم تكن خالية من السكان في هذا الوقت . كذلك لم تنهارْ صناعة الفخار في الفترة البابلية القديمة السابقة مع فترة الانهيار السياسي ، لكنه لم يستمر دون تغيير أيضًا. كما بقيت أواني التخزين الفخارية الكبيرة كما هي لكن إختفتْ الكؤوس والتي تُمثِّلُ الشكل الأكثر شيوعًا في الفترة البابلية القديمة لِتظهر مرة أخرى في العهد الكيشي . كما أنَّ الظاهرة نفسها موجودة في الخليج . هذا وعلى الرغم من وجود علاقة مع حضارة مدينة سوسة في ذلك الوقت كما هو موضح في السِجلات التاريخية والأسماء الشخصية إلا أنَّ الصناعة الفخارية لاتعكس ذلك إذ أنَّ الأمرَ مُختلفٌ تماماً هناك .

يحتوي أرشيفُ تل خيبر على ألواحٍ طينية مؤرخة لِملك سُلالة القطر البحري الثامن أياداراجالاما و الذي لم يتُمْ التأكُّد بعد من تأريخه الدقيق ، ولكن يبدو أن أسلافه قد اكتسبوا مناطق كبيرة من بابل ، وربما كان لهم نفوذ في أقصى الشمال حتى

اللفائِف للجزء العلوي منها . كما تمَّ ترقيق الجـدران بتقنية المِجداف والسندان .

هذا ويتمُ تلخيصُ هذه الطرق المختلفة في الشكل 4.2.1 . كانتْ هناك العديد من المعالجات السطحية بما في ذلك الكشط والتنعيم بالماء لتشكيل تسلسُلٍ ذاتي . كما تظهرُ الزخرفة المنقوشة والمُبهِرة أحيانًا في هذه العملية . كذلك كانتْ هناك درجة عالية من التوحيد في القياس أثناء عملية إنتاج الأشكال الفخارية .

تمَّ صُنع الفخار في مكان قريب جدًا ولكن ليس في تل خيبر في الحقيقة إذا حكمنا إعتماداً على نسيج البِناءِ ، حيث لا توجد أفران من فترة القُطر البحري أو مبددات والتي هي أشكال غير مستوية ومشتعلة أكثرمن المدة المطلوبة لإشتعالِها . هذا و يمكننا رُؤية أنَّ الفخار تمَّ حرقه في الفرن وحرق أواني الطهي على درجة حرارة منخفضة حوالي أقل من 700 درجة مئوية وحرقْ الأوعية الخزفية ذات اللون الأحمر عند 700-800 درجة مئوية والبرتقالي والأصفر عند 800-950 درجة مئوية ، أما الأواني الخزفية ذات الأنسجة الصلبة والخضراء فتَّم حرقها في درجةٍ تصلُ حتى 1000 درجة مئوية.

يمكننا التمييز بين 4 مجموعات تقنية من معلومات التشكيل وحرق الخزف :

تشمل المجموعة التقنية 1 الفئات 5 و 10 و 35 و 45 و 50 و 55 و 75 والنوع 85.1 ، وهي مصنوعة من الأنسجة H و E و D و C و B و A ملفوفة على عجلات وذات درجة حرق متوسطة.

وتشتمِلُ المجموعة التقنية 2 على الفِئاتِ 35 و 70 والأنواع 3-85.2 المصنوعة من الأنسجة H و F و E والتي تكون عن طريقِ لَفِّ العجلة والقالب وغالبا ماتكون درجة حرقها عالية .

تشتمل ُ المجموعة التقنية 3 على الفئات 25 و 30 ، المصنوعة من النسيج F عن طريق اللف والقالب وغالباً ماتكون درجة حرقها عالية .

أما المجموعة التقنية 4 هي فئة 60 مصنوعة من الأنسجة G و F عن طريق القالب واللف والمجداف والسِندان ودرجة حرقِها مُنخفِضة . كما يتُمُّ حرق الفُخار في ظروف مُؤكسدة غير كاملة على عكس المجموعات الأُخرى .

أنماطُ الإستخدام والإستبعاد

يسردُ اثنان من نصوص تل خيبر الأوعية الفُخارية التي وصلت إلى تل خيبر (الشكل 5.1) وتتطابق بعض الأسماء الأكدية مع بعض أوعيتنا الفخارية (انظر الجدول 3). بالطبع هناك أنواعٌ كثيرة لِلأوعية الفُخارية من تلك المذكورة هناك. يتُمُ تحليلُ الإستخدامات المُختلفة والمُحتملة لأوعيتنا الفخارية في الشكلين. 5.1 و 5.2 ووجودها في أجزاء مختلفة من المبنى المُحصّن كما في الشكل 5.3. هذا ونرى أنَّ في الغرفة 101 في الوحدة الشمالية العديدَ من أواني تقديم الطعام والأكل مما يدعمُ الإقتراح الذي ينُص بأنَّ صف الغرف المتشابهة في هذه المنطقة كان مكانًا لمجموعات من الأشخاص وربما جنود . كما إحتوتْ الغرفة 142 على العديد من الأكواب والأباريق مما يشيرُ إلى حدوثِ الكثير من حالات الشرب هناك . أما في الوحدة الجنوبية فقد إحتوتْ الغرفة 314 على أوعيةٍ للخدمةِ والأكلِ وزجاجات تخزين خاصة وربما كانتْ هذه الأدوات للزوارِ أو غيرهم من الأشخاص ذوي

أعلى تلة باقية في تل خيبر من بقايا الفترة الكيشية المبكرة . هذا ووجدنا واحدًا أو اثنين من أشكال الفترة الكيشية المتأخرة في مكانين في أعلى جزء من سطح الهضبة المُرتفعة خارج المبنى وفي الأماكن التي تعرّضتْ للتعريةِ عند المدخل الرئيسي (شكل 3.5) .

كذلك تمَّ العثورُ على أوجه تشابه لبعض الأنواع من تل خيبَر في موقِع تل بديري الواقِع في وادي نهر الخابور في سوريا ، ولكن لم يتمْ العثوْر على أوجه تشابه مُقنِعة للباحثين في مدينة سوسة . كما أنَّ هناك إعادة توطين حوالي 1650-1600 قبل الميلاد (الفترة 3 أ هناك) في جزيرة فيلكا في الكويت ، ولذلك أصبحتْ أشكال الأواني الفُخارية في بلاد ما بين النهرين شائعةً منذ ذلك الوقت ، كما أنَّ العديدَ من هذه الأشكال له أوجه تشابه جيدة جداً مغ الأشكال الموجودةِ في موقِع تلِّ خيبر. هذا وحدثَ الشيء نفسه في قلعة البحرين في الفترة قلعة البحرين في الفترة (IIIa) حوالي 1600-1450 قبل الميلاد .

مراحل تطور الانتاج

تتلخَّصُ العلاقة بين النسيج وشكل الوعاء في موقِع تل خيبر في الشكل(4.2) . يُتيحُ فحصُ المُحتويات بإستخدام المِجْهَر تحديدَ كيفية صُنعِ الأوعية الفخارية وتقسيمها إلى 5 مجموعات تشكيلية A-E . هذا وعلى الرغم من إظهارِ جميع الأنواع بِإستثناءِ أواني الطهي بعض الأستخدام للعجلةِ أي الطاقة الحركِية الدورانية إلا أنّه لايتُّمُ إلقاء عجلة بكاملها. لكن بدلاً من ذلك هناك إستخدامٌ كبيرٌ لِتقنية اللف لِصناعة الوعاء بما في ذلك إضافة اللمسات الأخيرة له والتي يتُّمُ إجراؤها على العجلة .

تتألفُ المجمو عة A من الفِئات 5 و10 (أوعية) و75 (فتحات أفواه) ونوع 85.1 (مناضِد صغيرة) . هذا وتكادُ تكونُ هذه الأوعية أنها مصنوعةٌ وبصورةٍ شبه مؤكَّدة عن طريق لف وتنعيم العجلة وقطعِ القواعد بخيطٍ أو سلكٍ .

المجموعة B عبارة عن 45 فِئة من القناني الزجاجية و 50 كوباً و 55 إبريقاً و 35 فنجاناً صغيراً. بدأتْ هذه الطريقة بنفسِ طريقة الأوعية ، حيث تمَّ بناءُ الجزء السفلي من جِسم الوعاء عن طريق اللفِ تاركاً فتحة في أساس الوعاء لربط القدم بها إذا لزم الأمر ، ثم إخراج الجزء العلوي من جِسمِ الوعاء من لفائف منفصلة وربط النصفين معًا. هذا وبالنسبة للأكوابِ فقد تمَّ صُنعِ القاعدة بشكلٍ مُنفصلٍ ودفعها في الحفرة ، وأحيانًا يتُّمُ إحاطته بِقطعة من الطين المخلوط بالقِش لمنع التشقق . تمَّ إستخدامُ هذه الطريقة أحيانًا في أشكال أخرى أيضًا (شكل 4.11) .

أما المجموعة C هي فِئة 70 (الجِرار) ، 35 (الفناجين الكبيرة) ، والنوع 85.2 (المناضِد الكبيرة) . تمَّ صُنعُ الأجسام السفلية لِلجِرارِ بدون إستخدام العجلة ، وربما بدلاً من ذلك قد تمَّ بعد الإنتهاء من بناء اللفائِف دفعُ الشكل داخِل قالب للانضمام إليها . هذا وتمَّ بعد ذلك صُنعُ الجزء العلوي من الجسم بنفس طريقة عمل المجموعة B كما تمَّ صُنع المناضِد الكبيرة عن طريق دفع اللفائِف معاً بواسطة اليد أيضاً .

المجموعة D هي الفئات 25 و30 Pithoi . تمَّ صُنعُ الهياكل السفلية لأوعية التخزين الكبيرة بِنفسِ طريقة صُنع جِرار المجموعةِ C . كما كانتْ الأجزاء العلوية مصنوعةً من لفائِف سميكة مُتصِّلة بالعجلةِ . بينما صُنِعتْ القواعِد والأضلاع بِشكلٍ مُنفصِل .

اما المجموعة E هي الفئات 80 أواني الطهي . تمَّ بناءُ الجزء السفلي من اللفائِف ثمَّ ضغطها في قالب لربطها ، ثمَّ أضافة

التسجيل والتصنيف

تمَّ غسلُ جميع قطع الأواني الفخارية ، وتمَّ تسجيلُ جميعَ القطع المكسورة المُشخَّصة مثل حافات الأواني والقواعد والقطع المكسورة ذات الطلاء أوالمِيزات الأخرى في قاعدةِ بياناتٍ وتَمَّ إعطاؤ ها رقم "p" المُميَّز وِفقاً للسياق. على سبيل المثال p3064-6 هي الشق السادِس من السياق 3064 .

بعد ذلك تمَّ القيام بِعملِ تصنيف نوعي للأشكالِ بإستخدامِ قِطع مكسورة مُشخَّصة مرسومة . هذا وتَمَّ رسمُ وتصويرُ جميع الأواني المكتملة أو شبه المكتملة والتي موجودٌ بعضها الآن في المتحفِ العراقي ، كذلك تمَّتْ إعادةُ جميعَ اواني الفخار الأُخرى إلى الموقع وتركها هناك .

التصنيفُ النوعي

يعتمدُ التصنيفُ النوعي على 9328 قطعة مكسورة مُشخَّصة وحوالي 400 صورة كاملة أو شبه كاملة لـلأواني الفخارية . تنقسمُ الأشكال إلى 18 فئةً (على سبيل المثال ، الفئة 5 - أوعية ذات حافة مستديرة عادية) ومُقسَّمة ثانية إلى 77 نوعاً (على سبيل المثال النوع 5.1 - بجسم متعرّج) . تمَّ وصفُ وتوضيح التصنيف النوعي للشكل بالكاملِ على الأطباق من 1 إلى 77. كذلك تمَّ تحديدُ ثمانية أنسجة ، A-H فقًا لما تحتويه من مواد معدنية أو عضوية ، ووِفقاً لمدى خشونة أو نعومة هذه الأنسجة . تُوضِّحُ الأشكال 2.45-2.52 هذه العملية.

التسلسل الزمني الداخلي والعلاقات بين الأقاليم

يشيرُالمستوى 1 في هذا المُجلّد إلى المبنى الأصلي المُحصَّن والذي كان الوحدة الجنوبية بالضبطِ . كما يعني المستوى 2 إعادة البناء الرئيسية للوحدة الجنوبية ، مضافاً إلى ذلك عملية الإضافة للوحدة الشمالية الكبيرة في الوقت نفسه .أنتجَ المستوى الأول والذي كان التنقيب محدودًا فيه حوالي 187 قطعة فقط من الأوعية الفخارية ، ولكن المستوى 2 المُقسَّم إلى المراحل 2.1 ، 2.2 ، 2.3 لديه 4688 وهناك 2759 من الودائع المختلطة. لم تكُنْ الاختلافات في الأنواع الموجودة وتكرار الأنواع ملحوظةً بشكل كبير بين المستويات والمراحل المختلفة عموماً ، وكان هذا الأمر أكثر صحة بالنسبة للأنسجة . هذا ويمكن رؤية المؤشرات الرئيسية في الجدولين 3.2 و 3.3. هناك بعض التشابه مع الأواني الفخارية الأولية من فترة الكيشيين مع الأطوار المُختلَطة والتي تتعلق بالنشاط في المبنى المُحصَّن بعد انتهاء فترة إستخدامه الرئيسية ، وكذلك المناطق خارج هذا المبنى . تتشابهُ الأواني الفخارية المأخوذة من المنازل الشرقية للمراحل الأخيرة من إستيطان المبنى المُحصَّن مع الأطوار المختلطة مع وجود بعض التداخل (شكل3.4) . من الواضِح تشابهُ العديد من الأنواعِ وخاصة الأوعية الفخارية الكبيرة مع أنواع الفترة البابلية المُتأخِرة وأنواع الفترة الكيشية المُبكرة من بِلاد مابين النهرين . ومع ذلك ، تُظهِرُ أنواع الأوعية الصغيرة بعض الاختلافات ، ونادِراً ماتوجد أواني مُسطحة مُنحنية في مُختلف المناطِق . لاتظهرْ العديدُ من ألأشكال التي تعتبرُ نموذجيةً للغاية في مواقع بلاد مابين النهرين في هذه الفترة في موقِع تل خيبر ولاسيما القدح البابلي المُميَّز . كما أنَّ أكواب الشرب الصغيرة المُنتشرة في كل مكان مُتشابهةٌ جداً في شكلها العام ولكن تجِدُ العديدُ منها في تلِّ خيبر لها قاعدة غير مُستقِرة .

إنَّ لأشكالِ الفترة الكيشية المبكرة من المراحل المختلطة أوجهُ تشابه في موقِع تل يلخي في منطقة حمرين ، ولكن هذه هي المرة الأولى التي يتم فيه تسجيلُ هذه الأشكال من جنوب بلاد ما بين النهرين . من المحتمل أن تكون بعض المدافن المأخوذة من قمة

الأواني الفُخارية من موقِع تل خيبر : الحِرفْ اليدوية التُراثية من عهدِ سُلالة القطر البحري الأولى

المُقدِّمة

كانتْ فترةُ مُنتصف الألفية الثانية قبل الميلاد بالنسبةِ لِجنوبِ بلاد مابين النهرين فترةَ صعود وإنهيار الدولة . قامتْ سُلالة حمورابي البابلية الأولى التي إمتدت من حوالي 1792 - 1595 بتوحيد ِ شمال وجنوب بلاد مابين النهرين تحت حكم بابل ، ثُمَّ تلاها عصرٌ مُظلِم من الإنهيار السياسي . تمَّ الإستيطان في تل خيبر في عهد ملوك سُلالة القطر البحري حوالي 1732-1450 والذين كانوا يمتلكون بعض السيطرة على الأهوار في الجنوب خلال معظم هذه الفترة قبل صعود حكم سُلالة الكيشيين حوالي 1450-1150 والذين لايُعرَف الكثير عنهم حتى الآن . قامَ فريقُ مشروع آثار منطقة أُور التابع لِجامعة مانشستر بالتنقيبِ في تلِّ خيبر في الفترة من 2013-2017 مما وفَّرَ أول مادة طبقية مُحكَمَة بما في ذلك النصوص المُتعلِّقة بهذه الفترة . يُقدِّمُ هذا المُجلَّد الأدلة الخزفية بِإستخدام منهجٍ شامِلٍ لِفحص طُرق التصنيع و الإستِخدام وتقديمِ رُؤى حولَ السياسة والإقتصاد في عهد سُلالة القطرالبحري بالإضافة إلى التواريخ . سيتُّمُ نشرُ باقي تفاصل العمل في بحث مون المنقّح الذي سيصدُرُ قريباً .

تركَّزتْ التنقيبات في موقِع تل خَيْبَر على المبنى الكبير المُحصَّن الذي يشغلُ مُعظم مساحة التَل . تَمَّ التنقيبُ في حوالي 10% من مساحة هذا المبنى وباقي العمل هو عبارةٌ عن عملية كَشطْ سطح المبنى . كما كانتْ هناك أيضاً بعض الأعمال التنقيبية في المساحة الصغيرة من البيوت الشرقية .

التسلسُل الزمني والتأريخ

نستخدمُ في هذا المُجلَّد التسلسلَ الزمني الأوسط . كان يُعتقدُ حتى هذه اللحظة أنَّ مُعظم المدن الجنوبية كانتْ مهجورةً خلال فترة القطر البحري ، كما كان هناك الكثير من الصراع والاضطراب في تلك المُدن بكُلِّ تأكيد . مع ذلك يُظهِر العمل التنقيبي في موقِع تَل خَيْبَر أنَّه كانتْ هناك وبِشكلٍ مُؤكَّدٍ حكومة إدارية تعملُ بِشكلٍ مُتطوّر . هناك القليلُ جداً من المواد التي تتضمن معلومات كافية نسبياً فيما يتعلّق بالأواني الفُخارية من فترة القُطر البحري لكنها تكون مُساعدةٌ لنا إذا أخذنا بنظر الإعتبار بعض المواد من منطقة الخليج ، لإنَّ ملوك سُلالة عهد القُطر الذهبي كانت لهم عِلاقات متواصِلة هناك . كان العمل الرئيسي حول هذا الموضوع قبل عملنا هذا هو لArmstrong and Gasche 2014 والذي يستخدمُ أوعية كامِلة فقط ولايتضمَّن أي أدِلّة من منطقة الخليج ويعتمِدُ على التسلسل الزمني المُعقَّد الموجود في مدينة سوسة .

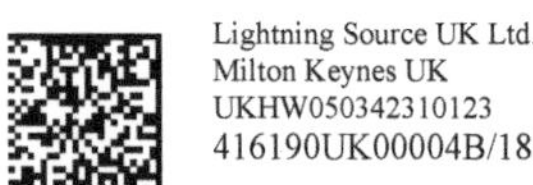

Lightning Source UK Ltd.
Milton Keynes UK
UKHW050342310123
416190UK00004B/188